Introduction

D1788566

In 1990, May 5 was the date on which the average American worker's income, since the beginning of the year, equaled his or her tax obligation to federal, state and local governments. In 1989, "Tax Freedom Day" was May 4. On a day-to-day basis, 2 hours and 45 minutes (1 hour and 47 minutes for federal taxes) of each 8-hour workday are used to pay for the deduction of government taxes of all varieties. These tax deductions and employee-authorized deductions have significantly increased the volume of clerical work and the complexity of accounting entries necessary in connection with payroll operations. Payroll accounting has emerged as one of the most important components of the organization's total accounting system.

This year taxes for old-age, survivors, and disability and hospital insurance will require a total employer-employee tax of 15.3% of the first $53,400 in wages paid each employee covered by the act. In addition to these social security taxes are federal and state unemployment taxes, and state and local income taxes in many states. The total federal and state payroll taxes for which an employer is liable may now exceed 10% of the wages paid to most employees. Payroll taxes, obviously, have come to represent a considerable portion of the operating costs of doing business.

At the federal, state, and local levels, frequent changes are made in the laws that affect a company's payroll tax structure. Recent changes in the federal income tax withholding law have had a significant impact on every worker's take-home pay. Thus, payroll accounting has become an active field of endeavor that requires a constant updating on the part of the persons charged with planning and organizing the payroll system. The steady increase in the portion of a company's operating expenses that payroll, payroll taxes, and fringe benefits occupy has dictated that each business exercise adequate control over every detail of its payroll system in order to improve the accuracy, reliability, and timeliness of the payroll information being processed. This includes not only the calculation of the payroll and the payroll taxes but also the preparation of those records and reports that form the foundation of an efficient payroll system.

The major objectives of this course may be summarized as follows:

1. To develop an appreciation and an understanding of the personnel and payroll records that provide the information required under the numerous laws affecting the operations of a payroll system.
2. To familiarize students with the payroll-record life of employees from their initial applications for employment to their applications for the first social security benefits checks.
3. To introduce students to the various aspects of the Fair Labor Standards Act and the other laws that affect payroll operations and employment practices.
4. To describe the basic payroll accounting systems and procedures used in computing wages and salaries and the timekeeping methods used to record time worked.
5. To acquaint students with the various phases of the Social Security Act, the federal income tax withholding law, and other laws relating to the payment of wages and salaries. Anyone involved in clerical or accounting work relating to payroll systems must have an understanding of the various federal, state, and local laws as they affect payroll accounting.
6. To provide practice in all payroll operations, the preparation of payroll registers, the recording of accounting entries involving payroll, and the preparation of payroll tax returns that are required of businesses.
7. To offer the instructors and students the option of completing the payroll project through the use of microcomputers. Students can use the optional diskette package to update employee files, to complete payroll registers, and to use computer-generated output for completing the accounting records and the various tax forms and reports that are part of the final project.
8. To introduce various types of automated equipment and data processing systems that eliminate many of the repetitive operations that are common to payroll accounting.

Each of the seven units in the textbook opens with a listing, GOALS OF THIS UNIT, which gives the reader a preview of what is to be accomplished in that unit. In addition, each of the first six units ends with a GLOSSARY of important terms that are introduced and defined in that unit. Social security benefits and automated payroll accounting systems are presented as optional topics in Appendixes A and B respectively. Depending upon the availability of time, the instructor may wish to assign one, both, or neither of the appendixes. Also, a testing program (a test for each of the first six units) is available in quantity, free of charge, from the publisher (Stock No. AH60AG).

Throughout this text, we have illustrated many of the currently used tax forms and reports. Because of the time lag between the writing of the text and its publication, some of the forms and reports to be used in 1991 could be slightly different from the illustrations.

We express our appreciation to the many instructors and students who have contributed suggestions to make this course more understandable and more practical to those who pursue the study of payroll accounting. We would especially like to thank Dan Biagi of Walla Walla Community College. As a result of these very helpful recommendations, each new edition has better satisfied the learning needs of students and the teaching needs of instructors.

Bernard J. Bieg
B. Lewis Keeling

PAYROLL ACCOUNTING

1991 EDITION

Bernard J. Bieg, C.P.A.
Professor, Business Studies
Bucks County Community College
Newtown, Pennsylvania

B. Lewis Keeling
Professor Emeritus
Bucks County Community College
Newtown, Pennsylvania

COLLEGE DIVISION South-Western Publishing Co.

CINCINNATI DALLAS LIVERMORE

AH60AB
Copyright © 1991
by SOUTH-WESTERN PUBLISHING CO.
Cincinnati, Ohio

ALL RIGHTS RESERVED

The text of this publication, or any part thereof, may not be reproduced or transmitted in any form or by any means, electronic or mechanical, including photocopying, recording, storage in an information retrieval system, or otherwise, without the prior written permission of the publisher.

ISBN: 0-538-80218-9

Library of Congress Catalog Card Number: 81-642522

1 2 DH 2 1

Printed in the United States of America

Sponsoring Editor: Mark Hubble
Editor: Judy Toland
Software Editor: Ellen Camm
Photo Researcher: Diana Fears
Senior Quality Control Associate: Tim Butz
Marketing Manager: Skip Wenstrup

As We Go To Press

After this 1991 Edition had been written, Congress passed the deficit-reduction budget and the Social Security Administration announced its social security tax rate and the taxable wage base. As a result, several topics, such as the social security taxable wage base discussed on page 71, need to be updated. Each of these topics, with reference to the appropriate unit, is briefly described below.

UNIT 3

FICA Tax Rate and Base

Commencing January 1, 1991, the *combined* FICA tax rate (old-age, survivors, disability insurance, and hospital insurance) and taxable wage base are 7.65% of the first $53,400.

However, note that the taxable wage base to be used in calculating the tax liability for the *Hospital Insurance (Medicare)* portion of the combined FICA tax rate increases to $125,000. The tax rate for the Hospital Insurance portion remains at 1.45%. For calendar years after 1991, the $125,000 figure will be adjusted for inflation.

Payroll Tax Deposits

For 1991 and future years, the deposit requirements will be consistent for all employers who have accumulated $100,000 or more of payroll taxes on any payday. Thus, if the amount of employee and employer FICA taxes and income taxes withheld on any payday total $100,000 or more, a deposit must be made by the close of the next working day.

Employer-Provided Educational Assistance

The exclusion for employer-provided educational assistance was reinstated for taxable years beginning after September 30, 1990, and extending through taxable years beginning before January 1, 1992. In the past, the exclusion did not apply to payment for any graduate-level courses taken by employees pursuing a program leading to a law, business, medical, or similar advanced academic or professional degree. However, this restriction on graduate-level courses has been repealed for taxable years beginning after December 31, 1991.

Social Security Coverage for State and Local Government Employees

Social security retirement coverage has been extended to all state and local government employees who are not currently covered by a public employee retirement program.

UNIT 4

Earned Income Credit

The earned income credit was increased for the taxable years beginning after December 31, 1990, to 18.5% for 1991; to 19% for 1992 and 1993; and to 20% for 1994 and thereafter.

Personal Exemptions and Standard Deductions

The personal exemption will rise to $2,150. The standard deduction will go to $5,700 on a joint return and to $3,400 on a single return.

Phase-Out of Personal Exemptions

The personal exemption allowed for a taxpayer and each dependent will be phased out as the adjusted gross income rises above $100,000 for a single person and $150,000 for a couple.

UNIT 5

FUTA Tax Rate

The gross 6.2% FUTA tax rate, which was scheduled to revert to 6% for wages paid after 1990, has been extended through 1995.

CONTENTS

UNIT 3 SOCIAL SECURITY TAXES/65

UNIT 4 WITHHOLDING FOR INCOME TAXES/109

UNIT 5 UNEMPLOYMENT COMPENSATION TAXES/163

UNIT 6 ANALYZING AND JOURNALIZING PAYROLL TRANSACTIONS/203

UNIT 7 PAYROLL PROJECT/247

APPENDIX A SOCIAL SECURITY BENEFITS/311

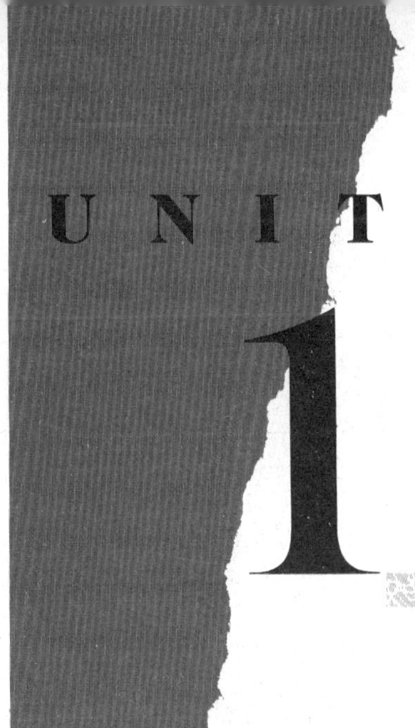

UNIT 1 The Need for Payroll and Personnel Records

GOALS OF THIS UNIT

After completing your study of this unit, you should be able to:

1. Identify the various laws that affect employers in their payroll operations.
2. Know the record-keeping requirements of these laws.
3. Realize the importance of a thorough record-keeping system.
4. Describe the procedures that are generally followed in a Human Resources or Personnel Department.
5. Recognize the various personnel records that are used by businesses and know the type of information shown on each form.
6. Understand the procedures employed in a typical payroll accounting system.
7. Identify the *payroll register* and the *employee's earnings record.*

With the increased capabilities of today's computer technology, the demands on payroll professionals have been magnified. Their skills as administrators and technicians are being challenged with every new payroll processing. Their work is being monitored by all who are affected by the payroll—the employees, the employer, and the government.

A payroll accounting system is the only operation in a business that is almost completely governed by various federal, state, and local laws and regulations. Regulations establish who is an employee, when to pay an employee, when overtime is to be paid, what deductions are made, and when taxes are paid. Lack of compliance with these laws and regulations can result in both fines and back-pay awards.

The preparation and processing of payroll data have become more difficult as changes in legislation have been enacted. With each new year, rates and taxable amounts vary so that payroll administrators must keep abreast of the changes that affect their firms' payroll record keeping.

The increased complexity of payroll operations is true in small businesses as well as in large companies. Certain records of time worked, regular earnings, overtime earnings, deductions from wages, and personnel information are needed. Likewise, information is needed to prepare numerous reports that must be completed accurately and filed promptly.

Only by understanding the requirements of the various laws affecting payroll operations can you know which payroll and personnel records and procedures are necessary. This unit examines briefly the various laws that affect employers in their payroll operations. You will be shown the payroll and personnel records that employers use to meet the requirements of the laws. First, however, let's take a brief look at payroll accounting as a profession.

THE PAYROLL PROFESSION

With the increased responsibilities of payroll specialists, the profession has seen a significant increase in salary compensation. As with other highly trained specialists, their places on the organizational chart have moved closer to the top echelon. It is, therefore, important that payroll professionals keep abreast of the changes in their field so that they can remain technically proficient. This need has spurred the development of an association of payroll practitioners—The American Payroll Association (APA).[1]

Membership in the association is open to anyone interested in or engaged in the support of payroll accounting. The APA offers professional training seminars and various publications to its members. In addition, each year the APA administers an examination for the payroll accountant, and those who pass the exam are awarded a certificate (Certified Payroll Professional). This testing and certification process has helped the payroll profession to gain its needed recognition in the business community.

FAIR LABOR STANDARDS ACT

In the processing of payrolls, the first step is to determine gross pay. The act that affects this calculation is the Fair Labor Standards Act (FLSA) of 1938. Commonly referred to as the Federal Wage and Hour Law, this law sets up minimum wage and overtime pay requirements. Amendments to the act in 1989 provided for increases in the minimum wage rates. The first change took effect on April 1, 1990; and it is to be followed by another increase on April 1, 1991, which will bring the minimum wage rate to $4.25 an hour. The amendments have also provided for a new subminimum training wage.

Other provisions of this law concern equal pay for equal work regardless of sex, restrictions upon the employment of child labor, public service contracts, and wage garnishment.

These basic provisions apply to employers individually engaged in interstate commerce or in the production of goods and services for interstate commerce and to employees in certain enterprises which are so engaged, unless specifically exempted.

The FLSA also imposes record-keeping requirements on employers. However, no specific form of record is prescribed. The basic requirements imposed on the employer concerning payroll and personnel records are shown in Illustration 1-1. In addition to satisfying those demands, employers of white-collar workers who are exempt from federal minimum wage and overtime pay standards must keep records that permit the calculation of such employees' total remuneration for each pay period. *Total remuneration* includes not only the payment for services rendered but also employee benefits and perquisites of employment such as board, lodging, or other facilities provided the worker.

All employers are required to keep records explaining the basis of wage differentials paid to employees of opposite sex for equal work performed in the same establishment. Included in such records are those relating to job evaluations, job descriptions, merit systems, seniority systems, and union contracts.

The employer is also required to display a poster, available from the regional office of the Wage and Hour Division, that informs employees of their minimum wage, equal pay, overtime pay, and wage-collection rights, as well as of child-labor restrictions.

A detailed discussion of this act and the standards established will be presented in Unit 2.

STATE MINIMUM WAGE AND MAXIMUM HOURS LAWS

Most states have established minimum wage rates for covered employees either by legislation or by administrative order of the legislature whereby minimum wage rates are fixed for specific industries. As noted earlier, there are also minimum wage and maximum hour provisions applicable to employers under the Fair Labor Standards Act, a federal law. Where both federal and state regulations cover the same employee, the higher of the two rates prevails. For example, the federal minimum wage was $3.80 an hour in 1990. However, the minimum hourly wage in Oregon was $4.25, or 45¢ greater than the federal minimum wage. All workers covered by that state's legislation would receive the higher state rate. During 1990, there were 10 states with rates that exceeded the federal minimum of $3.80 an hour.

As payroll managers, you must be familiar with the administrative orders of your particular states since the wage orders not only set minimum wages but also contain provisions affecting pay periods, pay for call-in time and waiting time, rest and meal periods, absences, meals and lodging, tips, uniforms, and other matters dealing with wages and hours. The state wage orders usually provide that the employer must keep records showing the wages paid, the hours worked, and such other information that will aid enforcement by state officials.

FAIR EMPLOYMENT LAWS

Federal and state legislation has been enacted to enforce fair employment practices. Many of these laws

---

[1]For more information on the organization, write to: American Payroll Association, New York Educational Division, P.O. Box 2344, Grand Central Station, New York, New York 10163.

	Item	Fair Labor Standards Act	Social Security	Income Tax Withholding	Unemployment Tax
EMPLOYEE DATA	Name	Yes	Yes	Yes	Yes
	Address	Yes	Yes	Yes	Yes
	Sex	Yes	....	....	....
	Date of birth	Yes	....	....	....
	Social security number	Yes	Yes	Yes	Yes
	Withholding allowances claimed	....	....	Yes	....
	Occupation	Yes	Yes	Yes	Yes
	Period employed	....	Yes	Yes	Yes
	State where services rendered	....	Yes	....	Yes
EMPLOYMENT DATA	Day and time of day when workweek begins	Yes	....	....	....
	Regular hourly rate of pay	Yes	....	....	....
	Basis of wage payments; e.g. $5 per hour; $40 per day	Yes	....	....	....
	Hours worked each day	Yes	....	....	....
	Hours worked each week	Yes	....	....	....
	Daily or weekly straight-time pay, exclusive of overtime pay	Yes	....	....	....
	Amount and nature of exempt pay	Yes	....	....	....
	Weekly overtime pay	Yes	....	....	....
	Total additions to or deductions from wages	Yes	....	....	....
	Total remuneration for payroll period	Yes	Yes	Yes	....
	Total remuneration for calendar year	....	Yes	....	Yes
	Date of payment	Yes	Yes	Yes	Yes
	Payroll period	Yes	Yes	Yes	Yes
TAX DATA	Employees' wages subject to tax for payroll period	....	Yes	Yes	....
	Employee's wages subject to tax for calendar year	....	Yes	....	Yes
	Taxable remuneration — if different from total remuneration, reason for difference	....	Yes	Yes	Yes
	Tax deductions from employees' wages	....	Yes	Yes	Yes
	Date tax collected if other than date of payment	....	Yes	Yes	....
	Tax paid by employer but not deducted from employee's wages	....	Yes	Yes	Yes
GEN'L	Specific form of records	No	No	No	No
	No. of years records must be kept	2–3	4	4	4

Illustration 1-1. Summary of Information Required by Major Federal Payroll Laws

deal with discrimination on the basis of age, race, color, religion, sex, or national origin as a condition of employment.

Civil Rights Act of 1964

Several fair employment practices are provided for in Title VII of the Civil Rights Act of 1964, entitled "Equal Employment Opportunity." The act, as amended, forbids employers to discriminate in hiring, firing, promoting, or in any other condition of employment on the basis of race, color, religion, sex, or national origin. Guidelines, established by the Equal Employment Opportunity Commission (EEOC), also include physical characteristics in the definition of national origin discrimination. For example, unnecessary height or weight requirements could exclude some individuals on the basis of their national origin. The EEOC has also declared that sexual harassment is a violation of the Civil Rights Act. Unwelcome sexual advances, requests for sexual favors, and other verbal or physical conduct of a sexual nature can constitute sexual harassment.

Employment agencies may not refer or refuse to refer applicants for employment on the basis of race, color, religion, sex, or national origin. Unions are prohibited from including or segregating their members on these bases, and unions may not cause employers to discriminate on these bases.

This act covers all employers who engage in an industry "affecting commerce" and who employ 15 or more workers for each working day in each of 20 or more weeks in the current or preceding calendar year. Employers specifically excluded from coverage of the fair employment practices legislation include: the United States government (state and local governments are covered), a corporation that is wholly owned by the United States, Indian tribes, private membership clubs (other than labor unions) that are exempt from federal income tax, and religious societies in the employment of members of a particular religion to work on the societies' religious activities. Although the United States government is classed as an exempt employer, the act states that it is the policy of the United States government to provide equal employment opportunities without discrimination, and that the President should use his existing authority to implement this policy.

To accomplish the purpose of eliminating discrimination, the Equal Employment Opportunity Commission tries to obtain voluntary compliance with the law before a court action for an injunction is filed. Where a state or local law forbids discriminatory practices, relief must first be sought under the state or local law before a complaint is filed with the Commission. The EEOC is authorized to institute court proceedings for an injunction if there is reason to believe that any person or group of persons is not complying with the law.

In addition to federal fair employment legislation, more than half the states and some cities have laws that prohibit employers from discriminating on the basis of race, creed, color, or national origin. In most of the states the laws are administered by a special commission or the state Department of Labor, which may authorize cease and desist orders that are enforceable in the courts.

Executive Orders

Employers not subject to Title VII coverage discussed above may come within the scope of the Civil Rights Act by reason of a contract or subcontract involving federal funds. In a series of *executive orders*, the federal government has banned, in employment on government contracts, discrimination that is based on race, color, religion, sex, or national origin. More significantly, the orders have been held to require that some contractors take affirmative action to ensure equal opportunity.

Affirmative Action. Affirmative action is designed to eliminate employment barriers to minorities, women, persons of various religious and ethnic groups, handicapped persons, and veterans. The concept of affirmative action was developed to clarify what firms seeking to conduct business with the federal government must do to be truly equal opportunity employers.

An *affirmative action plan* prescribes a specific program to eliminate, limit, or prevent discriminatory treatment on the basis of race, ethnic group, and sex. Some plans are required by law, while others are developed voluntarily. Often the affirmative action plan is designed to remedy the effects of past discrimination and prevent its recurrence. Usually the plan involves an analysis of the work force utilization; the establishment of attainable results-oriented goals and timetables for recruiting, hiring, training, and promoting any underrepresented classes; an explanation of the methods to be used to eliminate discrimination; and the establishment of responsibility for implementing the program. Under the federal government's drive to eliminate unnecessary paperwork, only companies with more than 250 employees and a federal contract exceeding $1 million have to write a formal affirmative action plan.

Executive Order 11246. This is the major antidiscrimination regulation for government contractors and subcontractors who perform work under a federal construction contract exceeding $10,000, and for the United States government itself. Examples of discrimination forbidden by Executive Order 11246 include a contractor's refusal to hire women for certain jobs because of overtime requirements or weightlifting requirements.

In their affirmative action plans, covered contractors are required to scrutinize tests and other screening procedures and to make all changes necessary to assure that they are nondiscriminatory. Contractors must post notices announcing their nondiscrimination responsibilities in places conspicuous to employees, applicants, and representatives of each labor union with which the contractors deal. In all advertisements for employment, contractors must state that there will be no discrimination in hiring for any position.

Age Discrimination in Employment Act (ADEA)

Under the Age Discrimination in Employment Act of 1967 (ADEA), employers, employment agencies, and labor unions are prohibited from discriminating on the basis of age in their employment practices. Only employers (those who employ 20 or more workers), employment agencies, and labor unions engaged in an industry affecting interstate commerce are covered. The act also covers federal, state, and local government employees, other than elected officials and certain aides not covered by civil service.

Under the ADEA, protection is provided for virtually all workers over 40. There is no longer an upper age cap. A key exception involves executives who are 65 or over and who hold high policymaking positions. If such an employee is entitled to an annual retirement benefit from the employer of at least $44,000, the employee can be forcibly retired.

In order to prove compliance with the various fair employment laws, employers must keep accurate personnel and payroll records. All employment applications, along with notations as to their disposition and the reasons for the disposition, should be retained. A complete file of job descriptions and copies of employment tests should be kept. All records pertaining to promotions, discharges, seniority plans, merit programs, incentive payment plans, etc., should also be retained.

FEDERAL INSURANCE CONTRIBUTIONS ACT (FICA)

The Federal Insurance Contributions Act (FICA) is part of the social security program planned by the federal government to provide economic security for workers and their families. Under the act, a tax is levied on employers and employees in certain industries to be paid to the federal government and credited to the Federal Old-Age and Survivors' Trust Fund and the Federal Disability Insurance Trust Fund. From these funds payments are made to persons who are entitled to benefits under the Social Security Act. The tax levied on employees by this act is a set percent of their gross wages, and it must be withheld from their pay.

Social security benefits are also available to the self-employed person under the provisions of the Self-Employment Contributions Act (SECA). This act imposes a tax on the net earnings from self-employment derived by an individual from any trade or business carried on by that person.

FICA also provides a two-part health insurance program, commonly known as Medicare, for the aged and the disabled. The Hospital Insurance plan is financed by a separate tax on both employers and employees. The Supplementary Medical Insurance plan is voluntary and is financed by those who desire coverage, with a matching payment by the federal government.

Detailed information about FICA and exemptions from its coverage is given in Unit 3, and the benefits available are briefly discussed in Appendix A.

Although no specific form of records is recommended for employers under FICA, the act requires that employers keep records providing certain specific information. The information needed and the period of time for which it is to be retained are shown in Illustration 1-1 on page 3.

INCOME TAX WITHHOLDING LAWS

With the passage of the 16th Amendment in 1913, taxation of income became constitutional. Today, an *income tax* is levied on the earnings of most employees and is deducted from their gross pay. In some cases, this may involve three separate deductions from the employee's gross pay—a federal income tax, a state income tax, and a local (city) income or wage tax. All of the acts that levy these various income taxes provide for the collection of taxes at the source of the wages paid (payroll withholding).

Federal Income Tax Withholding Law

The collection of federal income taxes at the source of wages paid came into being with the enactment of the Current Tax Payment Act of 1943. This act is commonly referred to as a withholding tax law. A percentage formula is used in an attempt to collect the approximate tax on wages or salaries by requiring the employer to withhold a specified amount from each wage or salary payment. These withholdings are then turned over to the federal government for the employee's tax account. Over the years many changes have been made in the tax rates, exemptions, and allowable deductions. The present requirements are discussed in detail in Unit 4.

Employers are required to keep records showing the information referred to in Illustration 1-1 on page 3. However, the law does not prescribe any specific forms to be used for such record keeping.

Because of the increased use of microimage systems that produce microfilm directly from computer files, the Internal Revenue Service (IRS) permits the microfilm reproduction (including microfiche) of general books of account, such as cash books, journals, voucher registers, ledgers, and supporting records of detail within the meaning of the Internal Revenue Code.

State and Local Income Tax Withholding Laws

State income taxes are imposed on individuals in most states. The laws vary from state to state as to the amount to be withheld, exemptions from withholding, and the time for withholding reports to be filed. Employers may also be required by *local* income tax laws to deduct and withhold local income taxes on salaries or wages paid. The withholding of state and local income taxes is further discussed in Unit 4.

UNEMPLOYMENT TAX ACTS

The purpose of *unemployment insurance taxes* is to provide funds at the state level for compensating unemployed workers. The employer is affected by taxes levied both by the federal government (Federal Unemployment Tax Act) and by the state government (State Unemployment Tax Acts).

Federal Unemployment Tax Act (FUTA)

Like the Federal Insurance Contributions Act, the Federal Unemployment Tax Act is incorporated in the Internal Revenue Code. If an employer employs one or more individuals in each of 20 or more weeks in occupations covered by FUTA or pays wages of $1,500 or more during any calendar quarter in the current or preceding calendar year, a federal unemployment insurance tax must be paid. The tax paid to the federal government is used for paying state and federal administrative expenses of the unemployment program. Employers subject to FUTA receive credit against most of the federal tax when they contribute to their state unemployment compensation funds. Detailed information as to employers and employees who are subject to the requirements of the act is given in Unit 5.

Employers subject to FUTA must keep permanent records that provide the information listed in Illustration 1-1 on page 3. No particular form is prescribed for these records. However, each employer must use forms and accounting systems that will enable the District Director of the Internal Revenue Service to ascertain whether the tax is correctly computed and paid.

State Unemployment Tax Acts (SUTA)

All the states and the District of Columbia have enacted unemployment insurance laws. Each employer receives a credit against the FUTA tax because of the contribution (tax) to a state's unemployment compensation program. The taxes paid to the individual states by employers are used primarily for the payment of unemployment benefits.

The Social Security Act specifies certain standards that each state had to meet in passing an unemployment compensation law. These standards have resulted in a fairly high degree of uniformity in the requirements of state unemployment laws and in the records that must be kept by businesses. State laws do differ, however, making it necessary for employers to be familiar with the laws of the states in which they operate.

The state unemployment compensation laws require employers to keep payroll records similar to those required under the federal law. Penalties may be imposed for failure to keep the required records or for failure or delinquency in making the required returns or for default or delinquency in paying the contributions. The required period for retaining records varies in different states, but in no case should the records be kept for a period of less than four years because of the federal requirement.

State unemployment compensation and tax acts are discussed in Unit 5.

OTHER FEDERAL LAWS AFFECTING THE NEED FOR PAYROLL AND PERSONNEL RECORDS

Generally the payroll and personnel records and reports that a business prepares and retains to meet the requirements of the laws already discussed provide sufficient information needed under the laws which are outlined in Illustration 1-2 and discussed below.

Employee Retirement Income Security Act of 1974 (ERISA)

This act covers employee pension and welfare plans that are established or maintained (1) by any employer engaged in commerce or in any industry or activity affecting commerce and (2) by any employee organization representing employees engaged in commerce or in any industry or activity affecting commerce. The legislation insures that workers will earn pension rights, and safeguards those pension funds by regulating how the funds are to be raised, how they are to be disbursed, who controls them, and what is to be done when funds are insufficient to pay promised benefits. However, the law *does not* require any employer to establish a pension plan.

ERISA was primarily designed to insure that workers who are covered by private pension plans receive benefits from those plans in accordance with their credited years of service with their employers. *Vesting* is the process of conveying to employees the right to share in a retirement fund in the event they are terminated before the normal retirement age. The vesting process is linked to the number of years needed for workers to earn an equity in their retirement plans and to become entitled to full or partial benefits at some future date if they leave the company before retirement. Once vested, a worker has the right

Law	Coverage	Contract Dollar Minimum	Major Provisions
Davis-Bacon Act (1931)	Laborers for contractors or subcontractors on federal government contracts for construction, alteration, or repair of public buildings or works.	$2,000	Minimum wage set by Secretary of Labor (weight is given to union wage scale prevailing in the project area).
Walsh-Healey Public Contracts Act (1936)	Laborers for contractors who furnish materials, supplies, articles, and equipment to any agency of the United States.	$10,000	Single minimum wage determined by Secretary of Labor for all covered employees in a given industry.
McNamara-O'Hara Service Contract Act (1965)	Service employees on contracts with the United States or the District of Columbia for the furnishing of services.	$2,500	Minimum wage set by Secretary of Labor based on minimum wage found to be prevailing in that locality.
Occupational Safety and Health Act (OSHA) (1970)	Any business involved in interstate commerce.	-0-	Sets specific occupational and health standards for employers; requires that records be kept of work-related deaths, illnesses, and injuries.
Vocational Rehabilitation Act (1973)	Companies with federal agency contracts.	$2,500	Must include in the contract an affirmative action clause requiring that the handicapped applicant or employee will be given appropriate consideration.
Vietnam Era Veterans' Readjustment Act (1974)	Government contractors with federal contracts or subcontracts.	$10,000	Requires contractors to take affirmative action to employ and advance in employment qualified veterans of the Vietnam era and disabled veterans.

Illustration 1-2. Federal Laws Affecting the Need for Payroll and Personnel Records

to receive a pension at retirement age, based on years of covered service, even though the worker may not be working for the firm at that time. Most retirement plans provide for vesting after the worker has been covered under the plan for a specified number of years. Currently, the law provides for full vesting in five years or gradually over seven years (20% after three years and 20% a year for the next four).

The law establishes minimum vesting schedules whereby workers who participate in a plan do not lose all of their benefits because of punishing forfeiture standards of the pension plan or because of inadequate fund resources. To protect against potential benefit losses because of a plan's termination, ERISA set up a government insurance program (The Pension Benefit Guaranty Corporation) to pay any benefits that could not be met with funds from the plan.

Individual Retirement Account (IRA). An *individual retirement account (IRA)* is a pension plan established and funded by an individual employee. The employee's contributions to an IRA may be made through the employer or a union or placed in an individual retirement savings account specified in the law. *Under certain conditions,* employees may put aside each year the lesser of $2,000 or 100% of their compensation without paying federal income taxes on their contributions.

A more detailed discussion of IRA accounts is presented in Unit 4.

Simplified Employee Pension (SEP) Plan. By means of a *simplified employee pension (SEP) plan,* employers may make contributions to individual retirement accounts on behalf of their employees. Employers may make annual contributions of up to 15% of each employee's compensation, but in no case may the contribution exceed $30,000. The contributions are placed in an individual retirement account for the employee. The employee can also contribute to the plan. The employee's contribution is limited to $2,000, or the employee's gross annual pay, whichever is less. The tax status of the employee's contribution is subject to the conditions set forth for IRA accounts, as explained in Unit 4.

Employers must contribute for all employees who are 21 years of age or older and who have worked for the employer at least three of the past five years. The contributions made by the employer are fully and immediately vested.

Disclosure Requirements. The reporting and disclosure requirements set forth by ERISA have tremendous implications for the record-keeping requirements of employers. Informational reports must be filed with the U.S. Department of Labor, the IRS, and the government insurance program.

In general, the reports are composed of descriptions of the plans and the annual financial data. The plan descriptions include the eligibility requirements for participation and for benefits; provisions for nonforfeitable pension benefits; circumstances which may result in disqualification, loss, or denial of benefits; and procedures for presenting claims. The annual reports include financial statements and schedules showing the current value of plan assets and liabilities, receipts and disbursements, and employer contributions; the assets held for investment purposes; insurance data; and an opinion of an independent qualified public accountant.

Upon written request from the participants, the administrator must also furnish a statement, not more than once in a 12-month period, of the total benefits accrued, accrued benefits that are vested, if any, or the earliest date on which accrued benefits will become vested.

Immigration Reform and Control Act of 1986

This act bars employers from hiring aliens unauthorized to work in the United States. It also requires all employers to verify employment eligibility for all individuals hired after November 6, 1986. To do this, the employer must examine the employee's verification documents and have the employee complete Form I-9, Employment Eligibility Verification (not illustrated). The document or documents that the employee must furnish to the employer are listed on Form I-9. These documents are used for two purposes: to identify the employee, and, if an alien, to verify authorization to work in the United States.

Form I-9 must be completed within three business days of the date the employee starts to work. The form must be retained for three years after the date of hiring or for one year after the date the employment is terminated, whichever is longer.

The Immigration and Naturalization Service (INS) can levy fines if an audit uncovers record-keeping violations. Civil penalties range from $100 to $1,000 for each violation.

OTHER STATE LAWS AFFECTING THE NEED FOR PAYROLL AND PERSONNEL RECORDS

States have enacted other laws which have a direct bearing on the payroll and personnel records that an employer must maintain and on the rights that must be extended to employees.

Workers' Compensation Laws

By means of *workers' compensation insurance*, employees and their dependents are protected against losses due to injury or death incurred during employment. Most states have passed laws that require employers to provide workers' compensation insurance by one of the following plans:

1. Contribution to a state compensation insurance fund administered by an insurance department of the state.
2. Purchase of workers' compensation insurance from a private insurance company authorized by the state to issue this type of policy.
3. Establishment of a self-insurance plan, approved by the state, under which the company bears all risk itself.

The cost of the workers' compensation insurance premiums is borne by the employer, except in New Mexico, Oregon, and Washington, where both the employer and the employee contribute to the workers' compensation fund. Benefits are paid to the injured worker, or to the survivors in the event of death, by the state, by the insurance company, or by the risk-assuming employer according to the adopted plan.

The insurance premiums are often based upon the total gross payroll of the business and may be stated in terms of an amount for each $100 of weekly wages paid to employees. The premium rates vary among types of jobs and vary in amount with the pay rate involved.

EXAMPLE:

The rate for the office workers of the Volpe Parts Company is $0.60 per $100 of payroll, while the rate for machine-shop workers is $6 per $100 of payroll.

If the employer's accident experience is low, the rates may be reduced to a certain minimum. Because the premium rates vary according to the different degrees of danger in various classes of jobs, it is necessary that payroll records be planned and carefully maintained to indicate job classifications for rate purposes. Every business should determine whether it comes under a workers' compensation insurance law and should keep any records required in connection with the law.

State Disability Benefit Laws

California, Hawaii, New Jersey, New York, Rhode Island, and Puerto Rico have passed laws to provide *disability benefits* to employees who are absent from their jobs because of illness, accident, or disease *not arising out of their employment*. State disability benefit laws are further discussed in Unit 5.

State Time-Off-To-Vote Laws

In many states employees are allowed to take time off from work to vote, and the United States Supreme Court has upheld the validity of time-off-to-vote laws. Although the laws of the states vary, generally the legislation provides that if employees who are entitled to vote in an election are absent from work for a specified period, they will not be penalized nor will there be a deduction from their wages. In most states the employee is required to have applied for the time off prior to the date of the election. Usually penalties are provided if the employer refuses an employee the right-to-vote privileges that have been conferred by state law.

Legal Holidays

Payroll administration requires that we know what holidays are legally recognized by our state. For example, the due dates for returns and tax payments are extended by the federal government and many states when the scheduled due date falls on a Saturday, a Sunday, or a legal holiday.

The federal government has declared New Year's Day (January 1), Independence Day (July 4), Veterans Day (November 11), Thanksgiving Day (fourth Thursday in November), and Christmas Day (December 25) to be legal public holidays. In addition, the following "Monday Holidays" are legal public holidays:

- Martin Luther King, Jr.'s Birthday, the third Monday in January.
- Presidents' Day, the third Monday in February.
- Memorial Day, the last Monday in May.
- Labor Day, the first Monday in September.
- Columbus Day, the second Monday in October.

Although almost all states have enacted legislation declaring most of the "Monday Holidays," we must be familiar with the legislation of our own state and those states wherein other employees of our firm may be working.

PERSONNEL SYSTEMS AND PAYROLL ACCOUNTING SYSTEMS

Up to this point in the unit, we have seen that a business must keep personnel and payroll records to meet the requirements of the various laws under which it is operating. In addition, these records form an integral part of an effective business system.

In developing its personnel system and payroll accounting system, a business should design basic forms and records that satisfy the requirements of all the laws applicable to that organization. Properly designed personnel and payroll accounting forms and records, as described in the closing pages of this unit, not only supply the information required by the various laws but also provide management with information needed in its decision-making process. Thus, properly designed personnel and payroll accounting forms and records result in savings in both time and work because the necessary information is recorded, stored, retrieved, and distributed economically, efficiently, and quickly.

PERSONNEL SYSTEMS

In most medium-size and large companies, the personnel systems require extensive record-keeping procedures in order to:

1. Provide data for considering promotions and changes in the status and earnings of workers.
2. Provide the information required by various federal, state, and local laws.
3. Justify company actions if investigated by national or state labor relations boards.
4. Justify company actions in discussions with local unions or plant committees.

Before the Payroll Department can pay newly hired employees, the Human Resources Department must process those employees. The procedure that the Human Resources Department follows in this hiring process is outlined below. Human Resources:

1. Receives a request from a department head, asking for additional or replacement employees.
2. Examines the application blanks.
3. Interviews applicants for the position.
4. Administers tests of various kinds to determine whether the applicant has the proper qualifications. A physical examination may also be required.
5. Checks references from previous employers, schools, or individuals.
6. Selects the proper person for the job.
7. Notifies the successful applicant and instructs him or her as to the starting date, time, and to whom to report.
8. Gives the necessary information for the new employee to the Payroll Department.
9. Prepares a personnel record for the new employee as a permanent record for the business.

A number of companies that manufacture business forms have available standard personnel forms and records that may be successfully used if a business does not care to design its own special forms.

In small companies it may not be necessary to keep such extensive personnel records. Frequently an application form or an employee history record may be the only document needed.

Throughout the remainder of this unit, the discussion of the various personnel and payroll records is augmented by the use of several illustrations. In the examples of these records, we shall follow Mary Louise Mosworth from her initial application for employment with the United Chemicals Company to her entry onto the company's payroll records.

Requisition for Personnel

The *requisition for personnel* form is used to notify the Employment Department or the Human Resources Department of the need for additional or replacement employees. The requisition for new employees can be initiated in a number of ways. In some companies a memo is sent to the Human Resources Department, stating the title of the position to be filled, a brief description of the duties of the job, and the salary range. Other companies may use preprinted forms. If a preprinted form is utilized, it should indicate the type and number of persons needed, the position to be filled, the rate of pay for the job, the salary range, the date the employee is needed, a summary of any special qualifications, and whether the position is permanent or temporary.

Illustration 1-3 shows a typical personnel requisition that is very suitable in businesses requiring a record of this kind. Usually, two copies of the form are prepared by the department head or other person making the request. The original copy is sent to the Employment Department or Human Resources Department, and the duplicate is retained by the person making the request.

In a small business, or in a business where the personnel turnover is small, personnel requisitions may not be needed. Where there are several departments, however, and one person is employing all personnel, a written requisition is highly desirable because the order is in writing and this helps to avoid confusion and needless questions.

Application for Employment

Every business, regardless of size, should have an application form to be filled out by a person seeking employment. The *application form* gives the applicant an opportunity to provide complete information as to personal qualifications, training, and experience. The form serves as a permanent record for the business and provides a means of obtaining information

United Chemicals

PERSONNEL REQUISITION

Department Accounting Position Payroll Clerk Date Wanted July 1, 19--

Name of person being replaced Martin W. Scruggs
(If addition, attach explanation)

Job Title Payroll Clerk Job Grade 4

*Name of person terminating ---

*Job Title --- *Job Grade ---

Date of Termination June 25, 19--

If temporary, for how long? ---

If part-time, what hours or days? ---

*Complete only if person being requested will not be performing the same job duties as the person terminating.

EDUCATION

HIGH SCHOOL ___ BUSINESS SCHOOL X

COLLEGE 1 (2) 3 4 YEARS

OTHER ___

LIST ANY SPECIAL QUALIFICATIONS NOT COVERED BY JOB DESCRIPTION:

Approval E. J. Dunn Date June 15, 19-- Signed Margaret T. Johnson
Supervisor—Department Head

(FOR HUMAN RESOURCES DEPARTMENT USE)

POSITION FILLED BY	CODE NO.	STARTING DATE	STARTING SALARY	PAYROLL NOTIFIED BY
Mary Louise Mosworth	33-4	7/1/--	$1,500 mo.	Vernon T. Hansen

Illustration 1-3. Personnel Requisition

needed for various purposes. When the people who interview the applicant have the information before them, as requested on the application blank, they are reminded of questions that should be asked of the applicant, and of facts that should be given the applicant.

Other purposes of the application form are to provide information for the checking of references, to serve as a guide to effective interviewing, and to provide information for correlation with data obtained from employment tests. The basic information that should be provided by the application for employment form is the following:

1. Personal information including the name, address, telephone number, and social security account number of the applicant.
2. Educational background including a summary of the schools attended, whether the applicant graduated, and degrees conferred.
3. Employment and experience record.
4. Type of employment desired.
5. References.

Employers who are subject to fair employment laws must make certain that all aspects of the prehire inquiries are free of discrimination on the basis of race, color, religion, sex, national origin, or age. *Prehire inquiries* include questions asked in the employment interview and on application forms, resumes of experience or education required of an applicant, and any kind of written testing. None of the federal civil rights laws specifically outlaw questions concerning the race, color, religion, sex, national origin, or age of an applicant. However, if the employer can offer no logical explanation for asking such questions, the Equal Employment Opportunity Commission and the Wage and Hour Administrator view such questions as discriminatory. Of course, prehire questions pertaining to religion, sex, national origin, or age are allowed when these factors are bona fide occupational qualifications for a job.

Asking an applicant's age or date of birth may tend to deter the older worker. Thus, if such information is asked for on an application form, a statement should appear on that form notifying the applicant that discrimination on the basis of age with respect to individuals who are at least 40 is prohibited by the Age Discrimination in Employment Act. Some businesses have removed the "date of birth" and "year of graduation" questions from their application forms.

United Chemicals

PERSONAL

Name	Date
Mary Louise Mosworth	June 18, 19--
7 North Street	Phone Number: 555-5136
City: Huntington · State: WV · Zip: 25703-2234	Social Security Number: 293-77-1388

In case of emergency, who would we notify? Name: Robert Mosworth Address: 7 North Street, Huntington Phone Number: 555-5136

STATEMENT OF HEALTH

Is There Any Reason Why You Would Be Unable to Perform Any of the Duties of the Position for Which You Are Applying? No

If Yes, Explain:

EMPLOYMENT INFORMATION

Type Work Preferred	When Available for Work
Accounting - clerical	at once

Are You Now Employed?	Reasons for Desiring Change
No	

Have You Ever Supervised People	How Many	Where
No		

List Special Skill and Office Equipment You Operate Efficiently: typewriter, office copier, video display terminal

Present Typing Speed	No. Years in School?	In Experience?	Present Shorthand Speed	No. Years in School	In Experience?
65	3	1	—	—	—

PREVIOUS EMPLOYMENT

SHOW LAST POSITION FIRST. ANSWER ALL QUESTIONS

1 Name and Address of Company: White Transfer Co., P.O. Box 801, Huntington, WV 25701-2231

Date Employed	Date Terminated	Final Salary	Name of Supervisor
Feb 1, 19--	Dec. 31, 19--	$5.80/hr.	Jean Sanning

Reason for Termination: To enter Business College

Duties and Positions Held: Clerk-typist – Verify extensions and prepare waybills

2 Name and Address of Company: Palmer Drugs, Broad & Center, Huntington, WV 25701-2232

Date Employed	Date Terminated	Final Salary	Name of Supervisor
Aug. 10, 19--	Jan. 31, 19--	$4.25/hr.	William Palmer

Reason for Termination: To accept full-time job at higher hourly rate

Duties and Positions Held: Cash register operator at check-out counter

Illustration 1-4. Application Blank (page 1)

EDUCATION

	Name and Address of School	Years Attended	Average Grade	Major Course	Minor Course	Graduate?
High School	Valley High School Huntington, WV	19__To 19__	B	Business	English	Yes
College		19__To 19__				
		19__To 19__				
Business School	Huntington College of Business-Huntington, WV	19__To 19__	A	Accounting	Office Procedures	Yes
Other		19__To 19__				

Your Most Interesting Subjects in Last School Attended: Accounting and Law

Your Most Difficult Subjects in Last School Attended: Economics

Honors and Extracurricular Activities in Last School Attended: Vice-President, Young Business Executives Club

PROFESSIONAL CERTIFICATES

Type	Issuing State	Date	No.
None			

REFERENCES

List below three references not previously mentioned in application, and not related to you, who have known you at least three years.

Name	Address	Occupation or Profession
Rev. Stephen M. Keel	51 Parker Rd. Huntington, WV 25710-2237	Minister, Central Presbyterian Church
George P. Russell	163 21st Street Nitro, WV 25143-2139	Chemical Engineer
Mrs. Ethel Carson	416 Eighth Street Huntington, WV 25701-2236	Instructor

The above statements are true to the best of my knowledge and belief. I am willing to undergo a medical examination as a basis for further consideration of my application.

Signature Mary L. Mosworth

DO NOT WRITE IN SPACE BELOW

Employed? ☒ Yes ☐ No	Hold Application in Pending File ☐ Yes ☒ No
Date to Report to Work: July 1, 19–	Department: Accounting
Position: Payroll Clerk	Job Grade: 4 — Salary: $1,500/mo.

Remarks: Very pleasing personality, well poised. Excellent scholastic background. Anxious to advance in accounting-related position.

Interviewed By	Interviewed By	Interviewed By
		Vernon T. Hansen

Illustration 1-4. Application Blank (page 2)

Generally an employer may not require information of a minority, a female, or an older applicant that would not be required of another applicant. It has also been held by the EEOC that asking a job applicant to list arrests on the job application violates the Civil Rights Act. An employer may seek or use information concerning criminal convictions of applicants or employees and may refuse to hire a convicted criminal only if there is a valid business need for doing so. Thus, if in the employer's business the workers have access to the personal property of the employer's clients, the employer may refuse to hire an applicant who has a public record of conviction for theft. The employer is also prohibited from making inquiries about an applicant's honorable discharge from the military service unless it can be proved that there is a proper business interest that justifies the asking of such information.

As shown in Illustration 1-4 on pages 12 and 13, an application blank may provide space for an interview record. This section of the form is completed by the interviewer either while the interview is in process or after it has been completed. The comments appearing on the application blank in Illustration 1-4 were those of Vernon T. Hansen, the Director of Human Resources. Often the applicant is interviewed by the potential supervisor as well as by a member of the Human Resources Department.

In case an applicant is rejected, a notation on the application form enumerating the reasons for rejection will prove helpful in the future. This would simplify the restudy of the applicant's qualifications if the individual should later reapply. In addition, a record of the reasons for rejecting an applicant will be needed in the event the company is accused of unfair labor practices.

Reference Inquiry

Before an applicant is employed, a company may check some of the references given on the application blank. Many businesses use a standard *reference inquiry form*, which is usually mailed to the person or company given as a reference. In some cases, businesses do not use a specially designed form for inquiring about references but instead write special letters. Other companies prefer a telephone reference check because they feel that a more frank opinion of the candidate is received over the telephone than in a letter. Some companies prefer not to check on personal references given by the job applicant since these tend to be less objective than business references. Today, any type of reference checking has taken on new meaning—expensive litigation. Because of this, many personnel departments give references only a cursory glance.

Under the Fair Credit Reporting Act of 1968, employers are subject to certain disclosure obligations when they seek an investigative consumer report from a consumer reporting agency on a job applicant or in certain instances on present employees. An investigative consumer report usually contains information about the individual's character, general reputation, and mode of living. Generally, the employer must notify the applicant or the employee in writing that such a report is being sought. Also, the employer must notify the applicant or employee that he or she may request information from the employer about the nature and scope of the information sought. In the event employment is denied because of the consumer report information, the employer is required to inform the individual that this was the reason or part of the reason for denying employment. Also, the employer must furnish the applicant with the name and address of the consumer reporting agency that made the report.

Hiring Notice

After the successful applicant is notified of employment and is informed as to the starting date, time, and to whom to report, a *hiring notice* is sent to the Payroll Department so that the new employee can be added properly to the payroll. A hiring notice such as that shown in Illustration 1-5 usually gives the name, address, and telephone number of the new employee, the department in which employed, the starting date, the rate of pay, the number of withholding allowances claimed, and any other information pertaining to deductions that are to be made from the employee's wages. Usually two copies of this form are prepared, with the original going to the Payroll Department and the duplicate being kept by the Human Resources Department.

Employee History Record

Although many businesses keep no personnel records other than the application blank, there is need for a more detailed record such as the *employee history record*, which provides a continuous record of the relationship between the employer and the employee. The employee history record, in addition to providing personal and other information usually found on an application blank, provides space to record the employee's progress, attendance, promotions, and salary increases.

The employee history record may also contain the findings of performance appraisals, which most companies conduct periodically for each employee. An employee appraisal, usually made by the worker's immediate supervisor, is used at the time of salary re-

HIRING NOTICE

NO. 220

SOCIAL SECURITY NO. 293-77-1388

DATE June 28, 19--

NAME Mary Louise Mosworth		CLOCK NO. 418	
ADDRESS 7 North St., Huntington, WV	ZIP 25703-2234	PHONE NO. 555-5136	
OCCUPATION Payroll Clerk	DEPT. Accounting	GROUP NO. --	
STARTING DATE July 1, 19--	TIME 8:00	A.M. P.M.	RATE $1,500 mo.
MARRIED	SINGLE x	BIRTH DATE 8/1/--	
LAST EMPLOYMENT	White Transfer Co.	LOCATION Huntington, WV	
	DATE LEFT 12/31/--	REASON Enrolled in college	
NO. OF WITHHOLDING ALLOWANCES 1			
IN EMERGENCY NOTIFY Robert Mosworth		PHONE NO. 555-5136	
EMPLOYEE'S SIGNATURE IN FULL Mary Louise Mosworth			
SUPERVISOR'S SIGNATURE Margaret T. Johnson			
EMPLOYMENT DEPARTMENT			
ORIGINAL TO PAYROLL DEPT. DUPLICATE RETAINED BY HUMAN RESOURCES DEPT.			

Illustration 1-5. Hiring Notice

view, promotion opening, and termination. These appraisals provide an evaluation of the employee's knowledge of duties, the quantity and quality of work, effectiveness in working with others, relations with customers, attendance and punctuality, promotion potential, and overall performance.

Change in Payroll Rate

The *change in payroll rate form* is used to notify the proper departments of a change in the employee's rate of remuneration. The change in rate may originate in the Human Resources Department or with the head of the department in which the employee works. In either event, the Payroll Department must be informed of the change for the employee so that the rate change is put into effect at the proper time and so that the records reflect the new rate. Illustration 1-6 on page 16 shows a form that may be used for this purpose. Ordinarily one copy is sent to the Payroll Department, one to the Human Resources Department, and one to the employee's department.

PAYROLL ACCOUNTING SYSTEMS

A *payroll accounting system* embodies all those procedures and methods related to the disbursement of pay to employees. A typical payroll accounting system includes the following procedures:

1. Timekeeping of hours worked or production units completed for salary payrolls as well as for hourly and piece-rate payrolls.
2. Computation of the *gross pay* (the total regular earnings plus the total overtime earnings) and the *net pay* (the gross pay less the deductions taken from the employee's earnings).
3. Maintenance of payroll deduction records.
4. Writing of the payroll.
5. Preparation of employees' earnings statements.
6. Issuance of paychecks or pay envelopes or the electronic transfer of payroll funds.
7. Reconciliation of payroll bank account.
8. Distribution of labor costs.
9. Recording of payroll in the general accounting books.
10. Preparation of reports for employees, government agencies, unions, and management.

The methods involved in each of the procedures vary from company to company depending upon the type of payroll accounting system used. The nature of the payroll records depends to a great extent on the size of the work force and the degree to which the record keeping is automated. Throughout this course, manual payroll accounting systems are described and illustrated. Automated accounting systems are described in Appendix B of this text.

In most payroll systems—manual or automated—there are two basic records: the payroll register and the employee's earnings record.

Payroll Register

The *payroll register* is a multicolumn form used to assemble and summarize the data needed at the end of each payroll period. It is a detailed listing of a company's complete payroll for that particular pay period. Thus, the payroll register lists all the employees who earned remuneration, the amount of remuneration, the deductions, and the net amount paid. The information provided in the payroll register is used primarily to meet the requirements of the Fair Labor Standards Act. However, the register is also used to provide information for recording the payroll entries in the journal and to prepare reports required by other federal, state, and local laws.

One form of payroll register is shown in Illustration 1-7 on page 17. Another form, which is used in the Continuing Payroll Problem at the end of Units 2 through 6, is shown in the fold-out at the back of this book. Further discussion of the payroll register is presented in Unit 6.

CHANGE OF STATUS

Please enter the following change(s) as of January 1, 19--

Name Mary L. Mosworth — Clock or Payroll No. 418

Soc. Sec. Number 293-77-1388

FROM

Job	Dept.	Shift	Rate
Payroll Clerk	Acct.	---	$1,500

TO

Job	Dept.	Shift	Rate
Accounting Clerk (A)	Acct.	---	$1,750

REASON FOR CHANGE:

- ☐ Hired
- ☐ Re-hired
- ☒ Promotion
- ☐ Demotion
- ☐ Transfer
- ☐ Merit Increase
- ☐ Length of Service Increase
- ☐ Re-evaluation of Existing Job
- ☐ Resignation
- ☐ Retirement
- ☐ Layoff
- ☐ Discharge

☐ Leave of Absence to ____________ Date

Other reason or explanation: ____________

AUTHORIZED BY Margaret T. Johnson APPROVED BY E. J. Dunn

Prepare in triplicate: (1) Human Resources (2) Payroll (3) Employee's Department

Illustration 1-6. Change of Status Form

Employee's Earnings Record

In addition to the information contained in the payroll register, businesses are required to provide more complete information about the accumulated earnings of each employee. For that reason, it is necessary to keep a separate payroll record on each employee—the *employee's earnings record*. This earnings record is kept for each employee whose wages are recorded in the payroll register. Each payday, after the information has been recorded in the payroll register, the information for each employee is transferred, or posted, to the employee's earnings record.

The employee's earnings record provides the information needed to prepare periodic reports required by the withholding tax laws, the FICA tax law, and state unemployment or disability laws. Employers also use the employee's earnings record in preparing *Form W-2, Wage and Tax Statement*. This form is used by the employer to report the amount of wages paid each worker in the course of the trade or business of the employer. An example of the employee's earnings record is shown in Illustration 1-8. A more detailed discussion of the preparation and use of the earnings record is presented in Unit 6.

PAYROLL REGISTER

FOR WEEK ENDING January 19 19--

No.		Name	Total Hours Worked	Regular Earnings Hrs.	Regular Earnings Rate	Regular Earnings Amount	Overtime Earnings Hrs.	Overtime Earnings Rate	Overtime Earnings Amount	Total Earnings	Deductions FICA Tax	Deductions Fed. Income Tax	Deductions State Income Tax	Net Paid Check No.	Net Paid Amount
1	403	Springs, Carl A.	40	40	4.15	166.00				166.00	12.70	22.00	2.67	504	128.63
2	409	Wiegand, Sue T.	42	40	S	192.00	2	7.20	14.40	206.40	15.79	9.00	2.76	505	178.85
3	412	O'Neill, John B.	38	38	4.50	171.00				171.00	13.08	17.00	5.10	506	135.82
4	413	Bass, Marie S.	44	40	5.00	200.00	4	7.50	30.00	230.00	17.60	2.00	4.67	507	205.73
5	418	Mosworth, M.L.	41	40	S	403.85	1	15.15	15.15	419.00	32.05	53.00	13.14	508	320.81
47		Totals				3,895.75			317.20	4,212.95	322.29	808.00	124.24		2,958.42

Illustration 1-7. Payroll Register

EMPLOYEE'S EARNINGS RECORD

Week	Week Ending	Total Hours Worked	Regular Earnings Hrs.	Regular Earnings Rate	Regular Earnings Amount	Overtime Earnings Hrs.	Overtime Earnings Rate	Overtime Earnings Amount	Total Earnings	Deductions FICA	Deductions Fed. Inc. Tax	Deductions State Inc. Tax	Not Paid Check No.	Not Paid Amount	Cumulative Earnings
1	1/5	40	40	S	403.85				403.85	30.89	51.00	12.74	419	309.22	403.85
2	1/12	42	40	S	403.85	2	15.15	30.30	434.15	33.21	56.00	13.94	463	331.00	838.00
3	1/19	41	40	S	403.85	1	15.15	15.15	419.00	32.05	53.00	13.14	508	320.81	1,257.00

Sex	Department	Occupation	State Employed	S.S. Account No.	Name-Last First Middle	No. W/H Allow.
F ✓ M	ACCTG.	ACCTG. CLERK (A)	WV	293-77-1388	MOSWORTH, MARY LOUISE	1 Marital Status S

Illustration 1-8. Employee's Earnings Record

Paycheck

When employees are paid by check, a check is written for each worker, using as the amount of net pay that figure appearing in the Net Paid column of the payroll register. Most paychecks, such as that depicted in Illustration 1-9, carry a stub, or voucher, that shows the earnings and deductions. Paying workers in cash, by check, or by means of an electronic transfer of payroll funds is explained in the following unit.

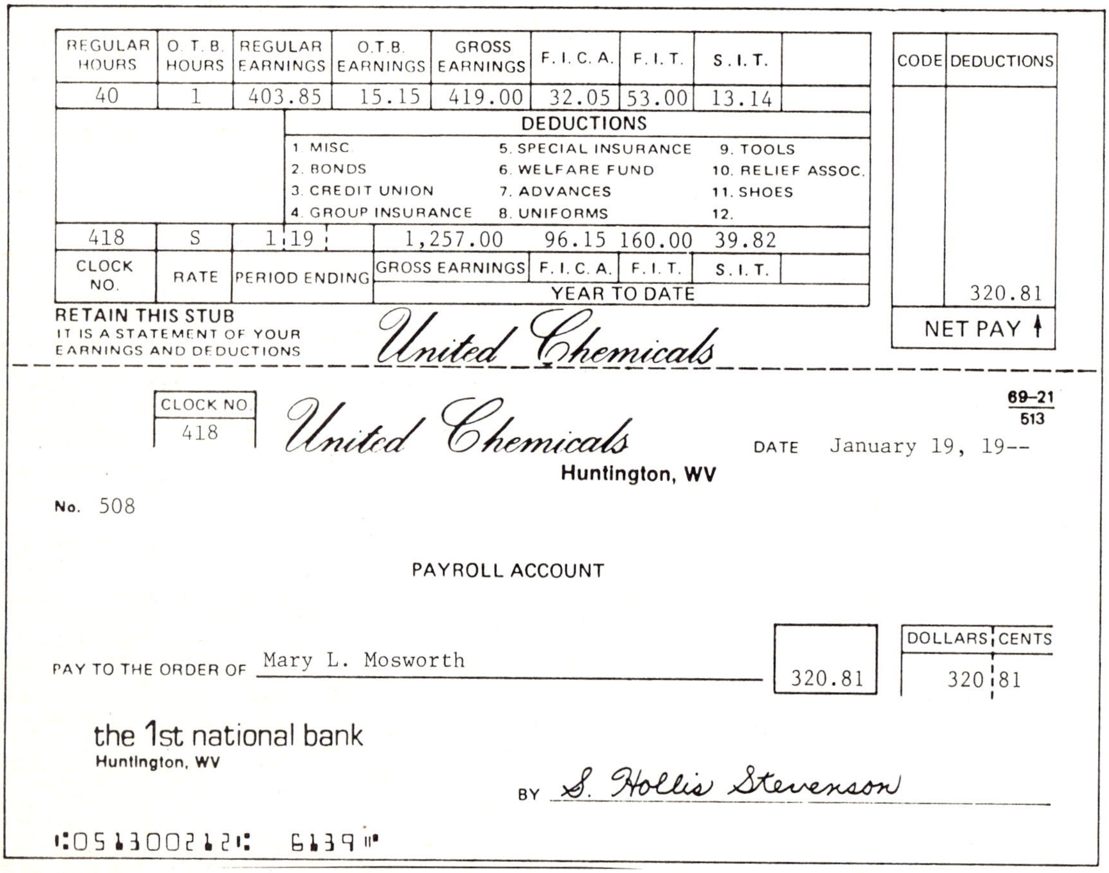

REGULAR HOURS	O. T. B. HOURS	REGULAR EARNINGS	O.T.B. EARNINGS	GROSS EARNINGS	F. I. C. A.	F. I. T.	S. I. T.	
40	1	403.85	15.15	419.00	32.05	53.00	13.14	

DEDUCTIONS

1. MISC.	5. SPECIAL INSURANCE	9. TOOLS
2. BONDS	6. WELFARE FUND	10. RELIEF ASSOC.
3. CREDIT UNION	7. ADVANCES	11. SHOES
4. GROUP INSURANCE	8. UNIFORMS	12.

CLOCK NO.	RATE	PERIOD ENDING	GROSS EARNINGS	F. I. C. A.	F. I. T.	S. I. T.
418	S	1 19	1,257.00	96.15	160.00	39.82
			YEAR TO DATE			

CODE	DEDUCTIONS
	320.81
NET PAY ↑	

RETAIN THIS STUB
IT IS A STATEMENT OF YOUR EARNINGS AND DEDUCTIONS

United Chemicals

CLOCK NO. 418

United Chemicals
Huntington, WV

DATE January 19, 19--

69–21
513

No. 508

PAYROLL ACCOUNT

PAY TO THE ORDER OF Mary L. Mosworth 320.81

DOLLARS	CENTS
320	81

the 1st national bank
Huntington, WV

BY *S. Hollis Stevenson*

⑆0513002121⑆ 6139⑈

Illustration 1-9. Paycheck with Stub Showing Current and Year-to-Date Earnings and Deductions

GLOSSARY

Affirmative action plan—a formal plan that prescribes a specific program to eliminate, limit, or prevent discriminatory treatment on the basis of race, ethnic group, and sex.

Application for employment form—personnel record which gives the applicant an opportunity to provide complete information as to personal qualifications, training, and experience.

Change in payroll rate form—document used to notify the proper departments of a change in the employee's rate of remuneration.

Disability benefits—payments to employees who are absent from their jobs because of illness, accident, or disease not arising out of their employment.

Employee history record—continuous record of the relationship between the employer and the employee.

Employee's earnings record—payroll record for each employee that is used to provide complete information about the accumulated earnings of each employee.

Executive order—regulation issued by the federal government that bans, in employment on government contracts, discrimination based on race, color, religion, sex, or national origin.

Fair employment legislation—laws that deal with discrimination on the basis of age, race, color, religion, sex, or national origin as a condition of employment.

Form W-2, Wage and Tax Statement—form used by the employer to report the amount of wages paid each worker in the course of the trade or business of the employer.

Gross pay—the total regular earnings plus the total overtime earnings.

Hiring notice—form that is sent to the Payroll Department so that new employees are properly added to the payroll.

Income tax—levy on the earnings of most employees that is deducted from their gross pay.

Individual retirement account (IRA)—employee's pension plan which is established and funded by the individual employee.

Investigative consumer report—study done by a consumer reporting agency on a job applicant or current employee concerning the individual's character, general reputation, and mode of living.

Net pay—the total earnings of the employee less the deductions from the earnings.

Payroll accounting system—those procedures and methods relating to the disbursement of pay to employees.

Payroll register—multicolumn form used to assemble and summarize the data needed at the end of each payroll period. It lists all employees who earned remuneration, the amount of remuneration, the deductions, and the net amount paid.

Prehire inquiries—questions asked in the employment interview and on application forms, resumes of experience or education required of an applicant, and any kind of written testing.

Reference inquiry form—document used by the employer to investigate the references given on the application blank by the job applicant.

Remuneration—payment for services rendered, including employee benefits and perquisites of employment such as board, lodging, or other facilities provided the worker.

Requisition for personnel—document submitted by a department head to the Employment Department or the Human Resources Department asking for additional or replacement employees.

Simplified employee pension (SEP) plan—formal plan by means of which employers may make contributions to individual retirement accounts on behalf of their employees.

Unemployment insurance taxes—the source of funds at the state level which are used to provide benefits for unemployed workers.

Vesting—the process of conveying to employees the right to share in a retirement fund in the event they are terminated before the normal retirement age.

Workers' compensation insurance—protection provided employees and their dependents against losses due to injury or death incurred during employment.

QUESTIONS FOR REVIEW

1. Under the FLSA, what information concerning employees' wages earned must be maintained by the employer?
2. Which act sets the minimum wage and what is that wage rate for the end of 1991?
3. What records must the employer who is subject to FLSA keep for white-collar workers who are exempt from federal minimum wage and overtime standards?
4. Under FLSA, what is included in the definition of employees' total remuneration?
5. What types of unfair employment practices are prohibited by the Civil Rights Act of 1964 as amended?
6. What is the purpose of the Age Discrimination in Employment Act (ADEA)?
7. Who pays the social security taxes that are levied by the Federal Insurance Contributions Act?
8. What are the two parts of the health insurance program provided by FICA?
9. What are the tax data requirements that an employer must meet in keeping payroll records that conform to the Federal Income Tax Withholding Law?
10. How are the funds used which are provided by FUTA and SUTA?
11. Who is covered by the Walsh-Healey Public Contracts Act?
12. Explain the concept of vesting.
13. What is the maximum amount of tax-free contributions that an eligible employee can place in his or her IRA account each year?
14. What is the purpose of workers' compensation insurance?
15. List the reasons why adequate personnel records are needed by most medium-size and large businesses.
16. Summarize the procedure that may be followed by the Human Resources Department in hiring new employees.
17. What kinds of information are commonly provided by the jobseeker on the application for employment form?

18. What is the significance of the Civil Rights Act of 1964 and the Age Discrimination in Employment Act in the employer's use of prehire inquiries?
19. What reasons can be advanced for including in the personnel file the records of applicants who were not hired?
20. What obligations are imposed upon the employer by the Fair Credit Reporting Act of 1968?
21. a. What is the purpose of a hiring notice?
    b. What information is usually included in this form?
22. What procedures are usually included in a typical payroll accounting system?
23. What is the purpose of the payroll register?
24. What use is made of the information contained in the employee's earnings record?

QUESTIONS FOR DISCUSSION

1. What personnel records would you suggest for a small retailer with three employees?
2. What kind of problem can be encountered when requesting references from previous employers of job applicants?
3. In staffing their offices, some firms encourage in-house referrals (recommendations of their present employees). What are some possible objections to this practice as a means of obtaining job applicants? What advantages may be realized by the firm that uses in-house referrals?
4. Some companies have every applicant for a job fill out an application blank, even though some are obviously not fitted for the position. Why is this done?
5. The main office of a large bank has an annual turnover of 500 office workers. As an employment officer of this bank, discuss the sources you would use in obtaining replacement employees.
6. Among the questions asked on the application for employment form of Horner Company are the following:
   a. Have you ever worked for Horner Company under another name?
   b. Give the name of your church and list the religious holidays you observe.
   c. Indicate the name of your birthplace.
   d. Are you a citizen of the United States?
   e. Indicate the foreign languages you can read, write, or speak fluently.

   In view of federal and state civil rights laws, do you believe that Horner Company is acting legally or illegally in asking each of the questions listed above?

CASE PROBLEM

Case 1-1 Streamlining Payroll Records

After working in the accounting department of the Brooher Steel Company for the past year, Claire Gieber has been promoted to head payroll clerk. In a recent meeting, the controller of the company, Matthew Watson, tells Gieber that he is very concerned over the time that is being spent in processing the weekly payroll. Top on his list of priorities for her is a review of the entire payroll accounting system and the implementation of any changes that can save the company time and money.

The company's payroll is presently being prepared manually. Earlier this year the company evaluated the use of computers for the processing of its payroll. In this evaluation the purchase and the leasing of a computer, as well as the use of an outside data processing company, were analyzed. In each of these proposals, the cost was considered too high.

Gieber's first step in her investigation is to study the payroll records that are currently used by the company. In reviewing the information presented on the company's three main records (the payroll register, the employee's earnings record, and the paycheck), Gieber finds, that in addition to the usual payroll data, space is provided for recording the following deductions from each weekly gross pay:

FICA tax
Federal income tax
State income tax
Union Dues
Blue Cross/Blue Shield
U.S. savings bonds
Group life insurance

Further, Gieber discovers that the data recorded on each form are, for the most part, exactly the same. Since each of the forms is written individually, most of the data are being separately recorded three times.

In order to alleviate this duplication, Gieber feels that by using carbonless paper (paper that reproduces on the following sheet of paper without the use of carbon paper) for the three records, the data could be entered on all of them at the same time with only one manual writing. However, in order to convert to records made of carbonless paper, the three forms will have to be redesigned so that data recorded on the top record will be correctly lined up on all forms lying below.

Prepare a new format for each of the three payroll records (the payroll register, the employee's earnings record, and the paycheck) that will permit use of a "one-write" manual recording on the carbonless paper. Particular attention should be devoted to the category headings that are listed at the top of each of these payroll records, so that they will be lined up on each sheet. In addition, prepare an instruction sheet on the steps that are to be followed in preparing the weekly payroll. In these instructions, the mechanics of placing the forms in proper sequence and entering the information on the top form should be explained.

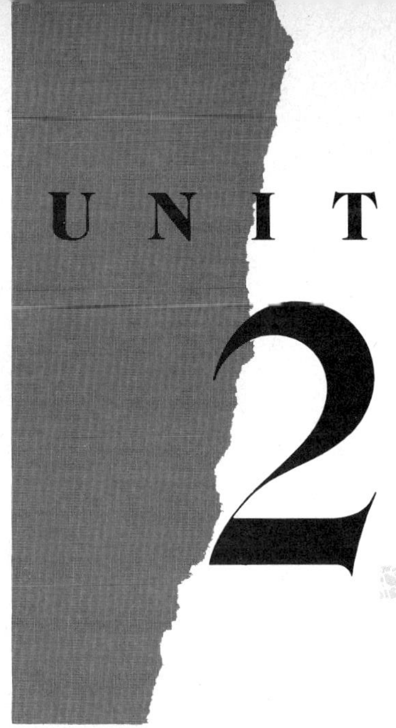

UNIT 2 Computing and Paying Wages and Salaries

GOALS OF THIS UNIT

After completing your study of this unit, you should be able to:

1. Understand the major provisions of the Fair Labor Standards Act that affect: (a) minimum wages, (b) equal pay for equal work regardless of sex, (c) overtime pay, (d) record keeping, and (e) child labor.
2. Distinguish between the employees' *principal* activities and their *preliminary* and *postliminary* activities.
3. Describe the main types of time records—time sheets and time cards—and indicate the kind of payroll data collected on each.
4. Perform the following arithmetic operations:
   a. Convert weekly wage rates to hourly rates.
   b. Convert monthly and annual salary rates to hourly rates.
   c. Calculate regular earnings and overtime earnings to arrive at total gross earnings.
   d. Apply two different methods in calculating overtime payment for pieceworkers.
   e. Calculate earnings under incentive and commission plans.
5. Describe how wages and salaries are paid (a) in cash, (b) by check, and (c) by electronic transfer of funds.

In this unit, we shall investigate the major provisions of the Fair Labor Standards Act and show how to determine the hours worked by employees. In addition, we shall examine in detail the records that are commonly used to record time worked, the major methods of computing salaries and wages, and the methods of paying employees. First, however, let us take a look at some findings revealed by a survey of work schedules in the United States:[1]

1. The number of multiple jobholders—those persons working at more than one job—is increasing.
2. Saturday work is the usual routine for one-fourth of all workers.
3. Work outside the typical daylight hours (usually in the evening) is the usual routine for about one-sixth of full-time workers and one-half of part-time workers.
4. Home-based work of at least 8 hours a week is reported by over 8 million workers, most of whom are full-time employees doing only a small part of their work at home.
5. About 12% of wage and salary workers with full-time jobs vary the start and end of their workday.

[1] Paul O. Flaim, "Work Schedules of Americans: An Overview of New Findings," *Monthly Labor Review* (November 1986): 3-6. Shirley J. Smith, "The Growing Diversity of Work Schedules," *Monthly Labor Review* (November 1986): 7-9. This issue contains a special section with several articles dealing with "Time Spent at Work."

6. More than half of all nonfarm wage and salary workers and nearly two-thirds of those working full time report they work exactly 40 hours each week.
7. Nearly three-quarters of the work force and more than four-fifths of those employed full time report schedules of 5 working days.

Even though we find that the 40-hour, 5-day workweek is the most common work schedule, the schedules of American workers have been changing and becoming increasingly diverse. To improve declining productivity, to decrease job dissatisfaction, and to reduce absenteeism, many firms are investigating alternative work schedules such as those briefly described in Illustration 2-1.

FAIR LABOR STANDARDS ACT

The Fair Labor Standards Act (FLSA), commonly known as the Federal Wage and Hour Law, contains provisions and standards concerning minimum wages, equal pay for equal work regardless of sex, overtime pay, record keeping, and child labor. The act is administered by the Wage and Hour Division of the U.S. Department of Labor. Since its enactment in 1938, the FLSA has been amended several times to broaden the definition of employees and enterprises that are covered by the law.

Type of Work Schedule	Description	Example(s)	Advantages	Disadvantages
Compressed Workweek	The usual number of full-time hours are worked in fewer than 5 days (the regular workweek).	4/40 workweek (4 workdays during the week, with each day 10 hours in duration).	1) Improves employee morale by providing more flexible leisure time, thus enabling workers to schedule commitments such as dental appointments outside work time. 2) Boosts productivity. 3) Reduces absenteeism.	1) Employees not available full workweek or at critical times. 2) Nonlabor costs (heating and cooling) increase as the result of longer hours of operation. 3) Employees become more fatigued. 4) Increases stress on supervisors.
Staggered Work Schedule	Fixed work schedule under which groups of employees arrive at their workplaces at different times and work a predetermined number of hours each workday.	Group A works 7:30 a.m. to 3:30 p.m., overlapping with Group B, which works 10:00 a.m. to 6:00 p.m.	1) Alleviates commuter tie-ups. 2) Reduces waiting time for elevators and lessens lobby congestion.	1) Increased scheduling problems. 2) Nonlabor costs increase as the result of longer hours of operation.
Flexible Work Schedule	Workday is divided into *core time* (those hours during which all employees must be present for work) and *flexible time* (those hours from which employees choose their arrival and departure times); also known as *flextime*.	In a workday with a span of 12 hours, employees working a regular 8-hour shift must be on the job during the peak workload hours 9:00 a.m. to 3:00 p.m. (core time). During the hours 6:00 a.m. to 9:00 a.m. and 3:00 p.m. to 6:00 p.m. (flexible time), employees select their arrival and departure times.	1) Improves customer service. 2) Increases employee performance by strengthening motivation and improving employee morale and attitudes toward jobs. 3) Eases rush-hour traffic peaks. 4) Decreases tardiness. 5) Attracts and retains employees having outside commitments, such as child care and elder care.	1) Added need for managers and supervisors to schedule and plan the work flow and ensure the coverage of critical functions. 2) Possible lack of supervision during all hours of work. 3) Increased nonlabor costs associated with more hours of operation.

Illustration 2-1. Types of Work Schedules (Continued)

Type of Work Schedule	Description	Example(s)	Advantages	Disadvantages
Job Sharing	One full-time job is shared by two people who generally split their working hours, job responsibilities, and employee benefits.	Employee A works from 8:00 a.m. to 12:00 p.m. Employee B works on the same job from 12:00 p.m. to 4:00 p.m.	1) Strengthens employee motivation by allowing larger blocks of leisure time, thus accommodating persons having outside commitments. 2) Improves employee attitudes toward their jobs and the organization, thus boosting employee morale. 3) Reduces turnover and increases job performance.	1) Increased costs of employee benefits such as group health insurance, social security taxes, and on-site child care. 2) Increases training costs. 3) Supervisory difficulties in relating to two different persons in one job, with possibility of communication breakdowns. 4) Possible conflicts of responsibility between two workers holding same job.
Telecommuting	Employees work off site, such as in their homes, rather than in offices.	Data-entry personnel, secretaries, typists, programmers, researchers, forms processors.	1) Working during off hours improves turnaround time and increases around-the-clock use of computer facilities. 2) Reduces workers' costs and problems associated with day care and baby-sitting services. 3) Offers productive outlet to persons who have had their mobility restricted by illness or accident but who are otherwise able and willing to work.	1) Difficulties in effectively managing and supervising telecommuters. 2) Loss of information because of unreliable communication units linking off-site units to firm's central computer. 3) Off-site workers feel socially isolated and thus unable to build rapport with peer office workers.
Permanent Part-Time Employment	Regular employment (not temporary or casual) is carried out during working hours that are shorter than normal.	Telemarketers who sell by phone several hours each day, and employees staffing departments where workload is not sufficient to warrant full-time staffs.	1) Appeals to workers attending school and those having family responsibilities and physical handicaps. 2) Part-timers may obtain job security and employee rights that full-time employees have.	Increased administrative problems related to managing and supervising a predominantly part-time staff.
Work Sharing	Employees work a shorter than normal week, have their salaries reduced accordingly, and receive partial state unemployment compensation benefits for lost days' pay.	In the dozen or so states having unemployment insurance programs that legally allow workers to receive partial temporary unemployment benefits in the event workers suffer moderate reductions in their work hours.	1) Enables employer to reduce employee hours rather than lay off workers. 2) Employer realizes savings on severance pay and other labor turnover costs.	1) Possible lack of job dedication by employees. 2) Employers may be faced with increased unemployment insurance benefit charges.

Illustration 2-1. Types of Work Schedules (Concluded)

Coverage

The FLSA provides for two bases of coverage—enterprise coverage and individual employee coverage.

Enterprise Coverage. Under *enterprise coverage,* all employees of an enterprise are covered if:

1. At least two employees are engaged in interstate commerce or in producing goods for interstate commerce. *Interstate commerce* refers to the trade, transportation, or communication among several states or between a state and any place outside that state. Employees are also covered if they handle, sell, or otherwise work on goods or materials that have been moved in or produced for interstate commerce, and
2. The business has annual gross sales of at least $500,000.

Coverage has also been extended, *without regard to annual sales volume,* to those who operate:

1. A hospital.
2. A nursing home.
3. An institution for the mentally ill.
4. A school for mentally or physically handicapped or gifted children.
5. A preschool, elementary, or secondary school.
6. An institution of higher education. (Note that coverage applies to hospitals, institutions, and schools whether or not they are operated for profit.)
7. A public agency.

Family establishments, often referred to as "mom and pop stores," are not considered part of the enterprise coverage under the FLSA. Thus, if the only regular employees of an establishment are the owner and his or her parent, spouse, child, or other immediate family member, the establishment is exempt from FLSA coverage.

Individual Employee Coverage. Under *individual employee coverage,* a worker is covered by the FLSA if the employee is either engaged in interstate commerce or in producing goods for such commerce. Employment in a fringe occupation closely related and directly essential to the production of goods for interstate commerce is sufficient to constitute engagement in the production of goods for interstate commerce.

Coverage depends on the activities of the individual employee and not on the work of fellow employees, nor the nature of the employer's business, nor the character of the industry as a whole. Thus, we find that even though a business does not meet the enterprise coverage test, it must pay FLSA wages to those workers eligible for individual coverage.

EXAMPLE:

James Rineheart works for a small manufacturing firm that has an annual sales volume of $370,000. Thus, the firm does not meet the $500,000 volume-of-sales requirement for enterprise coverage. However, Rineheart is individually covered since he operates machinery used to produce goods for interstate commerce.

Individual employee coverage has also been extended to *domestics* (maids, day workers, housekeepers, chauffeurs, cooks, full-time babysitters, gardeners, etc.) in private households. To be covered, the domestic must either receive cash wages of at least $50 from an employer during a calendar quarter, or work a total of 8 hours during a workweek, whether for one or more employers.

Wages

Under the FLSA, *wages* includes the remuneration or compensation paid employees—salaries, commissions, vacation pay, overtime pay, severance or dismissal pay, earned bonuses, and any other amounts agreed upon by the employer and the employee. Wages also includes the reasonable cost or fair value to the employer of board, lodging, or other facilities ordinarily furnished the employee.

You will find that the terms wages and salaries are commonly used interchangeably. However, the term *wage* refers to remuneration paid on an hourly, weekly, or piecework basis. The remuneration paid on a monthly, *biweekly* (every two weeks), *semimonthly* (twice a month), or yearly basis is ordinarily called *salary.* In either event, the employer agrees to pay the employees a certain amount for their time, whether it is by the hour, the week, the month, or the year, or based on output under a piece-rate system.

Minimum Wages

The FLSA of 1938 established a minimum wage of 25¢ an hour for a straight-time workweek of 44 hours. Following the first year of operation, the law provided for graduated rises in the minimum-wage figure and graduated decreases in the maximum weekly straight-time hours. Two years later when the standard workweek had decreased to 40 hours, the minimum wage had risen to 30¢. Several years later the minimum hourly wage rose to 40¢. With the objective of improving the purchasing power of covered workers, succeeding amendments to the FLSA increased the minimum hourly rate.

In 1989, the FLSA was amended to increase the minimum hourly wage as follows:

1. *Beginning April 1, 1990,* the minimum hourly wage was raised to $3.80. This was a 45¢ an hour increase over the $3.35 minimum wage that had prevailed since 1981.
2. *Beginning April 1, 1991,* the minimum hourly wage increases to $4.25.

Minimum Wage for Trainees. The Minimum Wage Law of 1989 also requires that *trainees* be paid minimum wages under the following conditions:

1. The subminimum training wage was set at not less than $3.35 an hour beginning April 1, 1990.
2. The training wage is available only to individuals between the ages of 16 through 19 who are entering the labor market for the first time.
3. Eligible workers may receive the training wage for a period of 90 cumulative days. A second employer may hire the trainee at the same wage for an additional 90 days, if the employer applies to the Secretary of Labor for a certificate of employment for that worker. Thus, employers may not pay the training wage for a period that exceeds the maximum of 180 days allowed for training.
4. The number of hours worked by the employees receiving training wages may not exceed one-fourth of the total hours that all workers are employed in an establishment during any one month.
5. By April 1, 1991, trainees will receive a minimum hourly wage of $3.6125, which, when rounded, by regulation is $3.61.
6. The 90-day training wage provisions are set to expire no later than April 1, 1993.

Paying Other Workers Less Than the Minimum Wage. Under certain conditions, we may find that wages lower than the minimum wage are paid some employees.

EXAMPLES:

---

1. **Retail or service establishments and farms may employ full-time students at 85% of the minimum wage.**
2. **Institutions of higher education may employ their own full-time students at 85% of the minimum wage.**
3. **Student-learners may be employed at 75% of the minimum wage if they are participating in a bona fide vocational training program conducted by an accredited school.**
4. **Persons whose earning capacity is impaired by age, physical or mental deficiency, or injury may be employed at special minimum wage rates. However, a certificate authorizing employment at such rates must first be obtained. The handicapped workers are entitled to the full benefits of the law, which requires premium pay for overtime hours and equal pay for equal work regardless of sex.**

Tips

A *tip* (to insure promptness) is a gift or gratuity given by a customer in recognition of some service performed for him or her. A *tipped employee* is one who is engaged in an occupation in which tips of more than $30 a month are customarily and regularly received.

An employer may consider, within prescribed limits, the tips received by a tipped employee as part of the employee's wages. During the year beginning April 1, 1990, an employer could credit up to 45% of a tipped employee's minimum wage as coming from tips actually received. After March 31, 1991, the tip credit percentage increases to 50%, at which time a tipped employee will have to be paid a minimum hourly wage of $2.13.

EXAMPLE:

In July, 1991, Barbara Rivera, a hair stylist, is paid $120 plus tips for a 40-hour workweek. The weekly wage paid Rivera is $50 less than the minimum wage for a 40-hour workweek ($4.25 x 40 = $170). Rivera regularly receives at least $250 in tips each week. Thus, each week her employer claims a credit of $50 from her tips in order to meet the weekly minimum wage requirement of $170. The maximum weekly credit that could have been available to the employer is $85 ($170 x 50%). Therefore, her employer could have paid Rivera as little as $85 a week and not have violated the provisions of the FLSA.

If, after March 31, 1991, the tips received by a worker are less than 50% of the minimum wage rate, the amount received is the maximum permissible tip credit. In such a case, the employer must pay the balance so that a combination of the tips received and of the wages paid in cash (or in the form of board, lodging, or other facilities) equals the minimum wage.

EXAMPLE:

In November, 1991, Bill Hunt, a waiter, is paid a weekly wage of $85 plus tips for a 40-hour workweek. The weekly wage paid Hunt is $85 less than the minimum wage requirement for a 40-hour workweek ($170 – $85). Over the past few months, Hunt has received tips totaling $80 each week. Each week his employer claims a credit for the

tips that Hunt receives. However, the amount of tips received, $80, is less than the 50% tip credit taken ($170 x 50% = $85). Thus, the maximum credit that the employer may take is $80, the tips received by Hunt. The employer must pay the balance, $5, along with the weekly wage of $85 so that the combined wages paid and the tip credit taken equal $170.

The rules for the reporting of tips by employees and employers are discussed in Unit 3.

Workweek

The FLSA defines a *workweek* as a fixed and regularly recurring period of 168 hours—7 consecutive 24-hour periods. The individual employee's workweek is the statutory or contract number of hours to be worked regularly during that period. The workweek may begin on any day of the week and need not coincide with the calendar week. An employer may establish the same workweek for the business operations as a whole or assign different workweeks to individual workers or groups of workers.

An employer may change the day a workweek begins if the change is intended to be permanent and not to evade the overtime pay requirements of the FLSA. If, however, the workweek is fixed by union contract, the employer's right to change the workweek depends upon the wording in the contract. Each workweek is considered to stand alone, and the overtime hours worked in one week may not be shifted to another workweek. Thus, each workweek is a separate unit for the purpose of computing overtime pay.

Overtime Hours and Overtime Pay

The FLSA states that overtime pay is required for all hours worked in excess of 40 in a workweek. Under the law the overtime pay required is time and one half the employee's regular hourly rate of pay. The regular hourly rate of pay at which the worker is employed may in no event be less than the statutory minimum. If the employee's regular rate of pay is higher than the statutory minimum, overtime compensation must be computed at a rate not less than one and one-half times such higher rate.

EXAMPLE:

Marcia Averre's regular rate of pay is $4.40 an hour. Her overtime rate must be at least $4.40 x 1.5, or $6.60, an hour.

Over the years, as the result of union contracts, hours beyond a certain number each day have become known as overtime. Work on Saturdays, Sundays, or on the sixth and seventh days of the workweek, holidays, and days of rest is thought of as overtime because this work often commands overtime pay. The FLSA, however, generally requires no overtime pay for daily hours worked in excess of any given number or for work on Saturdays, Sundays, holidays, or other special days.

Exceptions to Overtime Hours and Overtime Pay Provisions. An exception to the preceding statement regarding overtime hours and overtime pay is available for *hospital employees.* Hospitals are authorized to enter into an agreement with their employees under which a 14-day period, rather than a workweek, becomes the basis for computing overtime pay. Employees with whom such an agreement exists must receive overtime pay at not less than one and one-half times their regular hourly rate for hours worked in excess of 8 hours in any workday or in excess of 80 hours in a 14-day period, whichever is the greater number of overtime hours. Although employers have the option of using the normal workweek or the 14-day period, they cannot change from one method to the other arbitrarily.

EXAMPLE:

Pam Valenti, a lab technician at Metro Hospital, agreed that a 14-day period would be used to figure her overtime pay. She works 12 hours in one day during the period and 8 hours in each of the 9 other days during the period, a total of 84 hours. Valenti is entitled to 80 hours of straight-time pay and 4 hours of overtime pay for the 14-day period.

Let's say that Valenti worked only 7 hours in each of the 9 other days during the period, or a total of 75 hours. In this case, she would be entitled to 71 hours of straight-time pay and 4 hours of overtime pay for the 14-day period.

The minimum wage legislation of 1989 provides an exception for *employees who are receiving remedial education.* Under this law, employees who are receiving remedial education offered by their employers would be permitted to work up to 10 hours overtime each week without receiving overtime compensation. To qualify as *remedial* education, it must be provided to employees who lack a high school diploma or educational attainment at the eighth-grade level. The remedial training, which does not include training for a specific job, must be designed to provide reading and other basic skills at an eighth-grade level or below.

Compensatory Time Off. The employees of a state, a political subdivision of a state, or an interstate governmental agency are allowed use of compensatory time off in lieu of overtime compensation. Thus, we find that employees whose work includes public safety, emergency response, or seasonal activities are allowed to accumulate compensatory time off up to 480 hours. (The 480-hour limit represents 320 hours of overtime actually worked at the one and one-half overtime rate.) These employees may "bank" their hours and use them later as time off at time and one-half during the course of their employment.

Employees whose work does not include the preceding activities are allowed to bank 240 hours for compensatory time off. (The 240-hour limit represents 160 hours of overtime actually worked at the one and one-half overtime rate.) Upon reaching the 480- or 240-hour limit, an employee must receive either cash for additional hours of overtime worked or use some compensatory time before receiving further overtime compensation in the form of compensatory time off. Note that not all 480 or 240 hours have to be accrued before compensatory time off may be used.

State and local government employers must continue to pay their employees not less than the statutory minimum wage. (Note that employees of private employers or of the federal government are not affected by the amendments.) Volunteers of state and local governments are exempted from both the wage and hour provisions of the FLSA.

Equal Pay Law

The Equal Pay Act, effective in 1964, amended the FLSA to require that men and women performing equal work must receive equal pay. Any employer having workers subject to the minimum pay provisions of the Wage and Hour Law is subject to the Equal Pay Law. The law applies to *any establishment* wherein such workers are employed. The equal-pay requirements also apply to white-collar workers, including outside salespersons, even though they are exempt from the minimum wage standards.

The Equal Pay Law states that an employer must not discriminate by paying wages to employees of one sex at a lower rate than is paid the opposite sex for equal work on jobs that require equal skill, effort, and responsibility, and that are performed under similar working conditions. However, wage differentials between sexes are allowable if the differences are based on a seniority system, a merit system, a payment plan that measures earnings by quantity or quality of production, or any factor other than sex. If there is an unlawful pay differential between men and women, the employer is required to raise the lower rate to equal the higher rate.

Exemptions from FLSA Requirements

Exempt employees are those workers who are exempt from some, or all, of the FLSA requirements such as minimum wages, equal pay, and overtime pay. As you see in Illustration 2-2 on page 30, many workers are exempt from one or more of these requirements.

Some workers, such as executive, administrative, and professional employees, are exempt from the minimum wage and overtime pay provisions of the FLSA if certain tests regarding their duties and salaries are satisfied. In order for an employee to be granted this exemption as an *executive*, all of the following requirements must be met:

1. The primary duty must be that of managing an enterprise or department or subdivision thereof.
2. The employee must customarily and regularly direct the work of two or more full-time employees.
3. The employee can hire and fire and suggest changes in the status of other employees.
4. The employee must customarily and regularly exercise discretionary powers.
5. The nonexempt work must be no more than 20% of the executive's weekly hours worked, or 40% in the case of executives of retail or service establishments.
6. The employee's salary must be at least $155 a week exclusive of board, lodging, or other facilities.

A shorter test of exemption status may be applied to higher salaried employees who earn $250 or more each week. In this test, most highly paid employees need meet only the first two requirements listed above so long as their weekly salary (exclusive of board, lodging, or other facilities) is $250 or more.

Employees *who are paid by the hour* are not exempt from the minimum wage and overtime pay requirements and thus do not qualify for the salary test even if their total weekly compensation exceeds the limits specified.

Child-Labor Restrictions

A business is prohibited from the interstate shipment of its goods or services if it employs child labor unlawfully. Under the FLSA, the Secretary of Labor issues regulations that restrict the employment of individuals under the age of 18. The restrictions on child employment are divided into nonfarm occupations and agricultural occupations.

Employee Job Description	Minimum Wage Exemption	Equal Pay Exemption	Full Overtime Exemption
Agricultural employees.			X
Agricultural workers who are members of the employer's immediate family.	X	X	X
Air carrier employees if the carrier is subject to Title II of the Railway Labor Act.			X
Amusement or recreational establishment employees, provided the business has seasonal peaks.	X	X	X
Announcers, news editors, and chief engineers of radio or television stations in small communities.			X
Babysitters (casual) and companions to ill or aged persons unable to care for themselves.	X	X	X
Drivers and drivers' helpers who make local deliveries and are paid on a trip-rate or similar basis following a plan approved by the government.			X
Executive, administrative, and professional employees including teachers and academic administrative personnel in schools.	X		X
Fruit and vegetable employees who are engaged in the local transportation of these items or of workers employed or to be employed in the harvesting of fruits or vegetables.			X
Household domestic service employees who reside in the household.			X
Motion picture theater employees.			X
Motor carrier employees if the carrier is subject to regulation by the Secretary of Transportation.			X
Newspaper employees if the newspaper is published on a weekly, semiweekly, or daily basis and if the circulation is less than 4,000 copies, with the major circulation in the county of publication or contiguous counties.	X	X	X
Outside sales personnel.	X		X
Railroad, express company, and water carrier employees if the companies are subject to Part I of the Interstate Commerce Act.			X
Salespersons for automobile, truck, or farm implement dealers; parts stock clerks or mechanics; salespersons for boat, trailer, or aircraft dealers.			X
Taxicab drivers.			X

Illustration 2-2. Exemption Status of Workers under FLSA

Nonfarm Occupations. The basic minimum age for most jobs is 16 years. This is the minimum age for work in manufacturing and processing jobs or in any other occupations except those that are declared by the Secretary of Labor as hazardous for minors under 18. Some of the jobs classified as hazardous include occupations in: plants manufacturing or storing explosives, coal mines, operation of power-driven woodworking machines, slaughtering and meat-packing establishments, excavation work, and wrecking and demolition of buildings. In some hazardous occupations, the employment of a child under 18 as an apprentice, student learner, or trainee is permitted under narrowly restricted conditions.

Children under 16 years of age may *not* be employed in manufacturing, mining, or processing of goods; operating or tending power-driven machinery other than office machines; public messenger service; and jobs (other than office or sales work) connected with the transportation of persons or property by rail, highway, air, water, pipeline, or other means; warehousing and storage; communications and public utilities; construction, including demolition and repair.

Within certain limits 14- and 15-year-olds may be employed in retail, food service, and gasoline service establishments. For example, this age group may be employed in office and clerical work, including the operation of office machines; cashiering; selling; price marking and tagging by hand or by machine; errand and delivery work; kitchen work and other work involved in preparing and serving food and beverages; dispensing gasoline and oil; and car cleaning. The employment of minors between the ages of 14 and 16 is permitted only to the extent that it will not interfere with their schooling, health, and well-being. In addition, the following conditions must be met:

1. All work must be performed outside school hours.

2. There is a maximum 3-hour day and 18-hour week when school is in session (8 hours and 40 hours when not in session).
3. All work must be performed between 7 a.m. and 7 p.m. (9 p.m. during the summer).

Agricultural Occupations. The employment of children under age 12 is generally prohibited in agricultural occupations (1) during hours when school is in session, (2) outside school hours on farms, including conglomerates, that used more than 500 man-days of labor in any quarter of the preceding calendar year, and (3) outside school hours on noncovered farms without parental consent. However, children may work on farms owned or operated by their parents or guardians. Children 10 and 11 years old may be employed as hand harvest laborers outside school hours for up to eight weeks between June 1 and October 15, provided a number of strict conditions are met by the employer.

Children aged 12 and 13 are permitted to be employed only during hours when school is not in session provided there is parental consent or the employment is on a farm where the parents are employed.

Children aged 14 and 15 may be employed, but only during hours when school is not in session. No child under the age of 16 may be employed in a farm occupation that is declared hazardous, such as operating large tractors, corn pickers, cotton pickers, grain combines, and feed grinders.

Certificate of Age. Employers cannot be charged with having violated the child-labor restrictions of the law if they have on file an officially executed *certificate of age* which shows that the minor has reached the stipulated minimum age. In most states a state employment or age certificate, issued by the Federal Wage and Hour Division or by a state agency, is accepted as proof of age.

In some states a state or federal certificate of age, a state employment certificate, or a work permit may not be available. In such cases, the employer may rely on any one of the following documents as evidence of age for minor employees:

1. Birth certificate (or attested transcript thereof) or a signed statement of the recorded date and place of birth issued by a registrar of vital statistics or other officer charged with the duty of recording births.
2. Record of baptism (or attested transcript thereof) showing the date of birth of the minor.
3. Statement on the census records of the Bureau of Indian Affairs and signed by an administrative representative thereof showing the name and date and place of the minor's birth.

The employer should maintain a copy of the document or indicate in the payroll records which document was checked to verify the minor's age.

Penalties

The U.S. Government may bring civil or criminal actions against employers who violate the FLSA. Employers who willfully violate the wage and hour provisions of the law or the wage orders fixed by the Administrator of the Wage and Hour Division of the Department of Labor will be prosecuted and will be subject to a fine of not more than $10,000, or imprisonment for up to six months, or both. However, no person may be imprisoned for a first offense violation. If an imposed fine goes unpaid, however, the courts have the power to order imprisonment as an incident to the nonpayment. Violators of the child-labor provisions of the Act are subject to fines up to $1,000 for each violation.

Payroll managers should read the Fair Labor Standards Act and its amendments very carefully. If there is any question whether their companies are governed by the provisions of the law, managers should consult a representative of the Wage and Hour Division.

Areas Not Covered by the FLSA

As we saw earlier, the FLSA does not require employers to pay extra wages for work on Saturday, Sunday, or holidays. It does not require vacation, holiday, or severance pay; nor does it limit the number of hours of work for persons 16 years of age or over, as long as the overtime pay provisions are met.

In addition, the law does not require the employer to give employees the day off on holidays, nor to give them vacations. If the employee does work on a holiday, the employer is not required to pay the employee time and one-half. Thus, holidays, like Sundays, are treated the same as any other day. Whether time off is granted or overtime rates are paid depends on the employment agreement.

DETERMINING THE EMPLOYEE'S WORKING TIME

To avoid paying for time not actually spent on the job and to eliminate payment for unnecessary overtime work, we must know what types of employee activities should and should not be counted as working time under the law. Generally the hours that must be counted as working time include all the time that employees are actually at work or are required to be on duty.

A distinction must be made between an employee's principal activities and the preliminary and postliminary activities.

Principal Activities

The *principal activities* of employees are those tasks they are required to perform and include any work of consequence performed for the employer. Principal activities include those that are indispensable to the performance of productive work and those that are an integral part of a principal activity.

EXAMPLE:

Ted Jambro is a lathe operator who oils and cleans his machines at the beginning of each workday and installs new cutting tools. These activities performed by Jambro are part of his principal activity.

The test of compensability, with respect to principal activities, requires that there be physical or mental exertion, controlled or required by the employer and performed for the employer's benefit.

Clothes-Changing Time and Wash-Up. Because of the nature of their work, some employees are required to change clothes or to wash on the employer's premises. Statutes or ordinances may also require clothes changing or washing. When employees spend time in changing clothes or washing on the employer's premises, this time is regarded as part of their principal activities. However, even where the clothes changing or wash-up is required by the nature of the job or by law, it may be excluded from time worked either expressly or by custom and practice under a collective bargaining contract.

Travel Time. The time spent by employees in traveling to and from work need be counted as time worked only if contract, custom, or practice so requires. In some situations, however, travel time between home and work is counted as time worked.

EXAMPLE:

Lisa Rubini receives an emergency call outside her regular working hours and is required to travel a substantial distance to perform a job away from her usual work site for one of her employer's customers. The travel time is counted as time worked.

Also, if an employee who regularly works at a fixed location is given a special one-day work assignment in another city, the travel time is counted as time worked.

When travel is performed during the workday as part of an employee's principal activities, the travel time is treated as time worked.

EXAMPLE:

Reba Ferguson travels throughout the city from job site to job site during her working hours, 9 a.m. to 5 p.m., Mondays through Fridays. Such travel time is counted as part of her time worked.

Occasionally Ferguson is required to travel between workdays from one city to another. Her travel time is counted as working time when the hours involved correspond to her regular working hours, even though the hours may occur on days that are not normally her working days. The time spent in travel outside these regular working hours is not counted as time worked, however.

Let's say that Ferguson is sent on a trip that requires traveling on Saturday and Sunday in order to be at a job site the first thing Monday morning. Her travel time on Saturday and Sunday between the hours of 9 a.m. and 5 p.m. is counted as time worked, but travel time before 9 a.m. and after 5 p.m. is not counted.

Rest Periods and Coffee Breaks. The FLSA does not require that an employer give employees a rest period or a coffee break. However, the employer may grant such rest periods voluntarily; or the union contract or municipal or state legislation may require them. In these cases, if the time spent on a rest period is 20 minutes or less, the time must be counted as part of the hours worked. If the rest period is longer than 20 minutes, the compensability for the time depends upon the employee's freedom during that time or upon the provisions of the union contract.

Meal Periods. Bona fide meal periods (not including coffee breaks or snack times) during which the employee is completely relieved from duty are not considered working time. Lunch periods during which the employee is required to perform some duties while eating are not bona fide meal periods.

EXAMPLE:

Virginia Sherr, an office worker, is required to eat at the desk in order to operate the switchboard at lunch time. Sherr must be paid for the lunch period.

Training Sessions. Generally the time spent by employees in attending lectures and meetings for training purposes must be counted as working time.

EXAMPLE:

The working time spent by postal clerks in learning mail-distribution practices and the operation of letter-sorting machines counts as compensable time under the FLSA. The study and training time put in by the employees constitutes compensable work because it is (a) controlled and required by the employer, (b) for the primary benefit of the employer, and (c) an integral and indispensable part of the employees' principal work activities.

However, time spent in training sessions need not be counted as working time if *all* the following conditions are met:

1. Attendance by the employee is voluntary.
2. The employee does not produce any goods or perform any other productive work during the meeting or lecture.
3. The meeting or lecture takes place outside regular working hours.
4. The meeting or lecture is not directly related to the employee's work.

Preliminary and Postliminary Activities

Activities regarded as *preliminary* and *postliminary* need not be counted as time worked unless required by contract or custom. Some examples of activities regarded as preliminary and postliminary are: walking, riding, or traveling to or from the actual place where employees engage in their principal activities; checking in and out at the plant or office and waiting in line to do so; changing clothes for the convenience of the employee; washing up and showering unless directly related to the specific type of work the employee is hired to perform; and waiting in line to receive paychecks.

Absences

The FLSA does not require an employer to pay an employee for hours not worked because of illness. In the case of employees on an hourly wage basis, the time card shows the exact hours worked; and the time off is *not* counted toward the 40 hours for overtime pay purposes even if the employee is paid for the absences.

Employees on a salary basis are frequently paid for a certain number of days of excused absences after they have been employed by their company for a certain length of time. When the employee is absent from work, the department head usually is required to approve the time card for payment of salaries for hours not worked.

Tardiness

We find that employers handle tardiness in many ways. Frequently when an employee is late or leaves early, causing the time clock to print in red, the supervisor must O.K. the time card. Some companies require the employee to sign a special slip indicating the reason for being late or leaving early.

In some cases, time is kept according to the decimal system whereby each hour is divided into units of tens (6 minutes times 10 periods in each hour). An employee who is late 1 through 6 minutes is penalized or "docked" one tenth of an hour. One who is 7 through 12 minutes late is "docked" one fifth of an hour, etc. Many businesses following this procedure claim that when employees are "docked" each one-tenth hour, there is a tendency to reduce tardiness.

Working During Daylight-Saving Time

Under the Uniform Time Act, daylight-saving time is observed in most of the United States and its territories.[2] Daylight-saving time is in effect from the first Sunday in April until the last Sunday in October.

Shift workers on duty when daylight-saving time goes into effect will work an hour less. Giving such workers a full 8 hours' pay causes some questions under the FLSA. The additional hour's pay given to an employee who works a 7-hour shift need not be included in figuring the worker's regular rate of pay for the purpose of any overtime due that week. On the other hand, the extra hour's pay may not be credited toward any overtime compensation due.

EXAMPLE:

John Yetter is a nighttime clerk for a national hotel chain. His schedule requires him to work the first Saturday night in April from 11:00 p.m. to 7:00 a.m. Because daylight-saving time went into effect early Sunday morning, Yetter had to work only 7 hours. He will be paid for 8 hours of work, however. Further, Yetter's employer may not deduct the extra hour's pay from any overtime compensation due.

In the fall, when daylight-saving time ends, an employee who works a 9-hour shift must be paid for

[2] Areas that do not observe daylight-saving time include Arizona, Hawaii, Puerto Rico, Virgin Islands, American Samoa, and that portion of Indiana within the Eastern Time Zone.

all 9 hours. This time must be counted in determining the hours worked in that week.

KEEPING A RECORD OF TIME WORKED

As you saw in Illustration 1-1, page 3, the FLSA requires that certain time and pay records be kept by employers subject to the law. For example, employers must keep records that indicate the hours each employee worked each workday and each workweek. Most of the information required by the FLSA is the kind that a company would usually keep in following ordinary business practices.

The methods of keeping time records are left to the discretion of the employer. Selection of the type of record depends on the size of the company, and whether employees are paid on an hourly, weekly, biweekly, semimonthly, or monthly basis. Employees on a salary basis usually work a given number of hours each day, generally on a definite schedule. Employees on an hourly wage basis may work a varying number of hours with some "down time" and layoffs and some overtime work. All of this time must be recorded in some way. As you will learn in the following sections, time sheets or time cards may be used to keep this record.

Time Sheets

Many small businesses that must keep a record of time worked by each employee require each person to sign a *time sheet*, indicating the time of arrival for work and the time of departure. The time sheet can be found in many different forms. There may be a sheet used for each working day with employees signing their names on arrival in the morning and indicating the time they started and quit work. Some businesses have someone in each department serving in the capacity of a timekeeper, who uses a similar form to record the hours worked by each person in the department. Some businesses require a record of the exact time an employee arrives and leaves, while others require only the total hours worked each day. In any event, the time sheets provide the information required by law and the data used in computing the payroll. Illustration 2-3 shows a time sheet that contains the weekly work time information for an employee.

WEEKLY TIME REPORT

EMPLOYEE NAME Alma Chapman

DEPARTMENT Packing

REPORT FOR WEEK ENDING SATURDAY June 12, 19--

DAY	TIME IN	LUNCH PERIOD	TIME OUT	HOURS WORKED	EXCEPTIONS
Sunday	——	XXXXXXXXX	——	——	
Monday	8:00	– 45 minutes	10:05	2	S-6
Tuesday	7:50	– 45 minutes	4:40	8	
Wednesday	7:45	– 45 minutes	4:30	8	
Thursday	7:30	– 45 minutes	5:15	9	
Friday	8:00	– 45 minutes	4:45	8	
Saturday	——	XXXXXXXXX	——	——	
			WEEKLY TOTAL	35	6

Exception Code
S - Sickness H - Holiday
V - Vacation E - Other

EMPLOYEE'S SIGNATURE: Alma Chapman

APPROVED BY: James S. Malek

Illustration 2-3. Time Sheet

Time Cards

Under this timekeeping system, each employee is furnished a *time card* on which the time worked is recorded manually by the employee or automatically by a time clock. The time card is designed to fit various lengths of pay periods.

Illustration 2-4 shows one type of time card frequently used for a weekly pay period. The card provides space to record the hours worked, the rate of pay, deductions, and net pay. The handwritten figures are inserted by the payroll department to be used in computing total earnings, deductions, and net pay for the payroll period.

On some time clocks the *continental system* of recording time on the time card is used. Under this system, each day consists of one 24-hour period, instead of two 12-hour periods. The time runs from 12 midnight to 12 midnight. Eight o'clock in the morning is recorded as 800; 8 o'clock in the evening, as 2000; 5 o'clock in the evening, as 1700. Illustration 2-5 shows a time card that uses the continental system of recording time.

For many office workers the time card most commonly used is that which registers from 1 to 12 a.m. or p.m. with full minutes. However, for many mass-production jobs and in job shops, managers need additional information such as how and where each employee's time is spent. Accurate accounting of time spent enables managers and first-line supervisors to

No. **312** Pay Ending October 17, 19--

NAME GARY A. SCHNEIDER 262-09-7471

	Hours	Rate	Amount		DEDUCTIONS		
Reg.	40	10.75	430	00	FICA	40	30
O/T	6	16.13	96	78	FIT	81	00
					SIT	10	54
					CIT		
					Group Life Ins.	1	60
					Hospital Ins.	3	15
Total Earnings			526	78	U.S. Sav. Bonds	5	00
Less Deductions			141	59	Other		
NET PAY			385	19	Total	141	59

Days	MORNING IN	MORNING OUT	AFTERNOON IN	AFTERNOON OUT	OVERTIME IN	OVERTIME OUT	Daily Totals
1	M 759	M 1203	M 100	M 505			8
2	TU 750	TU 1204	TU 1259	TU 507			8
3	W 751	W 1201	W 1250	W 504	W 529	W 735	10
4	TH 800	TH 1202	TH 1258	TH 503			8
5	FR 800	FR 1205	FR 101	FR 506			8
6	SA 755	SA 1204					4
7							

Signature *Gary A. Schneider*

Illustration 2-4. Time Card

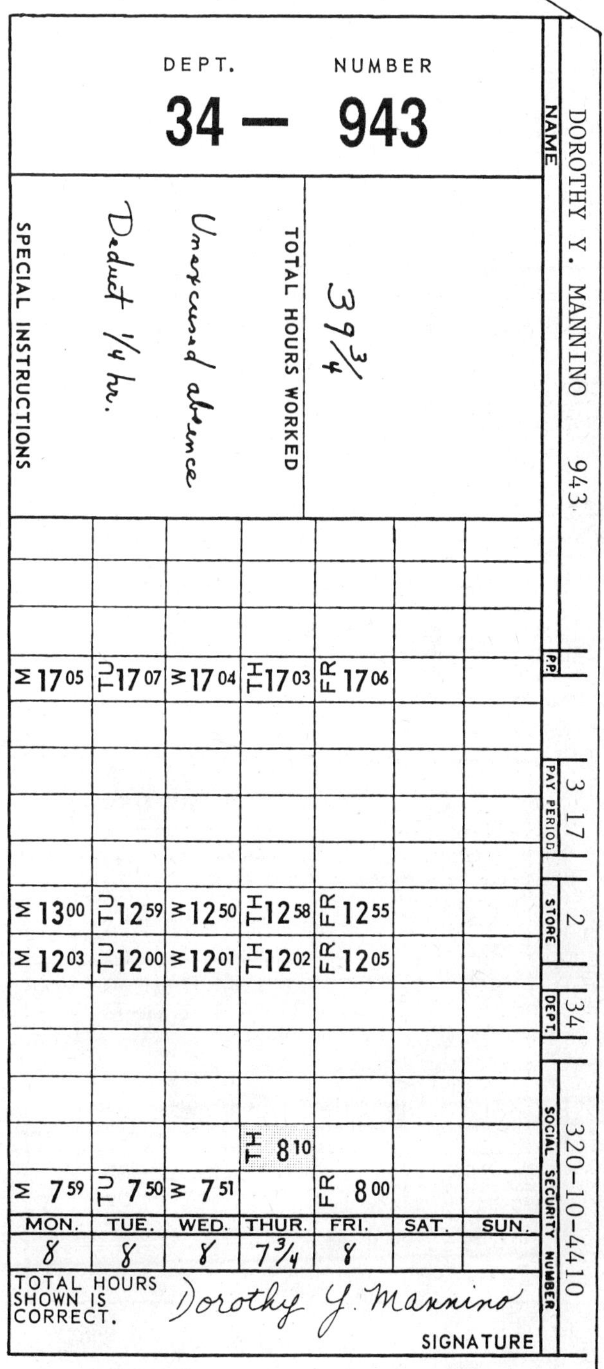

DEPT. NUMBER

34 — 943

NAME DOROTHY Y. MANNINO 943.

TOTAL HOURS WORKED 39¾

SPECIAL INSTRUCTIONS *Unexcused absence Deduct 1/4 hr.*

PAY PERIOD 3 17

STORE 2

DEPT. 34

SOCIAL SECURITY NUMBER 320-10-4410

MON.	TUE.	WED.	THUR.	FRI.	SAT.	SUN.
M 1705	TU 1707	W 1704	TH 1703	FR 1706		
M 1300	TU 1259	W 1250	TH 1258	FR 1255		
M 1203	TU 1200	W 1201	TH 1202	FR 1205		
			TH 810			
M 759	TU 750	W 751		FR 800		
8	8	8	7¾	8		

TOTAL HOURS SHOWN IS CORRECT. *Dorothy Y. Mannino* SIGNATURE

Illustration 2-5. Continental System Time Card

determine why certain materials were not available when needed in the production process, to learn what caused machine set-up or break-down time, and to investigate other factors relating to efficient operations. In mass-production operations, information is needed about how time was spent by an employee on a particular operation as the product passed along the line. In a job shop such as an auto or appliance repair shop, information is needed on how employees allocate their time to a single job. Where incentive plans are used, standards must be compared with actual time for the purposes of determining pay as well as for cost analysis of the individual parts produced.

For job costing, the continental time system, with minutes indicated in fractional equivalents, may be effectively used. As shown in Illustration 2-6, the labor time or charge is made against a specific job. The *job cost card*, prepared in advance by the scheduling or production control department, identifies the job and may accompany the job throughout the shop. Each employee who works on the job signs his or her name or clock number on the card in the space provided, together with the time registration on and off the job. Such a time record gives a complete summation of time spent on the job as soon as the job is completed and allows a study of the total time spent on a particular job.

PART NO. A-14583 JOB NO. 1771

JOB COST CARD

DESCRIPTION SWITCH BRACKET

CARD NO. 1 EST. TIME 11 HRS.

Employee		Time	Clock Time Record
	OFF		
	ON		
	OFF		
	ON		
	OFF		
	ON		
	OFF		
	ON		
	OFF		
	ON		
	OFF		
	ON		
	OFF		17SEP1075
311 Max First	ON	.19	17SEP1056
	OFF		17SEP1056
247 J. Sharpe	ON	.54	17SEP1002
	OFF		17SEP1002
125 John Smith	ON	1.96	17SEP 806
	OFF		17SEP 806
109 H. Hinkle	ON	1.06	17SEP 700
	OFF		16SEP1530
109 H. Hinkle	ON	.76	16SEP1454
	OFF		16SEP1454
166 B. Brinkman	ON	2.54	16SEP1200
	OFF		16SEP1150
166 B. Brinkman	ON	1.52	16SEP 998
	OFF		16SEP 998
131 G. Davis	ON	2.98	16SEP 700

TOTAL TIME 11.55

Cincinnati Time

Illustration 2-6. Job Cost Card with Time Recorded in Hundredths of an Hour

Mechanical Time-Clock System

The following summary indicates how a mechanical time-clock works:

1. The number of time-clock stations used by an employer depends on the number of hourly employees, the number of employee entrances, etc. Usually each station has a centrally located time clock with an *In* rack on one side and an *Out* rack on the other. Before employees report for work on Monday morning, a card for each employee is placed in the rack. Each slot in the rack is identified by a clock number and the cards are arranged chronologically by clock number. The cards are kept in the *Out* rack when employees are not at work, and in the *In* rack when employees are at work.
2. Each employee's card shows the clock number, name of employee, and a record of the hours worked.
3. When employees arrive on Monday morning, they remove their time cards from the *Out* rack and place them in the slot provided in the time clock. The insertion of the card actuates a device that prints in the *Morning In* column of the card the day of the week and the exact starting time. The employees then place their cards in the proper place in the *In* rack. At noon when the employees go to lunch, they remove their cards from the *In* rack, register the time in the *Morning Out* column, and place the cards in the *Out* rack. When they return to work after lunch, they take the cards from the *Out* rack, register the *Afternoon In* time, and place the cards in the *In* rack. At closing time in the afternoon, they take the cards from the *In* rack, register the *Afternoon Out* time, and place the cards in the *Out* rack. Overtime is recorded in a similar manner. On each succeeding day during the week, a similar procedure is followed. Each day there is an automatic adjustment in the time clock which makes it print on the next lower line.

Although the time clock described here prints the time automatically when a time card is properly inserted in the machine, some time clocks require pressing a lever to record the time after the card has been inserted.

4. The time clock is equipped with a two-color ribbon. The clock can be set so that all regular time is printed in black, and irregular time in red. For example, if regular working hours were from 8:00 a.m. to 5:00 p.m., with an hour from noon to 1:00 p.m. for lunch, the regular working day would be eight hours. The clock would record as follows:
   a. Black when the person rings in before 8:00 a.m. or 1:00 p.m.; also when the person rings out after 12:00 p.m. and 5:00 p.m.
   b. Red when the person rings in after 8:00 a.m. or 1:00 p.m.; also when the person rings out before 12:00 p.m. and 5:00 p.m. In other words, when the clock prints red, the person arrived late or left early.
   c. Red for both in and out for overtime work, so that special attention is called to the extra hours worked. (In Illustrations 2-4 and 2-5, red is indicated by the shaded areas.)
5. Blank spaces on the card indicate that the employee was absent or had neglected to "punch in" that day. For example, if the *Morning In* and *Out* columns were blank but time was recorded in the afternoon columns, it might indicate that the employee was absent in the morning.
6. At the end of the week, a clerk in the payroll department collects the time cards. The total hours worked, including regular and overtime, during the week are computed. This information is needed in calculating payroll and in preparing the information for the payroll register.

Computerized Time and Attendance Recording Systems

The main kinds of computerized time and attendance recording systems include:

1. *Card-generated systems* in which employees use time cards similar to the traditional time cards illustrated earlier. Daily and weekly totals are calculated and printed on the time cards for data entry into the firm's computer system.
2. *Badge systems* in which employees are issued plastic laminated badges containing punched holes or having magnetic strips or bar codes. The badges are used with electronic time clocks that collect and store data, which later become input to the computer system.
3. *Cardless and badgeless systems* in which employees enter only their personal identification numbers (PIN) on a numerical or alphanumerical key pad. This system, like the badge system, uses time clocks to collect and store data for transmission to and processing by the firm's computer system.

For illustrative purposes, one kind of computerized time-clock system—a card-generated system—is explained below.

The Timekeeper is a self-contained, wall-mounted time clock that contains a computer system.[3] This time clock is capable of accepting time and attendance data from time cards and computing complex payroll and on-the-job information. By means of time-clock systems, such as the Timekeeper, most manual payroll processing operations are eliminated.

Employees are provided with their own time cards that show their daily attendance record, thus complying with federal, state, and union regulations. The Timekeeper also totals employee hours and rounds out employee time to fractions of an hour in accordance with the payroll practice of the firm.

The Timekeeper card, shown in Illustration 2-7, is similar to the time cards illustrated previously. However, in addition to recording time in and time out, the card prints total hours worked each day and total hours worked from the beginning of the pay period indicated on the time card. The mark sense field at the bottom of the card identifies each employee or supervisor and authorizes access to and use of the Timekeeper. Prior to the use of the card, the mark sense field is marked with the employee's identification number, the shift, and the department. This marking may be done by the Timekeeper or with a pencil. The supervisors' time cards are used to activate the keyboard of the Timekeeper to enter data or to print summary reports on blank time cards. Some of the typical summary reports prepared by the Timekeeper are:

1. List of employee's daily and/or cumulative hours worked by shift and/or department.
2. Absentee list.
3. Tardy list.
4. List of employees on premises.
5. List of employees off premises.

When an employee places the card in the time clock, the computer scans the card. The employee's number is optically verified in the computer memory,

[3]Information supplied the authors by Kronos, Incorporated.

and the last print line on the card is located. The time of entry is then printed on the next line. Simultaneously, the computer stores the punch-in time in the system's memory. When an employee punches out, the Timekeeper again verifies the employee's identification number and calculates and rounds off the daily and cumulative payroll hours. Next, the actual punch-out time and the calculated cumulative hours are printed on the card and stored within the Timekeeper for transmission to a computer for payroll processing.

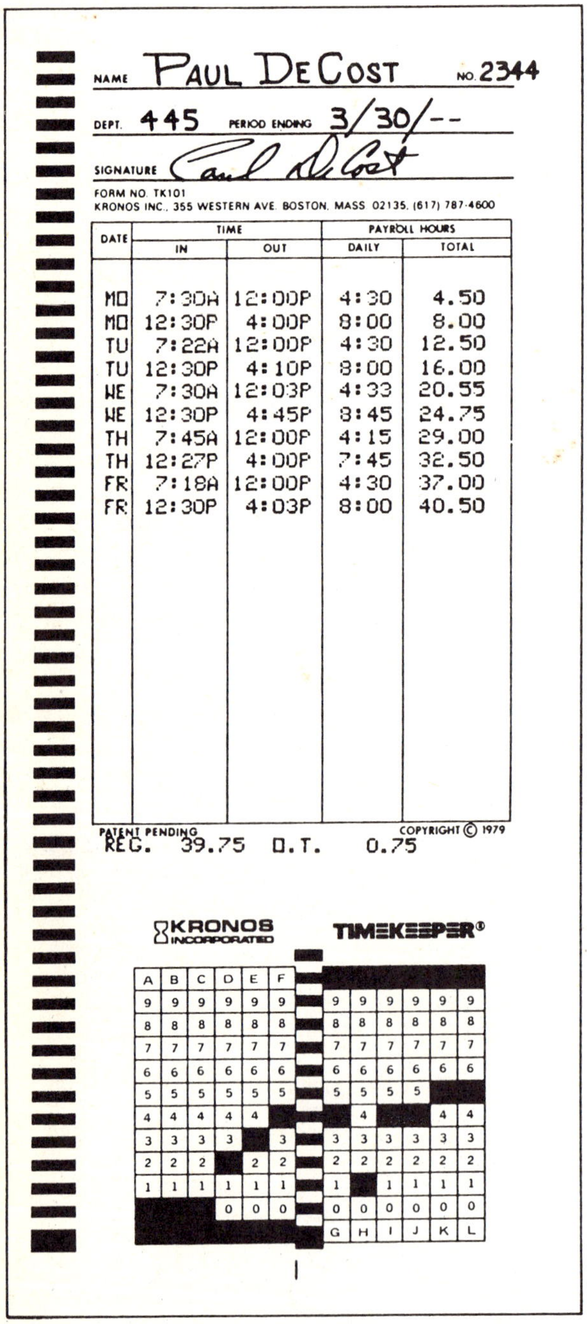

NAME PAUL DeCOST NO. 2344

DEPT. 445 PERIOD ENDING 3/30/--

SIGNATURE Paul DeCost

FORM NO. TK101
KRONOS INC., 355 WESTERN AVE. BOSTON, MASS 02135. (617) 787-4600

DATE	TIME IN	TIME OUT	PAYROLL HOURS DAILY	PAYROLL HOURS TOTAL
MO	7:30A	12:00P	4:30	4.50
MO	12:30P	4:00P	8:00	8.00
TU	7:22A	12:00P	4:30	12.50
TU	12:30P	4:10P	8:00	16.00
WE	7:30A	12:03P	4:33	20.55
WE	12:30P	4:45P	8:45	24.75
TH	7:45A	12:00P	4:15	29.00
TH	12:27P	4:00P	7:45	32.50
FR	7:18A	12:00P	4:30	37.00
FR	12:30P	4:03P	8:00	40.50

PATENT PENDING COPYRIGHT © 1979

REG. 39.75 O.T. 0.75

KRONOS INCORPORATED TIMEKEEPER®

Kronos, Inc.

Illustration 2-7. Mark-Sense Time Card Used in the Timekeeper Computerized Time-Clock System

(You will find a further discussion of computerized payroll accounting systems in Appendix B.)

Fractional Parts of an Hour

The FLSA requires that employees be paid for *all* time worked, including fractional parts of an hour. An employer cannot use an arbitrary formula or an estimate as a substitute for determining precisely the compensable working time which is part of an employee's fixed or regular hours. However, there is an exception to this rule. Employers may adopt the practice of recording an employee's starting and stopping time to the nearest five minutes, or the nearest tenth of an hour, or the nearest quarter of an hour. Nevertheless, the employer must be able to show that over a period of time the averages so recorded result in the employees being paid for all the time they actually worked.

Uncertain and indefinite working periods beyond the scheduled working hours cannot be practicably determined. Therefore, a few seconds or minutes may be disregarded since the law does not concern itself with trifles. Some courts have allowed from 10 to 20 minutes to be ignored, while other courts have refused to apply the law to periods as small as 10 minutes. Generally a few minutes of time spent by employees on the company premises for their own convenience before or after their workday are not included in the hours worked.

METHODS OF COMPUTING WAGES AND SALARIES

As you saw earlier, remuneration for time worked is usually at a time rate, that is, hourly, weekly, biweekly, semimonthly, or monthly; at a piece rate; at an incentive rate; on a commission basis; or a combination of one or more of these methods.

Time Rate

To calculate the wages of employees on an hourly basis, multiply the total regular hours worked by the regular hourly rate. If overtime is involved, multiply the total overtime hours by the overtime rate. By adding the total regular earnings and the total overtime earnings, we obtain the *gross earnings*.

EXAMPLE:

Nick Sotakos works a 40-hour week at $6.20 an hour with overtime hours paid at one and one-half times the regular rate. His regular weekly earnings are: 40 x $6.20, or $248.

Sotakos's overtime rate is: $6.20 x 1.5, or $9.30.

If Sotakos works 4 hours overtime, he has additional earnings for the 4 hours of $37.20 (4 x $9.30). His weekly gross earnings are: $248 + $37.20, or $285.20.

If Sotakos is paid only for time actually worked and works only 36 hours during a week, he earns: 36 x $6.20, or $223.20.

In many factories, we find that the actual time spent on a certain job is charged to that job.

EXAMPLE:

Sonja Butta spent 100 minutes on a certain job. Her wages chargeable to that job at the regular hourly rate of $5.58 would be computed as follows:

$$\$5.58 \times \frac{100}{60} = \$9.30$$

Converting Weekly Wage Rates to Hourly Rates. When an employee is paid on a weekly basis, sometimes we must convert the weekly wage rate to an hourly rate, especially to figure overtime earnings. To do this, we divide the weekly wage rate by the number of hours in the regular workweek.

EXAMPLE:

Joseph Gallo is paid $212 a week for a workweek consisting of 40 hours. If he worked 43 hours in a particular week, we compute his gross pay as follows:

$212.00 ÷ 40 hrs. = $5.30 Hourly Wage Rate

$5.30 Hourly Wage Rate x 1.5 = $7.95 Overtime Wage Rate

Gross Pay = $212 + (3 hrs. x $7.95) = $235.85

Illustration 2-8 shows a table of weekly wage rates with corresponding hourly wage rates based on a 40-hour week, and overtime wage rates at time and one-half for hours worked beyond 40. Practice varies as to the number of decimal places used in calculating overtime wage rates. In our illustration, the overtime wage rates have been rounded to two decimal places.

Converting Monthly Salary Rates to Hourly Rates. Many workers paid on a monthly basis earn overtime pay for work beyond a 40-hour week. In such cases, we must convert the monthly salary rate to an hourly rate in order to obtain the hourly overtime rate.

EXAMPLE:

Elaine Manera is paid a monthly salary of $900, and she receives overtime for hours worked beyond 40 in each workweek. During one weekly pay period she worked 6 hours overtime. We convert her monthly salary rate to its equivalent weekly salary by multiplying the monthly salary by 12 (the number of months) and dividing by 52 (the number of weeks), as follows:

$900 Monthly Rate x 12 Months = $10,800 Yearly Rate

$10,800 Yearly Rate ÷ 52 Weeks = $207.69 Weekly Rate

Next, we divide the weekly rate by the standard number of hours in the workweek to determine the equivalent hourly rate:

$207.69 Weekly Rate ÷ 40 Hours = $5.19 Hourly Rate

Then, we determine her hourly overtime rate:

$5.19 Hourly Rate x 1.5 = $7.79 Overtime Rate

Finally, we calculate Manera's weekly gross pay as follows:

6 Hrs. x $7.79 Overtime Rate = $46.74 (Overtime Earnings)

$207.69 (Regular Weekly Rate) + $46.74 (Overtime Earnings) = $254.43

Illustration 2-9 on page 40 shows a table of monthly salary rates with corresponding yearly rates, weekly rates, hourly rates based on a 40-hour week, and overtime rates at time and one half for hours worked beyond 40.

When employees are paid semimonthly, we follow the same plan in converting to an hourly basis except we must multiply the semimonthly earnings by 24 instead of by 12 to arrive at the yearly earnings. Similarly, if employees are paid biweekly, we multiply the biweekly earnings by 26 to arrive at the yearly earnings.

There are numerous tables of decimal equivalents, such as the one shown in Illustration 2-10, and other devices on the market to help in computing wages at

Weekly Wage Rate	Hourly Wage Rate (40-hr. week)	Overtime Wage Rate* (over 40 hrs.)
$160	$4.00	$ 6.00
170	4.25	6.38
180	4.50	6.75
190	4.75	7.13
200	5.00	7.50
210	5.25	7.88
220	5.50	8.25
230	5.75	8.63
240	6.00	9.00
250	6.25	9.38
260	6.50	9.75
270	6.75	10.13
280	7.00	10.50
290	7.25	10.88
300	7.50	11.25

*Rounded to two decimal places.

Illustration 2-8 Table of Weekly Wage Rates Converted to Hourly Rates

Monthly Salary Rate	Yearly Salary Rate	Weekly Salary Rate	Hourly Salary Rate* (40-hr. week)	Overtime Salary Rate* (over 40 hrs.)
$ 650	$ 7,800	$150.00	$3.75	$5.63
675	8,100	155.77	3.89	5.84
700	8,400	161.54	4.04	6.06
725	8,700	167.31	4.18	6.27
750	9,000	173.08	4.33	6.50
775	9,300	178.85	4.47	6.71
800	9,600	184.62	4.62	6.93
825	9,900	190.38	4.76	7.14
850	10,200	196.15	4.90	7.35
875	10,500	201.92	5.05	7.58
900	10,800	207.69	5.19	7.79
925	11,100	213.46	5.34	8.01
950	11,400	219.23	5.48	8.22
975	11,700	225.00	5.63	8.45
1,000	12,000	230.77	5.77	8.66
1,025	12,300	236.54	5.91	8.87
1,050	12,600	242.31	6.06	9.09

*Rounded to two decimal places.

Illustration 2-9 Table of Monthly Salary Rates Converted to Yearly, Weekly, and Hourly Rates

the hourly rate. Stationery and office supply firms usually sell such timesaving devices.

Fractional Cents. In computing the hourly and overtime rates shown in Illustrations 2-8 and 2-9, we ignored a fraction amounting to less than a half cent. We treated a fraction amounting to a half cent or more as a whole cent. Practice in the treatment of fractions varies with different employers. In the case of union and other employment contracts, the method of computing regular and overtime hourly rates may be prescribed in the contracts. Use of tables of decimal equivalents may yield weekly, hourly, and hourly overtime equivalents that differ by a cent or more from the amounts shown in Illustrations 2-8 and 2-9. Such differences are due to the process of rounding at various stages in the calculations.

Piece Rate

Under the *piece-rate system,* we pay workers according to their output or so much for each unit or piece produced. Thus, the wages increase as production increases.

EXAMPLE:

Jay White receives 14½¢ for every unit produced. He produces 450 units in an 8-hour workday. His daily wages are: 450 x .145, or $65.25.

The Fair Labor Standards Act specifies that under a piece-rate system, we compute the regular hourly rate of pay by adding together the total weekly earnings from piece rates and all other sources, such as production bonuses. Then, we divide this sum by the number of hours worked in the week for which such compensation was paid to arrive at the pieceworker's "regular hourly rate" for that week. This rate must *at least equal* the statutory minimum wage rate.

EXAMPLE:

Peggy Zagst earns daily wages of $47.20 during a 5-day, 40-hour workweek. Her weekly earnings, $236, divided by 40 hours, gives an average hourly earnings of $5.90. Zagst's average hourly earnings for nonovertime work in each workweek must at least equal the minimum wage.

	To convert into:		
	Weekly Salary Rate	Hourly Salary Rate*	Hourly Overtime Salary Rate*
Multiply the:			
Weekly salary rate by	. . .	.025	.0375
Semimonthly salary rate by	.4615	.01154	.0173
Monthly salary rate by	.2308	.00577	.00866
Yearly salary rate by	.01923	.00048	.000721

*Based on a 40-hour workweek.

Illustration 2-10. Table of Decimal Equivalents Used for Conversion into Weekly, Hourly, and Hourly Overtime Salary Rates

Overtime Earnings for Pieceworkers—Method A. For overtime work, the pieceworker is entitled to be paid, in addition to piecework earnings for the entire period, a sum equal to one-half the regular hourly rate of pay multiplied by the number of hours worked in excess of 40 in the week.

EXAMPLE:

Marge Adkins produced 3,073 pieces in a 44-hour workweek and is paid 14¾¢ for every unit produced. We calculate Adkins's total piecework and overtime earnings as follows:

3,073 Pieces x .1475 = $453.27 Piecework Earnings

$453.27 ÷ 44 Hours = $10.30 Regular Hourly Rate of Pay

.5 x $10.30 (Regular Hourly Rate of Pay) = $5.15 Overtime Rate Of Pay

4 Hours x $5.15 = $20.60 Overtime Earnings

$453.27 + $20.60 = $473.87 Piecework and Overtime Earnings

Overtime Earnings for Pieceworkers—Method B. There is another method of computing overtime payment for pieceworkers that complies with the requirements of the FLSA. Under this method, employees who are paid on the basis of a piece rate may agree with their employer in advance of the performance of the work that they shall be paid at a rate not less than one and one-half times the piece rate for each piece produced during the overtime hours. No additional overtime pay will be due the employees.

EXAMPLE:

Assume that in the preceding example, we paid Adkins overtime at a piece rate of one and one-half times the regular rate for all pieces produced during overtime hours. Of the total 3,073 pieces produced, 272 were produced in the 4 overtime hours. We calculate Adkins's total piecework and overtime earnings as follows:

2,801 pieces x .1475 = $413.15 Piecework Earnings

272 pieces x .2213 = $60.19 Overtime Earnings

$413.15 + $60.19 = $473.34 Piecework and Overtime Earnings

In some instances we may pay a worker an hourly rate for some hours and a piece rate for other hours during the week. In such cases the hourly rate must be at least the minimum rate and the piece-rate earnings for the piece-rate hours must average at least the minimum.

When the piece-rate system is used, production records are kept for each employee so that these records will be available in the payroll department when the time comes to compute the wages earned by each employee.

Special Incentive Plans

Most wage systems involving special incentives are modifications of the piece-rate system described previously.

EXAMPLE:

Le Tourneau pays its production workers according to the following incentive schedule:

Output	Rate
1st 100 units	$ 9.90 per C (hundred)
2d 100 units	10.05 per C
3d 100 units	10.25 per C
all units over 300	10.50 per C

On Monday, Adele Roche produced 410 pieces. We calculate her daily earnings as follows:

1st 100 units	$ 9.90
2d 100 units	10.05
3d 100 units	10.25
110 units over 300	11.55
Total daily earnings ...	$41.75

Under many incentive plans, the company determines a standard for the quantity that an average worker can produce in a certain period of time. Workers failing to reach the standard are paid at a lower piece rate, while those who produce more than the standard receive a higher rate for the quantity produced. When incentive plans are used, the computation of payroll is usually more complicated than under the time-rate or piece-rate systems. Records of time worked as well as the production of each employee must be available in computing wages under most incentive plans.

EXAMPLE:

Chu Wang, Inc., pays its blade polishers according to the following piece-rate incentive plan:

No. of Blades Polished Per 8-Hour Workday	Earnings Per Blade Polished
less than 1,850	$.0150
1,850 to 1,999	.0165
2,000 (Daily Standard)	.0180
2,001 to 2,100	.0198
2,101 to 2,250	.0217
over 2,250	.0240

For one regular 5-day workweek, we determine the gross pay of Lee Kum Choy from the company's production records as follows:

	No. of Blades Polished Daily	Earnings Per Blade Polished	Daily Earnings
M	2,097	.0198	$ 41.52
T	2,012	.0198	39.84
W	1,990	.0165	32.84
Th	2,253	.0240	54.07
F	1,992	.0165	32.87
Total weekly earnings			$201.14

Commissions

The entire remuneration, or at least part of the remuneration, of certain employees may be on a commission basis. A *commission* is a stated percentage of revenue paid an employee who transacts a piece of business or performs a service. Thus, a salesperson working in a certain territory may receive a fixed salary each year plus a bonus for sales in excess of a certain amount.

EXAMPLE:

Maria Fontana receives an annual $22,500 base salary for working a certain territory. A quota of $800,000 in sales has been set for that territory for the current year. It is agreed that Fontana will receive 6% commission on all sales in excess of $800,000. For the current year the sales in the territory are $830,000. The bonus paid Fontana would be 6% of $30,000, or $1,800. Her total earnings for the year would be $22,500 + $1,800, or $24,300.

There are numerous variations of the commission method of remuneration. Some businesses offer special premiums or bonuses for selling certain merchandise. For example, to help move merchandise in a ready-to-wear department, a department store will frequently pay a premium or a bonus to the salesperson who sells specific items of merchandise.

Commissions are considered to be payments for hours worked and must be included in determining the "regular" hourly rate. This is so regardless of whether the commission is the sole source of the employee's compensation or is paid in addition to a salary or hourly rate. It does not matter whether the commission earnings are computed daily, weekly, monthly, or at some other interval. However, in the case of outside salespeople who are exempt from the FLSA, commissions paid to them would not have to meet the minimum wage criteria. This also applies to all employees who are exempt because they are employed in establishments that meet the requirements for exemption.

Profit-Sharing Plans

Many businesses have developed *profit-sharing plans* whereby the employer shares with the employees a portion of the profits of the business. Generally, profit-sharing plans are of three types:

1. Cash payments are based upon the earnings of a specified period.
2. Profits are placed in a special fund or account to be drawn upon by employees at some future time. This plan may be in the form of a savings account, a pension fund, or an annuity.
3. Profits may be distributed to employees in the form of capital stock.

The payments made pursuant to a bona fide profit-sharing plan that meets the standards fixed by the Secretary of Labor's regulations are not deemed wages in determining the employee's regular rate of pay for overtime purposes.

METHODS OF PAYING WAGES AND SALARIES

The three main methods used in paying wages and salaries are (1) by cash, (2) by check, and (3) by electronic transfer. A small business may pay wages and salaries in cash, but most medium-size and large firms pay wages and salaries by check. As we look ahead to a "checkless society" in which the workers' pay is transferred electronically to bank accounts of their choice, the first two methods of paying wages and salaries may become obsolete for many business firms.

Paying Wages and Salaries in Cash

When a company pays wages and salaries in cash, a common procedure is:

1. Compute the total wages earned, the deductions, and the net amount to be paid and record this information in the payroll register, as shown in Illustration 1-7 on page 17. Later, we shall transfer this information to the employees' earnings records, such as that presented in Illustration 1-8 on page 17.

2. Prepare a supplementary payroll sheet that shows the various denominations of bills and coins needed to pay the salary of each employee. The form in Illustration 2-11 provides

HENDRIX, INC. SUPPLEMENTARY PAYROLL SHEET		Bills					Coins				June 30, 19--
Name of Employee	**Net Amount to Be Paid**	**$50**	**$20**	**$10**	**$5**	**$1**	**50¢**	**25¢**	**10¢**	**5¢**	**1¢**
Brandon, Paul C.	$ 268.62	5		1	1	3	1		1		2
Connor, Rose T.	271.40	5	1			1		1	1	1	
Day, Joseph R.	297.28	5	2		1	2		1			3
Gee, Margaret F.	204.92	4				4	1	1	1	1	2
Hawke, Sidney O.	271.64	5	1			1	1		1		4
Kirk, Evelyn A.	288.24	5	1	1	1	3			2		4
Lerro, Doris B.	268.12	5		1	1	3			1		2
Pesiri, Armand G.	378.80	7	1		1	3	1	1		1	
Topkis, Christine W.	284.65	5	1	1		4	1		1	1	
Vogel, John C.	224.10	4	1			4			1		
Total	$2,757.77	50	8	4	5	28	5	4	9	4	17

Illustration 2-11. Supplementary Payroll Sheet

columns to list the names of the employees, the net amount to be paid, the denominations needed to pay each employee, the total amount needed to pay all employees, and the total number of each denomination needed to pay all employees.

In determining the denominations needed to pay each employee in Illustration 2-11, we have followed the practice of giving employees the least possible number of denominations needed for their net pays. However, no employees will be given $100 bills.

3. Prepare a payroll slip by using the total amount of each denomination needed for the payroll. Illustration 2-12 on page 44 shows a payroll slip similar to one that many banks furnish to list the amount of each denomination needed for the payroll. The illustration shows the money needed to pay the payroll listed in Illustration 2-11.

4. Write a check for the total amount of the payroll and present it to the bank with the payroll slip so that we may obtain the proper denominations.

5. Place the amount due each employee in an envelope with a receipt showing the total earnings, the deductions, and the net amount paid. Next, we distribute the prepared envelopes to the employees.

Paying Wages and Salaries by Check

When we pay wages and salaries by check, we prepare and sign the checks in the usual way. The one preparing the checks should be sure that the names of the payees and the amounts are correct. The checks are made out for the net amounts to be paid employees.

Employers are required under the Social Security Act to give employees a periodic statement showing the deductions that have been made from their wages for social security tax purposes. We may distribute these statements each payday when the wages are paid, or we may give them out monthly, quarterly, or annually. Also, we give a statement to an employee at the time the person leaves the employ of the company. Most employers who pay wages and salaries by check indicate on each check issued or on the check stub or earnings statement the various deductions made. (See Illustration 2-13 on page 45.)

Many businesses maintain a payroll account at their bank in addition to their regular checking account. In such a case, we issue all checks to pay wages and salaries against the payroll account rather than against the regular checking account. When the company maintains a separate payroll account, a common procedure is:

1. Set up a payroll account with a certain balance to be maintained at all times. We do this by issuing a check against the regular check-

ing account and depositing the check in the payroll account. A small balance is desirable in the payroll account because it may be necessary to issue payroll checks before the regular payday. For example, if employees are leaving for vacation, we may give them their next payroll checks before the regular payday. Therefore, some balance will be needed in the payroll account to cover the payment of these checks.

2. After the payroll for each period has been computed, issue a check payable to *Payroll*, which will be drawn on the regular checking account and deposited in the special payroll account at the bank.
3. Prepare individual checks, which will be drawn against the special payroll account, and record the numbers of the payroll checks in the payroll register. Many companies having a large number of employees may use automatic means of signing the checks.

Bank of Middleton
PAYROLL WITHDRAWAL FROM THE ACCOUNT OF
HENDRIX, INC.

Date *June 30* 19--

Per *J. Stephens*

	DOLLARS		CENTS
BILLS: 100s			
50s	2	500	00
20s		160	00
10s		40	00
5s		25	00
1s		28	00
HALF DOLLARS		2	50
QUARTERS		1	00
DIMES			90
NICKELS			20
PENNIES			17
TOTAL	2	757	77

Illustration 2-12. Payroll Slip

By maintaining a separate payroll account at the bank, we simplify the reconciliation of the regular bank statement. The canceled payroll checks, accompanied by a statement of the payroll account balance, are returned separately from the canceled checks drawn upon the regular checking account. The payroll account balance as shown on the bank statement should always be equal to the sum of the total of the outstanding payroll checks and any maintained balance, less any service charge.

Paying Wages and Salaries by Electronic Transfer

The use of checks has expanded to the point where today about 40 billion checks are processed each year. To overcome their paperwork problems and mounting information processing costs, many banks, business firms, and government agencies are trying to eliminate payroll and other kinds of checks. Automatic payroll depositing is not new to the banking system or to employers. For many years employers have been able to send one check to each of the banks used by participating employees, along with a list of the amounts to be credited to the employees' specific accounts. Under such a plan the number of checks passing through the banking system is reduced, but the employees' banks are required to prepare numerous deposit slips or a computer tape to process the payroll, either of which is time consuming and costly.

Under an *electronic funds transfer system (EFTS)*, we do not issue a paycheck to each worker, although the worker is given a stub showing the amounts deducted. Instead, we create a computer tape that indicates for each employee: the employee's bank; account number at the bank; and net amount to be paid. A day or two before payday we send the tape to the company's bank where the amounts due any employees who also keep their accounts at that bank are removed from the tape and deposited to the appropriate accounts. That bank sends the remaining names to an automated clearinghouse which sorts out the other bank names and prepares a computer tape for each bank that is to receive funds electronically. For banks that are unable to receive entries in electronic form, the clearinghouse creates a printed statement showing the customers' names and the amounts for which their

EMPLOYEE'S NAME ARTHUR T. COCO

PENLAND EQUIPMENT COMPANY, SAN MATEO, FL 32088-2279

PAY PERIOD ENDING	HOURS	RATE	GROSS EARNINGS	F.I.C.A.	FED. WITH. TAX	STATE WITH. TAX	UNION DUES			NET EARNINGS PAID
5/16/--	REG. T. 40 O.T. 12	5.50 8.25	319.00	24.40	26.00		3.00			265.60

DEDUCTIONS

EMPLOYEE: THIS IS A STATEMENT OF YOUR EARNINGS AND DEDUCTIONS FOR PERIOD INDICATED. KEEP THIS FOR YOUR PERMANENT RECORD.

Illustration 2-13 Earnings Statement (Check Stub) Showing Payroll Deductions

accounts are to be credited. The actual crediting of accounts and the settlement occur on payday.

Under a "paperless" deposit and bill-paying system, we may deposit wages in bank accounts designated by the employees if the deposits are voluntarily authorized by the employees. Thus, no paper paychecks ever pass hands. Millions of written checks may be eliminated each month, partly by electronically transferring some payroll dollars directly from the accounts of the employers to those of employees. After we have electronically transferred each employee's net pay directly into the worker's account, the employee is able to authorize the bank to automatically transfer funds from that account to the accounts of creditors such as the utility company and the department store.

UNCLAIMED WAGES

Occasionally a worker may terminate employment or be terminated and not claim the final wage payment. The payroll manager is then faced with the question of what to do with the worker's unclaimed wages.

Even though there is a uniform law on the subject of unclaimed or abandoned property, varying practices are found in those states that provide for the disposition of unclaimed property, such as unclaimed wages. The uniform law, which is followed by most states, provides that the holder of any unclaimed property must file a report after a specified statutory period and then surrender the property to the state. The length of the statutory period varies widely from state to state. In other states the holder of unclaimed property files a report with the state and the state then files suit for possession of the property.

Because of the different practices among states, payroll managers must be well acquainted with the laws of their own states in the event they are faced with the difficult problem of disposing of unclaimed wages.

GLOSSARY

Biweekly—every two weeks.

Commission—stated percentage of revenue paid an employee who transacts a piece of business or performs a service.

Continental system—method of recording time on time cards in which the day is divided into one 24-hour period, with time running from 12 midnight to 12 midnight.

Electronic funds transfer system (EFTS)—system whereby the employer transfers employees' net pays to employees' bank accounts with electronic equipment rather than issuing paychecks.

Enterprise coverage—test applied to determine if employees of an enterprise are covered under the provisions of the Fair Labor Standards Act. The test criteria are: at least two employees engaged in interstate commerce, and an annual gross sales volume of at least $500,000.

Exempt employee—worker who is exempt from some, or all, of the FLSA requirements such as minimum wages, equal pay, and overtime pay.

Gross earnings—summation of total regular earnings and total overtime earnings; also known as *gross pay*.

Individual employee coverage—test applied to determine if an employee is covered under the provisions of the Fair Labor Standards Act. The test is that the employee is either engaged in interstate commerce or in producing goods for such commerce.

Job cost card—time card prepared for each job in process, showing the time spent by each employee on that particular job.

Piece-rate system—compensation plan under which workers are paid according to their output (units or pieces produced).

Principal activities—those tasks employees are required by the employer to perform.

Profit-sharing plan—compensation plan in which employer shares with employees a portion of the profits of the business.

Salary—remuneration paid on a monthly, biweekly, semimonthly, or yearly basis.

Semimonthly—twice a month.

Time card—form on which employee's time worked is recorded manually by the worker or automatically by a time clock.

Time sheet—form that indicates an employee's time of arrival and time of departure.

Tip—gift or gratuity given by a customer in recognition of service performed for him or her.

Tipped employee—one engaged in an occupation in which tips of more than $30 a month are customarily and regularly received.

Wage—remuneration paid on an hourly, weekly, or piecework basis.

Wages—remuneration or compensation paid employees plus the reasonable cost or fair value of any facilities furnished the employees by the employer.

Workweek—fixed and regularly recurring period of 168 hours—7 consecutive 24-hour periods.

QUESTIONS FOR REVIEW

1. What factors may cause a business organization to investigate alternative work schedules?
2. Explain the two bases of coverage provided by the FLSA.
3. Distinguish between the terms wage and salary.
4. Under what conditions may an employer pay training wages to newly employed workers?
5. What kinds of establishments may employ full-time students at 85% of the minimum wage?
6. To what extent are tips considered wages under the FLSA?
7. Explain the requirement set forth by the FLSA for overtime pay.
8. Explain how a state employee working in the area of public safety may use compensatory time off in lieu of overtime compensation.
9. What is the basic provision of the Equal Pay Law?
10. What requirements must be met by employees in order to be classified as an executive under the FLSA?
11. The following employees are exempt from various requirements of the FLSA. Indicate from which requirement or requirements each of the following employees is exempt:
    a. Amusement park employee
    b. Taxicab driver
    c. Casual babysitter
    d. Elementary school teacher
    e. Outside salesperson
12. Under what conditions may children under the age of 18 be employed in nonfarm occupations?
13. Why should an employer require a minor to furnish a state employment or age certificate at time of employment?
14. In determining the working time of employees, how are the principal activities of employees defined?
15. Under what conditions is travel time counted as time worked?
16. A company grants its employees a 15-minute rest period twice each workday. Must the employees be paid for each rest period?
17. When is time spent by employees in attending lectures and meetings for training purposes not counted as working time?
18. A production worker is employed on the third shift (usually 8 hours) when daylight-saving time goes into effect. Explain how the additional hour's pay given the worker is considered in determining the worker's regular pay rate and overtime compensation.
19. How may an employee's absence be indicated on a time card?
20. Explain how to calculate the overtime hourly rate for employees who are paid biweekly.
21. How are wages calculated under the piece-rate system?
22. Explain the two methods that may be used to calculate overtime wages for a pieceworker.
23. Outline the steps usually followed in paying wages and salaries (a) by cash and (b) by check.
24. How is the issuance of paychecks eliminated under an electronic funds transfer system?
25. What is the uniform law on the subject of unclaimed or abandoned property?

QUESTIONS FOR DISCUSSION

1. Peter Massey, a machinist for Star Motors, worked 4 hours overtime in the first week of a 2-week pay period. During the second week of the pay period, the company laid Massey off for 6 hours to offset the amount of overtime he worked during the first week. As a result, Massey's total earnings for the 2-week period were the same as they would have been had he worked no overtime hours. Did Star Motors violate any provision of the FLSA in this instance? Explain.
2. Along with many other companies, Gomez Printers observes the Friday after Thanksgiving as a paid holiday. The company requires each employee to make up Friday's lost hours in the following workweek by working extra hours without pay. Is Gomez Printers proceeding legally by requiring its employees to work extra hours without compensation to make up for the hours lost on the Friday holiday? Explain.
3. The cashiers at a drugstore like to make a preliminary count of the $50 "cash bank" in their registers before the store is opened for business. Is the time required to count the "cash bank" compensable under the overtime provisions of the FLSA?
4. Hearings have been held in Congress on a bill to shorten the workweek for wage earners from 40 hours to 35 hours. If the bill becomes law, employers would be required to pay double time for any work done over the new 35-hour limit. However, employers could no longer schedule overtime without first obtaining an employee's consent. Do you favor or oppose a 35-hour workweek? What arguments can you advance in favor of and against such a new law?
5. In the payroll department of DuMont, there is a policy of waiting one full week before correcting any paycheck errors of $30 or less. However, any pay shortages that exceed $30 are made up the same day. Also, any amounts less than $30 are made up the same day when the particular circumstances of the employees indicate that it would place an undue hardship on them to wait until the next pay one week later.

   Denise Harris, an order checker in DuMont's shipping department, discovered an error of $28.34 in her weekly check. Upon reporting the error, Harris was informed by a payroll clerk that she would have to wait until the next week's paycheck to recover the amount since the underpayment was less than $30.

   What is your reaction to DuMont's policy of providing for paycheck corrections? Assume that Harris protests the delay and in court argues that her earned wages should be paid on the date due. As the judge hearing the case, how would you decide?
6. In some companies employees are permitted to pick up the payroll check of another employee as a favor. What is your reaction to this practice?
7. Many banks in the United States participate in various types of *check truncation* or *check safekeeping* programs. Under such a program, instead of returning to a firm its canceled checks along with the monthly statement, the bank microfilms the checks and stores the truncated checks. For its customers participating in the program, the bank sends a periodic statement listing the numbers, dates, and amounts of checks posted to the customer's account during the previous month. If a customer should ask for a copy of a specific check, the bank sends a photograph or a computer image of the check reproduced from its microimage files.

   Assume that you are a payroll manager in a company participating in a check truncation program for the payroll checks written as well as for those written on your firm's commercial checking account. What advantages does the check truncation program offer your company? Do you see any disadvantages?
8. Consult the minimum wage and overtime law of your state, or of another state as directed by your instructor, and prepare a short report in which you discuss each of the following topics:
   a. Coverage and exceptions from coverage.
   b. Minimum wage.
   c. Overtime requirements.
   d. Subminimum wage rates.
   e. Gratuities and tips—how counted toward meeting the minimum wage.
   f. Requirements for publicly displaying certain items by the employer.
   g. Recordkeeping requirements.
   h. Penalties for violation of the law and its regulations.
   i. Remedies available to employees to recover unpaid wages.
   j. Existence of a statute of limitations, which imposes a time restriction on the starting of any action to recover a liability imposed by the law.
9. Consult your state law (or those of several states as directed by your instructor) to find out when termination payments must be made to workers who are discharged, who quit, or who are on strike.

Date ____________________ Name ____________________

PRACTICAL PROBLEMS

Special forms required to solve the Practical Problems are provided along with the problems in each unit.

NOTE: In this unit and in all succeeding work throughout the course, *unless instructed otherwise,* calculate hourly rates and overtime rates as follows:

1. **Carry the hourly rate and the overtime rate to 3 decimal places and then round off to 2 decimal places.**
2. **If the third decimal place is 5 or more, round to the next higher cent.**
3. **If the third decimal place is less than 5, simply drop the third decimal place.**

Examples: **$4.765 should be rounded to $4.77.**
$4.764 should be rounded to $4.76.

Also, use the minimum hourly wage of $4.25 in solving these problems and all that follow.

2-1. The hours worked and the hourly wage rates for five employees of the Cooley Company for the week ended September 10 follow.

a. For each employee, calculate the gross earnings.
b. Determine the total gross earnings for all employees.

Employee	Hours Worked	Regular Hourly Wage Rate	(a) Gross Earnings
Dempski, R.	38	$8.40	$ ________
Floyd, B.	40	5.25	$ ________
Iskin, J.	37	6.30	$ ________
Macintyre, H.	40	6.95	$ ________
Serock, P.	32½	4.25	$ ________
		(b) Total gross earnings	$ ________

2-2. The wages and hours information for five employees of Serbu Enterprises for the week ended July 5 is given below. Employees work a standard 40-hour workweek and are paid time and one-half for all hours over 40 in each workweek.

a. For each employee, calculate the regular earnings, overtime rate, overtime earnings, and total gross earnings.
b. Determine the total gross earnings for all employees.

			(a)			
Employee	**Hours Worked**	**Regular Hourly Wage Rate**	**Regular Earnings**	**Overtime Rate**	**Overtime Earnings**	**Total Gross Earnings**
Clay, T.	48	$6.45	$ 258—	$ 9.68	$ 77.44	$ 355.44
DeMusis, G.	44	6.25	$ 250	$ 9.38	$ 37.52	$ 296.90
Kliny, A. . . .	42	5.70	$ 228	$ 8.55	$ 17.10	$ 245.10
Ostrow, B. .	49	4.85	$ 194	$ 7.28	$ 65.52	$ 259.52
Wax, W. . . .	45½	7.40	$ 296	$ 11.10	$ 61.05	$ 357.05
			(b) Total gross earnings			$ 1514.01

2-3. Bruce Cabot is a waiter at the Towne House, where he receives a weekly wage of $80 plus tips for a 40-hour workweek. Cabot's weekly tips usually range from $180 to $200.

a. Under the Fair Labor Standards Act, the minimum amount of wages that Cabot must receive for a 40-hour workweek in August, 1991, is . . . . $__________

b. The maximum amount of tip credit that may be claimed that week by the Towne House is . . . . $__________

c. In addition to the $80 weekly wage, the amount the Towne House must pay Cabot each week is . . . . $__________

2-4. Tony Franco is a full-time student at Southern Junior College. After school hours he is employed by the college as a clerk at $3.50 per hour. One week in October, 1991, he worked 18½ hours.

a. Franco's earnings for the week are . . . . $__________

b. Is the hourly rate in violation of the FLSA? Explain.

c. If the hourly rate is in violation of the FLSA, the amount the college should pay Franco is . . . . $__________

2-5. May Kim, a full-time student at Central University, is employed by Gifford's Dress Shop as a salesperson. Her hourly rate is $3.25. One week in November, 1991, Kim worked 32¾ hours.

a. Kim's earnings for the week are . . . . $__________

b. Is the hourly rate in violation of the FLSA? Explain.

c. If the hourly rate is in violation of the FLSA, the amount the dress shop should pay Kim is . . . . $__________

2-6. Joe Vacca receives an hourly wage of $6.90 for a 40-hour week of 5 days, 8 hours daily. For Saturday work, he is paid one and one-half times the regular rate; for Sunday work, he is paid double the regular rate. During a certain week, he works the full 5-day week, plus 8 hours on Saturday and 4 hours on Sunday.

For this workweek, compute:

a. The regular earnings . . . . $__________

b. The overtime earnings . . . . __________

c. The total earnings . . . . $__________

2-7. Annette Henri is paid an hourly wage of $5.30 for a 32-hour workweek of 4 days, 8 hours daily. For any work on the fifth day and on Saturdays, she is paid one and one-half times her regular hourly rate. During a certain week, in addition to her regular 32 hours, Henri worked 6 hours on the fifth day and 5 hours on Saturday.

For this workweek, compute:

a. The regular earnings . . . . $__________

b. The overtime earnings . . . . __________

c. The total earnings . . . . $__________

Date ______________________ Name ______________________

2-8. Peter Romez receives $215 for a regular 40-hour week and time and one-half for overtime. For a workweek of 46 hours, compute:

a. The regular earnings . . . . $__________

b. The overtime earnings . . . . __________

c. The total earnings . . . . $__________

2-9. Chris Donato earns $1,450 each month and works 40 hours each week. Compute:

a. The hourly rate . . . . $__________

b. The overtime rate at time and one-half . . . . $__________

2-10. Richard Gentile is paid an annual salary of $18,900 by the Lett Company. Based on a 52-week year during which Gentile works 37½ hours each week, his hourly pay rate is . . . . $__________

2-11. Kathleen Otto, a medical secretary, is paid $1,075 monthly for a 35-hour week. For overtime work she receives extra pay at the regular hourly rate up to 40 hours, and time and one-half beyond 40 hours in any week. During one semimonthly pay period, Otto worked 10 hours overtime. Only 2 hours of this overtime were beyond 40 hours in any one week. Compute:

a. The regular semimonthly earnings . . . . $__________

b. The overtime earnings . . . . __________

c. The total earnings . . . . $__________

2-12. Cynthia Porrini receives $4.90 per hour for a workweek of 5 days, 7½ hours daily. She is paid time and one-half for overtime, but the overtime rate is not effective until she works 40 hours during the week. Porrini is not paid for time off. During a certain week, she is absent 2 hours on Monday and works 8 hours on Saturday. Compute:

a. The regular earnings . . . . $__________

b. The overtime earnings . . . . __________

c. The total earnings . . . . $__________

2-13. Refer to Problem 2-12. Assume that Porrini was paid for her absence on Monday and received time and one-half for all of her Saturday work. Compute:

a. The regular earnings . . . . $__________

b. The overtime earnings . . . . __________

c. The total earnings . . . . $__________

2-14. The time card below shows the time worked one week by Peter Van Horn. The employer disregards any time before 8:00 a.m. or 1:00 p.m. and after 5:00 p.m. Employees do not begin work until 8:00 a.m. or 1:00 p.m., and do not work beyond 5:00 p.m., unless they are asked to work overtime. Hours worked beyond the regular 8-hour day and on Saturday are paid at one and one-half times the regular rate. Hours worked on Sunday are paid double the regular rate.

No. 72							
Name Peter Van Horn							(a)
Day	Morning		Afternoon		Overtime		Hours Worked
	In	Out	In	Out	In	Out	
M	7:50	12:00	12:50	5:01			
T	7:56	12:01	12:49	5:02	5:30	7:31	
W	7:59	12:02	12:58	5:03			
T	7:45	12:00	12:55	5:00	5:29	8:02	
F	8:01	12:01	1:00	5:01	6:00	7:30	
S	7:48	12:02					
S			2:00	6:03			
(b)	Total Hours Worked						
Remarks							

Van Horn's regular wage rate is $4.78 per hour, and the regular workweek is 40 hours with five 8-hour days. Compute:

a. The hours worked each day. (Ignore the one-minute tardiness on Friday.)

b. The total hours worked.

c. The regular earnings . . . . $__________

d. The overtime earnings . . . . __________

e. The total earnings . . . . $__________

2-15. Under the decimal system of calculating time worked at the Silverman Company, production workers who are tardy are "docked" according to the schedule shown below.

Minutes Late in Ringing In	**Fractional Hour Deducted**
1 through 6	1/10
7 through 12	2/10
13 through 18	3/10
19 through 24	4/10
etc.	

DAY	AM		PM		(a) HRS WORKED
	In	Out	In	Out	
M	7:28	11:31	12:29	4:31	
T	7:35	11:30	12:30	4:30	
W	7:50	11:33	12:27	4:32	
Th	7:27	11:31	12:50	4:33	
F	7:28	11:32	12:40	4:30	

The regular hours of work, Monday through Friday, are from 7:30 to 11:30 a.m. and from 12:30 to 4:30 p.m. During one week Henry Vanderhoff, who earns $6.15 an hour, reports in and checks out as shown above. Employees are not paid for ringing in a few minutes before 7:30 and 12:30 nor for ringing out a few minutes after 11:30 and 4:30. Compute:

a. The hours worked each day.

b. The total hours worked . . . . __________

c. The gross earnings for the week . . . . $__________

Date ______________________ Name ______________________

2-16. Refer to Problem 2-15. Assume that Vanderhoff worked 5 hours overtime on Monday and that he is paid time and one-half for any hours over 8 each workday. Compute:

a. The regular earnings . . . . $__________

b. The overtime earnings . . . . __________

c. The gross earnings for the week . . . . $__________

2-17. The Toland Gear Company pays its employees according to the incentive schedule shown below.

Output	Rate per C (hundred)
1st 2,000 units	$1.95
next 100 units (2,001 to 2,100)	$2.00
all units over 2,100	$2.05

Using the following production data, compute:

a. The daily earnings for each employee.

b. The total daily earnings for all employees.

Employee	Units Produced		(a) Daily Earnings
Rocco D'Orazio	2,975	__________	$__________
John Ervin	2,480	__________	$__________
Kenneth Hicks	2,870	__________	$__________
Joseph Mylotte	2,710	__________	$__________
Thomas Wade	2,902	__________	$__________

(b) Total daily earnings . . . . $__________

2-18. Zeller Parts, Inc., pays its employees according to the incentive schedule shown below.

Output	Rate per C (hundred)
1st 500 units	$6.15
next 100 units (501 to 600)	$6.25
all units over 600 ..	$6.45

Using the following production data, compute:

a. The daily earnings for each employee.
b. The total daily earnings for all employees.

Employee	Units Produced		(a) Daily Earnings
Pauline Bonovitz	485	______	
		______	
		______	$______
Jose DeLaRosa	570	______	
		______	
		______	$______
Harlan Girard	730	______	
		______	
		______	$______
Anna Mayne	800	______	
		______	
		______	$______
Betty Shore	835	______	
		______	
		______	$______
	(b) Total daily earnings		$______

2-19. During the first week in November, Esther Coulter worked 45½ hours and produced 1,015 units under a piece-rate system. The regular piece rate is 18¢ a unit. Coulter is paid overtime according to the FLSA ruling for overtime work under a piece-rate system. Calculate:

a. The piecework earnings .... $______
b. The regular hourly rate .... $______
   The overtime hourly rate .... $______

   NOTE: In your calculations, carry the regular hourly rate and the overtime rate each to 4 decimal places and then round off each rate to 3 decimal places.

c. The overtime earnings .... ______
d. The total earnings .... $______

Date ______________________ Name ______________________

2-20. Refer to Problem 2-19. Assume that Coulter had agreed with her employer prior to the performance of the work that she shall be paid one and one-half times the regular piece rate for all pieces produced during the overtime hours. Assume that her production totals for the week were: 880 pieces during regular hours and 135 pieces during overtime hours. Calculate:

a. The piecework earnings .... $________

b. The overtime earnings .... ________

c. The total earnings .... $________

2-21. The hours worked and units produced by five production workers at the Charles Steel Company for the period ending December 12 are given below. The regular piece rate for each worker is 24¢ a unit. All workers are paid according to the FLSA ruling for overtime work under a piece-rate system. Calculate:

a. The piecework earnings for each employee.
b. The regular hourly rate.
c. The overtime rate.

NOTE: In your calculations, carry the regular hourly rate and the overtime rate each to 4 decimal places and then round off each rate to 3 decimal places.

d. The overtime earnings for each employee.
e. The total earnings for each employee.

Employee	Hrs. Worked	Units Produced	(a) Piecework Earnings	(b) Reg. Hrly. Rate	(c) Overtime Rate	(d) Overtime Earnings	(e) Total Earnings
M. Bell	44	1,322	$	$	$	$	$
E. Carter	40	1,175					
D. Erk	45	1,408					
F. Kitei	48½	1,555					
D. Soong	49¾	1,580					

2-22. The production record for Chu Wang, Inc., for the week ending April 16 is given on page 56. This record shows the weekly output for six of the firm's blade polishers. The company's piece-rate incentive plan is described on page 41.

For overtime work a premium is paid the employees. The premium rate for each piece produced during the overtime hours is one and one-half times the piece rate the employee earned that day for the total pieces produced. The production record shows that of the six blade polishers, only Correro worked overtime during the week. Of the total 2,757 blades polished by Correro on Wednesday, 584 were produced in two overtime hours.

On the production record, calculate:

a. The earnings per blade polished for each employee.
b. The daily earnings for each employee.
c. The weekly earnings for each employee.

CHU WANG, INC.

Production Record for Week Ending April 16, 19—

Employee	Day	No. of Blades Polished	(a) Earnings Per Blade Polished	(b) Daily Earnings
Luis Agosto	M	2,000	$______	$______
	T	2,170	______	______
	W	Absent	______	______
	T	2,116	______	______
	F	2,009	______	______
			(c) Total	$______
Ana Correro	M	2,240	$______	$______
	T	2,298	______	______
	W	2,173 (Regular)	______	______
		584 (Overtime)	______	______
	T	2,284	______	______
	F	2,069	______	______
			(c) Total	$______
Pearl Gaines	M	1,900	$______	$______
	T	1,950	______	______
	W	2,005	______	______
	T	2,107	______	______
	F	2,003	______	______
			(c) Total	$______
Thomas Kelman	M	1,980	$______	$______
	T	2,050	______	______
	W	2,010	______	______
	T	2,000	______	______
	F	2,007	______	______
			(c) Total	$______
Eloise Miller	M	2,217	$______	$______
	T	2,130	______	______
	W	2,020	______	______
	T	960	______	______
	F	2,010	______	______
			(c) Total	$______
David Rotberg	M	2,200	$______	$______
	T	2,195	______	______
	W	1,998	______	______
	T	2,090	______	______
	F	2,000	______	______
			(c) Total	$______

Date ______________________ Name ______________________

2-23. Refer to Problem 2-22. On the form given below, determine:

a. The average earnings per blade polished by each of the six workers during the week.
b. The average earnings per blade polished for all six workers during the week.
c. How the average earnings per blade polished for all six workers during the week compare with the daily standard earnings of $.0180 per blade.

Employee	Weekly Earnings	÷	No. Blades Polished	=	(a) Average Earnings Per Blade
Luis Agosto	$______		______		$______
Ana Correro	______		______		______
Pearl Gaines	______		______		______
Thomas Kelman	______		______		______
Eloise Miller	______		______		______
David Rotberg	______		______		______
Total	$______		______		

(b) $______ (Total weekly earnings) ÷ ______ (Total blades polished) = $______ (Average earnings per blade polished by all six workers)

(c) Average earnings per blade polished by all six workers: . . . . $______

Daily standard earnings per blade polished: 0180

The actual average for the week is (less than or greater than) the daily standard earnings by . . . . $______

2-24. Joan Sullivan, a sales representative, earns an annual salary of $17,750. She is also paid a commission on that portion of her annual sales that exceeds $60,000. The commission is 7% on all sales up to $45,000 above the quota. Beyond that amount, she receives a commission of 9½%. Her total sales for the past year were $128,000. Calculate:

a. The regular annual salary . . . . $______
b. The commission . . . . ______
c. The total annual earnings . . . . $______

2-25. Ferry Furriers pays its sales personnel a base salary plus commissions on sales that exceed a stated annual sales quota. From the information given below, calculate each salesperson's (a) commission and (b) total annual earnings.

Salesperson	Annual Sales	Annual Base Salary	Annual Sales Quota	Commission Percentage for Sales Above Quota	(a) Commission	(b) Total Annual Earnings
J. Fosco	$105,750	$25,700	$ 95,000	13½%	$______	$______
T. Glenn	150,540	27,500	135,000	10½%	______	______
A. Kehoe	97,220	20,000	90,000	8¾%	______	______
P. Luss	189,600	30,500	180,000	7%	______	______
J. Osti	87,290	24,375	70,000	12½%	______	______

2-26. Joyce Sand is employed as a salesperson in the men's department of Lukens Fashions. In addition to her weekly base salary of $240, Sand is paid a commission of 1% on her total net sales for the week (total gross sales less any customer returns). During the past week, to promote the sale of its fine cashmere sweaters, Lukens agreed to pay Sand an additional PM (push money) of 2% of the total net sales of cashmere sweaters. Sand's weekly sales tally is given below.

Item	Gross Sales	Customer Returns
Regular sweaters	$350	$48
Cashmere sweaters	995	75
Ties	180	-0-
Dress shirts	445	20
Sports shirts	185	15

Calculate Sand's total weekly earnings, showing her (a) weekly base salary, (b) commission, (c) PM, and (d) total weekly earnings.

(a) Weekly base salary . . . . $ 240.00
Weekly gross sales . . . . $________
Less customer returns . . . . ________
Weekly net sales . . . . $________
(b) Commission: $________ x 1% . . . . ________
Weekly gross sales of cashmere sweaters . . . . $________
Less customer returns . . . . ________
Weekly net sales of cashmere sweaters . . . . $________
(c) PM: $________ x 2% . . . . ________
(d) Total weekly earnings . . . . $________

2-27. Potts, Inc., recently converted from a 5-day, 40-hour workweek to a 4-day, 40-hour workweek, with overtime continuing to be paid at one and one-half times the regular hourly rate for all hours worked beyond 40 in the week. In this company, time is recorded under the continental system, as shown on the time card at the right.

Sue Ellen Boggs is part of the Group B employees whose regular workweek is Tuesday through Friday. The working hours each day are 800 to 1200; 1230 to 1630; and 1800 to 2000. The company disregards any time before 800, 1230, and 1800, and permits employees to ring in up to 10 minutes late before any deduction is made for tardiness. Deductions are made to the nearest 1/4 of an hour for workers who are more than 10 minutes late in ringing in.

No. 160 Hr. Rate $4.45
Name Sue Ellen Boggs O.T. Rate $6.675

Time		Mon	Tues	Wed	Thurs	Fri	Sat	
Evening	Out		2002	2001	2005	2000		
Evening	In		1801	1809	1802	1800		
Afternoon	Out		1630	1631	1630	1635		
Afternoon	In		1230	1231	1230	1238		
Morning	Out		1200	1202	1200	1203	1201	
Morning	In		755	750	813	759	800	Total for Week
Daily Totals		(a)						(b)

Remarks 13 minutes late Thursday - deduct 1/4 hr.

Refer to the time card and compute:

a. The daily total hours.
b. The total hours for the week.
c. The regular weekly earnings . . . . $________
d. The overtime earnings . . . . ________
e. The total weekly earnings . . . . $________

Date ______________________ Name ______________________

2-28. The job cost card used by Gamma Manufacturing Company to record the time spent in assembling its micro relays is illustrated below.

JOB COST CARD

Part No. B-640 Job No. 12

Description MICRO RELAY 640

Card No. 1 Estimated Time 6 Hrs.

No.	Employee	Time		Time Clock Record
		OFF		
		ON		
		OFF		
		ON		
		OFF		
		ON		
		OFF		
		ON		
		OFF		
		ON		
64	Bill Fleming	OFF		4 JUN 15[12]
		ON		4 JUN 15[00]
31	Laura Packard	OFF		4 JUN 14[74]
		ON		4 JUN 13[00]
44	HARRY O'NEILL	OFF		4 JUN 11[82]
		ON		4 JUN 10[00]
27	Ella Poole	OFF		4 JUN 09[75]
		ON		4 JUN 08[50]
47	Martha Ayers	OFF		4 JUN 08[48]
		ON		4 JUN 08[25]
19	Peter Wilson	OFF		4 JUN 08[20]
		ON		4 JUN 07[30]

TOTAL TIME ______________

On the form given below:

a. Determine the time spent on the job by each employee and the total time spent by all employees. *Note that the time is recorded in hundredths of an hour.*

b. Use the hourly wage rates given to calculate the total labor cost for producing the one relay. In your calculations, carry out the labor cost for each employee and the total labor cost to 4 decimal places.

No.	Employee	(a) Time	Hourly Wage Rate	(b) Labor Cost
64	Bill Fleming	________	$5.75	$________
31	Laura Packard	________	6.10	________
44	Harry O'Neill	________	6.30	________
27	Ella Poole	________	5.25	________
47	Martha Ayers	________	6.75	________
19	Peter Wilson	________	6.50	________
	Totals	________		$________

c. The company's time study engineer has determined that the standard labor cost for producing one micro relay is $36.5025. Calculate by what percentage (plus or minus) the actual labor cost on June 4 varied from the predetermined standard. . . . . ________

2-29. Hendrix, Inc., pays its employees' weekly wages in cash. A supplementary payroll sheet that lists the employees' names and their earnings for a certain week is shown below. Complete the payroll sheet by calculating the total amount of payroll and indicating the least possible number of denominations that can be used in paying each employee. However, no employees are to be given bills in denominations greater than $20.

HENDRIX, INC.

For Period Ending August 15, 19— | **Supplementary Payroll Sheet**

Name of Employee	Net Amount Paid	Bills				Coins				
		$20	$10	$5	$1	50¢	25¢	10¢	5¢	1¢
Chad T. Biskis	$251.75									
Nicole A. Cibik	256.52									
Domingo M. Diaz	184.94									
Laura B. Elias	202.59									
Ari M. Fleischer	253.64									
Diane Y. Germano	296.50									
Arnold B. Herst	194.26									
Edward C. Kenner	199.89									
Kathleen J. Marfia	234.01									
Kimberly A. Picket	195.80									
Total										

Date ______________________ Name ______________________

2-30. Refer to Problem 2-29. After you have completed the supplementary payroll sheet, prepare the payroll slip and check below. Sign your name on the "Per" line of the payroll slip. The check should be made payable to *Payroll* and signed with your signature below the company name.

Bank of Middleton

PAYROLL WITHDRAWAL FROM THE ACCOUNT OF

HENDRIX, INC.

Date ______________________ 19____

Per ______________________

	DOLLARS		CENTS
BILLS: 100s			
50s			
20s			
10s			
5s			
1s			
HALF DOLLARS			
QUARTERS			
DIMES			
NICKELS			
PENNIES			
TOTAL			

HENDRIX, INC.
PAYROLL ACCOUNT

No. 1915

56–456/422

______ 19____

PAY TO THE ORDER OF ______________________ $ ________

______________________ DOLLARS

Bank of Middleton

HENDRIX, INC.

____

CONTINUING PAYROLL PROBLEM

In the Continuing Payroll Problem, which is presented at the end of succeeding units, you will gain experience in computing wages and salaries and preparing a payroll register for the Steimer Company, Inc., a newly formed corporation. At the end of subsequent units, information will be presented so that the payroll register can be completed step by step as you proceed through the discussion material relating to that particular section of the payroll register.

The Steimer Company is a small manufacturing firm located in Philadelphia, PA. The company has a work force of both hourly and salaried employees. Each employee is paid for hours actually worked during each week, with the time worked being recorded in quarter-hour increments. The standard workweek consists of 40 hours, with all employees being paid time and one-half for any hours worked beyond the 40 regular hours.

Wages are paid every Friday, with one week's pay being held back by the company. Thus, the first payday for the Steimer Company is January 14 for the workweek ending January 7.

The information at the top of the next column will be used in preparing the payroll for the pay period ending January 7.

Ms. Nancy B. Costello prepares the time clerk's report for each pay period. Her report for the first week of operations is given below.

Using the payroll register for the Steimer Company, which is reproduced on a fold-out at the back of the book, proceed as follows:

Time Card No.	Employee Name	Hourly Wage or Salary
11	Mary L. Lopenski	$4.50 per hour
12	Anthony P. Wren	$3.95 per hour
13	Leroy A. Young	$5.10 per hour
21	Lester D. Hayes	$4.90 per hour
22	Meredith O. McGarry	$5.75 per hour
31	Nancy B. Costello	$215 per week
32	Gloria D. Hopstein	$1,700 per month
33	Vernon U. Porth	$1,350 per month
51	Marsha T. Stone	$1,510 per month
99	Harold Y. Steimer	$52,000 per year

1. Enter each employee's time card number and name in the appropriate columns.
2. Record the regular hours and the overtime hours worked for each employee, using the time clerk's report as your reference.
3. Complete the Regular Earnings columns (Rate Per Hour and Amount) and the Overtime Earnings columns (Rate Per Hour and Amount) for each employee.
4. Record the Total Earnings for each employee by adding the Regular Earnings and the Overtime Earnings.

Note: Retain your partially completed payroll register for use at the end of Unit 3.

TIME CLERK'S REPORT NO. 1
For Period Ending January 7, 19--

Badge No.	Employee	Time Record M	T	W	T	F	S	Time Worked	Time Lost
11	Mary L. Lopenski	8	8	8	8	8	—	40	
12	Anthony P. Wren	8	8	8	8	8	8	48	
13	Leroy A. Young	8	5½	8	8	8	—	37½	2½ hrs. tardy
21	Lester D. Hayes	10	10	8	8	10	—	46	
22	Meredith O. McGarry	8	8	8	8	8	—	40	
31	Nancy B. Costello	8	8	8	8	8	1¼	41¼	
32	Gloria D. Hopstein	8	8	8	8	8	—	40	
33	Vernon U. Porth	8	8	8	8	8	—	40	
51	Marsha T. Stone	8	8	8	8	8	4	44	
99	Harold Y. Steimer	8	8	8	8	8	—	40	

CASE PROBLEM

Case 2-1 Selecting A Computerized Time and Attendance Recording System

Assume you are the payroll clerk for Yours Truly, Inc., which employs 23 full-time workers. At the present time all of the company's employees record their time and attendance on one electromechanical time clock, which is adequate for the number of workers in your firm. As part of a feasibility study, you have been given the responsibility to investigate which kind of automated equipment will enable your company to process its payroll more efficiently and economically.

During your study you accumulate the following information:

1. Cost of the electromechanical time clock now in use, $1,000.
2. Cost of one calculating time clock that prints in and out times and automatically figures daily and weekly totals, $1,500.
3. Cost of one calculating time clock that will interface with your company's computer, $2,500. This system feeds all payroll data directly to the computer, thus eliminating the step of data entry from hard-copy time cards.
4. Cost of a badge-based system, for firms employing 50 or more employees, $5,000; for businesses with 1,000 employees or more, $50,000.

   This system, depending on the use of an employee's coded identification badge, eliminates time cards. The data are collected at a terminal, where the time is automatically recorded and sent to a central computer.
5. Estimated time required for you to process manually one time card, 7 minutes.
6. Your present hourly wage, $8.50.
7. Cost of an outside part-time bookkeeper to do the payroll work, $10 an hour.

Based upon the information you have obtained, prepare a report in which you recommend the type of equipment that should be installed to automate the payroll accounting operations, along with the estimated savings your company will realize during the first year.

Social Security Taxes

GOALS OF THIS UNIT

After completing your study of this unit, you should be able to:

1. Identify, for social security purposes, those persons covered under the law, those services that constitute employment, and the kinds of compensation that are defined as wages.
2. Apply the current tax rates for purposes of the Federal Insurance Contributions Act and the Self-Employment Contributions Act.
3. Understand the importance of obtaining and correctly using the Employer's Identification Number and the Employee's Social Security Number.
4. Complete accurately Form 941, the Employer's Quarterly Federal Tax Return, and Form 8109, the Federal Tax Deposit Coupon Book.
5. Understand the different requirements and procedures for depositing FICA taxes and income taxes withheld from employees' wages.
6. Recognize that, as collection agents for the government, employers may be subject to civil and criminal penalties if they fail to carry out their duties.

In this unit we center our discussion on the old-age, survivors, disability and health insurance program (OASDHI). This program provides monthly benefits to workers who qualify under the provisions of the Social Security Act. To cover the cost of this program, the act imposes taxes on employers and their employees. The statutes that provide the taxes are contained in the Internal Revenue Code of 1954, as amended. These statutes are:

1. The *Federal Insurance Contributions Act (FICA)*, which imposes two taxes on employers and two taxes on employees. One of the taxes that is levied on both is used to finance the *federal old-age, survivors, and disability insurance program (OASDI)*; the other is used to finance the *hospital insurance (HI), or Medicare,* program.
2. The *Self-Employment Contributions Act (SECA)*, which levies a tax upon the net earnings of the self-employed.

COVERAGE UNDER THE FICA

Today most workers in the United States are covered by the retirement and disability aspects of the social security program. Before individuals are considered to be "covered" for social security purposes, we must determine (a) if they are "employees," (b) whether the services they render are "employment," and (c) whether the compensation they receive is "wages" within the meaning of the law. The determination of a "covered" employee and "covered" employment is related to who pays the tax and who is entitled to benefits.

Employee

Every individual is an *employee* if that person performs services in a covered employment. As long as the common-law relationship of employer and employee exists and the employment is not exempt from the provisions of the law, both are covered and must observe its provisions.

A *common-law relationship* exists when the person for whom services are performed has the right to control and direct the individual who performs the services. The work performance pertains not only to the result to be accomplished but also to the details and means by which that result is to be accomplished. The employee is subject to the will and control of the employer as to *what* shall be done and *how* it should be done. Thus, the employer has the right to discharge the employee. Also, the employer furnishes the employee with tools and materials and a place in which to work.

There is no distinction between classes or grades of employees. Superintendents, supervisors, managers, department heads, and other executives are employees. All the officers of a corporation, such as the president, vice-presidents, the secretary, and the treasurer, are employees of the corporation. Their salaries are taxable the same as the wages paid to other employees. If, however, the corporation officers perform no services as such and receive no remuneration in any form, they are not considered employees of the corporation. Also, the definition of employee excludes a director of a corporation who performs no services other than attending and participating in meetings of the board of directors.

Partners generally are not employees of the partnership or of the other partners with regard to the business of the partnership. In some cases, however, a partnership may operate as an association that may be classified as a corporation. In such situations, any partner who renders services similar to those of corporate officers would be an employee.

The law also provides FICA coverage for the following four occupations:

1. Agent-drivers and commission-drivers who distribute food and beverage products, or handle laundry or dry cleaning.
2. Full-time life insurance salespersons.
3. Full-time traveling or city salespersons.
4. Homeworkers who receive at least $100 in cash by one employer in a calendar year. *Homeworkers* are persons who perform services for another, generally on a contract or piecework basis, and usually in their homes or in the home of another.

However, such persons are not covered by FICA if they have a substantial interest in the facilities used in connection with their jobs, or if the services consist of a single transaction.

Federal Government Employees. For many years, employees of the federal government were excluded from FICA coverage. However, all federal government employees who were hired on or after April 1, 1986, became covered under FICA. Before that date, coverage was extended only to specific groups of federal workers, as briefly noted below.

In 1983, all federal employees became subject to the *hospital insurance (HI)* portion of the FICA tax, with the exception of medical interns, student nurses, inmates of U.S. penal institutions, and those serving temporarily in case of fire, storm, earthquake, flood, and similar emergency.

Certain federal employees became subject to FICA taxes (both OASDI and HI) on or after January 1, 1984. As of that date, these groups included (1) all newly hired employees; (2) employees of the legislative branch and those not covered by the civil service retirement system; (3) members of Congress, the President, and the Vice President; and (4) sitting federal judges and political appointees at the executive level and in senior executive service. Still remaining exempt from FICA taxation (both OASDI and HI) are those workers listed above as exempt from the HI portion of the FICA tax.

State and Local Government Employees. The wages of state and local government employees hired after March 31, 1986, are subject only to the HI (Medicare) portion of the social security tax. Prior to 1986 state and local government employees were not subject to any portion of the FICA tax. However, all of the states have entered into voluntary agreements with the Secretary of Health and Human Services whereby certain groups of employees, such as teachers, may become covered by social security, including Medicare.

Exempt Employees. Employees of not-for-profit organizations became subject to FICA taxes on January 1, 1984. However, some services, such as those performed by duly ordained ministers of churches, remain exempt from FICA taxes. Ministers, certain members of religious orders, and Christian Science practitioners who had previously elected to be exempt from social security coverage may now be covered by filing a waiver form with the IRS. Once an election to be covered by social security is made, it is irrevocable.

Employer

Every person is an *employer* if the person employs one or more individuals for the performance of services in the United States, unless such services or employment are specifically excepted by the law. The term *person* as defined in the law means an individual, a trust or estate, a partnership, or a corporation.

Employment

The term *employment* means any service performed by employees for their employer, irrespective of the citizenship or residence of either. Most types of employment are covered under the Act, but we do find specific exclusions. Some types of employment are wholly exempt from coverage; others are exempt only if the cash wages received are less than a stipulated dollar amount. Among the kinds of employment *excluded* are:

1. *Agricultural services* when the remuneration paid *all* farm workers is less than $2,500 in any calendar year. Employers who do not meet the $2,500 annual payroll test may exclude remuneration for agricultural services when it amounts to less than $150 paid *each* worker in a calendar year. Payment for farm work with remuneration other than cash is not taxed.
2. *Domestic service* performed in a local college club, or local chapter of a college fraternity or sorority, or service performed in the employ of a school, college, or university by a *student* who is *enrolled* and *regularly attending classes* at the school, college, or university.
3. *Domestic service* in a private home (cooks, waiters, butlers, maids, babysitters, gardeners, etc.) if performed for *cash* remuneration of less than $50 a calendar quarter.
4. *Service performed by children under the age of 18* in the employ of their father or mother. This "under 18" exclusion applies to children employed by a father or a mother whose business is a sole proprietorship or by parents whose husband-wife business is organized as a partnership. However, the exclusion does *not* apply to children under age 18 who are employed by a family-owned corporation.
5. *Services performed by civilians for the United States government* or any of its instrumentalities (agencies) if such agencies are *specifically* exempt from the employer portion of the FICA tax, or if such services are covered by a retirement system established by law.
6. *Service performed by railroad workers* for employers covered by the Railroad Retirement Tax Act.
7. *Services performed in the employment of foreign governments,* such as ambassadors, ministers, and other diplomatic officers and employees.
8. *Services performed by student nurses* in the employ of a hospital or a nurses' training school if the nurses are *enrolled and regularly attending classes* in that school, which must be chartered or approved under state law.[1]
9. *Service performed by an individual under the age of 18* in the delivery or distribution of newspapers or shopping news, not including delivery or distribution to any point for subsequent delivery or distribution.

If the services performed during one-half or more of any pay period by an employee constitute covered employment, then all the services of the employee for that pay period must be counted as covered employment. On the other hand, if the services performed by an employee during more than one-half of a pay period do not constitute covered employment, then none of the services for that pay period are counted as covered employment. A pay period cannot exceed 31 consecutive days.

Voluntary Coverage

Coverage under FICA can be extended to certain classes of services that otherwise would be excluded. For example, prior to March 31, 1986, service in the employ of a state or local government had been exempt from the OASDI (old-age, survivors, and disability insurance) as well as the HI (hospital insurance) portion of the FICA tax. As noted earlier, however, state and local government employees are now subject to the HI portion of the tax. Coverage for the OASDI portion can also be extended to state and local government employees by means of a voluntary agreement entered into by the state and the Secretary of Health and Human Services. When a state elects voluntary coverage, it becomes responsible for the collection and payment of the FICA tax as if it were a covered employer.

Similarly, the District Director of the Internal Revenue Service may enter into an agreement with an American corporation to extend coverage to United States citizens who perform services outside the United States for the corporation's foreign affiliates. In the absence of such an agreement, this employment would be exempt from FICA coverage.

At one time not-for-profit organizations and state and local governments that had voluntarily been extended coverage had the right to withdraw from the Social Security System. However, the law was

[1]In 1989 the IRS ruled that the pay received by student nurses was *not* exempt from FICA taxes *unless* their pay is nominal and their work is part-time and an integral part of the curriculum.

amended so that voluntary coverage agreements can no longer be terminated, either in their entirety or for any specific groups covered by the agreements. This amendment was upheld by the Supreme Court, which ruled that a state may not withdraw its employees, or those of its political subdivisions, from the Social Security System.

Taxable Wages

OASDHI taxes are measured by the amount of wages paid by employers to their employees during the calendar year. In most instances the term *wages* includes not only the actual money received by employees but also the cash value of remuneration paid in other forms, such as meals and lodging provided *for the convenience of the employees*. The term *wages* is not the governing factor, since salaries, bonuses, fees, and commissions are all classified as wages if they are paid by an employer with respect to employment covered under the social security laws. Further, it does not matter upon what basis the payment is made. Wages may be paid hourly, daily, weekly, biweekly, semimonthly, monthly, annually, or on the basis of piecework or as a percentage of profits.

Other common types of payments made to workers that are considered wages under FICA are listed below:

1. *Advance payments* for work to be done in the future if the individual who receives the advance does the work or part of it and if the employer considers the work as satisfaction for the advance.
2. *Cash and noncash prizes and awards* made for doing outstanding work, for exceeding sales quotas, or for contributing suggestions that increase productivity or efficiency.
3. *Back pay awards* (pay received in one period for employment in an earlier period) unless the back pay is a settlement for a failure to employ the workers.
4. *Bonuses* if they are remuneration for services rendered by employees for an employer.
5. *Christmas gifts* unless the gifts are of nominal value such as a turkey or a ham.
6. *Commissions on sales or on insurance premiums* if paid as compensation for services performed.
7. *Death benefits*, or wage payments to an employee's dependents after the employee's death. However, if the payments are in the nature of a gratuity rather than compensation for services, the payments do not constitute wages. Payments made by an employer to an employee's estate or an employee's survivors after the calendar year in which the employee died are excluded from the definition of "wages" and are not taxed. Some employers provide a death-benefit plan for all employees generally or for certain classes of employees under which payments are made to the employee, or on behalf of an employee, or any of the employee's dependents at the time of the employee's death. Such death benefits are excluded from the term "wages" for FICA purposes.
8. *Dismissal pay*—payments made by an employer because of the involuntary separation of an employee from the employer's service.
9. *Guaranteed annual wage payments*, such as contained in union contract agreements whereby an employer guarantees that certain employees will either work during or be paid for each normal workweek in a calendar year.
10. *Idle time or standby payments*—amounts paid workers who are at the beck and call of an employer but who are performing no work.
11. *Jury duty pay*, where the difference between the employee's regular wages and the amount received for jury duty is paid by the employer. A similar situation exists when an employee is temporarily performing active duty with the armed forces or the state National Guard.
12. *Moving expense reimbursements* unless at time of payment it is reasonable to believe that the employee will be entitled to deduct these moving expenses in determining taxable income for federal income tax purposes. Present tax rules allow individuals, when they are transferred or move closer to work, to deduct (subject to limitations) all direct moving expenses and some indirect costs. (Indirect costs include the cost of house hunting before the move, temporary living expenses at the new location, and the cost of selling an old residence and buying a new one.) These same rules apply to the self-employed person who moves to be nearer a new work site. When employer reimbursements exceed the deduction limitations, the employee may have taxable income to report.
13. *Retroactive wage increases*.
14. *Stock payments* made by the employer, who transfers its stock to employees as remuneration for services. The transfers are taxed at the fair market value of the stock at the time of payment.
15. *Vacation pay*.
16. *Employees' federal income and social security taxes paid for by the employer*. However, payment of the employee portion of the FICA tax

by the employer for domestics working in the employer's home and for agricultural laborers is an exception to this rule.

17. *The first six months of sick pay* paid employees on account of sickness or accident disability. Payments made under a state temporary disability law are also subject to FICA taxes.
18. *Noncash fringe benefits*, such as personal use of company car, use of employer-provided vehicles for commuting (vanpooling), flights on employer-provided airplanes, and free or discounted flights on commercial airlines.
19. *Employer-paid premiums for an employee's group life insurance coverage* that exceeds $50,000.
20. *Payments to armed forces reservists* performing services on inactive duty training.

Tips. Under FICA, cash tips of $20 or more in a calendar month are looked upon as taxable wages. Employees must report their tips in writing to their employers by the 10th of the month following the month in which the tips were received. *Form 4070, Employee's Report of Tips to Employer*, shown in Illustration 3-1, may be used for this purpose. Form 4070 also contains an employee's daily record of tips (not illustrated) which provides workers a form for recording their daily tips conveniently and for retention in their personal files.

If employees receive tips of $20 or more in any month and do not report them to their employer, the employees must complete *Form 4137, Computation of Social Security Tax on Unreported Tip Income* (not illustrated). On this form, the employees compute the amount of FICA tax due on their unreported tip income. Later, the employees report the amount of FICA tax due when they file their personal income tax returns. Failure to report tips to their employers may subject employees to a penalty of 50% of the FICA tax due on the tips. Therefore, employees should attach a statement to their income tax returns explaining why they did not initially report the tips to their employers. Further, the Tax Court may rule that the nonreporting of tip income constitutes a fraud.

Employers must collect the employee's FICA tax on the tips that each employee reports. The employer deducts the employee's FICA tax from the wages due the employee or from other funds the employee makes available. The employer collects the employee's FICA tax throughout the year until the employee's combined wages and tips total the taxable wage base for that year. Employers are also liable for their share of the FICA tax on any tips that are subject to the employee's FICA tax.

Large food and beverage establishments (those with 11 or more employees and where tipping is customary) are required to allocate to their tipped employees the excess of 8% of the establishments' gross receipts over the tips reported by their employees.[2] However, employers withhold FICA taxes *only* from the tips reported by employees, not from the tips that are merely allocated. The amount of allocated tip income appears as a separate entry on the employee's *Wage and Tax Statement (Form W-2)*, as explained in Unit 4.

Every large food or beverage establishment must report annually to the IRS the amount of its receipts from food or beverage operations and the amount of tips reported by its employees. In some cases, as noted before, the establishment is required to allocate amounts as tips to its employees. *Form 8027, Employer's Annual Information Return of Tip Income and*

Form **4070** Department of the Treasury Internal Revenue Service	**Employee's Report of Tips to Employer** ▶ **For Paperwork Reduction Act Notice, see back of this form.**	OMB No. 1545-0065
Employee's name and address Morton O. Tanenbaum 1704 Elm St., San Diego, CA 92121-8837		**Social security number** 269 ⋮ 21 ⋮ 7220
Employer's name and address Holland House Inn 9 Fairway, San Diego, CA 92123-1369		
Month or shorter period in which tips were received from July 1, 19-- , to July 31, 19--		Tips $ 389.10
Signature *Morton O. Tanenbaum*		Date August 10, 19--

Illustration 3-1. Form 4070, Employee's Report of Tips to Employer

[2]Employers and employees of large food or beverage establishments where the tips average less than 8% of the gross receipts may petition the IRS to reduce the tip allocation. The tip allocation may be set as low as 2%. The IRS Revenue Procedure that provides the guidelines for petitioning states that more than one-half of the directly tipped employees must consent to the petition.

Allocated Tips, (not illustrated) is used. Detailed instructions for calculating the amount of allocated tips accompany this form.

Tax Savings for the Employer and the Employee. The payroll manager must be careful to apply the FICA tax only to those kinds of compensation that are regarded as taxable wages for social security purposes. Otherwise, both the company and the employee suffer when the tax is applied to exempt payments. Several examples of compensation that are *excluded* from the definition of wages for FICA tax purposes are described below.

Meals and Lodging. The value of meals or lodging furnished employees *for the convenience of the employer* is not wages for FICA purposes. If the meals and lodging do not meet the convenience-of-employer test, their value will be wages subject to FICA taxes.

The IRS has placed no specific value on meals or lodging furnished by employers to employees. Instead, the IRS relies on state valuations. Where a state has no law or regulation on the subject, fair value is defined as the reasonable prevailing value of the meals or lodging. In determining this value, some of the factors used are: (a) the value employers charge in their accounting records for meals or lodging, (b) any agreement between employer and employees as to the value, and (c) the specific type of meal or lodging provided.

Sick Pay. *Sick pay* is defined as any payment made to individuals, because of their personal injury or sickness, that does not constitute wages. The sick pay payments must be part of a plan to which the employer is a party. Further, sick pay must be paid for a period during which employees are *temporarily* absent from work because of injury or sickness. Sick pay does not include amounts paid under a plan if paid to individuals who are *permanently* disabled. As indicated earlier, the first six months of sick pay that employees receive are considered wages and thus are subject to withholding for FICA tax purposes. The period off the job must be continuous for six months. A relapse after a return to work starts a new six-month period. Payments made after the expiration of six calendar months following the last month in which the employee worked for the employer are not taxed.

Sick-pay payments may be made by a third party rather than by the employer. Typically, the third party is an insurance company. However, third parties also include trusts that provide incidental sick and accident benefits, and employers' associations funded to pay sickness and accident benefits. When sickness and accident benefits are paid by a third party, the third party is treated as a separate employer and is required to withhold and deposit the FICA taxes. However, the third party may be relieved of the liability for the employer's share of the FICA taxes. Thus, the employer may be charged with the liability for paying the employer portion of the FICA taxes if the third party fulfills each of these requirements:

1. Withholds the employee portion of the FICA tax.
2. Deposits the employee portion of the FICA tax.
3. Notifies the employer of the amount of wages or compensation involved.

For administrative convenience, an employer may contract with the third party to have it deposit the employer portion of the tax as well as the employee portion.

Generally payments made to employees or their dependents for medical or hospital expenses in connection with sickness or accident disability are not considered wages. However, these payments must be part of a system or a plan established by the employer for all employees or for a particular class of employees.

Simplified Employee Pension (SEP) Plans. Employers are permitted to contribute to individual retirement accounts and annuities that have been set up by or on behalf of employees. As indicated in Unit 1, such contribution arrangements are called *simplified employee pension (SEP) plans*. Employer contributions to SEP plans are *exempt* from FICA taxes if there is reason to believe that employees will be entitled to deduct the employer contributions for federal income tax purposes.

Payments for Educational Assistance. *Educational assistance* refers to the expenses that an employer pays for an employee's education, such as tuition, fees, and payments for books, supplies, and equipment. Also, educational assistance includes the cost of employer-provided courses of instruction (books, supplies, and equipment). Educational assistance *does not* include payment for tools or supplies that are kept by employees after they complete a course of instruction. Also, not included is any payment for courses or other education involving sports, games, or hobbies. The benefits received by employees under their employer's educational assistance plan are not includible in an employee's gross income. Further, these benefits are specifically excluded from "wages," as defined by FICA.

The Internal Revenue Code specifies that an employer's *nondiscriminatory educational assistance plan* must be in writing and designed for the exclusive purpose of providing employees with educational assistance. Further, the plan must not discriminate in favor of company officers, shareholders, owners, or highly compensated employees. The exclusion for employer-paid educational assistance does not apply to graduate-level courses nor to courses on sports, gardening, photography, etc.

Often employees take educational courses to improve their job skills or to meet the requirements for retaining their current jobs. If the employer pays the tuition costs to, or on behalf of, employees for such courses, the reimbursements are ordinary business expenses of the employer and thus are not subject to FICA taxes.

Up to October 1, 1990, the maximum amount of educational assistance benefits an employee could receive, free of FICA taxes during the year, was limited to $5,250. Any benefits in excess of this amount were subject to FICA taxes.[3]

In their annual income tax reporting, employers may deduct the educational assistance payments as business expenses, and employees may exclude the amounts from their gross income. If, however, the plan does not meet the requirements of the Code, the educational assistance payments must ordinarily be treated as wages subject to withholding for FICA tax purposes.

Taxable Wage Base

The *taxable wage base* is the maximum amount of wages during a calendar year that is subject to the FICA tax. Once this taxable wage base has been reached, all payments made to the employee during the remainder of the year, even though they are clearly wages, cease to be *taxable* wages. Thus, the collection of the FICA tax from that employee is no longer required. The wage base applies to amounts *paid* employees in a calendar year and not to the time when the services were performed by the employees.

EXAMPLE:

Renee Riley is paid on January 3, 1992, for work done during the last week of December, 1991. The wages would be taxed as income in the calendar year 1992, using 1992 tax rates.

The taxable wage base is subject to *escalator* increases whereby it is automatically adjusted whenever a *cost-of-living adjustment (COLA)* in social security benefits becomes available. The amount of the social security COLA each year is based on the growth from year to year in average annual wages in *all* employment.

Tax Rate

Under the Social Security Act as amended, taxes are imposed on employers and on employees for old-age, survivors, and disability insurance (OASDI) benefits, and for hospital insurance (HI) benefits. The 1991 social security tax rate is 7.65% for both the employer and the employee portions of the tax. A breakdown of the tax rate is given below:

OASDI Rate	6.20%
HI Rate	1.45
Combined Social Security Tax Rate	7.65%

Prior to 1951, taxable wages were limited to the first $3,000 earned in any year. By 1991 that wage base had increased to an estimated $54,300.[4] Along with this increase, the tax rate had climbed from 1.0% prior to 1950 to 7.65% in 1991.

Employees' FICA Taxes and Withholdings

Under FICA, employers are required to collect the FICA taxes from their employees and pay the taxes to the IRS at the same time they pay their own tax. The employee's portion of the tax is collected by deducting it from the wages at the time of payment. The amount of the tax to be withheld is computed by applying to the employee's taxable wages the tax rate in effect at the time that the wages are received. The rate to be applied is usually stated as a combined rate, 7.65%, for both types of insurance, rather than 6.20% for OASDI and 1.45% for HI. Thus, only one computation is needed in order to determine the tax to be withheld.

Employees are liable for the tax only until the employer has collected it from them. In other words, the liability for the tax extends to both the employee and the employer; but after the employer has collected the tax, the employee's liability ceases.

The following examples illustrate the computation of the FICA tax to be withheld.

[3]The exclusion of benefits paid under an employer's nondiscriminatory educational assistance plan expired September 30, 1990. At the time of this writing, the exclusion had not been reinstated beyond that date.

[4]At the time of this writing, it was estimated by the Social Security Board of Trustees that the taxable wage base for 1991 would be $54,300. However, in the past, the Trustees' projections have typically been a few hundred dollars low. The actual taxable wage base is not released until October or November each year. For future years, the Social Security Board's estimates of the taxable wage base are: 1992, $57,300; 1993, $60,300; 1994, $63,300; and 1995, $66,900.

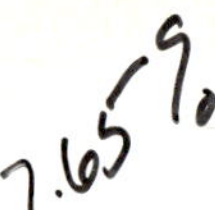

EXAMPLES:

1. **Anthony Winfield, who is employed by the Davis Company, earned $460 during the week ended February 1, 1991. He is paid for these earnings on February 8. Prior to this pay his cumulative gross earnings for the year were $1,895.70. The computation of the FICA tax to be withheld is:**

Taxable Wages	$ 460
Tax Rate	x 7.65%
FICA Tax to be Withheld	$35.19

2. **Alexia Mariano is a salaried employee of the Duncan Advertising Agency, and she is paid $1,250 every Friday. Prior to the pay of November 1, 1991, she had earned $53,750. The cumulative amount of FICA taxes withheld was $4,112.09 (43 weeks x $95.63 FICA taxes withheld weekly). The FICA tax to be withheld from Mariano's pay on November 1 is calculated as follows:**

Taxable Wage Limit	$54,300
Wages Paid to Date	53,750
Taxable Wages This Pay	$ 550
Tax Rate	x 7.65%
FICA Tax to be Withheld	$ 42.08[5]

3. **Edward Diaz is a waiter at the Uptowner Lounge. On April 1, 1991, he reported to his employer $240 of tips that he received during the month of March. On April 5, he was paid his regular salary of $200 for a 35-hour workweek. The FICA tax to be withheld from his pay would be:**

Taxable Wages	$ 200
Taxable Tips	240
Total Subject to FICA Tax	$ 440
Tax Rate	x 7.65%
FICA Tax to be Withheld	$33.66

In calculating the taxes, you may disregard any fractional part of a cent that results from applying the tax rate to the employee's taxable wages if it is less than half a cent. If the fractional part amounts to one-half cent or more, increase the amount of FICA tax withheld to the next whole cent.

Sometimes we find that an employee has paid FICA taxes on wages in excess of the taxable base because of having worked for more than one employer. If so, the employee is entitled to a refund for the overpayment. The amount of the overpayment is credited against the employee's federal income taxes for that year. Instructions are given on the *Individual Income Tax Return (Form 1040)* that explain how the overpayment should be treated.

Through error an employer may withhold too much FICA tax from employees' earnings and turn the money over to the IRS. In such a case the employer should repay the amount to the employees and make an adjustment on the quarterly tax return, as explained later in this unit.

Employer's FICA Taxes

In addition to withholding the correct amount of FICA tax from the employees' taxable earnings, the employer must make contributions to the program. The employer's portion of the tax is based on the wages paid to the employees. The tax is 7.65% of each employee's wages paid; however, as with employee withholdings, once the taxable wage base is reached, the employer no longer contributes for that particular employee. The employer's FICA tax, however, is not computed on the wages paid each employee but on the total taxable wages paid all employees.

EXAMPLE:

The Reardon Company has 100 employees, each earning $375.25 a week. The amount of tax withheld from each employee's paycheck each week is $28.71 (7.65% x $375.25). The total tax withheld from the 100 employees' wages is $2,871. The tax on the employer is 7.65% of the total payroll for the week, or $2,870.66 (7.65% x $37,525).

SELF-EMPLOYED PERSONS—THEIR INCOME AND TAXES

Coverage under the social security system was extended to the self-employed in 1951 under the *Self-Employment Contributions Act (SECA)*. Over the years we find that most self-employed persons have become covered by the law.

Self-Employment Income

An individual's self-employment income is the basis for levying taxes under SECA, and for determining the amount of income that may be credited toward old-age, survivors, and disability insurance

[5] In the design of many payroll accounting systems, the FICA taxable earnings are accumulated until the cut-off point ($54,300, maximum taxable earnings base) is reached. In other systems designs, the amount of FICA taxes withheld is accumulated until the cut-off point ($4,153.95, maximum FICA taxes withheld) is reached. Depending upon which cut-off point is used, there may be a few cents difference in the final amount of FICA taxes to be withheld. In this example, the FICA taxable earnings are accumulated until the $54,300 cut-off point is reached. For those using the $4,153.95 maximum FICA taxes withheld cut-off, the final amount to be withheld under this approach would be 22 cents less, or $41.86.

benefits or hospital insurance coverage. *Self-employment income* generally consists of the net earnings derived by individuals from a business or profession carried on by them as sole proprietors or by a partnership of which they are members.

We determine net earnings from self-employment by finding the sum of the following:

1. The gross income derived by an individual from any business or profession carried on, less allowable deductions attributable to such business or profession, and
2. The individual's distributive share (whether or not distributed) of the ordinary net income or loss from any business or profession carried on by a partnership of which the individual is a member.

Ordinarily the net business income of individuals as shown in their income tax returns constitutes their net earnings from self-employment for the purpose of the Social Security Act. Earnings of less than $400 from self-employment are ignored. The estimated maximum self-employment taxable income of any individual for 1991 is $54,300. If any wages are received, we reduce the maximum amount of taxable self-employment income by the amount of such wages. Thus, the aggregate amount of wages and self-employment income cannot exceed $54,300 in 1991.

EXAMPLE:

Terri Ripken receives wages in 1991 amounting to $54,600. Any earnings derived from self-employment do not constitute taxable self-employment income.

If the wages received in 1991 amount to less than $54,300, any self-employment earnings amounting to $400 or more must be counted as self-employment income up to an aggregate amount of $54,300.

EXAMPLE:

Anne Devereaux receives wages in 1991 amounting to $45,100. Her net earnings from self-employment amount to $10,200. Therefore, Devereaux must count $9,200 ($9,200 + $45,100 = $54,300) of her earnings in determining taxable self-employment income.

Taxable Year

In computing the taxes on self-employment income, the taxable year is the same as that used for income tax purposes. In the case of a partnership, the taxable year of the partners may not correspond with that of the partnership. In such instances the partners are required to include in computing net earnings from self-employment their distributive share of the income or loss of the partnership for any taxable year ending with or within their taxable year.

Reporting Self-Employment Income

Self-employment income is reported by individuals by transferring certain data from the *Profit or Loss From Business* schedule of their income tax return, *Schedule C*, Form 1040, to the *Social Security Self-Employment Tax* schedule, *Schedule SE*, on the same return.

Self-employed persons are required to include self-employment taxes in their quarterly payment of estimated income taxes. The taxpayer's estimated income tax is the sum of the estimated income taxes and self-employment taxes less any credits against the tax. Thus, each quarter the self-employed person is currently paying self-employment taxes into the social security and Medicare funds.

Self-Employment Taxes

The 1991 social security tax rate for self-employed persons is:

OASDI Rate	12.40%
HI Rate	2.90
Combined Social Security Tax Rate	15.30%

However, self-employed persons are able to reduce their taxable self-employment income in order to lessen the impact of the higher social security tax rates. This deduction is calculated according to the instructions that accompany Form 1040 and Schedule SE.

If self-employed persons report their earnings on a fiscal-year basis, they must use the tax rate that applies to the calendar year in which their fiscal year begins.

APPLICATION FOR EMPLOYER IDENTIFICATION NUMBER (FORM SS-4)

Every employer of one or more persons is required to file an application for an identification number (Form SS-4). A filled-in copy of Form SS-4 is shown in Illustration 3-2. The application form is available from any IRS or social security office.

An employer should file Form SS-4 early enough to allow for its processing, preferably four weeks before the number will be needed. The application must

Form **SS-4**

Department of the Treasury
Internal Revenue Service

Application for Employer Identification Number

(For use by employers and others. Please read the attached instructions before completing this form.) Please type or print clearly.

EIN

OMB No. 1545-0003

1 Name of applicant (True legal name) (See instructions.)
Montana Mining, Inc.

2 Trade name of business, if different from name in line 1

3 Executor, trustee, "care of name"
Care of Carla P. Ortiz

4a Mailing address (street address) (room, apt., or suite no.)
P.O. Box 447

5a Address of business. (See instructions.)
1200 High Gap

4b City, state, and ZIP code
Butte, MT 59701-0210

5b City, state, and ZIP code
Butte, MT 59701-1200

6 County and state where principal business is located
Silver Bow, MT

7 Name of principal officer, grantor, or general partner. (See instructions.) ▶
Grant X. Bilton, President

8a Type of entity (Check only one box.) (See instructions.)
☐ Individual SSN ____
☐ REMIC
☐ Personal service corp.
☐ State/local government
☐ National guard
☐ Other nonprofit organization (specify) ____
☐ Other (specify) ▶
☐ Estate
☐ Plan administrator SSN ____
☒ Other corporation (specify) Extraction
☐ Federal government/military
☐ Trust
☐ Partnership
☐ Farmers' cooperative
☐ Church or church controlled organization
If nonprofit organization enter GEN (if applicable) ____

8b If a corporation, give name of foreign country (if applicable) or state in the U.S. where incorporated ▶
Foreign country
State: Montana

9 Reason for applying (Check only one box)
☒ Started new business
☐ Hired employees
☐ Created a pension plan (specify type) ▶
☐ Banking purpose (specify) ▶
☐ Changed type of organization (specify) ▶
☐ Purchased going business
☐ Created a trust (specify) ▶
☐ Other (specify) ▶

10 Date business started or acquired (Mo., day, year) (See instructions.)
July 3, 19--

11 Enter closing month of accounting year. (See instructions.)
June

12 First date wages or annuities were paid or will be paid (Mo., day, year). **Note:** *If applicant is a withholding agent, enter date income will first be paid to nonresident alien. (Mo., day, year)*. . . . . ▶ July 12, 19--

13 Enter highest number of employees expected in the next 12 months. **Note:** *If the applicant does not expect to have any employees during the period, enter "0."* . . . . ▶

Nonagricultural	Agricultural	Household
450		

14 Does the applicant operate more than one place of business? . . . . ☐ Yes ☒ No
If "Yes," enter name of business. ▶

15 Principal activity or service (See instructions.) ▶ Copper Extraction

16 Is the principal business activity manufacturing? . . . . ☐ Yes ☒ No
If "Yes," principal product and raw material used ▶

17 To whom are most of the products or services sold? Please check the appropriate box. ☒ Business (wholesale)
☐ Public (retail) ☐ Other (specify) ▶ ☐ N/A

18a Has the applicant ever applied for an identification number for this or any other business? . . . . ☐ Yes ☒ No
Note: *If "Yes," please complete lines 18b and 18c.*

18b If you checked the "Yes" box in line 18a, give applicant's true name and trade name, if different than name shown on prior application.
True name ▶ Trade name ▶

18c Enter approximate date, city, and state where the application was filed and the previous employer identification number if known.

Approximate date when filed (Mo., day, year)	City and state where filed	Previous EIN

Under penalties of perjury, I declare that I have examined this application, and to the best of my knowledge and belief, it is true, correct, and complete.

Name and title (Please type or print clearly.) ▶ Carla P. Ortiz, V.P., Finance

Telephone number (include area code) 406-555-2400

Signature ▶ *Carla P. Ortiz* Date ▶ 7/3/--

Note: *Do not write below this line. For official use only.*

Please leave blank ▶	Geo.	Ind.	Class	Size	Reason for applying

Form SS-4

Illustration 3-2. Form SS-4, Application for Employer Identification Number

be filed with the IRS center where the federal tax returns are filed. (See page 86.) If the employer has no legal residence, or principal place of business, or principal office in any IRS district, the application should be filed with the IRS Service Center, Philadelphia, PA 19255.

An employer may not have received an identification number prior to the time the required returns are to be filed. In such a case, the employer should write "Applied for" and the date of the application in the space shown on the return for the identification number. Each employer receives but one identification number regardless of how many different establishments, offices, stores, factories, warehouses, or branches may be maintained or operated. If a business is sold or otherwise transferred and the new owner does not have an identification number, the number assigned to the former owner cannot be used. The new owner must file an application for a new identification number.

The employer must enter the identification number on all returns, forms, and correspondence relating to the taxes imposed under FICA that are sent to the District Director of Internal Revenue. The identification number should be used in any correspondence with the Social Security Administration (SSA) and should be entered on forms that are issued by the SSA. The penalty for failure to supply identification numbers is discussed later in this unit.

EMPLOYEE'S APPLICATION FOR A SOCIAL SECURITY CARD (FORM SS-5)

Under the Social Security Act every employee and every self-employed person must have an account number. The application for an account number is available at any social security or IRS office. The *Application for a Social Security Card (Form SS-5)* can be filed with any field office of the SSA. A filled-in copy of Form SS-5 is shown in Illustration 3-3 on page 76.

The application for an employee's social security card should be made far enough in advance of its first required use to allow for the processing of the application. The Social Security Act requires applicants for an account number card to furnish evidence of their age, identity, and U.S. citizenship or lawful alien status. Applicants may apply either by mailing the required documents and forms to their nearest Social Security office or by bringing them in person. However, individuals must apply *in person* at their Social Security office if they are age 18 or older and have never had a Social Security number card, or if they are aliens whose immigration documents should not be sent through the mail.

After filing Form SS-5, the employee will receive from the SSA a card showing the social security account number that has been assigned. See Illustration 3-4 on page 77.

Upon receipt of their account numbers, employees should advise their employers of the number assigned them. Care should be taken to see that employers are advised of the correct number. Should employees change positions, they must notify the new employer of their account number as soon as they commence employment. Should an employee change his or her name by court order or by marriage, the individual should request a new social security card by completing Form SS-5. Employees may have their account number changed at any time by applying to the SSA and showing good reasons for a change. Otherwise, only one account number is assigned to an employee and the employee will continue to use that number regardless of the number of changes in positions or the number of employers for whom service is rendered.

The Secretary of Health and Human Services is authorized to assure that social security numbers are issued to or on behalf of children who are below school age at the request of their parents or guardians and to children of school age when they first enroll in school. Further, Social Security account numbers must be obtained for children age two or over who are claimed as dependents on federal income tax returns. To thwart cheaters who claim dogs, cats, and nonexistent people as dependents, taxpayers are required to list the taxpayer identification numbers of any claimed dependents age two or over. The Secretary also insures that social security numbers are assigned to aliens when they are admitted to the United States under conditions that permit them to work.

Criminal penalties are provided (a) if one knowingly and willfully uses a social security number that was obtained with false information; (b) if one uses someone else's social security number; (c) if a person knowingly alters a social security card; buys or sells a card that is, or purports to be, a card issued by the Secretary; counterfeits a social security card; or possesses a social security card or counterfeit social security card with the intent to sell or alter it. The penalty involves a fine of up to $5,000 or imprisonment of up to 5 years, or both.

REQUEST FOR STATEMENT OF EARNINGS (FORM SSA-7004)

Each employee who has received taxable wages under the Social Security Act has an account with the SSA. This account shows the amount of wages credited to the employee's account. When employees or

SOCIAL SECURITY ADMINISTRATION
Application for a Social Security Card

Form Approved
OMB No. 0960-0066

INSTRUCTIONS
- Please read "How To Complete This Form" on page 2.
- Print or type using black or blue ink. DO NOT USE PENCIL.
- After you complete this form, take or mail it along with the required documents to your nearest Social Security office.
- If you are completing this form for someone else, answer the questions as they apply to that person. Then, sign your name in question 16.

1 NAME To Be Shown On Card: Bertha (FIRST) Mary (FULL MIDDLE NAME) Davis (LAST)

FULL NAME AT BIRTH IF OTHER THAN ABOVE: FIRST / FULL MIDDLE NAME / LAST

OTHER NAMES USED

2 MAILING ADDRESS Do Not Abbreviate: 18 Dundee Avenue (STREET ADDRESS, APT. NO., PO BOX, RURAL ROUTE NO.)
Akron (CITY) Ohio (STATE) 44320-2968 (ZIP CODE)

3 CITIZENSHIP (Check One): [X] U.S. Citizen [ ] Legal Alien Allowed To Work [ ] Legal Alien Not Allowed To Work [ ] Foreign Student Allowed Restricted Employment [ ] Conditionally Legalized Alien Allowed To Work [ ] Other (See Instructions On Page 2)

4 SEX: [ ] Male [X] Female

5 RACE/ETHNIC DESCRIPTION (Check One Only—Voluntary): [ ] Asian, Asian-American Or Pacific Islander [ ] Hispanic [X] Black (Not Hispanic) [ ] North American Indian Or Alaskan Native [ ] White (Not Hispanic)

6 DATE OF BIRTH: 8 1 66 (MONTH DAY YEAR)

7 PLACE OF BIRTH (Do Not Abbreviate): Lima (CITY) Ohio (STATE OR FOREIGN COUNTRY) FCI

Office Use Only

8 MOTHER'S MAIDEN NAME: Ruth (FIRST) Ann (FULL MIDDLE NAME) Archer (LAST NAME AT HER BIRTH)

9 FATHER'S NAME: Roger (FIRST) Paul (FULL MIDDLE NAME) Davis (LAST)

10 Has the person in item 1 ever applied for or received a Social Security number before?
[ ] Yes (If "yes", answer questions 11-13.) [X] No (If "no", go on to question 14.) [ ] Don't Know (If "don't know", go on to question 14.)

11 Enter the Social Security number previously assigned to the person listed in item 1.
☐☐☐-☐☐-☐☐☐☐

12 Enter the name shown on the most recent Social Security card issued for the person listed in item 1.
FIRST / MIDDLE / LAST

13 Enter any different date of birth if used on an earlier application for a card. MONTH DAY YEAR

14 TODAY'S DATE: 1 12 -- (MONTH DAY YEAR)

15 DAYTIME PHONE NUMBER: (419) 555-4321 (AREA CODE)

DELIBERATELY FURNISHING (OR CAUSING TO BE FURNISHED) FALSE INFORMATION ON THIS APPLICATION IS A CRIME PUNISHABLE BY FINE OR IMPRISONMENT, OR BOTH.

16 YOUR SIGNATURE: Bertha M Davis

17 YOUR RELATIONSHIP TO THE PERSON IN ITEM 1 IS: [X] Self [ ] Natural Or Adoptive Parent [ ] Legal Guardian [ ] Other (Specify)

DO NOT WRITE BELOW THIS LINE (FOR SSA USE ONLY)

NPN	DOC	NTI	CAN	ITV

PBC	EVI	EVA	EVC	NWR	DNR	UNIT

EVIDENCE SUBMITTED	SIGNATURE AND TITLE OF EMPLOYEE(S) REVIEWING EVIDENCE AND/OR CONDUCTING INTERVIEW
	DATE
	DCL DATE

Form SS-5

Illustration 3-3. Form SS-5, Application for a Social Security Card

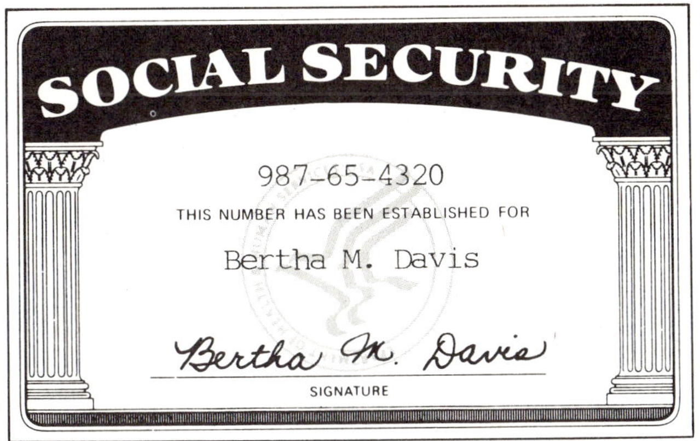

Illustration 3-4. Social Security Card

members of their family claim benefits, the wage credits in the employees' social security account are used to calculate the amount of benefits payable, as discussed in Appendix A.

The SSA makes it possible for employees to check the accuracy of the wage credits in their accounts. Form SSA-7004 (not illustrated) is the official form to use in requesting a statement of wages credited to an individual's account. Copies of this form are available by contacting the district office of the SSA or by calling the toll-free number, 1-800-937-2000.

After filing Form SSA-7004, workers will receive a statement of the social security covered wages earned each year since 1951 and an estimate of how much was paid in payroll taxes. For the years 1937-1950, a lump sum amount will be provided. Workers also receive an estimate of how much they would receive upon retirement at ages 62, 65, or 70. For younger workers, who will be expected to work until age 66 or 67 to draw full retirement benefits, that age is used instead of 65. Also, estimates are given for the amount of payments that widows or widowers and children under age 18 would receive upon the death or disability of the wage earner.

Because of errors that employers make in reporting wage information to the SSA and the IRS, from time to time workers should compare their wage records with those of the SSA. For example, in 1988, the SSA credited over $2 trillion in earnings to the accounts of 130 million workers. It is estimated that there were more than one million discrepancies between the reports received by the SSA and the IRS. Further, three million more wage reports are held in a suspense file while the agency tries to clear up missing or faulty employer and employee ID numbers and to correct other errors.[6] As a result, many workers lose credits for the social security taxes they have paid. If workers find any discrepancies between their records and the accounts kept by the SSA, claims can be made for adjustment. Errors will be corrected if they are reported within 3 years, 3 months, and 15 days following the close of any taxable year.

Beginning in 1995, statements of wages credited to employees' accounts will be provided automatically to persons who attain age 60. In 1999 the statements will be provided automatically to those under age 60 as well.

QUARTERLY RETURNS REQUIRED UNDER FICA

Employers covered under FICA are liable for their own FICA taxes and for their employees' FICA and income taxes that are withheld from the employees' wages. The withholding of income taxes is discussed in Unit 4. Every employer, except those employing agricultural workers, who is required to withhold income taxes from wages or who is liable for social security taxes must file a quarterly tax and information return. The quarterly return shows the total taxable wages (for FICA purposes) paid and the total amount of FICA taxes (employer and employee contributions) and income taxes withheld.

Generally an employer must deposit the income taxes and social security taxes withheld and the employer's FICA taxes in an authorized depositary or a Federal Reserve bank that serves the employer's geographic area. In other instances, as explained later in this section, the employer is not required to deposit the taxes but, instead, remits them with the quarterly return.

Any employer who fails to pay the withheld income taxes and FICA taxes, or fails to make deposits and payments, or does not file the tax returns as required by law may be required to deposit such taxes in a special trust account for the U.S. government and file monthly tax returns.

Forms Required Under FICA

The major forms used in preparing FICA tax returns and deposits are listed and briefly described in Illustration 3-5 on page 78.

Deposit Requirements for Employers of Nonagricultural Workers

The requirements for depositing FICA taxes and income taxes withheld from nonagricultural employees' wages vary according to the total amount of such taxes. Depending on the aggregate amount of

[6] *The Wall Street Journal*, 30 May 1990.

Form 941, Employer's Quarterly Federal Tax Return	Required of all covered employers, except employers of household employees and agricultural employees, subject to either income tax withholding or social security taxes, or both. (See Illustration 3-8, page 84.)
Form 941c, Statement to Correct Information	Used to correct income and social security tax information previously reported on Forms 941, 941E, 941-M, 941SS, 942, or 943.
Form 941E, Quarterly Return of Withheld Federal Income Tax and Hospital Insurance (Medicare) Tax	Required of employers who withhold federal income taxes *only* from remuneration such as wages, tips, annuities, and supplemental unemployment compensation benefits. Form 941E is also used by state and local government employers *not* covered by a voluntary agreement with the Secretary of Health and Human Services to provide social security coverage.
Form 941-M, Employer's Monthly Federal Tax Return	Required of employers who have not complied with the requirements for filing returns or paying or depositing all taxes reported on quarterly returns. Notification to file Form 941-M is received from the District Director, and preaddressed forms are mailed the employer monthly.
Form 941PR, Employer's Quarterly Federal Tax Return	Required of employers to report social security taxes for workers in Puerto Rico.
Form 941SS, Employer's Quarterly Federal Tax Return	Required of employers to report social security taxes for workers in American Samoa, Guam, the Northern Mariana Islands, and the Virgin Islands.
Form 942, Employer's Quarterly Tax Return for Household Employees	Used by employers of household workers for reporting FICA and income taxes on wages paid.
Form 943, Employer's Annual Tax Return for Agricultural Employees	Used by employers of agricultural workers for reporting FICA and income taxes on wages paid.
Form 8109, Federal Tax Deposit Coupon Book	A book containing coupons that are completed at the time of depositing various types of taxes such as withheld income and FICA (Form 941), agricultural withheld income and FICA (Form 943), and federal unemployment (Form 940, as discussed in Unit 5).

Illustration 3-5. Major Forms for Preparing FICA Tax Returns and Deposits

taxes involved (federal income tax and FICA tax withheld from employees' earnings plus the employer's portion of the FICA tax), employers may have to deposit their taxes several times a month, once each month, or quarterly. Further, as discussed below, some employers may not have to make any deposits.

Less Than $500 at End of Quarter. If at the end of the quarter the total undeposited taxes for the quarter are less than $500, no deposit is required. The taxes may be paid to the IRS at the time of filing the quarterly return, Form 941, which is discussed on pages 83-87. However, if the employer wishes, the taxes may be deposited by the end of the next month.

Less Than $500 at End of Month. If at the end of any month the total undeposited taxes are less than $500, no deposit is required. The amount of the undeposited taxes may be carried over to the following month within the quarter.

EXAMPLE:

The taxes on wages paid in October are $480. The taxes on wages paid in November are $570. No deposit is required for October, but the $480 is added to the $570 for November and the total ($1,050) must be deposited by December 15.

$500 or More But Less Than $3,000 at End of Any Month. If at the end of any month the total undeposited taxes are $500 or more but less than $3,000, the taxes must be deposited within 15 days after the end of the month. (This deposit requirement does not apply if the employer has made a deposit for an eighth-monthly period during the month under the $3,000 rule discussed below. See Example No. 3.)

$3,000 or More But Less Than $100,000 at the End of Eighth-Monthly Period. If the amount of employee and employer FICA taxes and income taxes withheld totals $3,000 or more, but less than $100,000, at the end of any eighth-monthly period, the taxes must be deposited within the next three banking days. Eighth-monthly periods end on the 3d, 7th, 11th, 15th, 19th, 22d, 25th, and the last day of each month. Nonbanking days are local banking holidays, Saturdays, Sundays, and legal holidays.

EXAMPLES:

---

1. **The taxes on wages paid from the 1st through the 3d of a month are $3,400. The taxes must be deposited within three banking days after the 3d of the month.**
2. **The taxes on wages paid from the 4th through the 7th of a month are $2,400. The taxes on wages paid from the 8th through the 11th are $1,800. No separate deposit is required for the $2,400. Instead, this amount is added to the $1,800 and the total ($4,200) must be deposited within three banking days after the 11th of the month.**
3. **The taxes on wages paid from the 23d through the 25th of January are $3,400. These taxes should be deposited within three banking days after the 25th of January. The taxes on wages paid from the 26th through the end of January are $2,300. A separate deposit is not required for the $2,300. Instead, this amount is carried over and added to the wages paid in February. (If, however, such a situation occurs in the last month of a quarter, any balance due of $500 or more but less than $3,000 should be deposited by the end of the next month.) If the undeposited liability reaches $3,000 or more before the 15th of the next month, this will require a deposit within 3 banking days after the applicable eighth-monthly period.**

The amount deposited by the employer can be affected by the *safe-haven rule*. Under this rule, employers required to make eighth-monthly deposits can at their option deposit at least 95% of their tax liability at the prescribed time without incurring any penalty for late deposits. Any underpayment for an eighth-monthly period in the first or second month of a quarter is due when the first deposit after the 15th of the next month comes due. Thus, if a deposit is required by the 18th of the next month, any underpayments for the preceding month are also due by that date. If the eighth-monthly period is in the last month of the quarter, any underpayment of $500 or more must be deposited by the end of the next month. Any underpayment less than $500 can be paid with Form 941. Employers using the 95% rule should be sure to check the appropriate box in the Record of Federal Tax Liability section on Form 941.

There is an exception to the three-banking-day deposit requirement if this is the *first* time employers are required to make a deposit within three banking days after the end of an eighth-monthly period. In such a case, employers may deposit the taxes by the 15th day of the next month (instead of within three banking days after the eighth-monthly period) if employers meet all of the following conditions:

1. Employers were not required to deposit taxes for any eighth-monthly period during the last four quarters.
2. Employers were not required to deposit taxes for any eighth-monthly period during earlier months of this quarter.
3. The total undeposited taxes at the end of any eighth-monthly period during this month are less than $10,000.

Employers qualifying for this exception should check the appropriate box in the Record of Federal Tax Liability section on Form 941 and attach a statement showing their net taxes for each of the last four calendar quarters.

$100,000 or More on Any Payday. If the amount of employee and employer FICA taxes and income taxes withheld *on any payday* in 1990 totaled $100,000, the taxes had to be deposited by the close of the next banking day. This requirement is effective even if the payday does not fall on the end of an eighth-monthly period. In 1991, the taxes must be deposited on the second banking day; in 1992, taxes are due on the third banking day. In 1993 and 1994, the taxes must be deposited on the first banking day after that day on which the employer has $100,000 or more to be deposited. For 1995 and thereafter, the Secretary of Treasury will announce the due date for the deposits.

EXAMPLES:

---

1. **At the end of business on Wednesday, May 15, 1991, the close of an eighth-monthly period, an employer has $60,000 of income tax withheld and FICA taxes. The $60,000 must be deposited within 3 banking days after May 15 in order to prevent a penalty for failure to deposit. On Thursday, May 16, the employer has an additional $70,000 of income tax**

withheld and FICA taxes. The employer is *not* required to deposit the $130,000 on the second banking day even though that amount of income tax withheld and FICA taxes is on hand. The obligation to deposit the $60,000 was fixed at the close of business on Wednesday, May 15, and that amount is taken into account for purposes of the $100,000 or more deposit rule. The $60,000 must be deposited by Monday, May 20, 1991, 3 banking days after Wednesday, May 15. The date by which the $70,000 must be deposited depends on what additional amounts, if any, are accumulated during the May 16-19 eighth-monthly period.

2. **Assume all the facts above, *except* the additional amount on hand on Thursday, May 16, is $108,000, not $70,000. The entire amount, $168,000, must be deposited by Monday, May 20, 1991. (The $60,000 deposit is required to be made within 3 banking days; the $108,000 must be deposited on the second banking day.)**

Some employers may have a tax liability of $100,000 or more for two consecutive eighth-monthly periods. In this case, employers are required to complete *Schedule B, Supplemental Record of Federal Tax Liability,* which is filed with Form 941. On Schedule B employers report their tax liability *day by day* for those periods. The tax liability by day must be reported even though an employer might not be subject to the next-banking-day deposit requirement.

Summary of Deposit Rules. The deposit rules for nonagricultural employers are summarized in Illustration 3-6.

Accumulated Unpaid Liability	Deposit Requirement
1. Less than $500 at the end of the calendar quarter—	1. Must be paid by the end of the following month, either as a deposit or with the quarterly tax return (Form 941).
2. Less than $500 at the end of any month—	2. No deposit is required. The amount of undeposited taxes is carried over to the following month within the quarter.
3. $500 or more but less than $3,000 at the end of any month—	3. Must deposit the accumulated liability by the 15th of the following month.
4. $3,000 or more but less than $100,000 at the end of any eighth-monthly period—	4. Must deposit the accumulated liability within three banking days after the close of the eighth-monthly period.
5. $100,000 or more on any payday—	5. In 1991, must deposit the accumulated liability by the close of the *second* banking day.

Illustration 3-6. Summary of Deposit Rules for Nonagricultural Employers

Deposit Requirements for Employers of Agricultural Workers

For the most part, the deposit-making rules that apply to employers of agricultural laborers (farm workers) are the same as those for employers of nonagricultural workers. However, there are a few exceptions, which are explained in the instructions accompanying *Form 943, Employer's Annual Tax Return for Agricultural Employees.*

The taxes reported on Form 943 include both income and FICA taxes. Thus, when employers of farm workers determine whether a deposit is due, they combine the FICA taxes due on wages paid with any federal income taxes withheld as a result of a voluntary agreement between them and their workers. If employers hire both agricultural and nonagricultural workers, generally they must combine the total taxes due for both kinds of workers in determining whether a deposit is due.

Employers of agricultural workers, as well as those who employ nonagricultural workers, must use the *Federal Tax Deposit Coupon Book (Form 8109).* The procedures to be followed in making deposits and completing Form 8109 are discussed in a later section.

Deposit Requirements for Employers of Household Employees

Household or domestic employees are usually not subject to federal income tax withholding, but they may voluntarily request that federal income taxes be withheld from their wages. Even though federal income taxes are not withheld from household employees' wages, their wages are subject to FICA taxes if each worker has been paid cash wages of $50 or more in a calendar quarter. The value of food, lodging, clothing, car tokens, and other noncash items given to household employees is not subject to FICA taxes. However, cash given in place of these items is considered wages.

Employers who withhold and pay FICA taxes or federal income taxes based on the wages paid domestic workers must file *Form 942, Employer's Quarterly*

Tax Return for Household Employees. On the quarterly return employers indicate the amount of wages paid and the amount of the income and FICA taxes collected. The return must be filed beginning with the first calendar quarter in which taxable wages are paid, either for FICA or federal income tax withholding purposes, and continuing, whether or not taxable wages are paid, until a final return is filed.

Employers must file Form 942 on or before the last day of the month following the close of each calendar quarter. So long as this form is used, the income and FICA taxes on wages paid domestic employees do not have to be counted in determining whether employers are required to make periodic tax deposits under the rules outlined earlier. Payment should accompany the return. If employers have both business and household employees, they may choose to report the wages and taxes applicable to their household workers on Form 941. In this case, the domestic workers' wages must be counted in determining the need for a periodic deposit.

Deposit Requirements for State and Local Government Employers

As you saw earlier, provision is made for the coverage of employees of state and local governments by means of voluntary agreement entered into between the state and the Secretary of Health and Human Services. Each state and local government employer covered under a voluntary agreement must file its return on Form 941 with the IRS and deposit its FICA taxes through the federal deposit system, as explained below. State and local government employers are required to make their tax deposits according to the same deposit schedule used by private employers.

Procedures for Making Deposits

Deposits of FICA taxes and employees' federal income taxes withheld are made by using one of the preprinted coupons included in the *Federal Tax Deposit Coupon Book, Form 8109.* This book is used for depositing various types of taxes in a Federal Reserve bank or in an authorized commercial depositary. Employers indicate on the coupon the type of tax being deposited and include a coupon with each deposit. To obtain additional coupons, employers should complete the Reorder Form, Form 8109A, that is provided in the coupon book.[7] A sample coupon form and part of the instructions for its completion are reproduced in Illustration 3-7 on page 82.

Employers who make their deposits at a Federal Reserve bank must make them at the Federal Reserve bank that serves their geographic area. Also, they must make payment with an "immediate credit item." An *immediate credit item* is a check or other instrument of payment for which immediate credit is given by the receiving bank in accordance with its check-collection schedule. If a deposit is not made with an immediate credit item, the bank stamps the coupon to reflect the name of the bank and the date on which the proceeds of the accompanying payment instrument are collected by the Federal Reserve bank. This date is used to determine the timeliness of the payment.

Authorized depositaries are required to accept cash, postal money orders drawn to the order of the depositary, or checks and drafts drawn on and to the order of the depositary. Employers may make a tax deposit by means of a check drawn on another financial institution only if the depositary is willing to accept that payment as a deposit of federal taxes.

The timeliness of deposits is determined by the date they are received by the commercial bank depositary or the Federal Reserve bank. However, a deposit of less than $20,000 received after the due date will be considered timely if the employer establishes that it was mailed on or before the second day before the prescribed date. A tax deposit of $20,000 or more must be at the depositary or the Federal Reserve bank on the due date.

When making a deposit, the employer enters the amount of the payment in the accounting records. The check or money order number is also recorded and serves as a source document for the entry. The employer may make a photocopy of the form if desired, but the canceled check may be used as a receipt. Form 8109 is not returned by the bank to the employer but is used as the basis for crediting the employer's tax account identified by the employer's identification number on the face of the form. The bank stamps the date and bank name on the form where indicated. The tax deposits are then forwarded by the bank to the IRS service center for posting to the taxpayer's account. When each employer's quarterly return is received, the IRS reconciles the tax deposits with the payments claimed on the return. At this point, settlement of the employer's tax liability is made.

[7] *Form 8109-B, Federal Tax Deposit Coupon,* is used by employers *only* if: (1) preprinted deposit coupons, Forms 8109, have been reordered but have not yet been received; or (2) the employer is a new entity and an employer identification number has been assigned but the initial supply of preprinted deposit coupons has not been received.

TAX YEAR MONTH →

AMOUNT OF DEPOSIT (Do NOT type; please print.)

DOLLARS	CENTS
3535	36

EMPLOYER IDENTIFICATION NUMBER → 89 1437003

BANK NAME/ DATE STAMP

Name Lopez Enterprises, Inc.

Address 25 Park Lane

City Columbus

State GA Zip 31902-2582

Telephone number (404) 555-3300

IRS USE ONLY

Darken only one TYPE OF TAX		and	Darken only one TAX PERIOD
● 941	○ Sch. A		● 1st Quarter
○ 990C	○ 1120		○ 2nd Quarter
○ 943	○ 990-T		○ 3rd Quarter
○ 720	○ 990PF		○ 4th Quarter
○ CT-1	○ 1042		
○ 940			

35

FOR BANK USE IN MICR ENCODING

Federal Tax Deposit Coupon
Form 8109-B

IMPORTANT

Read instructions carefully before completing Form 8109-B Federal tax deposit coupon.

Note: Except for the name, address, and telephone number, entries are processed by optical scanning equipment and must be completed by hand in the manner specified. Please use a soft lead pencil (for example, a # 2 pencil) so that the entries can be read more accurately by the optical scanning equipment. The name, address, and telephone number may be completed other than by hand. You **CANNOT** use photocopies of the coupons to make your deposits.

Paperwork Reduction Act Notice.–We ask for this information to carry out the Internal Revenue laws of the United States. We need it to ensure that taxpayers are complying with these laws and to allow us to figure and collect the right amount of tax. You are required to give us this information.

The time needed to complete and file this form will vary depending on individual circumstances. The estimated average time is 1 hour and 57 minutes. If you have comments concerning the accuracy of this time estimate or suggestions for making this form more simple, we would be happy to hear from you. You can write to the **Internal Revenue Service,** Washington, DC 20224, Attention: IRS Reports Clearance Officer TR:FP; or the **Office of Management and Budget,** Paperwork Reduction Project, Washington, DC 20503.

Purpose of Form.–Use Form 8109-B deposit coupons to make tax deposits **only** in the following two situations:

(1) You have reordered preprinted deposit coupons **(Form 8109)** but have not yet received them; or

(2) You are a new entity and have already been assigned an employer identification number (EIN), but have not yet received your initial supply of preprinted deposit coupons (Form 8109).

Note: ***You should get your reordered coupons (or your initial supply) within 5-6 weeks of the reorder (or receipt of your EIN). If you do not, please contact your local IRS office.***

If you have applied for an EIN, have not received it, and a deposit must be made, send your payment to your Internal Revenue Service Center. Make your check or money order payable to IRS and show on it your name (as shown on **Form SS-4,** Application for Employer Identification Number), address, kind of tax, period covered, and date you applied for an EIN. Also, attach an explanation to the deposit. Do **NOT** use Form 8109-B in this situation.

Do **not** use Form 8109-B to deposit delinquent taxes for which you have been assessed by the IRS. Pay those taxes directly to the IRS.

How To Complete Form 8109-B.–Enter your name exactly as shown on your return or other IRS correspondence, address, and employer identification number in the spaces provided. If you are required to file a Form 1120, Form 990-C, Form 990-PF (with net investment income), Form 990-T, or Form 2438, enter the month in which your tax year ends in the **"TAX YEAR MONTH"** boxes. For example, if your tax year ends in January, enter 01; if it ends in June, enter 06; if it ends in December, enter 12. Please make your entries for employer identification number and tax year month (if applicable) in the manner specified in *Amount of Deposit* below. Darken one box each in the "Type of Tax" and "Tax Period" columns as explained below.

Amount of Deposit–

Enter the amount of the deposit in the space provided. Enter amount legibly, forming the characters as shown below:

1	2	3	4	5	6	7	8	9	0

Handprint money amounts without using dollar signs, commas, a decimal point, or leading zeros. The commas and decimal point are already shown in the entry area.

For example, a deposit of $7,635.22 would be entered like this:

DOLLARS	CENTS
7635	22

If the deposit is for whole dollars only, enter "00" in the "CENTS" boxes.

Illustration 3-7. Form 8109-B, Federal Tax Deposit Coupon, and a Portion of the Accompanying Instructions

EMPLOYER'S QUARTERLY FEDERAL TAX RETURN (FORM 941)

Generally the employer must make a quarterly return of FICA taxes and withheld income taxes for the three months of each calendar quarter, using *Form 941, Employer's Quarterly Federal Tax Return.* A filled-in copy of Form 941 is shown in Illustration 3-8 on page 84. Once Form 941 has been filed, the employer receives preaddressed forms every three months. If the form is not received, the employer should request one from an IRS office in time to file the return when due.

Completing the Return

To complete Lines 1 through 19 of Form 941, employers may obtain the information from various sources, such as those listed in Illustration 3-9 on page 85.

Completing the Record of Federal Tax Liability

If the net taxes for the quarter (shown on Line 16) are less than $500, there is no need to complete the Record of Federal Tax Liability at the bottom of Form 941. (As noted earlier, the employer may pay the taxes at the time of filing Form 941 or deposit them by the due date of the form.) If, on the other hand, the taxes for the quarter are $500 or more, we *must* complete the Record.

If the taxes for every month are less than $3,000, we may show the amounts on the Total lines (I, II, and III) and skip the other lines. If, however, the taxes for any month are $3,000 or more, we must make an entry on each eighth-monthly period line that corresponds to our firm's payday. The entire tax liability (income taxes withheld plus both the employee and employer social security taxes less any advance EIC payments) must be shown for each eighth-monthly period during which there was a payday. Note that we do *not* show the amount of *federal tax deposits* on the Record. The IRS obtains the amount of federal tax deposits from the deposit coupons.

Depending upon the net amount of tax remaining due, the employer either remits the amount directly to the IRS with Form 941 or deposits the amount in an authorized depositary.

Signing Form 941

Form 941 must be signed by the employer or other person who is required to withhold and pay the tax, as follows:

1. If the employer is an *individual*, the return should be signed by that person.
2. If the employer is a *corporation*, the return should be signed by its president, vice president, or other principal officer given authority to sign the return.

   Corporate officers or duly authorized agents may use facsimile signatures under certain conditions. Each group of returns must be accompanied by a letter signed by the person authorized to sign the returns declaring (a) that the facsimile signature appearing on the returns is the signature adopted by him or her, and (b) that the signature was affixed to the returns by the officer or agent or at his or her direction.
3. If the employer is a *partnership* or *other unincorporated organization*, a responsible and duly authorized partner or officer having knowledge of the firm's affairs should sign the return.
4. If the employer is a *political body*, such as a state or territory, the return should be signed by the officer or employee who has control of the wage payments or an officer properly designated for that purpose.

Filing Form 941

The return is due on or before the last day of the month following the close of the calendar quarter for which the return is made. If, however, we have made timely deposits of the taxes for a quarter, we may file the quarterly return on or before the 10th day of the second month following the close of the calendar quarter for which the return is made. If no deposits have been made during the quarter, we may still obtain the 10-day extension by making a deposit of any taxes due on or before the last day of the first calendar month following the close of the quarter.

If the last day for filing a quarterly return falls on Saturday, Sunday, or a legal holiday, we may file the return on the next business day. If the return is filed by mailing, we should mail the return in sufficient time for it to reach the IRS Center no later than the next business day under ordinary handling of the mail.

Individual employers file their quarterly returns with the IRS Center of the region in which the employer's principal place of business or office or agency is located. The locations of the IRS Centers are given in Illustration 3-10 on page 86. Even though the IRS requires that a particular return be filed at a regional service center, the return may still be filed at the local office of the district director of the IRS if the return is hand delivered by the taxpayer.

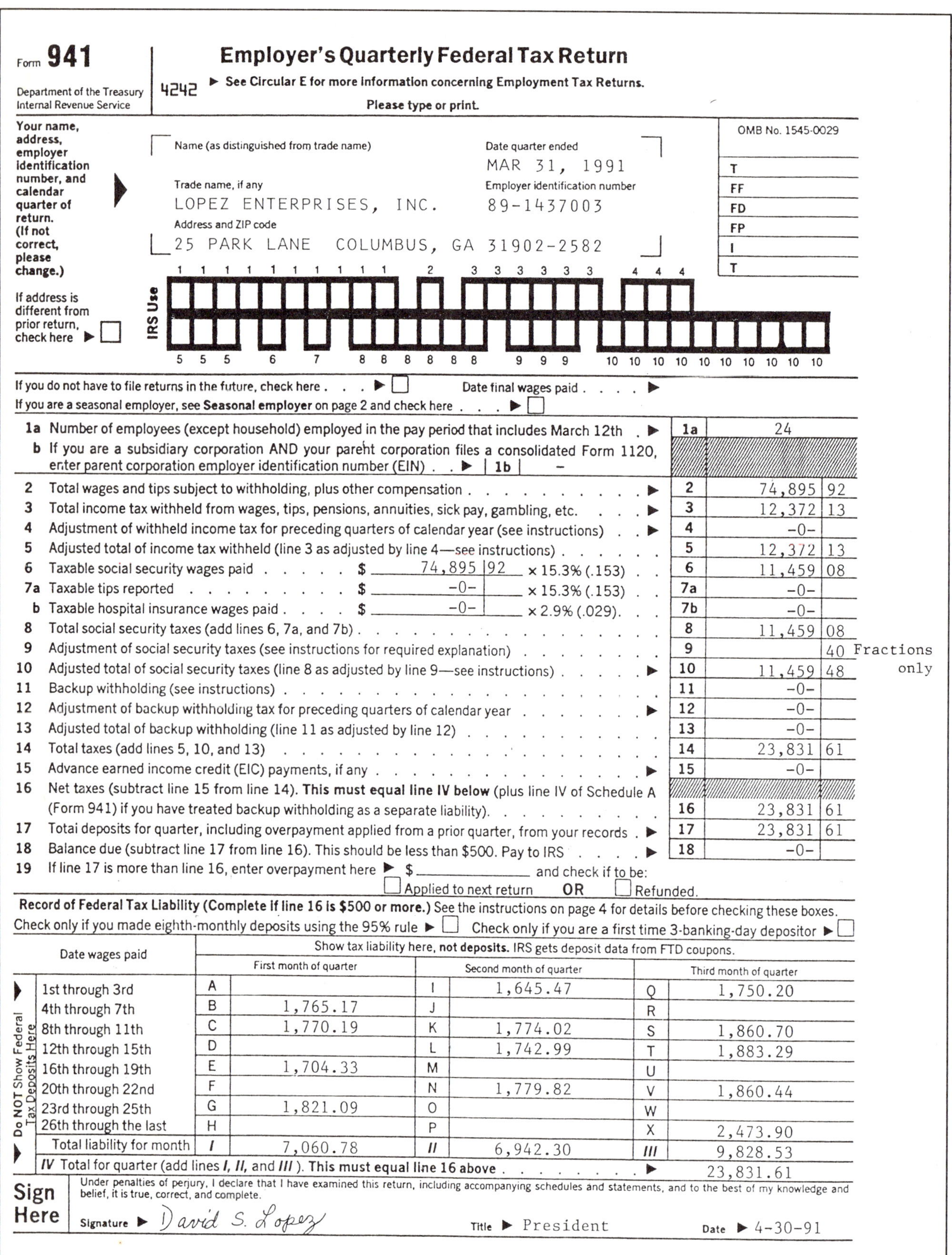

Form **941** Department of the Treasury Internal Revenue Service

4242

Employer's Quarterly Federal Tax Return

▶ See Circular E for more information concerning Employment Tax Returns.

Please type or print.

Your name, address, employer identification number, and calendar quarter of return. (If not correct, please change.)

Name (as distinguished from trade name) — Date quarter ended: MAR 31, 1991

Trade name, if any: LOPEZ ENTERPRISES, INC. — Employer identification number: 89-1437003

Address and ZIP code: 25 PARK LANE COLUMBUS, GA 31902-2582

OMB No. 1545-0029

T / FF / FD / FP / I / T

IRS Use: 1 1 1 1 1 1 1 1 1 1 2 3 3 3 3 3 3 4 4 4 / 5 5 5 6 7 8 8 8 8 8 8 9 9 9 10 10 10 10 10 10 10 10 10 10

If address is different from prior return, check here ▶ ☐

If you do not have to file returns in the future, check here . . . ▶ ☐ Date final wages paid . . . . ▶

If you are a seasonal employer, see **Seasonal employer** on page 2 and check here . . . ▶ ☐

1a	Number of employees (except household) employed in the pay period that includes March 12th . ▶	1a	24	
b	If you are a subsidiary corporation AND your parent corporation files a consolidated Form 1120, enter parent corporation employer identification number (EIN) . . ▶ 1b –			
2	Total wages and tips subject to withholding, plus other compensation . . . . ▶	2	74,895	92
3	Total income tax withheld from wages, tips, pensions, annuities, sick pay, gambling, etc. . . . ▶	3	12,372	13
4	Adjustment of withheld income tax for preceding quarters of calendar year (see instructions) . . ▶	4	-0-	
5	Adjusted total of income tax withheld (line 3 as adjusted by line 4—see instructions)	5	12,372	13
6	Taxable social security wages paid . . . . . $ 74,895 92 × 15.3% (.153) . .	6	11,459	08
7a	Taxable tips reported . . . . $ -0- × 15.3% (.153) . .	7a	-0-	
b	Taxable hospital insurance wages paid . . . . $ -0- × 2.9% (.029). . .	7b	-0-	
8	Total social security taxes (add lines 6, 7a, and 7b)	8	11,459	08
9	Adjustment of social security taxes (see instructions for required explanation)	9		40 Fractions only
10	Adjusted total of social security taxes (line 8 as adjusted by line 9—see instructions) . . . . ▶	10	11,459	48
11	Backup withholding (see instructions)	11	-0-	
12	Adjustment of backup withholding tax for preceding quarters of calendar year . . . . . . ▶	12	-0-	
13	Adjusted total of backup withholding (line 11 as adjusted by line 12)	13	-0-	
14	Total taxes (add lines 5, 10, and 13)	14	23,831	61
15	Advance earned income credit (EIC) payments, if any . . . . ▶	15	-0-	
16	Net taxes (subtract line 15 from line 14). **This must equal line IV below** (plus line IV of Schedule A (Form 941) if you have treated backup withholding as a separate liability).	16	23,831	61
17	Total deposits for quarter, including overpayment applied from a prior quarter, from your records . ▶	17	23,831	61
18	Balance due (subtract line 17 from line 16). This should be less than $500. Pay to IRS . . . . ▶	18	-0-	
19	If line 17 is more than line 16, enter overpayment here ▶ $ ______ and check if to be: ☐ Applied to next return OR ☐ Refunded.			

Record of Federal Tax Liability (Complete if line 16 is $500 or more.) See the instructions on page 4 for details before checking these boxes.

Check only if you made eighth-monthly deposits using the 95% rule ▶ ☐ Check only if you are a first time 3-banking-day depositor ▶ ☐

Do NOT Show Federal Tax Deposits Here

Date wages paid		First month of quarter		Second month of quarter		Third month of quarter
1st through 3rd	A		I	1,645.47	Q	1,750.20
4th through 7th	B	1,765.17	J		R	
8th through 11th	C	1,770.19	K	1,774.02	S	1,860.70
12th through 15th	D		L	1,742.99	T	1,883.29
16th through 19th	E	1,704.33	M		U	
20th through 22nd	F		N	1,779.82	V	1,860.44
23rd through 25th	G	1,821.09	O		W	
26th through the last	H		P		X	2,473.90
Total liability for month	*I*	7,060.78	*II*	6,942.30	*III*	9,828.53

IV Total for quarter (add lines *I*, *II*, and *III*). **This must equal line 16 above** . . . . ▶ 23,831.61

Sign Here Under penalties of perjury, I declare that I have examined this return, including accompanying schedules and statements, and to the best of my knowledge and belief, it is true, correct, and complete.

Signature ▶ David S. Lopez Title ▶ President Date ▶ 4-30-91

Illustration 3-8. Form 941, Employer's Quarterly Federal Tax Return

SOURCES OF INFORMATION FOR COMPLETING FORM 941

Line No.	Source of Information
1a	Payroll register
1b	Corporate records
2	General ledger account(s) for wages and salaries; Forms 4070, or employees' written statements to report cash tips
3	General ledger account(s)
4	Forms 941 previously filed and general ledger accounts—to determine amount of errors made in income tax withheld from wages paid in earlier quarters of the calendar year.
5	Add lines 4 and 3 if additional income tax withheld is being reported; subtract line 4 from line 3 if the amount of income tax withheld is being reduced.
6	Payroll register; include any social security taxes paid for employees, sick pay, and taxable fringe benefits subject to social security taxes. Do not include any tips. Do not report any employees' wages that exceed $54,300, the taxable wage base for 1991.
7a	Forms 4070, or employees' written statements to report cash tips. Enter all tips reported until tips and wages for each employee reach $54,300. Report this information even if you are unable to withhold the employee FICA tax. Do not include allocated tips, which should be reported on Form 8027.
7b	Payroll register; report amounts paid to certain federal, state, and local government employees who are subject only to the HI (Medicare) portion of the social security tax. Do not report more than $54,300 for each employee.
8	Add lines 6, 7a, and 7b.
9	Forms 941 previously filed. Correct errors in social security taxes reported on earlier return or correct errors in credits for overpayments of penalty or interest paid on tax for an earlier quarter. If you report both an underpayment and an overpayment, show only the difference.
	Use Form 941c to explain any amount on line 9, other than adjustments for fractions of cents or third-party sick pay. Or, you may attach a statement that shows the nature of error(s) being corrected.
	Use Form W-2c, Statement of Corrected Income and Tax Amount, to adjust an employee's social security wages, tips, or tax withheld for a prior year. Also, complete Form W-3c, Transmittal of Corrected Income and Tax Statements.
	To adjust for the tax on tips: Include the total uncollected employee social security tax for line 7a.
	To adjust for the tax on third-party sick pay: Deduct the social security tax on third-party sick pay for which you are not responsible. Write "Sick pay" in the margin.
	To adjust for fractions of cents: If there is a difference between the total tax on line 8 and the total deducted from your employees' wages or tips plus the employer's tax on those wages or tips (general ledger accounts) because of fractions of cents added or dropped in collecting the tax, report the difference. If this difference is the only entry, write "Fractions only" in the margin.
10	Add line 9 to line 8 if you are reporting additional taxes for an earlier quarter. Subtract line 9 from line 8 if you are reducing the amount of taxes reported for an earlier quarter or claiming credit for overpayments of penalty or interest paid on tax for an earlier quarter.
11	General ledger account(s). Payers of taxable interest, dividends, and certain other payments must withhold 20% of the amounts if the payees have failed to furnish the payers with correct taxpayer identification numbers. The amount of these income tax withholdings by the payers is known as *backup withholding.*
12	Payroll register and general ledger account(s); correct errors in backup withholding for earlier quarters of the year.
13	Add or subtract line 12 from line 11 to obtain adjusted total of backup withholding.
14	Record total taxes by adding lines 5, 10, and 13.
15	If applicable, show the amount of any *advance earned income credit (EIC)* payments made to low-income workers (payroll register). (As discussed in the next unit, in 1990, the maximum EIC per qualified worker was $953.) The credit may be paid out periodically as part of the workers' paychecks. The amount of the advance EIC payments does not change the amount you must deduct and withhold from employees' pay for income tax and employee FICA taxes. Advance EIC payments that you make are treated as made from the amounts withheld as income tax and employee FICA taxes, and your FICA tax contributions.
16	Determine net taxes by subtracting line 15 from line 14.
17	General ledger account(s), Schedule A of Form 941, previous Form 941; record the total deposits for the quarter, including backup withholding reported and any overpayment applied from previous quarter.
18	Calculate balance due by subtracting line 17 from line 16. Pay balance due to IRS.
19	Calculate overpayment by subtracting line 16 from line 17 and indicate if amount is to be applied to the next return or refunded.

Illustration 3-9. Sources of Information for Completing Form 941

If the Legal Residence, Principal Place of Business, Office, or Agency Is in	File with the Internal Revenue Service Center at
Florida, Georgia, South Carolina	Atlanta, GA 39901
New Jersey, New York (New York City and counties of Nassau, Rockland, Suffolk, and Westchester)	Holtsville, NY 00501
New York (all other counties), Connecticut, Maine, Massachusetts, New Hampshire, Rhode Island, Vermont	Andover, MA 05501
Illinois, Iowa, Minnesota, Missouri, Wisconsin	Kansas City, MO 64999
Delaware, District of Columbia, Maryland, Pennsylvania, Virginia	Philadelphia, PA 19255
Indiana, Kentucky, Michigan, Ohio, West Virginia	Cincinnati, OH 45999
Kansas, New Mexico, Oklahoma, Texas	Austin, TX 73301
Alaska, Arizona, California (counties of Alpine, Amador, Butte, Calaveras, Colusa, Contra Costa, Del Norte, El Dorado, Glenn, Humboldt, Lake, Lassen, Marin, Mendocino, Modoc, Napa, Nevada, Placer, Plumas, Sacramento, San Joaquin, Shasta, Sierra, Siskiyou, Solano, Sonoma, Sutter, Tehama, Trinity, Yolo, and Yuba), Colorado, Idaho, Montana, Nebraska, Nevada, North Dakota, Oregon, South Dakota, Utah, Washington, Wyoming	Ogden, UT 84201
California (all other counties), Hawaii	Fresno, CA 93888
Alabama, Arkansas, Louisiana, Mississippi, North Carolina, Tennessee	Memphis, TN 37501
If there is no legal residence or principal place of business in any state	Philadelphia, PA 19255

Illustration 3-10. Where to File Form 941

Paying the FICA Taxes

We may pay our FICA taxes directly to the IRS by check or money order, which should be made payable to the "Internal Revenue Service." Cash payments made in person are permissible, but we should not send cash through the mail. However, we may mail checks, drafts, and money orders.

Privately Printed Forms

Under certain conditions, Form 941 may be privately printed. However, since Form 941 is a quarterly return and may be revised each quarter, we must make sure we are using the current form. The forms must be exact facsimile reproductions of the officially printed Form 941 and meet other requirements contained in the Revenue Procedures, which are available from the IRS. In addition to providing specifications for substitute forms, the IRS provides reproduction proofs of its own forms at a prescribed per-page charge.

Reporting FICA Information on Magnetic Media

Firms that change from reporting their tax information on paper to magnetic media report a significant reduction in paperwork and storage space. For example, a reel of magnetic tape may contain the equivalent of 30,000 or more paper documents. Further, companies realize savings in handling and shipping expenditures.

The IRS permits reporting agents for groups of employers to furnish the information required for Form 941 on magnetic tape instead of paper documents. Agents who wish to file their returns on magnetic tape must first file a letter of application or submit *Form 8655, Reporting Agent Authorization.* Also, at the option of the employer, the IRS may permit the use of a composite employment tax return in lieu of Form 941. A single form, together with magnetic tapes or other approved media, is used for the returns of more than one employer.

Some states that require employers to file detailed quarterly wage reports authorize the combined reporting on magnetic tape of social security and state unemployment compensation reporting data. Using such combined reporting on tape enables employers to prepare and submit more easily the social security and state wage data. By means of the combined tape format, employers forward one tape or diskette to the SSA and a copy to the appropriate participating state unemployment insurance agency.

The magnetic media filing of Form 8027 (Employer's Annual Information Return of Tip Income and Allocated Tips) as well as other information returns is discussed in Unit 4.

PENALTIES

In this unit we have discussed only one of the employment taxes—FICA taxes on employees and employers. In the following unit, we shall examine the withholding of a second tax—employees' income taxes. Then, in Unit 5, we present another employment tax—unemployment compensation. *The following discussion of penalties applies to each of the employment taxes discussed in Units 3, 4, and 5.*

Employers act as collection agents for the government by collecting employment taxes and paying them to the appropriate governmental agency. If employers fail to carry out their duties as collection agents, they are subject to civil and criminal penalties. The penalties may take the form of additions to the tax, interest, and fines and imprisonment.

As you see in Illustration 3-11 on pages 88 and 89, penalties are imposed upon employers who fail to: (1) file employment tax returns, (2) pay over employment taxes when due, (3) make timely deposits, (4) furnish wage and tax statements, (5) file or furnish information returns, and (6) supply identification numbers. The severity of the penalty varies depending on the degree of willfulness present in the employer's conduct. The penalties may be assessed not only against the employer but may also be imposed on any person who has the duty or responsibility for collecting, accounting for, and paying over any tax. As we shall see, penalties are also imposed for passing bad checks.

FAILURE TO FILE EMPLOYMENT TAX RETURNS

The civil and criminal penalties facing employers who *fail to file employment tax returns* are discussed below.

Additions to Tax

If an employer *fails to file an employment tax return on the date prescribed for its filing*, a certain percentage of the amount of tax required to have been reported will be added to the tax. Such an addition to the tax is not applicable, however, when employers show to the satisfaction of the IRS that the failure to file was due to reasonable cause and not to willful neglect.

The amount to be added to the tax is 5% of the *net* amount of tax required to have been reported if the failure to report is for not more than one month. An additional 5% is levied for each additional month or fraction of a month during which the failure continues, not to exceed 25% in the aggregate. Thus, if a failure to file continued for four months, an employer would be liable for an addition to the tax equal to 20% of the net tax that should have been reported.

If the failure to file a return is *fraudulent*, the penalty is increased to 15% per month, not to exceed 75% in the aggregate.

Criminal Penalties

If employers *willfully* attempt to evade the payment of employment taxes by failing to file a return or by filing a false return, upon conviction, they may be fined up to $10,000 or imprisoned for not more than 5 years, or both.

Employment tax returns are signed under a statement declaring that the return is made under penalties of perjury. Thus, an employer who willfully signs a return knowing that it is not true and correct as to every material statement will, upon conviction, be subject to a fine of not more than $5,000, or imprisonment for not more than 3 years, or both.

FAILURE TO PAY OVER EMPLOYMENT TAXES

Employers who *fail to pay over the required amount of employment taxes when due* are faced with the following civil and criminal penalties.

Additions to Tax

Employers who fail to pay over the required amount of tax when due face a penalty of an additional tax amounting to ½% of the *net* amount due if the failure to pay lasts no longer than a month. For each month during which the failure to pay continues, an additional ½% penalty is levied, not to exceed 25% in the aggregate. Thus, if an employer's delinquency continues for six months, the addition will be equal to 3% of the net tax shown on the return or that should have been shown on the return. Along with any penalties that may be imposed, taxes due and unpaid will bear interest at the rate of 11% per year.[8]

If any part of a deficiency in the amount of taxes paid is due to *negligence or an intentional disregard* of the payment rules (but without intent to defraud), a penalty of 20% of any underpayment will be imposed.

In addition, an amount equal to 50% of the interest payable for that portion of the underpayment will be added to the amount due. *Negligence* includes any failure to make a reasonable attempt to comply with the provisions of the law. *Disregard* includes any careless, reckless, or intentional disregard of the law. However, the negligence penalty will not be imposed if it is shown that there was reasonable cause for the underpayment and that the taxpayer acted in good faith.

If any part of an underpayment is due to *fraud with an intent to evade* the tax, a penalty of 75% of the underpayment plus 50% of the amount of the interest due will be added to the tax due. In such a case, the fraud penalty will be imposed in place of the negligence penalty; the fraud penalty will also be imposed in place of the additions to the tax provided for failure to pay the tax.

The 100% Penalty

Employers who *willfully* fail to collect, account for or pay over employment taxes, or willfully attempt in any manner to evade or defeat the taxes, may be liable for a penalty equal to the total amount of the tax evaded, or not collected, or not accounted for and paid over. This *100% penalty* may be assessed on any person required to collect, account for, and pay over the tax. Thus, the penalty can be extended to corporate officers or employees, or to partnership members or employees who have the duty to withhold. If the 100% penalty is imposed, the 75% fraud penalty noted above may not be imposed for the same offense.

Tax Levies

If, within 10 days after notice and demand for payment, an employer fails to pay any tax for which he or she is liable, the IRS is authorized to levy and seize any property and property rights held by the employer at the time of the levy. If the IRS concludes that the collection of any tax is in jeopardy, it may immediately demand payment of the tax and, upon the employer's failure or refusal to pay, may levy and seize the employer's property without regard to the 10-day period.

Criminal Penalties

The *willful* failure to pay any tax constitutes a felony. Upon conviction of such a felony, the employer will be subject to a fine of not more than $10,000, or imprisonment for not more than 5 years, or both. These penalties are in addition to the 75% fraud penalty.

Illustration 3-11. Penalties That Apply to Employment Taxes (Continued)

[8]Each calendar quarter the Internal Revenue Service sets the interest rate to be charged for tax underpayments (and on refunds for tax overpayments). The rate is based on the short-term Treasury bill rate for the first month in each calendar quarter, plus 3 percentage points, and applies for the following calendar quarter.

FAILURE TO MAKE TIMELY DEPOSITS

Penalties are imposed for the *failure to make timely deposits of employment taxes*. These penalties are based on applicable percentages of the amount of the underpayment of a deposit as determined by the number of days the deposit is late. An *underpayment* is the excess of the amount of tax required to be deposited over the tax that was actually deposited.

If the failure to make a timely deposit is:

1. *Not more than 5 days late*, the penalty is 2% of the undeposited taxes.
2. *More than 5 days late but less than 15 days late*, the penalty is 5% of the undeposited taxes.
3. *More than 15 days late*, the penalty is 10%.

Also, a penalty of 15% may be imposed if the undeposited taxes are not paid on or before the earlier of:

1. 10 days after the first delinquency notice, or
2. The day on which notice and demand for immediate payment is given.

Any person who makes an overstated deposit claim is subject to a penalty of 25% of such claim. (This penalty is in addition to any other penalty imposed.) An *overstated deposit claim* refers to a claim of tax deposits in excess of the amount actually deposited. An overstated deposit claim also refers to claims for deposits not actually made. However, the penalty for overstated deposit claims does not apply if the overstated claims were due to reasonable cause and not due to willful neglect.

FAILURE TO FURNISH WAGE AND TAX STATEMENTS

If employers *willfully* fail to furnish their employees with properly executed wage and tax statements, or *willfully* furnish false or fraudulent statements, the civil penalty is $50 for each such statement. This fine is in addition to any criminal penalties that may be imposed. There is a maximum penalty of $100,000 in any calendar year. If such failures are due to *intentional disregard*, the penalty for each failure is $100 per statement or, if greater, 10% of the amount required to be shown on the statement. In this case there is no limit on the maximum penalty each calendar year.

The criminal penalty for the offenses noted, upon conviction, is a fine of not more than $1,000, or imprisonment for not more than 1 year, or both, for each offense.

FAILURE TO FILE OR FURNISH INFORMATION RETURNS

Employers who fail to timely file their information returns are subject to a penalty of $50 for each failure, with a maximum penalty of $250,000 in any calendar year. However, if a failure is *corrected within 30 days* after the required filing date, the penalty for each failure is $15 and the maximum penalty is $75,000. If a failure is corrected *after the 30th day but before August 1* of the calendar year in which the required filing date occurs, the penalty for each failure is $30 and the maximum penalty is $150,000.

If the failure to timely file information returns or to include all the information required to be shown on the returns, or the inclusion of incorrect information, is due to *intentional disregard*, the penalty is $100 per statement or, if greater, 10% of the amount required to be shown on the statement. In such cases, there is no limit on the maximum penalty for the calendar year.

FAILURE TO SUPPLY IDENTIFICATION NUMBER

Employers and employees are often required to include their identification number on tax returns, statements, and other documents. If any person fails to comply with such a requirement, a penalty of $5 is levied for each failure to include the identifying number.

Employers and employees may also be required to (a) furnish their identifying number to another person or (b) include another person's identifying number in the tax return, statement, or document made for that person. The penalty for failing to meet either requirement in (a) or (b) is $50 for each such failure. The total amount of penalty for all failures will not exceed $100,000.

BAD CHECKS

A specific penalty is imposed for giving the IRS a bad check or money order in payment of any employment taxes. The penalty is an amount equal to 2% of the amount of the check or money order. If the check is for less than $750, the penalty is $15 or the amount of the check, whichever is less. The penalty does not apply, however, if the check or money order was tendered in good faith and with reasonable cause to believe that it would be paid upon presentment.

Illustration 3-11. Penalties That Apply to Employment Taxes (Concluded)

GLOSSARY

Backup withholding—amount of income tax withheld by payers of taxable interest, dividends, and certain other payments made to payees who have failed to furnish the payers with correct identification numbers.

Common-law relationship—the state existing when the person for whom services are rendered has the right to control and direct the individual who performs the services, not only as to the result to be accomplished by the work but also as to the details and means by which that result is to be accomplished.

Educational assistance—the expenses that an employer pays for an employee's education, such as tuition, fees, and payments for books, supplies, and equipment.

Employee—any individual who performs services in covered employment.

Employer—any person who employs one or more individuals for the performance of services, unless such services or employment are specifically excepted by law.

Employment—any service performed by employees for their employer, irrespective of the citizenship or residence of either.

Immediate credit item—a check or other instrument of payment for which immediate credit is given the payee by the receiving bank in accordance with its check-collection schedule.

Person—an entity defined by law as an individual, a trust or estate, a partnership, or a corporation.

Safe-haven rule—rule that permits eighth-monthly-deposit employers to deposit at least 95% of their tax liability (employer-employee FICA taxes and employees' federal income taxes withheld) at prescribed times without incurring any penalty for late deposits.

Self-employment income—the net earnings derived by individuals from a business or profession carried on by them as sole proprietors or by a partnership of which they are members.

Sick pay—any payment made to individuals, because of their personal injury or sickness, that does not constitute wages.

Taxable wage base—the maximum amount of wages during a calendar year that is subject to a particular tax, such as FICA.

QUESTIONS FOR REVIEW

1. For social security purposes, what conditions must an individual meet to be classed as a:
   a. "Covered" employee?
   b. "Covered" employer?
2. What conditions must be present for a common-law relationship to exist between an employer and employee?
3. Jill Kravitz, 17 years of age, works in a grocery store for her father, who owns the store. Are the wages paid Jill subject to social security taxes? Why?
4. Explain what is meant by the term *voluntary coverage*.
5. For the purpose of determining the amount of wages subject to FICA taxes, how are wages defined?
6. Under what conditions are the following types of remuneration considered wages under FICA?
   a. Advances
   b. Christmas gifts
   c. Death benefits
   d. Sick pay
7. What are an employer's responsibilities for FICA taxes:
   a. On tips reported by tipped employees?
   b. On wages paid tipped employees?
8. The value of meals and lodging furnished employees may or may not represent wages for FICA tax purposes. Explain.
9. Under what condition is sick pay excluded from the definition of wages for FICA tax purposes?
10. What are (a) the social security tax rates on employees and on employers for 1991 and (b) the estimated taxable wage base for 1991?
11. How is the employee's portion of the FICA tax collected and paid to the IRS?
12. a. Peter Javier receives taxable wages from three employers during 1991. Is he entitled to a refund on the social security taxes paid on wages in excess of $54,300?
    b. If Javier is entitled to a refund on the excess social security taxes he has paid, how should he proceed in claiming such a refund?
13. Explain the procedure for calculating the employer's FICA tax.
14. From what sources may self-employment income be obtained?
15. What is the social security tax rate on self-employed persons for 1991?
16. What procedure should an employer follow in filing an application for an employer identification number?

17. Explain how individuals may check the accuracy of the wage credits in their social security insurance accounts.
18. Indicate the deposit requirement for each of the following nonagricultural employers:
    a. On payday, Thursday, April 18, the employee and employer FICA taxes and income taxes withheld total $3,490.
    b. At the end of July, the employee and employer FICA taxes and income taxes withheld total $455.
    c. On payday, Friday, November 15, the employee and employer FICA taxes and income taxes withheld total $101,230.
19. For what purpose does an employer complete Form 8109?
20. Explain how the timeliness of a $15,000 deposit of employment taxes is determined.
21. a. How often must an employer file Form 941?
    b. When must Form 941 be filed by an employer?
    c. For employers who have their legal residences in your city, with which IRS Center should they file Form 941?
22. What penalty is imposed on an employer who:
    a. Does not file Form 941 by the due date?
    b. Is 7 days late in making the monthly deposit of employment taxes?
    c. Gives the IRS a bad check for $1,250?

QUESTIONS FOR DISCUSSION

1. On Wednesday, August 15, 19—, the end of an eighth-monthly period, LaPoint Company had employment taxes of $25,000 that were required to be deposited within three banking days after the close of that eighth-monthly period. The deposit was mailed and postmarked on Monday, August 20, 19—, and was delivered on Tuesday, August 21, 19—. Was the tax deposit timely made by LaPoint Company? Explain.
2. The Downing Manufacturing Company, a newly formed corporation, pays its employees weekly. On January 6, a weekly payday, the company withheld $705.10 of income taxes and $289.27 of social security taxes from its employees' wages. The employer's social security taxes on the weekly pay are $289.26. Assume that each weekly payroll is the same amount as that on January 6. What requirement for depositing FICA taxes and income taxes withheld applies to this newly formed corporation?
3. When employees of the County Bank are summoned to serve on jury duty, the firm pays its workers the difference between their regular wages and the amount received for jury duty, even though the workers are absent from work.

   Amy Kane, a correspondence secretary with the bank, has been receiving a weekly salary of $365. Kane has just completed her first 5-day week of jury duty, for which she was paid $65 ($9 per day plus 20 cents per mile from her home to the court house, a 20-mile round trip).

   How much of Kane's earnings for this week is considered to be wages subject to FICA tax withholding?
4. During their first month of employment at Perez Company, all new workers are looked upon as probationary employees. During this period of time the new workers do not qualify for many employee benefits, such as the company-sponsored hospitalization-medical insurance program. Are the earnings received by the new workers during the probationary period properly defined as taxable wages for purposes of FICA?
5. During a recent strike at the Hulett Shoe Company, the union members were paid strike benefits by their union. One of the company workers, Tim Dopson, is employed by the union to serve as a union representative. In this capacity Dopson sits down at the bargaining table and represents the union in negotiating contracts with the company.
    a. Are the strike benefits paid by the union to its members subject to FICA tax withholding?
    b. Are the payments Dopson receives from the union for his services as union representative subject to FICA tax withholding?
6. Ivan McCullers, owner of a large retail store, has been making his deposits of FICA taxes and income taxes by mailing these amounts to his IRS service center. McCullers reasons that by making his deposits at the service center, he can have use of his money for several extra days during the delay required by the center to turn over his deposit to the Treasury Department. Is McCullers proceeding correctly in gaining more days' usage of his funds in his checking account? Explain.

Date ______________________ Name ______________________

PRACTICAL PROBLEMS

NOTE: In these and succeeding Practical Problems, the FICA tax rate is 7.65% on employers and employees on the first $54,300 of taxable wages.

3-1. The biweekly taxable wages for the employees of Barkan Graphics are given below. On the appropriate lines, record:

a. The FICA taxes that should be withheld from each employee's biweekly pay.
b. The total FICA taxes to be withheld.
c. The employer's FICA tax for the biweekly pay period.

BARKAN GRAPHICS

Employee No.	Employee Name	Biweekly Taxable Wages	(a) FICA Taxes
711	Bechette, Mel M.	$479.68	$________
512	Calderon, Karen T.	485.00	________
624	Fletcher, Rickey P.	394.55	________
325	Honeycuff, Eric X.	397.70	________
422	Lansford, William R.	778.00	________
210	Plunk, Floyd A.	775.50	________
111	Tolleson, Audrey S.	495.73	________
		(b) Total	$________

(c) Employer's FICA Tax = $________ (Total Taxable Wages) x ________ (FICA Tax Rate) = $________ (Employer's FICA Tax)

3-2. During 1991, Melido Canseco was paid a weekly salary of $1,085 by the Oak Company. Calculate the amount of FICA taxes that should be withheld from his pay:

a. For the 50th week . . . . $________
b. For the 51st week . . . . $________
c. For the 52d week . . . . $________

3-3. The annual salary paid each of the officers of Sabo, Inc., is given below. The officers are paid semimonthly on the 15th and the last day of the month. Determine the FICA taxes to be withheld from each officer's semimonthly pay on (a) June 30, (b) July 31, and (c) December 31.

SABO, INC.

Name and Title	Annual Salary	(a) June 30		(b) July 31		(c) December 31	
		Taxable Earnings	FICA Tax	Taxable Earnings	FICA Tax	Taxable Earnings	FICA Tax
Larkin, Andrew T. President	$100,200						
Oliver, Carla O. V-P, Finance	56,400						
Benzinger, Ryne J. V-P, Sales	56,160						
Armstrong, Sidney T. V-P, Manufacturing	56,000						
Winningham, Arlene C. V-P, Personnel ...	40,900						
Decker, Jessie R. V-P, Secretary ...	38,900						

3-4. Audrey Rucker and Jill Rodgers are partners engaged in operating the R&R Gift Shop, which employs the persons listed below. Paychecks are distributed every Friday to all employees. Based upon the information given, compute:

a. The amount of FICA tax to be withheld from the paychecks of March 22, 1991.
b. The amount of the employer's FICA taxes for the March 22 payroll.

R&R GIFT SHOP

Name and Position	Salary	Taxable Earnings	(a) FICA Tax
Jessica Palmer, general office worker ...	$335 per week	$	$
Brenda Whalen, salesperson	$1,980 per month		
Rob Stoll, part-time deliveryperson .	$285 per week		
Audrey Rucker, partner	$650 per week		
Jill Rodgers, partner	$650 per week		
	Totals	$	$

(b) Employer's FICA Taxes = $________ x ________ = $________

Taxable Earnings / FICA Tax Rate / FICA Taxes

Date ______________________ Name ______________________

3-5. Vicki DeVault began working as a part-time waitress on June 3, 1991, at Leonardo's Restaurant. The cash tips of $140 that she received during June were reported on Form 4070, which she submitted to her employer on July 1. During July, she was paid wages of $495 by the restaurant. Determine:

a. The amount of social security taxes that the employer should withhold from DeVault's wages during July . . . . $________

b. The amount of the employer's social security taxes on DeVault's wages and tips during July . . . . $________

3-6. Sue Ellen Stein was paid a salary of $32,800 during 1991 by the Farrell Company. In addition, during the year Stein started her own business as a public accountant and reported a net business income of $22,700 on her income tax return for 1991. Determine:

a. The amount of social security taxes that was withheld from her earnings during 1991 by the Farrell Company . . . . $________

b. Stein's social security taxes on the income derived from her public accounting business for 1991, assuming she receives a flat 50% reduction in her self-employment tax . . . . $________

3-7. The Bond Printing Company pays its salaried employees monthly on the last day of each month. The annual salary payroll for 1991 is given below. Compute:

a. The amount of FICA tax withheld from each employee's wages for January.
b. The total FICA taxes withheld from all employees' wages for January.
c. The amount of the employer's FICA tax on the taxable wages for January.
d. The amount of FICA tax withheld from each employee's wages for December.
e. The total FICA taxes withheld from all employees' wages for December.
f. The amount of the employer's FICA tax on the taxable wages for December.

BOND PRINTING COMPANY

Employee	Annual Salary	January		December	
		Taxable Wages	(a) FICA Tax on Employees	Taxable Wages	(d) FICA Tax on Employees
DAVIS, Sara	$20,160				
DAWSON, Martha	19,800				
FRANCO, Betty	20,400				
GLADDEN, Arthur	58,500				
HEATH, Maria	19,400				
KELLY, Laura	19,820				
KITTLE, Madge	17,990				
QUINTANA, Emilio	57,600				
RIPKEN, Elisa	19,980				
WASHINGTON, Teri	51,600				
Totals	. . .		(b)		(e)

Employer's FICA Tax . . . . (c)________________ (f)________________

3-8. The weekly and hourly wage schedule for the employees of Abrams, Inc., is given below. All employees work a full 40-hour week. Compute:

a. The taxable wages earned by each employee for a full week in February, 1991.
b. The FICA taxes withheld from each employee's wages.
c. The net wages paid each employee.
d. The total taxable wages, FICA taxes withheld, and net wages.
e. The employer's FICA taxes.

ABRAMS, INC.

Employee	Weekly (W) or Hourly (H) Wage	(a) Taxable Wages	(b) FICA Taxes	(c) Net Wages
Arlene Benedetti	$270 W	$________	$________	$________
Gary Combs	285 W	________	________	________
Bruce Earle	415 W	________	________	________
Joan Gill	450 W	________	________	________
Dwight Kaiser	$5.60 H	________	________	________
Joel Perkowski	5.85 H	________	________	________
Phillip Stieber	6.40 H	________	________	________
Chi Yee	6.80 H	________	________	________
(d) Total		$________	$________	$________

(e) Employer's FICA taxes: ________________________________

3-9. The monthly salaries and part-time hourly wage rates of the office employees of Thornton Payroll Service during 1991 are given on the next page. Assume that the monthly salaries were in effect during the entire year. In December, the part-time employees worked the number of hours and at the hourly rates as shown. None of the part-time employees have earned as much as $54,300 during the year. Compute:

a. The total wages of each part-time employee for December, 1991.
b. The taxable wages of each employee.
c. The FICA taxes withheld from the each employee's wages for December.
d. The total monthly payroll, the taxable wages, and the FICA taxes withheld.
e. The employer's FICA taxes for the month.

Date ____________________ Name ____________________

THORNTON PAYROLL SERVICE

Employees			(a) Total Monthly Salary Payroll	(b) Taxable Wages	(c) FICA Taxes
Full-Time Office:					
Asad, Gordon			$1,300		
Cella, Paul			1,300		
Essex, Joanna			1,875		
Gorzo, Marvin			1,875		
Lentini, Larry			1,800		
Price, Billie			4,200		
Ryan, Donna			2,400		
Sams, Richard			3,925		
Tona, Jeannette			4,625		
Wagner, Grace			1,500		
Part-Time Office:	**Hrs. Worked**	**Hourly Rate**			
Kaplan, Judy	170	$4.95			
Law, Sherri	170	4.95			
Miller, Sandy	140	6.00			
Quinn, Debra	145	5.00			
Stabinsky, Kim	162	5.50			
(d) Total					

(e) Employer's FICA Taxes: ____________________

3-10. Wayne P. Roney opened Wayne's Service Station on January 2, 1991. The business, whose fiscal year is the same as the calendar year, is subject to FICA taxes. At the end of the first quarter of 1991, Roney is required to file an Employer's Quarterly Federal Tax Return. Using Form 941, reproduced on page 99, prepare the return on the basis of the following information obtained from the payroll records of the company.

Employer's address: 114 Center Street, Sycamore, South Carolina 29846-3477
Employer's identification number: 61-0230450

The employees' names, occupations, social security numbers, and semimonthly wages are given below. Assume that the same amounts of wages were paid semimonthly during the quarter on the 15th and the last day of each month.

Employee's Name and Occupation	Soc. Sec. Account No.	Semimonthly Wage
Alan T. Frank, attendant	384-10-7233	$ 580.00
Patty R. Collett, attendant	345-90-8451	565.00
Patrick O. Hume, mechanic	528-09-3667	1,290.00
Denise B. Dow, cashier	766-43-6527	650.00
Total taxable wages		$3,085.00

None of the four employees reported tips during the quarter. No advance earned income credit (EIC) payments were made to the workers, and there were no backup withholdings.

The federal income taxes withheld from the employees' wages each semimonthly pay period totaled $412. All deposits of federal income taxes withheld and the employer-employee FICA taxes were timely made.

Note that on Line 6, the total taxable FICA wages are multiplied by a combined tax rate for both employer and employee. Often there is a small difference between (a) this total and (b) the total of FICA taxes withheld from employees each pay period and the amount of the employer's FICA tax calculated each pay period. This difference is attributable to the rounding of fractional parts of cents because the FICA tax calculated on Line 6 is based on the total taxable wages for the calendar quarter. When such a difference in amounts occurs, the difference is reported on Line 9 as a deduction or addition, as the case may be. The words "Fractions only" should be inserted in the margin of Form 941 to indicate the type of adjustment made.

Date ______________________ Name ______________________

Practical Problem 3-10

Form **941**

Department of the Treasury
Internal Revenue Service

4242

Employer's Quarterly Federal Tax Return

▶ **See Circular E for more information concerning Employment Tax Returns.**

Please type or print.

Your name, address, employer identification number, and calendar quarter of return. (If not correct, please change.)

Name (as distinguished from trade name) | Date quarter ended

Trade name, if any | Employer identification number

Address and ZIP code

OMB No. 1545-0029

T
FF
FD
FP
I
T

If address is different from prior return, check here ▶ ☐

IRS Use

1 1 1 1 1 1 1 1 1 1 2 3 3 3 3 3 3 4 4 4

5 5 5 6 7 8 8 8 8 8 8 9 9 9 10 10 10 10 10 10 10 10 10 10

If you do not have to file returns in the future, check here . . . ▶ ☐ Date final wages paid . . . . ▶

If you are a seasonal employer, see **Seasonal employer** on page 2 and check here . . . ▶ ☐

1a	Number of employees (except household) employed in the pay period that includes March 12th . ▶	**1a**	
b	If you are a subsidiary corporation AND your parent corporation files a consolidated Form 1120, enter parent corporation employer identification number (EIN) . . ▶ **1b** –		
2	Total wages and tips subject to withholding, plus other compensation . . . . ▶	2	
3	Total income tax withheld from wages, tips, pensions, annuities, sick pay, gambling, etc. . . . ▶	3	
4	Adjustment of withheld income tax for preceding quarters of calendar year (see instructions) . . ▶	4	
5	Adjusted total of income tax withheld (line 3 as adjusted by line 4—see instructions)	5	
6	Taxable social security wages paid . . . . . . $ ________ × 15.3% (.153) . .	6	
7a	Taxable tips reported . . . . $ ________ × 15.3% (.153) . .	7a	
b	Taxable hospital insurance wages paid . . . . $ ________ × 2.9% (.029). . .	7b	
8	Total social security taxes (add lines 6, 7a, and 7b)	8	
9	Adjustment of social security taxes (see instructions for required explanation)	9	
10	Adjusted total of social security taxes (line 8 as adjusted by line 9—see instructions) . . . . . ▶	10	
11	Backup withholding (see instructions)	11	
12	Adjustment of backup withholding tax for preceding quarters of calendar year . . . . ▶	12	
13	Adjusted total of backup withholding (line 11 as adjusted by line 12)	13	
14	Total taxes (add lines 5, 10, and 13)	14	
15	Advance earned income credit (EIC) payments, if any . . . . ▶	15	
16	Net taxes (subtract line 15 from line 14). **This must equal line IV below** (plus line IV of Schedule A (Form 941) if you have treated backup withholding as a separate liability).	16	
17	Total deposits for quarter, including overpayment applied from a prior quarter, from your records . ▶	17	
18	Balance due (subtract line 17 from line 16). This should be less than $500. Pay to IRS . . . . ▶	18	
19	If line 17 is more than line 16, enter overpayment here ▶ $ __________ and check if to be: ☐ Applied to next return **OR** ☐ Refunded.		

Record of Federal Tax Liability (Complete if line 16 is $500 or more.) See the instructions on page 4 for details before checking these boxes.

Check only if you made eighth-monthly deposits using the 95% rule ▶ ☐ Check only if you are a first time 3-banking-day depositor ▶ ☐

Do NOT Show Federal Tax Deposits Here

Date wages paid	Show tax liability here, **not deposits.** IRS gets deposit data from FTD coupons.					
	First month of quarter		Second month of quarter		Third month of quarter	
1st through 3rd	A		I		Q	
4th through 7th	B		J		R	
8th through 11th	C		K		S	
12th through 15th	D		L		T	
16th through 19th	E		M		U	
20th through 22nd	F		N		V	
23rd through 25th	G		O		W	
26th through the last	H		P		X	
Total liability for month	*I*		*II*		*III*	

IV Total for quarter (add lines ***I***, ***II***, and ***III***). **This must equal line 16 above** . . . . ▶

Sign Here

Under penalties of perjury, I declare that I have examined this return, including accompanying schedules and statements, and to the best of my knowledge and belief, it is true, correct, and complete.

Signature ▶ **Title** ▶ **Date** ▶

3-11. During the fourth calendar quarter of 1991, the Riverside Inn employed the persons listed below. Also given are the employees' salaries or wages and the amount of tips reported to the owner, Diane R. Peters, during the quarter.

Employee	Salary or Wage	Tips Reported
Grant P. Frazier, manager	$25,000/year	. . .
Joseph R. LaVanga, ass't. manager . . .	18,000/year	. . .
Susanne T. Ayers, waitress	$250/week	$2,240.90
Howard P. Cohen, waiter	225/week	2,493.10
Lee W. Soong, waitress	250/week	2,640.30
Mary E. Yee, waitress	250/week	2,704.00
Helen O. Woods, hostess/cashier	325/week	. . .
Koo C. Shin, ass't. chef	325/week	. . .
Aaron Y. Abalis, chef	400/week	. . .
David T. Harad, dishwasher	170/week	. . .

Employees are paid weekly on Saturday. During this calendar quarter, there were 13 weekly paydays. Tips were reported by the four tipped employees by the 10th of each month. The federal income taxes and FICA taxes to be withheld from the tips were estimated by Peters and withheld equally over the 13 weekly pay periods. For the employer's weekly FICA taxes on the tips reported, Peters used the same estimate as the amount of employees' FICA taxes withheld.

The total federal income taxes withheld during the quarter were $5,720. The total FICA taxes on *tips* reported during the quarter were $118.61 each week. The tax liability for each of the 13 paydays is shown on Form 941, page 101. All deposits of federal income taxes withheld and the employer-employee FICA taxes were timely made.

No advance earned income credit (EIC) payments were made to the workers, and there were no backup withholdings.

Based upon the information given above, complete Form 941, reproduced on page 101.

Date ______________ Name ______________

Practical Problem 3-11

Form **941** Department of the Treasury Internal Revenue Service

Employer's Quarterly Federal Tax Return

4242 ▶ See Circular E for more information concerning Employment Tax Returns.

Please type or print.

Your name, address, employer identification number, and calendar quarter of return. (If not correct, please change.)

Name (as distinguished from trade name) | Date quarter ended DEC 31, 1991

Trade name, if any RIVERSIDE INN | Employer identification number 65-4263607

Address and ZIP code 404 UNION AVE. MEMPHIS, TN 38112-1404

OMB No. 1545-0029

T / FF / FD / FP / I / T

If address is different from prior return, check here ▶ ☐

IRS Use

If you do not have to file returns in the future, check here . . . ▶ ☐ Date final wages paid . . . . ▶

If you are a seasonal employer, see **Seasonal employer** on page 2 and check here . . . ▶ ☐

1a	Number of employees (except household) employed in the pay period that includes March 12th . ▶	1a	
b	If you are a subsidiary corporation AND your parent corporation files a consolidated Form 1120, enter parent corporation employer identification number (EIN) . . ▶ 1b –		
2	Total wages and tips subject to withholding, plus other compensation . . . . ▶	2	
3	Total income tax withheld from wages, tips, pensions, annuities, sick pay, gambling, etc. . . . ▶	3	
4	Adjustment of withheld income tax for preceding quarters of calendar year (see instructions) . . ▶	4	
5	Adjusted total of income tax withheld (line 3 as adjusted by line 4—see instructions)	5	
6	Taxable social security wages paid . . . . . $ ______ × 15.3% (.153) . .	6	
7a	Taxable tips reported . . . . $ ______ × 15.3% (.153) . .	7a	
b	Taxable hospital insurance wages paid . . . . $ ______ × 2.9% (.029). . .	7b	
8	Total social security taxes (add lines 6, 7a, and 7b)	8	
9	Adjustment of social security taxes (see instructions for required explanation)	9	
10	Adjusted total of social security taxes (line 8 as adjusted by line 9—see instructions) . . . . . ▶	10	
11	Backup withholding (see instructions)	11	
12	Adjustment of backup withholding tax for preceding quarters of calendar year . . . . . . ▶	12	
13	Adjusted total of backup withholding (line 11 as adjusted by line 12)	13	
14	Total taxes (add lines 5, 10, and 13)	14	
15	Advance earned income credit (EIC) payments, if any . . . . ▶	15	
16	Net taxes (subtract line 15 from line 14). **This must equal line IV below** (plus line IV of Schedule A (Form 941) if you have treated backup withholding as a separate liability).	16	
17	Total deposits for quarter, including overpayment applied from a prior quarter, from your records . ▶	17	
18	Balance due (subtract line 17 from line 16). This should be less than $500. Pay to IRS . . . . ▶	18	
19	If line 17 is more than line 16, enter overpayment here ▶ $ ______ and check if to be: ☐ Applied to next return OR ☐ Refunded.		

Record of Federal Tax Liability (Complete if line 16 is $500 or more.) See the instructions on page 4 for details before checking these boxes.

Check only if you made eighth-monthly deposits using the 95% rule ▶ ☐ Check only if you are a first time 3-banking-day depositor ▶ ☐

Show tax liability here, **not deposits.** IRS gets deposit data from FTD coupons.

Do NOT Show Federal Tax Deposits Here

Date wages paid		First month of quarter		Second month of quarter		Third month of quarter
1st through 3rd	A		I	1,020.98	Q	
4th through 7th	B	1,020.98	J		R	1,020.98
8th through 11th	C		K	1,020.98	S	
12th through 15th	D	1,020.98	L		T	1,020.98
16th through 19th	E	1,020.98	M	1,020.98	U	
20th through 22nd	F		N		V	1,020.98
23rd through 25th	G		O	1,020.98	W	
26th through the last	H	1,020.98	P	1,020.98	X	1,020.98
Total liability for month	*I*	4,083.92	*II*	5,104.90	*III*	4,083.92

IV Total for quarter (add lines *I*, *II*, and *III*). **This must equal line 16 above** . . . . ▶

Sign Here Under penalties of perjury, I declare that I have examined this return, including accompanying schedules and statements, and to the best of my knowledge and belief, it is true, correct, and complete.

Signature ▶ Title ▶ Date ▶

3-12. The Trainer Company's tax liability (amount withheld from employees' wages for federal income tax and FICA tax plus the company's portion of the FICA tax) for the month of January, 1991, was $290, and for February, 1991, $216. The Trainer Company's employer identification number is 73-1456654.

Based on the information above and the instructions given in Illustration 3-7, page 82, complete the Federal Tax Deposit Coupon, Form 8109, shown below. In the space provided below the form, show the date by which the deposit must be made.

AMOUNT OF DEPOSIT (Do NOT type; please print.)

DOLLARS | CENTS

TAX YEAR MONTH →

EMPLOYER IDENTIFICATION NUMBER →

BANK NAME/ DATE STAMP

Name The Trainer Co.

Address 4713 Henderson Ave.

City South Bend

State IN Zip 46624-4530

Telephone number (219) 555-7331

IRS USE ONLY

Darken only one TYPE OF TAX		and	Darken only one TAX PERIOD
941	Sch. A		1st Quarter
990C	1120		2nd Quarter
943	990-T		3rd Quarter
720	990PF		4th Quarter
CT-1	1042		
940			

35

FOR BANK USE IN MICR ENCODING

Federal Tax Deposit Coupon
Form 8109-B

Date to be filed: ____________________

3-13. Assume that in Problem 3-12 no deposit was made by The Trainer Company until April 4. Determine the:

a. Penalty for failure to make timely deposit . . . . $__________

b. Penalty for failure to pay tax when due . . . . __________

c. Interest on taxes due and unpaid . . . . __________

d. Total penalty imposed . . . . $__________

3-14. At the Payne Die Company, office workers are employed for a 40-hour workweek on either an annual or a monthly salary basis. In the plant, most workers are paid according to a units-of-production (piece-rate) plan under which the overtime rate is equal to ½ the regular hourly pay rate.

Given on the form on page 103 are the current annual and monthly salary rates for five office workers and the number of units produced by six plant workers for the week ended November 8, 1991.

All workers are entitled to overtime pay for all hours worked beyond 40 each workweek at 1½ times the regular hourly rates.

a. For each worker calculate:

NOTE: In calculating all hourly rates, overtime rates, etc., carry out the cents to 3 decimal places and round back to 2 places.

(1) The regular earnings for the weekly payroll period ended November 8, 1991.
(2) The overtime earnings, if any.
(3) The total regular and overtime earnings.
(4) The FICA taxable wages for this pay period.
(5) The amount of FICA taxes to be withheld by the employer this pay period.
(6) The net pay for this pay period.

b. Determine the employer's FICA taxes for the week ended November 8, 1991.

Date ____________________ Name ____________________

Practical Problem 3-14

PAYNE DIE COMPANY

Weekly Payroll for Period Ending November 8, 1991

Employee	Salary or Unit Rate	Hrs Worked and Units Produced	Regular Earnings	Overtime Earnings	Total Reg. and O/T Earnings	Cum. FICA Taxable Wages as of Last Pay Period (11/1/91)	FICA Taxable Wages This Pay Period	FICA Taxes to be Withheld	Net Pay
a.			(1)	(2)	(3)		(4)	(5)	(6)
OFFICE:									
LENTZ, R.	$16,900 per yr.	40				$14,950.00			
STEYER, C.	$28,080 per yr.	40				$25,380.00			
LONG, S.	$4,900 per mo.	40				$53,815.52			
RICHEY, S.	$1,400 per mo.	48				$17,600.02			
TAVEAU, G.	$900 per mo.	40				$ 9,553.74			
PLANT:									
MANELLA, V.	$8.50/M (thousand)	40 hrs. 18,000 units				$ 8,380.00			
PLATT, R.	$12.50/M	46 hrs. 19,000 units				$17,570.10			
FLORA, L.	$11.80/M	48 hrs. 17,000 units				$10,418.13			
VALADEZ, M.	$12.50/M	40 hrs. 16,000 units				$11,603.90			
YAU, C.	$12.50/M	48 hrs. 19,500 units				$16,145.67			
KATZ, B.	$8.50/M	40 hrs. 16,500 units				$ 6,513.50			
Totals						. . . . . .			

b. Employer's FICA taxes for week ended November 8, 1991 . . . . $____________

CONTINUING PAYROLL PROBLEM

Refer to the partially completed payroll register which you started at the end of Unit 2. You will now determine the amount of FICA tax to be withheld from each employee's pay for the pay period ending January 7 by proceeding as follows:

1. In the Taxable Earnings—FICA column, record the amount of each employee's weekly earnings that is subject to the FICA tax.
2. Using the amounts that were recorded in step (1), determine the FICA tax for each employee by multiplying the taxable earnings by the current FICA tax rate. Record this amount in the appropriate Deductions column for each employee.

NOTE: Retain your partially completed payroll register for use at the end of Unit 4.

CASE PROBLEM

Case 3-1 Auditing Form 941

Ron Harte, payroll clerk for the Coastal Company, has just completed a rough draft of Form 941, the Employer's Quarterly Federal Tax Return, for the quarter ending March 31, 1991. The rough draft is shown on page 107. As Harte's supervisor and the person authorized to sign Form 941, you are auditing the form before it is mailed to make sure that the information on the form is accurate.

The information available to you in three of the company's general ledger accounts is shown on page 106. Employees are paid on the 15th and the last day of each month. When these days fall on Saturday or Sunday, employees are paid the previous Friday. Indicate what changes, if any, should be made on Form 941 before the final copy is prepared, signed, and mailed.

FICA TAXES PAYABLE Account No. 214

Date			Debit	Credit	Balance Debit	Balance Credit
1991						
Jan.	15			954.96		954.96
	15			954.96		1,909.92
	18		1,909.92			--------
	31			1,041.12		1,041.12
	31			1,041.10		2,082.22
Feb.	5		2,082.22			--------
	15			1,028.71		1,028.71
	15			1,028.71		2,057.42
	20		2,057.42			--------
	28			991.78		991.78
	28			991.76		1,983.54
Mar.	5		1,983.54			--------
	15			970.71		970.71
	15			970.74		1,941.45
	20		1,941.45			--------
	29			972.14		972.14
	29			972.11		1,944.25
Apr.	3		1,944.25			--------

EMPLOYEES FEDERAL INCOME TAXES PAYABLE Account No. 216

Date			Debit	Credit	Balance Debit	Balance Credit
1991						
Jan.	15			1,980.00		1,980.00
	18		1,980.00			--------
	31			2,217.00		2,217.00
Feb.	5		2,217.00			--------
	15			2,016.00		2,016.00
	20		2,016.00			--------
	28			2,007.00		2,007.00
Mar.	5		2,007.00			--------
	15			1,970.00		1,970.00
	20		1,970.00			--------
	29			1,887.00		1,887.00
Apr.	3		1,887.00			--------

WAGES AND SALARIES Account No. 511

Date			Debit	Credit	Balance Debit	Balance Credit
1991						
Jan.	15		12,483.16		12,483.16	
	31		13,609.40		26,092.56	
Feb.	15		13,447.13		39,539.69	
	28		12,964.43		52,504.12	
Mar.	15		12,689.02		65,193.14	
	29		12,707.69		77,900.83	

Form **941** Department of the Treasury Internal Revenue Service 4242

Employer's Quarterly Federal Tax Return

▶ See Circular E for more information concerning Employment Tax Returns.

Please type or print.

OMB No. 1545-0029

Your name, address, employer identification number, and calendar quarter of return. (If not correct, please change.)

Name (as distinguished from trade name) — Date quarter ended: MAR 31, 1991

Trade name, if any: COASTAL COMPANY — Employer identification number: 77-2267142

Address and ZIP code: 77 CASTRO SAN FRANCISCO, CA 94117-6903

T / FF / FD / FP / I / T

IRS Use

If address is different from prior return, check here ▶ ☐

If you do not have to file returns in the future, check here . . . ▶ ☐ Date final wages paid . . . . ▶

If you are a seasonal employer, see **Seasonal employer** on page 2 and check here . . . ▶ ☐

1a	Number of employees (except household) employed in the pay period that includes March 12th ▶	1a	19
b	If you are a subsidiary corporation AND your parent corporation files a consolidated Form 1120, enter parent corporation employer identification number (EIN) . . ▶ 1b –		
2	Total wages and tips subject to withholding, plus other compensation ▶	2	77,900 38
3	Total income tax withheld from wages, tips, pensions, annuities, sick pay, gambling, etc. ▶	3	12,077 00
4	Adjustment of withheld income tax for preceding quarters of calendar year (see instructions) ▶	4	-0-
5	Adjusted total of income tax withheld (line 3 as adjusted by line 4—see instructions)	5	12,077 00
6	Taxable social security wages paid $ 77,900 38 × 15.3% (.153)	6	11,918 76
7a	Taxable tips reported $ -0- × 15.3% (.153)	7a	-0-
b	Taxable hospital insurance wages paid $ -0- × 2.9% (.029)	7b	-0-
8	Total social security taxes (add lines 6, 7a, and 7b)	8	11,918 76
9	Adjustment of social security taxes (see instructions for required explanation)	9	04
10	Adjusted total of social security taxes (line 8 as adjusted by line 9—see instructions) ▶	10	11,918 80
11	Backup withholding (see instructions)	11	-0-
12	Adjustment of backup withholding tax for preceding quarters of calendar year ▶	12	-0-
13	Adjusted total of backup withholding (line 11 as adjusted by line 12)	13	-0-
14	Total taxes (add lines 5, 10, and 13)	14	23,995 80
15	Advance earned income credit (EIC) payments, if any ▶	15	-0-
16	Net taxes (subtract line 15 from line 14). **This must equal line IV below** (plus line IV of Schedule A (Form 941) if you have treated backup withholding as a separate liability).	16	23,995 80
17	Total deposits for quarter, including overpayment applied from a prior quarter, from your records ▶	17	23,977 80
18	Balance due (subtract line 17 from line 16). This should be less than $500. Pay to IRS ▶	18	18 00
19	If line 17 is more than line 16, enter overpayment here ▶ $ ______ and check if to be: ☐ Applied to next return OR ☐ Refunded.		

Record of Federal Tax Liability (Complete if line 16 is $500 or more.) See the instructions on page 4 for details before checking these boxes.

Check only if you made eighth-monthly deposits using the 95% rule ▶ ☐ Check only if you are a first time 3-banking-day depositor ▶ ☐

Do NOT Show Federal Tax Deposits Here

Show tax liability here, **not deposits.** IRS gets deposit data from FTD coupons.

Date wages paid		First month of quarter		Second month of quarter		Third month of quarter
1st through 3rd	A		I		Q	
4th through 7th	B		J		R	
8th through 11th	C		K		S	
12th through 15th	D	3,889.92	L	4,073.42	T	3,911.45
16th through 19th	E		M		U	
20th through 22nd	F		N		V	
23rd through 25th	G		O	3,990.54	W	
26th through the last	H	4,292.22	P		X	3,813.25
Total liability for month	*I*	8,189.14	*II*	8,063.96	*III*	7,724.70

IV Total for quarter (add lines *I*, *II*, and *III*). **This must equal line 16 above** ▶ 23,977.80

Sign Here Under penalties of perjury, I declare that I have examined this return, including accompanying schedules and statements, and to the best of my knowledge and belief, it is true, correct, and complete.

Signature ▶ Title ▶ Date ▶

Withholding for Income Taxes

GOALS OF THIS UNIT

After completing your study of this unit, you should be able to:

1. Determine coverage under the federal income tax withholding law by examining (a) the employer-employee relationship, (b) the kinds of payments defined as wages, and (c) those kinds of employment that are excluded under the law.
2. Complete Form W-2 and be familiar with other wage and tax statements.
3. Calculate the amount of federal income taxes to be withheld under the percentage method and the wage-bracket method.
4. Describe alternative methods of withholding federal income taxes such as quarterly averaging of wages, annualizing of wages, and cumulative withholding.
5. Calculate the withholding of federal income taxes on supplementary wage payments such as vacation pay, bonuses, commissions, dismissal pay, and tips.
6. Reinforce your knowledge of completing employers' returns such as Forms 941 and 8109, which we discussed in Unit 3.
7. Describe briefly the major kinds of information returns.
8. Understand how the task of payroll accounting is further complicated by the imposition of state and local income taxes.

The federal government has taxed our income since March 1, 1913, and over the years many tax statutes have been enacted. With the passage of the Current Tax Payment Act of 1943, employers were required to withhold federal income taxes from our wages and salaries on a "pay-as-you-go" basis. The amount of taxes withheld is not our exact tax liability because the amount withheld is based upon a system of graduated withholding rates that approximates the actual tax liability. If the actual tax is more or less than the amount withheld, when we file our annual income tax returns, we may have to pay more than the amount withheld or we may be entitled to a refund.

The Tax Reform Act of 1986 was possibly the most extensive overhaul of the U.S. tax code in almost 40 years. As a fundamental reform of the tax structure, the 1986 legislation contained many provisions that affect the withholding of federal income taxes. Those provisions that are of most significance to a firm's payroll accounting operations are discussed in this unit.[1] In this unit we describe the obligations of employers to withhold from each payment of wages and

[1]Those persons interested in tax planning and completing tax returns for individuals, partnerships, and corporations are directed to the many publications of the Internal Revenue Service. These publications and tax forms are available from the IRS Forms Distribution Center of the taxpayer's state and are in many public libraries that maintain reference sets of IRS publications.

salaries the amount required by law and to turn this amount over to the federal government for the employee's income tax account. After employers have remitted this amount, their responsibility for the collection of income taxes from their employees ends.

Payroll accounting is further complicated as a result of the number of states, cities, and counties that require the withholding of income taxes on wages and salaries. Thus, in order to avoid costly penalties, today's payroll managers, especially those in organizations having employees in many states, must have at their fingertips up-to-date information on laws and regulations such as those we describe in this unit.

COVERAGE UNDER FEDERAL INCOME TAX WITHHOLDING LAW

Before you may withhold any tax under the tax law, the following conditions must exist:

1. There must be, or must have been, an employer-employee relationship.
2. The payments received by the employee must be properly defined as wages.
3. The employment must not be exempted by the law.

We shall discuss each of these qualifying conditions in the following paragraphs.

Employers

An *employer* is any person or organization for whom an individual performs any service as an employee. Sole proprietors are employers regardless of whether they have one or more employees. Partners are also employers regardless of the number of employees and regardless of whether or not the partners draw compensation for services rendered. Corporations are employers, and the officers of a corporation including the president, vice-president, secretary, and treasurer are employees. Not-for-profit corporations, which are themselves exempt from income tax, are also employers and are subject to the withholding requirements. Such corporations include religious and charitable organizations, educational institutions, clubs, and social organizations. Employers also include the federal government, state governments, the governments of Puerto Rico and the District of Columbia, as well as any of their respective agencies, instrumentalities, or political subdivisions.

Employees

Every individual is an *employee* if the relationship between the employee and the person for whom the services are performed is the legal relationship of employer and employee. (See page 66.) In some cases it is rather difficult to determine whether the relationship of employer and employee exists. If such relationship exists, the designation of the relationship by the parties as anything other than that of employer and employee is immaterial. Thus, if such relationship exists, it is of no consequence that the employee is designated as a partner, agent, or independent contractor. Generally physicians, lawyers, dentists, veterinarians, public accountants, auctioneers, and others who follow an independent trade, business, or profession in which they offer their services to the public are *independent contractors* and not employees.

In defining the term employee, no distinction is made between classes or grades of employees. Thus, superintendents, managers, and other administrative and executive personnel are employees. As we stated above, the officers of a corporation are employees of that corporation. However, the directors of a corporation are not employees unless they perform services other than attending and participating in meetings of the board of directors. Partners are not considered employees even though they may draw compensation for services rendered the partnership. In the case of federal, state, or local governmental agencies, the term employee includes both officers and elected officials.

Wages

The term *wages* includes the total compensation paid for services whether in the form of wages, salaries, commissions, or bonuses, including the cash value of remuneration paid in a medium other than cash. When employers pay wages in the form of noncash property, they are not relieved of their duty to withhold. Rather, they must withhold on the fair value of the property.

Vacation allowances, dismissal payments, and other supplementary payments representing compensation for services rendered constitute wages. Any deductions from the wages paid employees are considered to be part of the employees' remuneration at the time the deductions are made. This means that the amount of federal income taxes to be withheld is determined from the *gross amount* of wages without regard to deductions made from gross wages for local, state, or federal taxes; insurance premiums; savings bond purchases; employee contributions to profit-sharing plans; and union dues.

Meals and Lodging. Generally the cash value of meals and lodging furnished employees is included in taxable wages. Under federal income tax withholding, however, the tax does *not* apply if employers furnish the meals and lodging on their premises and for their convenience, and require that employees accept the lodging.

EXAMPLE:

Jersey Hospital requires certain employees to live and to eat on the hospital's premises in order to be available for emergency calls. The hospital does *not* need to withhold federal income taxes on the cash value of the meals and lodging since the value of these items does not represent taxable income to employees.

If employees receive a cash allowance for their meals or lodging, the exclusion does not apply because only meals and lodging furnished *in kind* are free from withholding. An exception exists when employees receive supper money in cash for voluntarily working overtime. Generally the payment is regarded as for the employer's convenience and thus is not subject to federal income tax withholding.

Noncash Fringe Benefits. Examples of noncash fringe benefits that employers provide their employees include the personal use of company cars, use of vehicles for commuting (vanpooling), flights on employer-provided airplanes, and free or discounted flights on commercial airlines. Such fringe benefits are considered to be taxable income to employees and thus are subject to the withholding of federal income taxes.

Employers have much flexibility in deciding when to withhold federal income taxes on noncash fringe benefits so long as the withholding occurs in the calendar year in which the benefits are provided. For example, the withholding may be in the final paycheck in December, or the amount to be withheld may be spread over several pay periods. The timing of the withholding need not be the same for all employees nor for all benefits. However, if personal property such as securities or real estate is provided as a noncash fringe benefit, the withholding of federal income taxes must occur at the time of transferring the personal property.

The value of noncash fringe benefits that employers provide is looked upon as a payment of supplemental wages, which we describe later in this unit. As such, you may add the value of the fringe benefits to the employees' regular wages for a pay period and compute the withholding taxes on the total payment. Or you may withhold from the employees' regular wages a flat 20% of the value of the fringe benefits. Generally you must withhold federal income taxes and social security taxes on the date or dates the benefits are considered as having been paid. The amounts withheld from the employees' wages and the employer's payroll taxes are deposited in accordance with the rules for depositing taxes, which we shall discuss later.

Tips. *Cash* tips of $20 or more received in a calendar month, in the course of employment with a single employer, are treated as remuneration subject to income tax withholding.[2] *Noncash* tips, such as those in the form of passes, tickets, or other goods, are not considered wages and thus are not subject to federal income tax withholding.

An employee must furnish the employer with a statement of the cash tips received if they amount to at least $20 in a month. The employee must report the amount of the cash tips in writing to the employer by the tenth day of the following month. Failure on the part of the employee to make a timely report will subject the employee to a penalty. The Internal Revenue Service (IRS) issues a special pamphlet, consisting of Forms 4070 and 4070-A, that may be used by the employee in recording tips and reporting them to the employer. (See Illustration 3-1 on page 69.) The employer is not required to audit or verify the accuracy of the tip income reported for purposes of federal income tax withholding.

There are special reporting rules for large food and beverage establishments. A *large food or beverage establishment* is one that provides food or beverages for consumption on the premises, where tipping is customary, and where the employer normally employs more than 10 workers on a typical business day in all food or beverage operations.

If employees report tips that total 8% or more of the gross receipts (less carryout sales and sales with a 10% or more service charge added), no tip allocation is needed.[3] However, if the tips reported do not equal 8% of the gross receipts, the employer must allocate to the tipped employees an amount equal to the difference between 8% of the gross receipts and the total tips reported. The allocation may be made according to an agreement between the employer and the employees or in accordance with the method contained in the regulations issued by the IRS.

---

[2]The treatment of cash tips for the purpose of federal income tax withholding should not be confused with the definition of a tipped employee under the Fair Labor Standards Act. As noted in Unit 2, under the FLSA, a tipped employee is defined as a person engaged in an occupation in which tips of more than $30 a month are customarily received.

[3]The Deficit Reduction Tax Bill of 1984 provides that the employer or the majority of employees in large food and beverage establishments may petition the IRS District Director to reduce the percentage of gross receipts required to be allocated. The percentage of gross receipts to be allocated may be reduced from 8% to 2%.

EXAMPLE:

The tips reported during October by the employees of La Cruz Restaurant total $4,840. The gross receipts for that month are $78,500. The restaurant is required to allocate additional income of

($78,500 x .08) – $4,840, or $1,440,

among all of the tipped employees.

As we indicated earlier, federal income taxes are to be withheld *only* on the tips reported to the employer; no taxes are withheld on the tips that are merely allocated.

Employers who allocate tips are required to file annually with the IRS *Form 8027, Employer's Annual Information Return of Tip Income and Allocated Tips,* which contains information such as:

1. Total charged tips.
2. Total charged receipts (other than nonallocable receipts) on which there were charged tips.
3. Total amount of service charges less than 10% paid as wages to employees.
4. Total tips reported by indirectly tipped and directly tipped employees.
5. Gross receipts from food or beverage operations (other than nonallocable receipts).
6. Amount that must be allocated as tips and recorded on the employee's Wage and Tax Statement, Form W-2. (Form W-2 is described and illustrated later in this unit.)

Employers are also required to furnish a written statement to each employee to whom an amount is allocated. This statement contains the employer's name and address, employee's name, and the total amount allocated to the employee for the calendar year. This written statement is made on the employee's Wage and Tax Statement (Form W-2).

Regardless of whether employees receive an allocation, at the time of filing their personal income tax returns, employees are required to report as income all tips received. If employees fail to report the full amount of allocation as gross income, they must be able to furnish adequate records to substantiate the lesser amount reported.

Payments Exempt from Withholding

The law excludes from the definition of "wages" certain payments such as those described below. Thus, persons making such payments are *not* required to withhold federal income taxes.

Advances. Amounts paid in advance or reimbursements made to employees for traveling or other business expenses incurred or reasonably expected to be incurred are not subject to withholding. Any reasonable segregation of wages paid will be acceptable. Thus, you may issue one check indicating the amount that represents wages and the amount that represents reimbursed expenses, or you may issue a separate check covering the expenses.

Educational Assistance. Many employers reimburse their employees for the cost of tuition, fees, books, and supplies that is incurred when the employees are attending school. Such amounts are excluded from the definition of wages and thus are not subject to federal income tax withholding. In 1990, the maximum amount of educational assistance that could be excluded was $5,250.[4] However, withholding *is* required from employer-paid tuition payments for courses in graduate school that are *not* job related and for hobby-type courses such as photography and gardening.

The employer's educational assistance plan must be in writing and limited to providing employees with educational assistance. The plan must not discriminate in favor of employees who are officers, shareholders, self-employed individuals, or highly compensated employees or their dependents.

Note that employer-paid tuition for *job-related* courses are tax free and thus not subject to withholding. These tuition payments are one of several fringe benefits that employees may receive. To be considered job-related, a course must maintain or improve the employee's skills required for the job, or be required by the employer as a condition of continuing employment in the employee's current job. Courses that are needed by the employee to meet the minimum education requirements for a job or that prepare an employee for a new trade or business do *not* qualify as job-related.

Other Payments Exempt from Withholding. Some other types of employment and payments excluded for income tax *withholding* purposes are:

1. Agricultural workers, *all* of whom are paid cash remuneration *less* than $2,500 in any calendar year. Employers who do not meet the $2,500 annual payroll test may exclude remu-

[4]The exclusion of benefits paid under an employer's nondiscriminatory educational assistance plan expired on September 30, 1990. At the time of this writing, no provision had been made to extend the exclusion.

neration for agricultural services when it amounts to less than $150 paid *each* worker in a calendar year. Payment for farm work with remuneration other than cash is not taxed.

2. Domestic service in a private home, local college club, or local chapter of a college fraternity or sorority.
3. Persons not employed in the course of the employer's trade or business (casual laborers) provided the cash remuneration paid for service performed in the calendar quarter is less than $50 and employees work on fewer than 24 days in that or the preceding quarter.
4. Citizens or residents of the United States employed by a foreign government or an international organization such as the United Nations.
5. U.S. citizens residing abroad if (a) they have been bona fide residents of a foreign country or countries for an uninterrupted period that includes an entire taxable year, or (b) they show that they have been present in a foreign country or countries for at least 330 full days during a period of 12 consecutive months.
6. Ministers of churches and members of religious orders performing duties as such.
7. Public officials (fees only, not salaries).
8. Individuals under age 18 for delivery or distribution of newspapers or shopping news and vendors of newspapers and magazines whose remuneration consists of difference between purchase and sales price.
9. Deceased person's wages paid to the employee's beneficiary or estate.
10. Sickness or injury payments made under workers' compensation law or contract of insurance. (However, as we explain later, employees receiving sick pay may voluntarily authorize insurers and other third parties to withhold federal income taxes on the payments.)
11. Tips if less than $20 a month.
12. Moving expenses reimbursed by the employer if at time of payment it is reasonable to believe that the employee will be entitled to a deduction for these expenses on the individual's federal income tax return. When moving expenses are reimbursed (whether to the employee, to a third party for the employee, or by providing services in kind to the employee), the employee should be given a completed *Form 4782, Employee Moving Expense Information* (not illustrated).
13. Employer's cost of group term life insurance on the life of an employee. However, the cost of group term life insurance in excess of $50,000 is includible in the employee's gross income and must be reported by the employer as part of the employee's "wages, tips, and other compensation" on the worker's Wage and Tax Statement (Form W-2).
14. Strike benefits and lockout benefits paid by a union to its members.
15. Amounts received by service personnel on active service in an area declared by the President to be a combat zone.
16. Supper money paid occasionally to employees who work overtime, if the amounts can be classified as a *de minimis* fringe benefit. (*De minimis* fringe benefits are those of so little value as to make accounting for the benefits unreasonable or administratively impracticable.)
17. Employer contributions to cash or deferred arrangements, such as salary-reduction agreements (Code Sec. 401[k] plans). In such plans, an employee elects to have the employer contribute an amount to the plan on the employee's behalf or to receive the amount directly from the employer in cash. The amounts contributed to the plan following the employee's election are treated as employer contributions to the plan and are not subject to federal income tax withholding. In 1990, the amount an employee could defer under these arrangements was limited to $7,979.
18. Employer contributions to employer-sponsored individual retirement accounts (IRA) and simplified employee pension plans (SEP). Employees must include in their gross income the employer's contributions, but income tax withholding is not required if the employer reasonably expects that the employees will be able to deduct such contributions on their income tax returns. In 1990, employees could elect to defer up to $7,979 of employer contributions into a qualified SEP plan. In a qualified plan, employers must have 25 or fewer employees at the beginning of the year, and at least 50% of the employees must elect to contribute to the SEP plan.

Under certain conditions federal income tax withholding is permitted from some wage payments that are ordinarily exempt from withholding, as described above. For example, domestic workers and members of the clergy may request their employers to withhold federal income taxes from their wage payments during the year. Such a procedure is of particular benefit to these workers who are thus able to decrease their year-end tax liability.

WITHHOLDING ALLOWANCES AND WITHHOLDING CERTIFICATES

For purposes of computing the withholding tax, employees are entitled to personal allowances and allowances for dependents provided the employees properly furnish their employers with a claim for the allowances. In addition to the personal allowances and allowances for dependents, employees may claim other allowances such as a special withholding allowance and allowances for itemized deductions and tax credits.

Personal Allowances

A *personal allowance* (sometimes called a *personal exemption*) is a deduction allowed in computing taxable income. For the calendar year 1990, a personal allowance of $2,050 was permitted in computing an employee's taxable income, provided the employee was not claimed as a dependent on another person's tax return. Commencing in 1990, the exemption amount is annually adjusted, or indexed, for inflation.

If an employee is *married* and the spouse is not claimed as a dependent on another person's tax return, the employee may also claim one personal allowance for the spouse. (The additional personal allowances that were allowed for age and blindness in the past have been replaced with additional standard deductions for age and blindness, as we discuss later.)

If employees hold more than one job, they may not claim the *same* withholding allowances with more than one employer at the same time. They may claim all of their allowances on one job, or they may divide their allowances among jobs. Generally employees will find the amounts withheld to be more accurate if they claim all withholding allowances on the job with the largest wages and claim zero allowances on all other jobs.

An employee who is divorced or legally separated by a decree of separate maintenance is not to be treated as married. Also, if an employee is a nonresident alien (other than a resident of Canada, Mexico, or Puerto Rico), he or she may claim only *one* withholding allowance.

Allowances for Dependents

Employees may claim one allowance for each dependent (other than a spouse) who can be claimed on their federal income tax returns. To qualify as a dependent, the person must meet specific requirements that are listed in the instructions accompanying the individual's federal income tax return.

Special Withholding Allowance

To insure that wages below the level to which income taxes apply will not be subject to withholding, a worker may claim an additional allowance. This *special withholding allowance* may be claimed by workers whether or not they plan to itemize deductions on their tax returns. Note that the special withholding allowance is used *only* to figure the employee's income tax withholding; the allowance is *not* claimed when the employee files his or her tax return.

A special withholding allowance can be claimed by a person under any *one* of the following situations:

1. The person is single and has only one job.
2. The person is married and has only one job, and the spouse is not working.
3. The person has two jobs, only one of which paid more than $2,500.
4. The person is married and has two jobs or a working spouse, if only one job paid more than $2,500.

The special withholding allowance may be claimed by workers when they complete the Employee's Withholding Allowance Certificate, which we shall discuss and illustrate in a later section.

Other Withholding Allowances

Withholding allowances are designed to reduce the overwithholding of income taxes of employees. In addition to personal allowances and allowances for dependents, employees may be entitled to withholding allowances based on estimated tax credits (such as child and dependent care credit) and estimated itemized deductions (such as medical expenses and charitable contributions).

Employees may take these credits and deductions when filing their federal income tax returns. The number of withholding allowances is determined on the worksheets that accompany the withholding allowance certificate and then reported on the certificate itself, as shown in Illustration 4-1.

Form W-4—Employee's Withholding Allowance Certificate

Employees are required to furnish their employers with a signed *Employee's Withholding Allowance Certificate, Form W-4*. This form sets forth the number of withholding allowances that an employee claims, which shall in no event exceed the number to which the employee is entitled.

Form W-4 contains the withholding allowance certificate and detailed instructions and worksheets for employees to use in completing the certificate. Illustration 4-1 shows a filled-in withholding allowance certificate, Form W-4, which the employee detaches and gives to the employer.

You must retain the withholding certificates as a supporting record of the withholding allowances used in deducting income taxes from the employees' salaries and wages. Once filed, the withholding allowance certificate remains in effect until an amended certificate takes effect. You must retain the withholding certificates for as long as the certificates are in effect and for four years thereafter.

If there is a change in the status of employees with respect to the number of withholding allowances to which they are entitled, they should file an amended Form W-4 with you. In case there is a *decrease* in the number of withholding allowances, the employee must furnish you with a new certificate within 10 days. If, however, the reduction in allowances results from the death of a dependent or a spouse, the amended certificate need not be filed until December 1 since the personal allowance is not lost by death of the dependent during the current taxable year. Should there be an *increase* in the number of withholding allowances to which an employee is entitled, he or she should file a new certificate. However, an employee is not required to do so, as the claiming of additional allowances is optional with the employee.

When an employee files an amended certificate as a result of a change in status, you may put the certificate into effect at any time. However, you must put the certificate into effect no later than the start of the first payroll period ending (or the first payment of wages) on or after the 30th day you receive the certificate.

If an employee furnishes you with an amended Form W-4, you may not repay or reimburse the employee for income taxes overwithheld before the effective date of the new certificate. However, you may repay or reimburse the employee for income taxes overwithheld on or after the effective date of the amended form if you failed to take the new certificate into account.

It is important that employees file Form W-4 to avoid having amounts withheld that are not close to the amount of tax due at the time they file their tax returns. If an employee does not file a withholding allowance certificate, you must withhold federal income tax as if the employee had claimed no allowances.

If married employees do not claim their marital status on Form W-4, you must withhold according to the withholding tables for single employees. Thus, to take advantage of the lower withholding provided for married employees, married workers must indicate their marital status in Box 3 of Form W-4. In this box, the marital status entitled "Married, but withhold at higher Single rate" appears. Married couples with both spouses employed or a married person with more than one employer may use this status to increase the amount of income taxes withheld.

Form **W-4** Department of the Treasury Internal Revenue Service

Employee's Withholding Allowance Certificate
▶ **For Privacy Act and Paperwork Reduction Act Notice, see reverse.**

OMB No. 1545-0010 **1990**

1 Type or print your first name and middle initial	Last name	2 Your social security number
Alberta V.	Barrera	173-68-3201

Home address (number and street or rural route): 550 South State Street

City or town, state, and ZIP code: Troy, ME 04987-0550

3 Marital status: [x] Single [ ] Married [ ] Married, but withhold at higher Single rate.
Note: *If married, but legally separated, or spouse is a nonresident alien, check the Single box.*

4 Total number of allowances you are claiming (from line G above or from the Worksheets on back if they apply) . . . **4** 5

5 Additional amount, if any, you want deducted from each pay . . . **5** $ 0

6 I claim exemption from withholding and I certify that I meet **ALL** of the following conditions for exemption:

- Last year I had a right to a refund of **ALL** Federal income tax withheld because I had **NO** tax liability; **AND**
- This year I expect a refund of **ALL** Federal income tax withheld because I expect to have **NO** tax liability; **AND**
- This year if my income exceeds $500 and includes nonwage income, another person cannot claim me as a dependent.

If you meet all of the above conditions, enter the year effective and "EXEMPT" here . . . . . ▶ **6** 19

7 Are you a full-time student? (**Note:** *Full-time students are not automatically exempt.*) . . . **7** [ ] Yes [x] No

Under penalties of perjury, I certify that I am entitled to the number of withholding allowances claimed on this certificate or entitled to claim exempt status.

Employee's signature ▶ Alberta V. Barrera **Date** ▶ January 4, 1990

8 Employer's name and address (**Employer:** Complete 8 and 10 **only if sending to IRS**)	9 Office code (optional)	10 Employer identification number

Illustration 4-1. Form W-4, Employee's Withholding Allowance Certificate

No-Tax-Liability Exemption

Employees who had no income tax liability in 1990 and do not expect to have any in 1991 qualify for exemption from withholding of federal income tax from their wages. Such employees include students working during the summer, retired persons, and other part-time workers. Single persons who made less than $5,300 in 1990 owed no federal income tax. During 1990 a married couple entitled to file a joint return could earn combined wages up to $9,550 without incurring any federal income tax liability. However, if someone else claimed the employee as a dependent on his or her tax return, the employee probably would have to pay some income tax. For example, in 1990, employees were not exempt from withholding if they had any nonwage income, such as interest on savings or dividends, and if their total income (wages and nonwage income) was more than $500.

Part-time and summer employees who are exempt from the withholding of federal income taxes should complete and submit to you their Form W-4 showing the no-tax-liability status. In such cases, you *must not* withhold federal income tax from their wages. (This exemption does not affect your liability for collecting the employee's share of FICA contributions.) Employees claiming the exemption from withholding must file Form W-4 with you each year.

Additional and Voluntary Withholding Agreements

In some instances, employees wish to have additional federal income tax withheld from their wages. For example, a person with two or more jobs or a married couple, both of whom are working, may need to have additional income tax withheld. The simplest way to increase the amount of tax withheld is to reduce the number of withholding allowances claimed. However, this approach may not be satisfactory for employees who claim only one or even zero allowances. Therefore, employees may request on Form W-4 that their employer withhold an additional amount from their wages.

In other cases, employees may have no income tax withheld from their wages because the payments received do not represent wages; or the relationship between the one making the payment and the payee is not that of employer and employee. For example, the person receiving remuneration for services may be a clergyman or a domestic worker in a private home. As we indicated earlier in this unit, these types of payments do not constitute wages for income tax withholding purposes. However, such persons may voluntarily request that you withhold federal income taxes from their payments. Employees who wish to enter into an additional or a voluntary withholding agreement with their employer need only furnish you with Form W-4. The filing of this form constitutes a request for withholding.

Other persons may need to have additional taxes withheld if they receive income other than wages, such as interest and dividends. Procedures are available for these persons to enter into voluntary withholding agreements under which federal income taxes will be withheld from payments not ordinarily subject to withholding.

Requests for additional and voluntary withholding become effective when you accept them and commence to withhold the tax. The agreements remain in effect until the stipulated termination date or until the termination is mutually agreed upon by you and the employee. Either you or the employee may terminate an agreement before its stipulated or mutually agreed-upon termination date by furnishing to the other party a signed, written notice of termination.

Withholding Less Than the Required Amount

The full amount of the income tax for which employees are liable must be withheld. You may not withhold a lesser amount than required under the law. In determining the amount of tax required to be withheld, you consider the number of withholding allowances that an employee claims on Form W-4. In no event may the number of allowances claimed be greater than the number to which the employee is entitled.

A civil fine of $500 may be charged for filing a Form W-4 that decreases the tax withheld with no reasonable basis at the time of the decrease. Also, criminal penalties apply for willfully supplying false or fraudulent information or failing to supply information in an attempt to evade the tax.

Invalid Withholding Certificates

The number of allowances that a worker claims is used in computing the amount of federal income taxes to be withheld. However, you are under no obligation to determine whether the number of allowances claimed is greater than the number to which the employee is entitled.

A withholding certificate is deemed to be invalid and void if:

1. The withholding certificate has been altered by the employee.
2. Extraneous unauthorized material has been added to the form.
3. The employee has otherwise indicated that the data on the form are false.

In such cases, the employee should be told that the form is invalid and that another one should be completed. If the employee does not complete a valid form, you must withhold federal income taxes at the rate for a single person claiming no exemptions. However, if there is a prior valid certificate in effect with respect to the employee, you must continue to withhold in accordance with the prior certificate.

Submitting Forms W-4 to IRS

To curb the practice of filing false Forms W-4 by claiming unreasonable numbers of allowances or total exemption from withholding, the IRS requires employers to submit a copy of each form on which:

1. An employee claims more than 11 withholding allowances, or
2. An employee, usually earning more than $200 a week at the time the certificate was filed, claims to be exempt from withholding.

Employers should submit such copies of Form W-4 at the time and place of filing Form 941, Employer's Quarterly Federal Tax Return, for the reporting period. You may submit the W-4 information on magnetic tape instead of filing paper returns if you first receive permission from the IRS. Employers may submit their Forms W-4 to the IRS more often if they wish. If so, employers should include a cover letter giving their name, address, employer identification number, and the number of forms included.

Employees who claim allowances inconsistent with the IRS regulations may submit new Forms W-4 with supporting statements either directly to the IRS or to the employer, who must then forward the forms to the IRS. Until receipt of notice from the IRS, you are required to withhold on the basis of the statements made in the certificates submitted. The IRS may find that the copies of the Forms W-4 submitted contain materially incorrect statements. If the IRS verifies that the forms are defective, it will furnish you the reasons for such a determination. The IRS will advise you that employees who submitted defective Forms W-4 cannot claim an exempt status nor can they claim the number of allowances that is in excess of the number specified by the IRS in the written notice.

You must give the employees a copy of the notice and ask them to furnish new Forms W-4. Until new forms are received, you must withhold on the basis of the maximum number of allowances set by the IRS in the written notice. If the employees' new forms claim more allowances than the number set by the IRS, you should disregard the amended forms and continue withholding on the basis of the number of allowances set by the IRS.

Other Withholdings

Federal income taxes are also withheld from other kinds of payments made to current and former employees. We briefly describe several of the different kinds of payments below. You will find additional information about the withholdings in the instructions accompanying each withholding allowance form.

Form W-4P—Withholding Certificate for Pension or Annuity Payments. Generally the withholding of federal income taxes applies to payments made from pension, profit-sharing, stock bonus, annuity, and certain deferred compensation plans and individual retirement arrangements. You treat the payments from any of these sources as wages for the purpose of withholding. Unless the recipients of pension or annuity payments elect *not* to have federal income taxes withheld from such payments, the taxes will be withheld. Payers must withhold on monthly pension and annuity payments exceeding $796 ($9,550 a year) unless the payees elect otherwise. If the recipients do not instruct the payers to the contrary, the payers are required to withhold income taxes as if the recipients were married and claiming three withholding allowances.

By completing Form W-4P or a substitute form furnished by the payer, an employee can elect to have no income tax withheld from the payments received. The form may also be used to change the amount of tax that would ordinarily be withheld by the payers. Once completed, Form W-4P remains in effect until the recipient changes or revokes the certificate. The payer must notify the recipients each year of their right to elect to have no taxes withheld or to revoke their election.

Form W-4S—Request for Federal Income Tax Withholding From Sick Pay. Form W-4S must be filed with the *payer of sick pay* if the employee wants federal income taxes withheld from the payments. The form should not be filed with the worker's employer who makes such payments since employers are already required to withhold income taxes from sick pay. *Thus, Form W-4S is filed only if the payer is a third party, such as an insurance company.*

Withholding for Child Support. To enforce the collection of child-support funds, legislation was passed to require the withholding of these amounts. Under the law, procedures are developed by state agencies for the automatic withholding of child-support payments from employees' wages. The Family Support Act of 1988 requires the *immediate* withholding for child-support payments for all cases supported by a court order. The amount withheld is equal to the amount of the delinquency, subject to the limits prescribed in the federal garnishment law, which we shall discuss in Unit 6. Also, employers are entitled to withhold a fee, set by each state, for the administrative costs they incur in relation to the withholding.

Withholding to Collect Delinquent Taxes. The collection of delinquent federal taxes by means of payroll deductions has been authorized by the IRS. Under this procedure, employees use the *Payroll Deduction Agreement, Form 2159*. On this form, employees authorize their employer to deduct specified amounts from their salaries or wages each payday. During the period that amounts are being deducted from the employees' wages, the amounts of the deductions are recorded on the back of the employer's copy of Form 2159. Amounts withheld are sent directly to the IRS in self-addressed envelopes supplied by the IRS.

THE MAIN METHODS OF WITHHOLDING

After the number of withholding allowances has been determined, your next step is to select the method of computing the amount of federal income tax to be withheld. Usually one of two main methods of withholding—the *percentage method* or the *wage-bracket method*—is used. Under both methods, unmarried persons (either single or head of household) are distinguished from married persons. Both methods provide for giving employees the full benefit of the allowances they claim. As you will see below, both methods use withholding tables to determine the amount to be withheld.

In making a choice between the two methods, you are primarily concerned with the number of employees and the type of payroll accounting system used. You may change from one method to another at will and may use one method for one group of employees and the other method for other groups.

The two withholding methods take into account the standard deduction amounts. A *standard deduction* is an amount of money that is used to reduce a person's adjusted gross income in arriving at the taxable income. The standard deduction varies according to the taxpayer's filing status. For 1990, the following standard deductions apply (whether or not an individual is age 65 or older or is blind):

Joint return filers and surviving spouses	$5,450
Married filing separately	2,725
Head of household filers	4,750
Single filers	3,250

These amounts are increased for single and married individuals or surviving spouses age 65 or older or blind.

The Tax Reform Act of 1986 provides that each year the standard deductions given above will be adjusted for inflation. The adjustment also applies to the additional standard deductions available to elderly or blind persons.

Percentage Method

To determine the tax under the percentage method, take the following steps:

Step 1: Determine the amount of gross wages earned. If the employee's wage ends in a fractional dollar amount, round the gross pay to the nearest dollar; if the gross pay ends in 50¢, the rounding off must be to the next higher dollar. Or, you may round the last digit of the gross pay to 0.

Step 2: Multiply the number of allowances claimed by the amount of one allowance for the applicable payroll period, as determined in the Table of Allowance Values shown in Illustration 4-2.

Step 3: Subtract the amount for the number of allowances claimed from the employee's gross pay to find the excess of wages over allowances claimed.

Step 4: Determine the withholding tax on the excess of wages over allowances claimed by referring to the appropriate Percentage Method Withholding Table. These tables, in effect January 1, 1990, are shown in Tax Table A at the end of the textbook.

TABLE OF ALLOWANCE VALUES FOR 1990

PAYROLL PERIOD	AMOUNT OF ONE WITHHOLDING ALLOWANCE
Weekly	$ 39.42
Biweekly	78.85
Semimonthly	85.42
Monthly	170.83
Quarterly	512.50
Semiannual	1,025.00
Annual	2,050.00
Daily or miscellaneous (per day of such period)	7.88

Illustration 4-2. Table of Allowance Values for Percentage Method

The percentage method of computation is further explained in the following illustrative examples.

EXAMPLES:

A. **Sean Yan is single and claims one allowance. His income for the taxable year is $19,320, payable at the rate of $805 semimonthly.**

Computation of Amount to be Withheld

Step 1:	Semimonthly wages	$805.00
Step 2:	Amount of one withholding allowance (from Allowance Table) ...	85.42
Step 3:	Excess of wages over allowance	$719.58
Step 4:	Amount to be withheld from Table 3(a) in Tax Table A: 15% of $719.58 less $50.00	$100.44

B. **Jose Fernandez, married with one dependent child, claims three allowances. Neither the wife nor the child has any separate income. Fernandez receives a salary of $42,765, payable at the rate of $822.40 each week.**

Computation of Amount to be Withheld

Step 1:	Weekly wages (rounded to nearest dollar)		$822.00
Step 2:	Amount of one withholding allowance (from Allowance Table)	$39.42	
	Number of allowances claimed	x 3	118.26
Step 3:	Excess of wages over allowances ...		$703.74
Step 4:	Amount to be withheld from Table 1(b) in Tax Table A: $93.60 + 4.13 (28% of $703.74 less $689.00)		$ 97.73

As we indicated before, to determine the amount of tax to be withheld under the percentage method, you may round the last digit of the wage amount to zero. Or, you may round the wage amount to the nearest dollar, as done in Example B. Thus, if an employee receives a weekly wage of $395.37, you may eliminate the last digit and determine the amount of the tax to be withheld on $395.30. Or, you may compute the amount to be withheld on $395. In other words, in such a case, you have the option of computing the amount of tax to be withheld on (a) $395.37, (b) $395.30, or (c) $395. If you decide to round wage payments ending in an even half dollar, you must compute the amount to be withheld on the higher dollar. Thus, if the wage payment amounted to $395.50, you must compute the amount to be withheld on $396. Where the amount to be withheld is determined on the basis of a miscellaneous payroll period, you may round only the aggregate wages for the period (not the average daily wage) to the nearest dollar.

To calculate more easily an employee's excess of wages over allowances claimed, you may use the table shown in Illustration 4-3. To use this table:

Step 1: Locate in the left-hand column the total number of withholding allowances claimed by the employee.

Step 2: Determine the total dollar amount of the employee's withholding allowances in the corresponding line in the payroll period column.

Step 3: Subtract the amount obtained in Step 2 from the total wages earned by the employee for the payroll period to arrive at the excess of wages.

Step 4: Determine the withholding tax on the excess of wages over allowances claimed by referring to the appropriate Percentage Method Withholding Table in Tax Table A.

If the number of allowances is	And wages are paid— Weekly	Bi-weekly	Semi-monthly	Monthly	Quarterly	Semi-annually	Annually	Daily or Misc.
	The total amount of withholding allowances for that payroll period is—							
0	$ 0	$ 0	$ 0	$ 0	$ 0	$ 0	$ 0	$ 0
1	39.42	78.85	85.42	170.83	512.50	1,025.00	2,050.00	7.88
2	78.84	157.70	170.84	341.66	1,025.00	2,050.00	4,100.00	15.76
3	118.26	236.55	256.26	512.49	1,537.50	3,075.00	6,150.00	23.64
4	157.68	315.40	341.68	683.32	2,050.00	4,100.00	8,200.00	31.52
5	197.10	394.25	427.10	854.15	2,562.50	5,125.00	10,250.00	39.40
6	236.52	473.10	512.52	1,024.98	3,075.00	6,150.00	12,300.00	47.28
7	275.94	551.95	597.94	1,195.81	3,587.50	7,175.00	14,350.00	55.16
8	315.36	630.80	683.36	1,366.64	4,100.00	8,200.00	16,400.00	63.04
9	354.78	709.65	768.78	1,537.47	4,612.50	9,225.00	18,450.00	70.92
10	394.20	788.50	854.20	1,708.30	5,125.00	10,250.00	20,500.00	78.80
11 or more	Multiply the amount of one withholding allowance for the specific payroll period by the number of allowances claimed							

Illustration 4-3. Easy-Reference Table for Computing Employee's Excess of Wages over Allowances Claimed

The IRS makes available formula tables and wage-bracket tables for percentage method withholding. These tables are especially useful in automated payroll systems.

Wage-Bracket Method

Under the wage-bracket method, the IRS provides statutory wage-bracket tables for weekly, biweekly, semimonthly, monthly, and daily or miscellaneous pay periods. You may obtain copies of the tables from the District Director of Internal Revenue. Tables for 10-day and 28-day payroll periods also are available at the office of the District Director and will be supplied upon request. The weekly, biweekly, semimonthly, monthly, and daily tables for married and single persons, in effect January 1, 1990, are reproduced in Tax Table B at the end of the textbook.

If the payroll period is quarterly, semiannual, or annual, you must use the percentage method of withholding since there are no wage-bracket withholding tables available for these payroll periods. You may also use the percentage method for payroll periods for which statutory tables are provided.

To use the wage-bracket method to determine the amounts to be withheld from the wages earned by employees, you should take the following steps:

Step 1: Select the withholding table that applies to the employee's marital status and the payroll period. (You can save time during this step by first separating all employees into groups of "Not Married" and "Married" according to the payroll period. Then determine the amount of federal income tax for all employees in the one group before selecting the appropriate withholding table to be used for the second group.)

Step 2: Locate the wage bracket (the first two columns of the table) in which the employee's gross wages fall.

Step 3: Follow the line for such wage bracket across to the right to the column headed by the figure that represents the number of withholding allowances claimed by the employee. This amount is the tax to be withheld.

NOTE: If the amount of an employee's wages exceeds the amount shown in the last bracket of the table, use the percentage method of withholding. Before using the percentage method tables, however, be sure to reduce the employee's wages by the value of the total withholding allowances claimed.

If, instead of using the percentage method to compute the amount to be withheld from the semimonthly wages of Yan (Example A, page 119), you had elected to use the wage-bracket method, you would have withheld $101 each payday instead of $100.44. (Refer to semimonthly, not married table in Tax Table B.)

If, instead of using the percentage method to compute the amount to be withheld from the weekly wages of Fernandez (Example B, page 119), you had elected to use the wage-bracket method, you would have withheld $98 each payday instead of $97.73. (Refer to weekly, married table in Tax Table B.)

OTHER METHODS OF WITHHOLDING

In addition to the two principal methods of withholding we have described above, you may use other methods such as quarterly averaging of wages, annualizing wages, cumulative withholding, and withholding for part-year employment. Of these four alternative procedures, two methods—cumulative withholding and withholding for part-year employment—may be initiated only upon an employee's request. If you should find the alternative methods unsatisfactory for your particular payroll operations, you may devise your own withholding procedure, as we discuss later in the section, "Substantially Similar" Methods.

We discuss the features of the four alternative methods in this section. You may round to the nearest dollar the tax withheld under any of the alternative methods, following the rounding rules given on page 119.

Quarterly Averaging of Wages

Under this method of withholding, proceed as follows:

Step 1: Estimate the wages that will be paid the employee in the calendar quarter.

Step 2: Calculate an appropriate average payment.

Step 3: Withhold an amount based on the average payment instead of on the actual payment.

During the quarter you should make any needed adjustment to bring the amount of tax withheld on the basis of average payments into line with the amount required to be withheld without any averaging.

EXAMPLE:

Ortiz, Inc., estimates that Helene Ligonnier will be paid $6,000 during the second quarter of the year. Ligonnier's W-4 shows that she is married and claims seven withholding allowances. Divide the estimated quarterly wages by six—the number of semimonthly pay periods in the quarter—to determine the average payment of $1,000. From Tax Table B, you will find that the amount of federal income taxes to withhold from each semimonthly pay is $41.

The quarterly averaging of wages method works best where there is steady employment and little fluctuation in wages between pay periods. Thus, you can estimate a reasonably accurate average wage. If the only wage payments involved are tips, you cannot use the quarterly averaging method.

Annualizing Wages

For withholding purposes, you may annualize the wage payments and prorate the income tax applicable to those wage payments. Under the annualizing method, proceed as follows:

Step 1: Multiply the wages for one payroll period by the number of payroll periods in the year.

Step 2: Determine the annual amount of withholding required on the total wages.

Step 3: Divide the annual withholding amount by the number of payroll periods to arrive at the amount of withholding for one payroll period.

EXAMPLE:

Marc Field, a married employee with three allowances, is paid $1,050 semimonthly. Under the annualizing method, multiply the $1,050 semimonthly wage by 24 to arrive at an annual wage of $25,200. Next, subtract the withholding allowances of $6,150 (3 x $2,050) from the $25,200 annual wage to arrive at $19,050, the amount of wages subject to tax.

Table 7(b) in Tax Table A indicates that the tax to be withheld on $19,050 is 15% of the excess over $3,400. The excess, computed to be $15,650 ($19,050 – $3,400) and multiplied by .15, equals $2,347.50, the total amount to be withheld on an annual basis. Prorate this amount over the 24 semimonthly payrolls to arrive at $97.81, the amount to withhold from each semimonthly paycheck.

The annualizing method is especially advantageous if you wish to conserve computer memory, since only the rates, brackets, and allowance values for an annual payroll period need be stored in the computer.

Cumulative Withholding

Upon an employee's written request, you may withhold income taxes on the basis of the employee's cumulative wages. This method of withholding is primarily used when the amount of the employee's wage payments is very irregular and when the percentage method or the wage-bracket method would cause overwithholding. The cumulative withholding method may be used, however, only when the employee's wages since the beginning of the current calendar year have been paid in payroll periods that are all of the same length. Employees who may benefit from use of this method include commission salespeople and those working on a piece-rate basis.

Under the cumulative withholding method, proceed as follows:

Step 1: Add the wages for the payroll period to the total wages already paid during the calendar year.

Step 2: Divide the aggregate amount of wages by the number of payroll periods to which it pertains.

Step 3: Compute the total taxes on the average amount of wages just as if that amount had been paid to the employee in each of the payroll periods to which the total amount relates.

Step 4: Subtract from this amount of tax any amount already withheld during the preceding payroll periods.

Step 5: Deduct any excess tax from the current payment of wages.

EXAMPLE:

Roger Samuel, a salesperson for Drury Motors, is single and claims one withholding allowance. Samuel has been paid $28,000 in commissions during the first three quarters of this year (19 biweekly pay periods). Because he surpassed his quota of new cars to be sold, Samuel's next commission check at the beginning of the fourth quarter amounts to $3,700. Calculate the amount of federal income taxes to be withheld under the cumulative withholding method as follows:

1. **$28,000 (commissions paid in 19 biweekly pay periods of the past three quarters) + $3,700 (commissions for first biweekly pay in fourth quarter) = $31,700.**
2. **$31,700 ÷ 20 (biweekly pay periods) = $1,585 (average biweekly wages).**
3. **Using the percentage method, from Table 2(a), the income taxes on $1,585 are $311.60.**

$311.60 x 20 pay periods = $6,232 (total income taxes).

4. **$6,232 less $5,480.36 (actual taxes withheld during the first three quarters) = $751.64.**
5. **From his commissions of $3,700 during the 20th biweekly pay period, deduct $751.64 for federal income taxes.**

Note: **Had Samuel's employer used the percentage method instead of cumulative withholding, the federal income taxes to withhold on commissions of $3,700 would be $992.06.**

Part-Year Employment

Upon the request of an employee who works only part of a year, you may withhold according to a complicated averaging method that reduces the amount to be withheld. To be eligible for this alternative method, the employee must reasonably expect that he or she will be employed for a total of no more than 245 calendar days in all terms of continuous employment during the calendar year. The employee must also use a calendar-year accounting method.

"Substantially Similar" Methods

If your firm has a computerized payroll accounting system, possibly none of the withholding methods described above may be entirely satisfactory. In such cases you may devise any withholding method that will meet the needs of your organization. However, that method must yield deductions substantially similar to those withheld under the percentage method for the payroll period involved. A "substantially similar" method is defined as one that provides for amounts withheld that are within $10 either way of the amounts required to be withheld annually under the percentage method.

You need not submit your alternative method to the IRS for approval before putting it to use. However, you should make sure that the alternative method is tested against the full range of wage and allowance situations to make sure that the method meets the tolerances prescribed by the IRS.

WITHHOLDING TAX ON SUPPLEMENTAL WAGE PAYMENTS

Those responsible for payroll preparation are often faced with the problem of properly handling additional compensation known as supplemental wage payments. *Supplemental wage payments* include items such as vacation pay, bonuses, commissions, and dismissal pay. The problem arises since supplemental wages often are paid at a different time than the regular wage payments. Then, too, supplemental wages may be based on a different wage rate or for a wage period that differs from the regular wage period. Further, supplemental wages may be related to no particular payroll period.

When a supplemental wage payment is involved in payroll preparation, you should decide whether the payment must be lumped together with a regular wage payment or whether the supplemental wages may be treated separately. If the supplemental wages must be lumped together with a regular payment, the amount of tax withheld may be disproportionately high when compared with the effect of the payment on the employee's actual tax liability. This problem is created by the nature of the graduated withholding system.

To aid in solving problems such as those described above, the IRS has issued tax computation rules that indicate when supplemental wage payments must be lumped together with regular wage payments and when they may be treated separately. Generally the tax computation rules apply to any kind of supplemental wages. However, in the case of vacation pay, as we discuss below, different rules apply depending upon whether or not the vacation pay is paid at the same time as an employee's regular wages.

Supplemental Wages Paid Along with Regular Wages

When you pay supplemental wages at the same time as regular wages, the method of calculating the withholding tax depends on whether the payment is vacation pay or some other kind of supplemental wage.

Vacation Pay. When employees receive vacation pay along with their regular pay for a payroll period, the vacation pay is subject to withholding as though it were a regular payment made for the payroll period or periods occurring during the vacation.

EXAMPLE:

Josh Gayle, who is married, claims two allowances and is paid $620 biweekly. According to the wage-bracket table in Tax Table B, his usual withholding amount is $51. Gayle schedules his three weeks' vacation from Saturday, August 19, through Friday, September 8. For this period, his vacation pay is $930 ($310 each week for three weeks) and is paid him *with his regular pay* on the second biweekly payroll period on Friday, August 18. For withholding purposes, the first two weeks' vacation pay are deemed to be paid on Friday, September 1, and the third week is considered to be paid on Friday, September 15. Given below are the details of Gayle's paychecks for the

second payroll period in August and the two payroll periods in September:

Payday	Pay	Withholding
August 18	$1,550	$127.50
September 1	-0-	-0-
September 15	310	25.50

The $127.50 withheld on August 18 consists of $51 on Gayle's regular biweekly wages, $51 on two weeks' vacation pay (deemed paid on September 1), and $25.50 (one half of $51) on one week's vacation pay. The $25.50 withheld from the September 15 check relates to Gayle's regular pay for the week of September 11-15, his first week back from vacation.

If you had lumped the vacation pay with the regular wages and treated the entire amount as a single payment, the tax withheld, according to the wage-bracket table in Tax Table B, would have been $191, or $63.50 greater than the amount properly withheld under the procedure described above.

Other Supplemental Wages. You may pay a supplemental wage other than vacation pay at the same time as a regular wage payment. In such cases, you must combine the supplemental wages with the wage payment. Then, you determine the amount to be withheld from the aggregate payment as if the combined payment were a single payment for the payroll period involved.

EXAMPLE:

Jenny Wright, a married sales representative with three withholding allowances, is employed at a monthly salary of $1,800. She also receives an annual bonus of 10% of her total annual sales in excess of $50,000. Her sales for the current year amount to $96,000, on which the bonus is $4,600. The total of her bonus for the year and her salary for December amounts to $6,400. According to Table 4(b) in Tax Table A, the amount to withhold from her December paycheck is $1,217.61.

When you combine the regular wages and supplemental wages in a single payment, you may wish to indicate specifically the amount of each payment. In such cases, you may withhold federal income taxes at a flat 20% rate on the supplemental wages, if the tax is withheld on the employee's regular wages at the appropriate rate.

EXAMPLE:

Referring to the preceding example, you may indicate separately on Wright's paycheck stub the amount of each payment. In this case, calculate the amount of federal income taxes withheld as follows:

		Federal Income Taxes Withheld
Regular monthly earnings	$1,800	$ 150.68*
Annual bonus	4,600	920.00
Totals	$6,400	$1,070.68

*Using the percentage method.

Under this approach, the amount of federal income taxes withheld from Wright's last monthly pay is $146.93 less than under the preceding example.

Supplemental Wages Paid Separately from Regular Wages

In those situations where supplemental wages are not paid at the same time as regular wage payments, you need to determine whether or not federal income tax was withheld from the employee's prior wage payment. The computation rules we describe below pertain to all types of supplemental wage payments—vacation pay as well as other supplemental wage payments.

Federal Income Tax Not Withheld from Prior Wage Payment. In some instances federal income taxes are not withheld from employees' regular wages because their allowances exceed their wages. In these cases you must combine the supplemental wages with the wages paid for the last preceding payroll period or with the wages to be paid for the current payroll period. Then, determine the amount of tax to be withheld as if the aggregate of the supplemental wages and the regular wages were a single wage payment for the payroll period involved.

EXAMPLE:

Heng May, single with eight allowances, received his last weekly paycheck for the year on December 29. Since his total regular wages were $335, according to the wage-bracket table in Tax Table B, no federal income taxes were withheld. Two days later, May is paid a year-end bonus amounting to $600. Add the amount of this supplemental wage ($600) to the wages paid for the last preceding payroll period ($335), and withhold federal income taxes of $118 on the aggregate, $935.

Federal Income Tax Already Withheld from Regular Wages. When the federal income tax has already been withheld from the employee's regular wages, you may select one of two alternative methods for withholding the tax on the supplemental wages.

Method A. Under this method combine the supplemental wage with the wages for the last preceding or the current payroll period. Then, determine the amount to be withheld as if the supplemental wages and the regular wages were a single payment. However, since the federal income tax has already been withheld from the regular wages, subtract that amount from the tax due on the aggregate. Deduct only the excess federal income tax from the payment of the supplemental wages.

EXAMPLE:

Brent Einstein, married with two allowances, is paid $985 semimonthly. The tax to be withheld under the wage-bracket method on each semimonthly pay is $102. Einstein is paid his regular wage on June 15. On June 18 he receives a bonus of $500. The tax on the bonus is calculated as follows:

Regular wage payment	$ 985	
Bonus	500	
Total	$1,485	
Tax on total from wage-bracket table in Tax Table B		$177
Less tax already withheld on $985		102
Tax to be withheld from $500 bonus		$ 75

Method B. Under this alternative method for withholding federal income taxes, withhold a flat 20% of the supplemental wages. As indicated above, this method may be used only if you have already withheld federal income taxes from the employee's regular wages. Further, if you elect to withhold at the 20% rate, this must be done without considering any withholding allowances claimed by the employee. Thus, referring to the example given above, under this method you would withhold 20% of the $500 bonus payment, or $100, from the June 18 bonus paid Einstein.

WITHHOLDING TAX ON TIPS

As we noted earlier in this unit, tips amounting to $20 or more in a calendar month must be reported by employees to their employers. When reported, the tips are subject to federal income tax withholding. When employees report tips in connection with employment in which they also receive regular wages, calculate the amount of tax to be withheld on the tips as if the tips were a supplemental wage payment. Generally the rules for withholding federal income tax on tips are the same as those given in the preceding section for withholding taxes on supplemental wage payments.

You must withhold the employee's income tax and FICA tax on the reported tip income, but this withholding is made from the wages (other than tips) that are under the employer's control. The amount of tax due on the employee's tip income may exceed the amount of wages under the employer's control and available for making a deduction (or the amount of additional funds supplied by the employee). In such a case, the employee must pay the uncollected portion of the taxes directly to the IRS when the annual income tax return is filed.

ADVANCE PAYMENT OF EARNED INCOME CREDIT (EIC)

The *earned income credit (EIC)* is a reduction in the computation of the federal income taxes for workers who have dependent children and maintain a household. In 1990, the earned income credit provided payments of up to $953 to taxpayers who had earned incomes (wages, salaries, and other compensation plus earnings from self-employment) under $20,264. The maximum amount of the credit is adjusted annually for inflation.

Eligible employees may elect to receive payment of their earned income credit in advance of filing their annual personal income tax returns. To be eligible for the EIC payments, employees must meet the criteria given in the instructions accompanying Form W-5, which is discussed below.

Form W-5

Eligible employees who want to receive advance EIC payments must file *Form W-5, Earned Income Credit Advance Payment Certificate,* with their employer. A filled-in Form W-5 is shown in Illustration 4-4. If employees choose not to get the advance payments, they will still obtain the full benefit of the EIC when filing their annual personal income tax returns. Employees who have had no income taxes withheld must be informed about refundable earned income credits, unless the employees have filed Form W-4 claiming full exemption from withholding. To meet this requirement, employers have three options: (a) give employees IRS Notice 797, "You May Be Eligible for a Refund on Your Federal Income Tax Return Because of the Earned Income Credit," (b) supply employees with a written notice containing an exact reproduction of the wording in Notice 797, or (c) furnish employees with Forms W-2, or a substitute that contains the exact wording found on the back of Copy C of Form W-2.

When completing Form W-5, employees must show if they are married and if their spouse has a

Form W-5 in effect that year with an employer. The form remains in effect until the end of the calendar year. Thereafter, eligible employees must file a new certificate annually. The signed form should be made effective with the first payroll period ending on or after the date the certificate is given to the employer.

After an employee has given you a signed Form W-5, circumstances may change that make the employee ineligible for the credit. Or the employee's spouse may file a Form W-5. In such cases, the employee must, within 10 days after such a change, either revoke the previously filed form or file a new Form W-5 showing that the spouse has a Form W-5 in effect with an employer.

An employee may have filed a Form W-5 certifying that his or her spouse has a Form W-5 in effect, and the spouse later ceases to have a form in effect. In such an instance, the employee should file a new Form W-5 with you to certify that the spouse no longer has a Form W-5 in effect.

Computing the Advance Payment of the EIC

Employers must include the advance EIC payment with wages paid their eligible employees who have filed Form W-5. For purposes of the advance payment, wages are defined as amounts subject to income tax withholding. For employers of domestic and agricultural workers, wages mean amounts subject to FICA taxes.

In determining the amount of the advance payment, the following factors are taken into account:

1. Wages paid—including tips reported.
2. Whether a married employee's spouse has a Form W-5 in effect with an employer.

The amount of the payment to include in eligible employees' wage payments is determined from either the percentage method or wage-bracket tables provided by the IRS (not reproduced in this textbook). Separate tables are available for married employees whose spouses have a certificate in effect.

Paying the Advance EIC to Employees

The advance EIC payments do not affect the amount of income taxes or FICA taxes that is withheld from employees' wages and paid over to the IRS. Since the advance EIC payments are not compensation for services rendered, they are not subject to payroll taxes.

Generally employers will pay the amount of the advance EIC payments from withheld income taxes and FICA taxes. As indicated in Unit 3, these taxes are usually paid over to the IRS either through federal tax deposits or along with the employer's tax returns.

It is possible that for a payroll period the advance EIC payments may be more than the withheld income taxes and the FICA taxes. In such a case, you have the option of:

1. Reducing each advance EIC payment proportionately, or
2. Electing to make full payment of the advance EIC amount and treating such full amounts as an advance payment of your company's tax liability.

Employer's Returns and Records

As you saw above, the amount of the advance EIC payments does not change the amount that employers must deduct and withhold from their employees' pay

Form **W-5**
Department of the Treasury
Internal Revenue Service

Earned Income Credit
Advance Payment Certificate
This certificate expires on December 31, 1990.

1990

Type or print your full name: Jean Claude LaFitte
Your social security number: 227 09 2413
Home address (number and street or rural route): 25 Rudyard Lane
Apt. no.: 3A
City or town, state, and ZIP code: Mackinac Island, MI 49757-2500

Note: *If you file Form W-5 with an employer to receive advance payments of the earned income credit for 1990, you must file Form 1040 or Form 1040A for 1990. If married, you must file a joint return (unless you qualify to file as head of household).*

		Yes	No
1	I expect to be eligible for the earned income credit for 1990, I have no other certificate in effect with any other current employer, and I choose to receive advance payment of the earned income credit	X	
2	Are you married?		X
3	If you are married, does your spouse have a certificate in effect for 1990 with any employer?		

Under penalties of perjury, I declare that the information I have furnished above is, to the best of my knowledge, true, correct, and complete.

Signature ▶ Jean Claude LaFitte   Date ▶ March 1, 1990

Illustration 4-4. Form W-5, Earned Income Credit Advance Payment Certificate

for income taxes and FICA taxes. Advance EIC payments made by the employer are treated as having been made from amounts withheld as income tax and employee FICA taxes, and from the employer's FICA taxes. The amount of advance EIC payments is treated as if the employer had paid over the amount of the payments to the IRS on the day the wages are paid employees.

Employers take into account the amount of their advance EIC payments when completing their quarterly employment tax returns, Form 941. The amount of the advance EIC payments is subtracted from the total amount of income taxes and FICA taxes in order to determine the net taxes for the quarter.

All records of advance EIC payments should be retained four years and be available for review by the IRS. These records include: (a) copies of employees' Forms W-5, (b) amounts and dates of all wage payments and advance EIC payments, (c) dates of each employee's employment, (d) dates and amounts of tax deposits made, and (e) copies of returns filed.

INDIVIDUAL RETIREMENT ACCOUNTS (IRA)

As we pointed out in Unit 1, an individual retirement account (IRA) is a pension plan that is established and funded by an individual employee. Depending upon the existence of a company-funded retirement plan, employees may authorize that either one of two types of contributions—*deductible* or *nondeductible*—be withheld by their employer or union. Or employees may place their contributions in individual retirement savings accounts as specified in the law.

Deductible Contributions

The Tax Reform Act of 1986 provides that, under certain conditions, employees may put aside each year the lesser of $2,000 or 100% of their compensation *without paying federal income taxes on their contributions.* To be eligible for such *deductible* (tax-free) contributions, either of the following two conditions must be met:

1. The individual does not belong to a company-funded retirement plan. (In the case of a married person filing a joint return, neither the person nor the person's spouse belongs to the employer's maintained retirement plan.)
2. The individual has adjusted gross income that is less than $25,000. (A married couple filing a joint return must have adjusted gross income of less than $40,000.)

For a married individual entitled to take a tax-free IRA deduction, an additional benefit is allowed where the spouse has no earned income or only income less than $250. Thus, another $250 may be added to the couple's individual retirement accounts to permit a total contribution as great as $2,250.

EXAMPLE:

Frank and Connie Rivera file a joint tax return in 1991. In 1990, Frank earned $20,000 and Connie earned $220. In 1990, the couple contributed $2,250 to their IRA accounts and took the deductions on their joint return. Since Connie had earned less than $250 compensation in 1990, she will be treated as having no compensation for the year. Thus, Frank and Connie may take advantage of the spousal deduction.

The only restriction on the division between the employee's IRA and the spouse's IRA is that at least $250 must be placed in the spouse's account. The tax advantage of these IRAs is lost if the worker withdraws the money prematurely.

If the employee does belong to a company-funded retirement plan, *partial* tax-free deductions are allowed if:

1. The employee has adjusted gross income less than $35,000.
2. A married couple files a joint return with adjusted gross income less than $50,000.
3. A married couple files separately with one spouse having adjusted gross income less than $10,000.

Nondeductible Contributions

A person who is ineligible to make a deductible IRA contribution is permitted to make *nondeductible* contributions to a separate IRA account. The earnings on the nondeductible contributions are not subject to federal income tax until they are withdrawn. The limit on such nondeductible contributions for a taxable year is the lesser of $2,000 or 100% of the employee's compensation.

WAGE AND TAX STATEMENTS

You are required to furnish *wage and tax statements* to your firm's employees informing them of the wages paid during the calendar year and the amount of taxes withheld from those wages. You are also required to send copies of these statements to the federal government and in most cases to state, city, and local governments.

Form W-2

Form W-2, Wage and Tax Statement, shown in Illustration 4-5, is prepared if *any* of the following items applied to an employee during the calendar year:

1. Income tax or social security (FICA) tax was withheld.
2. Income tax would have been withheld if the employee had not claimed more than one withholding allowance or had not claimed exemption from withholding on Form W-4.
3. *Any* amount was paid for services, if the employer is in a trade or business. The cash value of any noncash payments made should be included.
4. Any advance EIC (earned income credit) payments were made.

In Illustration 4-6 on pages 128 and 129, we have summarized the instructions for completing each of the boxes on Form W-2. If an entry does not apply to your firm or the employee, leave the box blank.

You must give employees Form W-2 on or before January 31 following the close of the calendar year. When employees leave the service of your employer, you may give them Form W-2 any time after employment ends. If employees ask for Form W-2, you should give it to them within 30 days of their request or the final wage payment, whichever is later. In some instances the services of workers will be terminated but there is a reasonable expectation that they may be rehired at some time before the year ends. In such a situation you need not give Form W-2 to the employees. Instead, you may delay furnishing the form until January 31 following the close of the calendar year.

Copies of the six-part Form W-2 are distributed as follows:

1. *Copy A* → to the Social Security Administration by the end of February following the year for which Form W-2 is applicable.
2. *Copy 1* → to the state, city, or local tax department.
3. *Copy B* → to employees for filing with their federal income tax returns.
4. *Copy C* → to employees for retention in their personal records.
5. *Copy 2* → to employees for filing with their state, city, or local income tax returns.
6. *Copy D* → retained by employer.

1 Control number: 22222	For Paperwork Reduction Act Notice, see separate instructions. OMB No 1545-0008	For Official Use Only ▶	
2 Employer's name, address, and ZIP code Stone Metal Products 600 Third Avenue Philadelphia, PA 19103-5600		6 Statutory employee ☐ Deceased ☒ Pension plan ☒ Legal rep. ☐ 942 emp. ☐ Subtotal ☐ Deferred compensation ☐ Void ☐	
		7 Allocated tips	8 Advance EIC payment
		9 Federal income tax withheld 4,610.00	10 Wages, tips, other compensation 29,360.18
3 Employer's identification number 13-5407221	4 Employer's state I.D. number 46-8-0013	11 Social security tax withheld 2,246.05	12 Social security wages 29,360.18
5 Employee's social security number 382-13-7478		13 Social security tips	14 Nonqualified plans
19a Employee's name (first, middle, last) Henry T. Tate		15 Dependent care benefits	16 Fringe benefits incl. in Box 10
483 Monroe Street Philadelphia, PA 19119-4821 19b Employee's address and ZIP code		17 See Instr. for Forms W-2/W-2P B 78.00	18 Other Union dues w/h: 196.00
20	21	22	23

24 State income tax	25 State wages, tips, etc.	26 Name of state	27 Local income tax	28 Local wages, tips, etc.	29 Name of locality
616.56	29,360.18	PA	1,456.26	29,360.18	Phila.

Copy A For Social Security Administration   Dept. of the Treasury—Internal Revenue Service

Form **W-2 Wage and Tax Statement 1990**

Illustration 4-5. Form W-2, Wage and Tax Statement

HOW TO COMPLETE FORM W-2

NOTE: Type or print all entries, using black ink if possible. Do not make any erasures, whiteouts, or strikeovers on Copy A. Also, do not use script type. Make all dollar entries without the dollar sign but with the decimal point (000.00).

Box 1: The control number is for the employer to identify the individual Forms W-2. Up to 7 digits may be assigned the control number, which is used by the employer when writing the Social Security Administration about the form. This box need not be used if the employer prefers not to use a control number. The form Identifying Number 22222 is used by optical scanning equipment in the Social Security Administration to tell which information document (Form W-2) is being "read."

Box 2: Show the employer's name, address, and ZIP code. State and local government employers must show the employer SSA number (a 9-digit number starting with 69) below the employer's address for those employers covered under Section 218 of the Social Security Act.

Box 3: Show the identification number assigned by the IRS (00-0000000). Do not use a prior owner's number.

Box 4: The employer's state identification number is assigned by the state. You need not use the number unless copies of the form are used for state returns. This box is separated into two parts by a dotted line so that you may report two state I.D. numbers if you are reporting wages for two states. If you are reporting for only one state, enter the number above the dotted line.

Box 5: *Employee's social security number.* Give the number shown on the employee's social security card. If the employee does not have a number, he or she should apply for one at any SSA office.

Box 6: *Statutory employee.* Check this box for all statutory employees whose earnings are subject to social security tax but *not* subject to federal income tax withholding.

Deceased. Check this box if the employee is now deceased.

Pension plan. Check this box if the employee was an active participant (for any part of the year) in a retirement plan, including a simplified employee pension (SEP) plan.

Legal representative. Check this box when the employee's name is the only name shown but is shown as a trust account (John Doe Trust), or another name is shown in addition to the employee's name and the other person or business is acting on behalf of the employee.

942 employee. This box is to be used for household employers only. See Form 942 for instructions on when to check this box.

Subtotal. Employers who submit 41 or fewer individual Forms W-2 need not give subtotals. Other employers should place an X in the square on Form W-2 that shows the subtotal dollar amounts for the preceding 41 Forms W-2. The subtotal amounts to be shown are Boxes 7 through 15 and 17. A final subtotal is needed for statements that exceed multiples of 41. The subtotal statement should always be the last Form W-2.

Deferred compensation. Check this box if contributions were made on behalf of the employee to a section 401(k), 403(b), 408(k)(6), 457, or 501(c)(18)(D) retirement plan.

Void. Place an X in this square to show that an error has been made. Be sure the amounts shown on void forms are *not* included in the subtotals.

Box 7: *Allocated tips.* If you are a large food or beverage establishment, show the amount of tips allocated to the employee. Since this is an information item only, do *not* include the amount of tips allocated in Box 10 (wages, tips, other compensation) or in Box 13 (social security tips).

Box 8: Show the total paid to the employee as advance earned income credit (EIC) payments.

Box 9: Record the federal income tax withheld.

Box 10: Show, before any payroll deductions, the total of (1) wages paid; (2) noncash payments (including fringe benefits); (3) tips reported; (4) certain employee business expense reimbursements; and (5) all other compensation, including certain scholarships and fellowship grants and payments for moving expenses. Other compensation is what you paid the employee but from which you did not withhold federal income taxes. If you prefer, you may show the other compensation on a separate Form W-2.

Box 11: Show the total employee social security (FICA) tax you withheld or paid for the employee.

Box 12: Record the total wages paid (before payroll deductions) subject to employee social security tax. Do *not* include tips deemed to be wages, social security tips, or allocated tips. Generally noncash payments are considered wages. Include employee business expenses reported in Box 10. Include employer contributions to a qualified cash or deferred compensation plan, even though the contributions are not includible in Box 10 as wages, tips, and other compensation. Include any employee social security tax and employee state unemployment compensation tax you paid for the employee rather than deducting it from wages. Do not enter more than the maximum FICA taxable wage base for the year.

Box 13: Show the amount the employee reported even if you did not have sufficient employee funds to collect the social security (FICA) tax for the tips. Do *not* show any tips in this box after tips and wages equal the maximum FICA taxable wage base for the year. But show all tips reported in Box 10 along with wages and other compensation.

Box 14: Show the total amount of distributions to your employee from a nonqualified compensation plan or a section 457 plan. Also include this amount as wages in Box 10.

Box 15: Show the total amount of dependent care benefits that you paid or incurred for your employee, including any amount in excess of the $5,000 exclusion. Also, include in Box 10 any amount in excess of the $5,000 exclusion.

Box 16: Show the total value of the taxable fringe benefits included in Box 10 as other compensation. If you provided a vehicle and included 100% of the value in the employee's income, you must separately report this value to the employee in Box 16 or on a separate statement.

Box 17: Complete and code this box if one or more of (a) through (g) below applies. Use Box 18 to report other information you want to give your employee. Do not enter more than three codes in this box. If you are reporting more than three items, use a separate Form W-2.

(a) The amount of employee social security tax on tips not collected because the employee did not have enough funds from which to make the deduction. Do *not* include this amount in Box 11. Use **code A** for uncollected social security tax on tips.

(b) The cost of group term life insurance coverage in excess of $50,000 that you provided the employee. Also, include this amount in Boxes 10 and 12. Use **code B** for the cost of group term life insurance coverage over $50,000.

Illustration 4-6. Instructions for Completing Form W-2 (Continued)

(c) The amount of sick pay *not* includible in the employee's income because the employee contributed to the sick pay plan. Or, you may use a separate Form W-2 for sick pay by labeling Box 17, "Sick pay." Use **code C** for sick pay *not* includible as income.

(d) Use the following codes for contributions made to the plans listed below. (Also check the "Deferred compensation" checkbox in Box 6.)
D—section 401(k)
E—section 403(b)
F—section 408(k)(6)
G—section 457
H—section 501(c)(18)(D)

(e) If you are a federal, state, or local agency with employees paying the Medicare portion of the social security tax, show the social security wages and the Medicare tax withheld in Boxes 12 and 11. Use **Code J** for employees paying the Medicare portion of the social security tax.

(f) Excess "golden parachute" payments made to key corporate employees. If the excess payments are considered wages, treat the 20% excise tax as income tax withheld and include it in Box 9. Use **code K** for excess golden parachute payments.

(g) Amounts you reimbursed your employee for employee business expenses using the standard mileage rate or the per diem or high-low substantiation methods and the amount you reimbursed that exceeds the amounts specified under these methods. Enter in Box 17 the portion of the reimbursement that is equal to the amounts allowed under the government specified rates. Use **code L** for the amount of employee business expenses equal to the government specified rate. In Box 10, show the portion of the reimbursement that is *more than* that allowed under the government specified rates. Do *not* include in Box 17 any per diem or mileage allowance reimbursements if the total reimbursement is less than or equal to the amounts allowed under government specified rates.

Box 18: Use this box for any other information you want to give your employee. Label each item. Examples are union dues, health insurance premiums deducted, moving expenses paid, and educational assistance payments.

Box 19a: Enter the employee's name as shown on the employee's social security card (first, middle initial, last). If the name has changed, have the employee get a corrected card from any SSA office. Use the name on the original card until you see the corrected one.

Box 19b: This box is combined with Box 19a on all copies except Copy A to allow you to mail employees' copies in a window envelope or as a self-mailer.

Boxes 24 through 29: Use these boxes to report state or local income tax information. The state and local information boxes can be used to report wages and tax on two states and two localities. Keep each state's and locality's information separated by the broken line.

Illustration 4-6. Instructions for Completing Form W-2 (Concluded)

If Form W-2 has been lost or destroyed, you are authorized to furnish substitute copies to the employee. The substitute form should be clearly marked REISSUED STATEMENT. Do *not* send Copy A of the reissued statement to the Social Security Administration.

Occasionally you will prepare Forms W-2 which, after reasonable effort, you are unable to deliver to employees. Do *not* send the forms to the Social Security Administration, but instead retain them for a four-year period. You are deemed to have made a "reasonable effort" to deliver the Forms W-2 if you mailed them to the last known address of the employee.

Form W-2P

As you read earlier, federal income taxes are withheld from annuity or pension payments unless the recipients of such payments elect not to have the taxes withheld. Use *Form W-2P, Statement for Recipients of Annuities, Pensions, Retired Pay, or IRA Payments,* to report to payees the amounts of annuity or pension payments and the amount of federal income taxes withheld.

Form W-2P (not illustrated in this textbook) provides for the reporting of the gross amount of annuity payments made during the calendar year whether or not withholding was required on all payments; the total amount of federal income tax withheld; the payee's name, address, and social security number; and the payer's name, address, and identification number.

Form W-2c

Form W-2c, Statement of Corrected Income and Tax Amounts, is used to correct errors in previously filed Forms W-2 and W-2P. File Copy A of Form W-2c with the Social Security Administration and distribute the remaining copies of the form as noted on the bottom of each form. A separate form, Form W-3c (discussed later in this unit), is used to transmit each type of corrected wage and tax statement. However, if the correction is for only one employee or is to correct an employee's name and/or social security number only, you need not prepare a transmittal form.

Illustration 4-7 on page 130 shows how Form W-2c has been used to correct an error made in Tate's Form W-2 (Illustration 4-5, page 127).

1 Year being corrected 19 90	2 Employer's use	For Official Use Only ▶	
3 Form: ☒ W-2 ☐ W-2AS ☐ W-2NMI ☐ W-2P ☐ W-2GU ☐ W-2VI	4 Stat. emp. ☐ Deceased ☒ Pension plan ☒ Legal rep. ☐ 942 emp. ☐ Def'd. comp. ☐ Medicare gov't. emp. ☐		OMB No. 1545-0008
5 Employee's correct SSN 382-13-7478	6 Employer's SSA number 69-	7 Employer's Federal EIN 13-5407221	8 Employer's state I.D. number 46-8-0013
9 Employee's name, address, and ZIP code Henry T. Tate 483 Monroe Street Philadelphia, PA 19119-4821		10 Employer's name, address, and ZIP code Stone Metal Products 600 Third Avenue Philadelphia, PA 19103-5600	
Complete 11 and/or 12 **only** if **incorrect** on the last form you filed. Show **incorrect** item here ▶	11 Employee's **incorrect** SSN	12 Employee's name (as **incorrectly** shown on previous form)	

CHANGES Item	(a) As Previously Reported	(b) Correct Information	(c) Increase (decrease)—(b) less (a)
13 Social security wages			
14 Social security tips			
15 Social security tax withheld			
16 Wages, tips, other comp.			
17 Federal income tax withheld	4,610.00	4,160.00	(450.00)
18 Allocated tips			
19 *			
20 Gross annuity, etc. (W-2P)			
21 Taxable amount (W-2P)			
22 State wages			
23 State tax withheld			
24 Local wages			
25 Local tax withheld			

*See instructions. **For Paperwork Reduction Act Notice, see back of Copy D.** **Copy A for Social Security Administration**

Form **W-2c** **Statement of Corrected Income and Tax Amounts** Department of the Treasury Internal Revenue Service

Illustration 4-7. Form W-2c, Statement of Corrected Income and Tax Amounts

Privately Printed Forms

Some employers prefer to use their own privately printed forms, such as Forms W-2 and W-2P, rather than the ones provided by the IRS. To make sure that the same information is included on the substitute forms as that required by those provided by the IRS, specifications have been established for the private printing of forms. You may obtain "Specifications for Private Printing of Forms W-2, W-2P, and W-3" from any IRS center or district office. To the extent that the privately printed forms meet the specifications set forth, you may generally use them without prior approval of the IRS.

EMPLOYER'S RETURNS AND PAYMENTS

Beginning with the first quarter in which taxable wages are paid, you are required at prescribed times to file returns reporting the amount of wages paid and the amount of taxes withheld. Such reporting continues until you prepare a final return showing that your organization has gone out of business or otherwise has ceased to pay taxable wages.

Your accounting tasks and payroll procedures are further complicated as a result of rules that require different returns for different types of employees, differing deposit requirements, and different time periods for which the returns must be filed. The major returns completed by employers are briefly summarized in Illustration 4-8. The most recent information with regard to the withholding, deposit, payment and reporting of federal income taxes, FICA taxes, and FUTA taxes is available in Circular E, "Employer's Tax Guide." Circular E is available at the district offices of the IRS.

Form W-3

Form W-3, Transmittal of Income and Tax Statements, must be filed with the Social Security Administration

Form 941, Employer's Quarterly Federal Tax Return	For reporting federal income taxes withheld during the calendar quarter and the employer and employee portions of the FICA taxes. See Form 941 on page 84. Detailed information about the use of depositaries and the payment of taxes is given on pages 77-80.
Form 941E, Quarterly Return of Withheld Federal Income Tax and Hospital Insurance (Medicare) Tax	For reporting the federal income tax withheld from wages, tips, pensions, annuities, third-party sick pay, supplemental unemployment compensation benefits, certain gambling winnings, and backup withholding. Form 941E is also filed by certain state and local government employers to report income taxes withheld and the employer and employee hospital insurance tax.
Form 941-M, Employer's Monthly Federal Tax Return	For reporting federal income taxes withheld and social security taxes on a *monthly* basis. IRS may require monthly returns and payments of taxes from employers who have not complied with the requirements for filing returns or the paying or depositing of taxes reported on quarterly returns. You are not required to file monthly returns unless you receive written notification from the IRS.
Form 942, Employer's Quarterly Tax Return for Household Employees	For reporting federal income taxes withheld as a result of voluntary withholding agreements between employers and their domestic employees. Form 942 is also completed by employers who are liable for FICA taxes on wages paid domestic workers.
Form 943, Employer's Annual Tax Return for Agricultural Employees	For reporting the withholding of federal income taxes and FICA taxes on wages paid agricultural workers. Form 943 is used for agricultural employees even though the employer may employ nonagricultural workers.

Illustration 4-8. Summary of Major Returns Filed by Employers

by employers and other payers as a transmittal for information returns on Forms W-2 and W-2P. On Form W-3 you indicate the number of documents being transmitted. Form W-3 and the accompanying copies of the documents enable the Social Security Administration (and at a later date, the IRS) to compare the taxes withheld as reported on Forms W-2 and W-2P with the amount of taxes withheld as reported on the employers' Forms 941. A filled-in Form W-3 is shown in Illustration 4-9 on page 132.

Since Forms W-3 are read by optical scanning machines, type all entries if possible. Also, record all dollar entries without the dollar sign but with the decimal point (000.00). You should not staple Forms W-3 to the related Forms W-2 or W-2P since staple holes or tears cause the optical scanning equipment to jam.

File all Forms W-2 with one W-3 and all Forms W-2P with another W-3. When a large number of forms are to be transmitted, you may forward the forms in separate packages of convenient size, each of which is clearly identified with the payer's name and identifying number. Postal regulations require that all forms and packages sent by mail be sent by first-class mail.

You should file Form W-3 and the related documents with the Social Security Administration by the end of February each year at the locations shown in Illustration 4-10 on page 133.

Form W-3 is mailed to you during the fourth quarter as part of Publication 393, Federal Employment Tax Forms.

Form W-3c

The *Transmittal of Corrected Income and Tax Statements, Form W-3c,* (not illustrated in this textbook) is used to accompany copies of Form W-2c, Statement of Corrected Income and Tax Amounts, sent to the Social Security Administration. You must use a separate Form W-3c for each type of Form W-2 being corrected. You may also use Form W-3c to correct an employer identification number or establishment number.

Magnetic Media Reporting

The Secretary of the Treasury issues regulations that provide standards for determining which information returns must be filed on magnetic media or in other machine-readable form. The magnetic reporting

1 Control number	33333	For Official Use Only ▶ OMB No. 1545-0008	
☐ Kind of Payer	2 941/941E ☒ Military ☐ 943 ☐ CT-1 ☐ 942 ☐ Medicare gov't. emp. ☐	3 Employer's state I.D. number / 4	5 Total number of statements 132
6 Establishment number	7 Allocated tips	8 Advance EIC payments 778.00	
9 Federal income tax withheld 330,317.19	10 Wages, tips, and other compensation 2,620,736.40	11 Social security tax withheld 158,079.60	
12 Social security wages 2,066,400.00	13 Social security tips	14 Nonqualified plans	
15 Dependent care benefits	16 Adjusted total social security wages and tips	17 Deferred compensation 319,530.00	
18 Employer's identification number 88 — 1936281		19 Other EIN used this year	
20 Employer's name Grove Electronics		21 Gross annuity, pension, etc. (Form W-2P)	
33 Vista Road Vallejo, CA 94590-0033		23 Taxable amount (Form W-2P)	
22 Employer's address and ZIP code (If available, place label over boxes 18 and 20.)		24 Income tax withheld by third-party payer	

Under penalties of perjury, I declare that I have examined this return and accompanying documents, and to the best of my knowledge and belief, they are true, correct, and complete.

Signature ▶ Carl W. Toland Title ▶ President Date ▶ 2-28-91

Telephone number (optional) (415) 555-3200

Form **W-3 Transmittal of Income and Tax Statements 1990** Department of the Treasury Internal Revenue Service

Illustration 4-9. Form W-3, Transmittal of Income and Tax Statements

requirements are contained in Revenue Procedures, which may be obtained from the District Director's office and in publications of the Social Security Administration.

Form W-2 and Other Information Returns. If you file 250 or more information returns (Forms W-2, W-2P, W-2G, 1099 series, 5498, and 8027), you must use magnetic media instead of paper forms. Filers on magnetic media must obtain approval from the IRS for the media used to report information. Applications for such approval *(Form 4419, Application for Magnetic Media Reporting of Information Returns)* are due at the same time as requests for waiver. Generally you must file your requests for waiver and applications for approval with the IRS; however, you must file your applications concerning Forms W-2 and W-2P with the Social Security Administration.

If a firm seeks to obtain a waiver from the magnetic media requirements, the IRS will take into consideration several factors. One of these factors is the ability of the filer to comply with the requirements at a reasonable cost. In granting exemptions from the magnetic media filing requirements, the IRS also considers other instances of undue hardship, such as temporary equipment breakdowns or destruction of magnetic media equipment.

Form W-4. As you saw earlier, you must submit copies of Forms W-4 on which 11 or more withholding allowances are claimed. If you are filing on magnetic media, you must obtain a Transmitter Control Code (TCC) and submit the following: (a) a signed *Form 6466, Transmittal of Magnetic Tape of Form W-4, Employee's Withholding Allowance Certificate*; (b) a Form 6467 if submitting data for multiple employers; (c) a magnetic tape reel with a Form 6469 identifying label; and (d) a Form 4801 on the outside of the shipping container.

EMPLOYER'S RECORDS FOR INCOME TAXES WITHHELD

If you withhold federal income taxes from your employees' wages, you must keep the records required by the Director of Internal Revenue. The information required by the income tax withholding laws is summarized in Illustration 1-1, page 3.

If employer's residence, principal place of business, office, or agency is located in	File Form W-3 at this address
Alaska, Arizona, California, Colorado, Hawaii, Idaho, Iowa, Minnesota, Missouri, Montana, Nebraska, Nevada, North Dakota, Oregon, South Dakota, Utah, Washington, Wisconsin, Wyoming	Social Security Administration Salinas Data Operations Center Salinas, CA 93911
Alabama, Arkansas, Florida, Georgia, Illinois, Kansas, Louisiana, Mississippi, New Mexico, Oklahoma, South Carolina, Tennessee, Texas	Social Security Administration Albuquerque Data Operations Center Albuquerque, NM 87180
Connecticut, Delaware, District of Columbia, Indiana, Kentucky, Maine, Maryland, Massachusetts, Michigan, New Hampshire, New Jersey, New York, North Carolina, Ohio, Pennsylvania, Rhode Island, Vermont, Virginia, West Virginia	Social Security Administration Wilkes-Barre Data Operations Center Wilkes-Barre, PA 18769
If no legal residence or principal place of business in any state	Use address given above.

Illustration 4-10. Where to File Form W-3

There is no prescribed form in which you must keep the records. However, they must be maintained in a manner that will enable the IRS to determine whether any tax liability has been incurred and, if so, the extent of that liability. Although you may microfilm your general books of account, such as cash books, journals, and ledgers, the microfilm reproduction must be in accordance with procedures and standards set forth by the IRS. The IRS will grant permission to microfilm the general books of account only after it has examined your micrographic system.

To facilitate preparing the returns and reports for the federal, state, and local governments, you must keep certain payroll and earnings records, as indicated in the preceding units of this textbook. In most payroll accounting systems, a column is provided in both the payroll register and the employee's earnings record to show the amount of each kind of tax withheld from each employee's wages on each payday.

Your payroll records must be made available for inspection at all times by officers of the IRS. The records must be kept for a period of at least four years after the date the tax to which they relate becomes due, or the date the tax is paid, whichever is later.

INFORMATION RETURNS

You may be required to file an *information return* upon which you report the compensation paid to individuals who are not employees. Thus, you may need to file information returns in addition to preparing statements that reflect the amount of wages and other compensation paid to employees. The IRS requires that information returns be filed as an aid in determining whether the true income of a taxpayer has been reported; for, like Form W-2, copies of the information returns are filed with the IRS as well as being sent to the payee of the amount involved. We have briefly described several of the major information returns in Illustration 4-11, page 134. As an example of one type of information return, Form 1099-MISC is shown in Illustration 4-12, page 135.

Generally you must file an information return whenever payments totaling $600 or more are made in the form of (1) salaries, wages, commissions, fees, and other forms of compensation for services, or (2) interest, dividends, rents, royalties, annuities, pensions, and other gains, profits, and income paid by a person engaged in a trade or business in the course of that trade or business. When you pay employees any of the items listed in (1) above, your obligation to file an information return is satisfied by filing Form W-2.

Backup Withholding

Certain recipients of taxable interest, dividends, and other payments are required to provide the payers with correct Taxpayer Identification Numbers (TINs). The IRS uses the numbers for identification purposes to make sure that taxpayers are reporting accurately all sources of income received. Payers must be given the TINs whether or not the recipients are required to file tax returns.

Payers must generally withhold 20% of taxable interest, dividends, and certain other payments if the payees fail to furnish their correct TINs. As we pointed out in the previous unit, this type of withholding is called *backup withholding*. Generally payments are subject to backup withholding if:

1. The payees fail to furnish their TINs to the payers.
2. The IRS notifies the payers that the payees furnished incorrect TINs.

Form 1099-MISC, Statement for Recipients of Miscellaneous Income	For reporting miscellaneous types of income, such as rents, royalties, commissions, fees, prizes, and awards, of at least $600 paid to nonemployees, and any backup withholding. Gross royalty payments of $10 or more must also be reported on this form. (Life insurance companies may use either Form W-2 or 1099-MISC for reporting payments of commissions to full-time life insurance sales agents.) See Illustration 4-12.
Form 1099-INT, Statement for Recipients of Interest Income	For reporting payments of (a) interest of $10 or more paid or credited on earnings from savings and loan associations, credit unions, bank deposits, corporate bonds, etc.; (b) interest of $600 or more from other sources; (c) forfeited interest due on premature withdrawals of time deposits; (d) foreign tax eligible for the recipient's foreign tax credit withheld and paid on interest; and (e) payments of any interest on bearer certificates of deposit.
Form 1099-DIV, Statement for Recipients of Dividends and Distributions	For reporting payments of dividends totaling $10 or more to any person; foreign tax withheld and paid on dividends and other distributions on stock for a person; and distributions made by corporations and regulated investment companies (including money market funds) as part of a liquidation.
Form 1099-PATR, Statement for Recipients (Patrons) of Taxable Distributions Received from Cooperatives	For cooperatives to report patronage dividends paid and other distributions made that total $10 or more during the year.
Form 1099-R, Statement for Recipients of Total Distributions from Profit-Sharing, Retirement Plans, Individual Retirement Arrangements, Insurance Contracts, Etc.	For reporting total lump-sum distributions from profit-sharing, retirement plans, and individual retirement arrangements made by employees' trusts or funds; federal, state, or local government retirement systems; and life insurance companies.
Form 1099-G, Statement for Recipients of Certain Government Payments	For reporting unemployment compensation payments and state and local income tax refunds of $10 or more, taxable grants, income tax refunds, and agricultural subsidy payments.
Form 5498, Individual Retirement Arrangement Information	For reporting contributions received from each person to an individual retirement account (IRA) or a simplified employee pension plan (SEP) and qualified deductible voluntary employee contributions to a plan maintained by the employer.
Form 8027, Employer's Annual Information Return of Tip Income and Allocated Tips	For large food or beverage establishments to report the amount of receipts from food or beverage operations, the amount of tips reported by employees, and the amounts allocated as tips to employees.

Illustration 4-11. Major Information Returns

3. The payers are notified by the IRS that the payees are subject to backup withholding.
4. For interest or dividend accounts opened after December 31, 1983, the payees fail to certify to the payers that they are not subject to backup withholding or fail to certify their TINs.

Further information about those payments subject to backup withholding and the period of time for which the 20% should be withheld may be found in the instructions that accompany Form 1099.

Form 1096

Use *Form 1096, The Annual Summary and Transmittal of U.S. Information Returns,* to transmit to the IRS the information contained on Forms 1099. You must use a Form 1096 to transmit each separate type of in-

9595 ☐ VOID ☐ CORRECTED

Type or machine print PAYER'S name, street address, city, state, and ZIP code		1 Rents	OMB No. 1545-0115	Miscellaneous Income
Worldwide Publishing Co. 40 Fifth Avenue New York, NY 10011-4000		$ 2 Royalties $34,970.65 3 Prizes, awards, etc. $	1990 Statement for Recipients of	
PAYER'S Federal identification number 75-4013736	RECIPIENT'S identification number 461-91-4821	4 Federal income tax withheld $	5 Fishing boat proceeds $	Copy A For Internal Revenue Service Center
Type or machine print RECIPIENT'S name Laurie T. Musberger		6 Medical and health care payments $	7 Nonemployee compensation $	For Paperwork Reduction Act Notice and instructions for completing this form, see Instructions for Forms 1099, 1098, 5498, and W-2G.
Street address 1043 Maple Drive		8 Substitute payments in lieu of dividends or interest $	9 Payer made direct sales of $5,000 or more of consumer products to a buyer (recipient) for resale ▶ ☐	
City, state, and ZIP code Chicago, IL 60615-3443		10 Crop insurance proceeds $	11 State income tax withheld $	
Account number (optional)		12 State/Payer's state number 85-33378		

Form **1099-MISC** Department of the Treasury - Internal Revenue Service

Illustration 4-12. Form 1099-MISC, Miscellaneous Income

formation return. Thus, you must use a 1096 to transmit all Forms 1099-INT, and another 1096 to transmit all Forms 1099-MISC issued for the year. You must file Form 1096 and the accompanying information returns on or before the last day of February of the year following the payment.

Electronic Filing of Information Returns

By means of a dial-up modem, employers can electronically submit some of their information returns to the IRS. In 1990 the IRS began to accept electronically filed *original* Forms 5498 (Individual Retirement Arrangement Information) and all *corrected* returns for the Forms 1099 series, Form 5498, Form 1098 (Mortgage Interest Statement), and Form W-2G (Statement for Recipients of Certain Gambling Winnings).

According to the IRS, employers having compatible equipment may realize savings by electronically filing their information. In some instances, filing electronically is less costly than submitting returns on magnetic media. Those interested in obtaining information about electronic filing should contact the Electronic Filing Coordinator, Martinsburg Computing Center, at (304) 263-8700.

WITHHOLDING STATE INCOME TAXES

In 40 states, the District of Columbia, and Puerto Rico, employers must withhold income taxes on wage payments.[5] Thus, the payroll manager may be faced with the complex task of keeping informed of the latest tax developments at the state level. The problem becomes more acute if a firm has employees in several states. In this instance the payroll manager must know if there is an income tax in each of the states, if withholding from wages is required, how much must be withheld, what kinds of employees and payments are exempt from the state law, and how the tax is to be paid. Further, information may be needed about each state's regulations as to: (a) the required frequency with which you must make wage payments, (b) acceptable media of payment, (c) the maximum permissible interval between the end of a pay period and the payday for that pay period, (d) the time within which you must make a final wage payment to an employee who is discharged or laid off or who quits or goes on strike, (e) the frequency with which you must tell employees of the deductions made from their wage payments, and (f) the maximum amount of unpaid wages that you may pay to the surviving spouse or family of a deceased worker.

[5]Those states that do not have a personal income tax law requiring withholding from wage payments are: Alaska, Connecticut, Florida, Nevada, New Hampshire, South Dakota, Tennessee, Texas, Washington, and Wyoming.

Employers in most states use wage-bracket tables and percentage method formulas to determine the amount of state income taxes to withhold from their employees' wages. However, when the size of wage payments and the frequency of such payments are irregular, overwithholding may result. Thus, employees become dissatisfied with the amount of their take-home pay. Although the federal income tax law and regulations provide for the use of alternative withholding methods (see pages 120 to 122) in such situations, the methods are not automatically adopted by the states. Therefore, payroll managers must decide for their individually affected states which, if any, of the federal alternative withholding methods may be used to determine the amount of state income taxes to be withheld.

Withholding from Nonresidents or Residents or Both

In those states imposing personal income taxes, the laws vary as to the withholding of taxes from wages paid. For example, Arizona does not require the withholding of state income tax from *nonresidents* engaged in motion picture production in that state. In Hawaii, *nonresidents* who perform temporary services are not subject to withholding of the state income tax. In the District of Columbia, employers are required to withhold the tax from wages paid to *residents* only. In Oklahoma, *nonresidents* are exempt from state income tax withholding on the first $300 or less each calendar quarter. However, in most states having income tax laws, you are required to withhold the tax from *both nonresidents and residents*, unless, as described below, there is a reciprocal agreement with one or more states to the contrary. In most states a "covered employee" is any person from whose pay you are required to withhold federal income taxes under the Internal Revenue Code.

Other variations in state income tax laws result from *reciprocal agreements* among the states. For example, in Kentucky, reciprocal agreements have been entered into with Illinois, Indiana, Michigan, Ohio, West Virginia, and Wisconsin. Thus, if a resident of one of these states works in Kentucky, the employee will not be subject to withholding of Kentucky income tax if the other state grants an exemption from the withholding of its income tax to Kentucky residents who earn income in that state. Also, Kentucky has an agreement with Virginia whereby residents of Virginia who commute daily to work in Kentucky are not subject to Kentucky withholding, and vice versa.

Types of State Income Tax Returns or Reports

In connection with state income tax laws, there are four main types of returns or reports the payroll manager should be familiar with:

1. *Periodic withholding returns* on which you report the wages paid and the state tax withheld during the reporting period. Illustration 4-13 shows the *Employer Deposit Statement of Income Tax Withheld* used by employers in Pennsylvania. Depending on the amount of state income taxes withheld for each quarterly period, employers may be required to pay over the taxes semimonthly, monthly, or quarterly.

PA 501R
COMMONWEALTH OF PENNSYLVANIA
DEPARTMENT OF REVENUE

19--

EMPLOYER DEPOSIT STATEMENT OF INCOME TAX WITHHELD FOR USE ONLY BY EMPLOYERS WHO DO NOT HAVE PRE-PRINTED COUPONS.

EIN	QUARTER	PERIOD ENDING	DUE DATE
71-3456798	9-04	12/31/--	1/4/--

TYPE FILER:		EXPECTED 3-MONTH WITHHOLDING WILL BE:
QUARTERLY	☐	LESS THAN $300 TAX
MONTHLY	☐	$300 OR MORE BUT LESS THAN $1,000 TAX
SEMI-MONTHLY	☒	$1,000 OR MORE TAX

DATE WAGES WERE FIRST PAID 6/15/--

BUSINESS NAME AND ADDRESS

Weiner, Inc.
820 Allen Drive
Ambler, PA 19002-0882

1.	GROSS COMPENSATION	11,614 29
2.	INCOME TAX LIABILITY	243 90
3.	LESS CREDITS	-0-
4.	PLUS INTEREST	-0-
5.	PAYMENT	243 90

DATE	TELEPHONE NUMBER	SIGNATURE	TITLE
1/4/--	(215) 555-6700	Robert T. Rojas	Controller

Illustration 4-13. Form PA 501R, Pennsylvania Employer Deposit Statement of Income Tax Withheld

2. *Reconciliation returns* that compare the total amount of state tax paid as shown on the periodic returns with the amounts of state tax declared to have been withheld from employees' wages. The *Employer Quarterly Reconciliation Return of Income Tax Withheld* for use by employers in Pennsylvania is shown in Illustration 4-14. Employers who have computer systems may submit their information on magnetic tapes.
3. *Annual statements to employees* showing the amount of wages paid during the year and the state tax withheld from those wages. Form W-2, Wage and Tax Statement, was shown in Illustration 4-5.
4. *Information returns* used to report payments to individuals that are not subject to withholding and/or are not reported on the annual employee wage and tax statements. See Illustration 4-11 for a listing of the major information returns.

Since the requirements for transmitting returns and reports vary from state to state, you should be familiar with the tax regulations of the state in which your business firm is located and of the state or states in which your employees reside.

As a result of federal regulations that require the filing of information returns on magnetic media, many states permit you to submit your wage information on magnetic tape, disk, and diskette. Also, many states take part in the Combined Federal/State Filing Program. This program enables you to file information returns with the federal government and to authorize the release of the information to the applicable state rather than file a separate state return. To participate in this program, you must first obtain permission from the IRS.

WITHHOLDING LOCAL INCOME TAXES

In addition to state income tax laws, cities and counties in Alabama, California, Colorado, Delaware, Georgia, Indiana, Kentucky, Maryland, Michigan, Missouri, New Jersey, New York, Ohio, Oregon, and Pennsylvania have passed local income tax legislation requiring employers to deduct and withhold income taxes or license fees on salaries or wages paid.

As a few examples, in Alabama, several cities have license fee ordinances that require the withholding of the fees from employees' wages. Certain employees in Denver, Colorado, are subject to the withholding of the Denver Occupational Privilege Tax from their compensation. In Wilmington, Delaware, the Earned Income Tax is withheld from the taxable wages paid employees. In Kentucky, a license fee (payroll tax) is imposed by a number of cities and counties.

Illustration 4-15 on page 138 shows the return that must be completed by employers in Philadelphia, all of whom are required to withhold wage taxes from compensation paid their employees. Depending upon the amount of wage taxes withheld, employers may be required to make deposits weekly, semimonthly, monthly, or quarterly. For any late payment of the withheld tax, the city imposes a penalty on the underpayment. Employers are required to file annual summary returns with respect to the wage taxes deducted during the preceding calendar year. The annual reconciliation return and consolidated withholding statement is due January 31.

PA-W3R
COMMONWEALTH OF PENNSYLVANIA
DEPARTMENT OF REVENUE

19--

EMPLOYER QUARTERLY RECONCILIATION RETURN OF INCOME TAX WITHHELD
For Use ONLY When Employers Do Not Have Preprinted Coupons

EIN	QUARTER	QUARTER ENDING	DUE DATE	BUSINESS NAME AND ADDRESS
71-3456798	9-04	12/31/--	1/31/--	Weiner, Inc. 820 Allen Drive Ambler, PA 19002-0882

RECORD OF PA WITHHOLDING TAX BY PERIOD

Period	Semi-monthly Filer	Monthly Filer	Quarterly Filer
1	222 05		
2	230 13		
3	245 35		
4	285 70		
5	244 63		
6	243 90		
Total	1,471 76		

7. TOTAL COMPENSATION SUBJECT TO PA TAX	70,083 81
8. TOTAL PA WITHHOLDING TAX (FROM LEFT)	1,471 76
9. TOTAL DEPOSITS FOR QUARTER (INCLUDING PRIOR OVERPAYMENTS)	1,471 76
10. TAX DUE (IF LINE 9 IS LESS THAN THAN LINE 8)	-0-
11. OVERPAYMENT (IF LINE 9) IS GREATER THAN LINE 8)	-0-
12. PAYMENT	-0-

Under penalties of perjury, I declare that I have examined this return and to the best of my knowledge and belief, it is true, correct and complete.

Date	Telephone Number	Signature	Title
1/31/--	(215) 555-6700	Robert T. Rojas	Controller

Illustration 4-14. Form PA W-3R, Pennsylvania Employer Quarterly Reconciliation Return of Income Tax Withheld

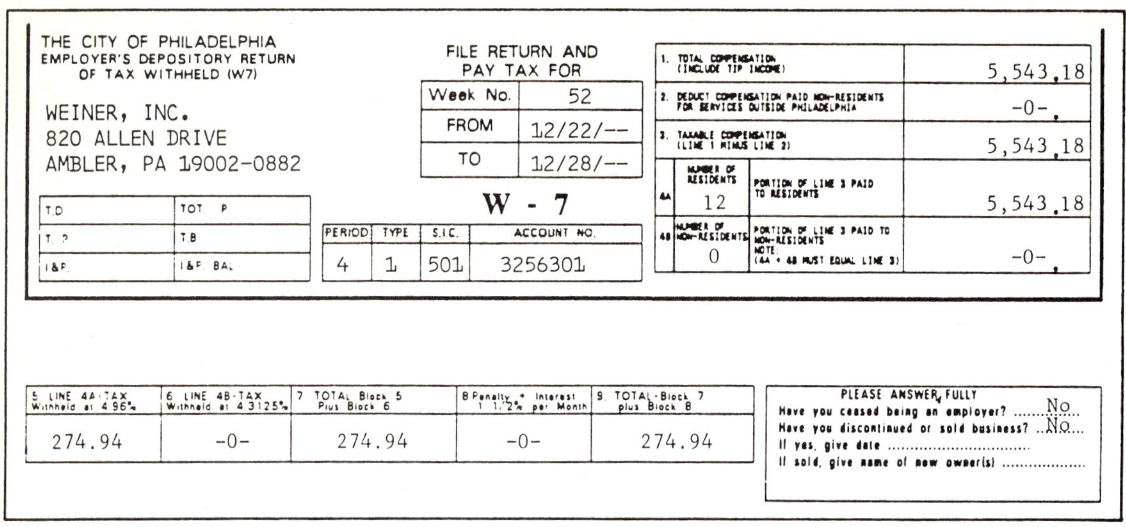

THE CITY OF PHILADELPHIA
EMPLOYER'S DEPOSITORY RETURN
OF TAX WITHHELD (W7)

WEINER, INC.
820 ALLEN DRIVE
AMBLER, PA 19002-0882

FILE RETURN AND PAY TAX FOR

Week No.	52
FROM	12/22/--
TO	12/28/--

W - 7

T.D	TOT. P
T. ?	T.B
I&P.	I&P. BAL

PERIOD	TYPE	S.I.C.	ACCOUNT NO.
4	1	501	3256301

1. TOTAL COMPENSATION (INCLUDE TIP INCOME)			5,543.18
2. DEDUCT COMPENSATION PAID NON-RESIDENTS FOR SERVICES OUTSIDE PHILADELPHIA			-0-.
3. TAXABLE COMPENSATION (LINE 1 MINUS LINE 2)			5,543.18
4A	NUMBER OF RESIDENTS 12	PORTION OF LINE 3 PAID TO RESIDENTS	5,543.18
4B	NUMBER OF NON-RESIDENTS 0	PORTION OF LINE 3 PAID TO NON-RESIDENTS NOTE: (4A + 4B MUST EQUAL LINE 3)	-0-.

5 LINE 4A-TAX Withheld at 4.96%	6 LINE 4B-TAX Withheld at 4.3125%	7 TOTAL Block 5 Plus Block 6	8 Penalty + Interest 1 1/2% per Month	9. TOTAL-Block 7 plus Block 8
274.94	-0-	274.94	-0-	274.94

PLEASE ANSWER FULLY
Have you ceased being an employer? ....No....
Have you discontinued or sold business? ..No...
If yes, give date ....
If sold, give name of new owner(s) ....

Illustration 4-15. Form W-7, City of Philadelphia Employer's Depository Return of Tax Withheld

GLOSSARY

Annualizing wages—plan of determining amount of income taxes to be withheld by multiplying the wages for one payroll period by the number of periods in the year, determining the annual amount of withholding required on the total wages, and dividing the annual withholding by the number of payroll periods.

Cumulative withholding—plan of determining amount of income taxes to be withheld by adding wages for a particular payroll period to total wages already paid during the year, dividing the aggregate by the number of payroll periods to which it pertains, computing the tax on the average amount of wages, subtracting the amount of tax already withheld during preceding payroll periods, and deducting any excess tax from current payment of wages.

Earned income credit (EIC)—reduction in the computation of the federal income taxes for workers who have dependent children and maintain a household.

Employee—any individual performing services for an employer in the legal relationship of employer and employee.

Employer—any person or organization for whom an individual performs any service as an employee.

Information return—form upon which an employer reports compensation paid to individuals who are not employees.

Percentage method—plan of determining amount of income taxes to be withheld through use of Table of Allowance Values and Percentage Method Withholding Table.

Personal allowance—a deduction allowed in computing taxable income; also known as a *personal exemption.*

Quarterly averaging of wages—plan of determining amount of income taxes to be withheld by estimating the employee's average wages for the calendar quarter, calculating an average payment, and withholding an amount based on the average payment.

Reciprocal agreement—arrangement entered into by two or more states whereby the resident of one state working in another state will not be subject to the withholding of income taxes by the state in which the person is employed if that state has entered into a similar agreement with the employee's resident state.

Special withholding allowance—allowance claimed by employees so that wages which are below the level subject to the income tax will not be subject to withholding.

Standard deduction—amount of money used to reduce a person's adjusted gross income in arriving at the taxable income.

Supplemental wage payments—additional compensation such as vacation pay, bonuses, and commissions paid to employees.

Wage and tax statement—statement furnished by employers to their employees informing them of the wages paid during the calendar year and the amount of taxes withheld from those wages.

Wage-bracket method—plan of determining amount of income taxes to be withheld by reading amount from tables provided by the IRS, which take into consideration length of payroll period, gross earnings, marital status, and number of withholding allowances claimed.

Wages—total compensation paid for services whether in the form of wages, salaries, commissions, or bonuses, including the cash value of remuneration paid in a medium other than cash.

QUESTIONS FOR REVIEW

NOTE: Tax Tables A and B at the back of this textbook and the tax regulations presented in this unit are to be used in answering all questions and solving all problems.

1. What three conditions must exist before any tax may be withheld under the federal income tax withholding law?

2. Define *wages* under the federal income tax law.

3. To what extent are cash tips treated as remuneration subject to federal income tax withholding?

4. Under what conditions must a large food establishment allocate tips to its tipped employees?

5. For each of the following kinds of wage payments, indicate whether or not the wages are exempt from the withholding of federal income taxes:
   a. Three weeks' vacation pay.
   b. Weekly advance to a sales representative for traveling expenses to be incurred.
   c. Weekly wages paid the housekeeper in a college fraternity.
   d. Monthly salary received by Rev. Cole Carpenter.
   e. Benefits paid by a union to its members who are on strike.

6. a. What is a personal allowance?
   b. What was the amount of a personal allowance in 1990?

7. Brock Armstrong is married and his only dependent is his wife, Norma. Norma is claimed as a dependent on her father's federal income tax return. Is Brock entitled to claim a personal allowance for Norma? Explain.

8. Are all employees entitled to claim one special withholding allowance? Explain.

9. For what purpose does an employer ask that a completed Form W-4 be on file for each employee?

10. On July 15, William Mitchell amended his Form W-4 to increase the number of withholding allowances from four to seven. Mitchell asked for a refund of the amount of overwithheld income taxes from January 1 to July 15 when the number of allowances was only four. Should Mitchell be reimbursed for the income taxes overwithheld before the effective date of the amended Form W-4?

11. a. Under what conditions may employees be exempt from the withholding of federal income taxes during 1991?
   b. How do such employees indicate their no-tax-liability status?

12. a. May an employee agree with the employer to withhold income tax *in excess of* that required under the law?
   b. May an employee agree with the employer to withhold income tax *less than* that required under the law?

13. Under what conditions are employers required to submit copies of Form W-4 to the IRS?

14. Commencing in June, Slade Exon is eligible to receive monthly payments from a pension fund. What procedure should Exon follow if he does not wish to have federal income taxes withheld from his periodic pension payments?

15. What is a standard deduction?

16. a. Rhonda Gramm is single and her wages are paid weekly. What is the amount of her withholding allowance?
   b. Howard Heinz, married, claims two withholding allowances and his wages are paid semimonthly. What is the total amount of his withholding allowance?

17. Max Lieberman, a married employee, fails to furnish his employer with a withholding allowance certificate. His weekly wages amount to $445. Under the percentage method, will any portion of his wages be subject to withholding? If so, indicate what portion.

18. Compare the percentage method and the wage-bracket method of withholding federal income taxes.

19. What steps should be taken by an employer to calculate the amount of income tax to be withheld by the annualizing of wages method?

20. Nancy Wallop is to receive her two weeks' vacation pay along with her regular semimonthly pay this Friday. Wallop's employer has decided to combine her two weeks' vacation pay with her regular semimonthly pay and withhold federal income taxes on the aggregate payment. Is the employer properly following the computation rules issued by the IRS? Explain.

21. The Baucus Company has just completed the processing of its year-end payroll and distributed all the weekly paychecks. The payroll department is now calculating the amount of the annual bonus to be given each worker. What methods may be used by the company in determining the amount of federal income taxes to be withheld from the annual bonus payments?

22. Gerry Jeffords is eligible to receive advance earned income credit (EIC) payments. How should she proceed to obtain her payments?

23. From what source do employers obtain the funds needed to make advance EIC payments to their eligible employees?

24. Orrin D'Amato, single, participates in his firm's pension retirement plan. This year his adjusted gross income will be about $42,000. How much of his compensation may D'Amato contribute to an IRA this year without paying federal income taxes on the contribution?

25. a. For what purpose are employers required to prepare Form W-2?
    b. When are employers required to furnish their employees with copies of Form W-2?
26. An employer withholds $2,500 in federal income taxes from employees' wages each week. When and to whom should the amount withheld be paid?
27. For what purpose is Form W-3 completed by the employer?
28. For how long a period of time should employers retain their payroll records?
29. Why are certain organizations and persons required to file information returns?
30. What is backup withholding?
31. Why are some employers required to file Form 1096?
32. Identify the main types of returns or reports that an organization may be required to file under a state income tax law.

QUESTIONS FOR DISCUSSION

1. Virginia Skelton, a former office layout consultant and now a full-time homemaker, was recently elected to the board of directors of Lantos, Inc. In addition to attending monthly board meetings, Skelton has assumed a short-term responsibility, along with the office manager, for developing a new word processing center. For her consulting services, Skelton is to be paid $950. The company will furnish an office, clerical help, and all materials and supplies to be used by Skelton. Will her earnings of $950 be subject to federal income tax withholding? Explain.
2. Alex Oberstar, a cook in the Lagomarsino company cafeteria, is furnished two meals each day during his eight-hour shift. Oberstar's duties require him to have his meals on the company's premises. Should the cash value of Oberstar's meals be included as part of his taxable wages? Explain.
3. The Solomon Company ordinarily pays its employees on a weekly basis. Recently one of the employees, Bernard Nagle, was sent from the home office on a three-week trip. Nagle has now returned to the office and you are preparing a single check covering his three-weeks' services. Should you withhold federal income taxes on the total gross earnings for the three-week period or should you calculate the federal income taxes as if Nagle were receiving three separate weekly wage payments?
4. Investigate your state's income tax withholding law (or that of some other state assigned by your instructor) and find the answers to the following questions:
    a. Who must withhold the tax?
    b. How are covered employers and covered employees defined?
    c. Are there any reciprocal agreements the state has entered into? If so, describe them.
    d. How is the withholding rate determined?
    e. What payments are subject to withholding?
    f. What payments are not subject to withholding?
    g. Are there any employee withholding exemptions?
    h. What methods of withholding are permitted?
    i. Describe each of the returns required by the state.
    j. What kinds of information must be retained by employers in their withholding tax records?
    k. What penalties are imposed for failure to comply with the withholding law?
5. Janice Sikorski, one of your firm's workers, has just come into the Payroll Department and says to you: "I am thinking of amending my Form W-4 so that an additional $10 is withheld each week. That way I will get a fat refund next year. What do you think of my idea?" How would you reply to Sikorski?
6. Anita Leland, a waitress in the Atlantis Casino, reported tips of $467 to her employer last year. Two months after she filed her federal income tax return, Leland received a letter from the IRS informing her that she had earned $5,260 in tips rather than the $467 reported. She was notified that she owed the government $1,872.94 in back taxes.
    a. How is the IRS able to determine the amount of tips received by a waitress in a casino?
    b. If the IRS is correct in its determination of the tips received, is Atlantis subject to a penalty for not having withheld payroll taxes on all the tips Leland received during the year?
7. Research the regulations your state may have issued regarding the filing of information returns to learn: (a) whether your state *permits* or *requires* the use of magnetic media, (b) which forms may be filed on magnetic media, and (c) whether your state participates in the Combined Federal/State Filing Program.

Date ______________________ Name ______________________

PRACTICAL PROBLEMS

4-1. Use the percentage method to determine the federal income taxes to withhold from the wages and salaries of each employee listed below.

Employee's Name	Marital Status	No. of W/H Allow.	Gross Wage or Salary	Amount to be Withheld
1. Amoroso, A.	Married	4	$610 weekly	$__________
2. Dorbuck, J.	Single	0	$825 biweekly	__________
3. Gleason, R.	Single	5	$9,630 quarterly	__________
4. Quinto, K.	Married	8	$925 semimonthly	__________
5. Sweeney, R.	Married	3	$1,975 monthly	__________

4-2. Use the (a) percentage method and (b) wage-bracket method to determine the federal income taxes to withhold from the wages and salaries of each employee listed below.

Employee's Name	Marital Status	No. of W/H Allow.	Gross Wage or Salary	Amount to be Withheld (a) Percentage Method	Amount to be Withheld (b) Wage-Bracket Method
1. Anastasi, B. ..	Single	2	$475 weekly	$__________	$__________
2. Caplan, J.	Single	1	$960 weekly	__________	__________
3. Jones, H.	Married	6	$1,775 biweekly	__________	__________
4. Schiff, W.	Married	4	$1,480 semimonthly	__________	__________
5. Yarrow, K.	Married	9	$5,350 monthly	__________	__________

4-3. Donato Bakery uses the wage-bracket method in determining the amount of federal income taxes to withhold from the wages of its employees. Calculate the amount to withhold from the wages paid each employee listed below.

DONATO BAKERY

Employee	Marital Status	No. of W/H Allow.	Payroll Period W=Weekly S=Semimonthly M=Monthly D=Daily	Wage	Amount to be Withheld
William Bowen ..	M	1	W	$1,550	$__________
Elizabeth Carden	S	1	W	490	__________
Mel Jergensen ..	S	3	W	575	__________
Jessie Kelley	M	6	M	4,095	__________
Rose Lechner ...	M	2	M	2,830	__________
Catherine Marcus	M	8	S	850	__________
Sarah Schartz ...	S	1	D	96	__________
Jeffrey Singer ...	S	4	S	1,925	__________
Manuel Torres ...	M	10	M	3,225	__________

4-4. The names of the employees of the Lambright Music Shop are listed on the payroll register illustrated below. The payroll register also shows the marital status, number of withholding allowances claimed, and the total weekly earnings for each employee. Complete the payroll register for the payroll period ending October 4, showing the following:

a. Amount to withhold from each employee's earnings under FICA. This pay period ending October 4 is the 40th weekly pay period of the year. Assume that during the year the employees received the same weekly pay.
b. Amount to withhold from each employee's earnings for federal income taxes (FIT). Use the wage-bracket method to compute the amount to withhold.
c. Amount to withhold from each employee's earnings for the state income tax (SIT). In this state the entire amount of earnings is subject to a 2% tax.
d. Amount to withhold from each employee's earnings for the city income tax (CIT). In this city the entire amount of earnings is subject to a 1½% tax.
e. Net pay for each employee.

LAMBRIGHT MUSIC SHOP

PAYROLL REGISTER

FOR PERIOD ENDING 19

EMPLOYEE'S NAME	MARITAL STATUS	NO. OF W/H ALLOW.	TOTAL EARNINGS	DEDUCTIONS (a) FICA	(b) FIT	(c) SIT	(d) CIT	(e) NET PAY
Blue, Marion E.	M	4	1 380 00					
Good, Ralph C.	S	1	275 00					
Irwin, Robert A.	M	0	195 00					
Larue, Stella V.	S	3	302 50					
Mayers, Charles D.	S	1	365 70					
Nash, Donald L.	S	2	464 80					
Syler, John T.	S	1	470 10					
Yost, Robert J.	M	5	360 00					
Totals								

Calculate the employer's FICA taxes for the pay period ending October 4.

Taxable earnings . . . . $________

FICA taxes . . . . $________

(Practical Problems continued on page 144.)

Date ______________________ Name ______________________

4-5. The names of the employees of Cox Security Systems and their regular salaries are shown in the payroll register below. Note that Hill and Van Dyne are paid monthly on the last day, while all others are paid weekly.

In addition to the regular salaries, the company pays an annual bonus based on the amount of earnings for the year. For the current year, the bonus amounts to 8% of the annual salary paid each employee. The bonus is to be paid along with the regular salaries on December 31, but the amount of the bonus and the amount of the regular salary will be shown separately on each employee's earnings statement. Assume that all employees received their regular salary during the entire year.

Prepare the payroll for the pay period ending December 31, showing the following for each employee:

a. Supplementary earnings.
b. Total earnings.
c. FICA taxes to withhold.
d. Federal income taxes (FIT) to withhold. Use the wage-bracket method to compute the amount to withhold from the regular salary. Withhold a flat 20% of the annual bonus.
e. State income taxes (SIT) to withhold. In this state the entire amount of earnings is subject to a 2% tax.
f. City income taxes (CIT) to withhold. In this city the entire amount of earnings is subject to a 1% tax.
g. Net pay.

COX SECURITY SYSTEMS

PAYROLL REGISTER

FOR PERIOD ENDING ______________________ 19 ____

EMPLOYEE'S NAME	MARITAL STATUS	NO. OF W/H ALLOW.	EARNINGS			DEDUCTIONS				(g) NET PAY
			REGULAR	(a) SUPP'L.	(b) TOTAL	(c) FICA	(d) FIT	(e) SIT	(f) CIT	
Hill, J. Harvey	M	5	4300 00							
Van Dyne, Joyce S.	M	2	2650 00							
Ackerman, Leslie N.	S	1	470 00							
Bunger, Russell L.	M	4	365 00							
Noblet, Thurman D.	M	2	280 00							
Short, Frank C.	S	1	350 00							
Toban, Harriette O.	M	2	375 00							
Wyeth, Amy R.	S	0	405 00							
Totals										

Calculate the employer's FICA taxes for the pay period ending December 31:

Taxable earnings . . . . $ ____________

FICA taxes . . . . $ ____________

Date ____________________ Name ____________________

4-6. During the quarter ending December 31 of the current year, Cox Security Systems had 13 weekly paydays and three monthly paydays. Using the data given in Problem 4-5, complete the form below to show the:

a. Total earnings paid during the quarter, including both the regular and the supplementary earnings.
b. Total amount of FICA taxes withheld during the quarter.
c. Total amount of federal income taxes (FIT) withheld during the quarter.
d. Total amount of state income taxes (SIT) withheld during the quarter.
e. Total amount of city income taxes (CIT) withheld during the quarter.
f. Total net amount paid each employee during the quarter.

COX SECURITY SYSTEMS

19

EMPLOYEE'S NAME	(a) TOTAL EARNINGS	DEDUCTIONS (b) FICA	(c) FIT	(d) SIT	(e) CIT	(f) NET PAY
Hill, J. Harvey						
Van Dyne, Joyce S.						
Ackerman, Leslie N.						
Bunger, Russell L.						
Noblet, Thurman D.						
Short, Frank C.						
Toban, Harriette O.						
Wyeth, Amy R.						
Totals						

4-7. The employees of Talbott Hosiery, Inc., are paid biweekly. The names of five employees of the company are given on the payroll register illustrated below. The payroll register also shows the marital status, number of withholding allowances claimed, and the total biweekly earnings for each worker. Assume that each employee is paid the same biweekly wage on each payday in 1991. Also shown below is the Wage-Bracket Table for Advance Earned Income Credit (EIC) Payments for a Biweekly Payroll Period. Each of the employees listed on the payroll register has completed a Form W-5 indicating that the worker is not married.

Complete the payroll register for the biweekly payroll period ending December 6, 1991, showing the following:

a. Amount to withhold from each employee's earnings under FICA.
b. Amount to withhold from each employee's earnings for federal income taxes (FIT). Use the wage-bracket method to compute the amount to be withheld.
c. Amount to withhold from each employee's earnings for the state income tax (SIT). In this state the entire amount of earnings is subject to a 1½% tax.
d. Amount of advance EIC payments to be paid each employee. Use the wage-bracket table below.
e. Net pay for each employee.

TALBOTT HOSIERY, INC.

PAYROLL REGISTER

FOR PERIOD ENDING 19

EMPLOYEE'S NAME	MARITAL STATUS	NO. OF W/H ALLOW.	TOTAL EARNINGS	DEDUCTIONS (a) FICA	(b) FIT	(c) SIT	(d) ADVANCE EIC PAYMENT	(e) NET PAY
Allen, Neil A.	S	4	393 00					
Diehl, Marcella O.	S	1	347 00					
McDowell, John T.	S	2	473 50					
Ronsini, Joan R.	S	3	522 00					
Wheeler, Debra S.	S	5	454 00					
Totals								

Wage-Bracket Table for Advance EIC Payments

BIWEEKLY Payroll Period

SINGLE or MARRIED Without Spouse Filing Certificate

And the wages are— At least	But less than	Payment to be made	And the wages are— At least	But less than	Payment to be made	And the wages are— At least	But less than	Payment to be made	And the wages are— At least	But less than	Payment to be made
$0	$8	$0	$129	$136	$18	$257	$419	$36	$589	$599	$18
8	15	1	136	143	19	419	429	35	599	609	17
15	22	2	143	150	20	429	439	34	609	619	16
22	29	3	150	158	21	439	449	33	619	629	15
29	36	4	158	165	22	449	459	32	629	639	14
36	43	5	165	172	23	459	469	31	639	649	13
43	50	6	172	179	24	469	479	30	649	659	12
50	58	7	179	186	25	479	489	29	659	669	11
58	65	8	186	193	26	489	499	28	669	679	10
65	72	9	193	200	27	499	509	27	679	689	9
72	79	10	200	208	28	509	519	26	689	699	8
79	86	11	208	215	29	519	529	25	699	709	7
86	93	12	215	222	30	529	539	24	709	719	6
93	100	13	222	229	31	539	549	23	719	729	5
100	108	14	229	236	32	549	559	22	729	739	4
108	115	15	236	243	33	559	569	21	739	749	3
115	122	16	243	250	34	569	579	20	749	759	2
122	129	17	250	257	35	579	589	19	759	769	1
									769	....	0

Date ______________________ Name ______________________

4-8. During the fourth quarter of 1991 there were six biweekly pay periods (October 11, 25; November 8, 22; and December 6, 20) for Talbott Hosiery, Inc. Assume that each of the six biweekly payments was the same as that calculated in Problem 4-7.

Using the forms supplied on pages 149-153, complete the following for the fourth quarter, 1991:

a. Federal Tax Deposit Coupons, Forms 8109. Below each coupon, indicate the due date of the deposit. The employer's telephone number is: (501) 555-7331.

b. Employer's Quarterly Federal Tax Return, Form 941. The form is to be signed by the company's president, Wilbur B. Kroft.

   Each pay period the amount of the advance EIC payments is subtracted from the employer's liability for the federal income taxes withheld, the employees' FICA taxes, and the employer's FICA taxes. Thus, for the October 11 pay, the tax liability is calculated as follows:

Federal income taxes withheld	$118.00
Employees' FICA taxes	167.49
Employer's FICA taxes	167.50
Total	$452.99
Less advance EIC payments	159.00
Tax liability to be recorded on Form 941 for first month of quarter, 8th through 11th day	$293.99

c. Employer's Quarterly Report of State Income Taxes Withheld. The report, due on or before January 31, 1992, is to be signed by Kroft.

Date ______________________ Name ______________________

Practical Problem 4-8

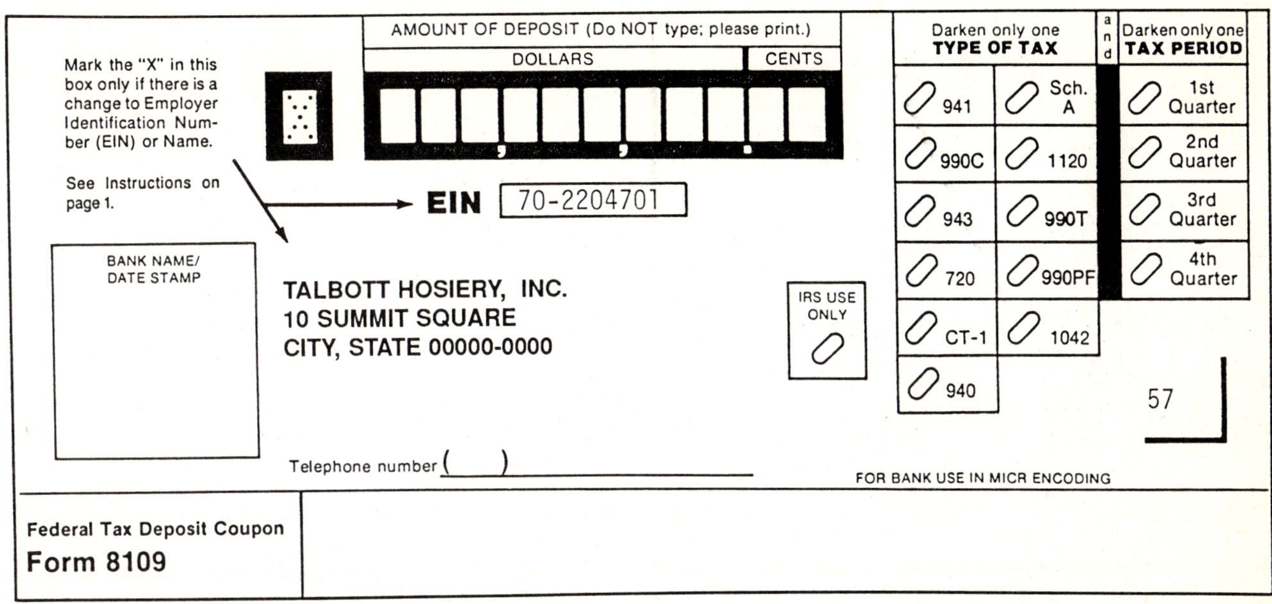

AMOUNT OF DEPOSIT (Do NOT type; please print.)

DOLLARS | CENTS

Mark the "X" in this box only if there is a change to Employer Identification Number (EIN) or Name.

See Instructions on page 1.

EIN 70-2204701

BANK NAME/ DATE STAMP

TALBOTT HOSIERY, INC.
10 SUMMIT SQUARE
CITY, STATE 00000-0000

IRS USE ONLY

Telephone number ( ) ______________

Darken only one TYPE OF TAX: 941, Sch. A, 990C, 1120, 943, 990T, 720, 990PF, CT-1, 1042, 940

and

Darken only one TAX PERIOD: 1st Quarter, 2nd Quarter, 3rd Quarter, 4th Quarter

57

FOR BANK USE IN MICR ENCODING

Federal Tax Deposit Coupon
Form 8109

To be deposited on or before ______________________

AMOUNT OF DEPOSIT (Do NOT type; please print.)

DOLLARS | CENTS

Mark the "X" in this box only if there is a change to Employer Identification Number (EIN) or Name.

See Instructions on page 1.

EIN 70-2204701

BANK NAME/ DATE STAMP

TALBOTT HOSIERY, INC.
10 SUMMIT SQUARE
CITY, STATE 00000-0000

IRS USE ONLY

Telephone number ( ) ______________

Darken only one TYPE OF TAX: 941, Sch. A, 990C, 1120, 943, 990T, 720, 990PF, CT-1, 1042, 940

and

Darken only one TAX PERIOD: 1st Quarter, 2nd Quarter, 3rd Quarter, 4th Quarter

57

FOR BANK USE IN MICR ENCODING

Federal Tax Deposit Coupon
Form 8109

To be deposited on or before ______________________

Date ______________________ Name ______________________

Practical Problem 4-8

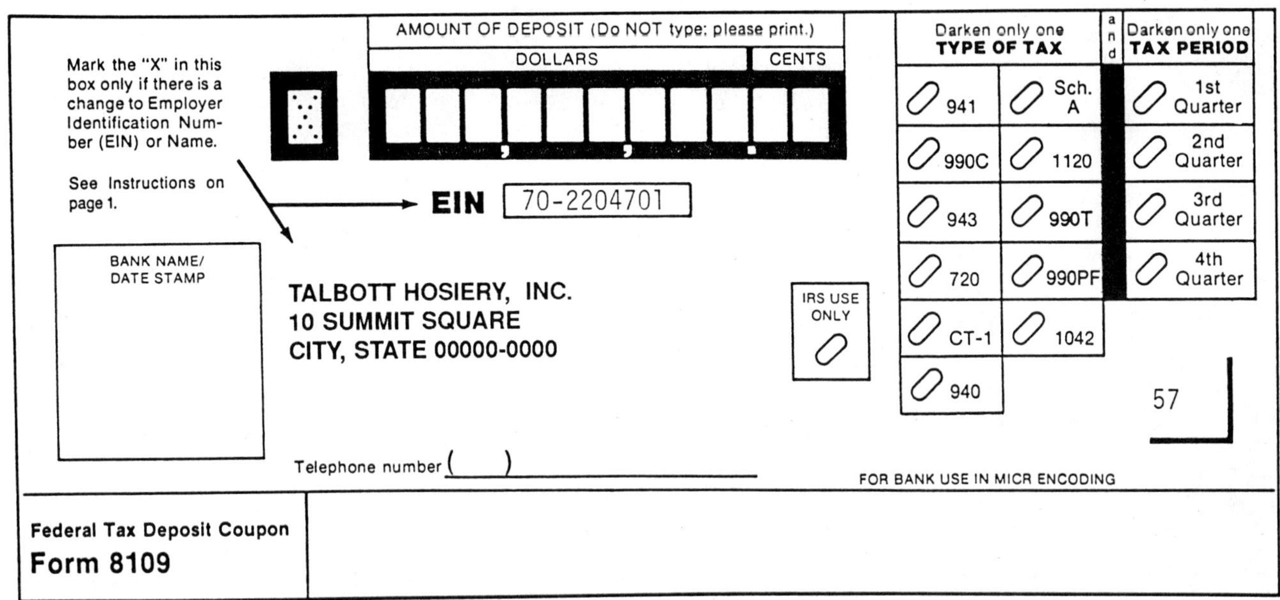

Mark the "X" in this box only if there is a change to Employer Identification Number (EIN) or Name.

See Instructions on page 1.

AMOUNT OF DEPOSIT (Do NOT type; please print.)

DOLLARS | CENTS

EIN 70-2204701

BANK NAME/ DATE STAMP

TALBOTT HOSIERY, INC.
10 SUMMIT SQUARE
CITY, STATE 00000-0000

IRS USE ONLY

Telephone number ( ) ______________

Darken only one TYPE OF TAX: 941, Sch. A, 990C, 1120, 943, 990T, 720, 990PF, CT-1, 1042, 940

and

Darken only one TAX PERIOD: 1st Quarter, 2nd Quarter, 3rd Quarter, 4th Quarter

57

FOR BANK USE IN MICR ENCODING

Federal Tax Deposit Coupon
Form 8109

To be deposited on or before ______________________

EMPLOYER'S REPORT
OF STATE INCOME TAX WITHHELD

(DO NOT WRITE IN THIS SPACE)

IMPORTANT: PLEASE REFER TO THIS NUMBER IN ANY CORRESPONDENCE →

WITHHOLDING IDENTIFICATION NUMBER	MONTH OF OR QUARTER ENDING
42-7-3301	DEC. 91

TALBOTT HOSIERY, INC.
10 SUMMIT SQUARE
CITY, STATE 00000-0000

IF YOU ARE A SEASONAL EMPLOYER AND THIS IS YOUR FINAL REPORT FOR THIS SEASON, CHECK HERE ☐ AND SHOW THE NEXT MONTH IN WHICH YOU WILL PAY WAGES.

IF NAME OR ADDRESS IS INCORRECT, PLEASE MAKE CORRECTIONS.

THIS REPORT MUST BE RETURNED EVEN IF NO AMOUNT HAS BEEN WITHHELD

1. GROSS PAYROLL THIS PERIOD	$
2. STATE INCOME TAX WITHHELD	$
3. ADJUSTMENT FOR PREVIOUS PERIOD(S). (ATTACH STATEMENT)	$
4. TOTAL ADJUSTED TAX (LINE 2 PLUS OR MINUS LINE 3)	$
5. PENALTY (25% OF LINE 4)	
6. INTEREST	
7. TOTAL AMOUNT DUE AND PAYABLE	$

MAIL THIS REPORT WITH CHECK OR MONEY ORDER PAYABLE TO THE DEPT. OF REVENUE ON OR BEFORE DUE DATE TO AVOID PENALTY.

Under penalties prescribed by law, I hereby affirm that to the best of my knowledge and belief this return, including any accompanying schedules and statements, is true and complete. If prepared by a person other than taxpayer, his affirmation is based on all information of which he has any knowledge.

SIGNATURE: ______________ TITLE: ______________ DATE: ______________

Date ____________________ Name ____________________

Practical Problem 4-8

Form **941** Department of the Treasury Internal Revenue Service

4242

Employer's Quarterly Federal Tax Return

► See Circular E for more information concerning Employment Tax Returns.

Please type or print.

Your name, address, employer identification number, and calendar quarter of return. (If not correct, please change.)

Name (as distinguished from trade name) | Date quarter ended: DEC 31, 1991

Trade name, if any: TALBOTT HOSIERY, INC. | Employer identification number: 70-2204701

Address and ZIP code: 10 SUMMIT SQUARE CITY, STATE 00000-0000

OMB No. 1545-0029

T / FF / FD / FP / I / T

IRS Use

If address is different from prior return, check here ► ☐

If you do not have to file returns in the future, check here . . . ► ☐ Date final wages paid . . . . ►

If you are a seasonal employer, see **Seasonal employer** on page 2 and check here . . . ► ☐

1a	Number of employees (except household) employed in the pay period that includes March 12th . ►	1a	
b	If you are a subsidiary corporation AND your parent corporation files a consolidated Form 1120, enter parent corporation employer identification number (EIN) . . ► 1b –		
2	Total wages and tips subject to withholding, plus other compensation . . . . ►	2	
3	Total income tax withheld from wages, tips, pensions, annuities, sick pay, gambling, etc. . . . ►	3	
4	Adjustment of withheld income tax for preceding quarters of calendar year (see instructions) . . ►	4	
5	Adjusted total of income tax withheld (line 3 as adjusted by line 4—see instructions)	5	
6	Taxable social security wages paid . . . . . $ ______ × 15.3% (.153) . .	6	
7a	Taxable tips reported . . . . $ ______ × 15.3% (.153) . .	7a	
b	Taxable hospital insurance wages paid . . . . $ ______ × 2.9% (.029). . .	7b	
8	Total social security taxes (add lines 6, 7a, and 7b)	8	
9	Adjustment of social security taxes (see instructions for required explanation)	9	
10	Adjusted total of social security taxes (line 8 as adjusted by line 9—see instructions) . . . . . ►	10	
11	Backup withholding (see instructions)	11	
12	Adjustment of backup withholding tax for preceding quarters of calendar year . . . . ►	12	
13	Adjusted total of backup withholding (line 11 as adjusted by line 12)	13	
14	Total taxes (add lines 5, 10, and 13)	14	
15	Advance earned income credit (EIC) payments, if any . . . . ►	15	
16	Net taxes (subtract line 15 from line 14). **This must equal line IV below** (plus line IV of Schedule A (Form 941) if you have treated backup withholding as a separate liability).	16	
17	Total deposits for quarter, including overpayment applied from a prior quarter, from your records . ►	17	
18	Balance due (subtract line 17 from line 16). This should be less than $500. Pay to IRS . . . . ►	18	
19	If line 17 is more than line 16, enter overpayment here ► $ ______ and check if to be: ☐ Applied to next return **OR** ☐ Refunded.		

Record of Federal Tax Liability (Complete if line 16 is $500 or more.) See the instructions on page 4 for details before checking these boxes.

Check only if you made eighth-monthly deposits using the 95% rule ► ☐ Check only if you are a first time 3-banking-day depositor ► ☐

Show tax liability here, **not deposits.** IRS gets deposit data from FTD coupons.

Do NOT Show Federal Tax Deposits Here

Date wages paid		First month of quarter		Second month of quarter		Third month of quarter
1st through 3rd	A		I		Q	
4th through 7th	B		J		R	
8th through 11th	C		K		S	
12th through 15th	D		L		T	
16th through 19th	E		M		U	
20th through 22nd	F		N		V	
23rd through 25th	G		O		W	
26th through the last	H		P		X	
Total liability for month	*I*		*II*		*III*	

IV Total for quarter (add lines *I*, *II*, and *III*). **This must equal line 16 above** . . . . ►

Sign Here Under penalties of perjury, I declare that I have examined this return, including accompanying schedules and statements, and to the best of my knowledge and belief, it is true, correct, and complete.

Signature ► Title ► Date ►

4-9. During the first two weeks of 1992 the payroll department of the Figley Corporation is preparing the Forms W-2 for distribution to its workers along with their paychecks on January 10. In this problem you will complete six of the forms in order to gain some experience in recording the different kinds of information required.

Assume that each worker earned the same weekly salary for each of the 52 paydays in 1991. Each worker participates in the company's qualified pension plan, toward which the employees contribute 5% of their annual wages and salaries.

Using the following information obtained from the personnel and payroll records of the firm, complete Copy A of the six Forms W-2 that are reproduced on pages 155 to 159.

Company Information:

Address: 4800 River Road
Philadelphia, PA 19113-5548
Federal identification number: 13-7490972
State identification number: 46-3-1066

Income Tax Information:

1. The wage-bracket method is used to determine the amount of federal income taxes to withhold each week.
2. The state tax rate in Pennsylvania is 2.1% of the worker's weekly gross earnings.
3. The city tax rate for residents of Philadelphia is 4.96% of the worker's weekly gross earnings.

Personnel and Payroll Information:

a. Patricia A. Grimes
54 Gradison Place
Philadelphia, PA 19113-4054

Single 1 allowance
$415/week
SS#: 376-72-4310

b. Roberta P. Kurtz
56 Andrews Court, Apt. 7
Philadelphia, PA 19103-3356
Dependent care payments, $950

Married 1 allowance
$485/week
SS#: 272-33-8804

c. David P. Markle
770 Camac Street
Philadelphia, PA 19101-3770

Single 0 allowance
$365/week
SS#: 178-92-3316

d. Harold W. Rasul
338 North Side Avenue
Philadelphia, PA 19130-6638
Cost of Rasul's group insurance exceeding $50,000: $262.75

Married 7 allowances
$1,200/week
SS#: 269-01-6839

e. Christine A. Shoemaker
4900 Gladwynne Terrace
Philadelphia, PA 19127-0049
Advance EIC payments made to Shoemaker: $6 each week

Married 2 allowances
$320/week
SS#: 368-14-5771

f. Angelo Zickar
480-A Hopkinson Tower
Philadelphia, PA 19101-3301
Educational assistance payments, $675

Single 1 allowance
$390/week
SS#: 337-99-8703

Date ______________________ Name ______________________

Practical Problem 4-9

1 Control number	22222	For Paperwork Reduction Act Notice, see separate instructions OMB No 1545-0008	For Official Use Only ▶

2 Employer's name, address, and ZIP code	6 Statutory employee ☐ Deceased ☐ Pension plan ☐ Legal rep ☐ 942 emp ☐ Subtotal ☐ Deferred compensation ☐ Void ☐	
	7 Allocated tips	8 Advance EIC payment
	9 Federal income tax withheld	10 Wages, tips, other compensation
3 Employer's identification number / 4 Employer's state I.D. number	11 Social security tax withheld	12 Social security wages
5 Employee's social security number	13 Social security tips	14 Nonqualified plans
19a Employee's name (first, middle, last)	15 Dependent care benefits	16 Fringe benefits incl. in Box 10
19b Employee's address and ZIP code	17 See Instr. for Forms W-2/W-2P	18 Other
20 / 21	22	23

24 State income tax	25 State wages, tips, etc.	26 Name of state	27 Local income tax	28 Local wages, tips, etc.	29 Name of locality

Copy A For Social Security Administration

Dept. of the Treasury—Internal Revenue Service

Form **W-2 Wage and Tax Statement 1991**

1 Control number	22222	For Paperwork Reduction Act Notice, see separate instructions OMB No 1545-0008	For Official Use Only ▶

2 Employer's name, address, and ZIP code	6 Statutory employee ☐ Deceased ☐ Pension plan ☐ Legal rep ☐ 942 emp ☐ Subtotal ☐ Deferred compensation ☐ Void ☐	
	7 Allocated tips	8 Advance EIC payment
	9 Federal income tax withheld	10 Wages, tips, other compensation
3 Employer's identification number / 4 Employer's state I.D. number	11 Social security tax withheld	12 Social security wages
5 Employee's social security number	13 Social security tips	14 Nonqualified plans
19a Employee's name (first, middle, last)	15 Dependent care benefits	16 Fringe benefits incl. in Box 10
19b Employee's address and ZIP code	17 See Instr. for Forms W-2/W-2P	18 Other
20 / 21	22	23

24 State income tax	25 State wages, tips, etc.	26 Name of state	27 Local income tax	28 Local wages, tips, etc.	29 Name of locality

Copy A For Social Security Administration

Dept. of the Treasury—Internal Revenue Service

Form **W-2 Wage and Tax Statement 1991**

Date ______________________ Name ______________________

Practical Problem 4-9

1 Control number 22222

For Paperwork Reduction Act Notice, see separate instructions
OMB No. 1545-0008

For Official Use Only ▶

2 Employer's name, address, and ZIP code

6 Statutory employee ☐ Deceased ☐ Pension plan ☐ Legal rep ☐ 942 emp ☐ Subtotal ☐ Deferred compensation ☐ Void ☐

7 Allocated tips

8 Advance EIC payment

9 Federal income tax withheld

10 Wages, tips, other compensation

3 Employer's identification number

4 Employer's state I.D. number

11 Social security tax withheld

12 Social security wages

5 Employee's social security number

13 Social security tips

14 Nonqualified plans

19a Employee's name (first, middle, last)

15 Dependent care benefits

16 Fringe benefits incl. in Box 10

17 See Instr. for Forms W-2/W-2P

18 Other

19b Employee's address and ZIP code

20

21

22

23

24 State income tax

25 State wages, tips, etc.

26 Name of state

27 Local income tax

28 Local wages, tips, etc.

29 Name of locality

Copy A For Social Security Administration

Dept. of the Treasury—Internal Revenue Service

Form **W-2 Wage and Tax Statement 1991**

1 Control number 22222

For Paperwork Reduction Act Notice, see separate instructions
OMB No. 1545-0008

For Official Use Only ▶

2 Employer's name, address, and ZIP code

6 Statutory employee ☐ Deceased ☐ Pension plan ☐ Legal rep ☐ 942 emp ☐ Subtotal ☐ Deferred compensation ☐ Void ☐

7 Allocated tips

8 Advance EIC payment

9 Federal income tax withheld

10 Wages, tips, other compensation

3 Employer's identification number

4 Employer's state I.D. number

11 Social security tax withheld

12 Social security wages

5 Employee's social security number

13 Social security tips

14 Nonqualified plans

19a Employee's name (first, middle, last)

15 Dependent care benefits

16 Fringe benefits incl. in Box 10

17 See Instr. for Forms W-2/W-2P

18 Other

19b Employee's address and ZIP code

20

21

22

23

24 State income tax

25 State wages, tips, etc.

26 Name of state

27 Local income tax

28 Local wages, tips, etc.

29 Name of locality

Copy A For Social Security Administration

Dept. of the Treasury—Internal Revenue Service

Form **W-2 Wage and Tax Statement 1991**

Date ______________________ Name ______________________

Practical Problem 4-9

1 Control number	22222	For Paperwork Reduction Act Notice, see separate instructions OMB No. 1545-0008	For Official Use Only ►
2 Employer's name, address, and ZIP code		6 Statutory employee ☐ Deceased ☐ Pension plan ☐ Legal rep ☐ 942 emp ☐ Subtotal ☐ Deferred compensation ☐ Void ☐	
		7 Allocated tips	8 Advance EIC payment
		9 Federal income tax withheld	10 Wages, tips, other compensation
3 Employer's identification number	4 Employer's state I.D. number	11 Social security tax withheld	12 Social security wages
5 Employee's social security number		13 Social security tips	14 Nonqualified plans
19a Employee's name (first, middle, last)		15 Dependent care benefits	16 Fringe benefits incl. in Box 10
19b Employee's address and ZIP code		17 See Instr. for Forms W-2/W-2P	18 Other
20	21	22	23

24 State income tax	25 State wages, tips, etc.	26 Name of state	27 Local income tax	28 Local wages, tips, etc.	29 Name of locality

Copy A For Social Security Administration

Dept. of the Treasury—Internal Revenue Service

Form **W-2 Wage and Tax Statement 1991**

1 Control number	22222	For Paperwork Reduction Act Notice, see separate instructions OMB No. 1545-0008	For Official Use Only ►
2 Employer's name, address, and ZIP code		6 Statutory employee ☐ Deceased ☐ Pension plan ☐ Legal rep ☐ 942 emp ☐ Subtotal ☐ Deferred compensation ☐ Void ☐	
		7 Allocated tips	8 Advance EIC payment
		9 Federal income tax withheld	10 Wages, tips, other compensation
3 Employer's identification number	4 Employer's state I.D. number	11 Social security tax withheld	12 Social security wages
5 Employee's social security number		13 Social security tips	14 Nonqualified plans
19a Employee's name (first, middle, last)		15 Dependent care benefits	16 Fringe benefits incl. in Box 10
19b Employee's address and ZIP code		17 See Instr. for Forms W-2/W-2P	18 Other
20	21	22	23

24 State income tax	25 State wages, tips, etc.	26 Name of state	27 Local income tax	28 Local wages, tips, etc.	29 Name of locality

Copy A For Social Security Administration

Dept. of the Treasury—Internal Revenue Service

Form **W-2 Wage and Tax Statement 1991**

CONTINUING PAYROLL PROBLEM

Refer to the partially completed payroll register upon which you were working at the end of Unit 3. You will now determine the amount of income taxes to withhold for each employee, proceeding as follows:

(1) In the appropriate columns of your payroll register, record the marital status and number of withholding allowances claimed for each employee, using the information given at the right.

(2) Record the amount of:

a. Federal income taxes (FIT) to withhold, using the wage-bracket method.

b. State income taxes (SIT). In Pennsylvania, the state tax rate is 2.1% of the worker's weekly gross earnings.

c. City income taxes (CIT). In Philadelphia, the city tax rate on residents is 4.96% of the worker's weekly gross earnings. All employees reside in Philadelphia.

Time Card No.	Marital Status	No. of Allowances
11	S	1
12	S	0
13	M	2
21	M	4
22	S	2
31	M	3
32	M	6
33	S	1
51	M	5
99	M	7

NOTE: Retain your partially completed payroll register for use at the end of Unit 5.

CASE PROBLEM

Case 4-1 Processing the Pay for a Deceased Worker

On June 1 Bill Melville called his supervisor and indicated that he was not feeling well. Later that day Melville was admitted to a hospital, where two weeks later he died. Melville's last monthly payday was on May 31. Under his company's policy Melville was entitled to full pay during the period of his absence; and upon his death, any unpaid salary was to be paid his beneficiary or estate. At the time of Melville's death, his beneficiary was given $950 representing Melville's salary for the month of June in which his death occurred, plus $750 representing the vacation allowance earned by Melville prior to his death.

a. Should federal income taxes be withheld on (1) the $950 monthly salary and (2) the $750 vacation allowance?

b. Assume that the paycheck for the month ending May 31 (from which federal income taxes had been withheld) was not cashed by Melville prior to his death. Should the employer prepare a new paycheck? If so, should the new paycheck reflect any deduction for federal income taxes?

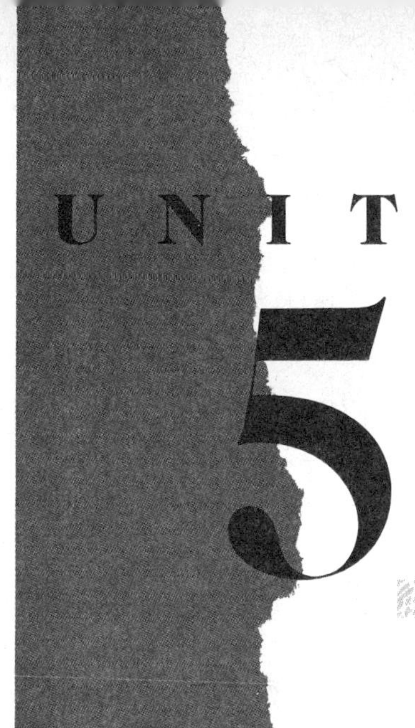

UNIT 5 Unemployment Compensation Taxes

GOALS OF THIS UNIT

After completing your study of this unit, you should be able to:

1. Describe the basic requirements for an individual to be classified as an employer or an employee under the Federal Unemployment Tax Act.
2. Understand the factors considered in determining the coverage of interstate employees.
3. Identify generally what is defined as taxable wages by the Federal Unemployment Tax Act.
4. Calculate the federal unemployment tax and the credit against this tax.
5. Describe how an experience rating system is used in determining employers' contributions to state unemployment compensation funds.
6. Complete the reports required by the Federal Unemployment Tax Act.
7. Describe the types of information reports under the various state unemployment compensation laws.
8. Understand the factors that determine eligibility for unemployment compensation benefits.

Under the Social Security Act of 1935, every state was mandated to set up an unemployment compensation program in order to provide payments to workers during periods of temporary unemployment. This unemployment insurance program is a coordinated federal-state program that is funded by payroll taxes at both federal and state levels.

Under the Federal Unemployment Tax Act (FUTA), a tax is imposed on employers and is based on wages paid for covered employment. It is not collected or deducted from employees' wages. The funds collected by the federal government as a result of this tax are used primarily to pay the cost of administering both the federal and the state unemployment insurance programs. The FUTA tax is not used for the payment of weekly benefits to unemployed workers. Such benefits are paid by the states in accordance with each state's unemployment tax law (SUTA). These unemployment benefits are paid out of each state's trust fund, which is financed by unemployment taxes levied on employers. Because all states conform to standards specified in FUTA, there is considerable uniformity in the provisions of the state unemployment compensation laws. However, there are many variations in eligibility requirements, rates of contributions, benefits paid, and duration of benefits. All the states, Puerto Rico, the Virgin Islands, and the District of Columbia have enacted unemployment compensation laws that have been approved by the Social Security Administration.

You can realize the extent of the federal-state unemployment insurance program in terms of the people involved by the fact that in October, 1990, the number of unemployed persons was 7.1 million out of a civilian labor force of about 124.8 million. At that time the jobless rate was 5.7%. *Unemployed persons* include young people seeking positions for the first time, seasonal workers unemployed a part of each year, and workers who lost their jobs through various causes and cannot find other suitable employment.

COVERAGE UNDER FUTA AND SUTA

Other than a few significant exceptions as explained in this section, the coverage under FUTA is similar to that under FICA, as described in Unit 3.

Employers—FUTA

The federal law levies a payroll tax on employers for the purpose of providing more uniform administration of the various state unemployment compensation laws. A person or a business is considered an employer if *either* of the following two tests is met:

1. Pays wages of $1,500 or more during any calendar quarter in the current or preceding calendar year.
2. Employs one or more persons, on at least some portion of one day, in each of 20 or more calendar weeks during the current or preceding taxable year.

If an individual qualifies as an employer under one of the tests, it is not necessary to meet the requirements of the alternative test.

A number of points serve to clarify the meaning of the two alternative tests: (a) a calendar week is defined as seven successive days beginning with Sunday; (b) it is not necessary that the 20 weeks be consecutive; (c) the employees need not be the same employees; (d) regular, part-time, and temporary workers are considered to be employees; (e) individuals on vacation or sick leave are counted as employees in determining the employer's status; and (f) members of a partnership are not considered to be employees.

As soon as an employer meets either test, the employer becomes liable for the FUTA tax for the entire calendar year.

EXAMPLE:

In the Vemor Company, the 20th week of having one or more employees does not occur until November of 1991. The company is liable for FUTA tax on all taxable wages paid beginning with January 1, 1991.

Once the employer status is attained, it continues for two calendar years. Thus, an employer may be covered in the second calendar year even though the coverage requirements are not met for that year. Once the second calendar year has ended, the employer's FUTA liability terminates until the coverage requirements are once again met.

Generally the nature of the business organization has no relevance in determining who is an employer. Thus, the employer may be an individual, corporation, partnership, company, association, trust, or estate. There may be instances where it is difficult to determine which of two entities is the employer for purposes of FUTA. As under FICA, the question is answered by determining which entity has the ultimate right to direct and control the employees' activities. It is not necessary that the employer actually direct or control the manner in which the services are performed; it is sufficient if the employer has the right to do so. The right to discharge is also an important factor indicating that the person possessing that right is an employer. Another factor characteristic of an employer is the furnishing of tools and a place to work for the individual who performs services.

Employers—SUTA

In general, employers specifically excluded under the federal law are also excluded under the state laws. However, as a result of variations found in state unemployment compensation laws, not all employers covered by the unemployment compensation laws of one or more states are covered by FUTA. For example, the services performed by some charitable organizations may be covered by a state's unemployment compensation act, but these same services may be exempt from FUTA coverage.

In order to have their state unemployment insurance laws approved by the federal government, the states must provide coverage for most state and local government workers, including employees in nonprofit elementary and secondary schools. In addition, coverage is extended to employers of domestic workers who pay $1,000 or more for such services in any calendar quarter of the current or preceding year. Also covered are employers of farm workers (a) who employ 10 or more farm workers during any 20 different weeks, or (b) who pay $20,000 or more in quarterly wages for farm services during the current or preceding calendar year.

Employees—FUTA

Every individual is considered an employee if the relationship between the worker and the person for whom the services are performed is the legal common-law relationship of employer and employee. This individual would then be counted in determining whether the employer is subject to FUTA. The nature of this common-law relationship is discussed in Unit 3, page 66.

No distinction is made between classes or grades of employees. Thus, superintendents, managers, and other supervisory personnel are employees. An officer of a corporation is an employee of the corporation, but a director, as such, is not.

For the purpose of the FUTA tax, the term "employee" also means any of the following who perform service for remuneration:

1. An agent-driver or a commission-driver who distributes food or beverages (other than milk) or laundry or dry-cleaning services for the principal.
2. A traveling or a city salesperson engaged in full-time soliciting and transmitting to the principal orders for merchandise for resale or supplies for use in business operations.

If a person in one of these categories has a substantial investment in facilities used to perform the services (not including transportation facilities), the individual is an independent contractor and not a covered employee. Also, individuals are not covered if their services are a single transaction that is not part of a continuing relationship with the persons for whom they are performed.

The work performed by the employee for the employer includes any services of whatever nature performed within the United States, regardless of the citizenship or residence of either. FUTA coverage also includes service of any nature performed outside the United States by a citizen of the United States for an American employer. The major exception is that service performed in Canada or in any other adjoining country with which the United States has an agreement relating to unemployment does not constitute covered employment.

An employee may perform both included and excluded employment for the same employer during a pay period. In such a case, the services which predominate in the pay period determine the employee's status with that employer for the period. Thus, where half or more of a worker's services for such pay period constitute employment, all of the services are deemed employment; if less than half of the services during the pay period constitute employment, none of the worker's services are deemed employment.

Under FUTA some services are wholly exempt from coverage. In other cases the services are exempt from coverage until the cash wages paid for the services reach a certain level. Once this level is exceeded, the services become covered employment.

Among those *excluded* from coverage in 1991 are the following:

1. Independent contractors, such as physicians, lawyers, dentists, veterinarians, contractors, subcontractors, public stenographers, auctioneers, and others who follow an independent trade, business, or profession in which they offer their services to the public.
2. Directors of corporations, unless they perform services for the corporation other than those required by attending and participating in meetings of the board of directors.
3. Members of partnerships.
4. Insurance agents or solicitors paid solely on a commission basis.
5. Agricultural laborers; however, if the employer employs 10 or more during any 20 different weeks in a year or pays $20,000 or more in a quarter during the current or preceding year, the exemption is lost.
6. Casual laborers, unless cash remuneration paid for such service is $50 or more in a calendar quarter, and the person to whom it is paid is regularly employed by the one for whom the services were performed during that period.[1]
7. Domestic workers, students or nonstudents, rendering service in a private home, local college club, or local chapter of a college fraternity or sorority. If the work is performed for an employer who paid $1,000 or more for such services in any calendar quarter of the current or preceding year, the exemption is lost.
8. Foreign students and exchange visitors who are carrying out the purposes for which they are admitted into the United States, such as in studying, teaching, or conducting research. If employed for other purposes, they would not be excluded.
9. Students enrolled full-time in a work-study or internship program, for work that is an integral part of the student's academic program.
10. Service performed by an individual for a son, daughter, or spouse, or by a child under the age of 21 for a parent.
11. Services performed by individuals in fishing and related activities if the vessel is less than ten net tons.
12. Service performed in the employ of foreign, federal, state, or local governments and certain of their instrumentalities. However, taxes imposed by FUTA apply to these federal instrumentalities: federal reserve banks, federal loan banks, and federal credit unions.
13. Government employees of international organizations, such as the United Nations.

[1]If a person works for an employer on some part of at least 24 days during the calendar quarter, he or she is considered to be regularly employed.

14. Individuals under 18 years of age who deliver or distribute newspapers or shopping news (other than delivery or distribution to any point for subsequent delivery and distribution) and retail vendors of any age who sell and distribute newspapers and magazines to the ultimate consumer.
15. Services performed by employees or employee representatives for employers covered by either the Railroad Retirement Tax Act or the Railroad Unemployment Insurance Act.
16. Services performed by a student who is enrolled and regularly attending classes at a school, college, or university, if service is performed for school, college, or university.
17. Student nurses and hospital interns.
18. Services performed in the employ of a religious, educational, or charitable organization that is exempt from federal income tax. This exemption includes service in church-sponsored elementary and secondary schools.

Employees—SUTA

The definition of "employee" as established by FUTA applies to a majority of the states, although minor variations exist in the state laws. One variation involves firms that employ persons who work in more than one state. In these cases, we must determine which state covers the workers for unemployment compensation purposes.

Coverage of Interstate Employees. An *interstate employee* is an individual who works in more than one state. To prevent duplicate contributions on the services of interstate employees, all states have adopted a uniform definition of employment in terms of where the work is localized. Under this definition, the entire services of an interstate worker are covered in one state only—that state in which the worker will most likely look for a job if he or she becomes unemployed.

The several factors that must be considered in determining coverage of interstate employees, in their order of application, are:

1. Place where the work is localized.
2. Location of base of operations.
3. Location of place from which operations are directed or controlled.
4. Location of employee's residence.

Place Where the Work is Localized. Under this main criterion of coverage adopted by the states, if all the work is performed within one state, it is clearly "localized" in that state and constitutes "employment" under the law of that state. In some cases, however, part of the person's work may be performed outside the state. In such instances the entire work may be treated as localized within the state if the services performed in other states are temporary or transitory in nature.

EXAMPLE:

Carson Thomson is a sales representative whose regular sales territory lies within Arizona. Thomson is covered by the laws of Arizona, with respect to his total employment, even though he makes frequent trips to the firm's showrooms in Los Angeles to attend sales meetings and to look over new lines of goods.

Location of Base of Operations. Often a worker may perform services continually in two or more states. In such situations it cannot be said that the employment in one state is incidental to the employment in the other state. Thus, the test of localization is not applicable since the services cannot be considered as localized within one state. Therefore, the base of operations test must be considered.

Under this test, the employee's services may be covered by the laws of a single state even though the services are not localized within that state. The base of operation is the place of a more or less permanent nature from which the employee starts work and to which he or she customarily returns. It could be a particular place where his or her (a) instructions are received, (b) business records are maintained, (c) supplies are sent, or (d) office is maintained (may be in the employee's home).

EXAMPLE:

Mitch Goldman travels through four southern states for the Irwin Company, which is headquartered in Georgia. His work is equally divided among the four states. When working in Georgia, he reports to the main office for instructions. The location of his base of operations is clearly Georgia, and his services are subject to the Georgia laws.

Location of Place from Which Operations Are Directed or Controlled. Often it may be impossible to say that an employee's services are localized in any state. Or it may be impossible to determine any base of operations of such services. If it is possible to fix the place of control in a particular state in which some service is performed, that will be the state in which the individual is covered.

EXAMPLE:

Joyce Mendes is a sales representative whose sales territory is so widespread that she does not retain any fixed business address or office. All of her orders or instructions are received by mail or wire wherever she may happen to be. Clearly the work is not localized in any state, and there is no fixed base of operations. However, the services performed by Mendes may still come under the provisions of a single state law—the law of that state in which is located the place of direction or control, provided that some of Mendes's work is also performed in that state.

Location of Employee's Residence. If an employee's coverage cannot be determined by any of the three tests described above, a final test, that of the employee's residence, is used. Thus, the worker's service is covered in its entirety in the state in which the employee lives, provided some of the service is performed in that state.

EXAMPLE:

Robert Donald is employed by the Prang Company of Indiana. He lives in Iowa, and his work territory includes Iowa, Minnesota, and Wisconsin. Since neither the base of operations nor the place from which his work is directed is in a state in which he works, he is covered in his state of residence (Iowa).

Reciprocal Arrangements and Transfers of Employment. The states have entered into several types of interstate agreements to provide unemployment insurance coverage and payment of benefits to interstate workers. These agreements are known as *reciprocal arrangements*. The most widely accepted type of interstate coverage arrangement is the Interstate Reciprocal Coverage Arrangement. Under this arrangement, an employer is permitted to elect to cover all of the services of a worker in any one state in which (a) any work is performed by the employee, or (b) the employee has his or her residence, or (c) the employer maintains the place of business. Thus, if an individual performs services for one employer in more than one state, even though some of the service is localized in one state and some in another, the worker's services may be covered under the law of one state. Once the employer chooses the state in which all the services of the interstate workers are to be covered, this state approves the election of coverage. Then, the appropriate agencies of the other states in which services are performed are notified so that they can agree to the coverage in the state of election. Over forty states subscribe to this arrangement.

Another aspect of reciprocal arrangements concerns the transfer of an employee from one state to another during the same calendar year. In all the states, an employer can include, for purposes of determining the taxable wage base, wages paid an employee with respect to employment covered by the unemployment compensation law of the previous state.

EXAMPLE:

The Karlson Company has paid wages of $4,000 to an employee in State A. During the year the employee is transferred to State B, which has a $7,000 taxable salary limitation for its state unemployment tax. The company has a credit of $4,000 against this $7,000 limit. Thus, the company has to pay State B's unemployment tax on only the next $3,000 of wages earned by that worker in State B during the remainder of the calendar year.

Wages—FUTA

As a payroll administrator, you should be familiar with the types of payments that are defined as taxable wages under FUTA since this tax is levied directly upon the employer. You may realize a direct savings in tax dollars by knowing which payments to workers constitute taxable wages.

Generally *wages* means all remuneration for employment, including the cash value of all remuneration paid in any medium other than cash, with certain exceptions.

EXAMPLE:

An exemption from FUTA exists for commissions paid to insurance agents and solicitors who are paid solely by commission.

During 1991, only the first $7,000 of remuneration paid by an employer to an employee with respect to employment during any calendar year is included in computing taxable wages. The basis upon which the remuneration is paid is immaterial. It may be paid on a piece-work basis or it may be a percentage of profits; it may be paid hourly, daily, weekly, biweekly, semimonthly, monthly, or annually.

Some of the more common types of payments made to employees and the taxability status of these payments are:

Taxable Wages for Unemployment Purposes

1. Advance payment for work to be done in the future.
2. Cash and noncash prizes and awards for doing outstanding work, for exceeding sales quotas, or for contributing suggestions that increase productivity or efficiency.
3. Bonuses as remuneration for services.
4. Christmas gifts, excluding noncash gifts of nominal value.
5. Commissions as compensation for covered employment.
6. Payments representing compensation for services by an employee which are paid to the dependents of an employee after his or her death. If the payments are in the nature of a gratuity rather than compensation for services, the payments are nontaxable. Any payments made by an employer to an employee's estate or to the employee's survivors after the calendar year in which the employee died are excluded from the definition of wages and thus may not be taxed.
7. Dismissal payments.
8. Idle time and standby payments.
9. Retroactive wage increases.
10. Transfer of stock by an employer to the employees as remuneration for services. (The fair market value of the stock at the time of payment is the taxable base.)
11. Payments under a guaranteed annual wage plan.
12. Contributions by an employer to a supplemental unemployment individual-account plan, to which the employee has a fully vested and nonforfeitable right.
13. All tips, including charged tips, reported by the employee to the employer.
14. Vacation pay.
15. Payment by the employer of the employee's FICA tax or the employee's share of any state unemployment compensation tax without deduction from the employee's wages.
16. Payments to employees or their dependents on account of sickness or accident disability. These payments are *not* taxable after the expiration of six months following the last calendar month in which the employee worked. Payments for work missed due to pregnancy are not classified as taxable wages during the first six months of absence.
17. Employer contributions to cash or deferred arrangements to the extent that the contributions are not included in the employees' gross income.

Nontaxable Wages for Unemployment Purposes

1. Advances or reimbursement of ordinary and necessary business expenses incurred in the business of the employer.
2. Bonuses under a supplemental compensation plan paid upon retirement, death, or disability of an employee.
3. Caddy fees.
4. Commissions paid to insurance agents and solicitors who are paid solely by commission. Such persons are classified as independent contractors, not employees.
5. Courtesy discounts to employees and their families.
6. Payments made by an employer under a plan established by the employer for health, accident, or life insurance, or retirement benefits on behalf of the employees or their dependents.
7. Reimbursement of an employee's moving expenses if at the time of payment, it is reasonable to believe that the employee will be entitled to a deduction for those expenses at the time of filing his or her federal income tax return.
8. Allowances made to an individual by a prospective employer for expenses incurred in connection with interviews for possible employment.
9. Retirement pay.
10. Payments made to employees from supplemental unemployment benefit funds.
11. Strike benefits paid by a union to its members.
12. Workers' compensation payments.
13. Educational assistance payments to workers. However, up to October, 1990, the maximum excludable amount for the year was $5,250. At the time of this writing, the exclusion had not yet been extended by Congress beyond October.
14. Value of meals and lodging furnished employees for the convenience of the employer.

Wages—SUTA

The definition of taxable wages is fairly uniform under the various state unemployment compensation laws. However, there are some variations among the states as to the status of particular kinds of payments. For example, about one sixth of the states have ruled that Christmas bonuses or gifts are "wages" where they are substantial, contractual, or where they are based on a percentage of the employee's wages or length of service. New Hampshire, however, provides that gifts or gratuities of $25 or less are not wages, unless paid under a contract related to past or future employment.

A further variation in defining taxable wages among the states arises in the treatment of *dismissal payments*, sometimes called payments in lieu of notice, separation pay, or terminal leave pay. Generally such payments are considered wages whether or not the employer is legally obligated to make the payments. However, in some states dismissal payments do not constitute wages unless the employer is legally required to make them. In Puerto Rico, no type of dismissal payment is considered to be wages.

UNEMPLOYMENT COMPENSATION TAXES AND CREDITS

The base of the unemployment compensation tax is wages *paid* rather than *wages payable*. Thus, an employer is liable for the unemployment compensation tax in the year in which wages are paid employees, not necessarily in the year in which the services are rendered. Thus, if an employee performs services in 1991 but is not paid for them until 1992, the employer is liable for the tax in 1992 and the 1992 tax rates apply.

Wages are considered paid when they are actually paid or when they are *constructively paid*. Wages are considered constructively paid when credited to the account of, or set apart for, an employee so that they may be drawn upon at any time, even though they are not actually possessed by the employee.

Tax Rate—FUTA

Under FUTA, all employers, as defined earlier, are subject to a tax with respect to having individuals in their employ. For 1991, the employer's tax rate is 6.2% of the first $7,000 wages paid each employee during the calendar year. Thus, an employer is liable for the FUTA tax on wages paid each employee until the employee's wages reach the $7,000 level. If an employee has more than one employer during the current year, the taxable wage base applies separately to each of those employers, unless one employer has transferred the business to the second.

EXAMPLE:

Assume that in 1991 an employer had charged the wages account for $63,910. Of this amount, $720 will not be paid until the first payday in 1992. Further, the wages actually paid to employees in 1991 in excess of $7,000 each amounted to $19,840. The gross FUTA tax imposed on the employer is computed as follows:

Total amount charged to wages during 1991		$63,910.00
Less:		
Wages not to be paid until 1992	$ 720	
Wages paid in excess of $7,000 limit	19,840	20,560.00
Total taxable wages		$43,350.00
Rate of tax		6.2%
Amount of gross FUTA tax		$ 2,687.70

Credits Against FUTA Tax. Employers are entitled to a credit against their FUTA tax liability for contributions made under approved state unemployment compensation laws. The maximum credit permitted is 5.4%. Thus, in the preceding example where the *gross* FUTA tax rate is 6.2%, the *net* FUTA rate would be .8% if the full 5.4% credit applied. The net FUTA tax may be calculated in two ways:

EXAMPLES:

1. Total taxable earnings (above example)		$43,350.00
Net rate of tax (6.2% – 5.4%)		.8%
Amount of net FUTA tax		$ 346.80
2. Amount of gross FUTA tax		$ 2,687.70
Total taxable wages	$43,350	
Credit against tax	5.4%	
Total credit		2,340.90
Amount of net FUTA tax		$ 346.80

To obtain the maximum credit of 5.4% against the federal tax, the employer must make the state contributions on or before the due date for filing the annual return under FUTA (see page 175). If the employer is tardy in paying the state contributions, the maximum credit that the employer may claim against the federal tax is 95% of 5.4%, or 5.13%.

EXAMPLE:

The Sutcliffe Company had taxable wages totaling $87,500 in 1991. During the year the company was late in paying its state contributions. The penalty for tardiness is shown in the following calculation of the firm's net FUTA tax for 1991:

Amount of gross FUTA tax ($87,500 x 6.2%)		$5,425.00
Total taxable wages	$87,500	
Credit against tax	5.13%	
Total credit		4,488.75
Amount of net FUTA tax ($87,500 x 1.07%)		$ 936.25

If the company had made timely payments of its state contributions, the amount of its net FUTA tax would have

been reduced to $700, for a savings of $236.25, as shown below.

Amount of gross FUTA tax ($87,500 x 6.2%)		**$5,425.00**
Total taxable wages	**$87,500**	
Credit against tax	**5.4%**	
Total credit		**4,725.00**
Amount of net FUTA tax ($87,500 x .8%) ...		**$ 700.00**

$936.25 – $700.00 = $236.25, savings

Experience Rating. In some cases, employers are permitted to pay contributions into their state unemployment fund at a rate lower than 5.4%. The method by which the employer contributions may be adjusted because of a favorable employment record is referred to as *experience rating* or *merit rating*. Thus, an employer's favorable experience rate (employment record) qualifies the employer for a SUTA rate lower than 5.4%. In such a case, FUTA provides for a credit equal to the employer's SUTA rate plus an additional credit so that the full 5.4% credit still applies. In this way, employers who have steady employment histories and, therefore, lower SUTA tax rates, are not penalized when the FUTA tax is paid.

EXAMPLE:

The Jaro Company pays taxable wages of $88,000 during 1991. The state's unemployment compensation law sets a range of unemployment tax rates from 2.7% to 6.8% under its experience rating system. Because of its past employment record, the Jaro Company is taxed at the rate of 4.4% by the state for 1991. The computation of the net FUTA and SUTA taxes is:

SUTA tax: 4.4% of $88,000 = $3,872		
Gross federal tax: 6.2% of $88,000		**$5,456**
Less credits against tax:		
Contributions actually paid to state	**$3,872**	
Additional credit*	**880**	**4,752**
Remainder of tax (net FUTA) ($88,000 x .8%)		**$ 704**

***The additional credit is computed as follows:**

SUTA tax, had the rate been 5.4%	**$4,752**
Contributions at experience rate (4.4%)	**3,872**
Additional credit allowed	**$ 880**

The Jaro Company is entitled to the maximum credit of 5.4%, even though the contributions paid to the state amounted to only 4.4%. Since the Jaro Company paid only $3,872 to the state fund and $704 to the federal fund, the total unemployment tax amounted to $4,576, or 5.2% of taxable wages. Thus, due to the experience rating of the employer, there was a savings of 1.0% (6.2% – 5.2%) in the combined tax.

Where contributions are paid into more than one state unemployment compensation fund, the credit against the federal tax is based on the contributions paid to each state. In some states the contribution rate might be less than 5.4%; however, the employer would receive the 5.4% credit against the gross FUTA tax. In those states where the employer's SUTA contribution is more than 5.4%, the credit against the gross FUTA tax is limited to 5.4%.

EXAMPLE:

The contribution rate of Domski Supply in Kansas is 5.5% and in Missouri, 2%. The credit against the gross FUTA tax on the wages paid is 5.4% in each state.

Under the unemployment compensation laws of certain states, the taxable wage base is set at a figure higher than the first $7,000 paid to each employee. For example, in Arkansas, the wage base for 1991 was the first $8,000. In such states, the total contributions that the employer is required to pay into the state fund may exceed 5.4% of the taxable wages as established by FUTA (first $7,000 of each employee's earnings). However, the maximum credit that can be claimed against the gross FUTA tax for the state contributions is 5.4% of the first $7,000 of each individual employee's earnings.

Title XII Advances. States, who due to financial difficulties cannot pay their unemployment compensation benefits, may borrow funds from the federal government under Title XII of the Social Security Act. These funds, called *Title XII advances*, are used by the states to pay their regular unemployment benefits.

Under the repayment provisions established by the federal government, if a state defaults in its payments, the credit against the gross FUTA tax is reduced by 5% beginning the second taxable year after the advance. This penalty is increased by an additional 5% for each succeeding year in which there is a balance due the federal government. Thus, employers in the affected states have their gross FUTA tax rate increased by 0.3% (5% of 5.4%) the second year after the advance, then by 0.6%, 0.9%, etc.

However, a cap—a limitation on the amount the federal credit may be reduced—has been established for states that meet certain solvency requirements as determined by the Secretary of Labor. The determination of the credit reduction is made on or before November 10 of each year. The credit reduction (cap) applicable to employers in the affected states is limited to 0.6%. In 1983, legislation was enacted that enabled other states that did not qualify for the total cap to have their annual credit reduction decreased by 0.1% or 0.2% if they met some of the solvency requirements. In 1990, the credit reduction did not apply to any state.

2. **John Garrison works in Puerto Rico, and earns $450 each week. He would contribute $1.35 (.3% of $450) of each pay to a disability fund. This .3% deduction would continue until his cumulative pay for the year reached $9,000.**

Tax Rates—SUTA

A summary of each state's 1990 unemployment compensation laws, including the tax rates and the wage limitations, is presented in Illustration 5-1 on pages 172 and 173.

The tax rate applied to each employer within a particular state yields the funds used by that state in paying benefits to its unemployed workers. Currently, all states have enacted *pooled-fund laws* as a basis for their unemployment insurance systems. By means of pooled funds, the cost of unemployment benefits is spread among all the employers in a particular state.

Employer Contributions. Every state has its own unemployment compensation law with varying tax rates and taxable wage bases. To minimize the impact of unemployment insurance taxes on newly covered employers, each state sets an initial contributions rate for new employers that will apply for a specific period of time. During this period of time the new employer's employment record can be developed and an experience rating later established. A state may assign a contributions rate of not less than 1% to newly covered employers on some "reasonable basis" other than employment experience. Once the new employer has accumulated the experience required under the provisions of the state law, a new rate will be assigned. For example, in Pennsylvania, the rate applied to certain new employers in the construction industry is 9.7%; other newly liable employers pay 3.5%.

Employee Contributions. Some states, as shown in Illustration 5-1, impose a contributions requirement on employees in addition to the contributions made by the employer.

EXAMPLES:

1. **Fay Nannen earns $320 during the first week of February while working for Dango, Inc. Since the company is located in New Jersey, Nannen would have $3.60 deducted from her pay (1.125% of $320). This 1.125% tax would be deducted on the first $13,900 paid to her during the year. (In New Jersey, .5% of the employees' contributions is for the disability benefit plan and .625% for the unemployment insurance fund.)**

Experience Rating. As indicated earlier, the concept of experience rating is based upon the payment of state unemployment taxes according to the employer's stability of employment. As an employer experiences a lower employee turnover, generally the state unemployment tax rate is lower. Similarly, a high employee turnover generally leads to a higher tax rate. By qualifying for reduced state unemployment contributions, an employer can realize substantial tax savings.

In all states, some type of experience-rating plan provides for a reduction in the employer's tax contributions based on the employer's experience with the risk of unemployment. Of the several formulas used to determine the contribution rates, the most commonly used is the *reserve-ratio formula*:

$$\text{Reserve Ratio} = \frac{\text{Contributions less Benefits Paid}}{\text{Average Payroll}}$$

The amount of the unemployment compensation contributions (taxes paid), the benefits paid by the state, and the employer's payroll are entered by the state on each employer's record. The benefits paid are subtracted from the contributions, and the balance of the employer's account is divided by the average payroll for a stated period of time to determine the reserve ratio.

Under this plan, the balance carried forward each year is the difference between the employer's total contributions and the total benefits paid to former employees by the state. Employers must accumulate and maintain a specified reserve before their contribution rate can be reduced. The contribution rates are established according to a schedule under which the higher the reserve ratio, the lower the tax rate. The formula is designed to make sure that no employers are granted a rate reduction unless during the year they contribute more to the fund than has been withdrawn.

Employers who have built up a balance in their reserve account (contributions paid in less benefits charged) are sometimes referred to as *positive-balance employers*. The larger the positive balance in a company's reserve account, the lower will be its tax rate. Employers whose reserve accounts have been charged for more benefits paid out than contributions paid in are referred to as *negative-balance employers*, and their high tax rates reflect this fact.

SUMMARY OF STATE UNEMPLOYMENT COMPENSATION LAWS (1990)

Warning: The provisions of the state laws are subject to change at any time.

State	Size of Firm (1 employee in specified time and/or size of payroll[1])	Contributions (On first $7,000 unless otherwise indicated)		Benefits (Excluding dependency allowances)			
		Employer Min.-Max.	Employee	Waiting Period (weeks)	Max. per Week	Min. per Week	Max. Duration (weeks)
ALABAMA	20 weeks	0.5%-5.4% on first $8,000		none	$145	$22	26
ALASKA	any time	2.2%-6.25% on first $20,900	.7% on first $20,900	1	212	44	26
ARIZONA	20 weeks	0.1%-5.4%		1	165	15	26
ARKANSAS	10 days	0.5%-6.4% on first $7,500		1	220	39	26
CALIFORNIA	over $100 in any calendar quarter	0.4%-5.5%	0.9% on first $21,900 (disability ins.)	1	166	30	26
COLORADO	any time	0.2%-5.4% on first $10,000		1	229	25	26
CONNECTICUT	20 weeks	1.2%-6.1% on first $7,100		none	270	15	26
DELAWARE	20 weeks	1.0%-9.5% on first $8,500		none	225	20	26
DISTRICT OF COLUMBIA	any time	0.8%-5.4% on first $8,000		1	293	13	26
FLORIDA	20 weeks	0.1%-5.4%		1	225	10	26
GEORGIA	20 weeks	0.06%-8.64% on first $7,500		1	165	37	26
HAWAII	any time	0.0%-5.4% on first $18,600	.5% of weekly wages, not to exceed $2.32 per week (disability ins.)	1	239	5	26
IDAHO	20 weeks or $300 in any calendar quarter	0.5%-5.4% on first $16,800		1	206	44	26
ILLINOIS	20 weeks	0.6%-6.9% on first $9,000		1	199	51	26
INDIANA	20 weeks	0.3%-5.4%		1	96	40	26
IOWA	20 weeks	0.6%-8.46% on first $11,500		1	186	27	26
KANSAS	20 weeks	0.06%-6.4% on first $8,000		1	222	55	26
KENTUCKY	20 weeks	0.3%-9.0% on first $8,000		none	186	22	26
LOUISIANA	20 weeks	0.27%-5.59% on first $8,500		1	181	10	26
MAINE	20 weeks	1.7%-5.8%		1	188	29	26
MARYLAND	any time	0.1%-6.0%		none	215	25	26
MASSACHUSETTS	13 weeks or more than $200 per quarter	1.8%-6.0%		1	282	14	30
MICHIGAN	20 weeks or $1,000 in calendar year	1.0%-10.0% on first $9,500		none	275	59	26
MINNESOTA	20 weeks	0.2%-9.1% on first $13,300		1	260	38	26
MISSISSIPPI	20 weeks	0.1%-5.4%		1	145	30	26
MISSOURI	20 weeks	0.0%-6.0%		1	150	33	26
MONTANA	over $1,000 in current or preceding year	0.3%-6.4% on first $13,200		1	193	48	26
NEBRASKA	20 weeks	0.1%-5.4%		1	144	20	26

[1]$1,500 in any calendar quarter in current or preceding calendar year unless otherwise specified.

Illustration 5-1. Summary of State Unemployment Compensation Laws (1990)

SUMMARY OF STATE UNEMPLOYMENT COMPENSATION LAWS (1990)

Warning: The provisions of the state laws are subject to change at any time.

State	Size of Firm (1 employee in specified time and/or size of payroll[1])	Contributions (On first $7,000 unless otherwise indicated)		Benefits (Excluding dependency allowances)			
		Employer Min.-Max.	Employee	Waiting Period (weeks)	Max. per Week	Min. per Week	Max. Duration (weeks)
NEVADA	$225 in any quarter	0.25%-5.4% on first $12,600		none	$202	$16	26
NEW HAMPSHIRE	20 weeks	0.01%-6.5%		none	156	39	26
NEW JERSEY	$1,000 in any year	0.4%-5.4% on first $13,900	1.125% (.5% for disability ins.; .625% for unempl. comp.)	1	258	51	26
NEW MEXICO	20 weeks or $450 in any quarter	0.6%-5.4% on first $11,100		1	170	34	26
NEW YORK	$300 in any quarter	0.3%-5.4%	.5% of weekly wages, not to exceed 60¢ per week (disability ins.)	1	245	80	26
NORTH CAROLINA	20 weeks	0.012%-6.84% on first $11,100		1	245	21	26
NORTH DAKOTA	20 weeks	0.6%-6.6% on first $11,200		1	198	43	26
OHIO	20 weeks	0.1%-6.5% on first $8,000		1	184	10	26
OKLAHOMA	20 weeks	0.2%-8.3% on first $9,500		1	197	16	26
OREGON	18 weeks or $225 in any quarter	1.8%-5.4% on first $16,000		1	238	55	26
PENNSYLVANIA	any time	1.5%-9.2% on first $8,000		1	280	35	26
PUERTO RICO	any time	5.4%	.3% on first $9,000 (disability ins.)	1	120	7	20
RHODE ISLAND	any time	1.4%-7.3% on first $13,800	1.0% on first $22,500 (disability ins.)	1	269	37	26
SOUTH CAROLINA	20 weeks	1.3%-5.4%		1	175	20	26
SOUTH DAKOTA	20 weeks	0.05%-8.7%		1	140	28	26
TENNESSEE	20 weeks	0.5%-10.0%		1	155	30	26
TEXAS	20 weeks	0.29%-6.29% on first $9,000		1	224	37	26
UTAH	$140 in calendar quarter in current or preceding calendar year	0.6%-8.0% on first $14,000		1	214	10	26
VERMONT	20 weeks	0.65%-5.95% on first $8,000		1	169	25	26
VIRGIN ISLANDS	any time	0.1%-9.0% on first $17,000		1	163	15	26
VIRGINIA	20 weeks	0.1%-6.2% on first $8,000		none	198	60	26
WASHINGTON	any time	0.5%-5.42% on first $16,800		1	246	61	30
WEST VIRGINIA	20 weeks	0.5%-7.5% on first $8,000		1	251	24	28
WISCONSIN	20 weeks	0.05%-9.8% on first $10,500		none	225	42	26
WYOMING	$500 in current or preceding calendar year	1.25%-9.75% on first $10,400		1	200	38	26

[1] $1,500 in any calendar quarter in current or preceding calendar year unless otherwise specified.

Illustration 5-1. (Concluded) Summary of State Unemployment Compensation Laws (1990)

Calculating the Contribution Rate. In an experience-rating system, the rate of contributions for employers is based on the employment experience of the employer. The rate is determined by computing the total of the reserve built up by employer contributions over a certain period of time and by determining the ratio of the amount in the reserve account to the employer's average annual payroll as determined under the state's formula.

EXAMPLE:

The Parson Company is an employer located in a state with an unemployment compensation law containing merit-rating provisions for employers who meet certain requirements. Below is a summary of the total wages for the years 1987 to 1990, inclusive. For the purpose of the illustration, assume that the total wages and taxable wages are the same amount.

Quarter	1987	1988	1989	1990
1st	$11,000	$10,000	$ 8,500	$10,500
2d	10,000	9,000	9,500	11,000
3d	10,000	9,500	10,000	11,000
4th	10,500	9,750	9,500	9,500
Total	$41,500	$38,250	$37,500	$42,000

A separate account is maintained by the State Unemployment Compensation Commission for each employer. The account is credited with contributions paid into the unemployment compensation fund by the employer and is charged with unemployment benefits that are paid from the fund.

For 1991, the state law set up the following contribution rate schedule for employers:

Reserve Ratio	Rate
Negative reserve balance	6.7%
0.0% to less than 8%	5.9%
8% to less than 10%	5.0%
10% to less than 12%	4.1%
12% to less than 15%	3.2%
15% and over	2.5%

The state law under discussion defines "annual payroll" as the wages paid during a 12-month period ending with the last day of the third quarter of any calendar year. The average annual payroll is the average of the last three annual payrolls.

The following computations show the state contributions made by the Parson Company for the calendar years 1987 to 1990, inclusive, the federal tax imposed under FUTA, and the method of arriving at the contribution rate for the calendar year 1991:

1987

Taxable wages	$41,500	
Rate (SUTA)	x 2.7%	
State contributions:		$1,120.50
Federal tax: .8% of $41,500		332.00
Total unemployment tax		$1,452.50

1988

Taxable wages	$38,250	
Rate (SUTA)	x 2.7%	
State contributions:		$1,032.75
Federal tax: .8% of $38,250		306.00
Total unemployment tax		$1,338.75

1989

Taxable wages	$37,500	
Rate (SUTA)	x 3.4%	
State contributions:		$1,275.00
Federal tax: .8% of $37,500		300.00
Total unemployment tax		$1,575.00

1990

Taxable wages	$42,000	
Rate (SUTA)	x 3.7%	
State contributions:		$1,554.00
Federal tax: .8% of $42,000		336.00
Total unemployment tax		$1,890.00

In computing the average annual payroll and the ratio of the balance in the reserve account to the average annual payroll, you must remember that the average annual payroll is the average of the last three annual payrolls, with each annual payroll period running from October 1 to September 30.

Assume that the Parson Company paid state contributions of $960 in 1985 and $1,010 in 1986 and that $1,850 was charged to the employer's account for unemployment compensation benefits during 1989 and 1990. The contribution rate for 1991 is computed as follows:

Computation of rate for 1991:

Annual payroll period ending 9/30/88	$ 39,000
Annual payroll period ending 9/30/89	37,750
Annual payroll period ending 9/30/90	42,000
Total of last 3 annual payroll periods	$118,750

Average annual payroll:

$118,750 divided by 3 = $39,583

Contributions for 1985	$ 960.00
Contributions for 1986	1,010.00
Contributions for 1987	1,120.50
Contributions for 1988	1,032.75
Contributions for 1989	1,275.00
Contributions for 1990 (first nine months)	1,202.50
Total contributions	$6,600.75
Less amount of benefits paid	1,850.00
Balance in reserve account 9/30/90	$4,750.75

$4,750.75, divided by average annual payroll, $39,583 = 12%

Since the reserve is 12% of the average annual payroll, the tax rate for 1991 is 3.2% (the ratio is between 12% and 15%).

Voluntary Contributions. In about half the states, employers may obtain reduced unemployment compensation rates by making *voluntary contributions* to the state fund. These contributions are deliberately made by employers in addition to their regularly required payments of state unemployment taxes. The purpose of voluntary contributions is to increase the balance in the employer's reserve account so that a lower contributions rate may be assigned for the following year. Thus, the new lower tax rate will save the employer more in future state unemployment tax payments than the amount of the voluntary contribution itself.

EXAMPLE:

To illustrate the tax saving that may be realized as a result of making voluntary contributions, consider the following case of the Werner Company, which is subject to the unemployment compensation law of a state that uses the reserve-ratio formula to determine experience ratings. The following contribution rate schedule will be in effect for 1992:

Reserve Ratio	Rate
0.0% to less than 1%	6.2%
1.0% to less than 1.4%	5.6%
1.4% to less than 1.8%	5.0%
1.8% to less than 2.2%	4.4%
2.2% to less than 2.6%	3.8%
2.6% to less than 3.0%	3.2%
3.0% and over	2.6%

For the three 12-month periods ending on June 30, 1991, the company had an average annual taxable payroll of $330,000. This is the base that the state uses as the average payroll. As of June 30, 1991, the credits to the employer's account exceeded the benefits paid by $6,800. Thus, the 1992 reserve ratio is 2.06% ($6,800 ÷ $330,000), which would result in the assignment of a 4.4% tax rate, as shown in the preceding table. If the employer's 1992 total taxable payroll were $390,000, the SUTA contribution would amount to $17,160.

If the Werner Company makes a voluntary contribution into the state fund within the time period specified by the state law, the tax for 1992 will be less. For example, if a $460 contribution is made, the reserve ratio will be 2.2% ($7,260 ÷ $330,000). As a result, the tax rate will be reduced to 3.8%, with the following savings realized in 1992:

Tax Payment with No Voluntary Contribution (4.4% x $390,000) =		$17,160
Tax Payment with Voluntary Contribution	$ 460	
(3.8% x $390,000) =	14,820	15,280
Tax Savings		$ 1,880

An employer who desires to make a voluntary contribution usually must determine without the aid of the state administrative agency the amount of the contribution needed in order to obtain a lower contribution rate. In some states, the agencies provide worksheets that aid employers in determining the amount of voluntary contributions required. If the amount of voluntary contribution is not sufficient to bring about a reduction in the employer's contribution rate, the contribution ordinarily will not be refunded. Instead, the state may give the employer credit against any future SUTA taxes due.

As with the regular contributions, the state must receive the voluntary contributions by a certain date before they can be credited to the employer's account and be used in computing a new tax rate. In some states, the employer may have a certain number of days following the mailing of the tax rate notice to make the voluntary contributions. For instance, in Arizona and New York, the voluntary contributions must be paid by January 31. In West Virginia, the contribution must be sent in within 30 days of the mailing of the tax notice.

UNEMPLOYMENT COMPENSATION REPORTS REQUIRED OF THE EMPLOYER

Employers liable for both the FUTA and the SUTA tax must file periodic reports with both the federal and the state governments. For FUTA tax reporting, there is an annual return (either Form 940 or 940-EZ) and a tax deposit form (Form 8109). Employers covered by state unemployment compensation laws are also generally required to submit two major kinds of reports. One is a tax return, on which the employer reports the tax due the state. The other is a wage report, which reflects the amount of taxable wages paid to each of the employer's covered employees.

Annual FUTA Return—Form 940

Form 940, Employer's Annual Federal Unemployment (FUTA) Tax Return, is the prescribed form for making the return required of employers in reporting the tax imposed under FUTA. A filled-in copy of this form is reproduced in Illustration 5-2 on page 176.

Completing the Return. All employers complete Questions A and B and Part I. Part II of the form is completed by employers:

1. Who pay contributions to only one state unemployment fund.
2. Who paid all contributions to the state by the due date of Form 940.
3. Whose total FUTA wages were subject to the unemployment fund of the one state.

Other employers complete Parts III and V.

Form **940**
Department of the Treasury
Internal Revenue Service

Employer's Annual Federal Unemployment (FUTA) Tax Return

▶ For Paperwork Reduction Act Notice, see page 2.

OMB No. 1545-0028
1991

T	
FF	
FD	
FP	
I	
T	

If incorrect, make any necessary change. ▶

Name (as distinguished from trade name)
Calendar year 1991

Trade name, if any
SHANNON HEATING COMPANY

Address and ZIP code
P.O. BOX 1803 LANSDOWNE, PA 19019-3636

Employer identification number 79 - 2360320

A Did you pay all required contributions to state unemployment funds by the due date of Form 940? (See instructions if none required.) . . . . ☒ Yes ☐ No
If you checked the "Yes" box, enter the amount of contributions paid to state unemployment funds . . . . ▶ $ 1,382|33

B Are you required to pay contributions to only one state? . . . . . . ☐ Yes ☒ No
If you checked the "Yes" box: (1) Enter the name of the state where you are required to pay contributions . . . . ▶ ________
(2) Enter your state reporting number(s) as shown on state unemployment tax return. ▶ ________

C If any part of wages taxable for FUTA tax is exempt from state unemployment tax, check the box. (See the Specific Instructions on page 2.). . . . . . ☐

Note: *If you checked the "Yes" boxes in both questions A and B and did not check the box in C above, you may be able to use Form 940-EZ.*

Part I Computation of Taxable Wages (to be completed by all taxpayers)

			Amount paid		
1	Total payments (including exempt payments) during the calendar year for services of employees			1	85,730 42
2	Exempt payments. (Explain each exemption shown, attaching additional sheets if necessary.) ▶ ________	2			
3	Payments for services of more than $7,000. Enter only the excess over the first $7,000 paid to individual employees not including exempt amounts shown on line 2. Do not use the state wage limitation.	3	25,317 62		
4	Total exempt payments (add lines 2 and 3)			4	25,317 62
5	Total taxable wages (subtract line 4 from line 1). (If any part is exempt from state contributions, see instructions.) ▶			5	60,412 80

Part II Tax Due or Refund (Complete if you checked the "Yes" boxes in both questions A and B and did not check the box in C above.)

1	Total FUTA tax. Multiply the wages in Part I, line 5, by .008 and enter here.	1	
2	Total FUTA tax deposited for the year, including any overpayment applied from a prior year (from your records) . .	2	
3	Balance due (subtract line 2 from line 1). This should be $100 or less. Pay to IRS . . . . ▶	3	
4	Overpayment (subtract line 1 from line 2). Check if it is to be: ☐ Applied to next return, or ☐ Refunded ▶	4	

Part III Tax Due or Refund (Complete if you checked the "No" box in either question A or B or you checked the box in C above. Also complete Part V.)

1	Gross FUTA tax. Multiply the wages in Part I, line 5, by .062			1	3,745 59
2	Maximum credit. Multiply the wages in Part I, line 5, by .054	2	3,262 29		
3	Credit allowable: Enter the smaller of the amount in Part V, line 11, or Part III, line 2 . .	3	3,262 29		
4	Total FUTA tax (subtract line 3 from line 1).			4	483 30
5	Total FUTA tax deposited for the year, including any overpayment applied from a prior year (from your records)			5	483 30
6	Balance due (subtract line 5 from line 4). This should be $100 or less. Pay to IRS . . . . ▶			6	-0-
7	Overpayment (subtract line 4 from line 5). Check if it is to be: ☐ Applied to next return, or ☐ Refunded ▶			7	

Part IV Record of Quarterly Federal Tax Liability for Unemployment Tax (Do not include state liability.)

Quarter	First	Second	Third	Fourth	Total for Year
Liability for quarter	203.42	159.95	98.83	21.10	483.30

Part V Computation of Tentative Credit (Complete if you checked the "No" box in either question A or B or you checked the box in C above—see instructions.)

Name of state	State reporting number(s) as shown on employer's state contribution returns	Taxable payroll (as defined in state act)	State experience rate period 4		State experience rate	Contributions if rate had been 5.4% (col. 3 x .054)	Contributions payable at experience rate (col. 3 x col. 5)	Additional credit (col. 6 minus col. 7) If 0 or less, enter 0.	Contributions actually paid to the state
1	2	3	From—	To—	5	6	7	8	9
PA	20747	40,000.00	1/1	12/31	2.4	2,160.00	960.00	1,200.00	960.00
IN	83-48032	7,040.58	1/1	12/31	2.2	380.19	154.89	225.30	154.89
KY	7321	13,372.22	1/1	12/31	2.0	722.10	267.44	454.66	267.44
10 Totals . . . . ▶		60,412.80						1,879.96	1,382.33

11 Total tentative credit (add line 10, columns 8 and 9 only—see instructions for limitations) . . . . . . ▶ 3,262 29

If you will not have to file returns in the future, write "Final" here (see general instruction "Who Must File") and sign the return. ▶

Under penalties of perjury, I declare that I have examined this return, including accompanying schedules and statements, and to the best of my knowledge and belief, it is true, correct, and complete, and that no part of any payment made to a state unemployment fund claimed as a credit was or is to be deducted from the payments to employees.

Signature ▶ J. D. Shannon   Title (Owner, etc.) ▶ Owner   Date ▶ 1/31/92

Form 940

Illustration 5-2. Form 940, Employer's Annual Federal Unemployment (FUTA) Tax Return

The specific information needed to complete Form 940 may be obtained from the sources listed in Illustration 5-3.

Payment of Balance Due. After calculating the final net FUTA tax (Line 1, Part II, or Line 4, Part III), the employer compares the net tax with the total deposits for the year in order to determine the balance due. Depending on the amount of the liability, the employer either deposits the balance due or remits it with Form 940 directly to the IRS.

SOURCES OF INFORMATION FOR COMPLETING FORM 940

Line No.	Source of Information
A	General ledger account for SUTA Taxes Payable
B	State unemployment tax forms
C	State unemployment tax forms
Part I—Computation of Taxable Wages	
1	General ledger account(s) for wages and salaries
2	Personnel records, time sheets, and employee earnings records
3	Employee earnings records
4	Follow directions for addition.
5	Follow directions for subtraction.
Part II—Tax Due or Refund	
1	Follow directions for multiplication.
2	General ledger account for FUTA Taxes Payable
3 and 4	Compare the net tax with the total deposits for the year.
Part III—Tax Due or Refund	
1 and 2	Follow directions for multiplication.
3	Determine the smaller of Part V, line 11, or Part III, line 2.
4	Follow directions for subtraction.
5	General ledger account for FUTA Taxes Payable
6 and 7	Compare the net tax with the total deposits for the year.
Part IV—Record of Quarterly Federal Tax Liability for Unemployment Tax	
1 through 5	From the appropriate states' unemployment tax returns
6 through 8	Follow mathematical instructions.
9	States' unemployment tax returns
10	Add Column 3.
11	Add totals of Columns 8 and 9.

Illustration 5-3. Sources of Information for Completing Form 940

Signing Form 940. Form 940 must be signed by:

1. The individual, if the employer is an individual.
2. The president, vice-president, or other principal officer, if the employer is a corporation.
3. A responsible and duly authorized member, if the employer is a partnership or other unincorporated organization.
4. A fiduciary, if the employer is a trust or estate.

Filing the Return. The employer must file the annual return not later than January 31 next following the close of the calendar year. If, however, the employer has made timely deposits that pay the FUTA tax liability in full, as discussed below, we may delay the filing of Form 940 until February 10. We must file the return on a calendar-year basis even though our company operates on a fiscal-year basis different from the calendar year. If January 31 falls on Saturday, Sunday, or a legal holiday, we may file the return on the following business day.

A mailed return bearing a postmark indicating it was mailed on or before the due date will be considered to have been timely filed even though it is received after the due date. If we send the return by registered mail, the date of registration is treated as the postmark date. If we send the return by certified mail, the postmark date on the employer's receipt is treated as the postmark date.

Upon application of the employer, the district director or the director of a service center may grant a reasonable extension of time in which to file the return, but not for payment of the tax. However, no extension will be granted for a period longer than 90 days. Generally, we must file the application for an extension in writing on or before the due date for filing the return.

We must file the return with the IRS center for the district in which our employer's principal place of business or office or agency is located. The locations of the IRS centers are given in Illustration 3-10, page 86.

If Form 940 is not available, the employer may make a statement disclosing the amount of wages paid and the amount of tax due. This statement will be accepted as a tentative return until the return is made on the proper form. A privately designed and printed or a computer-prepared substitute Form 940 is permitted if certain IRS specifications are met. For specific approval, a sample of the new form must be sent to the IRS.

Revenue Procedures have been issued for magnetic media filing of Form 940 by reporting agents. A letter of application must first be filed with the appropriate Internal Revenue Service Center if the agents desire to use this method of filing.

Once an employer has filed Form 940, the IRS will send the employer a preaddressed Form 940 near the close of each subsequent calendar year. In addition, a Federal Tax Deposit Coupon Book, Form 8109, will be mailed to the employer.

The IRS has undertaken a program to aid in ensuring that employers file their FUTA returns. Under this program the IRS matches its computer records to determine if employers who file Form 941, the Employer's Quarterly Federal Tax Return, have also filed Form 940. As a result of such comparisons, those employers who should have filed Form 940 but did not do so are then contacted by the IRS; for generally if an employer is required to file Form 941, Form 940 must also be filed.

Annual FUTA Return—Form 940-EZ

A streamlined Form 940 is available for employers who have uncomplicated tax situations. In order to use *Form 940-EZ, Employer's Annual Federal Unemployment (FUTA) Tax Return,* an employer must satisfy three simple tests:

1. Must have paid state unemployment taxes to only one state.
2. Must have made the state unemployment tax payments by the due date of Form 940-EZ.
3. All wages that were taxable for FUTA purposes were also taxable for state unemployment tax purposes.

As you can see from Illustration 5-4, Form 940-EZ, many payroll managers will have an easier time completing this year-end tax report than Form 940. This time-saving feature is apparent when you compare the IRS's estimates of the average time spent in completing the two forms:

	940	940-EZ
Recordkeeping	14 hours	5½ hours
Studying the form	18 minutes	7 minutes
Completing the form ..	32 minutes	26 minutes

Quarterly Deposit Form—FUTA

We compute the net FUTA tax on a quarterly basis during the month following the end of each calendar quarter. We determine the tax by multiplying .8% by that part of the first $7,000 of each of the employee's annual wages that the employer paid during the quarter. If the employer's tax liability is more than $100, we must deposit it with a Federal Reserve bank or an authorized commercial bank on or before the last day of the month following the end of the quarter. The deposit is considered timely if the bank receives it by the due date or if the employer can establish that it was mailed two days before the due date. We make a similar computation and deposit for each of the first three quarters of the year. Each quarterly deposit is to be accompanied by a preinscribed *Federal Tax Deposit Coupon (Form 8109).* A filled-in copy of this deposit form is reproduced in Illustration 5-5 on page 180.

If the tax liability for the first quarter is $100 or less, a deposit is not required; however, we must add the amount of the liability to the amount subject to deposit for the next quarter, in order to compare the tax due with the $100 minimum for that quarter.

EXAMPLE:

As shown in Illustration 5-2, page 176, the tax liability of the Shannon Heating Company for the 1st quarter of 1991 was $203.42; since the liability exceeded $100, a deposit was made on April 30, 1991. The tax liability for the 2d quarter was $159.95, and a deposit was made on July 31, 1991. The tax liability for the 3d quarter was $98.83, but since this amount was less than the $100 limit, no deposit was required. The tax liability for the 4th quarter was $21.10. Since the accumulated liability of $119.93 exceeded the $100 limit, a deposit of $119.93 was made on January 31, 1992, as shown on Form 8109 in Illustration 5-5 on page 180.

At the time of filing the annual return on Form 940, the employer pays the balance of tax owed for the prior year and not yet deposited. If the amount of tax reportable on Form 940 exceeds by more than $100 the sum of amounts deposited each quarter, the employer must deposit the total amount owed and undeposited (Form 8109) on or before January 31 following the year for which Form 940 is filed. If the amount owed is $100 or less, the employer may remit it with Form 940.

In the case of an employer in a state subject to the FUTA credit reduction because of Title XII advances, we calculate the deposits by multiplying the taxable wages by .8% during each of the first three quarters of the year. Since the penalty rate cannot be known with certainty until November of the current year, the procedure for the first three quarters is the same as that used by an employer in any state. However, since the amount of the penalty imposed for the year will be known during the fourth quarter, the deposit for the last quarter of the year will include the penalty for the entire year. This deposit is due by January 31 of the next year.

Form **940-EZ**
Department of the Treasury
Internal Revenue Service

Employer's Annual Federal Unemployment (FUTA) Tax Return

OMB No. 1545-1110
1991

T	
FF	
FD	
FP	
I	
T	

If incorrect, make any necessary changes.

Name (as distinguished from trade name)

Calendar year 1991

Trade name, if any
YANGO SUPPLY COMPANY

Address and ZIP code
13 M STREET SALEM, OR 97311-9595

Employer identification number
15 - 8590113

Before beginning, follow the chart under "Who Can Use Form 940-EZ" on page 2. If you cannot use Form 940-EZ, you must use Form 940 instead.

A Enter the amount of contributions paid to your state unemployment fund. (See instructions for line A on page 4.) . . . ▶ $ 12,410|00

B (1) Enter the name of the state where you have to pay contributions . . . ▶ Oregon

(2) Enter your state reporting number(s) as shown on state unemployment tax return ▶ 163-97557

Part I Taxable Wages and FUTA Tax

		Amount paid			
1 Total payments (including payments shown on lines 2 and 3) during the calendar year for services of employees . .			1	478,231	19
2 Exempt payments. (Explain all exempt payments, attaching additional sheets if necessary.) ▶	2				
3 Payments for services of more than $7,000. Enter only amounts over the first $7,000 paid to each employee. Do not include any exempt payments from line 2	3	303,231	19		
4 Total exempt payments (add lines 2 and 3) . . .			4	303,231	19
5 **Total taxable wages** (subtract line 4 from line 1) . . . ▶			5	175,000	00
6 **FUTA tax.** Multiply the wages on line 5 by .008 and enter here. (If the result is over $100, also complete Part II.) . .			6	1,400	00
7 Total FUTA tax deposited for the year, including any overpayment applied from a prior year (from your records) . .			7	1,400	00
8 **Amount you owe** (subtract line 7 from line 6). This should be $100 or less. Pay to IRS . . . ▶			8	-0-	
9 **Overpayment** (subtract line 6 from line 7). Check if it is to be: ☐ Applied to next return, or ☐ Refunded. ▶			9		

Part II **Record of Quarterly Federal Unemployment Tax Liability (Do not include state liability.) Complete only if line 6 is over $100.**

Quarter	First (Jan. 1 - Mar. 31)	Second (Apr. 1 - June 30)	Third (July 1 - Sept 30)	Fourth (Oct. 1 - Dec 31)	Total for Year
Liability for quarter	719.90	360.18	319.92	-0-	1,400.00

If you will not have to file returns in the future, write "Final" here (see *Who Must File a Return* on page 2) and sign the return. ▶

Under penalties of perjury, I declare that I have examined this return, including accompanying schedules and statements, and, to the best of my knowledge and belief, it is true, correct, and complete, and that no part of any payment made to a state unemployment fund claimed as a credit was, or is to be, deducted from the payments to employees.

Signature ▶ *William H. Yango* Title (Owner, etc.) ▶ President Date ▶ 1/31/92

Form **940-EZ**

Illustration 5-4. Form 940-EZ, Employer's Annual Federal Unemployment (FUTA) Tax Return

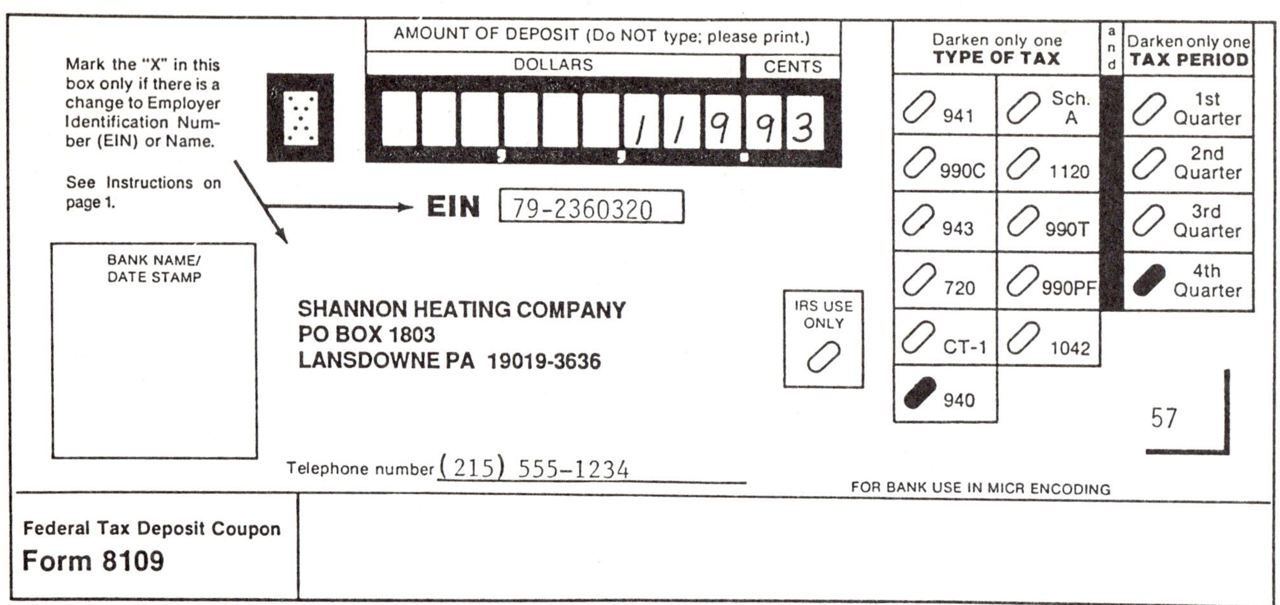
Mark the "X" in this box only if there is a change to Employer Identification Number (EIN) or Name.

See Instructions on page 1.

AMOUNT OF DEPOSIT (Do NOT type; please print.)

DOLLARS | CENTS

1,199.3

EIN 79-2360320

BANK NAME/ DATE STAMP

SHANNON HEATING COMPANY
PO BOX 1803
LANSDOWNE PA 19019-3636

IRS USE ONLY

Telephone number (215) 555-1234

Darken only one TYPE OF TAX: 941, Sch. A, 990C, 1120, 943, 990T, 720, 990PF, CT-1, 1042, 940 (darkened)

Darken only one TAX PERIOD: 1st Quarter, 2nd Quarter, 3rd Quarter, 4th Quarter (darkened)

57

FOR BANK USE IN MICR ENCODING

Federal Tax Deposit Coupon
Form 8109

Illustration 5-5. Form 8109, Federal Tax Deposit Coupon

Penalties—FUTA

As indicated in Unit 3, under the Internal Revenue Code, employers are subject to civil and criminal penalties for failing to file returns, pay the employment taxes when due, and make timely deposits. These penalties apply, generally, without regard to the type of tax or return involved. All of the penalties are discussed in Illustration 3-11, pages 88 and 89.

Information Reports—SUTA

There is wide variation in the official forms that the states provide for filing the reports required under the unemployment compensation laws. It is, therefore, necessary for us to become familiar with the law and regulations of each state in which liability might be incurred.

The reports that are required of the employers by the individual states are used to determine: (1) the employer's liability for the contributions, (2) the amount of the contribution due on a quarterly basis, and (3) the amount of benefits to which employees will be entitled if they become unemployed. The most important of the required reports are the following:

1. Status reports
2. Contribution reports
3. Wage information reports
4. Separation reports
5. Partial unemployment notices

Status Reports. Under the unemployment compensation laws of most states, new employers are required to register or file an initial statement or *status report.* The principal purpose of this report is to determine the employer's liability to make contributions into the state unemployment compensation fund. A status report may be required of employers regardless of whether they are liable for contributions under the state law.

Contribution Reports. All employers liable for contributions under the unemployment compensation law of any state are required to submit a quarterly *contribution report* or tax return. The purpose of this report is to provide a summary of the wages paid during the period and to show the computation of the tax or contribution. Usually, we must file this report on or before the last day of the month following the close of the calendar quarter, and the tax or contribution must be paid at the same time.

Wage Information Reports. In most states we are required to make *wage information reports* concerning individual employees. Usually we file these reports with the quarterly contribution reports. An example of a quarterly wage information report is shown in Illustration 5-6, page 181.

On the report we may list all employee names, social security account numbers, taxable wages, taxable tips, state in which worker was employed during the reported quarter, and employer's federal account number. We may also be required to list for each employee the number of credit weeks earned during the quarter. (A *credit week* is defined by the state's unemployment compensation law; for example, in Pennsylvania, a credit week is defined as any calendar week

MAIL TO:
COMMONWEALTH OF PENNSYLVANIA
DEPARTMENT OF LABOR AND INDUSTRY
OFFICE OF EMPLOYMENT SECURITY
HARRISBURG, PA 17121

EMPLOYER'S REPORT FOR UNEMPLOYMENT COMPENSATION
READ INSTRUCTIONS ON REVERSE SIDE OF EMPLOYER'S COPY
ANSWER EACH ITEM TYPE OR PRINT IN INK

FORM UC-2 QTR. 1ST YEAR 19 --

INV. OR R.D. CLEARANCE | EMPL. ALPHA INDEX | CASHIER'S TRANSMITTAL NUMBER

1. TOTAL NUMBER OF COVERED EMPLOYES IN PAY PERIOD INCL. 12TH OF MONTH → INCLUDE EMPLOYES WHOSE WAGES EXCEED TAXABLE LIMIT. IF NONE ENTER "0"	FIRST MONTH	SECOND MONTH	THIRD MONTH
	6	6	7

I CERTIFY THAT THE INFORMATION ON FORMS UC-2/2A/2B IS TRUE AND CORRECT TO THE BEST OF MY KNOWLEDGE AND BELIEF. NO PART OF THE AMOUNT OF EMPLOYER CONTRIBUTIONS REPORTED ON TAXABLE WAGES WAS DEDUCTED OR IS TO BE DEDUCTED FROM THE EMPLOYE'S WAGES.

SIGN HERE DO NOT PRINT: *Jack B. Kiel* — SIGNATURE OF OWNER, PARTNER, RESPONSIBLE OFFICER OR AUTHORIZED AGENT

TITLE: President (GIVE EXACT TITLE) DATE: 4-30-91

EMPLOYER CONTRIBUTION RATE: .041

EMPLOYER'S CODED ACCOUNT NO. ONLY: 79-16093-0

Please Type or Print EMPLOYER'S NAME AND ADDRESS

KIELSO COMPANY
8101 ARCHER LANE
NORRISTOWN, PA 19401-1936

IF ADDRESS HAS CHANGED, PLEASE CORRECT UC-2B PORTION OF THIS FORM

2. GROSS WAGES FOR EMPLOYE CONTRIBUTIONS	$	-0-
2A. EMPLOYE CONTRIBUTIONS DUE (.001 X ITEM 2)	$	-0-
3. TAXABLE WAGES FOR EMPLOYER CONTRIBUTIONS	$	29,290 00
4. EMPLOYER CONTRIBUTIONS DUE (RATE X ITEM 3)	$	1,200 89
4A. TOTAL CONTRIBUTIONS DUE (ITEM 2A + 4)	$	1,200 89
5. INTEREST DUE SEE INSTRUCTIONS	$	-0-
6. PENALTY DUE SEE INSTRUCTIONS	$	-0-
7. TOTAL REMITTANCE (ITEM 4A + 5 + 6)	$	1,200 89

DO NOT WRITE IN THIS SPACE — FOR OES USE

EXAMINED BY | UC-2A'S | SUBJECTIVITY DATE | POST CASH CREDIT: WE $, C $, I $, P $ | AUDITED BY
DATE PAYMENT RECEIVED | REPORT TIMELY | REPORT DELINQUENT DATE

EMPLOYER CONTRIBUTION RATE: .041

Please Type or Print EMPLOYER'S NAME AND ADDRESS

EMPLOYER'S CODED ACCOUNT NO. ONLY: 79-16093-0

KIELSO COMPANY
8101 ARCHER LANE
NORRISTOWN, PA 19401-1936

EMPLOYER'S QUARTERLY REPORT OF WAGES PAID TO EACH EMPLOYE

FORM UC-2A QTR. 1ST YEAR 19 --

7A. TEL. NO. OF PREPARER: 215-555-8210

FOR OES USE

8. TOTAL NUMBER OF PAGES IN THIS REPORT	1
9. GROSS WAGES (MUST AGREE WITH ITEM 2 ABOVE AND TOTALS OF ITEM 14) $	31,790 00
10. TOTAL NUMBER OF EMPLOYES LISTED IN ITEM 13 ON ALL PAGES	7
11. PLANT NUMBER	N/A

12. EMPLOYE'S SOC. SEC. ACCT. NO.			13. NAME OF EMPLOYE (TYPE OR PRINT IN INK) FIRST NAME	INITIAL	LAST NAME	14. GR. WAGES PD. THIS QTR.	15. CREDIT WEEKS
111	09	8271	Janet	L	Carroll	6,300 00	13
095	19	1918	Carson	H	Long	1,900 00	5
212	16	3790	Heidi	M	Dorsey	2,990 00	13
091	78	6510	Mary	F	Ernst	2,100 00	13
109	05	0093	Jack	B	Kiel	10,500 00	13
170	91	9008	Alan	W	Pinkett	4,100 00	13
089	87	1792	Lawrence	B	Golic	3,900 00	13
LIST ANY ADDITIONAL EMPLOYES ON FORM UC-2A SUPPLEMENT OR ON CONTINUATION SHEETS APPROVED BY OES. TOTAL FOR THIS PAGE						31,790 00	

Illustration 5-6. Pennsylvania Form UC-2, Employer's Report for Unemployment Compensation

in the quarter during which the person earned remuneration of not less than $50). Commercially printed forms may also be used provided the form includes all the necessary information required by the state.

About three fourths of the states permit the use of the same magnetic tape for reporting state wage information that is used for federal social security reporting purposes. By using the same magnetic tape and reporting specifications to satisfy both state and federal requirements, we eliminate the need to transcribe information from the tape prepared for the federal government to paper forms or punched cards for submission to the state. The payroll manager should contact the state agency to determine whether federal-state combined magnetic tape reporting is acceptable.

Separation Reports. Whenever a worker becomes separated from employment, we may be required to furnish a *separation report* providing a wage and employment record of the separated employee and the reason for leaving. Usually we must give a copy of the report to the worker in order that the individual may be informed of any entitlement to unemployment insurance benefits.

Partial Unemployment Notices. Most states require employers to give partial unemployment notices to those workers who become "partially unemployed" so that they are informed of their potential eligibility for partial unemployment benefits. *Partial unemployment* refers to employment by the individual's regular employer but on a reduced scale because of lack of work. In most states the notice must be given to the worker immediately after a week of partial employment has been completed. After that, the employer ordinarily furnishes the worker with some kind of low-earnings report during each week of partial employment so that the worker will be assured of the receipt of supplemental or partial benefits.

Penalties—SUTA

In all states there is some form of penalty for failure to pay, or for the late payment of, contributions, and also for failure to file reports. Some states impose a 10% penalty if the failure to pay the tax is due to negligence, and in a few states, a 50% penalty is imposed if the failure to pay is due to fraud. Many states also deny experience rates to employers who are delinquent in filing reports or paying contributions. In some states employers who have been delinquent in paying their contributions may be required to pay the contributions monthly rather than quarterly.

An employer's failure to file reports or pay contributions when due may, in addition to subjecting the employer to penalties and interest, result in paying contributions at a higher rate than would have been required otherwise. Where contributions are one of the factors used in the experience-rating formula, only payments made by a certain date may be used in figuring the new tax rates.

UNEMPLOYMENT COMPENSATION BENEFITS

Unemployment compensation benefits, which are payments made to workers who are temporarily unemployed, are provided primarily under the unemployment compensation law of each state. Each state specifies the qualifications to be met by the unemployed worker in order to be eligible for benefits, the amount of the benefits to be paid each individual, and the duration of the period for which benefits will be paid.

As discussed in Unit 4, payers of unemployment compensation benefits must send copies of Form 1099-G to the Internal Revenue Service and to the person receiving the benefits. This form is used only when the total benefits paid are $10 or more. These benefits are includable in the recipient's gross income for federal income tax purposes if the unemployment benefits plus the individual's adjusted gross income exceed certain dollar limits.

Employee Benefits—SUTA

There is no uniform rate of unemployment benefits payable by all states. The amount of the benefits that an unemployed worker is entitled to receive usually is about 50% of the regular weekly wages subject to minimum and maximum amounts specified by law. Maximum weekly benefits vary widely among states, from 50% to 70% of average weekly wages. Illustration 5-1 on pages 172 and 173 shows the minimum and maximum amounts of benefits (excluding dependency allowances) provided under the laws of each state.

Under the laws of all the states there is a limit to the total amount of benefits an unemployed worker may receive in any year. Usually the limit is expressed in the terms of amounts rather than weeks. Thus, the maximum amount of benefits allowed under the various state laws ranges from 26 to 30 times the individual's weekly benefit amount. Therefore, if a certain employee should qualify for weekly benefits of $150 and the maximum benefits payable during the year are $4,500, the employee would be entitled to receive benefits during a period of 30 weeks.

Dependency Allowances. The state unemployment compensation laws often provide for payment of a *dependency allowance,* which is an additional weekly benefit to unemployed workers with dependents. For example, the law in Connecticut provides for a weekly dependency allowance of $10 each for the claimant's nonworking spouse and each child and stepchild (but for no more than five dependents). However, the total dependency allowance cannot exceed 50% of the benefit otherwise payable to the claimant. In those states that provide dependency allowances, the allowances are sometimes made only to workers with dependent children of a stipulated age.

Eligibility for Benefits. The unemployment compensation laws of all the states require that a claimant meet certain conditions before becoming eligible to receive benefits. An analysis of the required qualifications in most states reveals that the claimant must:

1. File a claim for benefits.
2. Be able to work.
3. Be available for work.
4. Be actively seeking work or make a reasonable effort to obtain work.
5. Have earned a certain amount of wages or worked a certain number of weeks in covered employment.
6. Have registered at the local state employment office.
7. Have served the required waiting period.
8. Not be disqualified under any of the other provisions of the law.

Disqualification of Benefits. Certain disqualifications are set up in the state laws to conserve the funds and to insure the intended purpose of unemployment insurance, which is to compensate for involuntary unemployment. While there is wide variation in the state laws, the following are some of the more common reasons for disqualification:

1. Discharge for misconduct.
2. Voluntarily leaving work without good cause.
3. Unemployment due to a labor dispute.[2]
4. Leaving work to attend school.
5. Commitment to penal institution.
6. False or fraudulent representation to obtain benefits.
7. Refusal of suitable employment.
8. Receipt of certain kinds of remuneration.

Most state laws provide that an unemployed individual shall not be entitled to unemployment compensation benefits during any week in which the person receives remuneration from other sources such as workers' compensation for temporary partial disability, old-age benefits under the Social Security Act, vacation allowances, dismissal wages, earnings from self-employment, or unemployment compensation benefits from another state. In some cases, however, it is provided that if such remuneration is less than the benefits due the individual, the person shall receive the amount of the benefits less such remuneration.

An individual otherwise qualified may receive unemployment compensation benefits regardless of age. Thus, minors and persons over the age of 65 may qualify for unemployment compensation benefits.

Benefits for the Unemployed as a Result of Major Disaster. Under the *Disaster Relief Act*, unemployment benefits are provided to persons who become unemployed as a result of a major disaster. The benefits will be available so long as the individual's unemployment caused by a major disaster continues or until the individual is reemployed in a suitable position. In no event, however, will the benefits be paid for longer than one year after the disaster has been declared.

Benefits for Federal Employees. Under the *Federal Employee Unemployment Compensation* program of the Social Security Act, unemployment insurance is provided for federal civilian employees. If a federal civilian worker becomes unemployed, eligibility for benefits is determined under the unemployment law of the state in which the person last worked in federal civilian employment. If eligible, the person is entitled to unemployment benefits in the amounts and under the conditions provided by the state unemployment insurance law. Upon request by the state, the federal employing agencies make available their findings pertaining to federal civilian employment, wages, and reasons for job separation.

Benefits for Ex-Service Personnel. Unemployment compensation benefits for ex-service personnel are provided by the *Federal Unemployment Compensation for Ex-Servicemen* program of the Social Security Act. The benefits are determined by the unemployment insurance law of the state in which the person first files a claim that establishes a benefit year as the most recent separation from active military service.

Disability Benefits. Five states—California, Hawaii, New Jersey, New York, and Rhode Island—and Puerto Rico provide for the payment of *disability benefits* to workers who suffer wage losses through unemployment due to nonoccupational disease or injury. The programs in these states have developed in re-

[2]Most states provide benefits to strikers who have been replaced by nonstriking employees, and many states allow strikers to collect benefits in cases where their employers continue to operate.

sponse to the need for protecting workers who are not eligible for either workers' compensation or unemployment insurance. The programs are not health insurance as such, for benefits are paid only to offset the wage loss of an employee who becomes sick or suffers an accident not connected with work.

Payment of disability benefits under the state laws are, for the most part, financed by employee contributions. In Hawaii, New Jersey, New York, and Puerto Rico, however, employers are required to contribute. In California, New Jersey, and Puerto Rico, the benefits are provided under a state-administered plan; but employers may substitute their own plans if they so wish. However, such "private" or "voluntary" plans must provide benefits at least as favorable as those payable under the state plan. Rhode Island does not provide for the use of private plans, and all employees covered by the law are insured under the state fund. In Hawaii, the employer may provide for the benefits by means of private insurance, by deposit of securities or bonds with the State Director of Finance, by furnishing proof of ability to pay, or by private plans.

Supplemental Unemployment Benefits (SUB). Many union contracts provide for the private supplementation of state unemployment compensation benefits to provide payments to employees during periods of layoff. In nearly all of the states that have investigated the *Supplemental Unemployment Benefits (SUB)* plan benefits in relation to state unemployment compensation benefits, it has been ruled that workers who receive SUB may also simultaneously be paid unemployment compensation benefits. A SUB plan is usually one of two types: (a) the pooled-fund plan or (b) the individual-account plan.

Pooled-Fund Plan. This plan, which is also known as the "auto" or "Ford-type" plan, is the most common type of SUB plan. Under this plan employers contribute to a general fund a certain number of cents for each hour worked by employees currently on the job. Employees usually have a right to benefits from the fund only upon layoff and only after meeting stipulated eligibility requirements.

Individual-Account Plan. Under this plan, found mainly in the plate glass industry, contributions are paid to separate trusts for each employee and the employee has a vested and nonforfeitable right to the amount in the fund. Workers are entitled to the fund upon layoff and have a right to the fund when their employment is terminated. In the event the worker dies, the designated beneficiary is paid the content of the trust.

FUTA Funds

As indicated earlier, the net FUTA tax the employer pays to the federal government is used primarily to pay the state and federal administrative expenses of the total unemployment insurance program. However, there is a program of *federal-state extended unemployment compensation benefits* for employees who exhaust their regular state unemployment insurance benefits. Generally, under this program, the regular state benefits are extended by one half (covering the 27th to 39th week). However, the extended benefits are payable in a state only when the following two requirements are met:

1. The state unemployment rate is at least 5%.
2. The state unemployment rate is at least 20% above the average rate for the corresponding 13-week periods in the two prior calendar years.

The second requirement can be waived by state law, and extended benefits will still be paid if the state's unemployment rate is at least 6%.

As indicated earlier, the FUTA provides that when a state's unemployment compensation fund is insufficient to meet its benefit obligations, the state may obtain an advance from its federal account in the unemployment trust fund. Such advances constitute loans that must be repaid. If the loans (Title XII advances) are not repaid within the specified period, the net FUTA tax on employers in the *affected state* is increased until the loan has been recaptured through the increased taxes (see page 170).

Summary of Sources and Duration of Benefits

The chart on page 185 shows how the federal-state unemployment insurance system operates in a state in which the basic duration of benefits is 26 weeks. In addition to the kinds of benefits listed in the chart, legislation may be enacted that extends the federal-state benefits program.

Weeks of Unemployment	Source of Benefits	Starting Point	Life of Program
1st to 26th	Regular state program (funded entirely from state unemployment accounts)	Operates continuously	Permanent
27th to 39th	Federal-State Extended Benefits program (funded in equal parts from state accounts and the FUTA funds and advances from general revenues if needed)	Unemployment rate 6% in state, or 5% or more in state if rate is 20% higher than rate for corresponding 13-week periods in two prior calendar years	Permanent

GLOSSARY

Constructively paid wages—remunerations that are credited to the account of, or set apart for, an employee so that they may be drawn upon at any time, even though they are not actually possessed by the employee.

Contribution report—quarterly tax return filed with the state by the employer to provide a summary of the wages paid during the period and to show the computation of the tax or contribution.

Dependency allowance—an additional weekly benefit paid to unemployed workers with dependents.

Disability benefits—payments to workers who suffer wage losses through unemployment due to nonoccupational disease or injury.

Dismissal payments—amounts paid by employers to workers who have been separated from employment; also known as *payments in lieu of notice, separation pay*, or *terminal leave pay*.

Experience rating—method by which employer contribution payments may be adjusted because of a favorable employment record; also known as *merit rating*.

Federal-state extended benefits program—a plan for the payment of extended benefits to employees who exhaust their regular state unemployment insurance benefits.

Individual-account plan—supplemental unemployment benefits plan in which the employer's contributions are paid into a separate trust for each employee.

Interstate employee—an individual who works in more than one state.

Merit rating—*see* experience rating.

Negative-balance employers—those whose reserve accounts have been charged for more benefits paid out than contributions paid into the fund.

Partial unemployment—employment by the individual's regular employer on a reduced scale because of lack of work.

Partial unemployment notice—form completed by employer and given to partially unemployed workers so that supplemental unemployment benefits may be obtained.

Pooled-fund laws—unemployment insurance system wherein the cost of unemployment benefits is spread among all employers in a particular state.

Pooled-fund plan—supplemental unemployment benefits plan financed by employers' contributions into a general fund; also known as the *auto* or *Ford-type plan.*

Positive-balance employers—those who have built up a balance in their reserve accounts (contributions paid in less benefits charged).

Reciprocal arrangements—agreements between states to provide unemployment insurance coverage and payment of benefits to interstate workers.

Reserve-ratio formula—experience-rating plan used in most states, based on: Contributions less Benefits Paid ÷ Average Payroll.

Separation report—report that provides a wage and employment record of the separated employee and the reason for leaving.

Status report—initial statement filed by new employers with their state unemployment office, which determines their liability to make contributions into the state unemployment compensation fund.

Supplemental unemployment benefits—private supplementation of state unemployment compensation benefits to employees during periods of layoff.

Title XII advances—funds borrowed from the federal government by states who, due to financial difficulties, cannot pay their unemployment compensation benefits.

Unemployment compensation benefits—payments made to workers who are temporarily unemployed.

Unemployment insurance—a federal-state program that provides economic security for workers during periods of temporary unemployment.

Voluntary contributions—payments deliberately made by employers to their state funds in order to qualify for a lower unemployment compensation tax rate.

Wage information report—statement filed by the employer, usually with the quarterly contribution report, which lists employee names, social security account numbers, taxable wages, taxable tips, state in which worker was employed during the reported quarter, and employer's federal account number.

QUESTIONS FOR REVIEW

1. How are the employer's contributions to FUTA used by the federal government?
2. What are the two alternative tests that are applied to a business in order to judge whether it is an "employer" and, therefore, subject to the FUTA tax?
3. Explain how one of two entities is determined to be the employer for purposes of FUTA.
4. Under what conditions are agricultural laborers included in the coverage of FUTA?
5. To what extent does FUTA coverage extend to services that a citizen of the United States performs for an American employer outside the United States?
6. Explain how an employee who works in more than one state may be covered under the state unemployment compensation law of one state.
7. As far as SUTA is concerned, how does an employer account for the wages that are paid to an employee who is transferred to another plant location in a different state during the same calendar year?
8. Which of the following types of payments are taxable under FUTA:
   a. Commissions as compensation for covered employment.
   b. Christmas gifts of nominal value.
   c. Courtesy discounts to employees.
   d. Reimbursement of ordinary and necessary business expenses.
   e. Dismissal payments.
9. a. What is the basis upon which the FUTA tax is calculated?
   b. What portion of each employee's annual wages is subject to the FUTA tax?
   c. What is the current gross FUTA tax rate?
   d. What is the maximum credit an employer may claim for state contributions in computing the net FUTA tax?
10. Explain how experience rating allows an employer to pay an overall unemployment tax (FUTA and SUTA) of less than 6.2%.
11. An employer, because of a favorable experience rating, is permitted to pay a state contribution at a reduced rate of 1.5%. What percentage of taxable wages must be paid in the aggregate to the federal and state governments?
12. What are two situations in which an employer could be liable for a net FUTA tax greater than .8%?
13. What is the purpose of Title XII advances?
14. How is the SUTA tax rate determined for a new employer?
15. In 1990:
    a. Which state(s) had the widest range of SUTA tax rates for employers?
    b. Which state(s) paid the highest weekly maximum benefit (excluding dependency allowances) to qualified unemployed workers?
    c. Which state(s) had the highest taxable wage base for the SUTA tax?
16. Describe briefly the formula most commonly used to calculate the experience-rating contributions of an employer.
17. How might an employer's payroll taxes be reduced by means of voluntary contributions to the state's unemployment compensation plan?
18. Which employers can file Form 940-EZ?
19. a. For an employer who is subject to FUTA, what are the basic forms that must be filed with the federal government?
    b. When must these forms be filed?
    c. How are taxable wages computed on the annual return?
20. For 1991, the Baxter Company paid a 2.2% state unemployment tax to Rhode Island. What percentage of taxable wages would be paid in the aggregate to the federal and state governments for unemployment?
21. How may an employer obtain an extension of time in filing Form 940?
22. What is a separation report?
23. Why do some states require employers to furnish partial unemployment notices to workers?
24. Why might an unemployed worker be disqualified from receiving unemployment compensation benefits?
25. a. What is the purpose of the federal-state extended benefits program?
    b. How is this program financed?

QUESTIONS FOR DISCUSSION

1. Can the owner of a small business receive unemployment compensation? Explain.
2. Past unemployment legislation extended the duration of benefits to jobless persons through 65 weeks. What arguments could be used against proposals to re-extend the maximum period to, and even beyond, 65 weeks?
3. What arguments could be made for raising the upper limits of the SUTA tax rates?
4. Check the unemployment compensation law of your state and determine the answers to the following questions:
   a. How do nonprofit organizations, subject to coverage, make payments to the unemployment compensation fund?
   b. Can part-time teachers collect unemployment compensation between school terms?
   c. Can professional athletes receive unemployment compensation?
   d. Are aliens covered by the unemployment compensation law?
   e. How do employers protest or appeal benefit determinations and charges against their accounts?
   f. Briefly describe how a person's weekly benefit rate and maximum benefit amount are determined.
   g. Can an unemployed worker collect additional benefits if he or she has dependents? If so, how much is paid for each dependent?
   h. Does the state provide payment of partial benefits?
   i. Are benefits payable to a female during pregnancy?
   j. Can employers make voluntary contributions to their state unemployment reserve accounts?
   k. For what reasons may an unemployed worker be disqualified from receiving unemployment benefits?
   l. What steps are taken by the state unemployment agency to prevent the improper payment of claims?
5. As a way of curbing the unemployment rate, California has instituted a "shared-work compensation" program. Under this program, a company faced with a layoff of its workers may place its entire work force on a four-day workweek during the period of hardship. During this period of reduced workweeks, the employees collect partial unemployment benefits. When business rebounds, the firm returns to its normal five-day workweek, and the unemployment compensation benefits cease. Participation in the program must be approved by both the employer and the unions. If, however, the firm is not unionized, management has the discretion of putting the plan into effect.
   a. What are the benefits of such a shared-work compensation program to (1) the employer and (2) the employees?
   b. What disadvantages do you see in the operation of a shared-work compensation program, especially from the viewpoint of organized labor?

Date ______________________ Name ______________________

PRACTICAL PROBLEMS

5-1. During the year, the Hernandez Company is required to pay FUTA and SUTA taxes. The state's tax rate for the company is 3.8%. The taxable payroll for the year for FUTA and SUTA is $45,000. Compute:

a. The net FUTA tax . . . . $__________
b. The net SUTA tax . . . . __________
c. The total unemployment taxes . . . . $__________

5-2. During the year, the Nanchez Company has a SUTA tax rate of 5.9%. The taxable payroll for the year for FUTA and SUTA is $67,000. Compute:

a. The net FUTA tax . . . . $__________
b. The net SUTA tax . . . . __________
c. The total unemployment taxes . . . . $__________

5-3. The Parrett Company's payroll for the year is $737,910. Of this amount, $472,120 is for wages paid in excess of $7,000 to each individual employee. The SUTA rate in the state in which the Parrett Company is located is 2.9% on the first $7,000 of each employee's earnings. The FUTA tax also applies to the company. Determine:

a. The net FUTA tax . . . . $__________
b. The net SUTA tax . . . . __________
c. The total unemployment taxes . . . . $__________

5-4. The Garrison Shops had a SUTA tax rate of 3.7%, and their state's taxable limit was $8,000 of each employee's earnings. For the year, the Garrison Shops had FUTA taxable wages of $67,900 and SUTA taxable wages of $83,900. Determine:

a. The net FUTA tax . . . . $__________
b. The net SUTA tax . . . . $__________

5-5. Due to its experience rating, Ianelli, Inc., is required to pay unemployment taxes on its payroll as follows:

1. Under SUTA for state X on taxable wages of $18,000, the contribution rate is 4%.
2. Under SUTA for state Y on taxable wages of $24,000, the contribution rate is 2.65%.
3. Under SUTA for state Z on taxable wages of $79,000, the contribution rate is 2.9%.
4. Under FUTA, the taxable wages are $103,500.

Determine:

a. SUTA taxes paid to state X .... $__________
b. SUTA taxes paid to state Y .... $__________
c. SUTA taxes paid to state Z .... $__________
d. FUTA taxes paid .... $__________

5-6. The Brooks Company began its operations in August of the current year. During August and September, the company paid wages of $6,950. For the last quarter of the year, the taxable wages paid amounted to $12,910. None of the employees were paid more than $7,000 this year.

a. Is the Brooks Company liable for FUTA tax this year? Explain.

b. If so, what is the amount of the *gross* FUTA tax before any credit is granted for the SUTA tax? .... $__________

5-7. In September, 1991, the Haley Paint Company began operations in a state that requires new employers of one or more individuals to pay a state unemployment tax of 3.5% of the first $7,000 of wages paid each employee.

An analysis of the company's payroll for the year shows total wages paid of $177,610. The salaries of the president and the vice-president of the company were $20,000 and $15,000, respectively, for the four-month period; but there were no other employees who received wages in excess of $7,000 for the four months. Included in the total wages were $900 paid to a director who only attended director meetings during the year, and $6,300 paid to the factory superintendent.

Besides the total wages of $177,610, there was a payment of $2,430 made to the O'Hara Accounting Company for an audit they performed on the company's books in December, 1991. Determine:

a. The net FUTA tax .... $__________
b. The SUTA tax .... $__________

5-8. In April of the current year, the Korn Steel Company transferred Harry Marsh from its factory in Tennessee to its plant in South Carolina. The company's SUTA tax rates based on its experience ratings are 3.2% in Tennessee and 3.8% in South Carolina. Both states base the tax on the first $7,000 of each employee's earnings. This year the Korn Steel Company paid Harry Marsh wages of $9,900; $2,800 were paid in Tennessee and the remainder in South Carolina. Compute:

a. The amount of SUTA tax the company must pay to Tennessee on Marsh's wages .... $__________
b. The amount of SUTA tax the company must pay to South Carolina on Marsh's wages .... $__________
c. The amount of the net FUTA tax on Marsh's wages .... $__________

Date ______________________ Name ______________________

5-9. The partnership of Edward and Farnam paid the following wages during this year:

M. Edward (partner)	$21,000
S. Farnam (partner)	19,000
N. Pearson (supervisor)	12,500
T. Grunhart (factory worker)	9,700
R. Rice (factory worker)	9,200
D. Brown (factory worker)	7,900
S. Koenig (bookkeeper)	10,900
C. Chang (maintenance)	4,500

In addition, the partnership owed $200 to Chang for work he performed during December. However, payment for this work will not be made until January of the following year.

a. The *gross* FUTA tax for the partnership for this year is .... $__________

b. The *net* FUTA tax for this year is .... $__________

5-10. This year Katherine Thomason was paid wages of $9,340 by the Wexter Company. Due to its experience rating, the company's SUTA tax rate is 2.5%. The state's tax rate applies to the first $8,000 paid each employee. Determine:

a. The amount that the Wexter Company must pay for net FUTA and SUTA taxes in connection with Thomason's salary this year .... $__________

b. The net FUTA and SUTA taxes on Thomason's salary if the Wexter Company's tax rate was a less favorable 3.6% on the first $8,000 of each employee's earnings .... $__________

5-11. The Demigold Company paid wages of $170,900 this year. Of this amount, $114,000 was taxable for net FUTA and SUTA purposes. The state's contribution tax rate is 3.1% for the Demigold Company. Due to cash flow problems, the company was late in making its SUTA payments throughout the year. Compute:

a. The amount of credit the company would receive against the FUTA tax for its SUTA contributions .... $__________

b. The amount that the Demigold Company would pay to the federal government for their FUTA tax .... $__________

c. The amount that the company lost because of their late payments .... $__________

5-12. During 1991, the Jordan Company was subject to the Alaska state unemployment tax of 4.2%. The company's taxable earnings for FUTA were $86,700 and for SUTA, $101,000. Determine:

a. The SUTA tax that the Jordan Company would pay to the State of Alaska ..... $__________

b. The net FUTA tax for 1991 .... $__________

c. The amount of the employees' disability insurance tax for 1991 (use the employee's tax rate that is shown in Illustration 5-1 on page 172) .... $__________

5-13. The following unemployment tax-rate schedule is in effect during the calendar year 1991 in State A, which uses the reserve-ratio formula in determining employer contributions:

Reserve Ratio	Contributions Rate
0.0% or more, but less than 1%	6.7%
1.0% or more, but less than 1.2%	6.4%
1.2% or more, but less than 1.4%	6.1%
1.4% or more, but less than 1.6%	5.8%
1.6% or more, but less than 1.8%	5.5%
1.8% or more, but less than 2.0%	5.2%
2.0% or more, but less than 2.2%	4.9%
2.2% or more, but less than 2.4%	4.6%
2.4% or more, but less than 2.6%	4.3%
2.6% or more, but less than 2.8%	4.0%
2.8% or more, but less than 3.0%	3.7%
3.0% or more, but less than 3.2%	3.4%
3.2% or more	3.1%

The Grant Company, which is located in State A, had an average annual payroll of $850,000 for the three 12-month periods ending on June 30, 1990 (the computation date for the tax year 1991). As of June 30, 1990, the total contributions that had been made to the Grant Company's reserve account, in excess of the benefits charged, amounted to $17,440. Compute:

a. The Grant Company's reserve ratio for 1991 . . . . ______%

b. The 1991 contributions rate for the company . . . . ______%

c. The smallest contribution that the company can make in order to reduce its tax rate if State A permits voluntary contributions . . . . $______

d. The tax savings realized by the company taking into consideration the voluntary contribution made in "c" if the taxable payroll in 1991 is $980,000 . . . . $______

5-14. As of June 30, 1990 (the computation date for the 1991 tax rate), the Zimfer Company had a negative balance of $867 in its unemployment reserve account in State A. The company's average payroll over the last three 12-month periods amounted to $360,000. The unemployment compensation law of State A provides that the tax rate of an employer who has a negative balance on the computation date shall be 7.2% during the following calendar year. Using the tax-rate schedule presented in Problem 5-13, determine:

a. The smallest voluntary contribution that the Zimfer Company should make in order to effect a change in its tax rate . . . . $______

b. The amount of the tax savings as a result of the voluntary contribution if the Zimfer Company's taxable payroll for 1991 is $420,000 . . . . $______

5-15. Marlene Grady and Pauline Monroe are partners engaged in operating the MGM Doll Shop, a partnership, which has employed the following persons since the beginning of the year:

V. Hoffman (general office worker)	$1,700 per month
A. Drugan (saleswoman)	$15,000 per year
G. Beiter (stock clerk)	$180 per week
S. Egan (deliveryman)	$220 per week
B. Lin (cleaning and maintenance)	$160 per week

Grady and Monroe are each allowed a weekly salary of $450.

The doll shop is located in a state that requires unemployment compensation contributions of employers of one or more individuals. The company is subject to state contributions at a rate of 3.1% for wages not in excess of $8,100. Determine each of the following amounts based upon the 41st weekly payroll period for the week ending October 11, 1991:

Date ______________________ Name ______________________

a. The amount of FICA tax to be withheld from the earnings of each person.

M. Grady .... $__________
P. Monroe .... $__________
V. Hoffman .... $__________
A. Drugan .... $__________
G. Beiter .... $__________
S. Egan .... $__________
B. Lin .... $__________

b. The amount of the employer's FICA taxes for the weekly payroll .... $__________

c. The amount of state unemployment contributions for the weekly payroll .... $__________

d. The amount of the net FUTA tax on the payroll .... $__________

e. The total amount of the employer's payroll taxes for the weekly payroll .... $__________

5-16. The Glavine Steel Company is located in State H, which enables employers to reduce their contribution rates under the experience-rating system. During 1977 to 1986, inclusive, the company's total contributions to state unemployment compensation amounted to $14,695. For the calendar years 1987 to 1990, inclusive, the contribution rate for employers was 2.7%.

The contributions of each employer are credited to an account maintained by the State Unemployment Compensation Commission. This account is credited with contributions paid into the account by the employer and is charged with unemployment benefits that are paid from the account.

Starting January 1, 1991, the contributions rate for all employers in State H will be based on the following tax-rate schedule:

Reserve Ratio	Contributions Rate
Contributions falling below benefits paid	7.0%
0.0% to 7.9%	5.5%
8.0% to 9.9%	4.5%
10.0% to 11.9%	3.5%
12.0% to 14.9%	2.5%
15.0% or more	1.5%

The annual payroll is the total wages payable during a 12-month period ending with the last day of the third quarter of any calendar year. The average annual payroll is the average of the last three annual payrolls. The SUTA tax rate for the year is computed using the information available as of September 30 of the preceding year.

The schedule below shows the total payroll and the taxable payroll for the calendar years 1987 to 1990.

GLAVINE STEEL COMPANY

CALENDAR YEAR	1987		1988		1989		1990	
	Total Payroll	Taxable Payroll	Total Payroll	Taxable Payroll	Total Payroll	Taxable Payroll	Total Payroll	Taxable Payroll
First Quarter	$12,000	$12,000	$11,000	$11,000	$13,000	$13,000	$10,000	$10,000
Second Quarter	11,750	11,750	11,500	11,400	12,750	12,700	9,300	9,300
Third Quarter	12,500	12,250	12,750	12,400	12,200	12,000	9,350	9,350
Fourth Quarter	13,000	12,500	12,500	12,200	14,000	13,750	—	—

Unemployment benefits became payable to the company's qualified unemployed workers on January 1, 1978. Between that time and September 30, 1990, total benefits amounting to $15,100.90 were charged against the employer's account. Compute:

a. The contribution rate for 1991 .... ________%

b. The rate for 1991 if $2,000 additional benefits had been charged by mistake to the account of the Glavine Steel Company by the State Unemployment Compensation Commission .... ________%

5-17. As the accountant for the Monroe Trucking Company, you are preparing the company's annual return, Form 940. Use the following information to complete Form 940 on page 195.

The net FUTA tax liability for each quarter of 1991 was as follows: 1st, $97; 2d, $87; 3d, $69.70; and 4th, $59.50. Since the net FUTA tax liability did not exceed $100 until the end of the 2d quarter, the company was not required to make its first deposit of FUTA taxes until July 31, 1991. The second deposit was not required until January 31, 1992. Assume that the federal tax deposit coupons (Form 8109) were completed and the deposits made on these dates.

a. State F's reporting number: 73902.
b. The Monroe Trucking Company has one employee who performs all of his duties in another state—State P. The employer's identification number for this state is 7-115180.
c. Total payments made to employees during calendar year 1991:

State F	$53,450
State P	9,100
Total	$62,550

d. Payments made to employees in excess of $7,000: $23,400.
e. Amount contributed to unemployment compensation fund of State F under merit rating, 1.8% of $32,150, or $578.70, for calendar year 1991. For State P, the contribution was 3.6% of $7,000 (the taxable salary limit), or $252.
f. Form is to be signed by Elmer P. Lear, Vice-President.

Date ______________________ Name ______________________

Practical Problem 5-17

Form **940** Department of the Treasury Internal Revenue Service

Employer's Annual Federal Unemployment (FUTA) Tax Return

► For Paperwork Reduction Act Notice, see page 2.

OMB No. 1545-0028

1991

T	
FF	
FD	
FP	
I	
T	

If incorrect, make any necessary change. ►

Name (as distinguished from trade name)

Calendar year 1991

Trade name, if any

MONROE TRUCKING COMPANY

Address and ZIP code

423 BRISTOL PIKE, NEWTOWN, STATE F 18940-4523

Employer identification number

54- 0663793

A Did you pay all required contributions to state unemployment funds by the due date of Form 940? (See instructions if none required.) . . . ☐ Yes ☐ No

If you checked the "Yes" box, enter the amount of contributions paid to state unemployment funds . . . . ► $ ________

B Are you required to pay contributions to only one state? . . . . . ☐ Yes ☐ No

If you checked the "Yes" box: (1) Enter the name of the state where you are required to pay contributions . . . . ► ________

(2) Enter your state reporting number(s) as shown on state unemployment tax return. ► ________

C If any part of wages taxable for FUTA tax is exempt from state unemployment tax, check the box. (See the Specific Instructions on page 2.). . . . . ☐

Note: *If you checked the "Yes" boxes in both questions A and B and did not check the box in C above, you may be able to use Form 940-EZ.*

Part I Computation of Taxable Wages (to be completed by all taxpayers)

			Amount paid		
1	Total payments (including exempt payments) during the calendar year for services of employees			1	
2	Exempt payments. (Explain each exemption shown, attaching additional sheets if necessary.) ► ________	2			
3	Payments for services of more than $7,000. Enter only the excess over the first $7,000 paid to individual employees not including exempt amounts shown on line 2. Do not use the state wage limitation.	3			
4	Total exempt payments (add lines 2 and 3)			4	
5	**Total taxable wages** (subtract line 4 from line 1). (If any part is exempt from state contributions, see instructions.) ►			5	

Part II Tax Due or Refund (Complete if you checked the "Yes" boxes in both questions A and B and did not check the box in C above.)

1	**Total FUTA tax.** Multiply the wages in Part I, line 5, by .008 and enter here	1	
2	Total FUTA tax deposited for the year, including any overpayment applied from a prior year (from your records) . .	2	
3	**Balance due** (subtract line 2 from line 1). This should be $100 or less. Pay to IRS . . . . . . ►	3	
4	**Overpayment** (subtract line 1 from line 2). Check if it is to be: ☐ Applied to next return, or ☐ Refunded ►	4	

Part III Tax Due or Refund (Complete if you checked the "No" box in either question A or B or you checked the box in C above. Also complete Part V.)

1	Gross FUTA tax. Multiply the wages in Part I, line 5, by .062			1	
2	Maximum credit. Multiply the wages in Part I, line 5, by .054	2			
3	**Credit allowable:** Enter the smaller of the amount in Part V, line 11, or Part III, line 2 . .	3			
4	**Total FUTA tax** (subtract line 3 from line 1).			4	
5	Total FUTA tax deposited for the year, including any overpayment applied from a prior year (from your records)			5	
6	**Balance due** (subtract line 5 from line 4). This should be $100 or less. Pay to IRS . . . . ►			6	
7	**Overpayment** (subtract line 4 from line 5). Check if it is to be: ☐ Applied to next return, or ☐ Refunded ►			7	

Part IV Record of Quarterly Federal Tax Liability for Unemployment Tax (Do not include state liability.)

Quarter	First	Second	Third	Fourth	Total for Year
Liability for quarter					

Part V Computation of Tentative Credit (Complete if you checked the "No" box in either question A or B or you checked the box in C above—see instructions.)

Name of state	State reporting number(s) as shown on employer's state contribution returns	Taxable payroll (as defined in state act)	State experience rate period 4		State experience rate	Contributions if rate had been 5.4% (col. 3 x .054)	Contributions payable at experience rate (col. 3 x col. 5)	Additional credit (col. 6 minus col. 7) If 0 or less, enter 0.	Contributions actually paid to the state
1	2	3	From—	To—	5	6	7	8	9
10 Totals . . . . ►									

11 Total tentative credit (add line 10, columns 8 and 9 only—see instructions for limitations) . . . . ► ________

If you will not have to file returns in the future, write "Final" here (see general instruction "Who Must File") and sign the return. ► ________

Under penalties of perjury, I declare that I have examined this return, including accompanying schedules and statements, and to the best of my knowledge and belief, it is true, correct, and complete, and that no part of any payment made to a state unemployment fund claimed as a credit was or is to be deducted from the payments to employees.

Signature ► ________ **Title (Owner, etc.)** ► ________ **Date** ► ________

Form 940

5-18. The information listed below refers to the employees of the Dumas Company for the year ended December 31, 1991. The wages are separated into the quarters in which they were paid to the individual employees.

DUMAS COMPANY

Name	Social Security #	1st Qtr.	2d Qtr.	3d Qtr.	4th Qtr.	Total
Robert G. Cramer	173-68-0001	$ 1,800	$ 2,000	$ 2,000	$ 2,200	$ 8,000
Daniel M. English (Foreman).....	168-95-0003	3,000	3,400	3,400	3,400	13,200
Ruth A. Small	199-99-1998	2,000	2,300	2,300	2,400	9,000
Harry B. Klaus	168-75-7413	1,600	1,700	1,700	1,700	6,700
Kenneth N. George (Mgr.)	179-18-6523	3,600	4,000	4,500	5,000	17,100
Mavis R. Jones	123-45-6789	1,600	1,700	1,700	-0-	5,000
Marshall T. McCoy	131-35-3334	1,400	1,400	-0-	-0-	2,800
Bertram A. Gompers (President) ..	153-00-1014	4,500	5,000	5,500	6,300	21,300
Arthur S. Rooks	171-71-7277	-0-	700	1,700	1,700	4,100
Mary R. Bastian	186-83-8111	3,000	3,200	3,200	3,200	12,600
Klaus C. Werner	143-21-2623	2,300	2,500	2,500	2,500	9,800
Kathy T. Tyler	137-36-3534	-0-	-0-	1,300	1,700	3,000
Totals		$24,800	$27,900	$29,800	$30,100	$112,600

For 1991, State D's contributions rate for the Dumas Company, based on the experience rating system of the state, was 2.8% of the first $7,000 of each employee's earnings. The state tax returns are due one month after the end of each calendar quarter. During 1991, the company paid $1,976.80 of contributions to State D's unemployment fund.

Employer's phone number: (613) 555-0029. Employer's State D reporting number: 80596.

Using the forms supplied on pages 197-200, complete the following for 1991:

a. Federal Tax Deposit Coupons—Form 8109
b. Employer's Report for Unemployment Compensation, State D—4th Quarter only
c. Employer's Annual Federal Unemployment (FUTA) Tax Return—Form 940-EZ

Indicate on each form the date that the form should be submitted and the amount of money that must be paid.

The president of the company signs all tax forms.

Date ______________________ Name ______________________

Practical Problem 5-18

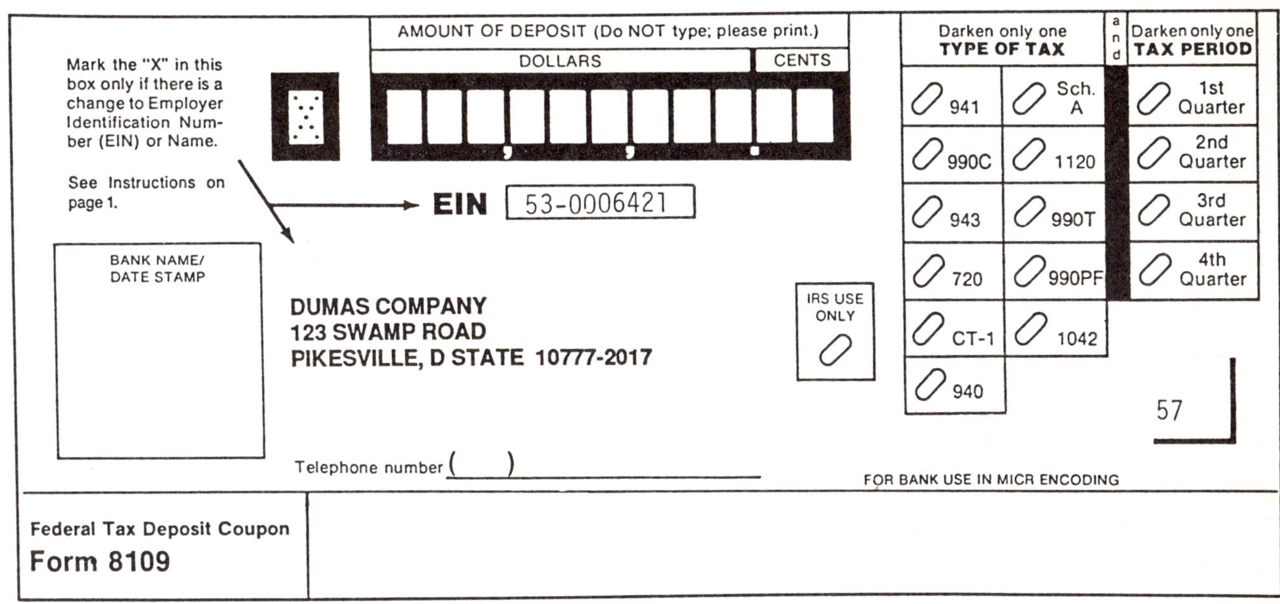

Mark the "X" in this box only if there is a change to Employer Identification Number (EIN) or Name.

See Instructions on page 1.

AMOUNT OF DEPOSIT (Do NOT type; please print.)

DOLLARS | CENTS

EIN 53-0006421

BANK NAME/ DATE STAMP

DUMAS COMPANY
123 SWAMP ROAD
PIKESVILLE, D STATE 10777-2017

IRS USE ONLY

Darken only one TYPE OF TAX: 941, Sch. A, 990C, 1120, 943, 990T, 720, 990PF, CT-1, 1042, 940

and

Darken only one TAX PERIOD: 1st Quarter, 2nd Quarter, 3rd Quarter, 4th Quarter

57

Telephone number ( )

FOR BANK USE IN MICR ENCODING

Federal Tax Deposit Coupon
Form 8109

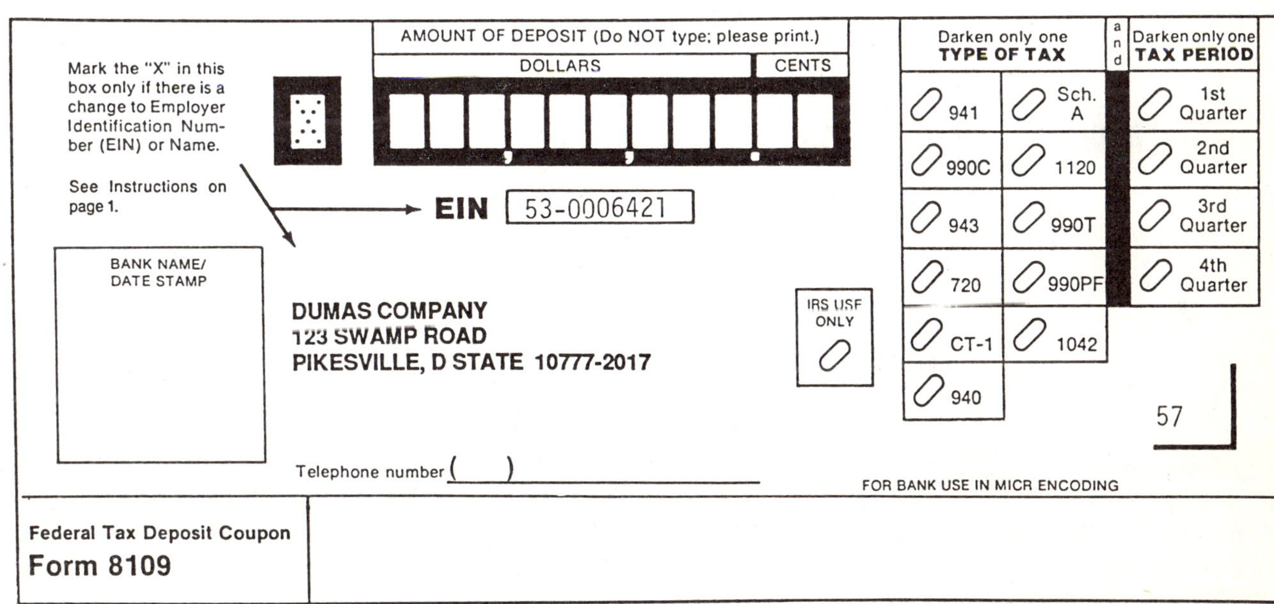

Mark the "X" in this box only if there is a change to Employer Identification Number (EIN) or Name.

See Instructions on page 1.

AMOUNT OF DEPOSIT (Do NOT type; please print.)

DOLLARS | CENTS

EIN 53-0006421

BANK NAME/ DATE STAMP

DUMAS COMPANY
123 SWAMP ROAD
PIKESVILLE, D STATE 10777-2017

IRS USE ONLY

Darken only one TYPE OF TAX: 941, Sch. A, 990C, 1120, 943, 990T, 720, 990PF, CT-1, 1042, 940

and

Darken only one TAX PERIOD: 1st Quarter, 2nd Quarter, 3rd Quarter, 4th Quarter

57

Telephone number ( )

FOR BANK USE IN MICR ENCODING

Federal Tax Deposit Coupon
Form 8109

Practical Problem 5-18

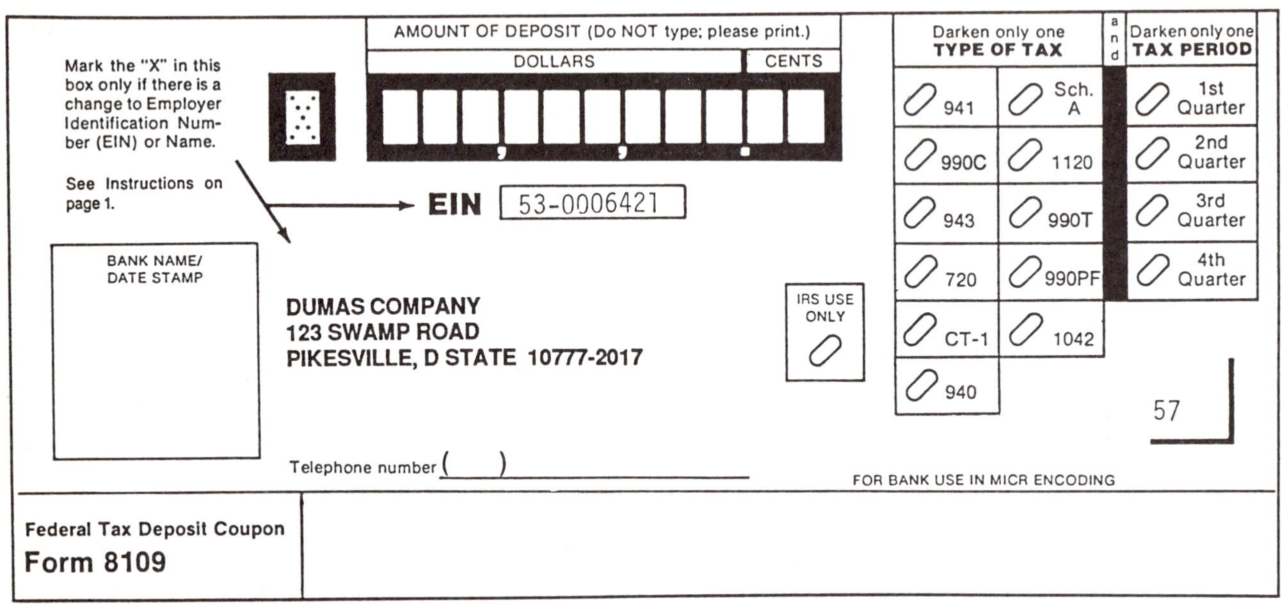

Mark the "X" in this box only if there is a change to Employer Identification Number (EIN) or Name.

See Instructions on page 1.

AMOUNT OF DEPOSIT (Do NOT type; please print.)

DOLLARS | CENTS

EIN 53-0006421

BANK NAME/ DATE STAMP

DUMAS COMPANY
123 SWAMP ROAD
PIKESVILLE, D STATE 10777-2017

IRS USE ONLY

Telephone number ( )

Darken only one TYPE OF TAX: 941, Sch. A, 990C, 1120, 943, 990T, 720, 990PF, CT-1, 1042, 940

and

Darken only one TAX PERIOD: 1st Quarter, 2nd Quarter, 3rd Quarter, 4th Quarter

57

FOR BANK USE IN MICR ENCODING

Federal Tax Deposit Coupon
Form 8109

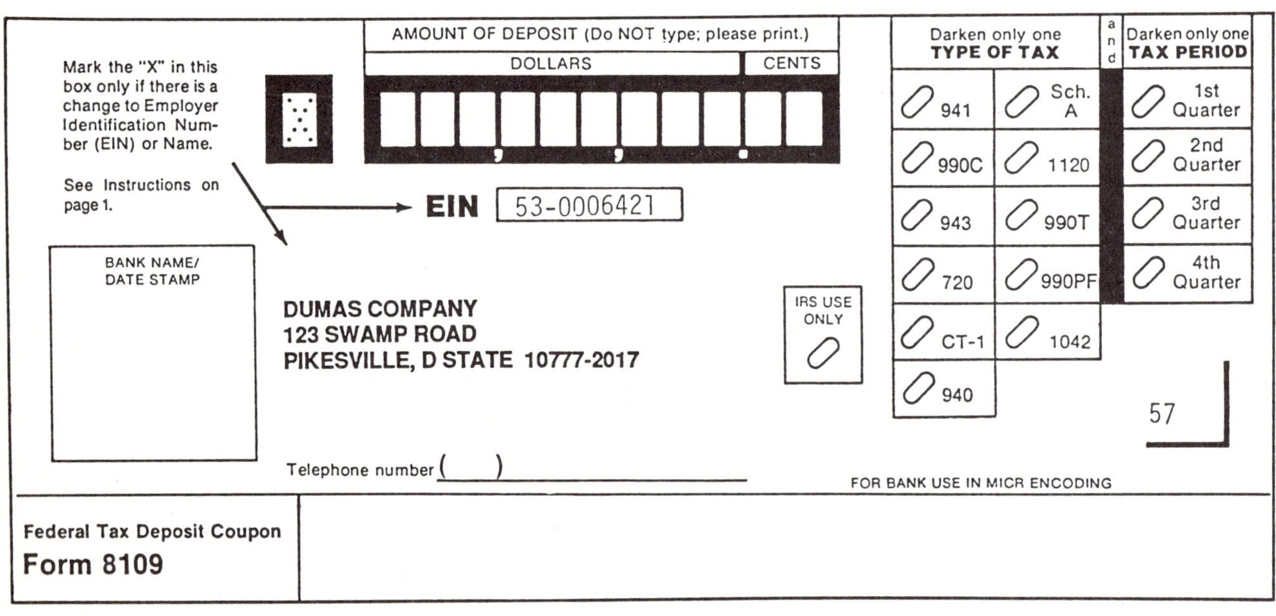

Mark the "X" in this box only if there is a change to Employer Identification Number (EIN) or Name.

See Instructions on page 1.

AMOUNT OF DEPOSIT (Do NOT type; please print.)

DOLLARS | CENTS

EIN 53-0006421

BANK NAME/ DATE STAMP

DUMAS COMPANY
123 SWAMP ROAD
PIKESVILLE, D STATE 10777-2017

IRS USE ONLY

Telephone number ( )

Darken only one TYPE OF TAX: 941, Sch. A, 990C, 1120, 943, 990T, 720, 990PF, CT-1, 1042, 940

and

Darken only one TAX PERIOD: 1st Quarter, 2nd Quarter, 3rd Quarter, 4th Quarter

57

FOR BANK USE IN MICR ENCODING

Federal Tax Deposit Coupon
Form 8109

Date ____________________ Name ____________________

Practical Problem 5-18

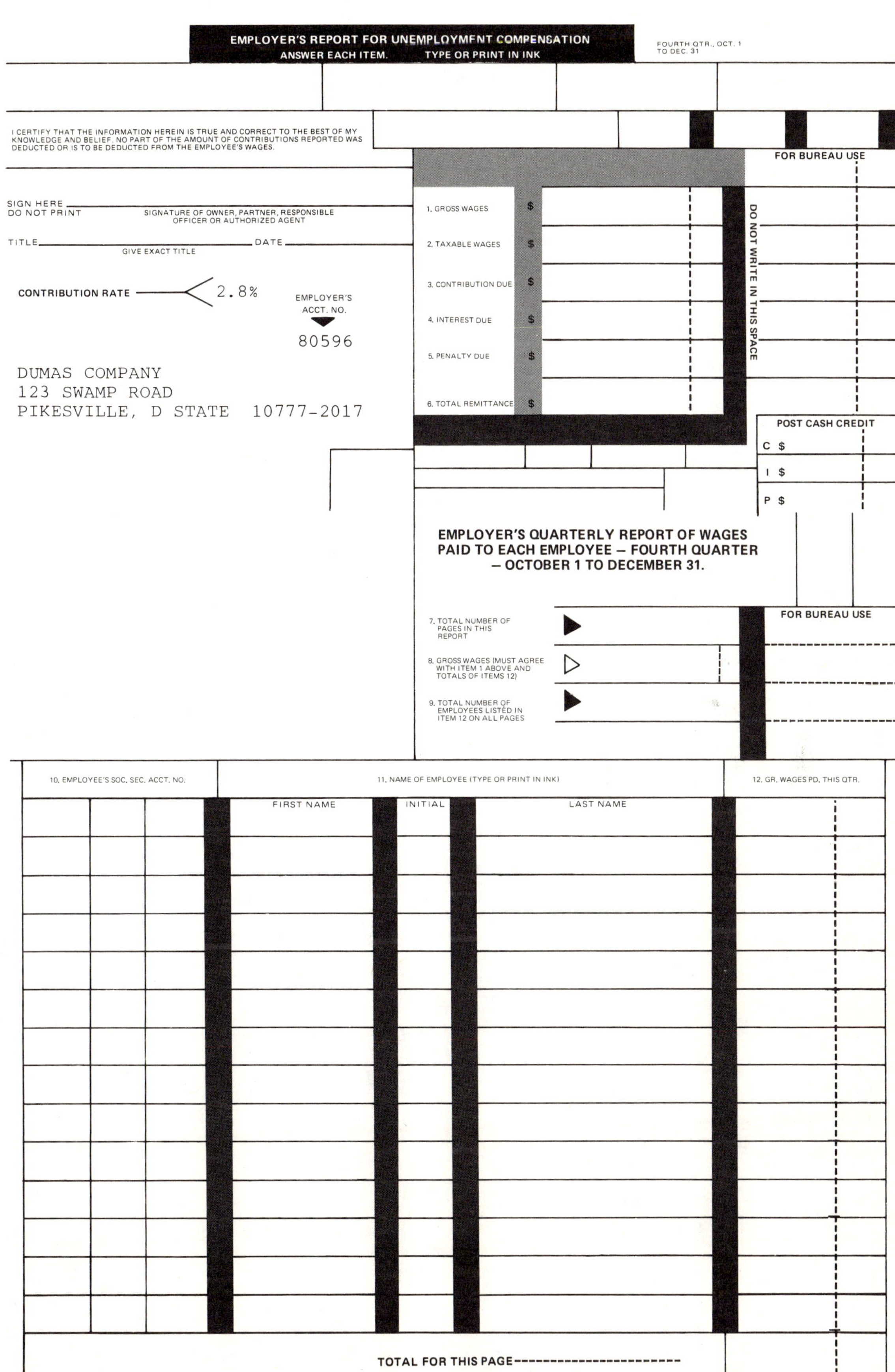

EMPLOYER'S REPORT FOR UNEMPLOYMENT COMPENSATION
ANSWER EACH ITEM. TYPE OR PRINT IN INK

FOURTH QTR., OCT. 1 TO DEC. 31

I CERTIFY THAT THE INFORMATION HEREIN IS TRUE AND CORRECT TO THE BEST OF MY KNOWLEDGE AND BELIEF. NO PART OF THE AMOUNT OF CONTRIBUTIONS REPORTED WAS DEDUCTED OR IS TO BE DEDUCTED FROM THE EMPLOYEE'S WAGES.

SIGN HERE DO NOT PRINT ____________________
SIGNATURE OF OWNER, PARTNER, RESPONSIBLE OFFICER OR AUTHORIZED AGENT

TITLE ____________________ DATE ____________
GIVE EXACT TITLE

CONTRIBUTION RATE 2.8%

EMPLOYER'S ACCT. NO. 80596

DUMAS COMPANY
123 SWAMP ROAD
PIKESVILLE, D STATE 10777-2017

FOR BUREAU USE

1. GROSS WAGES	$	
2. TAXABLE WAGES	$	
3. CONTRIBUTION DUE	$	
4. INTEREST DUE	$	
5. PENALTY DUE	$	
6. TOTAL REMITTANCE	$	

DO NOT WRITE IN THIS SPACE

POST CASH CREDIT
C $
I $
P $

EMPLOYER'S QUARTERLY REPORT OF WAGES PAID TO EACH EMPLOYEE — FOURTH QUARTER — OCTOBER 1 TO DECEMBER 31.

		FOR BUREAU USE
7. TOTAL NUMBER OF PAGES IN THIS REPORT		
8. GROSS WAGES (MUST AGREE WITH ITEM 1 ABOVE AND TOTALS OF ITEMS 12)		
9. TOTAL NUMBER OF EMPLOYEES LISTED IN ITEM 12 ON ALL PAGES		

10. EMPLOYEE'S SOC. SEC. ACCT. NO.	11. NAME OF EMPLOYEE (TYPE OR PRINT IN INK) FIRST NAME	INITIAL	LAST NAME	12. GR. WAGES PD. THIS QTR.
TOTAL FOR THIS PAGE				

Practical Problem 5-18

Form **940-EZ**

Department of the Treasury
Internal Revenue Service

Employer's Annual Federal Unemployment (FUTA) Tax Return

OMB No. 1545-1110

1991

T	
FF	
FD	
FP	
I	
T	

If incorrect, make any necessary changes.

Name (as distinguished from trade name)

Calendar year
1991

Trade name, if any
DUMAS COMPANY

Address and ZIP code
123 SWAMP ROAD PIKESVILLE,
D STATE 10777-2017

Employer identification number
53-0006421

Before beginning, follow the chart under "Who Can Use Form 940-EZ" on page 2. If you cannot use Form 940-EZ, you must use Form 940 instead.

A Enter the amount of contributions paid to your state unemployment fund. (See instructions for line A on page 4.) . . . ▶ $ ________

B (1) Enter the name of the state where you have to pay contributions . . . ▶ ________

(2) Enter your state reporting number(s) as shown on state unemployment tax return. ▶ ________

Part I Taxable Wages and FUTA Tax

			Amount paid			
1	Total payments (including payments shown on lines 2 and 3) during the calendar year for services of employees . .			1		
2	Exempt payments. (Explain all exempt payments, attaching additional sheets if necessary.) ▶ ________	2				
3	Payments for services of more than $7,000. Enter only amounts over the first $7,000 paid to each employee. Do not include any exempt payments from line 2	3				
4	Total exempt payments (add lines 2 and 3) . . .			4		
5	**Total taxable wages** (subtract line 4 from line 1) . . . ▶			5		
6	**FUTA tax.** Multiply the wages on line 5 by .008 and enter here. (If the result is over $100, also complete Part II.) . .			6		
7	Total FUTA tax deposited for the year, including any overpayment applied from a prior year (from your records) . .			7		
8	**Amount you owe** (subtract line 7 from line 6). This should be $100 or less. Pay to IRS . . . ▶			8		
9	**Overpayment** (subtract line 6 from line 7). Check if it is to be: ☐ Applied to next return, or ☐ Refunded. . ▶			9		

Part II Record of Quarterly Federal Unemployment Tax Liability (Do not include state liability.) Complete only if line 6 is over $100.

Quarter	First (Jan. 1 - Mar. 31)	Second (Apr. 1 - June 30)	Third (July 1 - Sept. 30)	Fourth (Oct. 1 - Dec. 31)	Total for Year
Liability for quarter					

If you will not have to file returns in the future, write "Final" here (see *Who Must File a Return* on page 2) and sign the return. ▶

Under penalties of perjury, I declare that I have examined this return, including accompanying schedules and statements, and, to the best of my knowledge and belief, it is true, correct, and complete, and that no part of any payment made to a state unemployment fund claimed as a credit was, or is to be, deducted from the payments to employees.

Signature ▶ Title (Owner, etc.) ▶ Date ▶

Form 940-EZ

CONTINUING PAYROLL PROBLEM

Refer to the partially completed payroll register that you worked on at the end of Unit 4. You will now calculate the employer's liability for unemployment taxes (FUTA and SUTA) for the pay of January 14. These computations will be used at the end of Unit 6 in recording the payroll tax entries.

To determine the employer's liability for unemployment taxes, proceed as follows:

1. Enter each employee's gross earnings in the Taxable Earnings—FUTA and SUTA columns.
2. Total the Taxable Earnings—FUTA and SUTA columns.
3. At the bottom of your payroll register, calculate the following for the total payroll:
   a. Net FUTA tax. Since this is the first pay period of the year, none of the employees are near the $7,000 ceiling; therefore, each employee's gross earnings is subject to the FUTA tax.
   b. Since the Steimer Company is a new employer, Pennsylvania has assigned the company a contribution rate of 3.5% on the first $8,000 of each employee's earnings.

NOTE: Retain your partially completed payroll register for use at the end of Unit 6.

CASE PROBLEM

Case 5-1 Reducing a High Unemployment Tax Rate

Over the past two years, Kermit Stone, the controller of the Hilton Company, has been concerned that the company has been paying a large amount of money for state unemployment taxes. On reviewing the "unemployment file" with the head accountant, Deborah Murtha, he learns that the company's tax rate is near the top of the range of the state's experience-rating system.

After calling the local unemployment office, Stone realizes that the turnover of employees at the Hilton Company has had an adverse effect on the company's tax rates. In addition, after consulting with Murtha, he discovers that the eligibility reports that come from the state unemployment office are just signed and sent back to the state without any review.

The eligibility reports are notices that an ex-employee has filed a claim for unemployment benefits. By signing these reports "blindly," the company, in effect, tells the state that the employee is eligible for the benefits. Any benefits paid are charged by the state against the Hilton Company's account.

Stone is convinced that the rates the company is paying are too high, and he feels that part of the reason is the "blind" signing of the eligibility reports. Besides this, he wonders what other steps the company can take to lower its contribution rate and taxes.

Submit recommendations that might help Stone reduce the "unfair" burden that the unemployment compensation taxes are leveling on the Hilton Company.

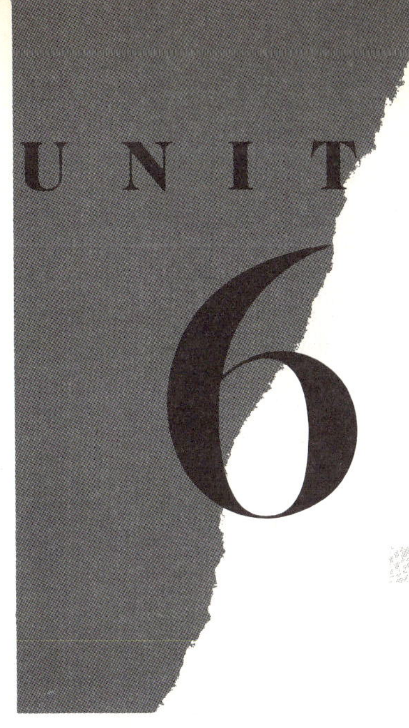

Analyzing and Journalizing Payroll Transactions

GOALS OF THIS UNIT

After completing your study of this unit, you should be able to:

1. Record payrolls in payroll registers and post to employees' earnings records.
2. Journalize the entries to record the payroll, amounts withheld from employees' gross earnings, and payroll taxes.
3. Post to the various general ledger accounts that are used to accumulate information from the payroll entries.
4. Understand the payment and the recording of the payroll tax deposits.
5. Use the information in the payroll registers and earnings records to prepare the various reports required by government agencies.

In this unit, we shall discuss with you the procedures for recording the payroll in a payroll register and for transferring information from the payroll register to the employees' earnings records. Also, we shall analyze typical transactions pertaining to a company's payroll, record these transactions in the company's book of original entry, and post them to the proper ledger accounts.

THE PAYROLL REGISTER

As you have seen in Illustration 1-7 on page 17 and in completing the Continuing Payroll Problem, the payroll register gives detailed information about the payroll for each pay period. To summarize, the payroll register may provide the following types of information:

1. The title of the form.
2. The period covered by the payroll and the date on which the pay period ends.
3. Department or branch. Some large businesses with many departments or branches prepare a separate sheet in the payroll register for each department or branch on each payday. Other firms provide "distribution" columns such as "Sales Salaries," "Office Salaries," and "Plant Wages" for classifying the gross wages and salaries according to the nature of the wage and salary expense. The total of each distribution column shows the total amount for that particular operating expense.
4. A column to record the name of each employee. Many businesses provide a column to record an identifying number such as the time clock number for each employee.
5. Marital status and number of withholding allowances. This information is used in determining the income tax deductions.
6. A record of time worked. Many companies show detailed information in the payroll register as to hours worked each day by each employee.
7. Some companies provide separate columns to show a total of regular hours worked and a total of overtime hours worked during the

pay period. This information may be of help in a business that schedules much overtime work.

8. The payroll register should show the regular rate of pay and the amount earned at the regular rate.
9. A space should be provided to record the overtime rate and the total earnings at the overtime rate.
10. A column should be provided to record the total earnings.
11. A section of the payroll register should provide information about deductions from total earnings. A separate column may be provided for each type of deduction. The various deductions will be discussed later in this unit.
12. A column to show the net amount paid, which is the total earnings less deductions. When wages or salaries are paid by check, a company usually provides a column for inserting the number of the check used in paying the employee.
13. Some firms provide special columns in the payroll register to indicate that portion of the employee's wages that is taxable under the Federal Insurance Contributions Act and other laws that require payment of the tax only on wages up to a certain amount.

The partial payroll register shown in Illustration 6-1 contains most of the information outlined above. This register is used to calculate the pay for hourly workers for a weekly pay period. The layout of the section devoted to time or hours worked will vary, depending on the payroll period and the work schedules of each individual business.

A payroll register may be a bound book with ruled sheets, or it may be a loose-leaf book with sheets to be inserted. Many companies that manufacture business forms design and produce payroll registers that are sold through stationery stores and office supply houses. Very often these forms can be adapted to meet the needs of a business without making any major change in the layout of the forms.

Although some small businesses still prepare the payroll by hand, most businesses use calculating machines and computers of various sizes to process their payrolls. We discuss the application of automated methods to the preparation of payrolls in Appendix B.

Proving the Totals of the Payroll Register

As shown later in this unit, the payroll register provides the information needed in preparing the *journal entries* to record (1) the wages earned, deductions from wages, and net amount paid each payday and (2) the employer's payroll taxes. Prior to making the journal entry to record the payroll, you must check the accuracy of the amounts entered in the payroll register by proving the totals of the money columns. The partial payroll register shown in Illustration 6-1 is proved as follows:

Proof:

Regular earnings . . .	$2,497.20	
Overtime earnings . .	265.50	
Total earnings		$2,762.70

PAYROLL REGISTER

FOR WEEK ENDING *January 17* 19--

	NO.	NAME	Marital Status	No. W/H Allow.	TIME RECORD						REGULAR EARNINGS			OVERTIME EARNINGS		
					M	T	W	T	F	S	Hours	RATE PER HOUR	AMOUNT	Hours	RATE PER HOUR	AMOUNT
1	10	Amand, Jorge L.	M	3	8	8	8	8	8	4	40	5 20	208 00	4	7 80	31 20
2	12	Basile, Carole O.	M	4	8	8	8	8	10		40	7 10	284 00	2	10 65	21 30
3	13	Darnell, Robert T.	S	1	8	8	8	8	8		40	6 30	252 00			
4	23	Gorbus, Glen A.	M	2	8	8	8	8	8	8	40	5 90	236 00	8	8 85	70 80
5	24	Granger, Mary I.	S	1	8	8	8	0	8		32	5 10	163 20			
36		Totals											2,497 20			265 50

Illustration 6-1. Payroll Register (left side)

FICA tax withheld ..	$ 211.35	
Federal income taxes withheld	215.00	
State income taxes withheld	55.25	
Group insurance withheld	14.70	
Total deductions		$ 496.30
Total net pay		2,266.40
Total earnings		$2,762.70

In preparing the journal entry to record a payroll, you do not need to make a separate journal entry to record the wages of each employee; instead, you make an entry each payday to record the aggregate amount of wages earned, deductions made, and net payments to all employees, as determined from the Totals line of the payroll register. Depending upon the nature of the accounting system in use, a business may record the journal entry in a two-column general journal, a cashbook, a cash payments journal, or a combined cash journal. After the journal entry has been made, you must transfer, or post, the information from the journal to the appropriate accounts in the general ledger.

Some companies use a formal *payroll journal* instead of a payroll register to record each payroll. When you record the payroll originally in a payroll journal, you post from the payroll journal to the general ledger accounts.

Using the Information in the Payroll Register

In addition to serving as the source of authority for preparing journal entries to record the payroll and the employer's payroll taxes, the payroll register provides information that meets the record-keeping requirements of the Fair Labor Standards Act. Also, the payroll register provides data that are used in preparing periodic reports required by various laws.

Besides the information contained in the payroll register, businesses are required to provide information about the accumulated earnings of each employee. For that reason it is necessary to keep a separate payroll record on each employee—the employee's earnings record. This record, which we introduced in Illustration 1-8 on page 17, is discussed in the following section.

THE EMPLOYEE'S EARNINGS RECORD

The employee's earnings record is a supplementary record that provides information for:

1. *Preparing the payroll register.* For example, the earnings record contains information such as the hourly rate, marital status, and number of withholding allowances claimed, which is needed to calculate gross earnings and to determine the amount to withhold for income tax purposes.
2. *Preparing reports* required by state unemployment compensation or disability laws.
3. *Determining when the accumulated wages of an employee reach the cutoff level* for purposes of FICA, FUTA, or SUTA. As shown in Illustration 6-2, a special "Cumulative Earnings" column is provided so that the total amount of accumulated wages can be recorded each pay period. Thus, when the FICA, FUTA, or SUTA cutoff has been reached, the record shows that the employee or the employer no longer has a

DEPT. ACCOUNTING — 10

TOTAL EARNINGS	DEDUCTIONS					NET PAID		TAXABLE EARNINGS			
	FICA TAX	FED. INCOME TAX	STATE INCOME TAX	GROUP INS.	OTHER	Check No.	AMOUNT	FICA	FUTA	SUTA	
239 20	18 30	8 00	4 78	9 00		898	199 12	239 20	239 20	239 20	1
305 30	23 36	12 00	6 11	9 00		899	254 83	305 30	305 30	305 30	2
252 00	19 28	29 00	5 04	3 90		900	194 78	252 00	252 00	252 00	3
306 80	23 47	24 00	6 14	9 00		901	244 19	306 80	306 80	306 80	4
163 20	12 48	15 00	3 26	3 90		902	128 56	163 20	163 20	163 20	5
2762 70	211 35	215 00	55 25	14 70			2266 40	2762 70	2762 70	2762 70	36

Illustration 6-1. Payroll Register (right side)

liability for that particular tax during the rest of the calendar year.

4. *Preparing payroll analyses* for governmental agencies and for internal management control. Information such as the department in which the employee works and the job title may be used as the basis for such analyses.
5. *Settling employee grievances* regarding regular pay and overtime pay calculations and the withholding of amounts for income taxes and other purposes.
6. *Completing Forms W-2,* which show for each employee the annual gross earnings, income taxes withheld, wages subject to FICA tax, and FICA taxes withheld.

An employee's earnings record is kept for each employee whose wages are recorded in the payroll register. Each payday, after the information has been recorded in the payroll register, the information for each employee is posted to the employee's earnings record. The columns are arranged so that the information can be transferred easily. The earnings record shown in Illustration 6-2 is arranged for weekly pay periods. You will note that totals are provided for each quarter so that you can enter information easily on the quarterly tax returns. At the bottom of page 1 of the earnings record, there is a line for semiannual totals. At the bottom of page 2 of the form, which is not illustrated, there is a line for annual totals that you will need in preparing Form 940 and other year-end reports.

If a business pays wages once a month, the employee's earnings record would need only one line for each month, or three lines for a quarter. Similarly, if a business paid wages semimonthly, the form would have six lines for each quarter.

RECORDING THE GROSS PAYROLL AND WITHHOLDINGS

After you have recorded the payroll in the payroll register and posted to the employees' earnings records, you must enter the information in the employer's accounting system. An entry for the totals of each payroll period should be made in the general journal and posted to the general ledger. You can obtain the amounts needed for this entry from the Totals line at the bottom of the last payroll register sheet.

EMPLOYEE'S EARNINGS RECORD

WEEK	19-- WEEK ENDING	TOTAL WORKED		REGULAR EARNINGS			OVERTIME EARNINGS			DEDUCTIONS					NET PAID		CUMULATIVE EARNINGS	TIME LOST
		DAYS	HOURS	HOURS	RATE	AMOUNT	HOURS	RATE	AMOUNT	FICA	FED. INC. TAX	STATE INC. TAX	GROUP INS.	OTHER DEDUCTIONS	CHECK NO.	AMOUNT		
1	1/3	5	44	40	5 20	208 00	4	7 80	31 20	18 30	8 00	4 78	9 00		510	199 12	239 20	
2	1/10	5	42	40	5 20	208 00	2	7 80	15 60	17 11	6 00	4 47	9 00		706	187 02	462 80	
3	1/17	6	44	40	5 20	208 00	4	7 80	31 20	18 30	8 00	4 78	9 00		898	199 12	702 00	
4																		
5																		
6																		
7																		
8																		
9																		
10																		
11																		
12																		
13																		
QUARTER TOTAL																		
1																		
2																		
13																		
QUARTER TOTAL																		
SEMIANNUAL TOTAL																		

SEX	DEPARTMENT	OCCUPATION	WORKS IN (STATE)	S. S. ACCOUNT NO.	NAME-LAST	FIRST	MIDDLE	NO. W/H ALLOW.
F M X	A-10	Clerk-Typist	XXX	204-43-1186	Amand	Jorge	Luis	3
								MARITAL STATUS M

Illustration 6-2. Employee's Earnings Record (page 1)

The following journal entry to record the payroll includes a debit to the appropriate expense account(s) for the gross payroll and credits to the various liability accounts for the withholdings from the pay and for the net amount to be paid employees:

	Debit	Credit
Salary Expense	XXX	
Liabilities (Withholdings) ...		XXX
Cash or Salaries Payable (Net Pay)		XXX
To record the payment of salaries and the liabilities for the employees' taxes withheld.		

Gross Payroll

You should record the total gross payroll (regular earnings and overtime earnings) as the debit portion of the payroll entry. The account to be used has a title such as *Wages Expense* or *Salaries Expense*. In the case of a company with many departments or cost centers, the accounts would have titles such as *Wages Expense—Department A, Wages Expense—Maintenance,* and *Wages Expense—Residential Services*. These accounts show the total gross earnings that the employer incurs as an *expense* each payday.

FICA Taxes—Employee

The employer is required by law to withhold social security taxes of 7.65% of the taxable wages of each employee. Since the employer has withheld these taxes from the pay of the employees and now owes this amount to the IRS, the taxes withheld represent a *liability* of the employer. When recording the payroll, you should credit an account entitled *FICA Taxes Payable* for the amount of FICA taxes withheld.

Federal Income Taxes

Employers are required to withhold a percentage of their employees' wages for income tax purposes. We explained in Unit 4 the methods of ascertaining the amounts to be withheld from wages for income tax purposes.

As with FICA taxes withheld, the employer also owes to the IRS the federal income taxes withheld from the employees' pay. You should keep a separate account in the general ledger for recording the employer's *liability* for the amount of federal income taxes withheld. A suitable title for this account is *Employees Federal Income Taxes Payable,* which may be abbreviated to read *Employees FIT Payable*. The account is credited for the total amount of federal income taxes withheld each payday and is subsequently debited for the amounts paid to a depositary or to the IRS.

State and City Income Taxes

Employers may be required to withhold state and city income taxes in addition to the federal income taxes that are withheld. You should keep a separate account in the general ledger for recording the employer's *liability* for the amount of each kind of income tax withheld. Account titles that may be used are: *Employees State Income Taxes (SIT) Payable* and *Employees City Income Taxes (CIT) Payable.*

Employees' Contributions to State Funds

A few states require employees to contribute to state unemployment compensation or disability funds. In states where employee contributions are required, the employer deducts the amount of the contributions from the employees' wages at the time the wages are paid. The *liability* for employees' contributions may be recorded in the same account as the employer's contributions; namely, *SUTA Taxes Payable.* Or, a separate ledger account, such as *SUTA Taxes Payable—State A* and *SUTA Taxes Payable—State B,* may be opened for each state. If the contributions of employees are to a disability benefit fund, this amount is usually reported separately to the state and should be recorded in a separate liability account such as *Employees Disability Contributions Payable.*

Net Pay

The total of the net amount paid to the employees each payday is credited to either the *Cash* account or the *Salaries Payable* account.

RECORDING PAYROLL TAXES

In this section we shall analyze the journal entries that are made to record the following kinds of payroll taxes, each of which has been discussed in preceding units:

1. *FICA*—taxes imposed under the Federal Insurance Contributions Act for old-age, survivors, and disability insurance and hospital insurance benefits.
2. *FUTA*—taxes imposed under the Federal Unemployment Tax Act.
3. *SUTA*—contributions to the unemployment compensation funds of one or more states.
4. *Workers' Compensation Insurance Expense*—cost of insurance that protects employees against losses due to injury or death incurred during employment.

The following accounts will be needed in the general ledger if the employer is subject to FICA taxes, FUTA taxes, SUTA taxes, and workers' compensation insurance expense:

1. *Payroll Taxes*—an expense account in which are recorded the FICA, FUTA, and SUTA taxes on the employer.
2. *FICA Taxes Payable*—a liability account in which is recorded the liability of the employer for the tax withheld from employees' wages plus the employer's portion of the tax.
3. *FUTA Taxes Payable*—a liability account showing the accumulation of the employer's federal unemployment taxes payable to the federal government.
4. *SUTA Taxes Payable*—a liability account showing the amount payable to state unemployment compensation fund(s).
5. *Workers' Compensation Insurance Expense*—an expense account in which are recorded the premiums paid by the company to provide coverage for employees against employment-related injury or death.

The following journal entry to record the payroll taxes includes a debit to the tax expense account for the total of the employer's payroll taxes and credits to the various tax liability accounts:

	Debit	Credit
Payroll Taxes	XXX	
Liabilities (Various Taxes) . .		XXX
To record the payroll taxes and liabilities of the employer.		

FICA Taxes—Employer

The law states specifically that deductions made from the wages of employees under FICA should be recorded immediately as a liability on the books of the company. The law does not require, however, that employers record their part of the FICA taxes at the time the *wages* are paid. While it is not necessary to record the employer's portion of the FICA taxes until the *taxes* are paid, many employers record their FICA tax liability each payday. This method of recording places the expense in the accounting period in which it was incurred.

The tax withheld from the employees' wages represents a liability of the employer. It does not constitute an expense of the employer since the employer simply withholds the amount of the tax. However, the tax on the employer represents both a business expense and a liability of the employer. Because the employer's FICA contribution is a *business expense*, it is deductible by the *employer* for federal income tax purposes (as are the costs of all other payroll taxes). However, the employee's contribution has the characteristics of an investment or a form of annuity, not an expense, and is therefore not deductible by the *employee* for federal income tax purposes.

SUTA Taxes

Under the state unemployment compensation laws, employers are required to pay contributions into one or more state unemployment compensation funds. When an employer is required to make contributions to the state unemployment compensation funds of more than one state, it may be advisable to keep a separate liability account for the contributions payable to each state. The employer may keep a single expense account in the general ledger with the title "SUTA Taxes" and a subsidiary ledger sheet for each state to which unemployment contributions are made.

FUTA Tax

An employer subject to the gross FUTA tax of 6.2% may be able to claim credit in paying the federal tax because of contributions made to state unemployment compensation funds. As discussed in Unit 5, the maximum credit that may be claimed is 5.4%, even though the amount of state contributions is more than or less than 5.4%. Thus, the net FUTA tax (6.2% - 5.4%) is .8%. Although you do not actually claim the credit against the FUTA tax until Form 940 is filed with the Internal Revenue Service, it is acceptable accounting practice to record the FUTA tax at the net amount (.8%) at the time you make the entry to record the employer's payroll taxes.

EXAMPLE:

The employees of the Absicon Company earn wages during the year amounting to $26,400, all of which is subject to the gross FUTA tax of 6.2%. The company is also required to make contributions to the unemployment compensation fund of the state in which the business is located at the rate of 2.8% of the wages paid each employee. The federal and state unemployment taxes are computed as follows:

SUTA tax, 2.8% of $26,400 =		**$739.20**	
Gross FUTA tax, 6.2% of $26,400 = ...	**$1,636.80**		
Less credit for SUTA tax, 5.4% of $26,400 = . .	**-1,425.60**	**211.20**	**(net FUTA tax)**
Total unemployment taxes . .		**$950.40**	

More simply, the net FUTA tax may be calculated by multiplying the taxable wages, $26,400, by the net FUTA tax rate, .8%, yielding $211.20.

The recording of the employer's FUTA tax for each pay period at .8% also applies to employers who, due to their state's liability for Title XII advances, have a net FUTA tax in excess of .8%. Since the exact rate is not known until November and the payment of the penalty is not made until the last deposit of the year, the FUTA tax expense for each payroll during the year is calculated at .8%. The extra FUTA tax, due to the penalty charge, can be recorded as a single adjusting entry at the end of the year:

	Debit	Credit
Payroll Taxes	XXX	
FUTA Taxes Payable		XXX
To record the employer's penalty for the year for the state's nonpayment of Title XII advances.		

The FUTA tax, like the FICA tax and the contributions to the state for unemployment compensation purposes, is a social security tax. Thus, the FUTA tax can be charged to the same expense account as the other payroll taxes on the employer, the Payroll Taxes account. However, since employers may be required to pay the net FUTA tax quarterly, and to pay the FICA taxes more frequently, it is advisable to keep separate accounts for recording these two liabilities of the employer.

Entries to Record Wages and Payroll Taxes

In the following illustrations of recording (or journalizing) wages and the payroll taxes imposed under both the federal and state laws, the employer is responsible for the following taxes:

1. FICA tax on employees: 7.65%.
2. FIT withheld from employees.
3. FICA tax on employers: 7.65%.
4. Net FUTA tax: .8%.
5. SUTA tax: 2.4%.

The weekly payroll amounts to $3,200, and the entire amount is subject to all social security and unemployment taxes. You may record this information in two separate journal entries. In the first entry, you might record the wages expense of the employer and the liabilities for the FICA taxes and FIT withheld in a two-column general journal as follows:

	Debit	Credit
Wages Expense	3,200.00	
FICA Taxes Payable		244.80
Employees FIT Payable		230.00
Cash		2,725.20
To record the payment of wages and the liability for the employees' FICA taxes and FIT withheld.		

We can analyze this entry in T-accounts as shown below:

WAGES EXPENSE

3,200.00 This debit represents the employees' gross earnings for the pay period. This results in an increase in the operating expenses of the employer.	

FICA TAXES PAYABLE

	244.80 This credit results in an increase in a liability of the employer.

The amount credited to FICA Taxes Payable is computed as follows:

7.65% of $3,200 = $244.80, amount deducted from employees' wages

EMPLOYEES FIT PAYABLE

	230.00 This credit results in an increase in a liability of the employer.

The amount credited to Employees FIT Payable is obtained by using one of the withholding methods explained in Unit 4.

CASH

	2,725.20 This credit results in a decrease in an asset.

The amount credited to Cash is computed as follows:

$3,200.00, gross wages earned
-474.80, employees' taxes withheld
$2,725.20, net amount paid employees

In the second entry, you can record the employer's payroll taxes as follows:

	Debit	Credit
Payroll Taxes	347.20	
FICA Taxes Payable		244.80
FUTA Taxes Payable		25.60
SUTA Taxes Payable		76.80
To record the payroll taxes and the employer's liability for the taxes.		

Let's analyze this entry by means of T-accounts as shown below:

PAYROLL TAXES

Debit	Credit
347.20 This debit results in an increase in the operating expenses.	

The amount debited to Payroll Taxes is computed as follows:

7.65% of $3,200 =	$244.80,	employer's FICA tax
.8% of $3,200 =	25.60,	employer's net FUTA tax
2.4% of $3,200 =	76.80,	employer's SUTA tax
Total payroll taxes	$347.20	

FICA TAXES PAYABLE

Debit	Credit
	244.80 244.80 The second credit amount, representing the employer's FICA tax, also increases the employer's liability. The amount is determined as shown in the computation of the payroll taxes.

FUTA TAXES PAYABLE

Debit	Credit
	25.60 This credit results in an increase in a liability of the employer. The amount is determined as shown in the computation of the payroll taxes.

SUTA TAXES PAYABLE

Debit	Credit
	76.80 This credit results in an increase in a liability of the employer. The amount is determined as shown in the computation of the payroll taxes.

In the preceding illustration no contributions were required of employees for state unemployment compensation purposes. Assume that the employees had been required to make contributions of 1% to state unemployment compensation funds. The entry would then appear as follows:

	Debit	Credit
Wages Expense	3,200.00	
FICA Taxes Payable		244.80
Employees FIT Payable		230.00
SUTA Taxes Payable		32.00
Cash		2,693.20
To record the payment of wages and the liability for the employees' FICA, FIT, and SUTA taxes withheld.		

In a small company with few employees, you can calculate the hours worked, determine net pay, and prepare the paychecks or pay envelopes in a relatively short period of time. For such companies, a journal entry wherein you directly credit the cash account for the total net pay is a logical, efficient procedure.

In larger companies, however, the calculation of hours worked, the determination of net pay, and the preparation of paychecks may extend over the greater part of a workday, or even longer. In such companies because of the workload involved in meeting each payroll, especially when the paychecks must be mailed to far-flung branch offices, the paychecks may be prepared several days in advance of their actual distribution to the workers. Further, the preparation of the workers' paychecks may occur in one accounting period, although the actual payment is made in the following accounting period. Thus, to show an accurate picture of the firm's liability for the payroll, at the time of recording the payroll the net pay is accrued and credited to a liability account such as Salaries Payable or Accrued Salaries Payable, instead of to the cash account. Later, when the paychecks are given to the workers, an entry is made to record the payment of the payroll. In this entry the liability account Salaries Payable is debited and the cash account is credited.

Recording Workers' Compensation Insurance Expense

As we indicated in Unit 1, most states have passed laws that require employers to provide workers' compensation insurance to protect their employees against losses due to injury or death incurred during employment. Usually the employer estimates and pays the premium in advance. The insurance premium, often based upon the total gross payroll of the business, may be stated in terms of an amount for each $100 of weekly wages paid to employees. At the end of the year, all the payrolls are audited and the company pays an additional premium or receives credit for an overpayment. Since the premium rate varies with the hazard involved in the work performed, your personnel and payroll records should provide for a careful classification of employees by kind or grade of work and a summary of labor costs according to the insurance premium classifications.

EXAMPLE:

In the McMahon Company there are only two different grades of work—office clerical and machine shop. The premium rates for 1991 are $.18 per $100 of payroll for the office clerical workers, and $2.90 per $100 of payroll for the machine-shop workers. Based upon past experience and budgetary projections for 1991, the company estimates its annual premium to be $8,900 and sends a check for that amount to the insurance carrier at the beginning of the year. The entry to record this transaction is:

Workers' Compensation Insurance Expense	8,900.00	
Cash		8,900.00

The effect of this entry, when posted to the ledger accounts, is an increase in the operating expenses of the company and a decrease in the assets.

At the end of 1991 the payrolls for the year are audited and analyzed and the current rates are applied to determine the actual premium as follows:

Work Grade	Total Payroll	Rate per $100	Premium
Office clerical ...	$ 81,000	$ .18	$ 145.80
Machine shop ...	312,000	2.90	9,048.00
Total	$393,000		$9,193.80
Less estimated premium paid in January ..			8,900.00
Balance due			$ 293.80

A check is written for the balance due the insurance company, and the following entry is made in the journal:

Workers' Compensation Insurance Expense	293.80	
Cash		293.80

RECORDING THE DEPOSIT OR PAYMENT OF PAYROLL TAXES

The journal entries required to record the deposit or payment of FICA taxes and income taxes withheld and the payment of FUTA and SUTA taxes are explained below.

Depositing FICA Taxes and Federal Income Taxes Withheld

As was explained to you in Unit 3, the requirements for depositing FICA taxes and federal income taxes withheld from employees' wages vary in relation to the total volume of such taxes.

EXAMPLE:

On April 15, the end of an eighth-monthly period, the ledger accounts FICA Taxes Payable and Employees FIT Payable of the Nannan Company appear as follows:

FICA TAXES PAYABLE

	4/15	860.09
	4/15	860.09
		1,720.18

EMPLOYEES FIT PAYABLE

	4/15	1,601.19

Since the total of these two account balances exceeds $3,000, the company is required to complete Form 8109 and to deposit the FICA and the federal income taxes within three banking days after April 15. The following journal entry is made to record this deposit:

FICA Taxes Payable	1,720.18	
Employees FIT Payable	1,601.19	
Cash		3,321.37

When this entry is posted, the debit of $1,720.18 to FICA Taxes Payable removes the liability for the employer's share, as well as the employees' share, of the FICA taxes imposed. The debit of $1,601.19 to Employees FIT Payable removes the liability for the total amount of federal income taxes withheld from the employees' wages during the period. The credit of $3,321.37 to the cash account reduces the assets of the company.

Paying State or City Income Taxes

When the employer turns over to the state or to the city the amount of income taxes withheld from employees' wages, the appropriate journal entry would be recorded as follows:

	Debit	Credit
Employees SIT Payable	XXX	
or		
Employees CIT Payable	XXX	
Cash		XXX

Paying FUTA and SUTA Taxes

At the time of completing Form 8109 and depositing the FUTA taxes that have accumulated during the preceding calendar quarter, an entry is made as follows:

	Debit	Credit
FUTA Taxes Payable	XXX	
Cash		XXX

Employers subject to the net FUTA tax plus a penalty for Title XII advances (see Unit 5, page 170) must make an adjusting entry prior to the last payment of the FUTA tax for the year. Since the amount of the penalty is not known until the fourth quarter, the penalty has not yet been recorded as a payroll tax expense. Therefore, an adjusting entry is made on December 31 to record the expense and the liability. This liability will be paid in January, in addition to the payment for the fourth quarter net FUTA tax.

The quarterly payment of state unemployment contributions is recorded as follows:

	Debit	Credit
SUTA Taxes Payable	XXX	
Cash		XXX

RECORDING THE ADJUSTMENT FOR END-OF-PERIOD WAGES

In most cases, the end of the fiscal (accounting) period does not coincide with the end of the payroll period. The wages for this last payroll period must be split between the fiscal period just ending (accrued wages) and the fiscal period just beginning. For instance, if the fiscal period ends on Wednesday and the employees are paid every Friday, the wages earned by the employees on Monday, Tuesday, and Wednesday are an expense of the fiscal period just ended. However, the wages earned on Thursday and Friday (payday) are an expense of the new fiscal period.

In order to record the wage expense properly for the fiscal period ended, an adjusting entry must be made on the last day of the fiscal period. However, since there is no actual wage payment, there is no need to credit any withholding accounts. The credit part of the entry is made to a single liability account for the total wage expense. In the case above, the wage expenses of Monday, Tuesday, and Wednesday would be recorded in the following adjusting entry:

	Debit	Credit
Wages Expense	XXX	
Wages Payable		XXX
To record wages incurred but unpaid as of the end of the fiscal period.		

RECORDING TRANSACTIONS PERTAINING TO OTHER PAYROLL DEDUCTIONS

Up to this point in our discussion of deductions that are made from wages and salaries, we have been limited to FICA taxes, state unemployment contributions, and income taxes. However, most companies have other deductions that must be taken into consideration when the payroll is prepared. Regardless of the number of deductions or the types of deductions that are made from employees' wages, we must provide a systematic means of keeping a record of the total wages for each employee, the deductions for each purpose, and the net amount paid. It is impossible to say that a certain type of record is satisfactory for every organization or even for each company doing a certain kind of business. Each business organization has its own problems and peculiarities that will affect the type of record needed. It is important, therefore, that we keep all the records required by law, as well as those needed for other purposes.

Although it is usually advisable to have a separate column in the payroll register for each deduction, the payroll register may become too cumbersome if there are too many columns for deductions. In many businesses, therefore, it is common practice to use a payroll register with a separate column for each of the major deductions, and to lump all other deductions together in one column headed "Other Deductions." Some companies use only one column for deductions and place the entire total in that column. If this practice is followed, it is usually necessary to have a supplementary record of deductions showing a detailed breakdown of the total for each employee. This supplementary record is then used as the basis for obtaining the figure for total deductions shown in the payroll register.

The deductions for FICA taxes, income taxes, disability benefits, and state unemployment benefits are required by law. Most other payroll deductions are the result of company policies, collective bargaining agreements, or court orders. Some of the purposes for which deductions may be made are:

1. Group insurance.
2. Hospitalization and surgical insurance.
3. Purchase of government bonds.
4. Union dues.

5. Garnishment of wages.
6. Pension and retirement benefits.

Group Insurance

Many companies have a *group insurance* program for employees. Such programs usually permit employees to obtain life insurance at a much lower rate than would be possible if the employee purchased the insurance as an individual. Under some group insurance plans, the employer and the employee share the cost of the insurance premium. The employees' share may be deducted from their wages every payday, every month, or every quarter.

When recording a payroll in which deductions are made from employees' wages for group insurance, the amount withheld from their wages is applied toward the payment of their share of the premium. The total amount withheld is recorded as a credit to a liability account with a title such as *Group Insurance Premiums Collected* or *Group Insurance Payments Withheld*. This general ledger account serves the same purpose as the accounts used to record payroll taxes withheld from employees' wages.

Hospital and Surgical Insurance

Many companies have developed their own hospital and surgical plans for employees, or are members of private insurance groups that provide coverage for employees of companies that are members of the group. If employees bear the cost or a portion of the cost of such insurance, the portion paid by the employees is usually deducted every payday, monthly, or quarterly from the wages of the employees. (This voluntary form of insurance protection should in no way be confused with the health insurance program for the aged. The latter program, Medicare, is discussed in Appendix A.)

The amounts withheld from the employees' wages for hospital and surgical insurance are credited to a liability account such as *Hospital and Surgical Insurance Premiums Collected*. Employers often pay the premium for hospital and surgical insurance in advance to the insurance carrier. At the time of paying the premium, a prepaid expense account such as *Prepaid Hospital and Surgical Insurance* is debited for the amount paid the carrier. Periodically this account is adjusted.

Purchase of Government Savings Bonds

Employees are encouraged to invest a certain amount of their wages in government savings bonds. Such plans or similar savings plans encourage employees to save a certain amount of each salary payment. The theory behind such deductions is that most employees will not miss a small amount that is set aside each payday, and over a period of time the deductions accumulate into a sizable amount.

Employees authorize their employer to make payroll deductions for the purchase of savings bonds by completing authorization forms that indicate how much is to be withheld and how frequently. The amounts that are withheld from the paychecks are set aside by the employer, acting in a trustee position, until a sufficient amount is available for the purchase of savings bonds for the employees. The minimum denomination for Series EE savings bonds for new participants in a payroll savings plan is $100. A $100 bond can be purchased as soon as the participant has accumulated the $50 purchase price in his or her withholding account.

EXAMPLE:

Wayne Richards has authorized his employer to withhold $10 from his pay every two weeks toward the purchase of a Series EE U.S. savings bond, which has a maturity value of $100. At the time of preparing each biweekly payroll, the employer credits the liability account *U.S. Savings Bond Deductions Payable* for $10. After the employer has recorded five similar entries, the balance of the liability account will be $50, the amount required for the purchase of one $100 Series EE U.S. savings bond. At this time the employer purchases the bond, which is later delivered to the employee. The journal entry to record this transaction includes a debit of $50 to the liability account *U.S. Savings Bonds Deductions Payable* and a corresponding credit to the cash account.

Union Dues

In companies in which employees are members of unions that require employees to pay dues to the union, many employees pay their dues, assessments, and initiation fees through deductions from wages. This withholding of union dues from employees' wages by the employer is known as a *check-off system*.

Amounts withheld from union members' wages are credited to a liability account such as *Union Dues Payable*. Monthly, or as agreed upon by the union and the employer, the amounts withheld are turned over to the treasurer of the union. At this time a journal entry is made in which the payment of union dues is recorded by debiting the liability account and crediting the cash account.

Garnishment of Wages

Garnishment refers to the legal or equitable procedure by means of which a portion of the wages of any person is required to be withheld for payment of a debt. Through the garnishment process, a creditor, with the aid of the courts, may require the employer to hold back wages and pay them to the court or to the creditor. In some companies the amounts to be held back are deducted each payday from the employee's wages.

Under the Consumer Credit Protection Act of 1968, the amount of wages subject to garnishment is limited to (a) 25% of a worker's disposable earnings or (b) the amount by which the weekly disposable earnings exceed by 30 times the minimum wages set by the Fair Labor Standards Act, whichever is less. *Disposable earnings* are the earnings remaining after withholding for income taxes and for other amounts required by law.

The provisions of the Consumer Credit Protection Act also prohibit an employer from discharging an employee simply because the employee's wages are subject to garnishment for one indebtedness. If another garnishment for a second indebtedness should arise, the worker could be discharged, provided a considerable amount of time had *not* elapsed between the two occasions of indebtedness. It is possible that the lapse of time could make the first garnishment immaterial. The payroll manager should also be aware that state garnishment laws that are more favorable to employees have priority over the federal law.

Pension and Retirement Benefits

Since in many instances social security benefits are inadequate for retired employees and their dependents, many firms provide pension and retirement plans that will supplement the government benefits. Although the benefit formulas and eligibility rules vary, the coverage is about the same for production workers, office employees, and managers. Many pension plans are financed solely by employer contributions, but other plans involve employee contributions.

Once these contributions are deducted from the employees' pay, they become a liability for the employer and are recorded as such in the payroll entry. The employer's contributions to a pension plan are recorded as an expense at the time of their payment.

Some employers also provide their employees with the opportunity to set up their own Individual Retirement Accounts (IRA) through a payroll deduction plan (see page 8). These voluntary contributions are deducted from the paychecks of the employees who desire to set up their own retirement accounts. These deductions are recorded as a liability in the payroll entry. This liability account will be cleared as the employer pays the contributions to the financial institution that is in charge of each employee's retirement account.

SUMMARY OF ACCOUNTS USED IN RECORDING PAYROLL TRANSACTIONS

The following listing summarizes the general ledger accounts that might be used by a company subject to FICA, FUTA, and one or more state unemployment compensation laws, and required to withhold federal and state income taxes and amounts for hospital insurance and union dues:

1. *Wages and Salaries*—an operating expense account in which the gross payroll is recorded.
2. *Payroll Taxes*—an operating expense account in which are recorded all payroll taxes on the employer under FICA, FUTA, and the various state unemployment compensation laws.
3. *FICA Taxes Payable*—a current liability account in which are recorded deductions made from employees' wages for FICA taxes. When the liability for the employer's portion of the FICA tax is recorded, the amount may also be credited to this account.
4. *FUTA Taxes Payable*—a current liability account in which is recorded the employer's federal unemployment taxes.
5. *SUTA Taxes Payable*—a current liability account in which are recorded the amounts due the states for the employer's unemployment compensation contributions. This account may also be credited for amounts deducted from employees' wages, if employees are required to contribute to state unemployment compensation funds.
6. *Employees FIT Payable*—a current liability account in which are recorded deductions made from employees' wages for federal income taxes.
7. *Employees SIT Payable*—a current liability account in which are recorded deductions made from employees' wages for state income taxes.
8. *Hospital Insurance Premiums Collected*—a current liability account in which are recorded deductions made from employees' wages for their share of the premiums paid for hospitalization and surgical coverage.
9. *Union Dues Payable*—a current liability account in which are recorded the deductions made from union members' wages for their union dues, assessments, or initiation fees.

ILLUSTRATIVE CASE

The following illustrative case shows the accounting procedures used by the Brookins Company in recording payroll transactions during the third quarter of its fiscal year. The fiscal year of the company ends on June 30, 1991. Employees are paid semimonthly on the 15th and the last day of the month. When the 15th or the last day of the month falls on Saturday or Sunday, employees are paid on the preceding Friday.

On January 1, 1991, the balances of the accounts used in recording payroll transactions are as shown below. These account balances are shown in the general ledger on pages 220 and 221.

Acct. No.	Account Title	Account Balance
11	Cash	$85,000.00
21	FICA Taxes Payable	906.02
22	FUTA Taxes Payable	122.00
23	SUTA Taxes Payable	40.50
25	Employees FIT Payable	1,472.00
26	Employees SIT Payable	474.42
28	Union Dues Payable	80.00
51	Wages and Salaries	46,500.00
55	Payroll Taxes	4,254.50

The first $54,300 in wages and salaries paid is subject to the FICA tax on both the employer (7.65%) and the employees (7.65%). The employer is also subject to a net FUTA tax of .8%, based on the first $7,000 in earnings paid each employee during a calendar year; and a SUTA tax of 2.3%, based on the first $7,000 in earnings paid during a calendar year. The state does not require contributions of employees for unemployment compensation or disability insurance.

The wage-bracket method is used to determine the amount of federal income taxes to be withheld from the employees' earnings. The state income tax law requires that a graduated percentage of the gross earnings of each employee be withheld each payday. Under the check-off system, union dues are withheld each payday from the union workers, who are employed in the plant. On or before the fourth of each month the dues collected during the preceding month are turned over to the treasurer of the union.

In the following narrative of transactions, the January 15 payroll transaction is explained in detail at the bottom of page 216. All other transactions are stated briefly. Adjacent to the narrative are the journal entries to record the transactions. The ledger accounts showing the transactions posted are on pages 220 and 221.

NARRATIVE OF TRANSACTIONS

JOURNAL **PAGE *15***

Jan. 2. Paid the treasurer of the union $80, representing the union dues withheld from the workers' earnings during the month of December

Date	Account	P.R.	Debit	Credit
1991 Jan. 2	Union Dues Payable	28	80.00	
	Cash	11		80.00
	To record the payment of the union dues withheld during December, 1990.			

Jan. 15. Paid total wages and salaries of all employees, $3,890. All the earnings are taxable under FICA. In addition to the social security taxes, the company withheld $455 from the employees' earnings for federal income taxes, $85.58 for state income taxes, and $45 for union dues. (See the explanation of the January 15 payroll transaction given at the bottom of this page.)

Date	Account	P.R.	Debit	Credit
15	Wages and Salaries	51	3,890.00	
	FICA Taxes Payable	21		297.59
	Employees FIT Payable	25		455.00
	Employees SIT Payable	26		85.58
	Union Dues Payable	28		45.00
	Cash	11		3,006.83
	To record the payment of wages and the liabilities for the employees' taxes withheld.			

Jan. 15. Recorded the employer's payroll taxes for the first pay in January. All the earnings are taxable under FICA, FUTA, and SUTA.

Date	Account	P.R.	Debit	Credit
15	Payroll Taxes	55	418.18	
	FICA Taxes Payable	21		297.59
	FUTA Taxes Payable	22		31.12
	SUTA Taxes Payable	23		89.47
	To record the payroll taxes and liabilities of the employer.			

Jan. 15. Completed Form 8109 and deposited with a Federal Reserve bank the FICA taxes and employees' federal income taxes withheld on the two December, 1990, payrolls. At the end of December the total liability for FICA taxes and federal income taxes withheld was $2,378.02. Since the undeposited payroll taxes totaled more than $500, the company is required under the *monthly* rule to deposit the taxes by the 15th day of the following month (see regulations for the monthly depositing of FICA taxes and federal income taxes withheld on page 79).

Date	Account	P.R.	Debit	Credit
15	FICA Taxes Payable	21	906.02	
	Employees FIT Payable	25	1,472.00	
	Cash	11		2,378.02
	To record the deposit of FICA taxes and federal income taxes withheld for the December 14 and 28, 1990, payrolls.			

The analysis of the January 15 payroll transaction is as follows:

1. Wages and Salaries is debited for $3,890, the total of the employees' gross earnings.
2. FICA Taxes Payable is credited for $297.59, the amount withheld from the employees' earnings.
3. Employees FIT Payable is credited for $455, the amount withheld from employees' earnings for federal income tax purposes.
4. Employees SIT Payable is credited for $85.58, the amount withheld from employees' earnings for state income taxes.
5. Union Dues Payable is credited for $45, the amount withheld from union members' earnings.
6. Cash is credited for $3,006.83, the net amount paid the employees ($3,890 gross earnings – $297.59 FICA – $455 FIT – $85.58 SIT – $45 union dues).
7. Payroll Taxes is debited for $418.18, the amount of taxes imposed on the employer under FICA, FUTA, and SUTA. The computation of the total payroll taxes is:

FICA:	7.65% of $3,890 =	$297.59
FUTA:	.8% of $3,890 =	31.12
SUTA:	2.3% of $3,890 =	89.47
Total payroll taxes		$418.18

8. FICA Taxes Payable is credited for the amount of tax on the employer, which is 7.65% of $3,890, or $297.59.
9. FUTA Taxes Payable is credited for $31.12, the liability incurred because of the taxes imposed on the employer under FUTA.
10. SUTA Taxes Payable is credited for $89.47, the amount of the contributions payable to the state.

NARRATIVE OF TRANSACTIONS | **JOURNAL** | **PAGE** *15*

Jan. 15. Paid the treasurer of the state $474.42, representing the amount of state income taxes withheld from the workers' earnings during the last quarter of 1990.

Date		Account	P.R.	Debit	Credit
1991					
Jan.	15	Employees SIT Payable	26	474.42	
		Cash	11		474.42
		To record the payment of the state income taxes withheld during the fourth quarter of 1990.			

Jan. 31. Paid total wages and salaries, $4,100. All of this amount constitutes taxable earnings under FICA. Withheld $483 for federal income taxes, $90.20 for state income taxes, and $45 for union dues

Date		Account	P.R.	Debit	Credit
	31	Wages and Salaries	51	4,100.00	
		FICA Taxes Payable	21		313.65
		Employees FIT Payable	25		483.00
		Employees SIT Payable	26		90.20
		Union Dues Payable	28		45.00
		Cash	11		3,168.15
		To record the payment of wages and the liabilities for the employees' taxes withheld.			

Jan. 31. Recorded the employer's payroll taxes for this payroll. All the earnings are taxable under FICA, FUTA, and SUTA.

Date		Account	P.R.	Debit	Credit
	31	Payroll Taxes	55	440.75	
		FICA Taxes Payable	21		313.65
		FUTA Taxes Payable	22		32.80
		SUTA Taxes Payable	23		94.30
		To record the payroll taxes and liabilities of the employer.			

Jan. 31. Completed Form 8109 and deposited $122 with a Federal Reserve bank to remove the liability for FUTA taxes for the fourth quarter, 1990.

Date		Account	P.R.	Debit	Credit
	31	FUTA Taxes Payable	22	122.00	
		Cash	11		122.00
		To record the deposit of FUTA taxes for the fourth quarter of 1990.			

Jan. 31. Filed the Employer's Annual Federal Unemployment (FUTA) Tax Return, Form 940, for the preceding calendar year. No journal entry is required since the 1990 liability for FUTA taxes was removed by the timely deposit on January 31, 1991. No taxes were paid at the time of filing the annual return.

Jan. 31. Filed the quarterly return (Form 941) with the IRS Center for the period ended December 31, 1990. No journal entry is required since the 1990 liability for FICA taxes and employees' federal income taxes withheld was removed by the timely deposit on January 15, 1991. No taxes were paid or deposited at the time of filing Form 941.

Jan. 31. Filed the state unemployment contributions return for the quarter ending December 31, 1990, and paid $40.50 to the state unemployment compensation fund.

Date		Account	P.R.	Debit	Credit
	31	SUTA Taxes Payable	23	40.50	
		Cash	11		40.50
		To record payment of contributions to state unemployment compensation fund for the fourth quarter of 1990.			

Feb. 1. Paid the treasurer of the union $90, representing the union dues withheld from the workers' earnings during the month of January.

Date		Account	P.R.	Debit	Credit
Feb.	1	Union Dues Payable	28	90.00	
		Cash	11		90.00
		To record the payment of the union dues withheld during January, 1991.			

Feb. 15. Paid total wages and salaries, $4,000. All of this amount is taxable under FICA. Withheld $470 for federal income taxes, $88 or state income taxes, and $45 for union dues.

Date		Account	P.R.	Debit	Credit
	15	Wages and Salaries	51	4,000.00	
		FICA Taxes Payable	21		306.00
		Employees FIT Payable	25		470.00
		Employees SIT Payable	26		88.00
		Union Dues Payable	28		45.00
		Cash	11		3,091.00
		To record the payment of wages and the liabilities for the employees' taxes withheld.			

NARRATIVE OF TRANSACTIONS | **JOURNAL** | **PAGE** *16*

Feb. 15. Recorded the employer's payroll taxes. All the earnings are taxable under FICA, FUTA, and SUTA.

Date		Account	P.R.	Debit	Credit
1991					
Feb.	15	Payroll Taxes	55	430.00	
		FICA Taxes Payable	21		306.00
		FUTA Taxes Payable	22		32.00
		SUTA Taxes Payable	23		92.00
		To record the payroll taxes and liabilities of the employer.			

Feb. 15. Completed Form 8109 and deposited $2,160.48 with a Federal Reserve bank to remove the liability for the FICA taxes and the employees' federal income taxes withheld on the January 15 and January 31 payrolls.

Date		Account	P.R.	Debit	Credit
	15	FICA Taxes Payable	21	1,222.48	
		Employees FIT Payable	25	938.00	
		Cash	11		2,160.48
		To record the deposit of FICA taxes and federal income taxes withheld for the January 15 and January 31, 1991, payrolls.			

Feb. 28. Paid total wages and salaries, $4,250. All of this amount is taxable under FICA. Withheld $502 for federal income taxes, $93.50 for state income taxes, and $50 for union dues.

Date		Account	P.R.	Debit	Credit
	28	Wages and Salaries	51	4,250.00	
		FICA Taxes Payable	21		325.13
		Employees FIT Payable	25		502.00
		Employees SIT Payable	26		93.50
		Union Dues Payable	28		50.00
		Cash	11		3,279.37
		To record the payment of wages and the liabilities for the employees' taxes withheld.			

Feb. 28. Recorded the employer's payroll taxes. All the earnings are taxable under FICA, FUTA, and SUTA.

Date		Account	P.R.	Debit	Credit
	28	Payroll Taxes	55	456.88	
		FICA Taxes Payable	21		325.13
		FUTA Taxes Payable	22		34.00
		SUTA Taxes Payable	23		97.75
		To record the payroll taxes and liabilities of the employer.			

Mar. 1. Paid the treasurer of the union $95, representing the union dues withheld from the workers' earnings during the month of February.

Date		Account	P.R.	Debit	Credit
Mar.	1	Union Dues Payable	28	95.00	
		Cash	11		95.00
		To record the payment of the union dues withheld during February, 1991.			

Mar. 15. Paid total wages and salaries, $4,300. All of this amount is taxable under FICA. Withheld $554 for federal income taxes, $94.60 for state income taxes, and $50 for union dues.

Date		Account	P.R.	Debit	Credit
	15	Wages and Salaries	51	4,300	
		FICA Taxes Payable	21		328.95
		Employees FIT Payable	25		554.00
		Employees SIT Payable	26		94.60
		Union Dues Payable	28		50.00
		Cash	11		3,272.45
		To record the payment of wages and the liabilities for the employees' taxes withheld.			

Mar. 15. Recorded the employer's payroll taxes. All the earnings are taxable under FICA, FUTA, and SUTA.

Date		Account	P.R.	Debit	Credit
	15	Payroll Taxes	55	462.25	
		FICA Taxes Payable	21		328.95
		FUTA Taxes Payable	22		34.40
		SUTA Taxes Payable	23		98.90
		To record the payroll taxes and liabilities of the employer.			

Mar. 15. Completed Form 8109 and deposited $2,234.26 with a Federal Reserve bank to remove the liability for FICA taxes and the employees' federal income taxes withheld on the February 15 and February 28 payrolls.

Date		Account	P.R.	Debit	Credit
	15	FICA Taxes Payable	21	1,262.26	
		Employees FIT Payable	25	972.00	
		Cash	11		2,234.26
		To record the deposit of FICA taxes and federal income taxes withheld for the February 15 and February 28, 1991, payrolls.			

NARRATIVE OF TRANSACTIONS	JOURNAL				PAGE 17
			P.R.	Debit	Credit
	1991				
Mar. 29. Paid total wages and salaries, $4,320. All of this amount is taxable under FICA. Withheld $570 for federal income taxes, $95.04 for state income taxes, and $50 for union dues.	Mar. 29	Wages and Salaries	51	4,320.00	
		FICA Taxes Payable	21		330.48
		Employees FIT Payable	25		570.00
		Employees SIT Payable	26		95.04
		Union Dues Payable	28		50.00
		Cash	11		3,274.48
		To record the payment of wages and the liabilities for the employees' taxes withheld.			
Mar. 29. Recorded the employer's payroll taxes. All of the earnings are taxable under FICA, FUTA, and SUTA.	29	Payroll Taxes	55	464.40	
		FICA Taxes Payable	21		330.48
		FUTA Taxes Payable	22		34.56
		SUTA Taxes Payable	23		99.36
		To record the payroll taxes and liabilities of the employer.			

After the transactions for January through March are journalized and posted, the general ledger payroll accounts as shown on the next two pages carry the following balances:

1. *FICA Taxes Payable:* $1,318.86, the amount of the liability for the tax imposed on both the employer and the employees with respect to wages and salaries paid on March 15 and March 29. This amount, along with the employees' federal income taxes withheld, must be deposited in a Federal Reserve bank by April 15.
2. *FUTA Taxes Payable:* $198.88, the accumulation of the amounts credited to this account each payday during the first three months of the calendar year. The balance of the account on March 31, 1991, must be deposited in a Federal Reserve bank by April 30, 1991.
3. *SUTA Taxes Payable:* $571.78, the amount due to the state unemployment compensation fund. This liability must be paid on or before April 30.
4. *Employees FIT Payable:* $1,124, the amount due for federal income taxes withheld from employees' earnings on March 15 and March 29. This amount, along with the balance of the FICA Taxes Payable account, represents a liability that must be deposited in a Federal Reserve bank by April 15.
5. *Employees SIT Payable:* $546.92, the amount due for state income taxes withheld from employees' earnings during the first three months of the calendar year. This amount must be paid to the treasurer of the state on the date specified in the state's income tax law.
6. *Union Dues Payable:* $100, amount due the treasurer of the union on or before April 4.
7. *Wages and Salaries:* $71,360, the total gross earnings for the three quarters of the company's fiscal year. The entire amount is an operating expense of the business.
8. *Payroll Taxes:* $6,926.96, the total payroll taxes for the three quarters imposed on the employer under FICA, FUTA, and SUTA. The entire amount is an operating expense of the business.

GENERAL LEDGER

CASH 11

Date		Item	P.R.	Dr.	Cr.	Balance Dr.	Balance Cr.
1991							
Jan.	1	Bal.	√			85,000.00	
	2		J15		80.00	84,920.00	
	15		J15		3,006.83	81,913.17	
	15		J15		2,378.02	79,535.15	
	15		J15		474.42	79,060.73	
	31		J15		3,168.15	75,892.58	
	31		J15		122.00	75,770.58	
	31		J15		40.50	75,730.08	
Feb.	1		J15		90.00	75,640.08	
	15		J15		3,091.00	72,549.08	
	15		J16		2,160.48	70,388.60	
	28		J16		3,279.37	67,109.23	
Mar.	1		J16		95.00	67,014.23	
	15		J16		3,272.45	63,741.78	
	15		J16		2,234.26	61,507.52	
	29		J17		3,274.48	58,233.04	

FICA TAXES PAYABLE 21

Date		Item	P.R.	Dr.	Cr.	Balance Dr.	Balance Cr.
1991							
Jan.	1	Bal.	√				906.02
	15		J15		297.59		1,203.61
	15		J15		297.59		1,501.20
	15		J15	906.02			595.18
	31		J15		313.65		908.83
	31		J15		3213.65		1,222.48
Feb.	15		J15		306.00		1,528.48
	15		J16		306.00		1,834.48
	15		J16	1,222.48			612.00
	28		J16		325.13		937.13
	28		J16		325.13		1,262.26
Mar.	15		J16		328.95		1,591.21
	15		J16		328.95		1,920.16
	15		J16	1,262.26			657.90
	29		J17		330.48		988.38
	29		J17		330.48		1,318.86

FUTA TAXES PAYABLE 22

Date		Item	P.R.	Dr.	Cr.	Balance Dr.	Balance Cr.
1991							
Jan.	1	Bal.	√				122.00
	15		J15		31.12		153.12
	31		J15		32.80		185.92
	31		J15	122.00			63.92
Feb.	15		J16		32.00		95.92
	28		J16		34.00		129.92
Mar.	15		J16		34.40		164.32
	29		J17		34.56		198.88

SUTA TAXES PAYABLE 23

Date		Item	P.R.	Dr.	Cr.	Balance Dr.	Balance Cr.
1991							
Jan.	1	Bal.	√				40.50
	15		J15		89.47		129.97
	31		J15		94.30		224.27
	31		J15	40.50			183.77
Feb.	15		J16		92.00		275.77
	28		J16		97.75		373.52
Mar.	15		J16		98.90		472.42
	29		J17		99.36		571.78

EMPLOYEES FIT PAYABLE 25

Date		Item	P.R.	Dr.	Cr.	Balance Dr.	Balance Cr.
1991							
Jan.	1	Bal.	√				1,472.00
	15		J15		455.00		1,927.00
	15		J15	1,472.00			455.00
	31		J15		483.00		938.00
Feb.	15		J15		470.00		1,408.00
	15		J16	938.00			470.00
	28		J16		502.00		972.00
Mar.	15		J16		554.00		1,526.00
	15		J16	972.00			554.00
	29		J17		570.00		1,124.00

EMPLOYEES SIT PAYABLE 26

Date		Item	P.R.	Dr.	Cr.	Balance Dr.	Balance Cr.
1991							
Jan.	1	Bal.	√				474.42
	15		J15		85.58		560.00
	15		J15	474.42			85.58
	31		J15		90.20		175.78
Feb.	15		J15		88.00		263.78
	28		J16		93.50		357.28
Mar.	15		J16		94.60		451.88
	29		J17		95.04		546.92

UNION DUES PAYABLE 28

Date		Item	P.R.	Dr.	Cr.	Balance Dr.	Balance Cr.
1991							
Jan.	1	Bal.	√				80.00
	2		J15	80.00		-------------	
	15		J15		45.00		45.00
	31		J15		45.00		90.00
Feb.	1		J15	90.00		-------------	
	15		J15		45.00		45.00
	28		J16		50.00		95.00
Mar.	1		J16	95.00		-------------	
	15		J16		50.00		50.00
	29		J17		50.00		100.00

WAGES AND SALARIES 51

Date		Item	P.R.	Dr.	Cr.	Balance Dr.	Balance Cr.
1991							
Jan.	1	Bal.	√			46,500.00	
	15		J15	3,890.00		50,390.00	
	31		J15	4,100.00		54,490.00	
Feb.	15		J15	4,000.00		58,490.00	
	28		J16	4,250.00		62,740.00	
Mar.	15		J16	4,300.00		67,040.00	
	29		J17	4,320.00		71,360.00	

PAYROLL TAXES 55

Date		Item	P.R.	Dr.	Cr.	Balance Dr.	Balance Cr.
1991							
Jan.	1	Bal.	√			4,254.50	
	15		J15	418.18		4,672.68	
	31		J15	440.75		5,113.43	
Feb.	15		J16	430.00		5,543.43	
	28		J16	456.88		6,000.31	
Mar.	15		J16	462.25		6,462.56	
	29		J17	464.40		6,926.96	

GLOSSARY

Business expense—cost of operating a business that is deductible by the employer for federal income tax purposes.

Check-off system—withholding of union dues from employees' wages by the employer.

Disposable earnings—the earnings remaining after withholding for income taxes and for other amounts required by law.

Garnishment—legal or equitable procedure by means of which a portion of the wages of any person is required to be withheld for payment of a debt.

Group insurance—life insurance program for employees at a low cost.

Journal entry—a transaction recorded in the accounting system of a business.

Payroll journal—book of original entry used for recording each payroll transaction and as the source for posting to appropriate general ledger accounts.

QUESTIONS FOR REVIEW

1. What are the main kinds of information contained in a payroll register?
2. For what reason are "distribution" columns sometimes provided in the payroll register?
3. Explain how to prove the accuracy of the totals of the payroll register.
4. What are the primary uses of the information contained in the payroll register?
5. Which payroll record is used by the employer in completing Forms W-2?
6. Explain the use of the "Cumulative" column in the employee's earnings record.
7. In Philadelphia, Pennsylvania, most workers are subject to three income taxes upon their earnings—federal, state, and city. Should an employer in Philadelphia record the liability for the withholding of all three income taxes in one liability account such as Income Taxes Payable?
8. What effect does the recording of the employer's portion of the FICA tax have on the accounts in the general ledger?
9. When is it necessary to provide the account, Employees Disability Contributions Payable?
10. What special accounts must usually be opened in the general ledger to record payroll transactions?
11. Does the recording of the social security taxes imposed on employers represent an increase or a decrease in owner's equity?
12. May the employer's FICA, FUTA, and SUTA taxes be deducted from gross income when the employer's federal income tax return is prepared?
13. Is it necessary for an employer who is subject to FICA and FUTA taxes to keep a separate expense account for the taxes under each act?
14. What is the effect of each of the following postings upon the assets, liabilities, and owner's equity of a company?
    a. A debit to Wages.
    b. A credit to FICA Taxes Payable.
    c. A debit to SUTA Taxes Payable.
    d. A credit to Cash.

15. Why is it necessary to classify employees by kind of work performed when calculating the cost of workers' compensation insurance?
16. What accounts are debited and credited when an employer records the deposit of FICA taxes and federal income taxes that have been withheld?
17. Does the payment of the social security taxes withheld from employees' wages represent an increase or a decrease in owner's equity?
18. Along with four payroll deductions required by law (FICA, Employees FIT, Employees SIT, and Employees CIT), five other deductions are typically made from the employees' earnings in the Cranston Company. What methods are available to the company in recording these nine deductions in the payroll register?
19. What journal entry is made at the time an employer turns over to the union treasurer the union dues that have been withheld under a check-off system?
20. What is meant by the *garnishment* of wages?

QUESTIONS FOR DISCUSSION

1. In what respect does an employee's earnings record resemble a ledger?
2. The Golic Corporation has undertaken a cost study of its operations. One area of concern to the company is the total cost of labor, particularly the cost of employee benefits. Prepare a list of the different kinds of costs that a company might incur as part of its "total package" salary cost.
3. A company subject to FICA taxes prepares a balance sheet at the end of each month. Which of the 12 monthly balance sheets will show a liability for social security taxes?
4. a. On which financial statement will a debit balance in the payroll taxes account appear?
   b. How should this account balance be classified on this financial statement?
5. Assume that an account is kept for Employees FIT Payable.
   a. On which financial statement will the account balance appear?
   b. How should the account balance be classified on this financial statement?

Date ______________________ Name ______________________

PRACTICAL PROBLEMS

Omit the writing of explanations for the journal entries.

6-1. a. An employer, Gail Winters, is subject to FICA taxes but exempt from FUTA and SUTA taxes. During the last quarter of the year, her employees earned monthly wages of $8,500, all of which is taxable. The amount of federal income taxes withheld each month is $1,040. Journalize the payment of wages and record the payroll tax on November 30.

JOURNAL

	DATE	DESCRIPTION	POST. REF.	DEBIT	CREDIT	
1						1
2						2
3						3
4						4
5						5
6						6
7						7

b. Prior to posting the November 30 payroll transaction, there were zero balances in the FICA Taxes Payable and the Employees FIT Payable accounts. After the November 30 transaction has been journalized and posted, the balances of these two accounts exceed $500. Thus, Winters is required to deposit with a Federal Reserve bank the FICA taxes and income taxes withheld on the November 30 payroll. Journalize the deposit of the payroll taxes on December 15.

JOURNAL

	DATE	DESCRIPTION	POST. REF.	DEBIT	CREDIT	
1						1
2						2
3						3
4						4

6-2. The employees of the Morton Music Company earn total wages of $4,690 during January. The total amount is taxable under FICA, FUTA, and SUTA. The state contribution rate for the company is 3.6%. The amount withheld for federal income taxes is $685. Journalize the payment of the monthly wages and record the payroll taxes.

JOURNAL

	DATE		DESCRIPTION	POST. REF.	DEBIT	CREDIT	
1							1
2							2
3							3
4							4
5							5
6							6
7							7
8							8
9							9

6-3. Tex, Inc., has a semimonthly payroll of $38,000 on May 15. Of this amount $32,850 is taxable under FICA and $29,300 under FUTA and SUTA. The state contribution rate for the company is 3.1%. The amount withheld for federal income taxes is $5,780. The amount withheld for state income taxes is $809. Journalize the payment of the wages and record the payroll taxes on May 15.

JOURNAL

	DATE		DESCRIPTION	POST. REF.	DEBIT	CREDIT	
1							1
2							2
3							3
4							4
5							5
6							6
7							7
8							8
9							9
10							10

Date ______________________ Name ______________________

6-4. Refer to Problem 6-3. Assume that the employees of Tex, Inc., are also required to pay state contributions (disability insurance) of 1% on the taxable payroll of $29,300, and that the employees' contributions are to be deducted by the employer. Journalize the May 15 payment of wages and record the payroll taxes, assuming that the state contributions of the employer and the employees are kept in separate accounts.

JOURNAL

	DATE		DESCRIPTION	POST. REF.	DEBIT	CREDIT	
1							1
2							2
3							3
4							4
5							5
6							6
7							7
8							8
9							9
10							10
11							11
12							12
13							13
14							14
15							15

6-5. The employees of the Pelter Company earn wages of $12,000 for the two weeks ending April 20. The entire amount of wages is subject to FICA, but only $9,800 is taxable under the federal and state unemployment compensation laws. The state contribution rate of the employer is 2.9%. Journalize the payment of the wages and record the payroll taxes on April 20. (Ignore employee income tax in this problem.)

JOURNAL

	DATE	DESCRIPTION	POST. REF.	DEBIT	CREDIT	
1						1
2						2
3						3
4						4
5						5
6						6
7						7
8						8

6-6. Refer to Problem 6-5. Assume that all employees are subject to state unemployment contributions of .5% on the taxable wages of $9,800, and that the employees' contributions are to be deducted by the employer. Journalize the payment of the wages and record the payroll taxes, assuming that the contributions of the employer and the employees are recorded in one account, SUTA Taxes Payable.

JOURNAL

	DATE	DESCRIPTION	POST. REF.	DEBIT	CREDIT	
1						1
2						2
3						3
4						4
5						5
6						6
7						7
8						8
9						9

Date ______________________ Name ______________________

6-7. The following information pertains to the payroll of the Furphy Textile Company on June 1:

a. The total wages earned by employees are $2,180.
b. The state unemployment insurance contribution rate is 2.5%.
c. The entire amount of wages is taxable under FICA, FUTA, and SUTA.
d. The amount withheld from the employees' wages for federal income taxes is $309; for state income taxes, $43.10; and for group insurance, $16.80.

Journalize the payment of wages and record the payroll taxes on June 1.

JOURNAL

	DATE		DESCRIPTION	POST. REF.	DEBIT	CREDIT	
1							1
2							2
3							3
4							4
5							5
6							6
7							7
8							8
9							9
10							10
11							11

6-8. On December 31, 1991, the Reuter Company has a balance of $98.75 in the FUTA Taxes Payable account. This represents the employer's liability for the fourth quarter taxes. Journalize the entry the Reuter Company should make in January, 1992, to record the last deposit of FUTA taxes for 1991.

JOURNAL

	DATE		DESCRIPTION	POST. REF.	DEBIT	CREDIT	
1							1
2							2
3							3

Date ______________________ Name ______________________

6-9. In Oregon, employers who are covered by the state Workers' Compensation Law must withhold employee contributions from the wages of covered employees at the rate of 14¢ for each day or part of a day that the worker is employed. Every covered employer is assessed 14¢ per day for each worker employed for each day or part of a day. The employer-employee contributions for workers' compensation are collected monthly, quarterly, or annually by the employer's insurance carrier, according to a schedule agreed upon by the employer and the carrier. The insurance carrier remits the contributions to the state's Workers' Compensation Department.

The Brunansky Company, a covered employer in Oregon, turns over the employer-employee workers' compensation contributions to its insurance carrier by the 15th of each month for the preceding month. During the month of July the number of full employee-days worked by the company's employees was 3,110; the number of part-time employee-days was 364.

a. The amount the company should have withheld from its full-time and part-time employees during the month of July for workers' compensation insurance is . . . $__________

b. The title you would give to the general ledger account to which the amount withheld from the employees' earnings would be credited is:

c. Journalize the entry on July 31 to record the employer's liability for workers' compensation insurance for the month.

JOURNAL

	DATE		DESCRIPTION	POST. REF.	DEBIT	CREDIT	
1							1
2							2
3							3

d. Journalize the entry on August 15 to record payment to the insurance carrier of the amount withheld from the employees' earnings for workers' compensation insurance and the amount of the employer's liability.

JOURNAL

	DATE		DESCRIPTION	POST. REF.	DEBIT	CREDIT	
1							1
2							2
3							3
4							4
5							5

6-10 In the form on page 231 are the amounts that appear in the Earnings to Date column of the employees' earnings records for 10 workers in the Unger Company. These amounts represent the cumulative taxable earnings for each worker as of October 18, the company's last payday. The gross amount of earnings to be paid each worker on the next payday, October 25, is also given in the form.

In the state where the Unger Company is located, the tax rates and bases are as follows:

Tax on Employees:

FICA	7.65% on first $54,300
SUTA	.5% on first $ 8,000

Tax on Employer:

FICA	7.65% on first $54,300
FUTA	.8% on first $ 7,000
SUTA	1.8% on first $ 8,000

In the appropriate columns of the form on page 231, do the following:

1. Calculate the amount to be withheld from each employee's earnings on October 25 for (a) FICA and (b) SUTA, and determine the total employee taxes.
2. Record the portion of each employee's earnings that is taxable under FICA, FUTA, and SUTA and calculate the total employer's payroll taxes on the October 25 payroll.

Date ____________________ Name ____________________

Practical Problem 6-10

THE UNGER COMPANY

	Employee	Earnings to Date	Gross Earnings Oct. 25	Taxes to Be Withheld from Employees' Earnings Under		Employer Taxes Portion of Employees' Earnings Taxable Under		
				FICA	SUTA	FICA	FUTA	SUTA
1.	Weiser, Robert A.	$54,090	$790					
2.	Stankard, Laurie C.	14,950	295					
3.	Grow, Joan L.	4,060	240					
4.	Rowe, Paul C.	8,190	235					
5.	Mc Namara, Joyce M.	7,460	195					
6.	O'Connor, Roger T.	54,510	810					
7.	Carson, Ronald B.	8,905	280					
8.	Kenny, Ginni C.	4,325	175					
9.	Devery, Virginia S.	53,790	590					
10.	Wilson, Joe W.	3,615	205					
	Total Employee Taxes			$	$			
				1.(a)	1.(b)			
	Total Taxable Earnings					$	$	$
	X Applicable Tax Rate							
	Totals					$	$	$
	Total Payroll Taxes						$ ______	
							2.	

6-11. In the Illustrative Case in this unit, payroll transactions for the Brookins Company were analyzed, journalized, and posted for the third quarter of the fiscal year. In this problem you are to record the payroll transactions for the last quarter of the firm's fiscal year. The last quarter begins on April 1, 1991.

Refer to the Illustrative Case on pages 215 to 221 and proceed as follows:

a. Analyze and journalize the transactions described in the following narrative. Use the two-column journal paper provided on pages 235 to 238. Omit the writing of explanations in the journal entries.
b. Post the journal entries to the general ledger accounts on pages 239 to 243.

Narrative of Transactions:

April 4. Paid the treasurer of the union the amount of union dues withheld from workers' earnings during March.

15. Payroll: $6,105. All wages and salaries taxable. Withheld $565 for federal income taxes, $107.32 for state income taxes, and $50 for union dues.

15. Paid the treasurer of the state the amount of state income taxes withheld from workers' earnings during the first quarter of 1991.

15. Completed Form 8109 and deposited funds in a Federal Reserve bank to remove the liability for FICA taxes and employees' federal income taxes withheld on the March payrolls.

30. Payroll: $5,850. All wages and salaries taxable. Withheld $509 for federal income taxes, $128.90 for state income taxes, and $55 for union dues.

30. Filed the Employer's Quarterly Federal Tax Return (Form 941) for the period ended March 31. No journal entry is required since the FICA taxes and federal income taxes withheld have been timely deposited in a Federal Reserve bank.

30. Completed the quarterly deposit (Form 8109) for the period ended March 31 and deposited the FUTA taxes in a Federal Reserve bank.

30. Filed the state contribution return for the quarter ended March 31 and paid the amount to the state unemployment compensation fund.

May 1. Paid the treasurer of the union the amount of union dues withheld from workers' earnings during April.

15. Payroll: $5,810. All wages and salaries taxable. Withheld $507 for federal income taxes, $125.05 for state income taxes, and $55 for union dues.

15. Completed Form 8109 and deposited funds with a Federal Reserve bank to remove the liability for FICA taxes and federal income taxes withheld on the April payrolls.

31. Payroll: $6,060. All wages and salaries taxable. Withheld $533 for federal income taxes, $119.00 for state income taxes, and $50 for union dues.

June 3. Paid the treasurer of the union the amount of union dues withheld from workers' earnings during May.

14. Payroll: $6,380. All wages and salaries taxable, except only $5,000 is taxable under FUTA and SUTA. Withheld $549 for federal income taxes, $128.70 for state income taxes, and $50 for union dues.

17. Completed Form 8109 and deposited funds with a Federal Reserve bank to remove the liability for FICA taxes and federal income taxes withheld on the May payrolls.

28. Payroll: $6,250. All wages and salaries taxable, except only $4,770 is taxable under FUTA and SUTA. Withheld $538 for federal income taxes, $127.60 for state income taxes, and $50 for union dues.

Date ______________________ Name ______________________

c. Answer the following questions:

(1) The total amount of the liability for FICA taxes and federal income taxes withheld as of June 28 is . . . . $__________

The date on which the company is required to deposit these amounts is:

(2) The total amount of the liability for state income taxes withheld as of June 28 is . . . . $__________

(3) The amount of FUTA taxes that must be paid to the federal government on or before July 31, 1991 is . . . . $__________

(4) The amount of contributions that must be paid into the state unemployment compensation fund on or before July 31, 1991 is . . . . $__________

(5) The total amount due the treasurer of the union is . . . . $__________

(6) The total amount of wages and salaries expense since the beginning of the fiscal year is . . . . $__________

(7) The total amount of payroll taxes expense since the beginning of the fiscal year is . . . . $__________

Date ______________________ Name ______________________

Practical Problem 6-11

JOURNAL

Page 18

DATE		DESCRIPTION	POST. REF.	DEBIT	CREDIT

Practical Problem 6-11

JOURNAL

Page 19

DATE		DESCRIPTION	POST. REF.	DEBIT	CREDIT

Date ____________________ Name ____________________

Practical Problem 6-11

JOURNAL

Page 20

DATE		DESCRIPTION	POST. REF.	DEBIT	CREDIT

Practical Problem 6-11

JOURNAL

Page 21

DATE		DESCRIPTION	POST. REF.	DEBIT	CREDIT

Date ______________________ Name ______________________

Practical Problem 6-11

ACCOUNT **CASH** ACCOUNT NO. 11

DATE		ITEM	POST. REF.	DEBIT	CREDIT	BALANCE	
						DEBIT	CREDIT
1991 Apr.	1	*Balance*	✓			5 8 2 3 3 04	

Practical Problem 6-11

ACCOUNT **FICA TAXES PAYABLE** ACCOUNT NO. 21

DATE		ITEM	POST. REF.	DEBIT	CREDIT	BALANCE DEBIT	BALANCE CREDIT
1991 Apr.	1	*Balance*	✓				1318 86

ACCOUNT **FUTA TAXES PAYABLE** ACCOUNT NO. 22

DATE		ITEM	POST. REF.	DEBIT	CREDIT	BALANCE DEBIT	BALANCE CREDIT
1991 Apr.	1	*Balance*	✓				198 88

Date ______________________ Name ______________________

Practical Problem 6-11

ACCOUNT **SUTA TAXES PAYABLE** ACCOUNT NO. 23

DATE		ITEM	POST. REF.	DEBIT	CREDIT	BALANCE DEBIT	BALANCE CREDIT
1991 Apr.	1	*Balance*	√				571 78

ACCOUNT **EMPLOYEES FIT PAYABLE** ACCOUNT NO. 25

DATE		ITEM	POST. REF.	DEBIT	CREDIT	BALANCE DEBIT	BALANCE CREDIT
1991 Apr.	1	*Balance*	√				1124 00

Practical Problem 6-11

ACCOUNT **EMPLOYEES SIT PAYABLE** ACCOUNT NO. 26

DATE		ITEM	POST. REF.	DEBIT	CREDIT	BALANCE DEBIT	BALANCE CREDIT
1991 Apr.	1	*Balance*	√				546 92

ACCOUNT **UNION DUES PAYABLE** ACCOUNT NO. 28

DATE		ITEM	POST. REF.	DEBIT	CREDIT	BALANCE DEBIT	BALANCE CREDIT
1991 Apr.	1	*Balance*	√				100 00

Date ____________________ Name ____________________

Practical Problem 6-11

ACCOUNT **WAGES AND SALARIES** ACCOUNT NO. 51

DATE		ITEM	POST. REF.	DEBIT	CREDIT	BALANCE DEBIT	BALANCE CREDIT
1991 Apr.	1	*Balance*	✓			71,360.00	

ACCOUNT **PAYROLL TAXES** ACCOUNT NO. 55

DATE		ITEM	POST. REF.	DEBIT	CREDIT	BALANCE DEBIT	BALANCE CREDIT
1991 Apr.	1	*Balance*	✓			6,926.96	

CONTINUING PAYROLL PROBLEM

In this last phase of your work on the Continuing Payroll Problem, you will record the amounts withheld for group insurance, hospital insurance, and purchase of savings bonds; and calculate the net pay for each employee. Refer to the partially completed payroll register upon which you were working at the end of Unit 5 and proceed as follows:

(1) In the appropriate column of the payroll register, record the amount to be withheld for group life insurance. Each employee contributes 85¢ each week toward the cost of group insurance coverage, with the exception of McGarry and Porth, who are not yet eligible for coverage under the company plan.
(2) Record the amount to be withheld for hospital insurance. Each employee contributes $1.65 each week toward the cost of hospital insurance.
(3) Record the amount to be withheld for the purchase of U.S. savings bonds. The following employees have signed authorization forms for weekly deductions for the purchase of savings bonds: Lopenski, $3; Young, $5; Hopstein, $2; and Stone, $7.50.
(4) Record the net pay for each employee. The net pay for each employee is obtained by subtracting the total amount of all deductions from the total earnings.
(5) Each worker is to be paid by check. Assign check numbers commencing with No. 313.
(6) Foot all money columns of the payroll register and prove the accuracy of the column totals.
(7) On a separate sheet of paper:
   (a) Prepare the journal entries as of January 12 to record the payroll and the payroll taxes for the week ending January 7. Credit Salaries Payable for the total net pay.
   Use the following tax rates and bases: employer's FICA, 7.65% on the first $54,300; FUTA, .8% on the first $7,000; and SUTA, 3.5% on the first $8,000.
   (b) Prepare the journal entry to record the payment of the payroll on January 14, when the paychecks are distributed to all workers.

Your work on the Continuing Payroll Problem is now completed and you may be asked to submit your payroll register to your instructor. The experience you have gained in working on each of the succeeding phases of the Continuing Payroll Problem will aid you in undertaking the payroll work involved in Unit 7. In Unit 7, the Comprehensive Payroll Project, you will be responsible for all aspects of payroll operations for a company for an entire calendar quarter.

CASE PROBLEM

Case 6-1 How to Meet the Need for Temporary Help

The Zettek Electronics Company is a small manufacturer that has been in operation for several years. During its existence, the company has maintained a core of approximately 60 assembly-line personnel. This work force has been able to complete all contracts without the need for additional employees. Periodically, when a rush order or a large-volume contract is received, the company is able to have the staff work overtime without employing additional personnel.

Recently, the company has secured a lucrative contract that will last approximately three months. Management feels that the present employees can complete the job, but to do so will require the use of extensive overtime. Mark Cramer, the Controller, has become concerned about the high cost of overtime for these types of contracts. He is presently evaluating other solutions to the company's short-term labor needs.

One alternative approach would be to hire about 20 temporary employees. These employees would work for the duration of the contract (three months) and then be terminated. When future contracts are obtained, the individuals could be rehired.

Cramer is also considering the use of Expert Help, Inc., a company that supplies temporary help. The people supplied are the employees of Expert Help, Inc., who pays their wages and all the taxes on the wages. The Zettek Company will be charged a set fee for each hour worked by each person supplied. The cost per hour is approximately 30% more than the comparable cost of hiring temporary help as employees of the Zettek Company.

The present method of working the staff overtime to meet the company's needs has not been ruled out. The four shop supervisors have met with Cramer and recommended that this method be continued.

As Controller of the Zettek Electronics Company, evaluate the three alternatives, analyzing the advantages and disadvantages of each.

Payroll Project

GOALS OF THIS UNIT

Unit 7 consists of a simulation, or practice set, for payroll accounting. After completing this unit, you will have applied the knowledge acquired in this course to practical payroll situations. This unit is a culmination of the information presented in the textbook.

After completing the simulation, you will have experienced the following:

1. Preparing payroll registers.
2. Maintaining employees' earnings records.
3. Journalizing and posting payroll and payroll tax entries.
4. Completing federal, state, and city tax deposit forms and journalizing the transactions.
5. Preparing various quarter-end and year-end payroll tax forms.
6. Making the accrual entry for the payroll at the end of a year.

The Payroll Project is designed to provide you with extended practice in keeping payroll records and accounting for payroll transactions. Your completion of this project involves an application of the information learned in the preceding units. The work provided is similar to that prevailing in the office of every employer in the United States who is subject to the provisions of the federal wage and hour law, income tax withholding laws, the social security laws, and the unemployment compensation laws.

In many large businesses with hundreds or thousands of employees, payroll records are often kept as subsidiary records of the general ledger accounts. Under such a system, the totals in the payroll ledger are transferred to the general ledger control account when the books are closed at the end of the fiscal period. The purpose of this course is to acquaint you with the effect of payroll transactions upon the general accounting records, as well as to present the details of recording payroll transactions. Therefore, general ledger accounts, rather than subsidiary payroll ledger accounts, will be used for all payroll transactions.

In this project you are employed by the Glo-Brite Paint Company. As the payroll clerk in the accounting department, you have been in charge of the payroll records since the company first began operations on January 5 of the current year. The company employs about 800 individuals; but for the purpose of this project, payroll records will be kept for only a dozen or so employees. This will avoid duplication and detailed work from which no additional learning experience would be gained. By understanding the principles of payroll accounting for a few employees, you should be able to keep similar records for several hundred employees since the principles involved are the same.

For purposes of this project, you will assume that the payroll records and tax reports have been completed and filed for the first three quarters of this year. Your work will involve the processing of the payrolls for the last quarter of the year and the completion of the last quarterly and annual tax reports and forms.

BOOKS OF ACCOUNT AND PAYROLL RECORDS

The books of account and payroll records that you will use in this project are described below.

Journal

You will use a two-column general journal to record all transactions affecting the accounts in the general ledger. This book of original entry serves as a posting medium for transactions affecting the payroll accounts.

General Ledger

A general ledger is used in keeping the payroll accounts. The ledger is ruled with balance-column ruling, which makes it possible to keep a continuous record of each account balance. Some of the ledger accounts will have beginning balances that were carried over from the first three quarters of the year.

The following chart of accounts has been used in opening the general ledger accounts on pages 273 to 280. The Glo-Brite Paint Company has other accounts in its general ledger, but those listed in the partial chart of accounts are the only accounts required in completing this project.

PARTIAL CHART OF ACCOUNTS

ACCOUNT TITLE	ACCOUNT NO.
Cash	11
Payroll Cash	12
FICA Taxes Payable	20
FUTA Taxes Payable	21
SUTA Taxes Payable	22
Employees Unemployment Taxes Payable[1]	23
Employees FIT Payable	24
Employees SIT Payable	25
Employees CIT Payable	26
Group Insurance Premiums Collected	27
Union Dues Payable	28
U.S. Savings Bonds Deductions Payable	29
Administrative Salaries	51
Office Salaries	52
Sales Salaries	53
Wages—Plant A	54
Wages—Plant B	55
Payroll Taxes	56

Payroll Register

The payroll register provides the information that is needed for journalizing each payroll and for posting to the employees' earnings records.

Employee's Earnings Record

The employee's earnings record provides a summary of each employee's earnings, deductions, and taxable wages. The information to be recorded in this record is posted from the payroll register.

From the personnel data given at the top of the next page, an employee's earnings record has been maintained for each employee on pages 282 to 288. On the first line of each of these records, the employee's cumulative figures for the first three quarters of the year are shown. Note that only one-half page has been used for each employee's earnings record. In actual practice, however, both sides of a complete sheet would be used for the same employee.

GENERAL INFORMATION

The home office and the manufacturing plants of the Glo-Brite Paint Company are located at 2215 Salvador Street, Philadelphia, PA 19175-0682. The company's federal identification number is 31-0450660; the state identifying number is 46-3-3300; the city identifying number is 501-6791855.

Regular Hours of Work

The workweek for all employees is 40 hours. The office is open from 8:00 a.m. to 5:00 p.m. each day, except weekends. One hour is allowed for lunch, 12:00 p.m. to 1:00 p.m.

The plants operate on a five-day workweek of eight hours per day. The normal working hours in the plants are from 7:00 a.m. to 11:00 a.m. and 12:00 p.m. to 4:00 p.m.

Overtime

All employees except the president, the sales manager, sales representatives, and supervisors are paid *time and a half* for any overtime exceeding 40 hours a week.

Workers in the plants are paid *time and a half* for any hours worked over eight each workday. The overtime rate for any work scheduled on Saturdays, Sundays, or holidays is *twice* the regular hourly rate of pay.

[1] During 1984 through 1988, all employees contributed to the state unemployment compensation fund without regard to any taxable wage limitation. In 1989 through 1991, there was no employee tax. However, since an employee tax may be levied in the future, a general ledger account is provided.

PERSONNEL DATA—October 1, 19—

BONNO, Anthony Victor, 694 Bristol Avenue, Philadelphia, PA 19135-0617. Married, claiming 4 withholding allowances. Telephone, 555-9827. Social Security No. 537-10-3481. Position, mixer operator in Plant B. Wages, $7.65 per hour. Group insurance, $24,000.

FERGUSON, James Claude, 808 Sixth Street, Philadelphia, PA 19106-0995. Married, claiming 5 withholding allowances. Telephone, 555-8065. Social Security No. 486-03-8645. Position, sales manager. Salary, $32,500 per year. Group insurance, $49,000. Department: Sales.

FORD, Catherine Louise, 18 Dundee Avenue, Philadelphia, PA 19151-1919. Divorced, claiming 2 withholding allowances. Telephone, 555-0235. Social Security No. 213-09-4567. Position, executive secretary. Salary, $975 per month. Group insurance, $18,000. Department: Office.

MANN, Dewey Wilson, 3007 Bisque Drive, Philadelphia, PA 19199-0718. Married, claiming 4 withholding allowances. Telephone, 555-0774. Social Security No. 282-37-9352. Position, sales representative. Salary, $1,950 per month. Group insurance, $35,000. Department: Sales.

O'NEILL, Joseph Tyler, 2100 Broad Street, Philadelphia, PA 19121-7189. Married, claiming 3 withholding allowances. Telephone, 555-2332. Social Security No. 897-04-1534. Position, president. Salary, $60,000 per year. Group insurance, $90,000. Department: Administrative.

RUSSELL, Virginia Aloise, 8004 Dowling Road, Philadelphia, PA 19135-9001. Single, claiming 1 withholding allowance. Telephone, 555-3681. Social Security No. 314-21-6337. Position, time clerk. Salary, $845 per month. Group insurance, $15,000. Department: Office.

RYAN, Norman Allen, 7300 Harrison Street, Philadelphia, PA 19124-6699. Married, claiming 4 withholding allowances. Telephone, 555-6660. Social Security No. 526-23-1223. Position, electrician in Plant A. Wages, $9.80 per hour. Group insurance, $31,000.

SOKOWSKI, Thomas James, 133 Cornwells Street, Philadelphia, PA 19171-5718. Married, claiming 2 withholding allowances. Telephone, 555-5136. Social Security No. 662-04-8832. Position, supervisor in Plant A. Salary, $450 per week. Group insurance, $35,000.

STUDENT, 7018 Erdrick Street, Philadelphia, PA 19135-8517. Single, claiming 1 withholding allowance. Position, accounting trainee. Salary, $650 per month. Group insurance, $12,000. Department: Office.

WILLIAMS, Ruth Virginia, 9433 State Street, Philadelphia, PA 19149-0819. Single, claiming 0 withholding allowances. Telephone, 555-5845. Social Security No. 518-30-6741. Position, programmer. Salary, $1,235 per month. Group insurance, $22,000. Department: Office.

Timekeeping

All office and plant employees, except the president, the sales manager, sales representatives, and supervisors, are required to ring in and out daily on a time clock. Those employees who ring in and out are required to notify the time clerk of the reason for lost time. (This information is required under the unemployment compensation laws of some states.) The time clerk prepares a weekly report of the hours worked by each employee.

Payday

Employees are paid biweekly on Friday. The first payday in the fourth quarter is Friday, October 9.

Since the weekly time clerk's report is not finished until the Monday following the end of each week, the first pay (October 9) will be for the two weeks, September 20—26 and September 27—October 3. The company, in effect, holds back one week's pay. This policy applies to all employees. The next payday (October 23) will cover the days worked in the weeks ending October 10 and October 17.

Payroll Taxes—Contributions and Withholdings

Payroll taxes are levied upon the Glo-Brite Paint Company and its employees as shown at the top of page 250.

Group Insurance

The company carries group life insurance on all its employees in an amount equal to one and one-half times the annual salary or wages paid each employee. Employees are fully covered under the group insurance program when they are employed full-time. A notation has been made on each employee's earnings record to show that each month 30¢ for each $1,000 of insurance coverage is deducted from the employee's earnings to pay a portion of the premium cost. This deduction is only made on the *last payday of each month.* The amount withheld is credited to a liability account entitled Group Insurance Premiums Collected.

The employer pays whatever additional premium is charged, which varies each year depending upon the average age of the employees and other factors.

PAYROLL TAXES LEVIED UPON THE GLO-BRITE PAINT COMPANY AND ITS EMPLOYEES	
Federal Income Taxes (FIT)	Withheld from each employee's gross earnings in accordance with information given on Form W-4 and employee's earnings record. Wage-bracket method is used to determine FIT withholding.
Pennsylvania State Income Taxes (SIT)	2.1% withheld from each employee's gross earnings during the calendar year.
Philadelphia City Income Taxes (CIT)	4.96% withheld from gross earnings of each employee.
Pennsylvania State Unemployment Taxes (SUTA)	*Employer:* 3.5% on first $8,000 gross earnings paid each employee during the calendar year.
Federal Unemployment Taxes (FUTA)	Net tax rate of .8% on first $7,000 gross earnings paid each worker in the calendar year.
Federal Insurance Contributions Act (FICA)	*Employer and Employee:* 7.65% on first $54,300 gross earnings paid each worker in the calendar year.

The employer is required to pay an estimated premium in advance at the beginning of the year. This amount is recorded as a debit to Prepaid Group Insurance in the general ledger. Prepaid Group Insurance is an asset account that will be adjusted at the end of the year by crediting it for the employees' share of the premium that was collected by withholding from their earnings during the year. The account is also credited for the company's share of the premium. At the same time, this amount will be charged to an appropriate expense account, after which the prepaid group insurance account will balance provided the insurance year is the same as the company's fiscal year. Otherwise, the balance of the account at the end of the fiscal year will represent a prepaid expense (asset).

Union Dues

All workers in the plants, except the supervisors, are union members. Under the check-off system, $8 is deducted *each payday* from the plant workers' earnings for union dues, assessments, and initiation fees. A notation to this effect has been made on each plant worker's earnings record. On or before the tenth of each month, the amounts withheld during the preceding month are turned over to the treasurer of the union.

Purchase of U.S. Savings Bonds

With the first pay in October, the company has started a payroll deduction plan for the purchase of U.S. savings bonds. Any employee who wishes to purchase bonds must sign an authorization form indicating how much is to be withheld from each paycheck. This information has been recorded on the appropriate employees' earnings records. The amounts withheld are retained by the company until the purchase price of a bond has been accumulated. At that time the company purchases the bond and delivers it to the employee. Those employees who have authorized a deduction from each paycheck for the purchase of U.S. savings bonds are:

Bonno	$ 5.00
Ferguson	5.00
O'Neill	10.00
Sokowski	5.00

Distribution of Labor Costs

The salaries and wages are to be charged to the labor cost accounts as follows:

PERSONNEL	ACCOUNT TO BE CHARGED
President	Administrative Salaries
Executive Secretary Programmer Time Clerk .... Student (Accounting Trainee)	Office Salaries
Sales Manager .... Sales Representatives	Sales Salaries
Workers .... Supervisors	Wages—Plant A or Wages—Plant B, depending upon plant in which the personnel are regularly employed.

NARRATIVE OF PAYROLL TRANSACTIONS

October 9, 19—

No. 1. The first payroll in October was for the two workweeks that ended on September 26 and October 3. This payroll transaction has been entered for you in the payroll register, the employees' earnings records, the general journal, and the general ledger. By reviewing the calculations of the wages and deductions in the payroll register and the posting of the information to the employees' earnings records, you can see the procedure to be followed each payday.

Wages and salaries are paid by issuing special payroll checks. When such checks are received at the bank on which they are drawn, they will be charged against the payroll cash account.

The following rules are observed in computing earnings each pay period:

1. Do not make any deduction from an employee's earnings if the employee loses less than 15 minutes of time in any day. Time lost that exceeds 15 minutes is rounded to the nearest quarter-hour and deducted. If the time lost by an employee is not to be deducted, the time clerk will make a notation to that effect on the Time Clerk's Report.
2. In completing the time record columns of the payroll register for all workers, you should place an 8 in the day column for each full day worked. If less than a full day is worked, show the actual hours for which the employee is being paid.
3. In the case of an employee who begins work during a pay period, compute the earnings by multiplying one full week worked, if any, by the weekly rate. For any partial week, compute the earnings for that week by multiplying the hours worked by the hourly rate of pay.
4. If time lost by a salaried employee is to be deducted from his or her pay, determine the employee's pay by multiplying the actual hours worked for that week by the hourly rate. The following schedule shows the weekly and hourly wage rates of the salaried employees:

EMPLOYEE	WEEKLY RATE	HOURLY RATE
Ferguson, James C. .	$ 625.00	$15.63
Ford, Catherine L. . .	225.00	5.63
Mann, Dewey W. . . .	450.00	11.25
O'Neill, Joseph T. . . .	1,153.85	28.85
Russell, Virginia A. . .	195.00	4.88
Sokowski, Thomas J.	450.00	11.25
Student	150.00	3.75
Williams, Ruth V. . . .	285.00	7.13

5. In the case of plant workers, other than supervisors, employment is on an hourly basis. Compute the wages by multiplying the number of hours worked during the pay period by the employee's hourly rate.

The information needed and the sequence of steps that are completed for the payroll are presented in the following discussion.

The time clerk prepared Time Clerk's Reports Nos. 38 and 39, as shown below, from the time cards used by the employees for these workweeks. Inasmuch as the president, sales manager, the sales representatives, and the supervisors do not ring in and out on the time clock, their records are not included in the time clerk's report; but their salaries must be included in the payroll.

① The following schedule shows the hourly wage rates of the two hourly employees that were used in preparing the payroll register for the payday on October 9.

EMPLOYEE	HOURLY RATE
Bonno, Anthony V.	$7.65
Ryan, Norman A.	9.80

TIME CLERK'S REPORT NO. 38

For the Week Ending September 26, 19--

EMPLOYEE	S	M	T	W	T	F	S	TIME WORKED	TIME LOST
Bonno, A. V. ...		8	8	8	8	8		40 hrs.	. . .
Ford, C. L.		8	8	8	8	8		40 hrs.	. . .
Russell, V. A. ..		8	8	8	8	8		40 hrs.	. . .
Ryan, N. A.		8	8	8	8	8		40 hrs.	. . .
Student		8	8	8	8	8		40 hrs.	. . .
Williams, R. V.		8	8	D	8	8		32 hrs.	8 hrs.*

*Time lost because of personal business; charged to personal leave; no deduction for this time lost.

D = lost full day

TIME CLERK'S REPORT NO. 39

For the Week Ending October 3, 19--

EMPLOYEE	S	M	T	W	T	F	S	TIME WORKED	TIME LOST
Bonno, A. V. ...		8	8	8	8	8		40 hrs.	. . .
Ford, C. L.		8	8	8	8	8		40 hrs.	. . .
Russell, V. A. ..		8	8	8	8	8		40 hrs.	. . .
Ryan, N. A.		8	8	8	8	8		40 hrs.	. . .
Student		8	8	8	8	8		40 hrs.	. . .
Williams, R. V.		8	8	8	8	8		40 hrs.	. . .

② The entry required for each employee is recorded in the payroll register (see page 290). The names of all employees are listed in alphabetical order, including yours as "Student." The fold-out payroll register forms that are needed to complete this project are bound at the back of the book on pages 290 to 292.

No deduction has been made for the time lost by Williams. Thus, the total number of hours (80) for which payment was made is recorded in the Regular Earnings Hours column of the payroll register. However, a notation of the time lost (D) was made in the Time Record column. When the absence is posted later to Williams' earnings record, 72 hours is recorded in the Total Hours Worked column, and 8 hours is recorded in the Time Lost column. In the Regular Earnings Hours column, 80 hours is recorded since there was no deduction for the time lost.

In computing the federal income taxes to be withheld, the wage-bracket tables in Tax Table B at the back of the book were used. Each payroll in the project requires the use of the tax tables for a *biweekly payroll period*. Note that the computation of the tax withholding for Joseph T. O'Neill from the wage-bracket table requires the use of the *Table of Allowance Values along with Tax Table A*. These tables are also presented at the back of the book.

Each payday $8 was deducted from the earnings of the plant workers, except the supervisor, for union dues.

Payroll check numbers were assigned beginning with check No. 672.

In the Labor Cost Distribution columns at the extreme right of the payroll register, each employee's gross earnings were recorded in that column which identifies the department in which the employee regularly works. The totals of the Labor Cost Distribution columns provide the amounts to be charged to the appropriate salary expense accounts and aid department managers and supervisors in comparing the actual labor costs with the budgeted amounts.

Once the net pay of each employee was determined, all the amount columns in the payroll register were footed, proved, and ruled.

③ An entry was made in the journal on page 264 transferring from the regular cash account to the payroll cash account the amount of the check issued to Payroll to cover the net amount of the payroll; next, the entry was posted.

④ Information from the payroll register was posted to the employees' earnings records (see pages 282-288).

Note that when posting the deductions for each employee, a column has been provided in the earnings record for recording each deduction for FICA, FIT, SIT, and CIT. All other deductions for each employee are to be totaled and recorded as one amount in the Other Deductions column. Subsidiary ledgers are maintained for Group Insurance Premiums Collected, Union Dues Withheld, and U.S. Savings Bonds Withholdings so that any question about the amounts withheld from an employee's earnings may be answered by referring to the appropriate subsidiary ledger. In this project your work will not involve any recording in or reference to the subsidiary ledgers.

⑤ The proper journal entry was made to record salaries, wages, taxes, and the net amount of cash paid. The journal entry to record the payroll for the first pay in the fourth quarter is shown below and in the general journal on page 264.

Account	Debit	Credit
Administrative Salaries	2,307.69	
Office Salaries	1,710.00	
Sales Salaries	2,150.00	
Wages—Plant A	1,684.00	
Wages—Plant B	612.00	
FICA Taxes Payable		647.50
Employees FIT Payable		915.00
Employees SIT Payable		177.73
Employees CIT Payable		419.80
Union Dues Payable		16.00
U.S. Savings Bonds Deductions Payable		25.00
Payroll Cash		6,262.66

The amounts charged the salary and wage expense accounts were obtained from the totals of the Labor Cost Distribution columns in the payroll register.

As shown in the listing of the distribution of labor costs on page 250, the salaries and wages were charged as follows:

ADMINISTRATIVE SALARIES

Joseph T. O'Neill (President)

OFFICE SALARIES

Catherine L. Ford (Executive Secretary)
Virginia A. Russell (Time Clerk)
Student (Accounting Trainee)
Ruth V. Williams (Programmer)

SALES SALARIES

James C. Ferguson (Sales Manager)
Dewey W. Mann (Sales Representative)

WAGES—PLANT A

Norman A. Ryan (Electrician)
Thomas J. Sokowski (Supervisor)

WAGES—PLANT B

Anthony V. Bonno (Mixer Operator)

FICA Taxes Payable was credited for $647.50, the amount deducted from employees' wages.

Employees FIT Payable, Employees SIT Payable, Employees CIT Payable, Union Dues Payable, and U.S. Savings Bonds Deductions Payable were credited for the total amount withheld for each kind of deduction from employees' wages. In subsequent payroll transactions, Group Insurance Premiums Collected will be credited for the amounts withheld from employees' wages for this type of deduction. Finally, Payroll Cash was credited for the sum of the net amounts paid all employees.

⑥ The payroll taxes for this pay were then recorded in the general journal on page 264 as follows:

Payroll Taxes	735.19	
FICA Taxes Payable		647.47
FUTA Taxes Payable		16.32
SUTA Taxes Payable		71.40

Payroll Taxes was debited for the sum of the employer's FICA, FUTA, and SUTA taxes. The taxable earnings used in calculating each of these payroll taxes was obtained from the appropriate column totals of the payroll register. The computation of the debit to Payroll Taxes was:

FICA:	7.65% of $8,463.69 =	$647.47
FUTA:	.8% of $2,040.00 =	16.32
SUTA:	3.5% of $2,040.00 =	71.40
Total Payroll Taxes		$735.19

FICA Taxes Payable was credited for $647.47, the amount of the liability for the employer's portion of the tax. FUTA Taxes Payable was credited for the amount of the tax on the employer for federal unemployment purposes ($16.32). SUTA Taxes Payable was credited for the amount of the contribution required of the employer under the state unemployment compensation law. This is the same amount, $71.40, that was charged as part of the debit to Payroll Taxes.

⑦ The journal entries were posted to the proper ledger accounts on pages 273-280.

October 14

***No.* 2.** Since the Glo-Brite Paint Company withholds the City of Philadelphia income tax, you are required to deposit the taxes with the Department of Revenue. The deposit rule that affects the Glo-Brite Paint Company states that if the withheld tax is $250 or more in any month, you must deposit the tax within three banking days subsequent to each pay date. The withheld tax for the October 9 payday was $419.80.

① Prepare the journal entry to record the deposit of the taxes and post to the appropriate ledger accounts.

② Complete one of the Philadelphia income tax depository forms (Form W-7) which appear on pages 296-298.

October 20

***No.* 3.** On this date the Glo-Brite Paint Company is required to deposit the Pennsylvania state income taxes withheld from the October 9 payroll.

The deposit rule states that if the employer expects the aggregate amount withheld each quarter to be $1,000 or more, the employer must pay the withheld tax semimonthly. The tax, along with the deposit statement (Form PA 501R), must be remitted within three banking days after the close of the semimonthly periods ending on the 15th and the last day of the month.

① Prepare the journal entry to record the deposit of the taxes and post to the appropriate ledger accounts.

② Complete one of the Pennsylvania deposit statements (Form PA 501R) which appear on pages 294-296. The company's telephone number is (215) 555-9559.

October 23

No. 4. Prepare the payroll for the last pay period of October from Time Clerk's Reports Nos. 40 and 41 below.

The proper procedure in recording the payroll is as follows:

① Complete the payroll register.

Inasmuch as only a portion of the payroll register sheet was used in recording the October 9 payroll, the October 23 payroll should be recorded on the same sheet to save space. On the first blank ruled line after the October 9 payroll, insert "Payday October 23—For Period Ending October 17, 19—." On the following lines record the payroll information for the last pay date of October. When recording succeeding payrolls, continue to conserve space by recording two payrolls on each separate payroll register sheet. In recording the payroll in actual practice, the payroll clerk might begin at the top of a new sheet.

The workers in the plants (Bonno and Ryan) are paid *time and a half* for any hours worked over eight each workday, and *twice* the regular hourly rate for work on Saturdays, Sundays, or holidays.

With this pay period, the *cumulative earnings* of several employees exceed the taxable income base set up by FUTA. This factor must be considered in preparing the payroll register and calculating the employer's payroll taxes. Refer to each employee's earnings record to see the amount of cumulative earnings.

Also, be sure to deduct 30¢ premium for each $1,000 of group insurance carried by each employee.

② Make the entry transferring from Cash to Payroll Cash the net amount of the total payroll, and post.

③ Post the required information from the payroll register to each employee's earnings record.

④ Record in the journal the salaries, wages, taxes withheld, group insurance premiums collected, union dues withheld, savings bonds deductions, and net amount paid, and post to the proper ledger accounts.

The entry required to record the October 23 payroll is the same as that to record the October 9 payroll, except it is necessary to record the liability for the amount withheld from the employees' wages to pay their part of the group insurance premium. The amount withheld should be recorded as a credit to Group Insurance Premiums Collected.

⑤ Record in the journal the employer's payroll taxes and the liabilities created, and post to the appropriate ledger accounts.

TIME CLERK'S REPORT NO. 40
For the Week Ending October 10, 19--

EMPLOYEE	S	M	T	W	T	F	S	TIME WORKED	TIME LOST
Bonno, A. V.		8	8	8	8	8	4	44 hrs.	. . .
Ford, C. L.		4	8	8	8	8		36 hrs.	4 hrs.*
Russell, V. A.		8	8	8	8	8		40 hrs.	. . .
Ryan, N. A.		8	8	8	8	8		40 hrs.	. . .
Student		8	8	8	8	8		40 hrs.	. . .
Williams, R. V.		8	8	8	8	8		40 hrs.	. . .

*Time lost on account of death of relative; charged against annual personal leave; no deduction for time lost.

TIME CLERK'S REPORT NO. 41
For the Week Ending October 17, 19--

EMPLOYEE	S	M	T	W	T	F	S	TIME WORKED	TIME LOST
Bonno, A. V.		8	8	8	8	8		40 hrs.	. . .
Ford, C. L.		8	8	8	8	8		40 hrs.	. . .
Russell, V. A.		8	8	8	8	8		40 hrs.	. . .
Ryan, N. A.		8	8	8	8	8	8	48 hrs.	. . .
Student		8	8	8	8	8		40 hrs.	. . .
Williams, R. V.		8	8	8	8	8		40 hrs.	. . .

October 28

No. 5. Deposited with the City Bank the amount of FICA taxes and federal income taxes for the October payrolls. Since the liability is greater than $3,000, the company must meet the three-banking day requirement as explained on page 79.

① Prepare the journal entry to record the deposit of the taxes and post to the appropriate ledger accounts.

② Complete the Federal Tax Deposit Coupon, Form 8109, to accompany the remittance, using one of the preinscribed forms on page 293. The company's telephone number is (215) 555-9559.

No. 6. Deposited with the City of Philadelphia the amount of city income taxes withheld from the October 23 payroll.

November 4

No. 7. Deposited with the State of Pennsylvania the amount of state income taxes withheld from the October 23 payroll.

No. 8. Virginia A. Russell completed an authorization form directing the payroll department to withhold $5 from each paycheck toward the purchase of U.S. savings bonds. Update Russell's earnings record accordingly.

No. 9. Thomas J. Sokowski completed a new Form W-4, showing that his marital status is now single and that the number of withholding allowances remains at 2. Sokowski's earnings record should be changed accordingly. Reflect this change in the November 6 pay.

November 6

No. 10. Paid the treasurer of the union the amount of union dues withheld during the month of October.

No. 11. Prepare the payroll for the first pay in November from Time Clerk's Reports Nos. 42 and 43 and record the paychecks issued to all employees. Record this payroll at the top of the second payroll register sheet.

Note: Virginia Russell worked only 38 hours in the week ending October 24. Therefore, her pay for that week will be calculated by multiplying 38 by $4.88 (her hourly rate). Ruth Williams worked only 39 hours in the week ending October 24. Therefore, her pay for that week will be calculated by multiplying 39 by $7.13 (her hourly rate).

Also, record the employer's payroll taxes.

November 11

No. 12. Deposited with the City of Philadelphia the amount of city income taxes withheld from the November 6 payroll.

November 13

No. 13. Because of her excessive tardiness and absenteeism, Ruth V. Williams was discharged today. For the week ending November 7, she was late a total of six hours; and for this week, she missed one

TIME CLERK'S REPORT NO. 42
For the Week Ending October 24, 19--

EMPLOYEE	S	M	T	W	T	F	S	TIME WORKED	TIME LOST
Bonno, A. V.		8	8	8	8	8		40 hrs.	. . .
Ford, C. L.		8	8	8	8	8		40 hrs.	. . .
Russell, V. A.		8	8	8	8	6		38 hrs.	2 hrs.*
Ryan, N. A.		8	8	8	8	8	1	41 hrs.	. . .
Student		8	8	8	8	8		40 hrs.	. . .
Williams, R. V.		8	8	8	7	8		39 hrs.	1 hr.†

*Time lost on account of auto accident; deduct 2 hours' pay.
†Time lost because of tardiness; deduct 1 hour's pay.

TIME CLERK'S REPORT NO. 43
For the Week Ending October 31, 19--

EMPLOYEE	S	M	T	W	T	F	S	TIME WORKED	TIME LOST
Bonno, A. V.		8	8	8	8	8		40 hrs.	. . .
Ford, C. L.		8	8	8	8	8		40 hrs.	. . .
Russell, V. A.		8	8	8	8	8		40 hrs.	. . .
Ryan, N. A.		8	8	8	8	8		40 hrs.	. . .
Student		8	8	8	8	8		40 hrs.	. . .
Williams, R. V.		8	8	8	8	8		40 hrs.	. . .

full day and was late two hours on another day. In lieu of two weeks' notice, Williams was given two full weeks' pay ($570.00).

Along with her dismissal pay ($570.00), she was paid for the week ending November 7 (34 hours, or $242.42) and the days worked this current week (30 hours, or $213.90). The total pay for the two partial weeks is $456.32.

① Record a separate entry in the payroll register to show Williams' total earnings, deductions, and net pay. The two weeks' dismissal pay is subject to all payroll taxes. Use the tax table for the biweekly payroll period for the total gross pay ($1,026.32) of Williams.

The deduction for group insurance premiums is $6.60. In the Time Record column make a note of Williams' discharge as of this date. Indicate the payroll check number used to prepare the final check for Williams. When posting to the earnings record, make a notation of Williams' discharge on this date.

② Prepare the journal entries to transfer the net cash and to record Williams' final pay and the employer's payroll taxes. Post to the ledger accounts.

③ Prepare a Wage and Tax Statement, Form W-2, which will be given to Williams with her final paycheck. Use the blank Form W-2 on page 303. Box No. 1 should be left blank since the Glo-Brite Paint Company does not use a control number to identify individual Forms W-2.

November 17

No. 14. Prepare an employee's earnings record for Beth Anne Woods, a new employee who began work today, Tuesday. Woods is single and claims one withholding allowance. She is employed as a programmer at a monthly salary of $1,300. Address, 8102 Franklin Court, Philadelphia, PA 19105-0915. Telephone, 555-1128. Social Security No. 724-03-1587. She is eligible for group insurance coverage of $23,000 immediately, although her first deduction for group insurance will not be made until December 18.

Department: Office.
Weekly rate: $300.00.
Hourly rate: $7.50.

November 18

No. 15. Deposited with the State of Pennsylvania the amount of state income taxes withheld from the November 6 and 13 (Ruth V. Williams) payrolls.

November 20

No. 16. Prepare the payroll for the last pay of November from Time Clerk's Reports Nos. 44 and 45 and record the paychecks issued all employees. Remember to deduct the premiums on the group insurance for each employee.

Also, record the employer's payroll taxes.

TIME CLERK'S REPORT NO. 44
For the Week Ending November 7, 19--

EMPLOYEE	TIME RECORD S	M	T	W	T	F	S	TIME WORKED	TIME LOST
Bonno, A. V.		8	8	8	8	8		40 hrs.	. . .
Ford, C. L.		8	8	8	8	8		40 hrs.	. . .
Russell, V. A.		8	8	8	8	8		40 hrs.	. . .
Ryan, N. A.		8	8	8	8	8		40 hrs.	. . .
Student		8	8	8	8	8		40 hrs.	. . .
Williams, R. V.		6	8	7	7	6		34 hrs.	6 hrs.*

*Time lost because of tardiness; deduct 6 hours' pay.

TIME CLERK'S REPORT NO. 45
For the Week Ending November 14, 19--

EMPLOYEE	TIME RECORD S	M	T	W	T	F	S	TIME WORKED	TIME LOST
Bonno, A. V.		...	...	8	8	8		24 hrs.	. . .
Ford, C. L.		8	8	8	8	8		40 hrs.	. . .
Russell, V. A.		8	8	8	8	8		40 hrs.	. . .
Ryan, N. A.		8	8	8	8	8	2	42 hrs.	. . .
Student		8	8	8	8	8		40 hrs.	. . .
Williams, R. V.		D	8	8	6	8		30 hrs.	10 hrs.*

*Time lost because of tardiness: deduct 2 hours' pay; and unexcused absence: deduct 8 hours' pay.

November 25

No. 17. Deposited with the City of Philadelphia the amount of city income taxes withheld from the November 13 and 20 payrolls.

No. 18. Salary increases of $26 per month, effective for the two weeks covered in the December 4 payroll, are given to Catherine L. Ford and Virginia A. Russell. The group insurance coverage for Ford will remain at $18,000; for Russell, it will be increased to $16,000. The employees' earnings records should be updated accordingly. The new wage rates are:

EMPLOYEE	WEEKLY RATE	HOURLY RATE
Ford, Catherine L. . .	$231.00	$5.78
Russell, Virginia A. . .	201.00	5.03

No. 19. Deposited with the City Bank the amount of FICA taxes and federal income taxes for the November payrolls.

November 30

No. 20. Prepare an employee's earnings record for Paul Winston Young, the president's nephew, who began work today. Young is single and claims one withholding allowance. He is training as a field sales representative in the city where the home office is located. His beginning salary is $1,000 per month. Address, 7936 Holmes Drive, Philadelphia, PA 19107-6107. Telephone, 555-2096. Social Security No. 432-07-6057. Young is eligible for group insurance coverage of $18,000.

Department: Sales.
Weekly rate: $230.77.
Hourly rate: $5.77.

December 3

No. 21. Deposited with the State of Pennsylvania the amount of state income taxes withheld from the November 20 payroll.

December 4

No. 22. Prepare the payroll for the first pay of December from Time Clerk's Reports Nos. 46 and 47 and record the paychecks issued all employees. Record this payroll at the top of the third payroll register sheet.

Note: Thursday, November 26, is a paid holiday for all workers.

Also, record the employer's payroll taxes.

No. 23. Anthony V. Bonno reports the birth of a son and completes an amended Form W-4, showing his total withholding allowances to be five. His earnings record should be changed accordingly, and the change in allowance status is to be reflected in the December 18 payroll.

No. 24. The subsidiary ledger for U.S. Savings Bonds Withholdings indicates that as of the December 4 payroll, $50, the purchase price of a $100 Series EE savings bond, has accrued in the account of Joseph T. O'Neill. Prepare the journal entry to record the purchase of the savings bond, which will be delivered to O'Neill. Post to the ledger accounts.

TIME CLERK'S REPORT NO. 46
For the Week Ending November 21, 19--

EMPLOYEE	S	M	T	W	T	F	S	TIME WORKED	TIME LOST
Bonno, A. V. ...		8	8	8	8	8		40 hrs.	. . .
Ford, C. L.		8	8	8	8	8		40 hrs.	. . .
Russell, V. A. ..		8	8	8	8	8		40 hrs.	. . .
Ryan, N. A.		8	8	8	4	8		36 hrs.	4 hrs.*
Student		8	8	8	8	8		40 hrs.	. . .
Woods, B. A. ...		...	8	8	8	8		32 hrs.	. . .

*Time lost on account of personal business; deduct 4 hours' pay.

TIME CLERK'S REPORT NO. 47
For the Week Ending November 28, 19--

EMPLOYEE	S	M	T	W	T	F	S	TIME WORKED	TIME LOST
Bonno, A. V. ...		8	8	8	PAID HOLIDAY	8	8	48 hrs.	. . .
Ford, C. L.		8	8	8	PAID HOLIDAY	8		40 hrs.	. . .
Russell, V. A. ..		8	8	8	PAID HOLIDAY	8		40 hrs.	. . .
Ryan, N. A.		9	10	8	PAID HOLIDAY	8		43 hrs.	. . .
Student		8	8	8	PAID HOLIDAY	8		40 hrs.	. . .
Woods, B. A. ...		8	8	8	PAID HOLIDAY	8		40 hrs.	. . .

December 9

No. 25. Paid the treasurer of the union the amount of union dues withheld during the month of November.

No. 26. Deposited with the City of Philadelphia the amount of city income taxes withheld from the December 4 payroll.

December 11

No. 27. The payroll department was informed that Virginia A. Russell was killed in an automobile accident on her way home from work Thursday, December 10.

December 14

No. 28. ① Make a separate entry in the payroll register to record the issuance of a check payable to the estate of Virginia A. Russell. This check covers Russell's work for the weeks ending December 5 and 12 ($361.96) plus her accrued vacation pay ($402.00).

Russell's final biweekly pay for time worked ($361.96) and the vacation pay ($402.00) are subject to FICA, FUTA, and SUTA taxes. Since Russell's cumulative earnings have surpassed the taxable earnings figures established by FUTA and SUTA, there will not be any unemployment tax on the employer. This final pay is not subject to withholding for FIT, SIT, or CIT purposes. The deduction for group insurance premiums is $4.80. No deduction is to be made from the final pay for the purchase of U.S. savings bonds.

② A notation of the death of Russell should be made in the payroll register and on her earnings record.

③ Prepare journal entries to transfer the net pay and to record Russell's final pay and the employer's payroll taxes. Post to the ledger accounts.

④ Prepare a Wage and Tax Statement, Form W-2, which will be given to the executor of the estate along with the final paycheck. The final gross pay ($763.96) is not reported in Box 10, but it is reported in Box 12. Use the blank Form W-2 on page 303.

In addition, the unpaid wages and vacation pay must be reported on Form 1099-MISC as nonemployee compensation. A Form 1096 must also be completed. These forms will be completed in February before their due date. (See Transaction Nos. 42 and 43.)

December 18

No. 29. Deposited with the State of Pennsylvania the amount of state income taxes withheld from the December 4 payroll.

No. 30. Wrote a check on the regular cash account, payable to the estate of Virginia A. Russell, for the amount that had accumulated in Russell's account toward the purchase of U.S. savings bonds.

No. 31. Prepare an employee's earnings record for Richard Lloyd Zimmerman, who was employed today as time clerk to take the place left vacant by the death of Virginia A. Russell last week. His beginning salary is $780 per month. Address, 900 South Clark Street, Philadelphia, PA 19195-6247. Telephone, 555-2104. Social Security No. 897-12-1502. Zimmerman is married and claims one withholding allowance. Zimmerman is eligible for group insurance coverage of $14,000, although no deduction for group insurance premiums will be made until the last payday in January.

Department: Office.
Weekly rate: $180.00.
Hourly rate: $4.50.

No. 32. Prepare the payroll for the latter pay of December from Time Clerk's Reports Nos. 48 and 49 and record the paychecks issued all employees. Also, record the employer's payroll taxes.

Note: After posting the information for this last pay to the employees' earnings records, calculate and enter the quarterly and yearly totals on each earnings record.

December 23

No. 33. Deposited with the City of Philadelphia the amount of city income taxes withheld from the December 18 payroll.

No. 34. Deposited with the City Bank the amount of FICA taxes and federal income taxes for the December payrolls.

NOTE: This completes the project insofar as recording the payroll transactions for the last quarter is concerned. The following additional transactions are given to illustrate different types of transactions arising in connection with the accounting for payrolls and payroll taxes. Record these transactions in the journal, but *do not* post to the ledger.

January 6

No. 35. Deposited with the State of Pennsylvania the amount of state income taxes withheld from the December 18 payroll.

January 8

No. 36. Paid the treasurer of the union the amount of union dues withheld during the month of December.

February 1

No. 37. Prepare Form 941, Employer's Quarterly Federal Tax Return, with respect to wages paid during the last calendar quarter. A blank Form 941 is reproduced on page 300. The information needed in preparing the return should be obtained from the ledger accounts, the payroll registers, the employees' earnings records, and the Federal Tax Deposit forms.

Form 941 and all forms that follow are to be signed by the president of the company, Joseph T. O'Neill.

No. 38. ① Complete Form 940-EZ, Employer's Annual Federal Unemployment (FUTA) Tax Return, using the blank form reproduced on page 301, and also Form 8109, Federal Tax Deposit Coupon, using the blank form reproduced on page 294. The information needed in preparing these forms can be obtained from the ledger accounts, the payroll registers, the employees' earnings records, and the following:

(a) Contributions paid to the Pennsylvania unemployment fund for the year amount to $2,833.17. (This amount includes the employer's contribution for the fourth quarter which will be determined and paid in Transaction No. 39.)

(b) FUTA taxable wages for the first three quarters: $65,490.00

(c) FUTA tax liability by quarter:
1st quarter—$272.71
2d quarter—$140.33
3d quarter—$110.88

(d) All deposits for the first three quarters were made on the dates they were due.

Journalize the entry to record the deposit included with Form 8109.

No. 39. ① Prepare Form UC-2, Employer's Report for Unemployment Compensation—Fourth Quarter, using the blank form reproduced on page 302. In Pennsylvania, a credit week is any calendar week during the quarter in which the employee earned at least $50 (without regard to when paid). The telephone

TIME CLERK'S REPORT NO. 48
For the Week Ending December 5, 19--

EMPLOYEE	S	M	T	W	T	F	S	TIME WORKED	TIME LOST
Bonno, A. V.		8	8	8	8	8	4	44 hrs.	. . .
Ford, C. L.		8	8	8	8	8		40 hrs.	. . .
Russell, V. A.		8	8	8	8	8		40 hrs.	. . .
Ryan, N. A.		8	9	9	9	9		44 hrs.	. . .
Student		8	8	7	8	8		39 hrs.	1 hr.*
Woods, B. A.		8	8	8	8	8		40 hrs.	. . .
Young, P. W.		8	8	8	8	8		40 hrs.	. . .

*Time lost because of tardiness; deduct 1 hour's pay.

TIME CLERK'S REPORT NO. 49
For the Week Ending December 12, 19--

EMPLOYEE	S	M	T	W	T	F	S	TIME WORKED	TIME LOST
Bonno, A. V.		8	8	8	8	8	8	48 hrs.	. . .
Ford, C. L.		4	8	8	8	8		36 hrs.	4 hrs.*
Russell, V. A.		8	8	8	8	D		32 hrs.	8 hrs.
Ryan, N. A.		10	8	8	9	8		43 hrs.	. . .
Student		4	8	8	8	8		36 hrs.	4 hrs.†
Woods, B. A.		8	8	8	8	8		40 hrs.	. . .
Young, P. W.		8	8	8	8	8		40 hrs.	. . .

*Time lost for dentist appointment; no deduction for this time lost.
†Time spent in training session; no deduction in pay.

number of the company is (215) 555-9559. All other information needed in preparing the form can be obtained from the ledger accounts, the payroll registers, and the employees' earnings records.

② Journalize the entry to record the payment of the taxes for the fourth quarter.

No. 40. Complete Form W-2, Wage and Tax Statement, for each employee, using the blank statements reproduced on pages 304-308. Use each employee's earnings record to obtain the information needed to complete the forms.

No. 41. Complete Form W-3, Transmittal of Income and Tax Statements, using the blank form reproduced on page 309. Use the information on Forms W-2 to complete this form.

No. 42. Complete Form 1099-MISC, Statement for Recipients of Miscellaneous Income, for the unpaid wages and vacation pay of Virginia A. Russell. The full amount of the December 14 payment must be reported as nonemployee compensation. The blank form is reproduced on page 310.

No. 43. Complete Form 1096, Annual Summary and Transmittal of U.S. Information Returns, using the blank form reproduced on page 310. Use the information on Form 1099-MISC to complete this form.

No. 44. Prepare Form PA W-3R, Employer Quarterly Reconciliation Return of Income Tax Withheld, using the blank form reproduced on page 298. The telephone number of the company is (215) 555-9559.

No. 45. Prepare the Annual Reconciliation of Wage Tax for Philadelphia, using the blank form reproduced on page 299.

QUESTIONS ON THE PAYROLL PROJECT

1. The total amount of expense incurred by the employer because of the payroll taxes imposed on salaries and wages paid during the quarter ended December 31 was . . . . . . $__________
2. The total amount of expense incurred by the employer because of payroll taxes imposed on the salary of Joseph T. O'Neill during the fourth quarter was . . . . . . $__________
3. The amount of the group insurance premiums collected from employees during the quarter ended December 31 was . . . . . . $__________
4. Assume that Bonno continues to authorize the withholding of $5 each payday for the purchase of savings bonds. On what payday will $50 have accumulated for the purchase of one $100 Series EE savings bond? . . . . . . __________
5. On the financial statements prepared at the end of its first year of operations, the company must show an accurate picture of all expenses and all liabilities incurred. The last payday of the year was December 18. However, the payment to the employees on that day did not include the weeks ending December 19 and 26 and the four days (December 28-31) in the following week. These earnings will be reflected in the January payrolls. Two-column journal paper is provided below for use in journalizing the following entry.

   Prepare the adjusting entry as of December 31 to record the salaries and wages that have accrued but remain unpaid as of the end of the year. When calculating the amount of the accrual for each hourly worker, assume each employee worked eight hours on each day during the period with no overtime. For each salaried worker, the accrual will amount to 14/10 of the worker's biweekly earnings, except for Zimmerman who worked only ten days.

   Each of the labor cost accounts should be debited for the appropriate amount of the accrual, and Salaries and Wages Payable should be credited for the total amount of the accrual. There is no liability for payroll taxes on the accrued salaries and wages until the workers are actually paid. Therefore, the company follows the practice of not accruing payroll taxes.

JOURNAL

PAGE

	DATE		DESCRIPTION	POST. REF.	DEBIT	CREDIT	
1							1
2							2
3							3
4							4
5							5
6							6
7							7
8							8
9							9
10							10

ACCOUNTING RECORDS AND REPORTS

Contents

JOURNAL

DATE		DESCRIPTION	POST. REF.	DEBIT	CREDIT
19–– Oct.	9	Payroll Cash	12	6262 66	
		Cash	11		6262 66
	9	Administrative Salaries	51	2307 69	
		Office Salaries	52	1710 00	
		Sales Salaries	53	2150 00	
		Wages — Plant A	54	1684 00	
		Wages — Plant B	55	612 00	
		FICA Taxes Payable	20		647 50
		Employees FIT Payable	24		915 00
		Employees SIT Payable	25		177 73
		Employees CIT Payable	26		419 80
		Union Dues Payable	28		16 00
		U.S. Savings Bonds Deductions Payable	29		25 00
		Payroll Cash	12		6262 66
	9	Payroll Taxes	56	735 19	
		FICA Taxes Payable	20		647 47
		FUTA Taxes Payable	21		16 32
		SUTA Taxes Payable	22		71 40

JOURNAL

PAGE

DATE		DESCRIPTION	POST. REF.	DEBIT	CREDIT

JOURNAL

PAGE

DATE		DESCRIPTION	POST. REF.	DEBIT	CREDIT

JOURNAL

PAGE

	DATE		DESCRIPTION	POST. REF.	DEBIT	CREDIT	
1							1
2							2
3							3
4							4
5							5
6							6
7							7
8							8
9							9
10							10
11							11
12							12
13							13
14							14
15							15
16							16
17							17
18							18
19							19
20							20
21							21
22							22
23							23
24							24
25							25
26							26
27							27
28							28
29							29
30							30
31							31
32							32
33							33
34							34

JOURNAL

PAGE

DATE	DESCRIPTION	POST. REF.	DEBIT	CREDIT

JOURNAL

PAGE

DATE		DESCRIPTION	POST. REF.	DEBIT	CREDIT

JOURNAL

PAGE

DATE		DESCRIPTION	POST. REF.	DEBIT	CREDIT

JOURNAL

PAGE

DATE		DESCRIPTION	POST. REF.	DEBIT	CREDIT

JOURNAL

PAGE

	DATE		DESCRIPTION	POST. REF.	DEBIT	CREDIT	
1							1
2							2
3							3
4							4
5							5
6							6
7							7
8							8
9							9
10							10
11							11
12							12
13							13
14							14
15							15
16							16
17							17
18							18
19							19
20							20
21							21
22							22
23							23
24							24
25							25
26							26
27							27
28							28
29							29
30							30
31							31
32							32
33							33
34							34

GENERAL LEDGER

ACCOUNT **CASH** ACCOUNT NO. 11

DATE		ITEM	POST. REF.	DEBIT	CREDIT	BALANCE DEBIT	BALANCE CREDIT
19-- Oct.	1	*Balance*	√			8 9 8 4 6 33	
	9		J41		6 2 6 2 66	8 3 5 8 3 67	

ACCOUNT **PAYROLL CASH** ACCOUNT NO. 12

DATE		ITEM	POST. REF.	DEBIT	CREDIT	BALANCE DEBIT	BALANCE CREDIT
19--							
Oct.	9		J41	6 2 6 2 66		6 2 6 2 66	
	9		J41		6 2 6 2 66	– – – –	– – – –

ACCOUNT **FICA TAXES PAYABLE** ACCOUNT NO. 20

DATE		ITEM	POST. REF.	DEBIT	CREDIT	BALANCE DEBIT	BALANCE CREDIT
19-- Oct.	9		J41		647 50		647 50
	9		J41		647 47		1294 97

ACCOUNT **FUTA TAXES PAYABLE** ACCOUNT NO. 21

DATE		ITEM	POST. REF.	DEBIT	CREDIT	BALANCE DEBIT	BALANCE CREDIT
19-- Oct.	9		J41		16 32		16 32

ACCOUNT **SUTA TAXES PAYABLE** ACCOUNT NO. 22

DATE		ITEM	POST. REF.	DEBIT	CREDIT	BALANCE DEBIT	BALANCE CREDIT
19-- Oct.	9		J41		71 40		71 40

ACCOUNT **EMPLOYEES UNEMPLOYMENT TAXES PAYABLE** ACCOUNT NO. 23

DATE		ITEM	POST. REF.	DEBIT	CREDIT	BALANCE DEBIT	BALANCE CREDIT

ACCOUNT **EMPLOYEES FIT PAYABLE** ACCOUNT NO. 24

DATE		ITEM	POST. REF.	DEBIT	CREDIT	BALANCE DEBIT	BALANCE CREDIT
19-- Oct.	9		J41		915 00		915 00

ACCOUNT **EMPLOYEES SIT PAYABLE** ACCOUNT NO. 25

DATE		ITEM	POST. REF.	DEBIT	CREDIT	BALANCE DEBIT	BALANCE CREDIT
19-- Oct.	9		J41		177 73		177 73

ACCOUNT ACCOUNT NO. 26

DATE		ITEM	POST. REF.	DEBIT	CREDIT	BALANCE DEBIT	BALANCE CREDIT
19-- Oct.	9		J41		419 80		419 80

ACCOUNT **GROUP INSURANCE PREMIUMS COLLECTED** ACCOUNT NO. 27

DATE		ITEM	POST. REF.	DEBIT	CREDIT	BALANCE DEBIT	BALANCE CREDIT

ACCOUNT **UNION DUES PAYABLE** ACCOUNT NO. 28

DATE		ITEM	POST. REF.	DEBIT	CREDIT	BALANCE DEBIT	BALANCE CREDIT
19-- Oct.	9		J41		16 00		16 00

ACCOUNT **U.S. SAVINGS BONDS DEDUCTIONS PAYABLE** ACCOUNT NO. 29

DATE		ITEM	POST. REF.	DEBIT	CREDIT	BALANCE DEBIT	BALANCE CREDIT
19-- Oct.	9		J41		25 00		25 00

ACCOUNT **ADMINISTRATIVE SALARIES** ACCOUNT NO. 51

DATE		ITEM	POST. REF.	DEBIT	CREDIT	BALANCE DEBIT	BALANCE CREDIT
19-- Oct.	1	*Balance*	√			4 2 6 9 2 27	
	9		J41	2 3 0 7 69		4 4 9 9 9 96	

ACCOUNT **OFFICE SALARIES** ACCOUNT NO. 52

DATE		ITEM	POST. REF.	DEBIT	CREDIT	BALANCE DEBIT	BALANCE CREDIT
19-- Oct.	1	*Balance*	√			2 8 3 5 0 00	
	9		J41	1 7 1 0 00		3 0 0 6 0 00	

ACCOUNT **SALES SALARIES** ACCOUNT NO. 53

DATE		ITEM	POST. REF.	DEBIT	CREDIT	BALANCE DEBIT	BALANCE CREDIT
19-- Oct.	1	*Balance*	√			2 8 5 2 5 00	
	9		J41	2 1 5 0 00		3 0 6 7 5 00	

ACCOUNT **WAGES — PLANT A** ACCOUNT NO. 54

DATE		ITEM	POST. REF.	DEBIT	CREDIT	BALANCE DEBIT	BALANCE CREDIT
19-- Oct.	1	*Balance*	√			3 1 3 3 5 30	
	9		J41	1 6 8 4 00		3 3 0 1 9 30	

ACCOUNT **WAGES — PLANT B** ACCOUNT NO. 55

DATE		ITEM	POST. REF.	DEBIT	CREDIT	BALANCE DEBIT	BALANCE CREDIT
19-- Oct.	1	*Balance*	√			1 1 3 2 2 00	
	9		J41	6 1 2 00		1 1 9 3 4 00	

ACCOUNT **PAYROLL TAXES** ACCOUNT NO. 56

DATE		ITEM	POST. REF.	DEBIT	CREDIT	BALANCE DEBIT	BALANCE CREDIT
19-- Oct.	1	*Balance*	√			1 3 9 0 6 21	
	9		J41	7 3 5 19		1 4 6 4 1 40	

EMPLOYEES' EARNINGS RECORDS

DEPARTMENT	OCCUPATION	WORKS IN (STATE)	SEX M	SEX F	S. S. ACCOUNT NO.	NAME-LAST	FIRST	MIDDLE
Plant B	Mixer Operator	PA	X		537-10-3481	BONNO	Anthony	Victor

DEDUCTIONS INFORMATION

SUTA	GROUP INSURANCE	UNION DUES	U.S. SAVINGS BONDS	OTHER		W/H ALLOW.	MARITAL STATUS
	$24,000—30¢/M	$8 each pay	$5.00 each pay		SALARY $ ____ WEEKLY RATE $ ____ HOURLY RATE $ 7.65 OVERTIME RATE $ 11.48	4	M

	19___ PAYDAY	TOTAL HOURS WORKED	REGULAR EARNINGS HRS.	REGULAR EARNINGS RATE	REGULAR EARNINGS AMOUNT	OVERTIME EARNINGS HRS.	OVERTIME EARNINGS RATE	OVERTIME EARNINGS AMOUNT	CUMULATIVE EARNINGS	DEDUCTIONS FICA	DEDUCTIONS	DEDUCTIONS FIT	DEDUCTIONS SIT	DEDUCTIONS CIT	OTHER DEDUCTIONS	NET PAID CK. NO.	NET PAID AMOUNT	TIME LOST
YEAR-TO-DATE TOTAL					10,293.40			1,028.60	11,322.00	866.13		610.00	237.76	561.66	216.80		8,829.65	
1	10/9	80	80	7.65	612.00				11,934.00	46.82		25.00	12.85	30.36	13.00	672	483.97	
2																		
3																		
4																		
5																		
6																		
QUARTER TOTAL																		
YEARLY TOTAL																		

DEPARTMENT	OCCUPATION	WORKS IN (STATE)	SEX M	SEX F	S. S. ACCOUNT NO.	NAME-LAST	FIRST	MIDDLE
Sales	Sales Manager	PA	X		486-03-8645	FERGUSON	James	Claude

DEDUCTIONS INFORMATION

SUTA	GROUP INSURANCE	UNION DUES	U.S. SAVINGS BONDS	OTHER		W/H ALLOW.	MARITAL STATUS
	$49,000—30¢/M		$5.00 each pay		SALARY $ 32,500/yr. WEEKLY RATE $ 625.00 HOURLY RATE $ 15.63 OVERTIME RATE $ ____	5	M

	19___ PAYDAY	TOTAL HOURS WORKED	REGULAR EARNINGS HRS.	REGULAR EARNINGS RATE	REGULAR EARNINGS AMOUNT	OVERTIME EARNINGS HRS.	OVERTIME EARNINGS RATE	OVERTIME EARNINGS AMOUNT	CUMULATIVE EARNINGS	DEDUCTIONS FICA	DEDUCTIONS	DEDUCTIONS FIT	DEDUCTIONS SIT	DEDUCTIONS CIT	OTHER DEDUCTIONS	NET PAID CK. NO.	NET PAID AMOUNT	TIME LOST
YEAR-TO-DATE TOTAL					23,125.00				23,125.00	1,769.06		2,191.00	485.63	1,147.00	132.30		17,400.01	
1	10/9	80	80		1,250.00				24,375.00	95.63		109.00	26.25	62.00	5.00	673	952.12	
2																		
3																		
4																		
5																		
6																		
QUARTER TOTAL																		
YEARLY TOTAL																		

DEPARTMENT	OCCUPATION	WORKS IN (STATE)	SEX M	SEX F	S. S. ACCOUNT NO.	NAME-LAST	FIRST	MIDDLE
Office	Executive Secretary	PA		X	213-09-4567	FORD	Catherine	Louise

DEDUCTIONS INFORMATION

SUTA	GROUP INSURANCE	UNION DUES	U.S. SAVINGS BONDS	OTHER	SALARY / RATES	W/H ALLOW.	MARITAL STATUS
	$18,000--30¢/M				SALARY $ 975/mo. WEEKLY RATE $ 225.00 HOURLY RATE $ 5.63 OVERTIME RATE $ 8.45	2	S

	19___ PAYDAY	TOTAL HOURS WORKED	REGULAR EARNINGS HRS.	RATE	AMOUNT	OVERTIME EARNINGS HRS.	RATE	AMOUNT	CUMULATIVE EARNINGS	FICA	FIT	SIT	CIT	OTHER DEDUCTIONS	NET PAID CK. NO.	AMOUNT	TIME LOST
YEAR-TO-DATE TOTAL					6300 00				6300 00	481 95	539 00	132 30	312 48	37 80		4796 47	
1	10/9	80	80		450 00				6750 00	34 43	38 00	9 45	22 32		674	345 80	
2																	
3																	
4																	
5																	
6																	
QUARTER TOTAL																	
YEARLY TOTAL																	

DEPARTMENT	OCCUPATION	WORKS IN (STATE)	SEX M	SEX F	S. S. ACCOUNT NO.	NAME-LAST	FIRST	MIDDLE
Sales	Sales Representative	PA	X		282-37-9352	MANN	Dewey	Wilson

DEDUCTIONS INFORMATION

SUTA	GROUP INSURANCE	UNION DUES	U.S. SAVINGS BONDS	OTHER	SALARY / RATES	W/H ALLOW.	MARITAL STATUS
	$35,000--30¢/M				SALARY $ 1,950/mo. WEEKLY RATE $ 450.00 HOURLY RATE $ 11.25 OVERTIME RATE $	4	M

	19___ PAYDAY	TOTAL HOURS WORKED	REGULAR EARNINGS HRS.	RATE	AMOUNT	OVERTIME EARNINGS HRS.	RATE	AMOUNT	CUMULATIVE EARNINGS	FICA	FIT	SIT	CIT	OTHER DEDUCTIONS	NET PAID CK. NO.	AMOUNT	TIME LOST
YEAR-TO-DATE TOTAL					5400 00				5400 00	413 10	432 00	113 40	267 84	31 50		4142 16	
1	10/9	80	80		900 00				6300 00	68 85	70 00	18 90	44 64		675	697 61	
2																	
3																	
4																	
5																	
6																	
QUARTER TOTAL																	
YEARLY TOTAL																	

DEPARTMENT	OCCUPATION	WORKS IN (STATE)	SEX M	SEX F	S. S. ACCOUNT NO.	NAME-LAST	FIRST	MIDDLE
Admin.	President	PA	X		897-04-1534	O'NEILL	Joseph	Tyler

DEDUCTIONS INFORMATION

SUTA	GROUP INSURANCE	UNION DUES	U.S. SAVINGS BONDS	OTHER
	$90,000--30¢/M		$10.00 each pay	

SALARY $ 60,000/yr.
WEEKLY RATE $ 1,153.85
HOURLY RATE $ 28.85
OVERTIME RATE $

W/H ALLOW.	MARITAL STATUS
3	M

	19___ PAYDAY	TOTAL HOURS WORKED	REGULAR EARNINGS HRS.	RATE	AMOUNT	OVERTIME EARNINGS HRS.	RATE	AMOUNT	CUMULATIVE EARNINGS	DEDUCTIONS FICA		FIT	SIT	CIT	OTHER DEDUCTIONS	NET PAID CK. NO.	AMOUNT	TIME LOST
YEAR-TO-DATE TOTAL					426 9 2 27				426 9 2 27	32 6 5 96		73 1 6 16	8 9 6 54	21 1 7 54	20 2 50		288 9 3 57	
1	10/9	80	80		23 0 7 69				449 9 9 96	1 7 6 54		3 8 1 00	4 8 46	1 1 4 46	1 0 00	676	15 7 7 23	
2																		
3																		
4																		
5																		
6																		
QUARTER TOTAL																		
YEARLY TOTAL																		

DEPARTMENT	OCCUPATION	WORKS IN (STATE)	SEX M	SEX F	S. S. ACCOUNT NO.	NAME-LAST	FIRST	MIDDLE
Office	Time Clerk	PA		X	314-21-6337	RUSSELL	Virginia	Aloise

DEDUCTIONS INFORMATION

SUTA	GROUP INSURANCE	UNION DUES	U.S. SAVINGS BONDS	OTHER
	$15,000--30¢/M			

SALARY $ 845/mo.
WEEKLY RATE $ 195.00
HOURLY RATE $ 4.88
OVERTIME RATE $ 7.32

W/H ALLOW.	MARITAL STATUS
1	S

	19___ PAYDAY	TOTAL HOURS WORKED	REGULAR EARNINGS HRS.	RATE	AMOUNT	OVERTIME EARNINGS HRS.	RATE	AMOUNT	CUMULATIVE EARNINGS	DEDUCTIONS FICA		FIT	SIT	CIT	OTHER DEDUCTIONS	NET PAID CK. NO.	AMOUNT	TIME LOST
YEAR-TO-DATE TOTAL					62 4 0 00				62 4 0 00	4 7 7 36		6 4 2 00	1 3 1 04	3 0 9 44	3 1 50		46 4 8 66	
1	10/9	80	80		3 9 0 00				66 3 0 00	2 9 84		4 1 00	8 19	1 9 34		677	2 9 1 63	
2																		
3																		
4																		
5																		
6																		
QUARTER TOTAL																		
YEARLY TOTAL																		

DEPARTMENT	OCCUPATION	WORKS IN (STATE)	SEX M	SEX F	S. S. ACCOUNT NO.	NAME-LAST	FIRST	MIDDLE
Plant A	Electrician	PA	X		526-23-1223	RYAN	Norman	Allen

DEDUCTIONS INFORMATION

SUTA	GROUP INSURANCE	UNION DUES	U.S. SAVINGS BONDS	OTHER	SALARY	WEEKLY RATE	HOURLY RATE	OVERTIME RATE	W/H ALLOW.	MARITAL STATUS
	$31,000—30¢/M	$8 each pay			$	$	$ 9.80	$ 14.70	4	M

	19___ PAYDAY	TOTAL HOURS WORKED	REGULAR EARNINGS HRS.	REGULAR EARNINGS RATE	REGULAR EARNINGS AMOUNT	OVERTIME EARNINGS HRS.	OVERTIME EARNINGS RATE	OVERTIME EARNINGS AMOUNT	CUMULATIVE EARNINGS	DEDUCTIONS FICA	FIT	SIT	CIT	OTHER DEDUCTIONS	NET PAID CK. NO.	NET PAID AMOUNT	TIME LOST
YEAR-TO-DATE TOTAL					132 8 7 50			13 9 7 80	146 8 5 30	11 2 3 42	10 7 0 00	3 0 8 39	7 2 8 34	2 3 5 70		112 1 9 45	
1	10/9	80	80	9 80	7 8 4 00				154 6 9 30	5 9 98	5 2 00	1 6 46	3 8 89	8 00	678	6 0 8 67	
2																	
3																	
4																	
5																	
6																	
QUARTER TOTAL																	
YEARLY TOTAL																	

DEPARTMENT	OCCUPATION	WORKS IN (STATE)	SEX M	SEX F	S. S. ACCOUNT NO.	NAME-LAST	FIRST	MIDDLE
Plant A	Supervisor	PA	X		662-04-8832	SOKOWSKI	Thomas	James

DEDUCTIONS INFORMATION

SUTA	GROUP INSURANCE	UNION DUES	U.S. SAVINGS BONDS	OTHER	SALARY	WEEKLY RATE	HOURLY RATE	OVERTIME RATE	W/H ALLOW.	MARITAL STATUS
	$35,000—30¢/M		$5.00 each pay		$	$ 450.00	$ 11.25	$	2	M

	19___ PAYDAY	TOTAL HOURS WORKED	REGULAR EARNINGS HRS.	REGULAR EARNINGS RATE	REGULAR EARNINGS AMOUNT	OVERTIME EARNINGS HRS.	OVERTIME EARNINGS RATE	OVERTIME EARNINGS AMOUNT	CUMULATIVE EARNINGS	DEDUCTIONS FICA	FIT	SIT	CIT	OTHER DEDUCTIONS	NET PAID CK. NO.	NET PAID AMOUNT	TIME LOST
YEAR-TO-DATE TOTAL					166 5 0 00				166 5 0 00	12 7 3 72	18 0 2 00	3 4 9 65	8 2 5 84	9 4 50		123 0 4 29	
1	10/9	80	80		9 0 0 00				175 5 0 00	6 8 85	9 3 00	1 8 90	4 4 64	5 00	679	6 6 9 61	
2																	
3																	
4																	
5																	
6																	
QUARTER TOTAL																	
YEARLY TOTAL																	

DEPARTMENT	OCCUPATION	WORKS IN (STATE)	SEX M F	S. S. ACCOUNT NO.	NAME-LAST	FIRST	MIDDLE
Office	Accounting Trainee	PA					

DEDUCTIONS INFORMATION

SUTA	GROUP INSURANCE	UNION DUES	U.S. SAVINGS BONDS	OTHER	SALARY / WEEKLY RATE / HOURLY RATE / OVERTIME RATE	W/H ALLOW.	MARITAL STATUS
	$12,000––30¢/M				SALARY $ 650/mo. WEEKLY RATE $ 150.00 HOURLY RATE $ 3.75 OVERTIME RATE $ 5.63	1	S

19__ PAYDAY	TOTAL HOURS WORKED	REGULAR EARNINGS HRS.	REGULAR EARNINGS RATE	REGULAR EARNINGS AMOUNT	OVERTIME EARNINGS HRS.	OVERTIME EARNINGS RATE	OVERTIME EARNINGS AMOUNT	CUMULATIVE EARNINGS	DEDUCTIONS FICA	FIT	SIT	CIT	OTHER DEDUCTIONS	NET PAID CK. NO.	NET PAID AMOUNT	TIME LOST
YEAR-TO-DATE TOTAL				55 5 0 00				55 5 0 00	4 2 4 58	5 0 9 00	1 1 6 55	2 7 5 28	3 2 40		41 9 2 19	
1 10/9	80	80		3 0 0 00				58 5 0 00	2 2 95	2 7 00	6 30	1 4 88		680	2 2 8 87	
2																
3																
4																
5																
6																
QUARTER TOTAL																
YEARLY TOTAL																

DEPARTMENT	OCCUPATION	WORKS IN (STATE)	SEX M F	S. S. ACCOUNT NO.	NAME-LAST	FIRST	MIDDLE
Office	Programmer	PA	F X	518-30-6741	WILLIAMS	Ruth	Virginia

DEDUCTIONS INFORMATION

SUTA	GROUP INSURANCE	UNION DUES	U.S. SAVINGS BONDS	OTHER	SALARY / WEEKLY RATE / HOURLY RATE / OVERTIME RATE	W/H ALLOW.	MARITAL STATUS
	$22,000––30¢/M				SALARY $ 1,235/mo. WEEKLY RATE $ 285.00 HOURLY RATE $ 7.13 OVERTIME RATE $ 10.70	0	S

19__ PAYDAY	TOTAL HOURS WORKED	REGULAR EARNINGS HRS.	REGULAR EARNINGS RATE	REGULAR EARNINGS AMOUNT	OVERTIME EARNINGS HRS.	OVERTIME EARNINGS RATE	OVERTIME EARNINGS AMOUNT	CUMULATIVE EARNINGS	DEDUCTIONS FICA	FIT	SIT	CIT	OTHER DEDUCTIONS	NET PAID CK. NO.	NET PAID AMOUNT	TIME LOST
YEAR-TO-DATE TOTAL				102 6 0 00				102 6 0 00	7 8 4 90	14 0 6 00	2 1 5 46	5 0 8 86	5 9 40		72 8 5 38	
1 10/9	72	80		5 7 0 00				108 3 0 00	4 3 61	7 9 00	1 1 97	2 8 27		681	4 0 7 15	8hrs.
2																
3																
4																
5																
6																
QUARTER TOTAL																
YEARLY TOTAL																

DEPARTMENT	OCCUPATION	WORKS IN (STATE)	SEX M F	S. S. ACCOUNT NO.	NAME-LAST	FIRST	MIDDLE

DEDUCTIONS INFORMATION							
SUTA	GROUP INSURANCE	UNION DUES	U.S. SAVINGS BONDS	OTHER	SALARY $____ WEEKLY RATE $____ HOURLY RATE $____ OVERTIME RATE $____	W/H ALLOW.	MARITAL STATUS

19____ PAYDAY	TOTAL HOURS WORKED	REGULAR EARNINGS HRS.	REGULAR EARNINGS RATE	REGULAR EARNINGS AMOUNT	OVERTIME EARNINGS HRS.	OVERTIME EARNINGS RATE	OVERTIME EARNINGS AMOUNT	CUMULATIVE EARNINGS	DEDUCTIONS FICA		FIT	SIT	CIT	OTHER DEDUCTIONS	NET PAID CK. NO.	NET PAID AMOUNT	TIME LOST
YEAR-TO-DATE TOTAL																	
1																	
2																	
3																	
4																	
5																	
6																	
QUARTER TOTAL																	
YEARLY TOTAL																	

DEPARTMENT	OCCUPATION	WORKS IN (STATE)	SEX M F	S. S. ACCOUNT NO.	NAME-LAST	FIRST	MIDDLE

DEDUCTIONS INFORMATION							
SUTA	GROUP INSURANCE	UNION DUES	U.S. SAVINGS BONDS	OTHER	SALARY $____ WEEKLY RATE $____ HOURLY RATE $____ OVERTIME RATE $____	W/H ALLOW.	MARITAL STATUS

19____ PAYDAY	TOTAL HOURS WORKED	REGULAR EARNINGS HRS.	REGULAR EARNINGS RATE	REGULAR EARNINGS AMOUNT	OVERTIME EARNINGS HRS.	OVERTIME EARNINGS RATE	OVERTIME EARNINGS AMOUNT	CUMULATIVE EARNINGS	DEDUCTIONS FICA		FIT	SIT	CIT	OTHER DEDUCTIONS	NET PAID CK. NO.	NET PAID AMOUNT	TIME LOST
YEAR-TO-DATE TOTAL																	
1																	
2																	
3																	
4																	
5																	
6																	
QUARTER TOTAL																	
YEARLY TOTAL																	

DEPARTMENT	OCCUPATION	WORKS IN (STATE)	SEX M F	S. S. ACCOUNT NO.	NAME-LAST	FIRST	MIDDLE

DEDUCTIONS INFORMATION

SUTA	GROUP INSURANCE	UNION DUES	U.S. SAVINGS BONDS	OTHER

SALARY $______
WEEKLY RATE $______
HOURLY RATE $______
OVERTIME RATE $______

W/H ALLOW.	MARITAL STATUS

19___ PAYDAY	TOTAL HOURS WORKED	REGULAR EARNINGS			OVERTIME EARNINGS			CUMULATIVE EARNINGS	DEDUCTIONS						NET PAID		TIME LOST
		HRS.	RATE	AMOUNT	HRS.	RATE	AMOUNT		FICA		FIT	SIT	CIT	OTHER DEDUC-TIONS	CK. NO.	AMOUNT	
YEAR-TO-DATE TOTAL																	
1																	
2																	
3																	
4																	
5																	
6																	
QUARTER TOTAL																	
YEARLY TOTAL																	

DEPARTMENT	OCCUPATION	WORKS IN (STATE)	SEX M F	S. S. ACCOUNT NO.	NAME-LAST	FIRST	MIDDLE

DEDUCTIONS INFORMATION

SUTA	GROUP INSURANCE	UNION DUES	U.S. SAVINGS BONDS	OTHER

SALARY $______
WEEKLY RATE $______
HOURLY RATE $______
OVERTIME RATE $______

W/H ALLOW.	MARITAL STATUS

19___ PAYDAY	TOTAL HOURS WORKED	REGULAR EARNINGS			OVERTIME EARNINGS			CUMULATIVE EARNINGS	DEDUCTIONS						NET PAID		TIME LOST
		HRS.	RATE	AMOUNT	HRS.	RATE	AMOUNT		FICA		FIT	SIT	CIT	OTHER DEDUC-TIONS	CK. NO.	AMOUNT	
YEAR-TO-DATE TOTAL																	
1																	
2																	
3																	
4																	
5																	
6																	
QUARTER TOTAL																	
YEARLY TOTAL																	

Transaction No. 5

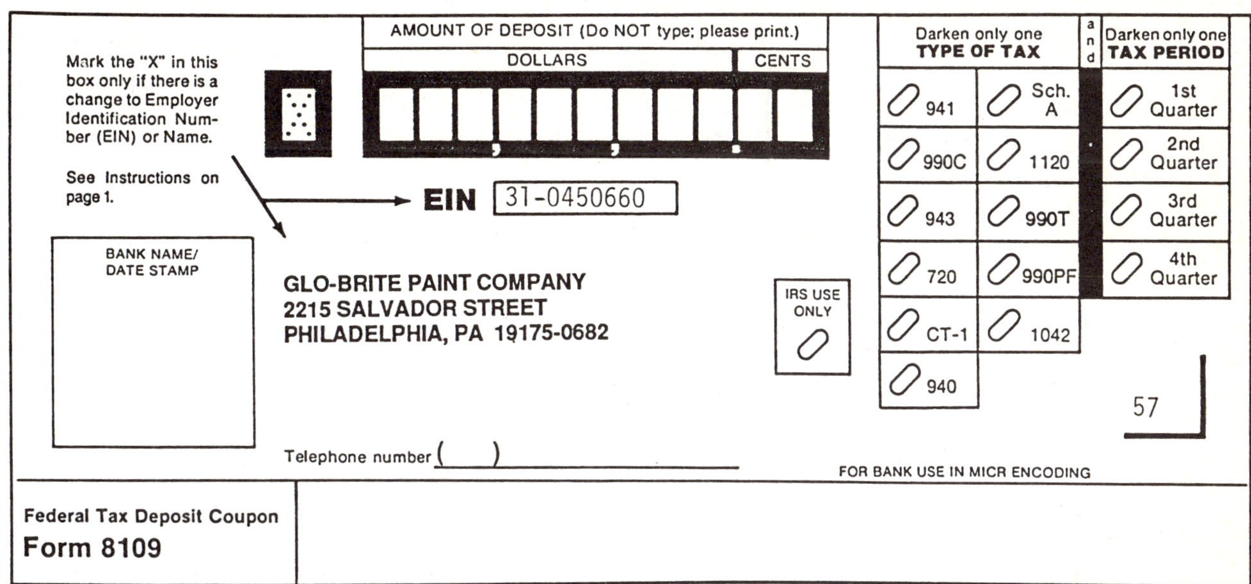

AMOUNT OF DEPOSIT (Do NOT type; please print.)

DOLLARS | CENTS

Mark the "X" in this box only if there is a change to Employer Identification Number (EIN) or Name.

See Instructions on page 1.

EIN 31-0450660

BANK NAME/ DATE STAMP

GLO-BRITE PAINT COMPANY
2215 SALVADOR STREET
PHILADELPHIA, PA 19175-0682

IRS USE ONLY

Darken only one TYPE OF TAX: 941, Sch. A, 990C, 1120, 943, 990T, 720, 990PF, CT-1, 1042, 940

and

Darken only one TAX PERIOD: 1st Quarter, 2nd Quarter, 3rd Quarter, 4th Quarter

57

Telephone number ( )

FOR BANK USE IN MICR ENCODING

Federal Tax Deposit Coupon
Form 8109

Transaction No. 19

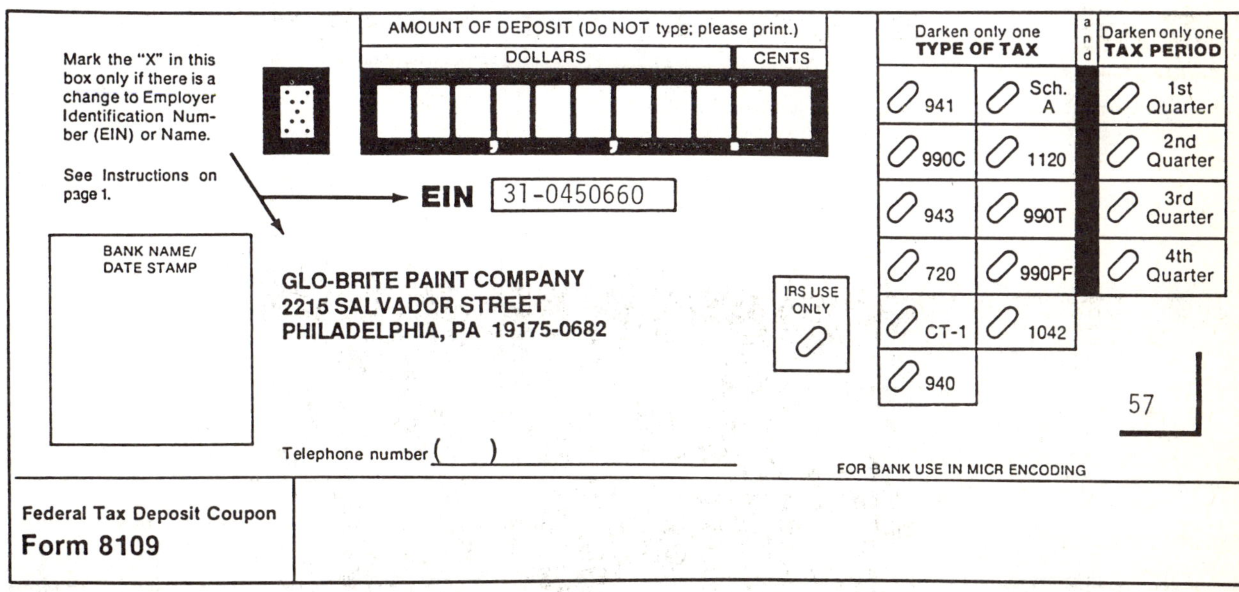

AMOUNT OF DEPOSIT (Do NOT type; please print.)

DOLLARS | CENTS

Mark the "X" in this box only if there is a change to Employer Identification Number (EIN) or Name.

See Instructions on page 1.

EIN 31-0450660

BANK NAME/ DATE STAMP

GLO-BRITE PAINT COMPANY
2215 SALVADOR STREET
PHILADELPHIA, PA 19175-0682

IRS USE ONLY

Darken only one TYPE OF TAX: 941, Sch. A, 990C, 1120, 943, 990T, 720, 990PF, CT-1, 1042, 940

and

Darken only one TAX PERIOD: 1st Quarter, 2nd Quarter, 3rd Quarter, 4th Quarter

57

Telephone number ( )

FOR BANK USE IN MICR ENCODING

Federal Tax Deposit Coupon
Form 8109

Transaction No. 34

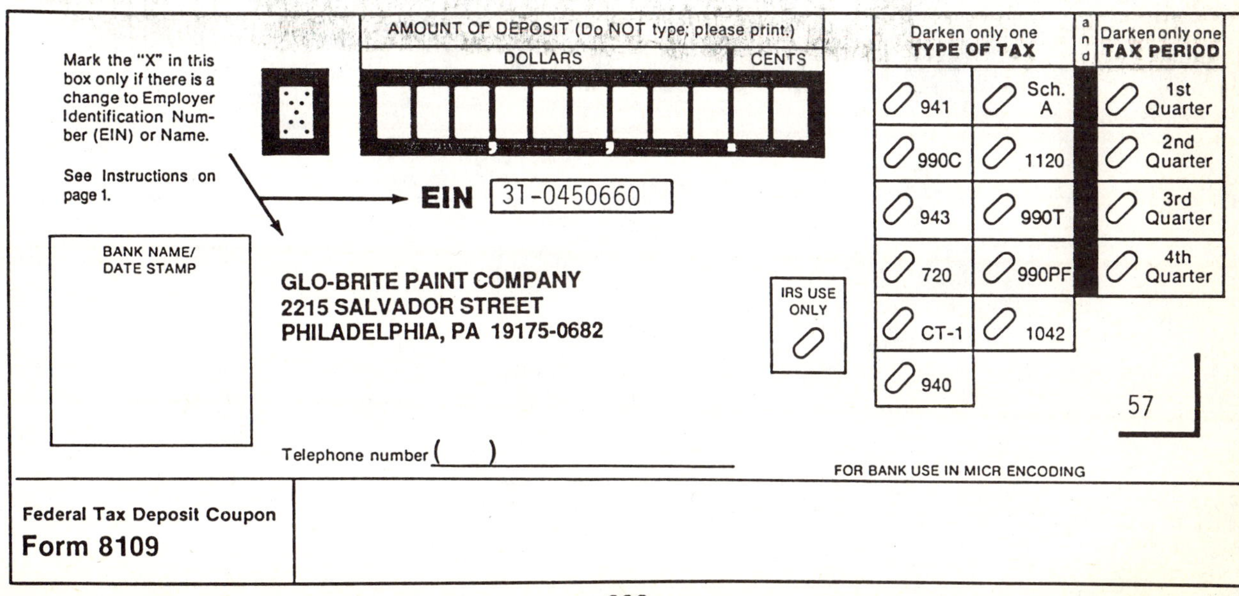

AMOUNT OF DEPOSIT (Do NOT type; please print.)

DOLLARS | CENTS

Mark the "X" in this box only if there is a change to Employer Identification Number (EIN) or Name.

See Instructions on page 1.

EIN 31-0450660

BANK NAME/ DATE STAMP

GLO-BRITE PAINT COMPANY
2215 SALVADOR STREET
PHILADELPHIA, PA 19175-0682

IRS USE ONLY

Darken only one TYPE OF TAX: 941, Sch. A, 990C, 1120, 943, 990T, 720, 990PF, CT-1, 1042, 940

and

Darken only one TAX PERIOD: 1st Quarter, 2nd Quarter, 3rd Quarter, 4th Quarter

57

Telephone number ( )

FOR BANK USE IN MICR ENCODING

Federal Tax Deposit Coupon
Form 8109

Transaction No. 38

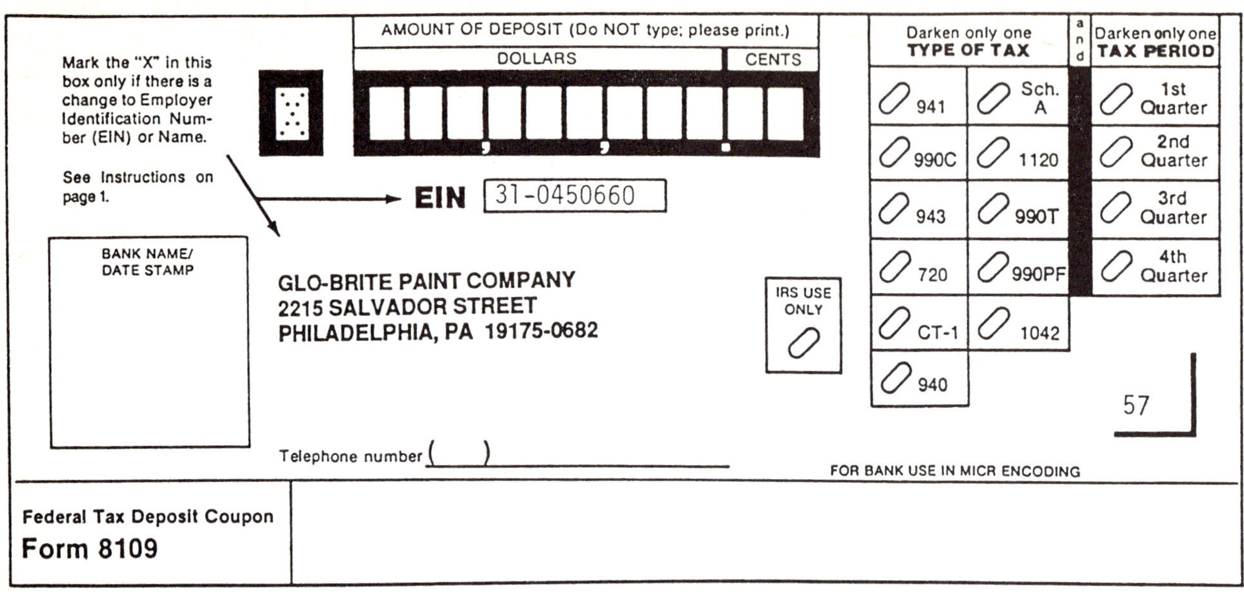

Mark the "X" in this box only if there is a change to Employer Identification Number (EIN) or Name.

See Instructions on page 1.

AMOUNT OF DEPOSIT (Do NOT type; please print.)

DOLLARS | CENTS

EIN 31-0450660

BANK NAME/ DATE STAMP

GLO-BRITE PAINT COMPANY
2215 SALVADOR STREET
PHILADELPHIA, PA 19175-0682

IRS USE ONLY

Telephone number ( )

Darken only one TYPE OF TAX		a n d	Darken only one TAX PERIOD
941	Sch. A		1st Quarter
990C	1120		2nd Quarter
943	990T		3rd Quarter
720	990PF		4th Quarter
CT-1	1042		
940			

57

FOR BANK USE IN MICR ENCODING

Federal Tax Deposit Coupon
Form 8109

Transaction No. 3

PA 501R
COMMONWEALTH OF PENNSYLVANIA
DEPARTMENT OF REVENUE

19 - -

EMPLOYER DEPOSIT STATEMENT OF INCOME TAX WITHHELD FOR USE ONLY BY EMPLOYERS WHO DO NOT HAVE PRE-PRINTED COUPONS.

EIN	QUARTER	PERIOD ENDING	DUE DATE
31-0450660	9-04	10/15/--	10/20/--

TYPE FILER: QUARTERLY ☐ MONTHLY ☐ SEMI-MONTHLY ☐

EXPECTED 3-MONTH WITHHOLDING WILL BE: LESS THAN $300 TAX; $300 OR MORE BUT LESS THAN $1,000 TAX; $1,000 OR MORE TAX

DATE WAGES WERE FIRST PAID ________

BUSINESS NAME AND ADDRESS

Glo-Brite Paint Company
2215 Salvador Street
Philadelphia, PA 19175-0682

1. GROSS COMPENSATION	
2. INCOME TAX LIABILITY	
3. LESS CREDITS	
4. PLUS INTEREST	
5. PAYMENT	

DATE	TELEPHONE NUMBER	SIGNATURE	TITLE
	( )		

Transaction No. 7

PA 501R
COMMONWEALTH OF PENNSYLVANIA
DEPARTMENT OF REVENUE

19 - -

EMPLOYER DEPOSIT STATEMENT OF INCOME TAX WITHHELD FOR USE ONLY BY EMPLOYERS WHO DO NOT HAVE PRE-PRINTED COUPONS.

EIN	QUARTER	PERIOD ENDING	DUE DATE
31-0450660	9-04	10/31/--	11/4/--

TYPE FILER: QUARTERLY ☐ MONTHLY ☐ SEMI-MONTHLY ☐

EXPECTED 3-MONTH WITHHOLDING WILL BE: LESS THAN $300 TAX; $300 OR MORE BUT LESS THAN $1,000 TAX; $1,000 OR MORE TAX

DATE WAGES WERE FIRST PAID ________

BUSINESS NAME AND ADDRESS

Glo-Brite Paint Company
2215 Salvador Street
Philadelphia, PA 19175-0682

1. GROSS COMPENSATION	
2. INCOME TAX LIABILITY	
3. LESS CREDITS	
4. PLUS INTEREST	
5. PAYMENT	

DATE	TELEPHONE NUMBER	SIGNATURE	TITLE
	( )		

Transaction No. 15

PA 501R
COMMONWEALTH OF PENNSYLVANIA
DEPARTMENT OF REVENUE

19 - -

EMPLOYER DEPOSIT STATEMENT OF INCOME TAX WITHHELD FOR USE ONLY BY EMPLOYERS WHO DO NOT HAVE PRE-PRINTED COUPONS.

EIN	QUARTER	PERIOD ENDING	DUE DATE
31-0450660	9-04	11/15/--	11/18/--

TYPE FILER: QUARTERLY ☐ MONTHLY ☐ SEMI-MONTHLY ☐

EXPECTED 3-MONTH WITHHOLDING WILL BE: LESS THAN $300 TAX; $300 OR MORE BUT LESS THAN $1,000 TAX; $1,000 OR MORE TAX

DATE WAGES WERE FIRST PAID ______.

BUSINESS NAME AND ADDRESS

Glo-Brite Paint Company
2215 Salvador Street
Philadelphia, PA 19175-0682

1. GROSS COMPENSATION	
2. INCOME TAX LIABILITY	
3. LESS CREDITS	
4. PLUS INTEREST	
5. PAYMENT	

DATE	TELEPHONE NUMBER	SIGNATURE	TITLE
	( )		

Transaction No. 21

PA 501R
COMMONWEALTH OF PENNSYLVANIA
DEPARTMENT OF REVENUE

19 - -

EMPLOYER DEPOSIT STATEMENT OF INCOME TAX WITHHELD FOR USE ONLY BY EMPLOYERS WHO DO NOT HAVE PRE-PRINTED COUPONS.

EIN	QUARTER	PERIOD ENDING	DUE DATE
31-0450660	9-04	11/30/--	12/3/--

TYPE FILER: QUARTERLY ☐ MONTHLY ☐ SEMI-MONTHLY ☐

EXPECTED 3-MONTH WITHHOLDING WILL BE: LESS THAN $300 TAX; $300 OR MORE BUT LESS THAN $1,000 TAX; $1,000 OR MORE TAX

DATE WAGES WERE FIRST PAID ______.

BUSINESS NAME AND ADDRESS

Glo-Brite Paint Company
2215 Salvador Street
Philadelphia, PA 19175-0682

1. GROSS COMPENSATION	
2. INCOME TAX LIABILITY	
3. LESS CREDITS	
4. PLUS INTEREST	
5. PAYMENT	

DATE	TELEPHONE NUMBER	SIGNATURE	TITLE
	( )		

Transaction No. 29

PA 501R
COMMONWEALTH OF PENNSYLVANIA
DEPARTMENT OF REVENUE

19 - -

EMPLOYER DEPOSIT STATEMENT OF INCOME TAX WITHHELD FOR USE ONLY BY EMPLOYERS WHO DO NOT HAVE PRE-PRINTED COUPONS.

EIN	QUARTER	PERIOD ENDING	DUE DATE
31-0450660	9-04	12/15/--	12/18/--

TYPE FILER: QUARTERLY ☐ MONTHLY ☐ SEMI-MONTHLY ☐

EXPECTED 3-MONTH WITHHOLDING WILL BE: LESS THAN $300 TAX; $300 OR MORE BUT LESS THAN $1,000 TAX; $1,000 OR MORE TAX

DATE WAGES WERE FIRST PAID ______.

BUSINESS NAME AND ADDRESS

Glo-Brite Paint Company
2215 Salvador Street
Philadelphia, PA 19175-0682

1. GROSS COMPENSATION	
2. INCOME TAX LIABILITY	
3. LESS CREDITS	
4. PLUS INTEREST	
5. PAYMENT	

DATE	TELEPHONE NUMBER	SIGNATURE	TITLE
	( )		

Transaction No. 35

PA 501R
COMMONWEALTH OF PENNSYLVANIA
DEPARTMENT OF REVENUE

19 - -

EMPLOYER DEPOSIT STATEMENT OF INCOME TAX WITHHELD
FOR USE ONLY BY EMPLOYERS WHO DO NOT HAVE PRE-PRINTED COUPONS.

EIN	QUARTER	PERIOD ENDING	DUE DATE
31-0450660	9-04	12/31/--	1/6/--

TYPE FILER:		EXPECTED 3-MONTH WITHHOLDING WILL BE:
QUARTERLY	☐	LESS THAN $300 TAX
MONTHLY	☐	$300 OR MORE BUT LESS THAN $1,000 TAX
SEMI-MONTHLY	☐	$1,000 OR MORE TAX

DATE WAGES WERE FIRST PAID ______________________

BUSINESS NAME AND ADDRESS

Glo-Brite Paint Company
2215 Salvador Street
Philadelphia, PA 19175-0682

1. GROSS COMPENSATION	
2. INCOME TAX LIABILITY	
3. LESS CREDITS	
4. PLUS INTEREST	
5. PAYMENT	

DATE	TELEPHONE NUMBER	SIGNATURE	TITLE
	( )		

Transaction No. 2

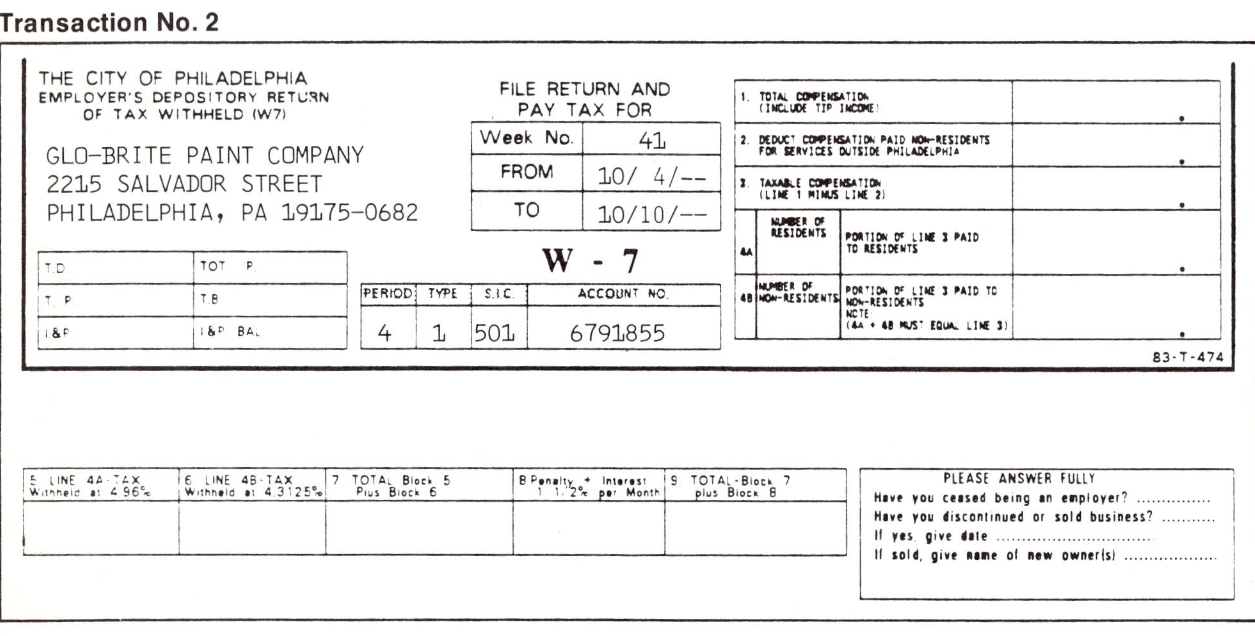

THE CITY OF PHILADELPHIA
EMPLOYER'S DEPOSITORY RETURN
OF TAX WITHHELD (W7)

GLO-BRITE PAINT COMPANY
2215 SALVADOR STREET
PHILADELPHIA, PA 19175-0682

FILE RETURN AND PAY TAX FOR

Week No.	41
FROM	10/ 4/--
TO	10/10/--

W - 7

T.D.	TOT. P.
T. P.	T.B.
I.&P.	I.&P. BAL.

PERIOD	TYPE	S.I.C.	ACCOUNT NO.
4	1	501	6791855

1. TOTAL COMPENSATION (INCLUDE TIP INCOME)	
2. DEDUCT COMPENSATION PAID NON-RESIDENTS FOR SERVICES OUTSIDE PHILADELPHIA	
3. TAXABLE COMPENSATION (LINE 1 MINUS LINE 2)	
4A NUMBER OF RESIDENTS — PORTION OF LINE 3 PAID TO RESIDENTS	
4B NUMBER OF NON-RESIDENTS — PORTION OF LINE 3 PAID TO NON-RESIDENTS NOTE: (4A + 4B MUST EQUAL LINE 3)	

83-T-474

5. LINE 4A-TAX Withheld at 4.96%	6. LINE 4B-TAX Withheld at 4.3125%	7. TOTAL Block 5 Plus Block 6	8. Penalty + Interest 1 1/2% per Month	9. TOTAL-Block 7 plus Block 8

PLEASE ANSWER FULLY
Have you ceased being an employer? ....
Have you discontinued or sold business? ....
If yes, give date ....
If sold, give name of new owner(s) ....

Transaction No. 6

THE CITY OF PHILADELPHIA
EMPLOYER'S DEPOSITORY RETURN
OF TAX WITHHELD (W7)

GLO-BRITE PAINT COMPANY
2215 SALVADOR STREET
PHILADELPHIA, PA 19175-0682

FILE RETURN AND PAY TAX FOR

Week No.	43
FROM	10/18/--
TO	10/24/--

W - 7

T.D.	TOT. P.
T. P.	T.B.
I.&P.	I.&P. BAL.

PERIOD	TYPE	S.I.C.	ACCOUNT NO.
4	1	501	6791855

1. TOTAL COMPENSATION (INCLUDE TIP INCOME)	
2. DEDUCT COMPENSATION PAID NON-RESIDENTS FOR SERVICES OUTSIDE PHILADELPHIA	
3. TAXABLE COMPENSATION (LINE 1 MINUS LINE 2)	
4A NUMBER OF RESIDENTS — PORTION OF LINE 3 PAID TO RESIDENTS	
4B NUMBER OF NON-RESIDENTS — PORTION OF LINE 3 PAID TO NON-RESIDENTS NOTE: (4A + 4B MUST EQUAL LINE 3)	

83-T-474

5. LINE 4A-TAX Withheld at 4.96%	6. LINE 4B-TAX Withheld at 4.3125%	7. TOTAL Block 5 Plus Block 6	8. Penalty + Interest 1 1/2% per Month	9. TOTAL-Block 7 plus Block 8

PLEASE ANSWER FULLY
Have you ceased being an employer? ....
Have you discontinued or sold business? ....
If yes, give date ....
If sold, give name of new owner(s) ....

Transaction No. 12

THE CITY OF PHILADELPHIA
EMPLOYER'S DEPOSITORY RETURN
OF TAX WITHHELD (W7)

GLO-BRITE PAINT COMPANY
2215 SALVADOR STREET
PHILADELPHIA, PA 19175-0682

T.D	TOT. P.
T. P	T.B
I&P	I&P BAL

FILE RETURN AND PAY TAX FOR

Week No.	45
FROM	11/1/--
TO	11/7/--

W - 7

PERIOD	TYPE	S.I.C.	ACCOUNT NO.
4	1	501	6791855

1. TOTAL COMPENSATION (INCLUDE TIP INCOME)		
2. DEDUCT COMPENSATION PAID NON-RESIDENTS FOR SERVICES OUTSIDE PHILADELPHIA		
3. TAXABLE COMPENSATION (LINE 1 MINUS LINE 2)		
4A NUMBER OF RESIDENTS	PORTION OF LINE 3 PAID TO RESIDENTS	
4B NUMBER OF NON-RESIDENTS	PORTION OF LINE 3 PAID TO NON-RESIDENTS NOTE: (4A + 4B MUST EQUAL LINE 3)	

83-T-474

5 LINE 4A-TAX Withheld at 4.96%	6 LINE 4B-TAX Withheld at 4.3125%	7 TOTAL Block 5 Plus Block 6	8 Penalty + Interest 1 1/2% per Month	9 TOTAL-Block 7 plus Block 8

PLEASE ANSWER FULLY
Have you ceased being an employer? ....
Have you discontinued or sold business? ....
If yes, give date ....
If sold, give name of new owner(s) ....

Transaction No. 17

THE CITY OF PHILADELPHIA
EMPLOYER'S DEPOSITORY RETURN
OF TAX WITHHELD (W7)

GLO-BRITE PAINT COMPANY
2215 SALVADOR STREET
PHILADELPHIA, PA 19175-0682

T.D	TOT. P.
T. P	T.B
I&P	I&P BAL

FILE RETURN AND PAY TAX FOR

Week No.	47
FROM	11/15/--
TO	11/21/--

W - 7

PERIOD	TYPE	S.I.C.	ACCOUNT NO.
4	1	501	6791855

1. TOTAL COMPENSATION (INCLUDE TIP INCOME)		
2. DEDUCT COMPENSATION PAID NON-RESIDENTS FOR SERVICES OUTSIDE PHILADELPHIA		
3. TAXABLE COMPENSATION (LINE 1 MINUS LINE 2)		
4A NUMBER OF RESIDENTS	PORTION OF LINE 3 PAID TO RESIDENTS	
4B NUMBER OF NON-RESIDENTS	PORTION OF LINE 3 PAID TO NON-RESIDENTS NOTE: (4A + 4B MUST EQUAL LINE 3)	

83-T-474

5 LINE 4A-TAX Withheld at 4.96%	6 LINE 4B-TAX Withheld at 4.3125%	7 TOTAL Block 5 Plus Block 6	8 Penalty + Interest 1 1/2% per Month	9 TOTAL-Block 7 plus Block 8

PLEASE ANSWER FULLY
Have you ceased being an employer? ....
Have you discontinued or sold business? ....
If yes, give date ....
If sold, give name of new owner(s) ....

Transaction No. 26

THE CITY OF PHILADELPHIA
EMPLOYER'S DEPOSITORY RETURN
OF TAX WITHHELD (W7)

GLO-BRITE PAINT COMPANY
2215 SALVADOR STREET
PHILADELPHIA, PA 19175-0682

T.D	TOT. P.
T. P	T.B
I&P	I&P BAL

FILE RETURN AND PAY TAX FOR

Week No.	49
FROM	11/29/--
TO	12/ 5/--

W - 7

PERIOD	TYPE	S.I.C.	ACCOUNT NO.
4	1	501	6791855

1. TOTAL COMPENSATION (INCLUDE TIP INCOME)		
2. DEDUCT COMPENSATION PAID NON-RESIDENTS FOR SERVICES OUTSIDE PHILADELPHIA		
3. TAXABLE COMPENSATION (LINE 1 MINUS LINE 2)		
4A NUMBER OF RESIDENTS	PORTION OF LINE 3 PAID TO RESIDENTS	
4B NUMBER OF NON-RESIDENTS	PORTION OF LINE 3 PAID TO NON-RESIDENTS NOTE: (4A + 4B MUST EQUAL LINE 3)	

83-T-474

5 LINE 4A-TAX Withheld at 4.96%	6 LINE 4B-TAX Withheld at 4.3125%	7 TOTAL Block 5 Plus Block 6	8 Penalty + Interest 1 1/2% per Month	9 TOTAL-Block 7 plus Block 8

PLEASE ANSWER FULLY
Have you ceased being an employer? ....
Have you discontinued or sold business? ....
If yes, give date ....
If sold, give name of new owner(s) ....

Transaction No. 33

THE CITY OF PHILADELPHIA
EMPLOYER'S DEPOSITORY RETURN
OF TAX WITHHELD (W7)

GLO-BRITE PAINT COMPANY
2215 SALVADOR STREET
PHILADELPHIA, PA 19175-0682

T.D.	TOT. P.
T. P.	T.B.
I.&P.	I.&P. BAL.

FILE RETURN AND PAY TAX FOR

Week No.	51
FROM	12/13/--
TO	12/19/--

W - 7

PERIOD	TYPE	S.I.C.	ACCOUNT NO.
4	1	501	6791855

1. TOTAL COMPENSATION (INCLUDE TIP INCOME)		.
2. DEDUCT COMPENSATION PAID NON-RESIDENTS FOR SERVICES OUTSIDE PHILADELPHIA		.
3. TAXABLE COMPENSATION (LINE 1 MINUS LINE 2)		.
4A NUMBER OF RESIDENTS	PORTION OF LINE 3 PAID TO RESIDENTS	.
4B NUMBER OF NON-RESIDENTS	PORTION OF LINE 3 PAID TO NON-RESIDENTS NOTE (4A + 4B MUST EQUAL LINE 3)	.

83-T-474

5 LINE 4A-TAX Withheld at 4.96%	6 LINE 4B-TAX Withheld at 4.3125%	7 TOTAL Block 5 Plus Block 6	8 Penalty + Interest 1 1/2% per Month	9 TOTAL-Block 7 plus Block 8

PLEASE ANSWER FULLY
Have you ceased being an employer? ....
Have you discontinued or sold business? ....
If yes, give date ....
If sold, give name of new owner(s) ....

Transaction No. 44

PA-W3R
COMMONWEALTH OF PENNSYLVANIA
DEPARTMENT OF REVENUE

EMPLOYER QUARTERLY RECONCILIATION RETURN OF INCOME TAX WITHHELD
For Use ONLY When Employers Do Not Have
Preprinted Coupons

19--

EIN	QUARTER	QUARTER ENDING	DUE DATE	BUSINESS NAME AND ADDRESS
31-0450660	9-04	12/31/--	2/1/--	Glo-Brite Paint Company 2215 Salvador Street Philadelphia, PA 19175-0682

RECORD OF PA WITHHOLDING TAX BY PERIOD

Period	Semi-monthly Filer	Monthly Filer	Quarterly Filer
1			
2			
3			
4			
5			
6			
Total			

7. TOTAL COMPENSATION SUBJECT TO PA TAX	
8. TOTAL PA WITHHOLDING TAX (FROM LEFT)	
9. TOTAL DEPOSITS FOR QUARTER (INCLUDING PRIOR OVERPAYMENTS)	
10. TAX DUE (IF LINE 9 IS LESS THAN THAN LINE 8)	
11. OVERPAYMENT (IF LINE 9) IS GREATER THAN LINE 8)	
12. PAYMENT	

Under penalities of perjury, I declare that I have examined this return and to the best of my knowledge and belief, it is true, correct and complete.

Date	Telephone Number	Signature	Title
	( )		

Transaction No. 45

ANNUAL RECONCILIATION OF WAGE TAX

Due Date:
2/28/--

19--

Print your numbers like this: 1 2 3 4 5 6 7 8 9 0

Glo-Brite Paint Company
2215 Salvador Street
Philadelphia, PA 19175-0682

Type Tax: W

SEE INSTRUCTIONS ON BACK

ACCOUNT NO. 6 7 9 1 8 5 5

If you had no taxable compensation in 19--, see instructions.

Note: "A" and "B" Denote Employees, Not Gross Wages

A. Number of Taxable Philadelphia Residents

B. Number of Taxable Non-Residents

1. Taxable Residents Compensation . 0 0

2. Line 1 times .0496 (4.96%)

3. Taxable Non-Residents Compensation

4. Line 3 times .043125 (4.3125%)

5. Total Tax Due (Line 2 plus Line 4)

6. Tax Previously Paid For 19--

--DO NOT DETACH--

NAME:

ACCOUNT NO.

If Line 5 is Greater Than Line 6, Use Line 7

7. Tax Due (Line 5 Minus Line 6)
Make Check Payable To: City of Philadelphia

If line 5 is less than line 6, use line 8

8. Tax Overpaid (Line 6 Less Line 5)

Signature:____

I hereby certify that I have examined this return and that it is correct to the best of my knowledge.

Transaction No. 37

Form **941**

Department of the Treasury
Internal Revenue Service

4242

Employer's Quarterly Federal Tax Return

▶ See Circular E for more information concerning Employment Tax Returns.

Please type or print.

Your name, address, employer identification number, and calendar quarter of return. (If not correct, please change.)

Name (as distinguished from trade name) — Date quarter ended: DEC 31, 19--

Trade name, if any: GLO-BRITE PAINT COMPANY — Employer identification number

Address and ZIP code: 2215 SALVADOR ST. PHILADELPHIA, PA 19175-0682

OMB No. 1545-0029

T
FF
FD
FP
I
T

If address is different from prior return, check here ▶ ☐

IRS Use

If you do not have to file returns in the future, check here . . . ▶ ☐ Date final wages paid . . . . ▶

If you are a seasonal employer, see **Seasonal employer** on page 2 and check here . . . ▶ ☐

1a	Number of employees (except household) employed in the pay period that includes March 12th . ▶	1a	
b	If you are a subsidiary corporation AND your parent corporation files a consolidated Form 1120, enter parent corporation employer identification number (EIN) . . ▶ 1b –		
2	Total wages and tips subject to withholding, plus other compensation . . . . ▶	2	
3	Total income tax withheld from wages, tips, pensions, annuities, sick pay, gambling, etc. . . . ▶	3	
4	Adjustment of withheld income tax for preceding quarters of calendar year (see instructions) . . ▶	4	
5	Adjusted total of income tax withheld (line 3 as adjusted by line 4—see instructions)	5	
6	Taxable social security wages paid . . . . . $ ________ × 15.3% (.153) . .	6	
7a	Taxable tips reported . . . . $ ________ × 15.3% (.153) . .	7a	
b	Taxable hospital insurance wages paid . . . . $ ________ × 2.9% (.029). . .	7b	
8	Total social security taxes (add lines 6, 7a, and 7b)	8	
9	Adjustment of social security taxes (see instructions for required explanation)	9	
10	Adjusted total of social security taxes (line 8 as adjusted by line 9—see instructions) . . . . . ▶	10	
11	Backup withholding (see instructions)	11	
12	Adjustment of backup withholding tax for preceding quarters of calendar year . . . . ▶	12	
13	Adjusted total of backup withholding (line 11 as adjusted by line 12)	13	
14	Total taxes (add lines 5, 10, and 13)	14	
15	Advance earned income credit (EIC) payments, if any . . . . ▶	15	
16	Net taxes (subtract line 15 from line 14). **This must equal line IV below** (plus line IV of Schedule A (Form 941) if you have treated backup withholding as a separate liability).	16	
17	Total deposits for quarter, including overpayment applied from a prior quarter, from your records . ▶	17	
18	Balance due (subtract line 17 from line 16). This should be less than $500. Pay to IRS . . . . ▶	18	
19	If line 17 is more than line 16, enter overpayment here ▶ $ ________ and check if to be: ☐ Applied to next return **OR** ☐ Refunded.		

Record of Federal Tax Liability (Complete if line 16 is $500 or more.) See the instructions on page 4 for details before checking these boxes.

Check only if you made eighth-monthly deposits using the 95% rule ▶ ☐ Check only if you are a first time 3-banking-day depositor ▶ ☐

Do NOT Show Federal Tax Deposits Here

Show tax liability here, **not deposits.** IRS gets deposit data from FTD coupons.

Date wages paid		First month of quarter		Second month of quarter		Third month of quarter
1st through 3rd	A		I		Q	
4th through 7th	B		J		R	
8th through 11th	C		K		S	
12th through 15th	D		L		T	
16th through 19th	E		M		U	
20th through 22nd	F		N		V	
23rd through 25th	G		O		W	
26th through the last	H		P		X	
Total liability for month	*I*		*II*		*III*	

IV Total for quarter (add lines *I*, *II*, and *III*). **This must equal line 16 above** . . . . ▶

Sign Here

Under penalties of perjury, I declare that I have examined this return, including accompanying schedules and statements, and to the best of my knowledge and belief, it is true, correct, and complete.

Signature ▶ Title ▶ Date ▶

Transaction No. 38

Form **940-EZ**

Department of the Treasury
Internal Revenue Service

Employer's Annual Federal Unemployment (FUTA) Tax Return

OMB No. 1545-1110

19--

T	
FF	
FD	
FP	
I	
T	

Name (as distinguished from trade name)

Calendar year
19--

If incorrect, make any necessary changes.

Trade name, if any
GLO-BRITE PAINT COMPANY

Address and ZIP code
2215 SALVADOR ST. PHILADELPHIA, PA 19175-0682

Employer identification number
31 - 0450660

Before beginning, follow the chart under "Who Can Use Form 940-EZ" on page 2. If you cannot use Form 940-EZ, you must use Form 940 instead.

A Enter the amount of contributions paid to your state unemployment fund. (See instructions for line A on page 4.) . . . ▶ $ ____________

B (1) Enter the name of the state where you have to pay contributions . . . . ▶ ____________

(2) Enter your state reporting number(s) as shown on state unemployment tax return. ▶ ____________

Part I Taxable Wages and FUTA Tax

			Amount paid		
1	Total payments (including payments shown on lines 2 and 3) during the calendar year for services of employees . .			1	
2	Exempt payments. (Explain all exempt payments, attaching additional sheets if necessary.) ▶ ____________	2			
3	Payments for services of more than $7,000. Enter only amounts over the first $7,000 paid to each employee. Do not include any exempt payments from line 2	3			
4	Total exempt payments (add lines 2 and 3)			4	
5	Total taxable wages (subtract line 4 from line 1) . . . . . ▶			5	
6	FUTA tax. Multiply the wages on line 5 by .008 and enter here. (If the result is over $100, also complete Part II.) . .			6	
7	Total FUTA tax deposited for the year, including any overpayment applied from a prior year (from your records) . .			7	
8	Amount you owe (subtract line 7 from line 6). This should be $100 or less. Pay to IRS . . . . ▶			8	
9	Overpayment (subtract line 6 from line 7). Check if it is to be: ☐ Applied to next return, or ☐ Refunded. . ▶			9	

Part II **Record of Quarterly Federal Unemployment Tax Liability (Do not include state liability.) Complete only if line 6 is over $100.**

Quarter	First (Jan. 1 - Mar. 31)	Second (Apr. 1 - June 30)	Third (July 1 - Sept. 30)	Fourth (Oct. 1 - Dec. 31)	Total for Year
Liability for quarter	272.71	140.33	110.88		

If you will not have to file returns in the future, write "Final" here (see *Who Must File a Return* on page 2) and sign the return. ▶

Under penalties of perjury, I declare that I have examined this return, including accompanying schedules and statements, and, to the best of my knowledge and belief, it is true, correct, and complete, and that no part of any payment made to a state unemployment fund claimed as a credit was, or is to be, deducted from the payments to employees.

Signature ▶ **Title (Owner, etc.)** ▶ **Date** ▶

Form **940-EZ**

Transaction No. 39

MAIL TO:
COMMONWEALTH OF PENNSYLVANIA
DEPARTMENT OF LABOR AND INDUSTRY
OFFICE OF EMPLOYMENT SECURITY
HARRISBURG, PA 17121

EMPLOYER'S REPORT FOR UNEMPLOYMENT COMPENSATION
READ INSTRUCTIONS ON REVERSE SIDE OF EMPLOYER'S COPY
ANSWER EACH ITEM TYPE OR PRINT IN INK

FORM UC-2

QTR. 4TH YEAR 19__

INV. OR R.D. CLEARANCE | EMPL. ALPHA INDEX | CASHIER'S TRANSMITTAL NUMBER

1. TOTAL NUMBER OF COVERED EMPLOYES IN PAY PERIOD INCL. 12TH OF MONTH → INCLUDE EMPLOYES WHOSE WAGES EXCEED TAXABLE LIMIT IF NONE ENTER "0"	FIRST MONTH	SECOND MONTH	THIRD MONTH

I CERTIFY THAT THE INFORMATION ON FORMS UC-2/2A/2B IS TRUE AND CORRECT TO THE BEST OF MY KNOWLEDGE AND BELIEF. NO PART OF THE AMOUNT OF EMPLOYER CONTRIBUTIONS REPORTED ON TAXABLE WAGES WAS DEDUCTED OR IS TO BE DEDUCTED FROM THE EMPLOYE'S WAGES.

SIGN HERE ____________________
DO NOT PRINT SIGNATURE OF OWNER, PARTNER, RESPONSIBLE OFFICER OR AUTHORIZED AGENT

TITLE ____________________ DATE ________
GIVE EXACT TITLE

EMPLOYER CONTRIBUTION RATE: .035

EMPLOYER'S CODED ACCOUNT NO. ONLY: 46-3-3300

Please Type or Print EMPLOYER'S NAME AND ADDRESS

GLO-BRITE PAINT COMPANY
2215 SALVADOR STREET
PHILADELPHIA, PA 19175-0682

IF ADDRESS HAS CHANGED, PLEASE CORRECT UC-2B PORTION OF THIS FORM

2. GROSS WAGES FOR EMPLOYE CONTRIBUTIONS * $

2A. EMPLOYE CONTRIBUTIONS DUE (.001 X ITEM 2) * $

3. TAXABLE WAGES FOR EMPLOYER CONTRIBUTIONS $

4. EMPLOYER CONTRIBUTIONS DUE (RATE X ITEM 3) $

4A. TOTAL CONTRIBUTIONS DUE (ITEM 2A + 4) $ *

5. INTEREST DUE SEE INSTRUCTIONS $

6. PENALTY DUE SEE INSTRUCTIONS $

7. TOTAL REMITTANCE (ITEM 4A + 5 + 6) $

DO NOT WRITE IN THIS SPACE

FOR OES USE

EXAMINED BY | UC-2A'S | SUBJECTIVITY DATE

DATE PAYMENT RECEIVED

REPORT TIMELY

REPORT DELINQUENT DATE

POST CASH CREDIT
WE $ ________
C $ ________
I $ ________
P $ ________
AUDITED BY

EMPLOYER CONTRIBUTION RATE: .035

Please Type or Print EMPLOYER'S NAME AND ADDRESS

EMPLOYER'S CODED ACCOUNT NO. ONLY: 46-3-3300

GLO-BRITE PAINT COMPANY
2215 SALVADOR STREET
PHILADELPHIA, PA 19175-0682

EMPLOYER'S QUARTERLY REPORT OF WAGES PAID TO EACH EMPLOYE

FORM UC-2A

QTR. 4TH YEAR 19__

7A. TEL. NO. OF PREPARER ____________________

8. TOTAL NUMBER OF PAGES IN THIS REPORT

9. GROSS WAGES (MUST AGREE WITH ITEM 2 ABOVE AND TOTALS OF ITEM 14) $

10. TOTAL NUMBER OF EMPLOYES LISTED IN ITEM 13 ON ALL PAGES

11. PLANT NUMBER

FOR OES USE

12. EMPLOYE'S SOC. SEC. ACCT. NO.	13. NAME OF EMPLOYE (TYPE OR PRINT IN INK) FIRST NAME	INITIAL	LAST NAME	14. GR. WAGES PD. THIS QTR.	15. CREDIT WEEKS

LIST ANY ADDITIONAL EMPLOYES ON FORM UC-2A SUPPLEMENT OR ON CONTINUATION SHEETS APPROVED BY OES.

TOTAL FOR THIS PAGE ____________________

*See the footnote on page 248.

Transaction No. 13

1 Control number | 22222 | For Paperwork Reduction Act Notice, see separate instructions OMB No 1545 0008 | For Official Use Only ►

2 Employer's name, address, and ZIP code

6 Statutory employee ☐ | Deceased ☐ | Pension plan ☐ | Legal rep ☐ | 942 emp ☐ | Subtotal ☐ | Deferred compensation ☐ | Void ☐

7 Allocated tips | 8 Advance EIC payment

9 Federal income tax withheld | 10 Wages, tips, other compensation

3 Employer's identification number | 4 Employer's state I D number

5 Employee's social security number

11 Social security tax withheld | 12 Social security wages

13 Social security tips | 14 Nonqualified plans

19a Employee's name (first, middle, last)

15 Dependent care benefits | 16 Fringe benefits incl in Box 10

17 See Instr for Forms W-2/W-2P | 18 Other

19b Employee's address and ZIP code

20 | 21 | 22 | 23

24 State income tax | 25 State wages, tips, etc | 26 Name of state | 27 Local income tax | 28 Local wages, tips, etc | 29 Name of locality

Copy A For Social Security Administration

Dept. of the Treasury—Internal Revenue Service

Form **W-2 Wage and Tax Statement 19--**

Transaction No. 28

1 Control number | 22222 | For Paperwork Reduction Act Notice, see separate instructions OMB No 1545 0008 | For Official Use Only ►

2 Employer's name, address, and ZIP code

6 Statutory employee ☐ | Deceased ☐ | Pension plan ☐ | Legal rep ☐ | 942 emp ☐ | Subtotal ☐ | Deferred compensation ☐ | Void ☐

7 Allocated tips | 8 Advance EIC payment

9 Federal income tax withheld | 10 Wages, tips, other compensation

3 Employer's identification number | 4 Employer's state I D number

5 Employee's social security number

11 Social security tax withheld | 12 Social security wages

13 Social security tips | 14 Nonqualified plans

19a Employee's name (first, middle, last)

15 Dependent care benefits | 16 Fringe benefits incl in Box 10

17 See Instr for Forms W-2/W-2P | 18 Other

19b Employee's address and ZIP code

20 | 21 | 22 | 23

24 State income tax | 25 State wages, tips, etc | 26 Name of state | 27 Local income tax | 28 Local wages, tips, etc | 29 Name of locality

Copy A For Social Security Administration

Dept. of the Treasury—Internal Revenue Service

Form **W-2 Wage and Tax Statement 19--**

Transaction No. 40

1 Control number	22222	For Paperwork Reduction Act Notice, see separate instructions OMB No 1545 0008	For Official Use Only ▶
2 Employer's name, address, and ZIP code		6 Statutory employee ☐ Deceased ☐ Pension plan ☐ Legal rep ☐ 942 emp ☐ Subtotal ☐ Deferred compensation ☐ Void ☐	
		7 Allocated tips	8 Advance EIC payment
		9 Federal income tax withheld	10 Wages, tips, other compensation
3 Employer's identification number	4 Employer's state I D number	11 Social security tax withheld	12 Social security wages
5 Employee's social security number		13 Social security tips	14 Nonqualified plans
19a Employee's name (first, middle, last)		15 Dependent care benefits	16 Fringe benefits incl in Box 10
19b Employee's address and ZIP code		17 See Instr. for Forms W-2/W-2P	18 Other
20	21	22	23

24 State income tax	25 State wages, tips, etc.	26 Name of state	27 Local income tax	28 Local wages, tips, etc.	29 Name of locality

Copy A For Social Security Administration

Dept. of the Treasury—Internal Revenue Service

Form **W-2 Wage and Tax Statement 19--**

1 Control number	22222	For Paperwork Reduction Act Notice, see separate instructions OMB No 1545 0008	For Official Use Only ▶
2 Employer's name, address, and ZIP code		6 Statutory employee ☐ Deceased ☐ Pension plan ☐ Legal rep ☐ 942 emp ☐ Subtotal ☐ Deferred compensation ☐ Void ☐	
		7 Allocated tips	8 Advance EIC payment
		9 Federal income tax withheld	10 Wages, tips, other compensation
3 Employer's identification number	4 Employer's state I D number	11 Social security tax withheld	12 Social security wages
5 Employee's social security number		13 Social security tips	14 Nonqualified plans
19a Employee's name (first, middle, last)		15 Dependent care benefits	16 Fringe benefits incl. in Box 10
19b Employee's address and ZIP code		17 See Instr. for Forms W-2/W-2P	18 Other
20	21	22	23

24 State income tax	25 State wages, tips, etc.	26 Name of state	27 Local income tax	28 Local wages, tips, etc.	29 Name of locality

Copy A For Social Security Administration

Dept. of the Treasury—Internal Revenue Service

Form **W-2 Wage and Tax Statement 19--**

Transaction No. 40

1 Control number	22222	For Paperwork Reduction Act Notice, see separate instructions OMB No 1545 0008	For Official Use Only ►
2 Employer's name, address, and ZIP code		6 Statutory employee ☐ Deceased ☐ Pension plan ☐ Legal rep ☐ 942 emp ☐ Subtotal ☐ Deferred compensation ☐ Void ☐	
		7 Allocated tips	8 Advance EIC payment
		9 Federal income tax withheld	10 Wages, tips, other compensation
3 Employer's identification number	4 Employer's state I D number	11 Social security tax withheld	12 Social security wages
5 Employee's social security number		13 Social security tips	14 Nonqualified plans
19a Employee's name (first, middle, last)		15 Dependent care benefits	16 Fringe benefits incl in Box 10
19b Employee's address and ZIP code		17 See Instr for Forms W-2/W-2P	18 Other
20	21	22	23

24 State income tax	25 State wages, tips, etc	26 Name of state	27 Local income tax	28 Local wages, tips, etc.	29 Name of locality

Copy A For Social Security Administration

Dept. of the Treasury—Internal Revenue Service

Form **W-2 Wage and Tax Statement 19--**

1 Control number	22222	For Paperwork Reduction Act Notice, see separate instructions OMB No 1545 0008	For Official Use Only ►
2 Employer's name, address, and ZIP code		6 Statutory employee ☐ Deceased ☐ Pension plan ☐ Legal rep ☐ 942 emp ☐ Subtotal ☐ Deferred compensation ☐ Void ☐	
		7 Allocated tips	8 Advance EIC payment
		9 Federal income tax withheld	10 Wages, tips, other compensation
3 Employer's identification number	4 Employer's state I D number	11 Social security tax withheld	12 Social security wages
5 Employee's social security number		13 Social security tips	14 Nonqualified plans
19a Employee's name (first, middle, last)		15 Dependent care benefits	16 Fringe benefits incl. in Box 10
19b Employee's address and ZIP code		17 See Instr for Forms W-2/W-2P	18 Other
20	21	22	23

24 State income tax	25 State wages, tips, etc.	26 Name of state	27 Local income tax	28 Local wages, tips, etc.	29 Name of locality

Copy A For Social Security Administration

Dept. of the Treasury—Internal Revenue Service

Form **W-2 Wage and Tax Statement 19--**

Transaction No. 40

1 Control number 22222 | For Paperwork Reduction Act Notice, see separate instructions OMB No 1545-0008 | For Official Use Only ►

2 Employer's name, address, and ZIP code

6 Statutory employee | Deceased | Pension plan | Legal rep | 942 emp | Subtotal | Deferred compensation | Void

7 Allocated tips | 8 Advance EIC payment

9 Federal income tax withheld | 10 Wages, tips, other compensation

3 Employer's identification number | 4 Employer's state I.D. number

11 Social security tax withheld | 12 Social security wages

5 Employee's social security number

13 Social security tips | 14 Nonqualified plans

19a Employee's name (first, middle, last)

15 Dependent care benefits | 16 Fringe benefits incl. in Box 10

17 See Instr. for Forms W-2/W-2P | 18 Other

19b Employee's address and ZIP code

20 | 21 | 22 | 23

24 State income tax | 25 State wages, tips, etc. | 26 Name of state | 27 Local income tax | 28 Local wages, tips, etc. | 29 Name of locality

Copy A For Social Security Administration

Dept. of the Treasury—Internal Revenue Service

Form **W-2 Wage and Tax Statement 19--**

1 Control number 22222 | For Paperwork Reduction Act Notice, see separate instructions OMB No 1545-0008 | For Official Use Only ►

2 Employer's name, address, and ZIP code

6 Statutory employee | Deceased | Pension plan | Legal rep | 942 emp | Subtotal | Deferred compensation | Void

7 Allocated tips | 8 Advance EIC payment

9 Federal income tax withheld | 10 Wages, tips, other compensation

3 Employer's identification number | 4 Employer's state I.D. number

11 Social security tax withheld | 12 Social security wages

5 Employee's social security number

13 Social security tips | 14 Nonqualified plans

19a Employee's name (first, middle, last)

15 Dependent care benefits | 16 Fringe benefits incl. in Box 10

17 See Instr. for Forms W-2/W-2P | 18 Other

19b Employee's address and ZIP code

20 | 21 | 22 | 23

24 State income tax | 25 State wages, tips, etc. | 26 Name of state | 27 Local income tax | 28 Local wages, tips, etc. | 29 Name of locality

Copy A For Social Security Administration

Dept. of the Treasury—Internal Revenue Service

Form **W-2 Wage and Tax Statement 19--**

Transaction No. 40

1 Control number	22222	For Paperwork Reduction Act Notice, see separate instructions OMB No 1545 0008	For Official Use Only ▶
2 Employer's name, address, and ZIP code		6 Statutory employee ☐ Deceased ☐ Pension plan ☐ Legal rep ☐ 942 emp ☐ Subtotal ☐ Deferred compensation ☐ Void ☐	
		7 Allocated tips	8 Advance EIC payment
		9 Federal income tax withheld	10 Wages, tips, other compensation
3 Employer's identification number	4 Employer's state I D number	11 Social security tax withheld	12 Social security wages
5 Employee's social security number		13 Social security tips	14 Nonqualified plans
19a Employee's name (first, middle, last)		15 Dependent care benefits	16 Fringe benefits incl. in Box 10
19b Employee's address and ZIP code		17 See Instr. for Forms W-2/W-2P	18 Other
20	21	22	23

24 State income tax	25 State wages, tips, etc.	26 Name of state	27 Local income tax	28 Local wages, tips, etc.	29 Name of locality

Copy A For Social Security Administration

Dept. of the Treasury—Internal Revenue Service

Form **W-2 Wage and Tax Statement 19--**

1 Control number	22222	For Paperwork Reduction Act Notice, see separate instructions OMB No 1545-0008	For Official Use Only ▶
2 Employer's name, address, and ZIP code		6 Statutory employee ☐ Deceased ☐ Pension plan ☐ Legal rep ☐ 942 emp ☐ Subtotal ☐ Deferred compensation ☐ Void ☐	
		7 Allocated tips	8 Advance EIC payment
		9 Federal income tax withheld	10 Wages, tips, other compensation
3 Employer's identification number	4 Employer's state I D number	11 Social security tax withheld	12 Social security wages
5 Employee's social security number		13 Social security tips	14 Nonqualified plans
19a Employee's name (first, middle, last)		15 Dependent care benefits	16 Fringe benefits incl. in Box 10
19b Employee's address and ZIP code		17 See Instr. for Forms W-2/W-2P	18 Other
20	21	22	23

24 State income tax	25 State wages, tips, etc.	26 Name of state	27 Local income tax	28 Local wages, tips, etc.	29 Name of locality

Copy A For Social Security Administration

Dept. of the Treasury—Internal Revenue Service

Form **W-2 Wage and Tax Statement 19--**

Transaction No. 40

1 Control number	22222	For Paperwork Reduction Act Notice, see separate instructions OMB No 1545-0008	For Official Use Only ►
2 Employer's name, address, and ZIP code		6 Statutory employee ☐ Deceased ☐ Pension plan ☐ Legal rep ☐ 942 emp ☐ Subtotal ☐ Deferred compensation ☐ Void ☐	
		7 Allocated tips	8 Advance EIC payment
		9 Federal income tax withheld	10 Wages, tips, other compensation
3 Employer's identification number	4 Employer's state I D number	11 Social security tax withheld	12 Social security wages
5 Employee's social security number		13 Social security tips	14 Nonqualified plans
19a Employee's name (first, middle, last)		15 Dependent care benefits	16 Fringe benefits incl in Box 10
19b Employee's address and ZIP code		17 See Instr for Forms W-2/W-2P	18 Other
20	21	22	23

24 State income tax	25 State wages, tips, etc	26 Name of state	27 Local income tax	28 Local wages, tips, etc	29 Name of locality

Copy A For Social Security Administration

Dept. of the Treasury—Internal Revenue Service

Form **W-2 Wage and Tax Statement 19--**

1 Control number	22222	For Paperwork Reduction Act Notice, see separate instructions OMB No 1545-0008	For Official Use Only ►
2 Employer's name, address, and ZIP code		6 Statutory employee ☐ Deceased ☐ Pension plan ☐ Legal rep ☐ 942 emp ☐ Subtotal ☐ Deferred compensation ☐ Void ☐	
		7 Allocated tips	8 Advance EIC payment
		9 Federal income tax withheld	10 Wages, tips, other compensation
3 Employer's identification number	4 Employer's state I D number	11 Social security tax withheld	12 Social security wages
5 Employee's social security number		13 Social security tips	14 Nonqualified plans
19a Employee's name (first, middle, last)		15 Dependent care benefits	16 Fringe benefits incl in Box 10
19b Employee's address and ZIP code		17 See Instr for Forms W-2/W-2P	18 Other
20	21	22	23

24 State income tax	25 State wages, tips, etc	26 Name of state	27 Local income tax	28 Local wages, tips, etc	29 Name of locality

Copy A For Social Security Administration

Dept. of the Treasury—Internal Revenue Service

Form **W-2 Wage and Tax Statement 19--**

Transaction No. 41

1 Control number | 33333 | For Official Use Only ▶ OMB No. 1545-0008

☐ Kind of Payer ▶

2 941/941E ☐ Military ☐ 943 ☐ CT-1 ☐ 942 ☐ Medicare gov't. emp. ☐

3 Employer's state I.D. number

4

5 Total number of statements

6 Establishment number	7 Allocated tips	8 Advance EIC payments
9 Federal income tax withheld	10 Wages, tips, and other compensation	11 Social security tax withheld
12 Social security wages	13 Social security tips	14 Nonqualified plans
15 Dependent care benefits	16 Adjusted total social security wages and tips	17 Deferred compensation

18 Employer's identification number

19 Other EIN used this year

20 Employer's name

21 Gross annuity, pension, etc. (Form W-2P)

23 Taxable amount (Form W-2P)

24 Income tax withheld by third-party payer

22 Employer's address and ZIP code (If available, place label over boxes 18 and 20.)

Under penalties of perjury, I declare that I have examined this return and accompanying documents, and to the best of my knowledge and belief, they are true, correct, and complete.

Signature ▶ Title ▶ Date ▶

Telephone number (optional) ____________

Form **W-3 Transmittal of Income and Tax Statements 19--**

Department of the Treasury
Internal Revenue Service

Transaction No. 42

9595 ☐ VOID ☐ CORRECTED

Type or machine print PAYER'S name, street address, city, state, and ZIP code

1 Rents $

2 Royalties $

3 Prizes, awards, etc $

OMB No. 1545-0115

19--

Statement for Recipients of

Miscellaneous Income

PAYER'S Federal identification number | RECIPIENT'S identification number

4 Federal income tax withheld $

5 Fishing boat proceeds $

Type or machine print RECIPIENT'S name

6 Medical and health care payments $

7 Nonemployee compensation $

Street address

8 Substitute payments in lieu of dividends or interest $

9 Payer made direct sales of $5,000 or more of consumer products to a buyer (recipient) for resale ▶ ☐

City, state, and ZIP code

10 Crop insurance proceeds $

11 State income tax withheld $

Account number (optional)

12 State/Payer's state number

Copy A For Internal Revenue Service Center

For Paperwork Reduction Act Notice and instructions for completing this form, see Instructions for Forms 1099, 1098, 5498, and W-2G.

Form 1099-MISC

Do NOT Cut or Separate Forms on This Page

Department of the Treasury - Internal Revenue Service

Transaction No. 43

DO NOT STAPLE 6969 ☐ CORRECTED

Form **1096** Department of the Treasury Internal Revenue Service

Annual Summary and Transmittal of U.S. Information Returns

OMB No. 1545-0108

19--

ATTACH IRS LABEL HERE

Type or machine print FILER'S name (or attach label)

Street address

City, state, and ZIP code

If you are not using a preprinted label, enter in Box 1 or 2 below the identification number you used as the filer on the information returns being transmitted. Do not fill in both Boxes 1 and 2.

Name of person to contact if IRS needs more information

Telephone number ( )

For Official Use Only

1 Employer identification number	2 Social security number	3 Total number of documents	4 Federal income tax withheld	5 Total amount reported with this Form 1096
			$	$

Check only one box below to indicate the type of form being transmitted. If this is your FINAL return, check here . . . . . ☐

☐	☐	☐	☐	☐	☐	☐	☐	☐	☐	☐	☐	☐
W-2G 32	1098 81	1099-A 80	1099-B 79	1099-DIV 91	1099-G 86	1099-INT 92	1099-MISC 95	1099-OID 96	1099-PATR 97	1099-R 98	1099-S 75	5498 28

Under penalties of perjury, I declare that I have examined this return and accompanying documents, and, to the best of my knowledge and belief, they are true, correct, and complete.

Signature ▶ .... Title ▶ .... Date ▶ ....

APPENDIX

A

Social Security Benefits

GOALS OF THIS APPENDIX

After completing your study of this appendix, you should be able to:

1. Understand terms such as quarter of coverage, fully insured, currently insured, average monthly wage, and primary insurance amount, the meaning of which is required when calculating the various kinds of benefits.
2. Describe the several different kinds of benefits provided under the social security system.
3. Advise workers on the procedure to be followed in applying for social security benefits.

Usually when we refer to *social security benefits,* we are speaking about old-age, survivors, or disability insurance benefits—those which are discussed in this appendix. Since these benefits are provided for under Title II of the Social Security Act, sometimes they are known as *Title II benefits.* Social security benefits, also called *OASDI benefits,* are paid to workers, their spouses, children, and parents, and to widows, widowers, and some divorced persons.

As the employees of a firm near retirement age, they may approach the payroll manager to find out what retirement benefits and hospital and medical benefits they are entitled to under their social security coverage. Then, too, if workers become disabled or die, their families may turn to the payroll manager for advice as to their rights to disability benefits or survivors benefits. Thus, this appendix discusses the benefits related to the two programs of old-age, survivors, and disability insurance and health insurance for the aged and disabled.

OLD-AGE, SURVIVORS, AND DISABILITY BENEFITS

Benefits payable under the old-age, survivors, and disability program may be classified as:

1. Old-age or disability benefits paid to the worker.
2. Benefits for dependents of a retired or disabled worker.
3. Benefits for surviving family members of a deceased worker.
4. Lump-sum death payments.

For individuals and their families to be eligible for most benefits, the person must be "fully insured." Lump-sum benefits and certain survivor benefits are payable, however, if the individual is only "currently insured." A knowledge of the meaning of such terms as quarter of coverage, fully insured, currently insured, and average monthly wage is needed to understand the method of computing the various benefits to which individuals, their dependents, or their survivors may be entitled.

Quarter of Coverage

A calendar quarter is a period of three consecutive calendar months ending on March 31, June 30, September 30, or December 31. A *quarter of coverage* refers to the minimum amount of wages or self-employment income with which individuals must be credited in a calendar quarter if they are to receive credit toward being insured for that period. Quarters of coverage are used in determining whether workers, as classified below, are fully insured, currently insured, or insured for disability benefits.

Wage-Earners. In 1991 a worker receives one quarter of coverage, up to a maximum of four, for each $540 of earnings in the calendar year.

Self-Employed Persons. The individual's net earnings from self-employment must amount to at least $400 for the taxable year before any quarters in that year can be credited with self-employment income. For 1991 a self-employed person is credited with one quarter of coverage for each calendar quarter in which $540 or more in self-employment income was allocated.

Farm Workers. The quarters of coverage earned by farm workers are based on wages received during the calendar year, not during the calendar quarter. A farm worker may earn a maximum of four quarters of coverage each year. For 1991 a farm worker is credited with one quarter of coverage, up to a total of four, for each $540 earned during the year.

Fully Insured Individual

To be eligible for most retirement and disability benefits, a worker must be fully insured. To be *fully insured*, a worker normally needs between six and 40 quarters of coverage. The number of quarters needed depends on when the person reaches a specified age or dies. When 40 quarters of coverage (10 years), have been obtained, the worker is fully insured for life and need not be concerned about counting the number of quarters of coverage.

Currently Insured Individual

Although individuals must be fully insured before they or their families can obtain retirement benefits, lump-sum benefits and certain survivor benefits are payable if the individuals are only currently insured.

To be *currently insured*, individuals must have at least six quarters of coverage during the 13-quarter period ending with (1) the quarter in which they died, or (2) the quarter in which they became entitled to old-age insurance benefits or most recently became entitled to disability benefits. The quarters of coverage need not have been consecutive within such 13-quarter period.

Primary Insurance Amount

The *primary insurance amount (PIA)* is a person's monthly retirement or disability benefit and the base upon which monthly benefits of the worker's family and survivors are calculated. Social security benefits are calculated according to one of several methods, depending, generally, on the year in which the worker reached age 62, died, or became disabled.

Under the 1977 amendments to the Social Security Act, a formula is used to determine the PIA of workers who reach age 62, become disabled, or die in 1979 or later. By means of the formula, benefits are kept up-to-date with increases in prices after a worker becomes eligible for benefits. In the formula, the PIA is derived from the worker's *averaged indexed monthly earnings*. By means of *indexing*, the worker's average monthly earnings are updated, or adjusted, to reflect changes in wage levels up to the time of entitlement to benefits.

Cost-of-Living Increases in Benefits

Generally automatic increases in social security benefits are tied to increases in the cost of living as measured by the Consumer Price Index. For example, starting with the benefit checks received in January, 1990, there was a 4.7% cost-of-living increase in the social security benefits. For those receiving benefit checks commencing in January, 1991, the estimated cost-of-living adjustment (COLA) in benefits is 5.4%.

Wage Credits for Veterans and Service Personnel

Prior to 1957 service personnel were given wage credits of $160 for each month of active service, although at that time they paid no social security tax. Beginning in 1957 service personnel are covered like other employees and pay FICA tax on their basic pay; but they receive additional wage credits up to $1,200 each year.

Reduced Benefits

The Social Security Amendments of 1983 provided that the age at which a person can retire with no reduction in benefits will eventually be raised to 67. However, this change, which will be phased in gradually, does not affect workers born in 1937 or earlier. Early retirement with reduced benefits will still be permitted at age 62, but workers who retire exactly at age 62 in the year 2022 or later will get only 70% of their full benefits.

In the meantime, for persons currently reaching retirement age, 65 is still the age at which full benefits may be received. If a worker chooses to claim old-age benefits before age 65, the amount of the monthly benefits will be permanently reduced. If employees commence to receive benefits at age 62, the earliest age at which they can qualify, the amount of reduction is about 20%. For each month after age 62 that the worker waits before applying for benefits, the reduction will be less.

Eligible widows or widowers may receive reduced benefits as early as age 60. If the worker at any time received a reduced benefit, the widow or widower may not receive more than the greater of (a) a benefit equal to the amount the worker would be getting if alive, or (b) 82.5% of the worker's PIA. For a widow or widower whose worker spouse was receiving an unreduced benefit, the age-60 benefit will be 71.5% of the worker's PIA. If the benefit is taken at age 62, it will be 82.9% of the worker's PIA.

Severely disabled widows and widowers and surviving divorced spouses may receive reduced benefits at age 50. The benefits for such a person age 50-59 equal 71.5% of the worker's unreduced benefit.

The spouse or divorced spouse of a worker who is getting benefits may also become entitled to reduced benefits on reaching age 62. The benefit payable to one whose benefits start at age 62 is reduced by about 25%.

Persons, such as a widowed mother, may be receiving benefits only because they are caring for a child of the deceased worker. In such cases, those persons are not subject to the reduction provisions, even though they may receive benefits at an early age.

The benefit payable to a husband, wife, mother, father, widow, or widower may be reduced by the amount of a government pension to which the person is entitled on the basis of his or her own work in government service not covered by social security. Thus, government workers are prevented from getting both a full public (government) pension and a social security benefit of a spouse, mother, or father. However, most persons who received, or were eligible to receive, a government pension before December, 1982, are not affected by this reduction or "offset." The reduction does currently apply to husbands who were not dependent on their wives for half or more of their support, to applicants for father's benefits, and to divorced spouses whose marriage did not last at least 20 years.

KINDS OF SOCIAL SECURITY BENEFITS

Several different kinds of benefits are provided under the social security system, each depending upon the relationship of the beneficiary to the retired, deceased, or disabled worker. As mentioned before, the worker, upon whose earnings record the benefits are based, must have attained a certain insured status and acquired quarters of coverage. In addition, an application for such benefits must be filed.

Illustration A-1 shows in summary form the kinds of benefits available and the qualifications needed by the insured worker or his or her beneficiary in order to receive these benefits.

Disability Benefits

Title II of the Social Security Act provides the following types of protection for the disabled worker:

1. Monthly cash benefits for disabled workers and their families.
2. Protection of the workers' wage records while they are disabled so that any low earnings obtained during the period of disability will have minimal effect upon the workers' wage records.
3. Monthly cash benefits for severely disabled widows and widowers and surviving divorced spouses who are age 50 and over.
4. Monthly cash benefits for a disabled child beneficiary age 18 or older.
5. Vocational rehabilitation services for social security disability beneficiaries who are capable of being restored to productive activity.

Workers who have become so severely disabled that they are unable to work can protect their rights to future benefits for themselves and their families by applying to have their social security records "frozen." Thus, after a five-month waiting period, monthly disability benefits are payable to workers and their families while the workers are disabled. Although the worker does not have to be completely helpless to be considered disabled, the disability must be so severe that it prevents the worker from doing any substantial gainful work. Further, the disability must last, or be expected to last, for at least 12 full months or result in death.

As we indicated earlier in this appendix, generally disabled workers must have enough quarters of coverage so that if the workers are already at retirement age, they would be fully insured and have 20 quarters of coverage in the 40-quarter period ending with the one in which the workers become disabled. There are exceptions, however. For example, blind persons need only be fully insured, and workers who are disabled at age 24-30 can qualify if they worked half of the time between age 21 and the onset of disability.

Family Benefits

The monthly payments to members of a retired or a disabled worker's family and the payments to the survivors of an insured worker are equal to a certain percentage of the worker's benefit. Family benefits are generally calculated in relation to the worker's PIA, even though benefits were obtained before age 65. However, there is a limit on the amount that one family may obtain in total benefits, and some of these benefits may be reduced if taken early.

The benefits payable to members of the worker's family, before any reductions are applied because of age or limitations upon total family benefits, are as follows:

Relationship of Family Member to Worker	Percentage of Worker's Benefit to Be Received
Wife, husband, divorced wife, or divorced husband	50% while worker is alive
Child	50% while worker is alive and 75% if worker is dead
Widow, widower, or surviving divorced spouse	100% if of full retirement age; 75% if he or she is caring for worker's child
Dependent grandchild	50% if worker is alive; 75% if worker is dead; child's parents must be dead or disabled
Dependent parent who outlives the worker	82½%; if both parents qualify, a total of 150% is received

Benefits for Divorced Persons

A divorced woman may receive a wife's or a widow's benefit if she was married to her former husband (the insured worker) for at least 10 years. Prior to 1983, these benefits were terminated upon her remarriage. Similar benefits are payable to divorced men.

Divorced spouses who have been divorced for at least 2 years may draw benefits at age 62 if the former spouse is eligible for retirement benefits. It is of no consequence whether the former spouse's benefits have been claimed or if they have been suspended because of substantial employment.

Students' Benefits

Generally benefits for a child end when the child reaches age 18 unless the child is a full-time student or has a disability. Benefits end for elementary or high school students when they reach age 19.

Benefits for Aliens and Prisoners

The Social Security Amendments of 1983 placed limitations on the benefits received by some aliens and prisoners. If an alien is receiving benefits as a dependent or a survivor of an insured worker and has been outside the United States for 6 consecutive months, the benefits will be suspended. Exceptions are made for young children and beneficiaries who lived in the United States for at least 5 years and had a relationship with the worker which established eligibility for benefits. Benefits may also be continued where international social security agreements are in force.

If a person is confined in jail for a felony, benefits may not be paid that person, except in limited circumstances where the felon is participating in an approved rehabilitation program. The benefits payable to a felon's spouse or child are not affected.

Benefits for the Self-Employed

Old-age, survivors, and disability benefits and hospital insurance benefits are payable to self-employed persons and their dependents or survivors under the same conditions as to wage earners and their dependents or survivors.

Benefits for Employees of Carriers

Companies engaged as carriers and employees of carriers are exempted under FICA, as indicated in Unit 3. To provide old-age and disability benefits for workers in these occupations, special legislation has been enacted governing railroads and other carriers, as well as the employees of carriers.

The Railroad Retirement Tax Act sets up the provisions under which employees of carriers subject to the Interstate Commerce Act may retire and become eligible for annuities. The term "annuity" is substituted for the term "benefit" used under the Social Security Act, but both terms have a similar meaning and are commonly referred to as old-age insurance. Details about benefits and taxes can be obtained from the Railroad Retirement Tax Act and the Carriers' Taxing Act.

Special Minimum Benefit

Special provision is made for persons who have worked in jobs covered by social security for many years but at rather low earnings levels. Such workers can qualify for a special benefit that is somewhat higher than that available to them under the regular benefit computation provisions of the law. Thus, workers can receive a benefit equal to $11.50 times the number of years over 10 (up to 30) that they have been covered by the law and have met certain minimum earnings requirements set forth in the law. The special benefits payable under these provisions will be automatically adjusted for cost-of-living increases in the future.

KINDS OF SOCIAL SECURITY BENEFITS

(1) *Old-Age or Disability Benefits*

Person to Receive Benefits	*Eligibility Requirements — The insured individual must be:*
Retired worker, age 62 or older	Fully insured
Disabled worker (except one who is blind), any age under 65	Both fully insured and insured for disability benefits

(2) *Benefits for Dependents of Retired or Disabled Workers*

Person to Receive Benefits	Eligibility Requirements
Spouse, or divorced spouse, age 62 or older Spouse, any age, if caring for child (except student age 18 or over) entitled to benefits Unmarried child, grandchild, or great-grandchild if — (a) under age 18, or (b) under age 19 and a full-time elementary or secondary school student, or (c) age 18 or older with a disability that began before age 22.	Fully insured for old-age benefits or insured for disability benefits, whichever is applicable.

(3) *Survivor Benefits*

Person to Receive Benefits	Eligibility Requirements
Widow, widower, or divorced person, age 60 or older or age 50–59 and able to meet a special definition of disability	Fully insured
Widow, widower, or divorced parent of deceased worker's child, any age, caring for a young child entitled to benefits Unmarried child, grandchild, or great-grandchild if child is — (a) under age 18, or (b) under age 19 and a full-time elementary or secondary school student, or (c) age 18 or older with a disability that began before age 22.	Either fully insured or currently insured
Dependent parents, 62 or older	Fully insured

(4) *Lump-Sum Death Payment ($255)*

Person to Receive Benefits	Eligibility Requirements
Paid only, in order of priority, to (1) worker's widow or widower living with worker at time of death, (2) worker's widow or widower not living with worker but eligible on worker's earnings record, or (3) eligible surviving child	Either fully insured or currently insured

Illustration A-1. Kinds of Social Security Benefits

Working after Benefits Start—the Retirement Test

Under the social security system, it is expected that workers will retire, at least partially, when they reach retirement age. If they do not retire, at least partially, they ordinarily are unable to collect their benefits. The *retirement test* or *annual earnings test,* which is provided by law, determines to what extent workers and self-employed persons may continue to have earnings and still collect their full social security benefits. The retirement test applies to a worker's earnings whether or not the work is covered by the Social Security Act. As explained below, different annual amounts of earnings are applied in the retirement test, depending on whether the retired worker is over or under age 65.

Retired Workers, Age 65 to 70. In 1991, workers who are 65 or older but under age 70 at any time during the year can earn $9,720 without losing any benefits. Commencing in 1990, $1 for each $3 in excess of the stipulated earnings limit is deducted from the benefits paid the worker and any family members who may be receiving benefits.[1] However,

[1]Prior to 1990, $1 in benefits was lost for every $2 in excess earnings for persons of full retirement age.

during the first year of eligibility only, a monthly earnings test is also applied to determine the amount of benefits to be received. Thus, in 1991, workers who reach age 65 and retire are paid a full benefit for any month in which they neither earned more than $810 nor were substantially self-employed, regardless of their total earnings. After the initial year of retirement, however, the monthly measure in the retirement test is eliminated.

When retired persons commence to work after receiving benefits, their wages are subject to social security and Medicare taxes, regardless of their age. Some who delay their retirement and work beyond age 65 receive extra benefit credits, as explained in a later section.

Retired Workers, Age 62 to 64. Workers retiring in 1991 at ages 62 to 64 can earn $7,080 without losing any benefits. *In the first year of eligibility only,* a monthly test applies whereby workers are paid full benefits for those months in which they neither earned more than $590 nor were substantially self-employed. In the second and succeeding years of eligibility, annual earnings tests are applied to determine any excess earnings. As we explained above, the retired worker loses $1 for each $3 in excess of the stipulated earnings limit.

Retired Workers, Age 70 and Over. At age 70 benefits are paid retired workers, no matter how much they earn.

Increased Benefits for Workers Who Delay Retirement

A person may earn increased social security benefits by working beyond the full retirement age (currently age 65). The amount of the increase is based on the credit the worker receives for each month of delayed retirement. In turn, the amount of credit allowed depends on the worker's birth date, as shown in the following listing:

Birth Date	Amount of Credit Received
1916 or earlier	1/12% per month (1% per year)
1917 through 1924	1/4% per month (3% per year)
1925 or later	3½% to 8% per year, depending on birth date

By deferring their claims for benefits, wage earners will generally be able to qualify for a higher primary insurance amount in the years ahead. Thus, the deferral of increased benefits will appeal to those workers who, beyond age 65, continue to enjoy not only good health but also good earnings.

MEDICAL CARE FOR AGED AND NEEDY

The 1965 amendments to the Social Security Act established a three-part program of medical care for the aged and the needy: (1) hospital insurance benefits for the aged and disabled, (2) supplementary medical insurance benefits for the aged and disabled, and (3) medical assistance to the needy.

The first of these programs, hospital insurance benefits for the aged and disabled, is sometimes called Basic Medicare, Part A Medicare, or hospital insurance. The *hospital insurance plan* provides protection against the costs of certain hospital and related services. The plan is financed by a separate hospital insurance tax paid by employees, employers, and the self-employed. The tax provisions are discussed on pages 71 and 73.

The second program, the *supplementary medical insurance benefits* for the aged and disabled, is often referred to as supplementary, voluntary, voluntary supplementary Medicare, the medical insurance program, or Part B Medicare. This voluntary supplementary program for the aged and disabled is designed to cover the costs of doctors' services and a number of other items and services not covered under the basic program. The program is largely financed by monthly premiums from those who enroll and by matching contributions from the federal government. Under this plan the federal government usually pays 80% of the reasonable costs or charges for covered services after the individual pays a deductible each year. The individual also pays the additional 20%.

The third program is popularly called *Medicaid.* Under this program medical assistance is provided to aged and needy persons by means of a joint federal-state program.

No social security taxes are imposed upon either the employer or the employee to provide for the latter two programs. Thus, the eligibility for benefits under only the first program, Part A Medicare, or the hospital insurance program, is discussed.

Those eligible for hospital insurance benefits include everyone over 65 who is entitled to monthly social security benefits or is a qualified beneficiary of the railroad retirement program. Even though workers have reached age 65 and do not receive benefit payments because of their earnings while still working, they should file applications for hospital insurance benefits.

Persons not entitled to social security or railroad retirement benefits are eligible for hospital insurance if they are resident citizens and were born before 1903. Further, those receiving disability benefits under social security or railroad retirement for not less than 24 months are also entitled to hospital insurance, even though under age 65.

Almost all persons age 65 or over who are ineligible for benefits can voluntarily enroll for hospital insurance coverage. The enrollee must pay a monthly premium based on the total cost of hospital insurance protection for the uninsured group. (Voluntary enrollees must also enroll for supplementary medical insurance and pay that premium too.)

As indicated in Unit 3, most federal employees have become entitled to coverage for Medicare tax and benefit purposes. Under a temporary provision, those who worked for the federal government during and before January, 1983, were given credit toward Medicare eligibility for their past federal employment. The dependents and survivors of qualified federal employees also became entitled to Medicare under this temporary provision if they were otherwise qualified.

The Medicare Catastrophic Coverage Act of 1988 expanded the benefits received under Part A Medicare, reduced the amount that beneficiaries are required to pay for Medicare benefits, and provided coverage for outpatient prescription drugs. However, the legislation does not cover all types of catastrophic health expenses, such as long and expensive stays in nursing homes. In addition, to help pay for the benefits provided by the Act, all Medicare-eligible individuals pay a surcharge, or supplemental premium, on their income tax liability.

APPLYING FOR SOCIAL SECURITY BENEFITS

Generally social security benefits are paid only if applied for by the person who is entitled to receive them. The application for benefits must be completed by the applicant if he or she is at least 18 years of age, mentally competent, and physically capable of filling out the form. In all other situations the application may be filed on behalf of the eligible person by a legal guardian, other legal representative, or by the person who is caring for the applicant.

Special application forms are available for applying for benefits under the old-age, survivors, and disability insurance program. The proper forms may be obtained from the nearest district office of the Social Security Administration, which will also give applicants any help they may need in preparing the application, including notary services, free of charge.

After the claimant has filed an application with the district office of the Social Security Administration, the application is forwarded to the appropriate payment center for final approval. If the claim is found correct, it is approved by the Social Security Administration, and the United States Treasury is notified that payment should be made. Benefits commence with the month in which the person meets the eligibility requirements, and the benefit checks are usually mailed so that they will be received on the third day of the month following the month for which payment is due. The entitlement to benefits ends with the month preceding the month in which an event occurs that causes the cessation of entitlement. Thus, if a beneficiary should die in April, the benefit entitlement would end with the preceding March.

It is important that claims for benefits be filed promptly. Generally, benefits are payable retroactively; however, some benefit payments may be limited or prohibited if application is made too late, especially by those age 62 to 64.

Proof of Age

Applicants for benefits may be required to give evidence of their right to receive benefits or the amount of such benefits. If age is a condition to entitlement, the applicant may be required to file a proof of age showing the date of birth. Evidence based on such records as those listed below may be acceptable:

1. Public records of birth (birth certificate)
2. Church records of birth or baptism established or recorded before the age of five
3. Census Bureau notification of registration of birth
4. Hospital birth record or certificate
5. Foreign records of birth
6. Physician's or midwife's birth record
7. Certification, on approved form, of Bible or other family record
8. Naturalization records
9. Immigration papers
10. Military records
11. Passports
12. School records
13. Vaccination records
14. Insurance policy
15. Labor union or fraternal organization records
16. Marriage records
17. Other evidence of probative value, such as employment records and voting records

Statement of Employer

The individual's wage record kept by the Social Security Administration may be several months in arrears since the posting of wages earned to the wage records of individuals is a tremendous task.[2] Therefore, the Administration may request the employer to complete a Statement of Employer, Form SSA-7011, in order to bring an individual's wage record up-to-date. Thus, the computation of the individual's benefits will include the most recent earnings.

Electronic Transfer of Social Security Benefits

Beneficiaries of social security benefits may elect to have their monthly benefits electronically transferred to their bank, savings and loan association, credit union, or other qualified financial organization. The beneficiary is aided by the electronic transfer of benefits in that the possibility of loss is reduced and the process of depositing is eliminated. The beneficiary is further assured that the deposit will be made while the beneficiary is absent from his or her home or is away during any temporary period of relocation.

Taxability and Assignability of Benefits

A portion of a worker's social security benefits is included in taxable income for federal income tax purposes. The amount of benefits taxable is determined by a complicated formula that relates the worker's adjusted gross income and 50% of the social security benefits to a base amount set by the government. In no case, however, will workers pay income taxes on more than one half of their benefits.

Social security benefits cannot be assigned and generally the benefits are not subject to levy, garnishment, or attachment. However, the benefits may be attached in order to collect delinquent federal taxes or to enforce an obligation to make child-support or alimony payments.

GLOSSARY

Average indexed monthly earnings—a worker's average monthly earnings which are updated, or adjusted, to reflect changes in wage levels.

Currently insured—criterion used to determine eligibility for social security benefits; persons must have at least six quarters of coverage during the 13-quarter period ending with (1) the quarter in which they died, or (2) the quarter in which they became entitled to old-age insurance benefits or most recently became entitled to disability benefits.

Fully insured—criterion used to determine eligibility for most retirement and disability benefits; generally, a worker needs between six and 40 quarters of coverage.

Hospital insurance plan—program of medical care that provides protection against costs of certain hospital and related services; also known as *Basic Medicare* or *Part A Medicare.*

Indexing—updating, or adjusting, a dollar amount over any particular time period (such as a calendar year) to reflect changes in wage levels that have occurred since a predetermined base time period.

Medicaid—program of medical assistance provided to aged and needy persons by means of a joint federal-state program.

Primary insurance amount (PIA)—a person's monthly retirement or disability benefit, which is the base upon which monthly benefits of the worker's family and survivors are calculated.

Quarter of coverage—criterion used to determine if workers are fully insured, currently insured, or insured for disability benefits; the minimum amount of wages or self-employment income with which individuals must be credited in a calendar quarter if they are to receive credit toward being insured for that period.

Retirement test—government-imposed test to determine to what extent workers and self-employed persons may continue to have earnings and still collect their full social security benefits.

Social security benefits—payments made under Title II of the Social Security Act to retired workers, their spouses, children, and parents, as well as widows, widowers, and some divorced persons; also known as *OASDI benefits* and *Title II benefits.*

Supplementary medical insurance plan—program of voluntary medical care for aged and disabled designed to cover costs of doctors' services and other items and services not covered under basic program; also known as *supplementary* or *voluntary Medicare* or *Part B Medicare.*

[2] As indicated in Unit 3, workers should check on the status of their social security accounts from time to time to make sure that their earnings have been properly credited. Form SSA-7004, used to request a statement of earnings, is described on pages 75 and 77. This form may be obtained by calling the toll-free number 1-800-937-2000.

APPENDIX B

Automated Payroll Accounting Systems

GOALS OF THIS APPENDIX

After completing your study of this appendix, you should be able to:

1. Compare the flow of information processing in manual payroll accounting systems with that in automated systems and visualize how the input and output media used in manual systems are adapted to automated systems.
2. Understand that the three basic payroll accounting records lying at the heart of manual systems—payroll register, payroll check and earnings statement, and earnings record—continue to serve as integral records in automated systems.
3. Identify the basic characteristics of computers and classify computers according to size.
4. Describe the technologies commonly found in computer systems.

The payroll accounting systems that you have read about in the seven units of this textbook are *manual* payroll systems. Such manual payroll accounting systems, relying upon the hand-recording of payroll data in a payroll register, employees' earnings records, and paychecks, are found in small business firms. However, larger business enterprises have modified and automated their manual payroll systems in order to process more quickly and more economically their payrolls for a greater number of employees.

In this appendix you will examine several examples of automated payroll accounting systems, ranging from an accounting board to computerized payroll processing. In these systems the major objective is to realize economy by applying the *write-it-once concept*. Under this concept, we initially record data such as hours worked and wage rates in such a way that they may be used over and over again without need for a costly rewriting or rekeyboarding of the data.

ACCOUNTING BOARD SYSTEMS

The *accounting board system*, also known as a *peg-board system* or a *write-it-once system*, is a handwritten system of accounting. The *accounting board* is a flat writing surface upon which a series of pegs is positioned along one or two edges, or in the center. Thus, we can bring together payroll forms, with punched holes running along the edges or in the middle, and properly align them on the accounting board for writing with ballpoint pen or pencil. By using carbon paper or no-carbon-required paper, we can record our data on the top form and simultaneously reproduce the same data on each form lying below it.

In Illustration B-1, you see that the payroll register, the individual employee's earnings record, and the employee's payroll check and statement are arranged in shingle-like fashion and held in place by means of

PLACE OVER FIRST PEG

PAYROLL REGISTER

NAME	PERIOD ENDING	HOURS WORKED	EARNINGS: REGULAR	OVERTIME	OTHER	TOTAL	DEDUCTIONS: FEDERAL INC. TAX	FICA	STATE INC. TAX	OTHER	TOTAL	NET PAY	ACCUMULATED EARNINGS	CHECK NUMBER	LINE NO.
TOTALS BROUGHT FORWARD →															
Paul Deasy	19-- 7/15	40	288.00	—	—	288.00	22.00	22.03	9.80	—	53.83	234.17	8646.40	3005	1
Connie Deshler	7/15	40	240.00	—	—	240.00	33.00	18.36	11.13	—	62.49	177.51	6840.10	3006	2

EMPLOYEE'S EARNINGS RECORD

NAME Robert F. Kohler SOCIAL SECURITY NO. 296-22-2273 NO. OF W/H ALLOW. 1

ADDRESS 44 Merion Dr. Wyandotte, MI 48192-2450 MARITAL STATUS S

RATE $8.20/hr.

NAME	PERIOD ENDING	HOURS WORKED	EARNINGS: REGULAR	OVERTIME	OTHER	TOTAL	DEDUCTIONS: FEDERAL INC. TAX	FICA	STATE INC. TAX	OTHER	TOTAL	NET PAY	ACCUMULATED EARNINGS	CHECK NUMBER	
TOTALS BROUGHT FORWARD →			8856.00	1251.80	—	10107.80	1146.00	773.25	420.42	—	2339.67	7768.13	10107.80		
Robert F. Kohler	19-- 7/1	44	328.00	49.20	—	377.20	47.00	28.86	15.62	—	91.48	285.72	10485.00	2947	1
Robert F. Kohler	7/8	43	328.00	36.90	—	364.90	45.00	27.91	15.07	—	87.98	276.92	10849.90	2973	2
Robert F. Kohler	7/15	32	262.40	—	—	262.40	30.00	20.07	10.28	—	60.35	202.05	11112.30	3014	3
TOTAL															
YEAR TO DATE															

WYANDOTTE FEDERAL SAVINGS AND LOAN — WYANDOTTE, MI 48192-3070

Wyandotte Federal Savings and Loan 3014 74-2/714

3757 West Columbus Street • Wyandotte, MI 48192-3070

TO THE ORDER OF ______ DATE ______ $ ______

PAY ______ DOLLARS

PAY CHECK

Wyandotte Federal Savings and Loan

WARREN NATIONAL BANK
WYANDOTTE, MI 48192-3074

BY ______

⑆07140204⑆ 0747312340⑈

NOTE

Detach and retain the remittance stub above. It is a record of your earnings and payroll deductions.

Detach and destroy this portion before cashing pay check.

4

EMPLOYEE'S EARNINGS RECORD

Illustration B-1. Payroll Register, Employee's Earnings Record, and Payroll Check and Employee Statement, Aligned for Payroll Posting on an Accounting Board

pegs along the edge of the board. When we enter data on the employee payroll check statement, we simultaneously record them on the proper lines of the payroll register and the employee's earnings record. We do not need carbon paper because the earnings records and the payroll register are printed on carbonless paper. Such a payroll system is designed primarily for small and medium-size businesses.

We can also use the accounting board in other accounting systems applications, such as accounts receivable and accounts payable, where several records using identical data are prepared at one writing. By using an accounting board system, small and medium-size businesses benefit from the economies and accuracies of mechanized accounting equipment without having to buy expensive machines or employ specially trained operators.

MECHANICAL PAYROLL SYSTEMS

Mechanical payroll systems are commonly illustrated by the electromechanical machines that make up the punched-card system. The *punched-card* or *unit-record system* is based upon a machine-language code in which alphabetic and numeric data are represented by holes punched in cards. Punched-card machines are then used to sort, collate, reproduce, and print the processed data in report form and to perform all types of arithmetic calculations. The processed data become the output that is printed on forms such as paychecks, payroll registers, deductions registers, and income tax reports.

The punched-card system was the principal pioneer system for processing data by a family of machines that could read and process data from one encoding (the keypunching operation). As the computer age dawned, the punched card became an important input document for automated systems. However, because of the fact that punched-card machines are too slow and costly for processing data in today's high-speed processing world, the punched-card system has diminished in importance.

COMPUTER SYSTEMS

A *computer* is an integrated electronic system in which mathematical operations are computed at the speed of light through the use of transistors, diodes, and microminiaturized circuits. As an information-systems machine, the computer provides incredible power for those businesses in which information is the principal product. When the computer processes words or numbers, some of its operations are automated. Others, however, are not since the computer operates under the direction of people. *Thus, people are still the dominant force in any computer system.*

A *computer system* typically is composed of the following elements:

1. *Equipment* that converts human-readable data (handwritten or typewritten/keyboarded) into a form that the computer can process. Also, equipment is needed for entering and storing data and for later converting the processed data into human language, the output of video display terminals (VDTs) and printers. Usually the equipment in a computer system is called *hardware.*
2. *Programs* or *software,* the instructions necessary to operate the computer system.
3. *Personnel,* who operate, program, and manage the system.

Computer technology is the basis for the automated systems that move information through the organization. Your ability to use the technology available for processing payrolls begins with an understanding of the basic characteristics of computers.

Basic Characteristics of Computers

In general, all computers receive and process information, retain information as needed in the future, and communicate that information to users. In order to do so, all computers share the following basic characteristics:

1. *Electronic circuitry* (switches) through which the computer routes data to be processed. Present-generation computers use *integrated circuits (ICs)* called *microprocessors* built on very small silicon *chips* (approximately 1/6" x 1/8"). These chips can hold more than one million electronic transistors that perform the many types of electronic switching functions necessary to computer operations. A digital watch, for example, holds about 5,000 ICs and a small computer, about 50,000. The number of ICs can be expanded in many computers which, in turn, increases their processing and storage powers. With such expansion, remarkable increases in operating speeds become possible. For example, many computers operate at the *nanosecond* level (one billionth of a second); and even faster speeds, such as *picoseconds* (trillionths of a second) and *femtoseconds* (quadrillionths of a second), are reported.
2. An *internal memory* that receives and stores the data to be processed and the *program* that contains the detailed instructions necessary to

process the data. The computer's internal memory is divided into many small sections called *storage locations*, each of which has a specific numeric address much like the address given to a residence in a city. When the address is known, we can easily access the data item "residing" in that storage location.

We measure the capacity of a computer by the number of bytes that can be stored in internal memory. A *byte* is a computer term for a basic data character, such as a letter, number, or symbol. One common byte format consists of eight bits plus a ninth bit that checks the accuracy of the data represented. (*Bit* is an abbreviation of the term *binary digit*, the basic value in a numeric system that uses two digits—0 and 1—to represent alphabetic, numeric, and related data within the computer.)

Usually we express memory in terms of thousands of bytes. For example, a computer with 640K has approximately 640,000 storage locations, since the letter *K*—an abbreviation of the word *kilo*—represents 1,000. However, in computer circles, K equals 1,024 bytes. A broader measure of computer memory is the *megabyte (MB)*—1,024 K or 1,048,576 bytes. For convenience, we frequently round and express this measure as one million; thus a computer with 40MB actually stores 41,943,040 or about 40 million characters.

3. The *ability to perform mathematical operations and machine logic*. For example, the computer can (a) perform arithmetic operations (addition, subtraction, multiplication, and division); (b) determine if a number is positive, negative, or equal to zero; and (c) "decide" whether one of two numbers, when compared, is equal to, higher than, or lower than the other. (We convert alphabetic characters to numeric codes and compare them in the same way as numeric data.) Thus, we say that the computer has a "logical" ability when it compares numbers and on the basis of such comparisons moves or advances from one set of instructions to another.

4. The *automated control of input, process, and output activities*. The computer is automated in that it self-regulates the flow of program instructions and data to be processed from the various input devices. It can also perform many processing steps and store or print out the processed information as the program directs without the need for human operators. As a result, we can lower labor costs and improve our productivity in payroll accounting systems.

Some computers, called *analog computers*, measure continuously changing conditions, such as temperature and atmospheric pressure, and convert them into quantities. You will commonly find analog computer applications in refineries, chemical plants, and utilities. The computers used in processing payrolls are typically *digital computers*, which count numbers, or digits, while processing numeric and alphabetic data that have been converted to a numeric code. Since most data processed in payroll operations are either numeric or alphabetic, we shall discuss only the digital computer in this appendix.

Sizes of Computers

The most common way to classify business computers is by *size*, which refers to their capacity for processing volumes of data. Usually computer size is described in terms of the number of storage locations in internal memory (64K, 128K, 256K, 640K, and so on). The largest computers are called *mainframes*; smaller computers, represented by *minicomputers* and *microcomputers*, have less internal memory, fewer input-output (I/O) units, and more limited storage capacity.

Mainframes. We refer to a large computer as a *mainframe* since it serves as the principal source of power and direction for complex company-wide data processing and telecommunication networks. Large computers provide millions of units of internal memory and process information at very high speed with millions—and, as indicated earlier, billions—of operations per second. You will also find that mainframes often serve as *host computers*, which direct the input, processing, output, and distribution of information to, from, and among a group of small computers. Mainframes, such as the type shown in Illustration B-2, are typically located in central data processing departments that are managed by specialists in computer science and data processing systems.

Minicomputers. A small computer equipped with integrated circuits and housed in a compact desk-size or desktop cabinet is called a *minicomputer*. (See Illustration B-3.) A minicomputer is a direct "descendant" of the mainframe and, with the addition of integrated circuits, is able to take over many mainframe responsibilities. Minicomputers are capable of supporting a large number of terminals that perform a variety of operations simultaneously. Typical of these operations are the following: payroll accounting, accounts receivable and accounts payable processing, sales systems reporting, interest computing, and word processing. In addition, minicomputers serve as standalone systems in departments or as I/O systems attached to mainframes.

Hewlett-Packard

Illustration B-2. A Mainframe System

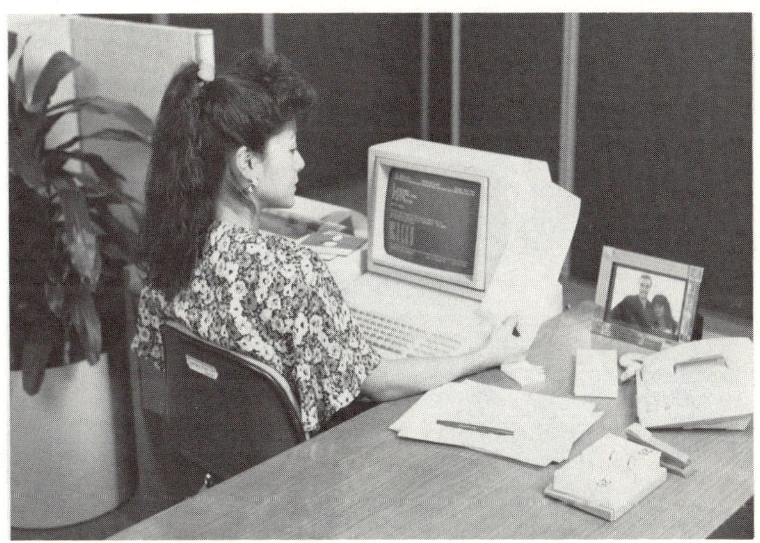

Illustration B-3. A Minicomputer

Microcomputers. The smallest and least expensive class of computers is the *microcomputer*. Today, as a result of microprocessor technology and the availability of peripheral devices for entering, storing, and printing data, microcomputers have become more powerful and fully operational. For these reasons, the lines of distinction separating minicomputers and microcomputers are fuzzy.

A microcomputer is designed for use by one person; hence, we often use the term *personal computer* or *PC*. A typical PC, shown in Illustration B-4, is placed on a desk and takes up about as much space as a typewriter and a portable television set.

Portable PCs are also available. For example, *transportables* (also called *luggables*) usually weigh 20 to 30 pounds, have a conventional TV-like display screen, and can be moved about easily. Smaller PCs, called *laptop*, or *briefcase*, computers, weigh from 6 to 20 pounds, have a flat display screen, and can operate up to 10 hours on rechargeable batteries. See Illustration B-5. Still smaller are the *notebook PCs*, which fit into coat pockets and generally weigh no more than 7 pounds. Another model of portable computer is the *box portable*, or *lunchbox machine*, that weighs 14 to 18 pounds and has more features and better displays than the laptop models.

Illustration B-4. A Typical Size Microcomputer

Illustration B-5. A Laptop Microcomputer

Portable computers are used by people whose jobs require them to travel extensively and to make computations, prepare reports, and store records en route. Most portable computers are compatible with the larger machines maintained in the home office. You may also find laptops being used by your peers who take notes in class and at the library and then write their reports at home.

The PC has revolutionized the computer industry; and because of its small size, ease of use, and relatively low cost (usually under $5,000), it has been successfully introduced into all types of offices and into millions of homes throughout the world. The PC system shown in Illustration B-4 consists of the following components, which are described in more detail in the following section:

1. A *central processing unit (CPU)* in which computing operations are performed. In the PC, the size of the CPU (measured by the amount of memory provided) ranges from 64K to 512K or more as needed. Microcomputers with 256K hold about 260,000 characters, or nearly 32,000 words of text.
2. A keyboard for entering instructions and data into the system and a display screen (monitor) for viewing the data. Some screens are capable of displaying 120 characters and 256 colors.

3. One or more *disk drive* units in which are placed the media (such as floppy disks) used to send information to, and store information produced by, the system. One drive unit may hold a hard disk, as described later.
4. A *printer* that produces reports, charts, letters, and memorandums.

In addition, a growing number of PC systems are equipped with modems. A *modem* is a communication device that links the computer to a telephone, thus allowing the computer to "talk" to another computer over standard telephone wires. This linkage permits you to access information in computer files thousands of miles away and to send or receive programs and files, such as letters, software, and graphics, to or from another computer.

We are finding that the desktop PC is becoming more sophisticated and its power greatly expanded through more powerful microprocessors, networking capabilities, and operating systems designed to handle many tasks. Computer experts refer to these powerful PCs as *workstations.* At one time these very expensive workstations were reserved for specific applications like engineering and design, which involve much work in graphics. Today, however, computer manufacturers are promoting a broader range of uses for these high-powered machines. As a result, the PC and the computer workstation are becoming more and more similar in their features and capability.

Personal computers are *user friendly;* that is, they are easy to operate since they require no technical knowledge. Application programs, which include payroll accounting, financial planning, graphics, inventory control, production control, and word processing, are readily available. Also, advances in telecommunications technology provide for the connection of PCs to telephone lines for transmitting data among networks of PCs or to minicomputers or mainframes. In addition, the use of PCs in homes has ushered in *telecommuting*—the application of telecommunications technology to the processing of information at a location other than the office.

COMPUTER SYSTEMS TECHNOLOGY

Illustration B-6 outlines the basic systems functions and the means by which they are performed in each of the phases of a computerized payroll accounting system. To understand the main concepts shown in this figure, let's examine briefly the most common technologies found in automated systems. (You will find more complex systems explained in detail in advanced references on computer science and data processing systems.)

Input Technology

Technology must be provided so that we may enter into the computer (input) the payroll data to be processed as well as the program that instructs the computer what operations to perform and in what order. Highly skilled technical personnel, known as *programmers,* write computer programs and plan the conversion of unprocessed data onto one or more media. The most common forms of input to the computer are achieved by using one or more of the following media:

1. *VDTs* (video display terminals), on which the data and the program are keyboarded.
2. *Magnetic tape,* upon which data are stored as magnetized spots. A typical reel of tape ½ inch by 2,400 feet is mounted on a device called a *tape drive* for use in a large computer system. From this device, the contents of the tape are sent as input to the internal memory of the computer.
3. *Magnetic disks,* which provide storage locations on both sides of the round magnetic medium. Data are recorded on a disk in the form of magnetized spots arranged in concentric (parallel) tracks on each recording surface. In large computer systems, disks are usually arranged in stacks called *disk packs* and placed in a disk drive unit that is used to transfer to the computer's memory the data maintained on the disks. Small computer systems use diskettes, which are discussed in a later section.
4. *Scanning devices* that read electronically the encoded characters on printed or handwritten documents and thus provide *source data automation (SDA)* whereby data are converted to machine-readable form. Thus, SDA bypasses the need for data entry by human operators. (Optical-character and magnetic-character recognition readers are examples of this type of device.)
5. *Speech* (the human voice), which is used to a limited extent as input to the computer. Two types of speech-recognition, or voice-recognition, systems have been developed: (a) isolated speech recognition in which the sender is restricted to a limited vocabulary with short pauses between words; and (b) continuous speech recognition in which words are spoken in a natural, connected speech pattern. One computer program, called Sphinx, under-

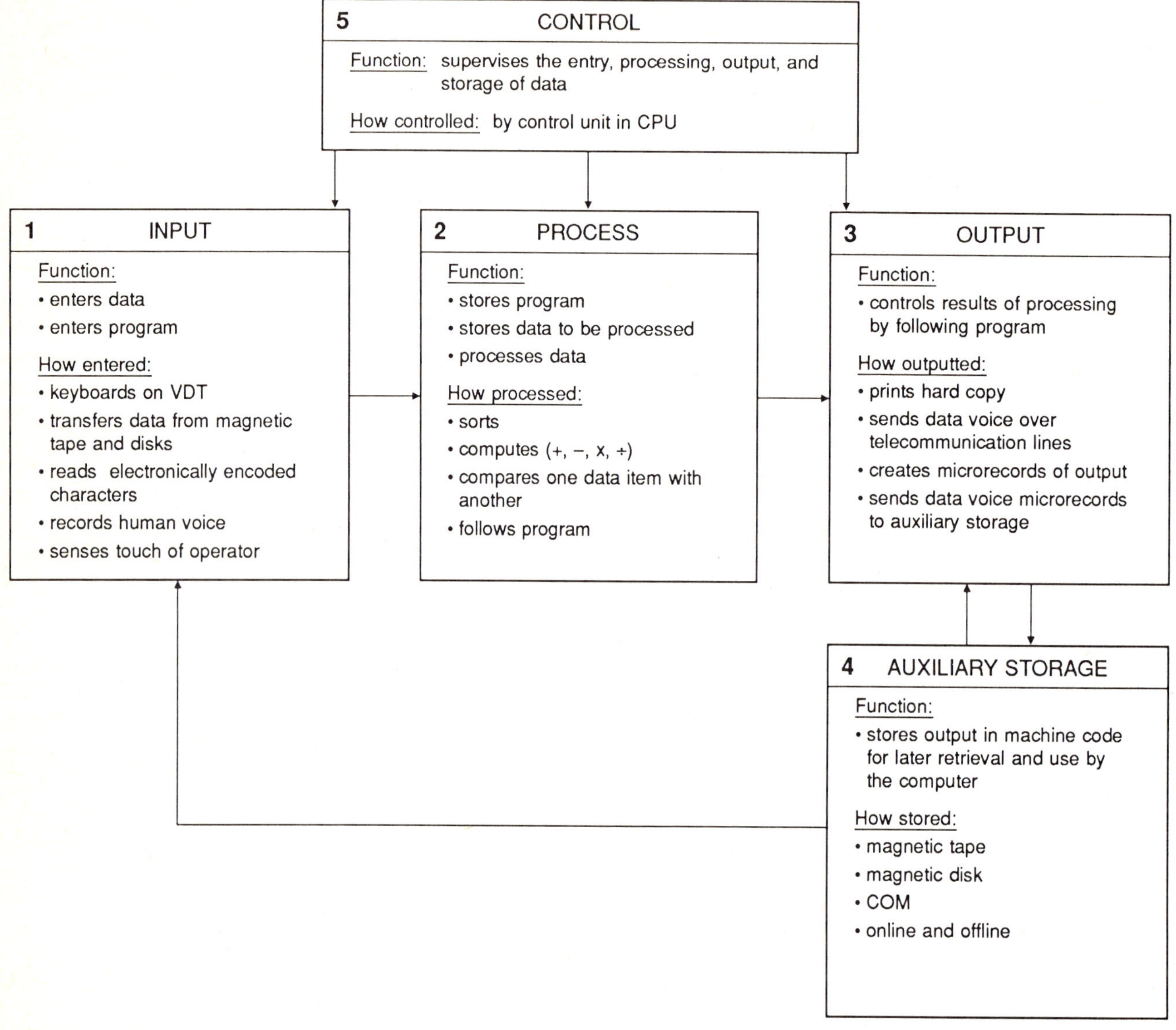

Illustration B-6. Phases of a Computerized Payroll Accounting System and Related Functions[1]

stands continuous human speech at 94% accuracy and does not have to be taught to recognize each user's voice.[2]

6. *Graphics and image devices,* such as:
   a. The *mouse,* a small plastic device with which the VDT operator controls the movement of the *cursor* (the blinking box symbol or blinking underscore) on the display screen. When you move the mouse, the movement of your hand is duplicated by the cursor on the screen through electrical impulses sent by the mouse to the computer.[3] A mouse is shown (next to the keyboard) in Illustration B-4.
   b. The *light pen,* an electrical device resembling a pen, that is used for writing or sketching on the display screen to provide input to the computer. As the pen reacts to the light from the screen, the image

[1]Adapted from Mina M. Johnson and Norman F. Kallaus, *Records Management,* 4th ed. (Cincinnati: South-Western Publishing Co., 1987), 335.

[2]"Those Computers Hear You Loud and Clear," *Business Week* (July 4, 1988): 112.

[3]Other input devices related to the mouse are the trackball and the joystick. For more information on these devices as well as an increasing number of off-the-shelf packages used in graphic design, consult an up-to-date computer systems/data processing textbook or a reference on office automation, such as David Barcomb, *Office Automation: A Survey of Tools and Technology,* 2d ed. (Bedford, MA: Digital Press, 1989), Chapter 4.

written or sketched is digitized (converted to a numeric code) by the computer for processing, storing, and printing in the system.

c. Other *touch-sensitive screens* such as the screen upon which you enter commands by pressing the designated areas with your finger. For example, by touching a file name listed on the screen, you can retrieve a desired file from computer storage.

7. *Handwriting,* which is emerging as a simple means of entering data into a PC. Through the use of an electronic pen, workers can fill in numbers and check boxes on a form displayed on a VDT. This type of "pen" technology may someday act as a popular alternative to the PC's keyboard.

Punched cards and punched paper tape, two other input media, have, for the most part, been replaced by more convenient, faster, and less troublesome input devices.

Processing Technology

The processing phase in the computer system involves the tasks of receiving input and performing arithmetic, logical, and output operations under program control. The data to be processed must be represented in some form so that the computer can manipulate the characters in line with the output desired. Prior to the advent of electronic circuitry, computing machines, such as adding machines and rotary calculators, were electromechanical and processed numeric data in the same way the office worker does—using the 10-position (0-9) decimal system to solve computational problems. Such a system was slow and when possible was replaced by a much more simplified numeric system using two states.

In computer systems, data are represented in a two-state form: either the presence (one state) or the absence (a second state) of electronic signals in certain sections of the circuitry. This is the so-called *binary code* in which all letters and numbers to be encoded are represented by two symbols, "0" and "1," in various combinations. Thus, a computer's electrical impulses may be either in a conducting or nonconducting state, while internal storage devices, such as magnetic cores, may be magnetized in either a clockwise or counterclockwise direction. More simply, the two symbols may be considered as indicating a "pulse," and "no pulse," or an "on" and "off" state. The "on" state indicates the presence of a number (1) while the absence of a pulse (the "off" state) indicates the absence of a value, or 0.

More detailed information on the various codes used in computer systems may be found in data processing textbooks and the technical manuals provided by the computer manufacturers.

Central Processing Unit (CPU).

The computer unit responsible for processing data is called the *central processing unit (CPU),* which, as the "brain" of the system, contains the circuits that control and execute the instructions. The equipment and devices that are directly connected to the computer are said to be *online.* This is in contrast with *offline,* which refers to the equipment and devices not directly connected to the computer.

In the CPU, we find these three main components: (1) the *memory,* (2) the *arithmetic-logic unit,* and (3) the *control unit,* which regulates all processing operations through built-in monitoring capabilities that are beyond the "reach" of the user. The memory unit and the arithmetic-logic unit are explained in this section along with a brief description of the process of programming a computer. The control unit is discussed in a later section.

Memory. *Memory,* or *primary storage,* is an area where the data and programs are temporarily stored before, during, and after processing. Whenever a program is entered into the computer, it is either stored in memory where it remains until processing is completed or it is retained in memory until needed for further computing operations. In a similar way, data entered from input devices are placed in memory to be available for processing. However, *no actual processing takes place in memory;* this function is reserved for the arithmetic-logic unit. As we shall see below, there are two major types of primary storage.

Random Access Memory (RAM). In the *random access memory (RAM),* the array of memory locations on one or more microchips is activated when electrical power reaches the unit. At this time, data can be entered into a memory location. *When the power is turned off, all data in RAM are lost.* For this reason, it is important that we store all processed data in the diskette file before turning off the power.

Read Only Memory (ROM). The special type of memory, *read only memory (ROM),* is permanently programmed with one group of frequently used instructions. No additional data or instructions may be stored in the ROM memory. Thus, the program residing in ROM cannot be changed by the user; only its contents can be read. In contrast to RAM, ROM does not lose its program when the computer's power is turned off.

Both RAM and ROM are *random access,* which means that the computer can go directly (at random) to any set of data without first "reading" each of the sets that have been stored in sequential order.

Arithmetic-Logic Unit. In microcomputers, the *arithmetic-logic unit* is often referred to as a microprocessor, a microchip on which reside the control and arithmetic-logic functions. In such computers, the data and the program are brought into the microprocessor and executed one step at a time, after which the results are returned to memory. The processing cycle is repeated until all program steps have been completed.

Programming the Computer. No computer can perform its processing tasks unless it is properly programmed. In order to write an effective program of *instructions*, the programmer follows these steps:

1. *Analyze the problem and chart the strategy for solving the problem.* Often a *general systems flowchart*, using standardized program charting symbols, is prepared.
2. *Write and test the program.* In computer systems, the most common programming languages are:
   a. *Business programming languages:*
      (1) *COBOL* (COmmon Business Oriented Language)—a high-level language developed for business applications, especially where large volumes of alphanumeric files are handled. (*High-level languages* allow users to write their own programs using terms with which they are familiar rather than using the computer's machine code.)
      (2) *RPG* (Report Program Generator)—a business-oriented language that is highly structured and relatively easy to learn. The language allows users to program many business operations as well as create reports.
   b. *Scientific programming languages:*
      (1) *BASIC* (Beginner's All-Purpose Symbolic Instruction Code)—an easy-to-learn, easy-to-use algebraic language with a small number of commands and simple statement formats. Even though the commands are written in a mathematical-equation format for reasons of simplicity, BASIC is widely used in programming instructions, in personal computing, and in business and industry.
      (2) *FORTRAN*, whose name was created from the two words **FOR**mula **TRAN**slator, was developed to aid in the programming of scientific, mathematical, and engineering problems. Although FORTRAN has application in business data processing since many business problems can be expressed in mathematical equations, FORTRAN is not suitable for the extensive processing of alphanumeric data files stored in secondary storage devices.
      (3) *Pascal*—a high-level language, named for the French mathematician, Blaise Pascal, which is easy to use and is taught widely in schools and colleges.[4]

An *application program*, or *application software*, refers to a computer program written to perform a specialized computer task. Application programs are available from vendors or software firms for many common applications, such as payroll, inventory control, and word processing. Software purchased from vendors is usually copyrighted and thus should not be reproduced without the vendor's permission. Users may also write their own application programs, using the programming languages discussed above.

Output Technology

The *output*, or the results of the computer processing operations, is prepared according to the program instructions residing in the computer. If the end use of the processed data is a report (text copy) or a completed business document, the results will be printed in planned report form or on a business form, such as a paycheck or a customer invoice. If the output is to be used in later computer processing, as in the case of preparing a payroll or updating inventory data, the output may be placed in secondary storage, as discussed later. In this case, the data contained in secondary storage are fed back as input to the system for executing another information-processing cycle.

The most common output devices used in computer systems are:

1. *VDTs (video display terminals)*, some of which have the capability for displaying copy in color to enhance the presentation of graphics.
2. *Printers* that produce in plain (decoded) language single or multiple copies of the infor-

[4]For detailed explanations of the nature and purpose of these programming languages, see James F. Clark and Judith J. Lambrecht, *Information Processing: Concepts, Principles, and Procedures* (Cincinnati: South-Western Publishing Co., 1985), Chapters 13-15.

mation processed by the computer. We find two types of printers, as explained below.

a. *Impact printers* that create the printed output by means of movable print heads that strike the paper through a ribbon, thus transferring the impression onto the paper.

b. *Nonimpact printers* that have no movable print heads; instead, these printers create characters on paper by means of a process (laser, heat, or chemical) similar to that used by office copying equipment.

3. *Voice (audio) response units* that create the human voice in two ways: (a) from a prerecorded set of words stored in memory; or (b) from sounds that the computer receives as input and converts to digitized (numeric) form.

4. *Special-purpose output devices*, such as *computer output microfilm (COM)* in which the computer's output is photographed on microfilm for later use in reader equipment. Another specialized output device is the *graph plotter*, which is used to make engineering drawings and graphics and charts that are to be reproduced in printed reports.

Storage Technology

Technology provides two types of data storage within the computer system: (1) primary storage in which the data and the program reside temporarily in the CPU's memory unit, and (2) secondary or auxiliary storage in which the processed data are stored outside the computer on an online or offline basis.

Primary Storage. In addition to the internal storage provided by integrated circuits, another form of primary storage—*bubble memory*—was developed as a type of miniaturized computer storage. When viewed under a microscope, each unit of storage appears as a small circle, or bubble. In order to represent binary data in bubble storage, the presence of a bubble represents the value of "1," and the absence of a bubble represents a binary value of "0." A 1-inch square bubble package stores 92,000 bits of data in the form of magnetic bubbles that move in thin films of magnetic material. This type of storage provides an economical medium for data storage and, unlike microchip storage, has the advantage of retaining the data in storage when the power is turned off.

Secondary Storage. *Secondary,* or *auxiliary, storage* is external storage provided in a computer system because the amount of data that can be stored in internal memory is limited. We find several forms of secondary storage, as explained below.

Magnetic Tape. *Magnetic tape* is commonly used in large computer systems to store serial (or sequential) information, such as payroll data, by employee number, for all persons in a firm. The magnetic tape must be placed on a tape drive before the data can be read onto, or read from, the tape. As is true of most magnetic media, magnetic tape may be erased and reused.

Magnetic Disk. By means of a *magnetic disk*, users have direct access to any portion of the tracks on the recording surface. For many operations, this feature is useful as compared with other media, such as magnetic tape, in which unwanted portions of the tape must be sorted through in order to locate the desired data.

Floppy Disk. The *floppy disk* is a flexible diskette made of mylar plastic that is encased in a paper or plastic jacket. The floppy disk resembles a small phonograph record. The data, stored in sectors much like storage on magnetic disks, can be retrieved randomly. Used widely with microcomputers and minicomputers, floppy disks provide storage at relatively low cost. These disks are available in three sizes: 3½",5 ¼", and 8". The popular 5¼" disk is, to some extent, being replaced by the more durable 3½" disk, which is permanently housed within a plastic casing and which can hold more data than the larger floppy disk.

Hard Disk. The *hard disk*, made of rigid aluminum, is usually encased within the computer. Since data are stored more closely together on hard disks than on floppy disks, more data can be stored in less space. Because hard disks rotate at a much faster speed than floppy disks, faster retrieval and storage capabilities are possible. Retrieval time is about ten times faster from a hard disk as compared with the floppy disk.

Optical Disk. Another type of secondary storage uses the *optical disk* (sometimes called the *video disk*). Optical disk storage is created when a laser-beam recorder scans a document, film, or slide and then copies it and transfers the image onto a metal disk. Between 50 and 100 times more data can be stored on optical disks than on magnetic disks. For example, a 5-inch compact optical disk has the storage capacity of about 1,500 floppy disks, or nearly 250,000 typed pages. A 20-volume encyclopedia of the entire parts list for all Honda cars can be stored on a compact disk similar to the CD you buy at a record store.

Control Technology

Technological controls are required to ensure an effective computer system. An effectively written and properly tested program is a major type of technological control, for without it, the goal of the system cannot be achieved. In addition, control resides in the control unit of the CPU, which operates in the following manner:

1. *The control unit processes the instructions recorded in the program.* It directs the various processing operations spelled out in the program and checks to see that the instructions are properly carried out.
2. *The control unit also "authorizes" the receipt of information from secondary storage units.* It stores the intermediate results of the operations in *buffer storage,* a temporary storage location, until such results are finally stored in auxiliary storage or are printed out.
3. *The control unit then instructs the computer to prepare the results on the appropriate output devices* (printing, plotting, computer output microfilm, and so on).

AN ILLUSTRATIVE COMPUTER SYSTEM

The following example, charted in Illustration B-7, shows how payroll data may be processed in a computer system. The weekly time cards, as original source documents, represent attendance and time records for all employees.

The payroll master file, in which all current payroll data regarding employees are recorded, is stored on magnetic tape or disk. The master file is the source for reproducing each week the constant data that appear on the time cards. As changes in personnel, such as new hires or transfers, take place, the changes are entered directly into the master file. Constant employee deductions such as hospital/medical insurance, savings bond purchases, and employee stock purchases, are also entered in the master file.

All variable, nonrepetitive deductions, payroll adjustments, hours worked, etc., are calculated and entered directly into on-line data-entry devices (or, alternatively, keyboarded on tape or disk). This information becomes the input used to update programs which in turn update the master files and calculate earnings, withholdings, etc.

The following information about each employee is contained in the payroll master file, which is updated each pay period:

1. Name and employee number
2. Social security account number
3. Hourly wage rate or weekly salary
4. Withholding allowances and other deductions
5. Quarterly and yearly earnings to date
6. Withheld taxes to date
7. Personnel data
8. Absences and other miscellaneous data

When the payroll master file is merged with another file containing variable information, such as vacation pays and salary increases, a new master file is created. At the same time, a current pay record is calculated and stored on tape or disk.

In another merging operation, the master file is combined with the current pay file to produce a labor file. The labor file becomes the source for all labor cost distribution and cost reports to be produced later on the computer. Files are also prepared to establish control totals and to produce a record of bond deductions. The current pay file contains the employee's gross pay, net pay, and deduction figures as well as year-to-date earnings and taxes. The current pay file is then processed and all checks and earnings statements are printed on a high-speed printer.

DATA SERVICE CENTERS

A *data service center,* or *service bureau,* is an organization that specializes in processing data for its customer firms. The center is used by firms with large-scale data processing equipment during peak-load periods when the firms' equipment is not adequate to handle all their needs. Also, small companies without the funds or staff required to operate their own data processing centers may use such a center to meet their major computing needs.

The services provided by a data service center range from specialized accounting systems, such as payroll, accounts receivable, order processing, sales analysis, and inventory control, to elaborate personnel record keeping and information retrieval. For the small business, data service centers fill a very crucial processing need. The advantages of using the services of such a center are:

1. No large investment in computers, auxiliary equipment, or other expensive hardware is required by the user.
2. The work is done accurately and according to a prearranged turnaround time by the center.
3. Frequently there is a savings in the unit cost of processing data because of skilled technical personnel, efficiently programmed procedures, and appropriate equipment. Accurate records on processing times and cost are provided, thereby furnishing the user with better information for controlling costs.
4. There is a savings in payroll taxes and the cost of employee benefits because the user's office staff is not increased.

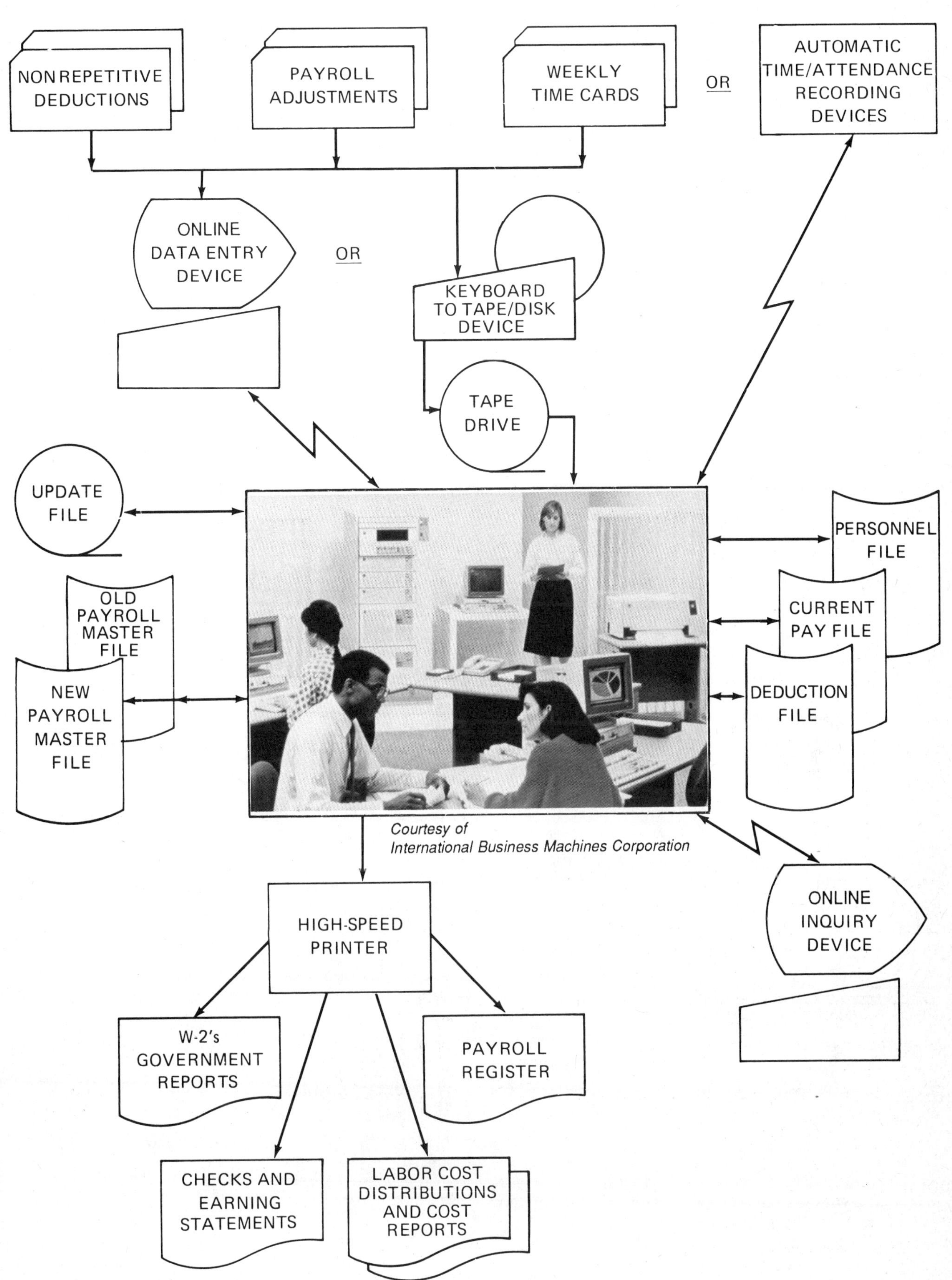

Illustration B-7. A Computer Payroll System

5. Maximum convenience is provided the user. In some cases, the data to be processed are picked up at the customer's office; and the processed output is delivered back to the office at a specified time. In other cases, the data are deposited in a drive-in type of facility; and the finished processed reports may be picked up later at the same facility. The input of the data to the center is usually simple and relatively inexpensive.

The costs of using data service centers vary, depending on the nature and extent of the work performed. Cost information may be obtained from the service centers and from representatives of machine manufacturers.

GLOSSARY

Accounting board—a flat writing surface upon which pegs are positioned along one or two edges, or in the center, for attaching and aligning specially designed business forms.

Accounting board system—a handwritten accounting system that uses an accounting board and specially designed forms; also known as a *pegboard system* or a *write-it-once system.*

Analog computer—a computer that measures continuously changing conditions, such as temperature and atmospheric pressure, and converts them into quantities.

Application program—a computer program written to perform a specialized computer task; also known as *application software.*

Arithmetic-logic unit—an operating unit of the CPU that performs arithmetic operations, shifts and moves data, and performs comparing operations on the data; also referred to as a *microprocessor.*

Auxiliary storage—*see* Secondary storage.

BASIC (Beginner's All-Purpose Symbolic Instruction Code)—an acronym for an easy-to-learn, easy-to-use algebraic language with a small number of commands and simple statement formats; widely used in programming instructions, in personal computing, and in business and industry.

Binary code—a coding system in which alphabetic and numeric data are represented in a two-state form, "0" and "1."

Binary digit—the basic value in the binary system, which uses two digits—0 and 1—to represent alphabetic, numeric, and related data within the computer; also known as *bit.*

Bit—*see* Binary digit.

Bubble memory—a type of computer storage in which data are stored in the form of magnetic bubbles that move in thin films of magnetic material.

Buffer storage—temporary storage within a computer that is used for storing intermediate results of operations until the results are finally stored in auxiliary storage or are printed out.

Byte—a computer term for a basic data character, such as a letter, number, or symbol.

Central processing unit (CPU)—the "brain" of the computer system that contains the circuits that control and execute the instructions.

COBOL (COmmon Business-Oriented Language)—an acronym for a high-level language developed for business applications, especially where large volumes of alphanumeric files are handled.

Computer—an integrated electronic system in which mathematical operations are computed at the speed of light through the use of transistors, diodes, and microminiaturized circuits.

Computer output microfilm (COM)—a special-purpose output device in which the computer's output is photographed on microfilm for later use in reader equipment.

Computer system—a group of interconnected machines, including the computer, that process data and provide many information-handling capabilities.

Control unit—an operating unit of the CPU that interprets the instructions recorded on the input media, directs the various processing operations, and checks to see that the instructions are properly carried out.

Cursor—the blinking box symbol or blinking underscore that appears on the screen of a video display terminal (VDT).

Data service center—an organization that specializes in processing data for its customer firms; also known as a *service bureau.*

Digital computer—a computer that counts numbers or digits.

Disk drive—a unit of the PC system in which are placed the media used to send information to, and store information produced by, the system.

Disk pack—a stack of magnetic disks mounted in a disk drive for entering and retrieving information.

Electronic circuitry—the switches through which the computer routes data to be processed.

Femtosecond—one quadrillionth of a second.

Floppy disk—a flexible diskette, made of mylar plastic and encased in a paper or plastic jacket, that serves as an input-output medium.

FORTRAN (FORmula TRANslation)—an acronym for a programming language used to solve scientific, mathematical, and engineering problems.

Graph plotter—a special-purpose output device used to make engineering drawings and graphics and charts that are to be reproduced in printed reports.

Hard disk—a magnetic medium, made of aluminum, that is usually encased within the computer.

High-level language—a synthetic programming language that allows users to write their own programs using terms with which they are familiar rather than using the computer's machine code.

Host computer—a mainframe that directs the input, processing, output, and distribution of information to, from, and among a group of small computers.

Impact printer—a printer that creates the printed output by means of movable print heads that strike the paper through a ribbon, thus transferring the impression onto the paper.

Integrated circuit (IC)—*see* microprocessor.

Internal memory—a component of the computer system that receives the data to be processed and the program containing detailed instructions necessary to process the data.

K—abbreviation for the word *kilo*, or 1,000; in computer circles, K equals 1,024 bytes.

Kilo—*see* K.

Laptop computer—a small, portable personal computer that weighs from 6 to 20 pounds, has a flat display screen, and operates up to 10 hours on rechargeable batteries; also known as a *briefcase computer.*

Light pen—an electrical device resembling a pen that is used for writing or sketching on the display screen to provide input to the computer.

Magnetic disk—a round, magnetic storage medium in which data are recorded in the form of magnetized spots arranged in concentric (parallel) tracks on each recording surface.

Magnetic tape—an input-output medium upon which data are recorded as magnetized spots.

Mainframe—a large computer that serves as the principal source of power and direction for complex company-wide data processing and telecommunication networks.

Megabyte—a measure of computer memory that equals 1,024 K or 1,048,576 bytes, usually rounded and expressed as one million bytes.

Memory—the area in the central processing unit (CPU) where the data and programs are temporarily stored before, during, and after processing; also referred to as *primary storage.*

Microcomputer—the smallest and least expensive class of computers, designed for use by one person; also known as a *personal computer (PC).*

Microprocessor—an integrated circuit (IC) built on a very small silicon chip containing transistors that perform many types of electronic switching functions.

Minicomputer—a small computer with integrated circuits and housed in a compact, desk-size or desktop cabinet.

Modem—a communication device that links the computer to a telephone and allows the computer to "talk" to another computer over standard telephone lines.

Monitor—the display screen of a computer system that is used for viewing the data.

Mouse—a small plastic device with which the VDT operator controls the movement of the cursor on the display screen.

Nanosecond—one billionth of a second.

Nonimpact printer—a printer, with no movable heads, that creates characters on paper by means of a process (laser, heat, or chemical) similar to that used by office copying equipment.

Notebook PC—a portable personal computer that fits into a coat pocket and generally weighs no more than 7 pounds.

Offline—the equipment and devices not directly connected to the computer.

Online—the equipment and devices directly connected to the computer.

Optical disk—a form of computer storage in which a laser-beam recorder scans a document, film, or slide and then copies it and transfers the image onto a metal disk; also known as a *video disk.*

Output—the results of computer processing operations recorded on formal reports and business documents or on media such as magnetic tapes and magnetic disks.

Pascal—a high-level programming language, named for the French mathematician, Blaise Pascal, which is easy to use and is taught widely in schools and colleges.

Pegboard system—*see* Accounting board system.

Personal computer (PC)—*see* Microcomputer.

Picosecond—one trillionth of a second.

Primary storage—*see* Memory.

Printer—an output device that produces in plain (decoded) language single or multiple copies of the information generated by the computer.

Program—the instructions necessary to operate the computer system; also known as *software.*

Programmer—a highly skilled technical person who plans the conversion of unprocessed data onto one or more media acceptable by the computer system.

Punched-card system—a system in which data are converted to machine-language code through the punching of holes in cards; also known as a *unit-record system.*

Random access memory (RAM)—a type of memory in which data are entered when electrical power activates the array of memory locations on one or more microchips.

Random access—the capability of a computer to go directly (at random) to any set of data without first "reading" each of the sets that have been stored in sequential order.

Read only memory (ROM)—a special type of memory that is permanently programmed with one group of frequently used instructions.

RPG (Report Program Generator)—a business-oriented programming language that is highly structured, relatively easy to learn, and allows users to program many business operations as well as create reports.

Scanning device—a machine that reads printed or handwritten documents and thus provides source data automation (SDA) whereby data are converted to machine-readable form.

Secondary storage—units such as magnetic tapes and magnetic disks that enlarge the storage capacity of the computer system; also known as *auxiliary storage.*

Service bureau—*see* Data service center.

Software—ready-made programs developed by computer manufacturers and other firms to direct the operations of the computer and its peripheral equipment.

Source data automation (SDA)—the process of converting printed or handwritten data to machine-readable form by means of scanning devices.

Storage location—one of the many small sections of the computer's internal memory.

Tape drive—a device that transmits the contents of a magnetic tape as input to the memory of the computer.

Terminal—*see* Video display terminal (VDT).

Transportable—a portable personal computer that usually weighs 20 to 30 pounds, has a conventional TV-like display screen, and can be moved about easily; also known as a *luggable.*

Unit-record system—*see* Punched-card system.

User friendly—a characteristic of personal computers that are easy to operate since they require no technical knowledge.

Video disk—*see* Optical disk.

Video display terminal (VDT)—an input device used for keyboarding the data and the program.

Voice (audio) response unit—an output device that creates the human voice from a prerecorded set of words stored in memory or from sounds the computer receives as input, which is converted to digitized (numeric) form.

Workstation—a personal computer with greatly expanded power by means of more powerful microprocessors, networking capabilities, and operating systems designed to handle many tasks.

Write-it-once concept—the initial recording of data in such a way that they may be used over and over again without need for a costly manual rewriting or rekeyboarding of the data.

Write-it-once system—*see* Accounting board system.

TAX TABLE
A

Percentage Method Withholding Table

Payroll period	Amount of one withholding allowance:
Weekly	$ 39.42
Biweekly	78.85
Semimonthly	85.42
Monthly	170.83
Quarterly	512.50
Semiannual	1,025.00
Annual	2,050.00
Daily or miscellaneous (per day of such period)	7.88

TABLES FOR PERCENTAGE METHOD OF WITHHOLDING
(Effective January 1, 1990)

TABLE 1—If the Payroll Period With Respect to an Employee is Weekly

(a) SINGLE person—including head of household:

If the amount of wages (after subtracting withholding allowances) is: Not over $23 — The amount of income tax to be withheld shall be: 0

Over—	But not over—		of excess over—
$23	—$397	15%	—$23
$397	—$928	$56.10 plus 28%	—$397
$928	—$2,121	$204.78 plus 33%	—$928
$2,121		$598.47 plus 28%	—$2,121

(b) MARRIED person—

If the amount of wages (after subtracting withholding allowances) is: Not over $65 — The amount of income tax to be withheld shall be: 0

Over—	But not over—		of excess over—
$65	—$689	15%	—$65
$689	—$1,573	$93.60 plus 28%	—$689
$1,573	—$3,858	$341.12 plus 33%	—$1,573
$3,858		$1,095.17 plus 28%	—$3,858

TABLE 2—If the Payroll Period With Respect to an Employee is Biweekly

(a) SINGLE person—including head of household:

If the amount of wages (after subtracting withholding allowances) is: Not over $46 — The amount of income tax to be withheld shall be: 0

Over—	But not over—		of excess over—
$46	—$794	15%	—$46
$794	—$1,856	$112.20 plus 28%	—$794
$1,856	—$4,242	$409.56 plus 33%	—$1,856
$4,242		$1,196.94 plus 28%	—$4,242

(b) MARRIED person—

If the amount of wages (after subtracting withholding allowances) is: Not over $131 — The amount of income tax to be withheld shall be: 0

Over—	But not over—		of excess over—
$131	—$1,379	15%	—$131
$1,379	—$3,146	$187.20 plus 28%	—$1,379
$3,146	—$7,716	$681.96 plus 33%	—$3,146
$7,716		$2,190.06 plus 28%	—$7,716

TABLE 3—If the Payroll Period With Respect to an Employee is Semimonthly

(a) SINGLE person—including head of household:

If the amount of wages (after subtracting withholding allowances) is: Not over $50 — The amount of income tax to be withheld shall be: 0

Over—	But not over—		of excess over—
$50	—$860	15%	—$50
$860	—$2,010	$121.50 plus 28%	—$860
$2,010	—$4,596	$443.50 plus 33%	—$2,010
$4,596		$1,296.88 plus 28%	—$4,596

(b) MARRIED person—

If the amount of wages (after subtracting withholding allowances) is: Not over $142 — The amount of income tax to be withheld shall be: 0

Over—	But not over—		of excess over—
$142	—$1,494	15%	—$142
$1,494	—$3,408	$202.80 plus 28%	—$1,494
$3,408	—$8,359	$738.72 plus 33%	—$3,408
$8,359		$2,372.55 plus 28%	—$8,359

TABLE 4—If the Payroll Period With Respect to an Employee is Monthly

(a) SINGLE person—including head of household:

If the amount of wages (after subtracting withholding allowances) is: Not over $100 — The amount of income tax to be withheld shall be: 0

Over—	But not over—		of excess over—
$100	—$1,721	15%	—$100
$1,721	—$4,021	$243.15 plus 28%	—$1,721
$4,021	—$9,192	$887.15 plus 33%	—$4,021
$9,192		$2,593.58 plus 28%	—$9,192

(b) MARRIED person—

If the amount of wages (after subtracting withholding allowances) is: Not over $283 — The amount of income tax to be withheld shall be: 0

Over—	But not over—		of excess over—
$283	—$2,988	15%	—$283
$2,988	—$6,817	$405.75 plus 28%	—$2,988
$6,817	—$16,718	$1,477.87 plus 33%	—$6,817
$16,718		$4,745.20 plus 28%	—$16,718

TABLES FOR PERCENTAGE METHOD OF WITHHOLDING
(Effective January 1, 1990)

TABLE 5—If the Payroll Period With Respect to an Employee is Quarterly

(a) SINGLE person—including head of household:

If the amount of wages (after subtracting withholding allowances) is: / The amount of income tax to be withheld shall be:

Not over $300 0

Over—	But not over—		of excess over—
$300	—$5,163......	15%	—$300
$5,163	—$12,063.....	$729.45 plus 28%	—$5,163
$12,063	—$27,575.....	$2,661.45 plus 33%	—$12,063
$27,575...............		$7,780.41 plus 28%	—$27,575

(b) MARRIED person—

If the amount of wages (after subtracting withholding allowances) is: / The amount of income tax to be withheld shall be:

Not over $850 0

Over—	But not over—		of excess over—
$850	—$8,963......	15%	—$850
$8,963	—$20,450.....	$1,216.95 plus 28%	—$8,963
$20,450	—$50,153.....	$4,433.31 plus 33%	—$20,450
$50,153...............		$14,235.30 plus 28%	—$50,153

TABLE 6—If the Payroll Period With Respect to an Employee is Semiannual

(a) SINGLE person—including head of household:

If the amount of wages (after subtracting withholding allowances) is: / The amount of income tax to be withheld shall be:

Not over $600 0

Over—	But not over—		of excess over—
$600	—$10,325.....	15%	—$600
$10,325	—$24,125.....	$1,458.75 plus 28%	—$10,325
$24,125	—$55,150.....	$5,322.75 plus 33%	—$24,125
$55,150...............		$15,561.00 plus 28%	—$55,150

(b) MARRIED person—

If the amount of wages (after subtracting withholding allowances) is: / The amount of income tax to be withheld shall be:

Not over $1,700......... 0

Over—	But not over—		of excess over—
$1,700	—$17,925.....	15%	—$1,700
$17,925	—$40,900.....	$2,433.75 plus 28%	—$17,925
$40,900	—$100,305....	$8,866.75 plus 33%	—$40,900
$100,305..............		$28,470.40 plus 28%	—$100,305

TABLE 7—If the Payroll Period With Respect to an Employee is Annual

(a) SINGLE person—including head of household:

If the amount of wages (after subtracting withholding allowances) is: / The amount of income tax to be withheld shall be:

Not over $1,200......... 0

Over—	But not over—		of excess over—
$1,200	—$20,650.....	15%	—$1,200
$20,650	—$48,250.....	$2,917.50 plus 28%	—$20,650
$48,250	—$110,300....	$10,645.50 plus 33%	—$48,250
$110,300..............		$31,122.00 plus 28%	—$110,300

(b) MARRIED person—

If the amount of wages (after subtracting withholding allowances) is: / The amount of income tax to be withheld shall be:

Not over $3,400......... 0

Over—	But not over—		of excess over—
$3,400	—$35,850.....	15%	—$3,400
$35,850	—$81,800.....	$4,867.50 plus 28%	—$35,850
$81,800	—$200,610....	$17,733.50 plus 33%	—$81,800
$200,610..............		$56,940.80 plus 28%	—$200,610

TABLE 8—If the Payroll Period With Respect to an Employee is a Daily Payroll Period or a Miscellaneous Payroll Period

(a) SINGLE person—including head of household:

If the amount of wages (after subtracting withholding allowances) divided by the numberof days in the payroll period is: / The amount of income tax to be withheld per day shall be:

Not over $4.60.......... 0

Over—	But not over—		of excess over—
$4.60	—$79.40......	15%	—$4.60
$79.40	—$185.60.....	$11.22 plus 28%	—$79.40
$185.60	—$424.20.....	$40.96 plus 33%	—$185.60
$424.20...............		$119.70 plus 28%	—$424.20

(b) MARRIED person—

If the amount of wages (after subtracting withholding allowances) divided by the numberof days in the payroll period is: / The amount of income tax to be withheld per day shall be:

Not over $13.10......... 0

Over—	But not over—		of excess over—
$13.10	—$137.90.....	15%	—$13.10
$137.90	—$314.60.....	$18.72 plus 28%	—$137.90
$314.60	—$771.60.....	$68.20 plus 33%	—$314.60
$771.60...............		$219.01 plus 28%	—$771.60

TAX TABLE
B

WAGE-BRACKET WITHHOLDING TABLES

WEEKLY Payroll Period— Employee NOT MARRIED—Effective January 1, 1990

And the wages are—		And the number of withholding allowances claimed is—										
At least	But less than	0	1	2	3	4	5	6	7	8	9	10 or more
		The amount of income tax to be withheld shall be—										
$0	$25	$0	$0	$0	$0	$0	$0	$0	$0	$0	$0	$0
25	30	1	0	0	0	0	0	0	0	0	0	0
30	35	1	0	0	0	0	0	0	0	0	0	0
35	40	2	0	0	0	0	0	0	0	0	0	0
40	45	3	0	0	0	0	0	0	0	0	0	0
45	50	4	0	0	0	0	0	0	0	0	0	0
50	55	4	0	0	0	0	0	0	0	0	0	0
55	60	5	0	0	0	0	0	0	0	0	0	0
60	65	6	0	0	0	0	0	0	0	0	0	0
65	70	7	1	0	0	0	0	0	0	0	0	0
70	75	7	2	0	0	0	0	0	0	0	0	0
75	80	8	2	0	0	0	0	0	0	0	0	0
80	85	9	3	0	0	0	0	0	0	0	0	0
85	90	10	4	0	0	0	0	0	0	0	0	0
90	95	10	5	0	0	0	0	0	0	0	0	0
95	100	11	5	0	0	0	0	0	0	0	0	0
100	105	12	6	0	0	0	0	0	0	0	0	0
105	110	13	7	1	0	0	0	0	0	0	0	0
110	115	13	8	2	0	0	0	0	0	0	0	0
115	120	14	8	2	0	0	0	0	0	0	0	0
120	125	15	9	3	0	0	0	0	0	0	0	0
125	130	16	10	4	0	0	0	0	0	0	0	0
130	135	16	11	5	0	0	0	0	0	0	0	0
135	140	17	11	5	0	0	0	0	0	0	0	0
140	145	18	12	6	0	0	0	0	0	0	0	0
145	150	19	13	7	1	0	0	0	0	0	0	0
150	155	19	14	8	2	0	0	0	0	0	0	0
155	160	20	14	8	2	0	0	0	0	0	0	0
160	165	21	15	9	3	0	0	0	0	0	0	0
165	170	22	16	10	4	0	0	0	0	0	0	0
170	175	22	17	11	5	0	0	0	0	0	0	0
175	180	23	17	11	5	0	0	0	0	0	0	0
180	185	24	18	12	6	0	0	0	0	0	0	0
185	190	25	19	13	7	1	0	0	0	0	0	0
190	195	25	20	14	8	2	0	0	0	0	0	0
At least	But less than	0	1	2	3	4	5	6	7	8	9	10 or more
195	200	26	20	14	8	3	0	0	0	0	0	0
200	210	27	21	15	10	4	0	0	0	0	0	0
210	220	29	23	17	11	5	0	0	0	0	0	0
220	230	30	24	18	13	7	1	0	0	0	0	0
230	240	32	26	20	14	8	2	0	0	0	0	0
240	250	33	27	21	16	10	4	0	0	0	0	0
250	260	35	29	23	17	11	5	0	0	0	0	0
260	270	36	30	24	19	13	7	1	0	0	0	0
270	280	38	32	26	20	14	8	2	0	0	0	0
280	290	39	33	27	22	16	10	4	0	0	0	0
290	300	41	35	29	23	17	11	5	0	0	0	0
300	310	42	36	30	25	19	13	7	1	0	0	0
310	320	44	38	32	26	20	14	8	2	0	0	0
320	330	45	39	33	28	22	16	10	4	0	0	0
330	340	47	41	35	29	23	17	11	5	0	0	0
340	350	48	42	36	31	25	19	13	7	1	0	0
350	360	50	44	38	32	26	20	14	8	2	0	0
360	370	51	45	39	34	28	22	16	10	4	0	0
370	380	53	47	41	35	29	23	17	11	5	0	0
380	390	54	48	42	37	31	25	19	13	7	1	0
390	400	56	50	44	38	32	26	20	14	8	3	0
400	410	58	51	45	40	34	28	22	16	10	4	0
410	420	61	53	47	41	35	29	23	17	11	6	0
420	430	64	54	48	43	37	31	25	19	13	7	1
430	440	67	56	50	44	38	32	26	20	14	9	3
440	450	70	58	51	46	40	34	28	22	16	10	4
450	460	72	61	53	47	41	35	29	23	17	12	6
460	470	75	64	54	49	43	37	31	25	19	13	7
470	480	78	67	56	50	44	38	32	26	20	15	9
480	490	81	70	59	52	46	40	34	28	22	16	10
490	500	84	72	61	53	47	41	35	29	23	18	12
500	510	86	75	64	55	49	43	37	31	25	19	13
510	520	89	78	67	56	50	44	38	32	26	21	15
520	530	92	81	70	59	52	46	40	34	28	22	16
530	540	95	84	73	62	53	47	41	35	29	24	18

WEEKLY Payroll Period— Employee NOT MARRIED—Effective January 1, 1990

And the wages are—		And the number of withholding allowances claimed is—										
At least	But less than	0	1	2	3	4	5	6	7	8	9	10 or more
		The amount of income tax to be withheld shall be—										
$540	$550	$98	$86	$75	$64	$55	$49	$43	$37	$31	$25	$19
550	560	100	89	78	67	56	50	44	38	32	27	21
560	570	103	92	81	70	59	52	46	40	34	28	22
570	580	106	95	84	73	62	53	47	41	35	30	24
580	590	109	98	87	76	65	55	49	43	37	31	25
590	600	112	100	89	78	67	56	50	44	38	33	27
600	610	114	103	92	81	70	59	52	46	40	34	28
610	620	117	106	95	84	73	62	53	47	41	36	30
620	630	120	109	98	87	76	65	55	49	43	37	31
630	640	123	112	101	90	79	68	56	50	44	39	33
640	650	126	114	103	92	81	70	59	52	46	40	34
650	660	128	117	106	95	84	73	62	53	47	42	36
660	670	131	120	109	98	87	76	65	55	49	43	37
670	680	134	123	112	101	90	79	68	57	50	45	39
680	690	137	126	115	104	93	82	70	59	52	46	40
690	700	140	128	117	106	95	84	73	62	53	48	42
700	710	142	131	120	109	98	87	76	65	55	49	43
710	720	145	134	123	112	101	90	79	68	57	51	45
720	730	148	137	126	115	104	93	82	71	60	52	46
730	740	151	140	129	118	107	96	84	73	62	54	48
740	750	154	142	131	120	109	98	87	76	65	55	49
750	760	156	145	134	123	112	101	90	79	68	57	51
760	770	159	148	137	126	115	104	93	82	71	60	52
770	780	162	151	140	129	118	107	96	85	74	63	54
780	790	165	154	143	132	121	110	98	87	76	65	55
790	800	168	156	145	134	123	112	101	90	79	68	57
800	810	170	159	148	137	126	115	104	93	82	71	60
810	820	173	162	151	140	129	118	107	96	85	74	63
820	830	176	165	154	143	132	121	110	99	88	77	66
830	840	179	168	157	146	135	124	112	101	90	79	68
840	850	182	170	159	148	137	126	115	104	93	82	71
850	860	184	173	162	151	140	129	118	107	96	85	74
860	870	187	176	165	154	143	132	121	110	99	88	77
870	880	190	179	168	157	146	135	124	113	102	91	80
880	890	193	182	171	160	149	138	126	115	104	93	82
At least	But less than	0	1	2	3	4	5	6	7	8	9	10 or more
890	900	196	184	173	162	151	140	129	118	107	96	85
900	910	198	187	176	165	154	143	132	121	110	99	88
910	920	201	190	179	168	157	146	135	124	113	102	91
920	930	204	193	182	171	160	149	138	127	116	105	94
930	940	207	196	185	174	163	152	140	129	118	107	96
940	950	210	198	187	176	165	154	143	132	121	110	99
950	960	214	201	190	179	168	157	146	135	124	113	102
960	970	217	204	193	182	171	160	149	138	127	116	105
970	980	220	207	196	185	174	163	152	141	130	119	108
980	990	224	211	199	188	177	166	154	143	132	121	110
990	1,000	227	214	201	190	179	168	157	146	135	124	113
1,000	1,010	230	217	204	193	182	171	160	149	138	127	116
1,010	1,020	233	220	207	196	185	174	163	152	141	130	119
1,020	1,030	237	224	211	199	188	177	166	155	144	133	122
1,030	1,040	240	227	214	202	191	180	168	157	146	135	124
1,040	1,050	243	230	217	204	193	182	171	160	149	138	127
1,050	1,060	247	234	221	208	196	185	174	163	152	141	130
1,060	1,070	250	237	224	211	199	188	177	166	155	144	133
1,070	1,080	253	240	227	214	202	191	180	169	158	147	136
1,080	1,090	257	244	231	218	205	194	182	171	160	149	138
1,090	1,100	260	247	234	221	208	196	185	174	163	152	141
1,100	1,110	263	250	237	224	211	199	188	177	166	155	144
1,110	1,120	266	253	240	227	214	202	191	180	169	158	147
1,120	1,130	270	257	244	231	218	205	194	183	172	161	150
1,130	1,140	273	260	247	234	221	208	196	185	174	163	152
1,140	1,150	276	263	250	237	224	211	199	188	177	166	155
1,150	1,160	280	267	254	241	228	215	202	191	180	169	158
1,160	1,170	283	270	257	244	231	218	205	194	183	172	161
1,170	1,180	286	273	260	247	234	221	208	197	186	175	164
1,180	1,190	290	277	264	251	238	225	212	199	188	177	166
1,190	1,200	293	280	267	254	241	228	215	202	191	180	169

$1,200 and over — Use Table 1(a) for a **SINGLE person.**

WAGE-BRACKET WITHHOLDING TABLES

WEEKLY Payroll Period — Employee MARRIED — Effective January 1, 1990

And the wages are—		And the number of withholding allowances claimed is—										
At least	But less than	0	1	2	3	4	5	6	7	8	9	10 or more
		The amount of income tax to be withheld shall be—										
$0	$70	$0	$0	$0	$0	$0	$0	$0	$0	$0	$0	$0
70	75	1	0	0	0	0	0	0	0	0	0	0
75	80	2	0	0	0	0	0	0	0	0	0	0
80	85	3	0	0	0	0	0	0	0	0	0	0
85	90	3	0	0	0	0	0	0	0	0	0	0
90	95	4	0	0	0	0	0	0	0	0	0	0
95	100	5	0	0	0	0	0	0	0	0	0	0
100	105	6	0	0	0	0	0	0	0	0	0	0
105	110	6	0	0	0	0	0	0	0	0	0	0
110	115	7	1	0	0	0	0	0	0	0	0	0
115	120	8	2	0	0	0	0	0	0	0	0	0
120	125	9	3	0	0	0	0	0	0	0	0	0
125	130	9	3	0	0	0	0	0	0	0	0	0
130	135	10	4	0	0	0	0	0	0	0	0	0
135	140	11	5	0	0	0	0	0	0	0	0	0
140	145	12	6	0	0	0	0	0	0	0	0	0
145	150	12	6	0	0	0	0	0	0	0	0	0
150	155	13	7	1	0	0	0	0	0	0	0	0
155	160	14	8	2	0	0	0	0	0	0	0	0
160	165	15	9	3	0	0	0	0	0	0	0	0
165	170	15	9	3	0	0	0	0	0	0	0	0
170	175	16	10	4	0	0	0	0	0	0	0	0
175	180	17	11	5	0	0	0	0	0	0	0	0
180	185	18	12	6	0	0	0	0	0	0	0	0
185	190	18	12	6	1	0	0	0	0	0	0	0
190	195	19	13	7	1	0	0	0	0	0	0	0
195	200	20	14	8	2	0	0	0	0	0	0	0
200	210	21	15	9	3	0	0	0	0	0	0	0
210	220	22	17	11	5	0	0	0	0	0	0	0
220	230	24	18	12	6	0	0	0	0	0	0	0
230	240	25	20	14	8	2	0	0	0	0	0	0
240	250	27	21	15	9	3	0	0	0	0	0	0
250	260	28	23	17	11	5	0	0	0	0	0	0
260	270	30	24	18	12	6	0	0	0	0	0	0
270	280	31	26	20	14	8	2	0	0	0	0	0
At least	But less than	0	1	2	3	4	5	6	7	8	9	10 or more
280	290	33	27	21	15	9	3	0	0	0	0	0
290	300	34	29	23	17	11	5	0	0	0	0	0
300	310	36	30	24	18	12	6	0	0	0	0	0
310	320	37	32	26	20	14	8	2	0	0	0	0
320	330	39	33	27	21	15	9	3	0	0	0	0
330	340	40	35	29	23	17	11	5	0	0	0	0
340	350	42	36	30	24	18	12	6	1	0	0	0
350	360	43	38	32	26	20	14	8	2	0	0	0
360	370	45	39	33	27	21	15	9	4	0	0	0
370	380	46	41	35	29	23	17	11	5	0	0	0
380	390	48	42	36	30	24	18	12	7	1	0	0
390	400	49	44	38	32	26	20	14	8	2	0	0
400	410	51	45	39	33	27	21	15	10	4	0	0
410	420	52	47	41	35	29	23	17	11	5	0	0
420	430	54	48	42	36	30	24	18	13	7	1	0
430	440	55	50	44	38	32	26	20	14	8	2	0
440	450	57	51	45	39	33	27	21	16	10	4	0
450	460	58	53	47	41	35	29	23	17	11	5	0
460	470	60	54	48	42	36	30	24	19	13	7	1
470	480	61	56	50	44	38	32	26	20	14	8	2
480	490	63	57	51	45	39	33	27	22	16	10	4
490	500	64	59	53	47	41	35	29	23	17	11	5
500	510	66	60	54	48	42	36	30	25	19	13	7
510	520	67	62	56	50	44	38	32	26	20	14	8
520	530	69	63	57	51	45	39	33	28	22	16	10
530	540	70	65	59	53	47	41	35	29	23	17	11
540	550	72	66	60	54	48	42	36	31	25	19	13
550	560	73	68	62	56	50	44	38	32	26	20	14
560	570	75	69	63	57	51	45	39	34	28	22	16
570	580	76	71	65	59	53	47	41	35	29	23	17
580	590	78	72	66	60	54	48	42	37	31	25	19
590	600	79	74	68	62	56	50	44	38	32	26	20
600	610	81	75	69	63	57	51	45	40	34	28	22
610	620	82	77	71	65	59	53	47	41	35	29	23
620	630	84	78	72	66	60	54	48	43	37	31	25

WEEKLY Payroll Period — Employee MARRIED — Effective January 1, 1990

And the wages are—		And the number of withholding allowances claimed is—										
At least	But less than	0	1	2	3	4	5	6	7	8	9	10 or more
		The amount of income tax to be withheld shall be—										
$630	$640	$85	$80	$74	$68	$62	$56	$50	$44	$38	$32	$26
640	650	87	81	75	69	63	57	51	46	40	34	28
650	660	88	83	77	71	65	59	53	47	41	35	29
660	670	90	84	78	72	66	60	54	49	43	37	31
670	680	91	86	80	74	68	62	56	50	44	38	32
680	690	93	87	81	75	69	63	57	52	46	40	34
690	700	95	89	83	77	71	65	59	53	47	41	35
700	710	98	90	84	78	72	66	60	55	49	43	37
710	720	101	92	86	80	74	68	62	56	50	44	38
720	730	104	93	87	81	75	69	63	58	52	46	40
730	740	106	95	89	83	77	71	65	59	53	47	41
740	750	109	98	90	84	78	72	66	61	55	49	43
750	760	112	101	92	86	80	74	68	62	56	50	44
760	770	115	104	93	87	81	75	69	64	58	52	46
770	780	118	107	95	89	83	77	71	65	59	53	47
780	790	120	109	98	90	84	78	72	67	61	55	49
790	800	123	112	101	92	86	80	74	68	62	56	50
800	810	126	115	104	93	87	81	75	70	64	58	52
810	820	129	118	107	96	89	83	77	71	65	59	53
820	830	132	121	109	98	90	84	78	73	67	61	55
830	840	134	123	112	101	92	86	80	74	68	62	56
840	850	137	126	115	104	93	87	81	76	70	64	58
850	860	140	129	118	107	96	89	83	77	71	65	59
860	870	143	132	121	110	99	90	84	79	73	67	61
870	880	146	135	123	112	101	92	86	80	74	68	62
880	890	148	137	126	115	104	93	87	82	76	70	64
890	900	151	140	129	118	107	96	89	83	77	71	65
900	910	154	143	132	121	110	99	90	85	79	73	67
910	920	157	146	135	124	113	102	92	86	80	74	68
920	930	160	149	137	126	115	104	93	88	82	76	70
930	940	162	151	140	129	118	107	96	89	83	77	71
940	950	165	154	143	132	121	110	99	91	85	79	73
950	960	168	157	146	135	124	113	102	92	86	80	74
960	970	171	160	149	138	127	116	105	94	88	82	76
970	980	174	163	151	140	129	118	107	96	89	83	77
At least	But less than	0	1	2	3	4	5	6	7	8	9	10 or more
980	990	176	165	154	143	132	121	110	99	91	85	79
990	1,000	179	168	157	146	135	124	113	102	92	86	80
1,000	1,010	182	171	160	149	138	127	116	105	94	88	82
1,010	1,020	185	174	163	152	141	130	119	107	96	89	83
1,020	1,030	188	177	165	154	143	132	121	110	99	91	85
1,030	1,040	190	179	168	157	146	135	124	113	102	92	86
1,040	1,050	193	182	171	160	149	138	127	116	105	94	88
1,050	1,060	196	185	174	163	152	141	130	119	108	97	89
1,060	1,070	199	188	177	166	155	144	133	121	110	99	91
1,070	1,080	202	191	179	168	157	146	135	124	113	102	92
1,080	1,090	204	193	182	171	160	149	138	127	116	105	94
1,090	1,100	207	196	185	174	163	152	141	130	119	108	97
1,100	1,110	210	199	188	177	166	155	144	133	122	111	100
1,110	1,120	213	202	191	180	169	158	147	135	124	113	102
1,120	1,130	216	205	193	182	171	160	149	138	127	116	105
1,130	1,140	218	207	196	185	174	163	152	141	130	119	108
1,140	1,150	221	210	199	188	177	166	155	144	133	122	111
1,150	1,160	224	213	202	191	180	169	158	147	136	125	114
1,160	1,170	227	216	205	194	183	172	161	149	138	127	116
1,170	1,180	230	219	207	196	185	174	163	152	141	130	119
1,180	1,190	232	221	210	199	188	177	166	155	144	133	122
1,190	1,200	235	224	213	202	191	180	169	158	147	136	125
1,200	1,210	238	227	216	205	194	183	172	161	150	139	128
1,210	1,220	241	230	219	208	197	186	175	163	152	141	130
1,220	1,230	244	233	221	210	199	188	177	166	155	144	133
1,230	1,240	246	235	224	213	202	191	180	169	158	147	136
1,240	1,250	249	238	227	216	205	194	183	172	161	150	139
1,250	1,260	252	241	230	219	208	197	186	175	164	153	142
1,260	1,270	255	244	233	222	211	200	189	177	166	155	144
1,270	1,280	258	247	235	224	213	202	191	180	169	158	147
1,280	1,290	260	249	238	227	216	205	194	183	172	161	150

$1,290 and over — Use Table 1(b) for a **MARRIED person.**

WAGE-BRACKET WITHHOLDING TABLES

BIWEEKLY Payroll Period— Employee NOT MARRIED—Effective January 1, 1990

And the wages are—		And the number of withholding allowances claimed is—										
At least	But less than	0	1	2	3	4	5	6	7	8	9	10 or more
		The amount of income tax to be withheld shall be—										
$0	$50	$0	$0	$0	$0	$0	$0	$0	$0	$0	$0	$0
50	55	1	0	0	0	0	0	0	0	0	0	0
55	60	2	0	0	0	0	0	0	0	0	0	0
60	65	2	0	0	0	0	0	0	0	0	0	0
65	70	3	0	0	0	0	0	0	0	0	0	0
70	75	4	0	0	0	0	0	0	0	0	0	0
75	80	5	0	0	0	0	0	0	0	0	0	0
80	85	5	0	0	0	0	0	0	0	0	0	0
85	90	6	0	0	0	0	0	0	0	0	0	0
90	95	7	0	0	0	0	0	0	0	0	0	0
95	100	8	0	0	0	0	0	0	0	0	0	0
100	105	8	0	0	0	0	0	0	0	0	0	0
105	110	9	0	0	0	0	0	0	0	0	0	0
110	115	10	0	0	0	0	0	0	0	0	0	0
115	120	11	0	0	0	0	0	0	0	0	0	0
120	125	11	0	0	0	0	0	0	0	0	0	0
125	130	12	0	0	0	0	0	0	0	0	0	0
130	135	13	1	0	0	0	0	0	0	0	0	0
135	140	14	2	0	0	0	0	0	0	0	0	0
140	145	14	3	0	0	0	0	0	0	0	0	0
145	150	15	3	0	0	0	0	0	0	0	0	0
150	155	16	4	0	0	0	0	0	0	0	0	0
155	160	17	5	0	0	0	0	0	0	0	0	0
160	165	17	6	0	0	0	0	0	0	0	0	0
165	170	18	6	0	0	0	0	0	0	0	0	0
170	175	19	7	0	0	0	0	0	0	0	0	0
175	180	20	8	0	0	0	0	0	0	0	0	0
180	185	20	9	0	0	0	0	0	0	0	0	0
185	190	21	9	0	0	0	0	0	0	0	0	0
190	195	22	10	0	0	0	0	0	0	0	0	0
195	200	23	11	0	0	0	0	0	0	0	0	0
200	205	23	12	0	0	0	0	0	0	0	0	0
205	210	24	12	1	0	0	0	0	0	0	0	0
210	215	25	13	1	0	0	0	0	0	0	0	0
215	220	26	14	2	0	0	0	0	0	0	0	0
At least	But less than	0	1	2	3	4	5	6	7	8	9	10 or more
220	225	26	15	3	0	0	0	0	0	0	0	0
225	230	27	15	4	0	0	0	0	0	0	0	0
230	235	28	16	4	0	0	0	0	0	0	0	0
235	240	29	17	5	0	0	0	0	0	0	0	0
240	245	29	18	6	0	0	0	0	0	0	0	0
245	250	30	18	7	0	0	0	0	0	0	0	0
250	260	31	20	8	0	0	0	0	0	0	0	0
260	270	33	21	9	0	0	0	0	0	0	0	0
270	280	34	23	11	0	0	0	0	0	0	0	0
280	290	36	24	12	0	0	0	0	0	0	0	0
290	300	37	26	14	2	0	0	0	0	0	0	0
300	310	39	27	15	3	0	0	0	0	0	0	0
310	320	40	29	17	5	0	0	0	0	0	0	0
320	330	42	30	18	6	0	0	0	0	0	0	0
330	340	43	32	20	8	0	0	0	0	0	0	0
340	350	45	33	21	9	0	0	0	0	0	0	0
350	360	46	35	23	11	0	0	0	0	0	0	0
360	370	48	36	24	12	1	0	0	0	0	0	0
370	380	49	38	26	14	2	0	0	0	0	0	0
380	390	51	39	27	15	4	0	0	0	0	0	0
390	400	52	41	29	17	5	0	0	0	0	0	0
400	410	54	42	30	18	7	0	0	0	0	0	0
410	420	55	44	32	20	8	0	0	0	0	0	0
420	430	57	45	33	21	10	0	0	0	0	0	0
430	440	58	47	35	23	11	0	0	0	0	0	0
440	450	60	48	36	24	13	1	0	0	0	0	0
450	460	61	50	38	26	14	2	0	0	0	0	0
460	470	63	51	39	27	16	4	0	0	0	0	0
470	480	64	53	41	29	17	5	0	0	0	0	0
480	490	66	54	42	30	19	7	0	0	0	0	0
490	500	67	56	44	32	20	8	0	0	0	0	0
500	520	70	58	46	34	22	10	0	0	0	0	0
520	540	73	61	49	37	25	13	2	0	0	0	0
540	560	76	64	52	40	28	16	5	0	0	0	0
560	580	79	67	55	43	31	19	8	0	0	0	0

BIWEEKLY Payroll Period— Employee NOT MARRIED—Effective January 1, 1990

And the wages are—		And the number of withholding allowances claimed is—										
At least	But less than	0	1	2	3	4	5	6	7	8	9	10 or more
		The amount of income tax to be withheld shall be—										
$580	$600	$82	$70	$58	$46	$34	$22	$11	$0	$0	$0	$0
600	620	85	73	61	49	37	25	14	2	0	0	0
620	640	88	76	64	52	40	28	17	5	0	0	0
640	660	91	79	67	55	43	31	20	8	0	0	0
660	680	94	82	70	58	46	34	23	11	0	0	0
680	700	97	85	73	61	49	37	26	14	2	0	0
700	720	100	88	76	64	52	40	29	17	5	0	0
720	740	103	91	79	67	55	43	32	20	8	0	0
740	760	106	94	82	70	58	46	35	23	11	0	0
760	780	109	97	85	73	61	49	38	26	14	2	0
780	800	112	100	88	76	64	52	41	29	17	5	0
800	820	117	103	91	79	67	55	44	32	20	8	0
820	840	122	106	94	82	70	58	47	35	23	11	0
840	860	128	109	97	85	73	61	50	38	26	14	2
860	880	133	112	100	88	76	64	53	41	29	17	5
880	900	139	117	103	91	79	67	56	44	32	20	8
900	920	145	123	106	94	82	70	59	47	35	23	11
920	940	150	128	109	97	85	73	62	50	38	26	14
940	960	156	134	112	100	88	76	65	53	41	29	17
960	980	161	139	117	103	91	79	68	56	44	32	20
980	1,000	167	145	123	106	94	82	71	59	47	35	23
1,000	1,020	173	151	128	109	97	85	74	62	50	38	26
1,020	1,040	178	156	134	112	100	88	77	65	53	41	29
1,040	1,060	184	162	140	118	103	91	80	68	56	44	32
1,060	1,080	189	167	145	123	106	94	83	71	59	47	35
1,080	1,100	195	173	151	129	109	97	86	74	62	50	38
1,100	1,120	201	179	156	134	112	100	89	77	65	53	41
1,120	1,140	206	184	162	140	118	103	92	80	68	56	44
1,140	1,160	212	190	168	146	124	106	95	83	71	59	47
1,160	1,180	217	195	173	151	129	109	98	86	74	62	50
1,180	1,200	223	201	179	157	135	113	101	89	77	65	53
1,200	1,220	229	207	184	162	140	118	104	92	80	68	56
1,220	1,240	234	212	190	168	146	124	107	95	83	71	59
1,240	1,260	240	218	196	174	152	129	110	98	86	74	62
1,260	1,280	245	223	201	179	157	135	113	101	89	77	65
At least	But less than	0	1	2	3	4	5	6	7	8	9	10 or more
1,280	1,300	251	229	207	185	163	141	119	104	92	80	68
1,300	1,320	257	235	212	190	168	146	124	107	95	83	71
1,320	1,340	262	240	218	196	174	152	130	110	98	86	74
1,340	1,360	268	246	224	202	180	157	135	113	101	89	77
1,360	1,380	273	251	229	207	185	163	141	119	104	92	80
1,380	1,400	279	257	235	213	191	169	147	124	107	95	83
1,400	1,420	285	263	240	218	196	174	152	130	110	98	86
1,420	1,440	290	268	246	224	202	180	158	136	114	101	89
1,440	1,460	296	274	252	230	208	185	163	141	119	104	92
1,460	1,480	301	279	257	235	213	191	169	147	125	107	95
1,480	1,500	307	285	263	241	219	197	175	152	130	110	98
1,500	1,520	313	291	268	246	224	202	180	158	136	114	101
1,520	1,540	318	296	274	252	230	208	186	164	142	120	104
1,540	1,560	324	302	280	258	236	213	191	169	147	125	107
1,560	1,580	329	307	285	263	241	219	197	175	153	131	110
1,580	1,600	335	313	291	269	247	225	203	180	158	136	114
1,600	1,620	341	319	296	274	252	230	208	186	164	142	120
1,620	1,640	346	324	302	280	258	236	214	192	170	148	125
1,640	1,660	352	330	308	286	264	241	219	197	175	153	131
1,660	1,680	357	335	313	291	269	247	225	203	181	159	137
1,680	1,700	363	341	319	297	275	253	231	208	186	164	142
1,700	1,720	369	347	324	302	280	258	236	214	192	170	148
1,720	1,740	374	352	330	308	286	264	242	220	198	176	153
1,740	1,760	380	358	336	314	292	269	247	225	203	181	159
1,760	1,780	385	363	341	319	297	275	253	231	209	187	165
1,780	1,800	391	369	347	325	303	281	259	236	214	192	170
1,800	1,820	397	375	352	330	308	286	264	242	220	198	176
1,820	1,840	402	380	358	336	314	292	270	248	226	204	181
1,840	1,860	408	386	364	342	320	297	275	253	231	209	187
1,860	1,880	414	391	369	347	325	303	281	259	237	215	193

$1,880 and over — Use Table 2(a) for a **SINGLE** person.

WAGE-BRACKET WITHHOLDING TABLES

BIWEEKLY Payroll Period — Employee MARRIED — Effective January 1, 1990

And the wages are—		And the number of withholding allowances claimed is—										
At least	But less than	0	1	2	3	4	5	6	7	8	9	10 or more
		The amount of income tax to be withheld shall be—										
$0	$135	$0	$0	$0	$0	$0	$0	$0	$0	$0	$0	$0
135	140	1	0	0	0	0	0	0	0	0	0	0
140	145	2	0	0	0	0	0	0	0	0	0	0
145	150	3	0	0	0	0	0	0	0	0	0	0
150	155	3	0	0	0	0	0	0	0	0	0	0
155	160	4	0	0	0	0	0	0	0	0	0	0
160	165	5	0	0	0	0	0	0	0	0	0	0
165	170	6	0	0	0	0	0	0	0	0	0	0
170	175	6	0	0	0	0	0	0	0	0	0	0
175	180	7	0	0	0	0	0	0	0	0	0	0
180	185	8	0	0	0	0	0	0	0	0	0	0
185	190	9	0	0	0	0	0	0	0	0	0	0
190	195	9	0	0	0	0	0	0	0	0	0	0
195	200	10	0	0	0	0	0	0	0	0	0	0
200	205	11	0	0	0	0	0	0	0	0	0	0
205	210	12	0	0	0	0	0	0	0	0	0	0
210	215	12	0	0	0	0	0	0	0	0	0	0
215	220	13	1	0	0	0	0	0	0	0	0	0
220	225	14	2	0	0	0	0	0	0	0	0	0
225	230	15	3	0	0	0	0	0	0	0	0	0
230	235	15	3	0	0	0	0	0	0	0	0	0
235	240	16	4	0	0	0	0	0	0	0	0	0
240	245	17	5	0	0	0	0	0	0	0	0	0
245	250	18	6	0	0	0	0	0	0	0	0	0
250	260	19	7	0	0	0	0	0	0	0	0	0
260	270	20	8	0	0	0	0	0	0	0	0	0
270	280	22	10	0	0	0	0	0	0	0	0	0
280	290	23	11	0	0	0	0	0	0	0	0	0
290	300	25	13	1	0	0	0	0	0	0	0	0
300	310	26	14	2	0	0	0	0	0	0	0	0
310	320	28	16	4	0	0	0	0	0	0	0	0
320	330	29	17	5	0	0	0	0	0	0	0	0
330	340	31	19	7	0	0	0	0	0	0	0	0
340	350	32	20	8	0	0	0	0	0	0	0	0
350	360	34	22	10	0	0	0	0	0	0	0	0
At least	But less than	0	1	2	3	4	5	6	7	8	9	10 or more
360	370	35	23	11	0	0	0	0	0	0	0	0
370	380	37	25	13	1	0	0	0	0	0	0	0
380	390	38	26	14	3	0	0	0	0	0	0	0
390	400	40	28	16	4	0	0	0	0	0	0	0
400	410	41	29	17	6	0	0	0	0	0	0	0
410	420	43	31	19	7	0	0	0	0	0	0	0
420	430	44	32	20	9	0	0	0	0	0	0	0
430	440	46	34	22	10	0	0	0	0	0	0	0
440	450	47	35	23	12	0	0	0	0	0	0	0
450	460	49	37	25	13	1	0	0	0	0	0	0
460	470	50	38	26	15	3	0	0	0	0	0	0
470	480	52	40	28	16	4	0	0	0	0	0	0
480	490	53	41	29	18	6	0	0	0	0	0	0
490	500	55	43	31	19	7	0	0	0	0	0	0
500	520	57	45	33	21	10	0	0	0	0	0	0
520	540	60	48	36	24	13	1	0	0	0	0	0
540	560	63	51	39	27	16	4	0	0	0	0	0
560	580	66	54	42	30	19	7	0	0	0	0	0
580	600	69	57	45	33	22	10	0	0	0	0	0
600	620	72	60	48	36	25	13	1	0	0	0	0
620	640	75	63	51	39	28	16	4	0	0	0	0
640	660	78	66	54	42	31	19	7	0	0	0	0
660	680	81	69	57	45	34	22	10	0	0	0	0
680	700	84	72	60	48	37	25	13	1	0	0	0
700	720	87	75	63	51	40	28	16	4	0	0	0
720	740	90	78	66	54	43	31	19	7	0	0	0
740	760	93	81	69	57	46	34	22	10	0	0	0
760	780	96	84	72	60	49	37	25	13	1	0	0
780	800	99	87	75	63	52	40	28	16	4	0	0
800	820	102	90	78	66	55	43	31	19	7	0	0
820	840	105	93	81	69	58	46	34	22	10	0	0
840	860	108	96	84	72	61	49	37	25	13	1	0
860	880	111	99	87	75	64	52	40	28	16	4	0
880	900	114	102	90	78	67	55	43	31	19	7	0
900	920	117	105	93	81	70	58	46	34	22	10	0

BIWEEKLY Payroll Period — Employee MARRIED — Effective January 1, 1990

And the wages are—		And the number of withholding allowances claimed is—										
At least	But less than	0	1	2	3	4	5	6	7	8	9	10 or more
		The amount of income tax to be withheld shall be—										
$920	$940	$120	$108	$96	$84	$73	$61	$49	$37	$25	$13	$2
940	960	123	111	99	87	76	64	52	40	28	16	5
960	980	126	114	102	90	79	67	55	43	31	19	8
980	1,000	129	117	105	93	82	70	58	46	34	22	11
1,000	1,020	132	120	108	96	85	73	61	49	37	25	14
1,020	1,040	135	123	111	99	88	76	64	52	40	28	17
1,040	1,060	138	126	114	102	91	79	67	55	43	31	20
1,060	1,080	141	129	117	105	94	82	70	58	46	34	23
1,080	1,100	144	132	120	108	97	85	73	61	49	37	26
1,100	1,120	147	135	123	111	100	88	76	64	52	40	29
1,120	1,140	150	138	126	114	103	91	79	67	55	43	32
1,140	1,160	153	141	129	117	106	94	82	70	58	46	35
1,160	1,180	156	144	132	120	109	97	85	73	61	49	38
1,180	1,200	159	147	135	123	112	100	88	76	64	52	41
1,200	1,220	162	150	138	126	115	103	91	79	67	55	44
1,220	1,240	165	153	141	129	118	106	94	82	70	58	47
1,240	1,260	168	156	144	132	121	109	97	85	73	61	50
1,260	1,280	171	159	147	135	124	112	100	88	76	64	53
1,280	1,300	174	162	150	138	127	115	103	91	79	67	56
1,300	1,320	177	165	153	141	130	118	106	94	82	70	59
1,320	1,340	180	168	156	144	133	121	109	97	85	73	62
1,340	1,360	183	171	159	147	136	124	112	100	88	76	65
1,360	1,380	186	174	162	150	139	127	115	103	91	79	68
1,380	1,400	190	177	165	153	142	130	118	106	94	82	71
1,400	1,420	196	180	168	156	145	133	121	109	97	85	74
1,420	1,440	202	183	171	159	148	136	124	112	100	88	77
1,440	1,460	207	186	174	162	151	139	127	115	103	91	80
1,460	1,480	213	191	177	165	154	142	130	118	106	94	83
1,480	1,500	218	196	180	168	157	145	133	121	109	97	86
1,500	1,520	224	202	183	171	160	148	136	124	112	100	89
1,520	1,540	230	207	186	174	163	151	139	127	115	103	92
1,540	1,560	235	213	191	177	166	154	142	130	118	106	95
1,560	1,580	241	219	197	180	169	157	145	133	121	109	98
1,580	1,600	246	224	202	183	172	160	148	136	124	112	101
1,600	1,620	252	230	208	186	175	163	151	139	127	115	104
At least	But less than	0	1	2	3	4	5	6	7	8	9	10 or more
1,620	1,640	258	235	213	191	178	166	154	142	130	118	107
1,640	1,660	263	241	219	197	181	169	157	145	133	121	110
1,660	1,680	269	247	225	203	184	172	160	148	136	124	113
1,680	1,700	274	252	230	208	187	175	163	151	139	127	116
1,700	1,720	280	258	236	214	192	178	166	154	142	130	119
1,720	1,740	286	263	241	219	197	181	169	157	145	133	122
1,740	1,760	291	269	247	225	203	184	172	160	148	136	125
1,760	1,780	297	275	253	231	208	187	175	163	151	139	128
1,780	1,800	302	280	258	236	214	192	178	166	154	142	131
1,800	1,820	308	286	264	242	220	198	181	169	157	145	134
1,820	1,840	314	291	269	247	225	203	184	172	160	148	137
1,840	1,860	319	297	275	253	231	209	187	175	163	151	140
1,860	1,880	325	303	281	259	236	214	192	178	166	154	143
1,880	1,900	330	308	286	264	242	220	198	181	169	157	146
1,900	1,920	336	314	292	270	248	226	203	184	172	160	149
1,920	1,940	342	319	297	275	253	231	209	187	175	163	152
1,940	1,960	347	325	303	281	259	237	215	193	178	166	155
1,960	1,980	353	331	309	287	264	242	220	198	181	169	158
1,980	2,000	358	336	314	292	270	248	226	204	184	172	161
2,000	2,020	364	342	320	298	276	254	231	209	187	175	164
2,020	2,040	370	347	325	303	281	259	237	215	193	178	167
2,040	2,060	375	353	331	309	287	265	243	221	199	181	170
2,060	2,080	381	359	337	315	292	270	248	226	204	184	173
2,080	2,100	386	364	342	320	298	276	254	232	210	188	176
2,100	2,120	392	370	348	326	304	282	259	237	215	193	179
2,120	2,140	398	375	353	331	309	287	265	243	221	199	182
2,140	2,160	403	381	359	337	315	293	271	249	227	204	185
2,160	2,180	409	387	365	343	320	298	276	254	232	210	188
2,180	2,200	414	392	370	348	326	304	282	260	238	216	194
2,200	2,220	420	398	376	354	332	310	287	265	243	221	199
$2,220 and over		Use Table 2(b) for a **MARRIED** person.										

WAGE-BRACKET WITHHOLDING TABLES

SEMIMONTHLY Payroll Period—Employee NOT MARRIED—Effective January 1, 1990

And the wages are—		And the number of withholding allowances claimed is—										
At least	But less than	0	1	2	3	4	5	6	7	8	9	10 or more
		The amount of income tax to be withheld shall be—										
$0	$55	$0	$0	$0	$0	$0	$0	$0	$0	$0	$0	$0
55	60	1	0	0	0	0	0	0	0	0	0	0
60	65	2	0	0	0	0	0	0	0	0	0	0
65	70	3	0	0	0	0	0	0	0	0	0	0
70	75	3	0	0	0	0	0	0	0	0	0	0
75	80	4	0	0	0	0	0	0	0	0	0	0
80	85	5	0	0	0	0	0	0	0	0	0	0
85	90	6	0	0	0	0	0	0	0	0	0	0
90	95	6	0	0	0	0	0	0	0	0	0	0
95	100	7	0	0	0	0	0	0	0	0	0	0
100	105	8	0	0	0	0	0	0	0	0	0	0
105	110	9	0	0	0	0	0	0	0	0	0	0
110	115	9	0	0	0	0	0	0	0	0	0	0
115	120	10	0	0	0	0	0	0	0	0	0	0
120	125	11	0	0	0	0	0	0	0	0	0	0
125	130	12	0	0	0	0	0	0	0	0	0	0
130	135	12	0	0	0	0	0	0	0	0	0	0
135	140	13	0	0	0	0	0	0	0	0	0	0
140	145	14	1	0	0	0	0	0	0	0	0	0
145	150	15	2	0	0	0	0	0	0	0	0	0
150	155	15	3	0	0	0	0	0	0	0	0	0
155	160	16	3	0	0	0	0	0	0	0	0	0
160	165	17	4	0	0	0	0	0	0	0	0	0
165	170	18	5	0	0	0	0	0	0	0	0	0
170	175	18	6	0	0	0	0	0	0	0	0	0
175	180	19	6	0	0	0	0	0	0	0	0	0
180	185	20	7	0	0	0	0	0	0	0	0	0
185	190	21	8	0	0	0	0	0	0	0	0	0
190	195	21	9	0	0	0	0	0	0	0	0	0
195	200	22	9	0	0	0	0	0	0	0	0	0
200	205	23	10	0	0	0	0	0	0	0	0	0
205	210	24	11	0	0	0	0	0	0	0	0	0
210	215	24	12	0	0	0	0	0	0	0	0	0
215	220	25	12	0	0	0	0	0	0	0	0	0
220	225	26	13	0	0	0	0	0	0	0	0	0
At least	But less than	0	1	2	3	4	5	6	7	8	9	10 or more
225	230	27	14	1	0	0	0	0	0	0	0	0
230	235	27	15	2	0	0	0	0	0	0	0	0
235	240	28	15	3	0	0	0	0	0	0	0	0
240	245	29	16	3	0	0	0	0	0	0	0	0
245	250	30	17	4	0	0	0	0	0	0	0	0
250	260	31	18	5	0	0	0	0	0	0	0	0
260	270	32	19	7	0	0	0	0	0	0	0	0
270	280	34	21	8	0	0	0	0	0	0	0	0
280	290	35	22	10	0	0	0	0	0	0	0	0
290	300	37	24	11	0	0	0	0	0	0	0	0
300	310	38	25	13	0	0	0	0	0	0	0	0
310	320	40	27	14	1	0	0	0	0	0	0	0
320	330	41	28	16	3	0	0	0	0	0	0	0
330	340	43	30	17	4	0	0	0	0	0	0	0
340	350	44	31	19	6	0	0	0	0	0	0	0
350	360	46	33	20	7	0	0	0	0	0	0	0
360	370	47	34	22	9	0	0	0	0	0	0	0
370	380	49	36	23	10	0	0	0	0	0	0	0
380	390	50	37	25	12	0	0	0	0	0	0	0
390	400	52	39	26	13	1	0	0	0	0	0	0
400	410	53	40	28	15	2	0	0	0	0	0	0
410	420	55	42	29	16	4	0	0	0	0	0	0
420	430	56	43	31	18	5	0	0	0	0	0	0
430	440	58	45	32	19	7	0	0	0	0	0	0
440	450	59	46	34	21	8	0	0	0	0	0	0
450	460	61	48	35	22	10	0	0	0	0	0	0
460	470	62	49	37	24	11	0	0	0	0	0	0
470	480	64	51	38	25	13	0	0	0	0	0	0
480	490	65	52	40	27	14	1	0	0	0	0	0
490	500	67	54	41	28	16	3	0	0	0	0	0
500	520	69	56	43	31	18	5	0	0	0	0	0
520	540	72	59	46	34	21	8	0	0	0	0	0
540	560	75	62	49	37	24	11	0	0	0	0	0
560	580	78	65	52	40	27	14	1	0	0	0	0
580	600	81	68	55	43	30	17	4	0	0	0	0

SEMIMONTHLY Payroll Period—Employee NOT MARRIED—Effective January 1, 1990

And the wages are—		And the number of withholding allowances claimed is—										
At least	But less than	0	1	2	3	4	5	6	7	8	9	10 or more
		The amount of income tax to be withheld shall be—										
$600	$620	$84	$71	$58	$46	$33	$20	$7	$0	$0	$0	$0
620	640	87	74	61	49	36	23	10	0	0	0	0
640	660	90	77	64	52	39	26	13	0	0	0	0
660	680	93	80	67	55	42	29	16	3	0	0	0
680	700	96	83	70	58	45	32	19	6	0	0	0
700	720	99	86	73	61	48	35	22	9	0	0	0
720	740	102	89	76	64	51	38	25	12	0	0	0
740	760	105	92	79	67	54	41	28	15	3	0	0
760	780	108	95	82	70	57	44	31	18	6	0	0
780	800	111	98	85	73	60	47	34	21	9	0	0
800	820	114	101	88	76	63	50	37	24	12	0	0
820	840	117	104	91	79	66	53	40	27	15	2	0
840	860	120	107	94	82	69	56	43	30	18	5	0
860	880	124	110	97	85	72	59	46	33	21	8	0
880	900	130	113	100	88	75	62	49	36	24	11	0
900	920	135	116	103	91	78	65	52	39	27	14	1
920	940	141	119	106	94	81	68	55	42	30	17	4
940	960	147	123	109	97	84	71	58	45	33	20	7
960	980	152	128	112	100	87	74	61	48	36	23	10
980	1,000	158	134	115	103	90	77	64	51	39	26	13
1,000	1,020	163	140	118	106	93	80	67	54	42	29	16
1,020	1,040	169	145	121	109	96	83	70	57	45	32	19
1,040	1,060	175	151	127	112	99	86	73	60	48	35	22
1,060	1,080	180	156	132	115	102	89	76	63	51	38	25
1,080	1,100	186	162	138	118	105	92	79	66	54	41	28
1,100	1,120	191	168	144	121	108	95	82	69	57	44	31
1,120	1,140	197	173	149	125	111	98	85	72	60	47	34
1,140	1,160	203	179	155	131	114	101	88	75	63	50	37
1,160	1,180	208	184	160	136	117	104	91	78	66	53	40
1,180	1,200	214	190	166	142	120	107	94	81	69	56	43
1,200	1,220	219	196	172	148	124	110	97	84	72	59	46
1,220	1,240	225	201	177	153	129	113	100	87	75	62	49
1,240	1,260	231	207	183	159	135	116	103	90	78	65	52
1,260	1,280	236	212	188	164	141	119	106	93	81	68	55
1,280	1,300	242	218	194	170	146	122	109	96	84	71	58
At least	But less than	0	1	2	3	4	5	6	7	8	9	10 or more
1,300	1,320	247	224	200	176	152	128	112	99	87	74	61
1,320	1,340	253	229	205	181	157	133	115	102	90	77	64
1,340	1,360	259	235	211	187	163	139	118	105	93	80	67
1,360	1,380	264	240	216	192	169	145	121	108	96	83	70
1,380	1,400	270	246	222	198	174	150	126	111	99	86	73
1,400	1,420	275	252	228	204	180	156	132	114	102	89	76
1,420	1,440	281	257	233	209	185	161	138	117	105	92	79
1,440	1,460	287	263	239	215	191	167	143	120	108	95	82
1,460	1,480	292	268	244	220	197	173	149	125	111	98	85
1,480	1,500	298	274	250	226	202	178	154	130	114	101	88
1,500	1,520	303	280	256	232	208	184	160	136	117	104	91
1,520	1,540	309	285	261	237	213	189	166	142	120	107	94
1,540	1,560	315	291	267	243	219	195	171	147	123	110	97
1,560	1,580	320	296	272	248	225	201	177	153	129	113	100
1,580	1,600	326	302	278	254	230	206	182	158	135	116	103
1,600	1,620	331	308	284	260	236	212	188	164	140	119	106
1,620	1,640	337	313	289	265	241	217	194	170	146	122	109
1,640	1,660	343	319	295	271	247	223	199	175	151	127	112
1,660	1,680	348	324	300	276	253	229	205	181	157	133	115
1,680	1,700	354	330	306	282	258	234	210	186	163	139	118
1,700	1,720	359	336	312	288	264	240	216	192	168	144	121
1,720	1,740	365	341	317	293	269	245	222	198	174	150	126
1,740	1,760	371	347	323	299	275	251	227	203	179	155	131
1,760	1,780	376	352	328	304	281	257	233	209	185	161	137
1,780	1,800	382	358	334	310	286	262	238	214	191	167	143
1,800	1,820	387	364	340	316	292	268	244	220	196	172	148
1,820	1,840	393	369	345	321	297	273	250	226	202	178	154
1,840	1,860	399	375	351	327	303	279	255	231	207	183	159
1,860	1,880	404	380	356	332	309	285	261	237	213	189	165
1,880	1,900	410	386	362	338	314	290	266	242	219	195	171

$1,900 and over — Use Table 3(a) for a **SINGLE person**.

SEMIMONTHLY Payroll Period—Employee MARRIED—Effective January 1, 1990

And the wages are—		And the number of withholding allowances claimed is—										
At least	But less than	0	1	2	3	4	5	6	7	8	9	10 or more
		The amount of income tax to be withheld shall be—										
$0	$145	$0	$0	$0	$0	$0	$0	$0	$0	$0	$0	$0
145	150	1	0	0	0	0	0	0	0	0	0	0
150	155	2	0	0	0	0	0	0	0	0	0	0
155	160	2	0	0	0	0	0	0	0	0	0	0
160	165	3	0	0	0	0	0	0	0	0	0	0
165	170	4	0	0	0	0	0	0	0	0	0	0
170	175	5	0	0	0	0	0	0	0	0	0	0
175	180	5	0	0	0	0	0	0	0	0	0	0
180	185	6	0	0	0	0	0	0	0	0	0	0
185	190	7	0	0	0	0	0	0	0	0	0	0
190	195	8	0	0	0	0	0	0	0	0	0	0
195	200	8	0	0	0	0	0	0	0	0	0	0
200	205	9	0	0	0	0	0	0	0	0	0	0
205	210	10	0	0	0	0	0	0	0	0	0	0
210	215	11	0	0	0	0	0	0	0	0	0	0
215	220	11	0	0	0	0	0	0	0	0	0	0
220	225	12	0	0	0	0	0	0	0	0	0	0
225	230	13	0	0	0	0	0	0	0	0	0	0
230	235	14	1	0	0	0	0	0	0	0	0	0
235	240	14	2	0	0	0	0	0	0	0	0	0
240	245	15	2	0	0	0	0	0	0	0	0	0
245	250	16	3	0	0	0	0	0	0	0	0	0
250	260	17	4	0	0	0	0	0	0	0	0	0
260	270	19	6	0	0	0	0	0	0	0	0	0
270	280	20	7	0	0	0	0	0	0	0	0	0
280	290	22	9	0	0	0	0	0	0	0	0	0
290	300	23	10	0	0	0	0	0	0	0	0	0
300	310	25	12	0	0	0	0	0	0	0	0	0
310	320	26	13	0	0	0	0	0	0	0	0	0
320	330	28	15	2	0	0	0	0	0	0	0	0
330	340	29	16	3	0	0	0	0	0	0	0	0
340	350	31	18	5	0	0	0	0	0	0	0	0
350	360	32	19	6	0	0	0	0	0	0	0	0
360	370	34	21	8	0	0	0	0	0	0	0	0
370	380	35	22	9	0	0	0	0	0	0	0	0
At least	But less than	0	1	2	3	4	5	6	7	8	9	10 or more
380	390	37	24	11	0	0	0	0	0	0	0	0
390	400	38	25	12	0	0	0	0	0	0	0	0
400	410	40	27	14	1	0	0	0	0	0	0	0
410	420	41	28	15	3	0	0	0	0	0	0	0
420	430	43	30	17	4	0	0	0	0	0	0	0
430	440	44	31	18	6	0	0	0	0	0	0	0
440	450	46	33	20	7	0	0	0	0	0	0	0
450	460	47	34	21	9	0	0	0	0	0	0	0
460	470	49	36	23	10	0	0	0	0	0	0	0
470	480	50	37	24	12	0	0	0	0	0	0	0
480	490	52	39	26	13	0	0	0	0	0	0	0
490	500	53	40	27	15	2	0	0	0	0	0	0
500	520	55	42	30	17	4	0	0	0	0	0	0
520	540	58	45	33	20	7	0	0	0	0	0	0
540	560	61	48	36	23	10	0	0	0	0	0	0
560	580	64	51	39	26	13	0	0	0	0	0	0
580	600	67	54	42	29	16	3	0	0	0	0	0
600	620	70	57	45	32	19	6	0	0	0	0	0
620	640	73	60	48	35	22	9	0	0	0	0	0
640	660	76	63	51	38	25	12	0	0	0	0	0
660	680	79	66	54	41	28	15	2	0	0	0	0
680	700	82	69	57	44	31	18	5	0	0	0	0
700	720	85	72	60	47	34	21	8	0	0	0	0
720	740	88	75	63	50	37	24	11	0	0	0	0
740	760	91	78	66	53	40	27	14	2	0	0	0
760	780	94	81	69	56	43	30	17	5	0	0	0
780	800	97	84	72	59	46	33	20	8	0	0	0
800	820	100	87	75	62	49	36	23	11	0	0	0
820	840	103	90	78	65	52	39	26	14	1	0	0
840	860	106	93	81	68	55	42	29	17	4	0	0
860	880	109	96	84	71	58	45	32	20	7	0	0
880	900	112	99	87	74	61	48	35	23	10	0	0
900	920	115	102	90	77	64	51	38	26	13	0	0
920	940	118	105	93	80	67	54	41	29	16	3	0
940	960	121	108	96	83	70	57	44	32	19	6	0

SEMIMONTHLY Payroll Period—Employee MARRIED—Effective January 1, 1990

And the wages are—		And the number of withholding allowances claimed is—										
At least	But less than	0	1	2	3	4	5	6	7	8	9	10 or more
		The amount of income tax to be withheld shall be—										
$960	$980	$124	$111	$99	$86	$73	$60	$47	$35	$22	$9	$0
980	1,000	127	114	102	89	76	63	50	38	25	12	0
1,000	1,020	130	117	105	92	79	66	53	41	28	15	2
1,020	1,040	133	120	108	95	82	69	56	44	31	18	5
1,040	1,060	136	123	111	98	85	72	59	47	34	21	8
1,060	1,080	139	126	114	101	88	75	62	50	37	24	11
1,080	1,100	142	129	117	104	91	78	65	53	40	27	14
1,100	1,120	145	132	120	107	94	81	68	56	43	30	17
1,120	1,140	148	135	123	110	97	84	71	59	46	33	20
1,140	1,160	151	138	126	113	100	87	74	62	49	36	23
1,160	1,180	154	141	129	116	103	90	77	65	52	39	26
1,180	1,200	157	144	132	119	106	93	80	68	55	42	29
1,200	1,220	160	147	135	122	109	96	83	71	58	45	32
1,220	1,240	163	150	138	125	112	99	86	74	61	48	35
1,240	1,260	166	153	141	128	115	102	89	77	64	51	38
1,260	1,280	169	156	144	131	118	105	92	80	67	54	41
1,280	1,300	172	159	147	134	121	108	95	83	70	57	44
1,300	1,320	175	162	150	137	124	111	98	86	73	60	47
1,320	1,340	178	165	153	140	127	114	101	89	76	63	50
1,340	1,360	181	168	156	143	130	117	104	92	79	66	53
1,360	1,380	184	171	159	146	133	120	107	95	82	69	56
1,380	1,400	187	174	162	149	136	123	110	98	85	72	59
1,400	1,420	190	177	165	152	139	126	113	101	88	75	62
1,420	1,440	193	180	168	155	142	129	116	104	91	78	65
1,440	1,460	196	183	171	158	145	132	119	107	94	81	68
1,460	1,480	199	186	174	161	148	135	122	110	97	84	71
1,480	1,500	202	189	177	164	151	138	125	113	100	87	74
1,500	1,520	207	192	180	167	154	141	128	116	103	90	77
1,520	1,540	213	195	183	170	157	144	131	119	106	93	80
1,540	1,560	219	198	186	173	160	147	134	122	109	96	83
1,560	1,580	224	201	189	176	163	150	137	125	112	99	86
1,580	1,600	230	206	192	179	166	153	140	128	115	102	89
1,600	1,620	235	211	195	182	169	156	143	131	118	105	92
1,620	1,640	241	217	198	185	172	159	146	134	121	108	95
1,640	1,660	247	223	201	188	175	162	149	137	124	111	98
At least	But less than	0	1	2	3	4	5	6	7	8	9	10 or more
1,660	1,680	252	228	204	191	178	165	152	140	127	114	101
1,680	1,700	258	234	210	194	181	168	155	143	130	117	104
1,700	1,720	263	239	216	197	184	171	158	146	133	120	107
1,720	1,740	269	245	221	200	187	174	161	149	136	123	110
1,740	1,760	275	251	227	203	190	177	164	152	139	126	113
1,760	1,780	280	256	232	208	193	180	167	155	142	129	116
1,780	1,800	286	262	238	214	196	183	170	158	145	132	119
1,800	1,820	291	267	244	220	199	186	173	161	148	135	122
1,820	1,840	297	273	249	225	202	189	176	164	151	138	125
1,840	1,860	303	279	255	231	207	192	179	167	154	141	128
1,860	1,880	308	284	260	236	212	195	182	170	157	144	131
1,880	1,900	314	290	266	242	218	198	185	173	160	147	134
1,900	1,920	319	295	272	248	224	201	188	176	163	150	137
1,920	1,940	325	301	277	253	229	205	191	179	166	153	140
1,940	1,960	331	307	283	259	235	211	194	182	169	156	143
1,960	1,980	336	312	288	264	240	217	197	185	172	159	146
1,980	2,000	342	318	294	270	246	222	200	188	175	162	149
2,000	2,020	347	323	300	276	252	228	204	191	178	165	152
2,020	2,040	353	329	305	281	257	233	209	194	181	168	155
2,040	2,060	359	335	311	287	263	239	215	197	184	171	158
2,060	2,080	364	340	316	292	268	245	221	200	187	174	161
2,080	2,100	370	346	322	298	274	250	226	203	190	177	164
2,100	2,120	375	351	328	304	280	256	232	208	193	180	167
2,120	2,140	381	357	333	309	285	261	237	214	196	183	170
2,140	2,160	387	363	339	315	291	267	243	219	199	186	173
2,160	2,180	392	368	344	320	296	273	249	225	202	189	176
2,180	2,200	398	374	350	326	302	278	254	230	206	192	179
2,200	2,220	403	379	356	332	308	284	260	236	212	195	182
2,220	2,240	409	385	361	337	313	289	265	242	218	198	185
2,240	2,260	415	391	367	343	319	295	271	247	223	201	188
$2,260 and over	Use Table 3(b) for a **MARRIED person**.											

WAGE-BRACKET WITHHOLDING TABLES

MONTHLY Payroll Period— Employee NOT MARRIED—Effective January 1, 1990

And the wages are–		And the number of withholding allowances claimed is—										
At least	But less than	0	1	2	3	4	5	6	7	8	9	10 or more
		The amount of income tax to be withheld shall be—										
$0	$105	$0	$0	$0	$0	$0	$0	$0	$0	$0	$0	$0
105	110	1	0	0	0	0	0	0	0	0	0	0
110	115	2	0	0	0	0	0	0	0	0	0	0
115	120	3	0	0	0	0	0	0	0	0	0	0
120	125	3	0	0	0	0	0	0	0	0	0	0
125	130	4	0	0	0	0	0	0	0	0	0	0
130	135	5	0	0	0	0	0	0	0	0	0	0
135	140	6	0	0	0	0	0	0	0	0	0	0
140	145	6	0	0	0	0	0	0	0	0	0	0
145	150	7	0	0	0	0	0	0	0	0	0	0
150	160	8	0	0	0	0	0	0	0	0	0	0
160	170	10	0	0	0	0	0	0	0	0	0	0
170	180	11	0	0	0	0	0	0	0	0	0	0
180	190	13	0	0	0	0	0	0	0	0	0	0
190	200	14	0	0	0	0	0	0	0	0	0	0
200	210	16	0	0	0	0	0	0	0	0	0	0
210	220	17	0	0	0	0	0	0	0	0	0	0
220	230	19	0	0	0	0	0	0	0	0	0	0
230	240	20	0	0	0	0	0	0	0	0	0	0
240	250	22	0	0	0	0	0	0	0	0	0	0
250	260	23	0	0	0	0	0	0	0	0	0	0
260	270	25	0	0	0	0	0	0	0	0	0	0
270	280	26	1	0	0	0	0	0	0	0	0	0
280	290	28	2	0	0	0	0	0	0	0	0	0
290	300	29	4	0	0	0	0	0	0	0	0	0
300	320	32	6	0	0	0	0	0	0	0	0	0
320	340	35	9	0	0	0	0	0	0	0	0	0
340	360	38	12	0	0	0	0	0	0	0	0	0
360	380	41	15	0	0	0	0	0	0	0	0	0
380	400	44	18	0	0	0	0	0	0	0	0	0
400	420	47	21	0	0	0	0	0	0	0	0	0
420	440	50	24	0	0	0	0	0	0	0	0	0
440	460	53	27	1	0	0	0	0	0	0	0	0
460	480	56	30	4	0	0	0	0	0	0	0	0
480	500	59	33	7	0	0	0	0	0	0	0	0
At least	But less than	0	1	2	3	4	5	6	7	8	9	10 or more
500	520	62	36	10	0	0	0	0	0	0	0	0
520	540	65	39	13	0	0	0	0	0	0	0	0
540	560	68	42	16	0	0	0	0	0	0	0	0
560	580	71	45	19	0	0	0	0	0	0	0	0
580	600	74	48	22	0	0	0	0	0	0	0	0
600	640	78	52	27	1	0	0	0	0	0	0	0
640	680	84	58	33	7	0	0	0	0	0	0	0
680	720	90	64	39	13	0	0	0	0	0	0	0
720	760	96	70	45	19	0	0	0	0	0	0	0
760	800	102	76	51	25	0	0	0	0	0	0	0
800	840	108	82	57	31	6	0	0	0	0	0	0
840	880	114	88	63	37	12	0	0	0	0	0	0
880	920	120	94	69	43	18	0	0	0	0	0	0
920	960	126	100	75	49	24	0	0	0	0	0	0
960	1,000	132	106	81	55	30	4	0	0	0	0	0
1,000	1,040	138	112	87	61	36	10	0	0	0	0	0
1,040	1,080	144	118	93	67	42	16	0	0	0	0	0
1,080	1,120	150	124	99	73	48	22	0	0	0	0	0
1,120	1,160	156	130	105	79	54	28	2	0	0	0	0
1,160	1,200	162	136	111	85	60	34	8	0	0	0	0
1,200	1,240	168	142	117	91	66	40	14	0	0	0	0
1,240	1,280	174	148	123	97	72	46	20	0	0	0	0
1,280	1,320	180	154	129	103	78	52	26	1	0	0	0
1,320	1,360	186	160	135	109	84	58	32	7	0	0	0
1,360	1,400	192	166	141	115	90	64	38	13	0	0	0
1,400	1,440	198	172	147	121	96	70	44	19	0	0	0
1,440	1,480	204	178	153	127	102	76	50	25	0	0	0
1,480	1,520	210	184	159	133	108	82	56	31	5	0	0
1,520	1,560	216	190	165	139	114	88	62	37	11	0	0
1,560	1,600	222	196	171	145	120	94	68	43	17	0	0
1,600	1,640	228	202	177	151	126	100	74	49	23	0	0
1,640	1,680	234	208	183	157	132	106	80	55	29	3	0
1,680	1,720	240	214	189	163	138	112	86	61	35	9	0
1,720	1,760	248	220	195	169	144	118	92	67	41	15	0

MONTHLY Payroll Period— Employee NOT MARRIED—Effective January 1, 1990

And the wages are–		And the number of withholding allowances claimed is—										
At least	But less than	0	1	2	3	4	5	6	7	8	9	10 or more
		The amount of income tax to be withheld shall be—										
$1,760	$1,800	$260	$226	$201	$175	$150	$124	$98	$73	$47	$21	$0
1,800	1,840	271	232	207	181	156	130	104	79	53	27	2
1,840	1,880	282	238	213	187	162	136	110	85	59	33	8
1,880	1,920	293	245	219	193	168	142	116	91	65	39	14
1,920	1,960	304	257	225	199	174	148	122	97	71	45	20
1,960	2,000	316	268	231	205	180	154	128	103	77	51	26
2,000	2,040	327	279	237	211	186	160	134	109	83	57	32
2,040	2,080	338	290	243	217	192	166	140	115	89	63	38
2,080	2,120	349	301	254	223	198	172	146	121	95	69	44
2,120	2,160	360	313	265	229	204	178	152	127	101	75	50
2,160	2,200	372	324	276	235	210	184	158	133	107	81	56
2,200	2,240	383	335	287	241	216	190	164	139	113	87	62
2,240	2,280	394	346	298	251	222	196	170	145	119	93	68
2,280	2,320	405	357	310	262	228	202	176	151	125	99	74
2,320	2,360	416	369	321	273	234	208	182	157	131	105	80
2,360	2,400	428	380	332	284	240	214	188	163	137	111	86
2,400	2,440	439	391	343	295	248	220	194	169	143	117	92
2,440	2,480	450	402	354	307	259	226	200	175	149	123	98
2,480	2,520	461	413	366	318	270	232	206	181	155	129	104
2,520	2,560	472	425	377	329	281	238	212	187	161	135	110
2,560	2,600	484	436	388	340	292	245	218	193	167	141	116
2,600	2,640	495	447	399	351	304	256	224	199	173	147	122
2,640	2,680	506	458	410	363	315	267	230	205	179	153	128
2,680	2,720	517	469	422	374	326	278	236	211	185	159	134
2,720	2,760	528	481	433	385	337	289	242	217	191	165	140
2,760	2,800	540	492	444	396	348	301	253	223	197	171	146
2,800	2,840	551	503	455	407	360	312	264	229	203	177	152
2,840	2,880	562	514	466	419	371	323	275	235	209	183	158
2,880	2,920	573	525	478	430	382	334	286	241	215	189	164
2,920	2,960	584	537	489	441	393	345	297	250	221	195	170
2,960	3,000	596	548	500	452	404	357	309	261	227	201	176
3,000	3,040	607	559	511	463	416	368	320	272	233	207	182
3,040	3,080	618	570	522	475	427	379	331	283	239	213	188
3,080	3,120	629	581	534	486	438	390	342	294	247	219	194
3,120	3,160	640	593	545	497	449	401	353	306	258	225	200
At least	But less than	0	1	2	3	4	5	6	7	8	9	10 or more
3,160	3,200	652	604	556	508	460	413	365	317	269	231	206
3,200	3,240	663	615	567	519	472	424	376	328	280	237	212
3,240	3,280	674	626	578	531	483	435	387	339	291	244	218
3,280	3,320	685	637	590	542	494	446	398	350	303	255	224
3,320	3,360	696	649	601	553	505	457	409	362	314	266	230
3,360	3,400	708	660	612	564	516	469	421	373	325	277	236
3,400	3,440	719	671	623	575	528	480	432	384	336	288	242
3,440	3,480	730	682	634	587	539	491	443	395	347	300	252
3,480	3,520	741	693	646	598	550	502	454	406	359	311	263
3,520	3,560	752	705	657	609	561	513	465	418	370	322	274
3,560	3,600	764	716	668	620	572	525	477	429	381	333	285
3,600	3,640	775	727	679	631	584	536	488	440	392	344	297
3,640	3,680	786	738	690	643	595	547	499	451	403	356	308
3,680	3,720	797	749	702	654	606	558	510	462	415	367	319
3,720	3,760	808	761	713	665	617	569	521	474	426	378	330
3,760	3,800	820	772	724	676	628	581	533	485	437	389	341
3,800	3,840	831	783	735	687	640	592	544	496	448	400	353
3,840	3,880	842	794	746	699	651	603	555	507	459	412	364
3,880	3,920	853	805	758	710	662	614	566	518	471	423	375
3,920	3,960	864	817	769	721	673	625	577	530	482	434	386
3,960	4,000	876	828	780	732	684	637	589	541	493	445	397
4,000	4,040	887	839	791	743	696	648	600	552	504	456	409
4,040	4,080	900	850	802	755	707	659	611	563	515	468	420
4,080	4,120	913	861	814	766	718	670	622	574	527	479	431
4,120	4,160	926	873	825	777	729	681	633	586	538	490	442
4,160	4,200	940	884	836	788	740	693	645	597	549	501	453
4,200	4,240	953	896	847	799	752	704	656	608	560	512	465
4,240	4,280	966	910	858	811	763	715	667	619	571	524	476
4,280	4,320	979	923	870	822	774	726	678	630	583	535	487
4,320	4,360	992	936	881	833	785	737	689	642	594	546	498

$4,360 and over — Use Table 4(a) for a **SINGLE person**.

WAGE-BRACKET WITHHOLDING TABLES

MONTHLY Payroll Period— Employee MARRIED—Effective January 1, 1990

And the wages are—		And the number of withholding allowances claimed is—										
At least	But less than	0	1	2	3	4	5	6	7	8	9	10 or more
		The amount of income tax to be withheld shall be—										
$0	$290	$0	$0	$0	$0	$0	$0	$0	$0	$0	$0	$0
290	300	2	0	0	0	0	0	0	0	0	0	0
300	320	4	0	0	0	0	0	0	0	0	0	0
320	340	7	0	0	0	0	0	0	0	0	0	0
340	360	10	0	0	0	0	0	0	0	0	0	0
360	380	13	0	0	0	0	0	0	0	0	0	0
380	400	16	0	0	0	0	0	0	0	0	0	0
400	420	19	0	0	0	0	0	0	0	0	0	0
420	440	22	0	0	0	0	0	0	0	0	0	0
440	460	25	0	0	0	0	0	0	0	0	0	0
460	480	28	2	0	0	0	0	0	0	0	0	0
480	500	31	5	0	0	0	0	0	0	0	0	0
500	520	34	8	0	0	0	0	0	0	0	0	0
520	540	37	11	0	0	0	0	0	0	0	0	0
540	560	40	14	0	0	0	0	0	0	0	0	0
560	580	43	17	0	0	0	0	0	0	0	0	0
580	600	46	20	0	0	0	0	0	0	0	0	0
600	640	51	25	0	0	0	0	0	0	0	0	0
640	680	57	31	5	0	0	0	0	0	0	0	0
680	720	63	37	11	0	0	0	0	0	0	0	0
720	760	69	43	17	0	0	0	0	0	0	0	0
760	800	75	49	23	0	0	0	0	0	0	0	0
800	840	81	55	29	4	0	0	0	0	0	0	0
840	880	87	61	35	10	0	0	0	0	0	0	0
880	920	93	67	41	16	0	0	0	0	0	0	0
920	960	99	73	47	22	0	0	0	0	0	0	0
960	1,000	105	79	53	28	2	0	0	0	0	0	0
1,000	1,040	111	85	59	34	8	0	0	0	0	0	0
1,040	1,080	117	91	65	40	14	0	0	0	0	0	0
1,080	1,120	123	97	71	46	20	0	0	0	0	0	0
1,120	1,160	129	103	77	52	26	0	0	0	0	0	0
1,160	1,200	135	109	83	58	32	6	0	0	0	0	0
1,200	1,240	141	115	89	64	38	12	0	0	0	0	0
1,240	1,280	147	121	95	70	44	18	0	0	0	0	0
1,280	1,320	153	127	101	76	50	24	0	0	0	0	0
At least	But less than	0	1	2	3	4	5	6	7	8	9	10 or more
1,320	1,360	159	133	107	82	56	30	5	0	0	0	0
1,360	1,400	165	139	113	88	62	36	11	0	0	0	0
1,400	1,440	171	145	119	94	68	42	17	0	0	0	0
1,440	1,480	177	151	125	100	74	48	23	0	0	0	0
1,480	1,520	183	157	131	106	80	54	29	3	0	0	0
1,520	1,560	189	163	137	112	86	60	35	9	0	0	0
1,560	1,600	195	169	143	118	92	66	41	15	0	0	0
1,600	1,640	201	175	149	124	98	72	47	21	0	0	0
1,640	1,680	207	181	155	130	104	78	53	27	2	0	0
1,680	1,720	213	187	161	136	110	84	59	33	8	0	0
1,720	1,760	219	193	167	142	116	90	65	39	14	0	0
1,760	1,800	225	199	173	148	122	96	71	45	20	0	0
1,800	1,840	231	205	179	154	128	102	77	51	26	0	0
1,840	1,880	237	211	185	160	134	108	83	57	32	6	0
1,880	1,920	243	217	191	166	140	114	89	63	38	12	0
1,920	1,960	249	223	197	172	146	120	95	69	44	18	0
1,960	2,000	255	229	203	178	152	126	101	75	50	24	0
2,000	2,040	261	235	209	184	158	132	107	81	56	30	4
2,040	2,080	267	241	215	190	164	138	113	87	62	36	10
2,080	2,120	273	247	221	196	170	144	119	93	68	42	16
2,120	2,160	279	253	227	202	176	150	125	99	74	48	22
2,160	2,200	285	259	233	208	182	156	131	105	80	54	28
2,200	2,240	291	265	239	214	188	162	137	111	86	60	34
2,240	2,280	297	271	245	220	194	168	143	117	92	66	40
2,280	2,320	303	277	251	226	200	174	149	123	98	72	46
2,320	2,360	309	283	257	232	206	180	155	129	104	78	52
2,360	2,400	315	289	263	238	212	186	161	135	110	84	58
2,400	2,440	321	295	269	244	218	192	167	141	116	90	64
2,440	2,480	327	301	275	250	224	198	173	147	122	96	70
2,480	2,520	333	307	281	256	230	204	179	153	128	102	76
2,520	2,560	339	313	287	262	236	210	185	159	134	108	82
2,560	2,600	345	319	293	268	242	216	191	165	140	114	88
2,600	2,640	351	325	299	274	248	222	197	171	146	120	94
2,640	2,680	357	331	305	280	254	228	203	177	152	126	100
2,680	2,720	363	337	311	286	260	234	209	183	158	132	106

MONTHLY Payroll Period— Employee MARRIED—Effective January 1, 1990

And the wages are—		And the number of withholding allowances claimed is—										
At least	But less than	0	1	2	3	4	5	6	7	8	9	10 or more
		The amount of income tax to be withheld shall be—										
$2,720	$2,760	$369	$343	$317	$292	$266	$240	$215	$189	$164	$138	$112
2,760	2,800	375	349	323	298	272	246	221	195	170	144	118
2,800	2,840	381	355	329	304	278	252	227	201	176	150	124
2,840	2,880	387	361	335	310	284	258	233	207	182	156	130
2,880	2,920	393	367	341	316	290	264	239	213	188	162	136
2,920	2,960	399	373	347	322	296	270	245	219	194	168	142
2,960	3,000	405	379	353	328	302	276	251	225	200	174	148
3,000	3,040	415	385	359	334	308	282	257	231	206	180	154
3,040	3,080	426	391	365	340	314	288	263	237	212	186	160
3,080	3,120	437	397	371	346	320	294	269	243	218	192	166
3,120	3,160	448	403	377	352	326	300	275	249	224	198	172
3,160	3,200	460	412	383	358	332	306	281	255	230	204	178
3,200	3,240	471	423	389	364	338	312	287	261	236	210	184
3,240	3,280	482	434	395	370	344	318	293	267	242	216	190
3,280	3,320	493	445	401	376	350	324	299	273	248	222	196
3,320	3,360	504	456	409	382	356	330	305	279	254	228	202
3,360	3,400	516	468	420	388	362	336	311	285	260	234	208
3,400	3,440	527	479	431	394	368	342	317	291	266	240	214
3,440	3,480	538	490	442	400	374	348	323	297	272	246	220
3,480	3,520	549	501	453	406	380	354	329	303	278	252	226
3,520	3,560	560	512	465	417	386	360	335	309	284	258	232
3,560	3,600	572	524	476	428	392	366	341	315	290	264	238
3,600	3,640	583	535	487	439	398	372	347	321	296	270	244
3,640	3,680	594	546	498	450	404	378	353	327	302	276	250
3,680	3,720	605	557	509	462	414	384	359	333	308	282	256
3,720	3,760	616	568	521	473	425	390	365	339	314	288	262
3,760	3,800	628	580	532	484	436	396	371	345	320	294	268
3,800	3,840	639	591	543	495	447	402	377	351	326	300	274
3,840	3,880	650	602	554	506	459	411	383	357	332	306	280
3,880	3,920	661	613	565	518	470	422	389	363	338	312	286
3,920	3,960	672	624	577	529	481	433	395	369	344	318	292
3,960	4,000	684	636	588	540	492	444	401	375	350	324	298
4,000	4,040	695	647	599	551	503	456	408	381	356	330	304
4,040	4,080	706	658	610	562	515	467	419	387	362	336	310
4,080	4,120	717	669	621	574	526	478	430	393	368	342	316
At least	But less than	0	1	2	3	4	5	6	7	8	9	10 or more
4,120	4,160	728	680	633	585	537	489	441	399	374	348	322
4,160	4,200	740	692	644	596	548	500	453	405	380	354	328
4,200	4,240	751	703	655	607	559	512	464	416	386	360	334
4,240	4,280	762	714	666	618	571	523	475	427	392	366	340
4,280	4,320	773	725	677	630	582	534	486	438	398	372	346
4,320	4,360	784	736	689	641	593	545	497	449	404	378	352
4,360	4,400	796	748	700	652	604	556	509	461	413	384	358
4,400	4,440	807	759	711	663	615	568	520	472	424	390	364
4,440	4,480	818	770	722	674	627	579	531	483	435	396	370
4,480	4,520	829	781	733	686	638	590	542	494	446	402	376
4,520	4,560	840	792	745	697	649	601	553	505	458	410	382
4,560	4,600	852	804	756	708	660	612	565	517	469	421	388
4,600	4,640	863	815	767	719	671	624	576	528	480	432	394
4,640	4,680	874	826	778	730	683	635	587	539	491	443	400
4,680	4,720	885	837	789	742	694	646	598	550	502	455	407
4,720	4,760	896	848	801	753	705	657	609	561	514	466	418
4,760	4,800	908	860	812	764	716	668	621	573	525	477	429
4,800	4,840	919	871	823	775	727	680	632	584	536	488	440
4,840	4,880	930	882	834	786	739	691	643	595	547	499	452
4,880	4,920	941	893	845	798	750	702	654	606	558	511	463
4,920	4,960	952	904	857	809	761	713	665	617	570	522	474
4,960	5,000	964	916	868	820	772	724	677	629	581	533	485
5,000	5,040	975	927	879	831	783	736	688	640	592	544	496
5,040	5,080	986	938	890	842	795	747	699	651	603	555	508
5,080	5,120	997	949	901	854	806	758	710	662	614	567	519
5,120	5,160	1,008	960	913	865	817	769	721	673	626	578	530
5,160	5,200	1,020	972	924	876	828	780	733	685	637	589	541
5,200	5,240	1,031	983	935	887	839	792	744	696	648	600	552
5,240	5,280	1,042	994	946	898	851	803	755	707	659	611	564
5,280	5,320	1,053	1,005	957	910	862	814	766	718	670	623	575

$5,320 and over — Use Table 4(b) for a **MARRIED person.**

WAGE-BRACKET WITHHOLDING TABLES

DAILY or MISC Payroll Period— Employee NOT MARRIED—Effective January 1, 1990

And the wages divided by the number of days in such period are—		And the number of withholding allowances claimed is—										
		0	1	2	3	4	5	6	7	8	9	10 or more
At least	But less than	The amount of income tax to be withheld shall be the following amount multiplied by the number of days in such period—										
$0	$9	$0	$0	$0	$0	$0	$0	$0	$0	$0	$0	$0
9	12	1	0	0	0	0	0	0	0	0	0	0
12	15	1	0	0	0	0	0	0	0	0	0	0
15	18	2	1	0	0	0	0	0	0	0	0	0
18	21	2	1	0	0	0	0	0	0	0	0	0
21	24	3	2	0	0	0	0	0	0	0	0	0
24	27	3	2	1	0	0	0	0	0	0	0	0
27	30	4	2	1	0	0	0	0	0	0	0	0
30	33	4	3	2	0	0	0	0	0	0	0	0
33	36	4	3	2	1	0	0	0	0	0	0	0
36	39	5	4	3	1	0	0	0	0	0	0	0
39	42	5	4	3	2	1	0	0	0	0	0	0
42	45	6	5	3	2	1	0	0	0	0	0	0
45	48	6	5	4	3	2	0	0	0	0	0	0
48	51	7	6	4	3	2	1	0	0	0	0	0
51	54	7	6	5	4	2	1	0	0	0	0	0
54	57	8	6	5	4	3	2	1	0	0	0	0
57	60	8	7	6	5	3	2	1	0	0	0	0
60	63	9	7	6	5	4	3	1	0	0	0	0
63	66	9	8	7	5	4	3	2	1	0	0	0
66	69	9	8	7	6	5	4	2	1	0	0	0
69	72	10	9	8	6	5	4	3	2	0	0	0
72	75	10	9	8	7	6	4	3	2	1	0	0
75	78	11	10	8	7	6	5	4	3	1	0	0
78	81	11	10	9	8	7	5	4	3	2	1	0
81	84	12	11	9	8	7	6	5	3	2	1	0
84	87	13	11	10	9	7	6	5	4	3	1	0
87	90	14	12	10	9	8	7	5	4	3	2	1
90	93	15	12	11	9	8	7	6	5	4	2	1
93	96	15	13	11	10	9	8	6	5	4	3	2
96	99	16	14	12	10	9	8	7	6	4	3	2
99	102	17	15	13	11	10	8	7	6	5	4	3
102	105	18	16	14	11	10	9	8	7	5	4	3
105	108	19	17	14	12	11	9	8	7	6	5	3
108	111	20	17	15	13	11	10	9	7	6	5	4
At least	**But less than**	**0**	**1**	**2**	**3**	**4**	**5**	**6**	**7**	**8**	**9**	**10 or more**
111	114	20	18	16	14	12	10	9	8	7	6	4
114	117	21	19	17	15	12	11	10	8	7	6	5
117	120	22	20	18	16	13	11	10	9	8	6	5
120	123	23	21	19	16	14	12	10	9	8	7	6
123	126	24	22	19	17	15	13	11	10	9	7	6
126	129	25	22	20	18	16	14	11	10	9	8	7
129	132	26	23	21	19	17	14	12	11	9	8	7
132	135	26	24	22	20	18	15	13	11	10	9	8
135	138	27	25	23	21	18	16	14	12	10	9	8
138	141	28	26	24	21	19	17	15	13	11	10	8
141	144	29	27	24	22	20	18	16	13	11	10	9
144	147	30	28	25	23	21	19	16	14	12	10	9
147	150	31	28	26	24	22	20	17	15	13	11	10
150	153	31	29	27	25	23	20	18	16	14	12	10
153	156	32	30	28	26	23	21	19	17	15	12	11
156	159	33	31	29	26	24	22	20	18	15	13	11
159	162	34	32	30	27	25	23	21	18	16	14	12
162	165	35	33	30	28	26	24	22	19	17	15	13
165	168	36	33	31	29	27	25	22	20	18	16	14
168	171	36	34	32	30	28	25	23	21	19	17	14
171	174	37	35	33	31	28	26	24	22	20	17	15
174	177	38	36	34	31	29	27	25	23	20	18	16
177	180	39	37	35	32	30	28	26	24	21	19	17
180	183	40	38	35	33	31	29	27	24	22	20	18
183	186	41	38	36	34	32	30	27	25	23	21	19
186	189	42	39	37	35	33	30	28	26	24	22	19
189	192	43	40	38	36	33	31	29	27	25	22	20
192	195	44	41	39	37	34	32	30	28	26	23	21
195	198	45	42	40	37	35	33	31	29	26	24	22
198	201	46	43	40	38	36	34	32	29	27	25	23
201	204	47	44	41	39	37	35	32	30	28	26	24
204	207	48	45	42	40	38	35	33	31	29	27	24
207	210	49	46	43	41	39	36	34	32	30	27	25
210	213	49	47	44	42	39	37	35	33	31	28	26
213	216	50	48	45	43	40	38	36	34	31	29	27

DAILY or MISC Payroll Period— Employee NOT MARRIED—Effective January 1, 1990

And the wages divided by the number of days in such period are—		And the number of withholding allowances claimed is—										
		0	1	2	3	4	5	6	7	8	9	10 or more
At least	But less than	The amount of income tax to be withheld shall be the following amount multiplied by the number of days in such period—										
$216	$219	$51	$49	$46	$44	$41	$39	$37	$34	$32	$30	$28
219	222	52	50	47	45	42	40	37	35	33	31	29
222	225	53	51	48	46	43	41	38	36	34	32	29
225	228	54	52	49	47	44	41	39	37	35	33	30
228	231	55	53	50	48	45	42	40	38	36	33	31
231	234	56	54	51	49	46	43	41	39	36	34	32
234	237	57	55	52	50	47	44	42	39	37	35	33
237	240	58	56	53	51	48	45	43	40	38	36	34
240	243	59	57	54	52	49	46	44	41	39	37	35
243	246	60	58	55	53	50	47	45	42	40	38	35
246	249	61	59	56	54	51	48	46	43	41	38	36
249	252	62	60	57	55	52	49	47	44	42	39	37
252	255	63	61	58	56	53	50	48	45	43	40	38
255	258	64	62	59	57	54	51	49	46	44	41	39
258	261	65	63	60	58	55	52	50	47	45	42	40
261	264	66	64	61	59	56	53	51	48	46	43	40
264	267	67	65	62	60	57	54	52	49	47	44	41
267	270	68	66	63	61	58	55	53	50	47	45	42
270	273	69	67	64	61	59	56	54	51	48	46	43
273	276	70	68	65	62	60	57	55	52	49	47	44
276	279	71	69	66	63	61	58	56	53	50	48	45
279	282	72	70	67	64	62	59	57	54	51	49	46
282	285	73	71	68	65	63	60	58	55	52	50	47
285	288	74	72	69	66	64	61	59	56	53	51	48
288	291	75	73	70	67	65	62	60	57	54	52	49
291	294	76	74	71	68	66	63	61	58	55	53	50
294	297	77	75	72	69	67	64	62	59	56	54	51
297	300	78	76	73	70	68	65	63	60	57	55	52
300	303	79	77	74	71	69	66	64	61	58	56	53
303	306	80	78	75	72	70	67	65	62	59	57	54
306	309	81	79	76	73	71	68	66	63	60	58	55
309	312	82	80	77	74	72	69	67	64	61	59	56
312	315	83	81	78	75	73	70	68	65	62	60	57
315	318	84	82	79	76	74	71	69	66	63	61	58
318	321	85	83	80	77	75	72	70	67	64	62	59
At least	**But less than**	**0**	**1**	**2**	**3**	**4**	**5**	**6**	**7**	**8**	**9**	**10 or more**
321	324	86	84	81	78	76	73	71	68	65	63	60
324	327	87	85	82	79	77	74	72	69	66	64	61
327	330	88	86	83	80	78	75	72	70	67	65	62
330	333	89	86	84	81	79	76	73	71	68	66	63
333	336	90	87	85	82	80	77	74	72	69	67	64
336	339	91	88	86	83	81	78	75	73	70	68	65
339	341	92	89	87	84	81	79	76	74	71	68	66
341	343	93	90	87	85	82	80	77	74	72	69	67
343	345	93	91	88	85	83	80	78	75	72	70	67
345	347	94	91	89	86	83	81	78	76	73	70	68
347	349	95	92	89	87	84	82	79	76	74	71	69
349	351	95	93	90	87	85	82	80	77	74	72	69
351	353	96	93	91	88	85	83	80	78	75	72	70
353	355	97	94	91	89	86	84	81	78	76	73	71
355	357	97	95	92	89	87	84	82	79	76	74	71
357	359	98	95	93	90	87	85	82	80	77	74	72
359	361	99	96	93	91	88	85	83	80	78	75	72
361	363	99	97	94	91	89	86	84	81	78	76	73
363	365	100	97	95	92	89	87	84	82	79	76	74
365	367	100	98	95	93	90	87	85	82	80	77	74
367	369	101	99	96	93	91	88	86	83	80	78	75
369	371	102	99	97	94	91	89	86	84	81	78	76
371	373	102	100	97	95	92	89	87	84	82	79	76
373	375	103	101	98	95	93	90	88	85	82	80	77
375	377	104	101	99	96	93	91	88	86	83	80	78
377	379	104	102	99	97	94	91	89	86	84	81	78
379	381	105	103	100	97	95	92	89	87	84	82	79
381	383	106	103	101	98	95	93	90	88	85	82	80
383	385	106	104	101	99	96	93	91	88	86	83	80
385	387	107	104	102	99	97	94	91	89	86	84	81
387	389	108	105	103	100	97	95	92	90	87	84	82

$389 and over — Use Table 8(a) for a **SINGLE person.**

WAGE-BRACKET WITHHOLDING TABLES

DAILY or MISC Payroll Period— Employee MARRIED—Effective January 1, 1990

And the wages divided by the number of days in such period are—		And the number of withholding allowances claimed is—										
		0	1	2	3	4	5	6	7	8	9	10 or more
At least	But less than	The amount of income tax to be withheld shall be the following amount multiplied by the number of days in such period—										
$0	$15	$0	$0	$0	$0	$0	$0	$0	$0	$0	$0	$0
15	18	1	0	0	0	0	0	0	0	0	0	0
18	21	1	0	0	0	0	0	0	0	0	0	0
21	24	1	0	0	0	0	0	0	0	0	0	0
24	27	2	1	0	0	0	0	0	0	0	0	0
27	30	2	1	0	0	0	0	0	0	0	0	0
30	33	3	2	0	0	0	0	0	0	0	0	0
33	36	3	2	1	0	0	0	0	0	0	0	0
36	39	4	2	1	0	0	0	0	0	0	0	0
39	42	4	3	2	1	0	0	0	0	0	0	0
42	45	5	3	2	1	0	0	0	0	0	0	0
45	48	5	4	3	1	0	0	0	0	0	0	0
48	51	5	4	3	2	1	0	0	0	0	0	0
51	54	6	5	4	2	1	0	0	0	0	0	0
54	57	6	5	4	3	2	0	0	0	0	0	0
57	60	7	6	4	3	2	1	0	0	0	0	0
60	63	7	6	5	4	3	1	0	0	0	0	0
63	66	8	7	5	4	3	2	1	0	0	0	0
66	69	8	7	6	5	3	2	1	0	0	0	0
69	72	9	7	6	5	4	3	2	0	0	0	0
72	75	9	8	7	6	4	3	2	1	0	0	0
75	78	10	8	7	6	5	4	2	1	0	0	0
78	81	10	9	8	6	5	4	3	2	1	0	0
81	84	10	9	8	7	6	5	3	2	1	0	0
84	87	11	10	8	7	6	5	4	3	1	0	0
87	90	11	10	9	8	7	5	4	3	2	1	0
90	93	12	11	9	8	7	6	5	3	2	1	0
93	96	12	11	10	9	7	6	5	4	3	2	0
96	99	13	11	10	9	8	7	6	4	3	2	1
99	102	13	12	11	10	8	7	6	5	4	2	1
102	105	14	12	11	10	9	8	6	5	4	3	2
105	108	14	13	12	10	9	8	7	6	5	3	2
108	111	14	13	12	11	10	9	7	6	5	4	3
111	114	15	14	13	11	10	9	8	7	5	4	3
114	117	15	14	13	12	11	9	8	7	6	5	4
At least	But less than	0	1	2	3	4	5	6	7	8	9	10 or more
117	120	16	15	13	12	11	10	9	8	6	5	4
120	123	16	15	14	13	12	10	9	8	7	6	4
123	126	17	16	14	13	12	11	10	8	7	6	5
126	129	17	16	15	14	12	11	10	9	8	7	5
129	132	18	16	15	14	13	12	11	9	8	7	6
132	135	18	17	16	15	13	12	11	10	9	7	6
135	138	19	17	16	15	14	13	11	10	9	8	7
138	141	19	18	17	15	14	13	12	11	10	8	7
141	144	20	18	17	16	15	14	12	11	10	9	8
144	147	21	19	17	16	15	14	13	12	10	9	8
147	150	22	19	18	17	16	14	13	12	11	10	8
150	153	23	20	18	17	16	15	14	12	11	10	9
153	156	23	21	19	18	16	15	14	13	12	11	9
156	159	24	22	20	18	17	16	15	13	12	11	10
159	162	25	23	21	19	17	16	15	14	13	11	10
162	165	26	24	21	19	18	17	15	14	13	12	11
165	168	27	25	22	20	18	17	16	15	14	12	11
168	171	28	25	23	21	19	18	16	15	14	13	12
171	174	28	26	24	22	20	18	17	16	14	13	12
174	177	29	27	25	23	20	18	17	16	15	14	13
177	180	30	28	26	23	21	19	18	17	15	14	13
180	183	31	29	27	24	22	20	18	17	16	15	13
183	186	32	30	27	25	23	21	19	17	16	15	14
186	189	33	30	28	26	24	22	19	18	17	16	14
189	192	33	31	29	27	25	22	20	18	17	16	15
192	195	34	32	30	28	25	23	21	19	18	16	15
195	198	35	33	31	29	26	24	22	20	18	17	16
198	201	36	34	32	29	27	25	23	21	19	17	16
201	204	37	35	32	30	28	26	24	21	19	18	17
204	207	38	35	33	31	29	27	24	22	20	18	17
207	210	38	36	34	32	30	27	25	23	21	19	17
210	213	39	37	35	33	31	28	26	24	22	19	18
213	216	40	38	36	34	31	29	27	25	23	20	18
216	219	41	39	37	34	32	30	28	26	23	21	19
219	222	42	40	37	35	33	31	29	26	24	22	20

DAILY or MISC Payroll Period— Employee MARRIED—Effective January 1, 1990

And the wages divided by the number of days in such period are—		And the number of withholding allowances claimed is—										
		0	1	2	3	4	5	6	7	8	9	10 or more
At least	But less than	The amount of income tax to be withheld shall be the following amount multiplied by the number of days in such period—										
$222	$225	$43	$40	$38	$36	$34	$32	$29	$27	$25	$23	$21
225	228	44	41	39	37	35	32	30	28	26	24	21
228	231	44	42	40	38	36	33	31	29	27	25	22
231	234	45	43	41	39	36	34	32	30	28	25	23
234	237	46	44	42	39	37	35	33	31	28	26	24
237	240	47	45	42	40	38	36	34	31	29	27	25
240	243	48	46	43	41	39	37	34	32	30	28	26
243	246	49	46	44	42	40	38	35	33	31	29	26
246	249	49	47	45	43	41	38	36	34	32	30	27
249	252	50	48	46	44	41	39	37	35	33	30	28
252	255	51	49	47	44	42	40	38	36	33	31	29
255	258	52	50	48	45	43	41	39	36	34	32	30
258	261	53	51	48	46	44	42	40	37	35	33	31
261	264	54	51	49	47	45	43	40	38	36	34	32
264	267	54	52	50	48	46	43	41	39	37	35	32
267	270	55	53	51	49	46	44	42	40	38	35	33
270	273	56	54	52	50	47	45	43	41	38	36	34
273	276	57	55	53	50	48	46	44	42	39	37	35
276	279	58	56	53	51	49	47	45	42	40	38	36
279	282	59	56	54	52	50	48	45	43	41	39	37
282	285	59	57	55	53	51	48	46	44	42	40	37
285	288	60	58	56	54	52	49	47	45	43	40	38
288	291	61	59	57	55	52	50	48	46	44	41	39
291	294	62	60	58	55	53	51	49	47	44	42	40
294	297	63	61	58	56	54	52	50	47	45	43	41
297	300	64	61	59	57	55	53	50	48	46	44	42
300	303	65	62	60	58	56	53	51	49	47	45	42
303	306	65	63	61	59	57	54	52	50	48	46	43
306	309	66	64	62	60	57	55	53	51	49	46	44
309	312	67	65	63	60	58	56	54	52	49	47	45
312	315	68	66	63	61	59	57	55	52	50	48	46
315	318	69	67	64	62	60	58	55	53	51	49	47
318	321	70	67	65	63	61	59	56	54	52	50	47
321	324	71	68	66	64	62	59	57	55	53	51	48
324	327	72	69	67	65	62	60	58	56	54	51	49
At least	But less than	0	1	2	3	4	5	6	7	8	9	10 or more
327	330	73	70	68	65	63	61	59	57	54	52	50
330	333	74	71	69	66	64	62	60	57	55	53	51
333	336	75	72	70	67	65	63	61	58	56	54	52
336	339	76	73	71	68	66	64	61	59	57	55	53
339	341	77	74	71	69	66	64	62	60	58	55	53
341	343	77	75	72	69	67	65	63	60	58	56	54
343	345	78	75	73	70	68	65	63	61	59	57	54
345	347	79	76	73	71	68	66	54	62	59	57	55
347	349	79	77	74	71	69	67	64	62	60	58	55
349	351	80	77	75	72	69	67	65	63	60	58	56
351	353	81	78	75	73	70	68	65	63	61	59	57
353	355	81	79	76	73	71	68	66	64	62	59	57
355	357	82	79	77	74	71	69	67	64	62	60	58
357	359	83	80	77	75	72	70	67	65	63	60	58
359	361	83	81	78	75	73	70	68	65	63	61	59
361	363	84	81	79	76	73	71	68	66	64	62	59
363	365	85	82	79	77	74	71	69	67	64	62	60
365	367	85	83	80	77	75	72	70	67	65	63	61
367	369	86	83	81	78	75	73	70	68	65	63	61
369	371	86	84	81	79	76	73	71	68	66	64	62
371	373	87	85	82	79	77	74	72	69	67	64	62
373	375	88	85	83	80	77	75	72	70	67	65	63
375	377	88	86	83	81	78	75	73	70	68	66	63
377	379	89	87	84	81	79	76	74	71	68	66	64
379	381	90	87	85	82	79	77	74	72	69	67	64
381	383	90	88	85	83	80	77	75	72	70	67	65
383	385	91	89	86	83	81	78	75	73	70	68	66
385	387	92	89	87	84	81	79	76	74	71	68	66
387	389	92	90	87	85	82	79	77	74	72	69	67
389	391	93	90	88	85	83	80	77	75	72	70	67
391	393	94	91	89	86	83	81	78	76	73	70	68

$393 and over — Use Table 8(b) for a **MARRIED person**.

INDEX

T

U